Kent & Jen —
may meaning
and joy be yours
always! Michele

Helping College Students Find Purpose

The Campus Guide to Meaning-Making

Robert J. Nash
Michele C. Murray

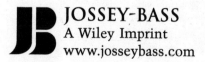

JOSSEY-BASS
A Wiley Imprint
www.josseybass.com

Published by Jossey-Bass

A Wiley Imprint

989 Market Street, San Francisco, CA 94103-1741—www.josseybass.com

Jossey-Bass books and products are available through most bookstores. To contact Jossey-Bass directly call our Customer Care Department within the U.S. at 800-956-7739, outside the U.S. at 317-572-3986, or fax 317-572-4002.

Jossey-Bass also publishes its books in a variety of electronic formats. Some content that appears in print may not be available in electronic books.

Library of Congress Cataloging-in-Publication Data
Nash, Robert J.
    Helping college students find purpose: the campus guide to meaning-making/Robert J. Nash, Michele C. Murray. – 1st ed.
        p. cm. – (Jossey-Bass higher and adult education series)
    Includes bibliographical references and index.
    ISBN 978-0-470-40814-8 (cloth)
    1. Education, Higher–United States.   2. Education, Humanistic–United States.
    3. Existentialism.   I. Murray, Michele C.   II. Title.
    LA227.4.N36 2010
    378.19'8–dc22   2009038858

Printed in the United States of America

FIRST EDITION

HB Printing 10 9 8 7 6 5 4 3 2 1

The Jossey-Bass Higher and
Adult Education Series

Contents

Foreword

It has been said that the future will belong to those who can tell the best story of the twenty-first century. We human beings all dwell within stories absorbed from our culture, mediated by family, friends, and associates, and ratified by conventional media, religious faith communities, scientific inquiry, political discourse, commercial advertising, and other institutions that shape our common life. These stories are inevitably recast as we continually twist and stretch them in our efforts to make sense of self, world, cosmos—demanding ways to maintain a firm grip on reality. The stories we live and tell provide coherence and meaning and orient our sense of purpose. The master stories—our personal and cultural myths—determine what we value and whom we love.

When the narrative becomes too thin or sketchy to stand up to the task of everyday meaning-making and begins to unravel, we drift into meaninglessness and grow vulnerable to isolation and desolation—or mere unthinking busyness. On the other hand, the story may be fiercely defended, yet if it is simply too tightly woven to embrace the fullness of a larger truth, it may constrain the potential of our lives and even become dangerous to others and ourselves.

Thus in every generation, a part of growing up is the development of the capacity to reflect on the meaning-making tales given to us and to critically examine the assumptions, biases, strengths, and viability of those stories. We discover that the journey into adulthood requires us to become conscious of the individual and collective meanings we make and to learn to compose over time a worthy story to live by. This is the deep purpose of the journey from ignorance to knowledge, and every society has a stake in whether and how our young discover and work this task.

This meaning-making is distinctively challenged in today's world. We live in a time "between stories." The great cultural myths—religious, political, economic—that have guided our societies are now under severe review as our generations are asked to live at one of those great hinge times in history. We are contending with unprecedented conditions (e.g., breaking open the human genome, climate change, a global economy), and we now stand on new moral and ethical frontiers.

Nash and Murray invite all who work in higher education to recognize that in every era the college years are a critical time in the life span for examining, testing, and re-creating the stories we live by. University students are ripe for discerning a narrative that is worthy of the potential of a young adult life and for doing so in ways that enable them to see themselves as an integral part of a larger communal reality—a shared dialogue at the heart of the human enterprise, a disciplined dialogue that must necessarily embrace both the wonderful and the terrible—a hard-headed, open-hearted, and difficult practice that has consequences for both self and world.

Providing persuasive evidence that too many of our students are bored, angry, driven, and mere consumers of courses and credentials without access to a worthy "Why?", Nash and Murray offer compelling descriptions of students' hunger for meaning and clear, practical approaches from their own teaching experience about how to respond as "meaning constructivist" educators. They make vivid the significance of the "quarter-life crises" in the lifelong journey of meaning-making, and illumine the power of the interdependent roles of faculty, administrators, and students affairs professionals who serve by intention or default as "meaning mentors."

At the same time, Nash and Murray know that most faculty and others who provide leadership within the academy typically do not perceive that questions of meaning lie within the domain of their personal and professional expertise. Indeed, much of today's professional training does not prepare people for "deep-meaning education," though the wider public could rightly presume that questions of meaning, purpose, and significance are central to the intellectual life, integral to the work of every discipline, and threaded throughout the shared life of the campus—on behalf of the wider culture. The particular approaches offered here will not be the mode for all, but the underlying principles that they make explicit will inform the imagination of every educator who embraces the dual vocation of higher education: to create and impart knowledge and to serve as a primary, privileged setting for the formation of adulthood, citizenship, and leadership.

The aspiration of this book is that we will find here a pathway into deeper reflection on the purposes of higher education and our roles within it. We are invited to rediscover our capacity to work with students in ways that do not impose a particular narrative upon them, but do create the space in which we may appropriately evoke, respond, inform, clarify, enrich, and even inspire the meaning-making process of our students—encouraging their capacity for curiosity, skepticism, and meaningful commitments.

As we move into the formidable challenges of the twenty-first century, it becomes increasingly evident that we have been far too naïve about the power and adequacy of the master narratives being offered to the next generations. This book invites us to reclaim the core of the intellectual life, inviting our students into a disciplined, far-reaching dialogue that begins with "Why...?" "How do we know...?" and "For what...?" Here faculty, administrators, and student affairs professionals are reminded that meaning-making is a domain that cannot be deferred to presumed cultural norms already in place. This call for a more adequate understanding of what we mean by higher education asks all of us to relinquish our tendency to defer the bigger questions to "experts"—be they philosophers or counselors. We are invited to a "crossover pedagogy" in which across the life of the campus, we may more effectively grapple with the reality of our students as whole persons and reclaim our necessary role in the human adventure of meaning-making—on behalf of the renewal of the vocation of higher education, its vital role in today's global commons, and in the individual lives we serve.

Sharon Daloz Parks
Author, *Big Questions, Worthy Dreams*

To all my students over a four-decade period, whose presence in my classes and in my life has been the major inspiration for this book. To Madelyn, my partner for almost five decades, who understands the indefatigable need I have to write in order to make sense of my world, my vocation, and my own ongoing quest for meaning. To Michele C. Murray, my brilliant and talented coauthor, colleague, and dear friend, who has taught me more about meaning-making than she might have thought possible.

Finally, to the best senior editor I have ever had, David Brightman, along with his expert team at Jossey-Bass—without whom there would be no book on meaning-making.

—Robert J. Nash

To the students I have had the privilege to know and whose journeys to meaning have inspired me. To Robert J. Nash, who invited me into this project and who has brightened my world. To my parents, Dwight and Elodie, who were my first teachers and meaning mentors. To my husband, Chris Lewers, who brings new meaning to my life and who is a source of great blessings.

—Michele C. Murray

Preface

We wrote this book with two major audiences in mind. Because Robert is a faculty member and an Official University Scholar in the social sciences and the humanities at his university, and Michele is a student affairs vice-president and innovator at hers, we obviously want to reach *both* the professoriate and higher education administrators. We believe strongly that when it comes to teaching for meaning-making, no single group in the academy owns the meaning-making or purpose-driven life. Nor does any single group on campus own the intellectual life. Education, when done well, is cross-disciplinary, collaborative, and student-centered. Faculty and administrators need one another as active, knowledgeable, passionate collaborators if we are to be successful in helping our students to discover, and to create, in Frankl's (Frankl, 1979) words, a "meaning to live for." (See Resource B, Crossover Pedagogy, in the Resources section for a fuller treatment of this type of collaboration.)

In this day and age, the old academic and administrative silos are imploding. All the campus constituencies, including our students, are looking for creative ways to save ourselves, to save one another, to save the best that knowledge and wisdom have to offer, and to save our institutions and our planet. As Rorty (1999) has said, in the absence of any metaphysical or political certainty that all of us can agree on in a troubled, strife-filled, postmodern world, the most that we can hope for is to "huddle together against the darkness" in order to produce some light. In other words, we are all struggling to make meaning of our existence, and sometimes it is wiser for us to do this together, if we are to survive as a human species. Faculty and administrators have unique and special contributions to make in the search for meaning, and when they make the effort to work together, everyone on a college campus benefits. For us, there is simply no alternative.

We hope that *faculty* in their individual disciplines will take away from our book a set of creative philosophical or psychological rationales, and pedagogical strategies, for teaching about meaning—in the classroom, lecture hall, and seminar room. We hope that *administrators* will discover inspiring and helpful ways to meet students where they are, anywhere on campus and beyond, in their meaning-making ventures. Most of all, though, we want faculty and student affairs administrators to collaborate actively and directly, when appropriate, both inside and outside the classroom. We are committed to the proposition that both groups have much to teach one another, and, in so doing, they will have that much more to teach students about how to make meaning.

Questions of Meaning

We are impressed with this quotation from Frankl (1979): "The truth is that as the struggle for survival has subsided, the question has emerged—survival for what? Ever more people today have the *means* to live, but no *meaning* to live for" (p. 77). As university educators, we witness firsthand every day the need for our students of all ages, both traditional and nontraditional, to have something coherent to believe in, some centering values and goals to strive for. They, like us, need strong background beliefs and ideals to shore them up during these times when religious and political wars plague entire societies; when the natural environment continues to deteriorate;

and when the fluctuations of the global economy result in recession, inflation, and the inequitable distribution of scarce resources. On a more personal level, students need to make sense of the turmoil that results when their personal relationships get turned upside-down, or their work grows tedious and unsatisfying, or they become disillusioned by a sense of being unfulfilled; or when they face a life-altering decision, or they learn that the person who means the most to them in the whole world no longer loves them; or especially on a dreaded occasion when they hear that someone they love suffers from the ravages of a metastatic malignancy. Sadly, there are few opportunities on most college campuses—either inside or outside the conventional classroom, and as curricula become more vocational and professionally driven—for students to develop these strong background beliefs and ideals.

Today's college students are asking their own existential questions of meaning. As Frankl suggested, they are in search of a "meaning to live for." Their questions are timeless, yet they reflect the age in which they live. These questions are a fascinating admixture of the abstract and the practical, the universal and the particular. They represent well the tensions that exist for so many college students who seek to find the delicate balance that exists in the difficult space between idealism and realism, between macro- and micro-meaning. Here is a sample of some of these questions:

- What does it mean to be successful?

- Is it bad to want to make a lot of money?

- How will I know what type of career is best for me?

- Why do I hurt so much when a relationship ends?

- How do I tell my parents that the career they have chosen for me is not the one I want?

- Why do innocent people have to suffer?

- Will the lifestyles I see reflected in popular culture really make me happy?

- Can I be a good person without religion?

- Is religion only a set of "thou shalts" and "thou shalt nots"?

- Where do my deepest passions lie, and can I really carve out a career that reflects these?

- Why am I so vulnerable?

- Why do I worry about the future so much?

- Why am I here in school when I could be doing something far more constructive in the world beyond my campus?

- How, if at all, can I clean up all the messes in the world caused by wars, environmental decay, corporate greed, social injustice, political corruption, and irrelevant education?

- Is it any use even to try, because, after all, I am only one person?

In response to these types of questions, and many others that come up in the book, we attempt to provide a series of concrete classroom and cross-campus strategies to help students successfully navigate their diverse meaning-making activities. We do this even as we admit, openly and honestly, that there is no magic bullet that will meet everyone's need for meaning-making. We address this caveat to all those students, faculty, and administrators who may be reading this book looking for the all-purpose blueprint. Meaning-making—as even this brief sample of questions suggests—is as multidimensional and complex as are each of the individual meaning-makers who pursue this quest throughout their lives. There is no one-size-fits-all template for meaning-making.

The Quarterlife Generation and the Malady of Meaninglessness

At one time in the academy, thinkers believed that the problem of meaninglessness required a strictly philosophical solution. During existentialism's heyday between the world wars, and for a long while thereafter, philosophers such as Sartre, Camus, Jaspers, and Marcel wrote frequently about the human struggle to make or find meaning amidst meaninglessness; to live a life of authentic freedom at a time when choices seemed limited. In an apparently absurd world—where hundreds of thousands of individuals lost their lives in two major wars, the United States dropped nuclear bombs on Hiroshima and Nagasaki, and the Nazi holocaust wiped out almost an entire generation of Jews and others—the loss of any credible meaning in life that could make sense of the human slaughter dominated many philosophical agendas.

Soon enough, though, meaninglessness got psychologized, and rightly so. It was not long before the clinicians got involved. Psychotherapists like Jung, Frankl, and Allport wrote many books on the topic. Existential therapists set up shop throughout the United States, especially in colleges and university settings. Today, however, meaninglessness has become the reigning malady of the medical profession. The loss of any sustainable meaning in many patients is now understood to be the result of a serotonin-depleted brain chemistry, and antidepressant medications are the solutions. All well and good, as far as they go, and they do go far for many. But do they go far enough?

Most of us—and this certainly includes the current quarterlife generation of students—experience, at the very least, intermittent reminders of life's meaninglessness (Yalom, 1980, 2002, 2008). Meaninglessness is the state of mind that says nothing we do really counts for anything lasting or worthwhile. A sense of meaningless-ness, for so many of our quarterlife students, is an entering wedge for overwhelming feelings of dread, anxiety, and sadness. It can sometimes result in a sense of nihilism, fatalism, or ennui.

We will talk at length about the quarterlife generation in Chapter One. But, for now, let us say that, in our experience in higher education collectively spanning over sixty years of service to students, the term *quarterlife generation* describes a transitional period between two developmental stages. This period can start as early as the years from age seventeen to twenty and last as long as into the early to mid-thirties. It is a transitional period of profoundly unsettling philosophical and existential questions, and in some ways it is age-independent. These vexing questions come up again and again for adults of all ages and stages, as well as for all ethnicities, races, religions, and other important types of differences (see Steinle, 2005). These quarterlife questions are universal (see Cupitt, 2005). Moreover, it is important to understand that these questions result in tasks that must be completed in order for adults to move on to other transitional periods in their lives. If the tasks do not get completed, then they continue on into the next transitional period and then into the next period after that. Both of us have seen traditional and nontraditional students who wrestle with these tasks throughout the age and life stage continuum. These questions tend to get recycled until they find answers, and if they do not, they follow us to the grave (see Baggini, 2005; de la Chaumiere, 2004; Yalom, 2008).

The quarterlife period is frequently a tumultuous time for most of our students, because it triggers an overwhelming anxiety about the past, present, and future. So many of our quarterlife students are plagued with worry about failure—living up to others' expectations, letting go of the comfortable securities of childhood, coming to terms with the growing tension between freedom and responsibility, and constantly comparing themselves to peers and coming up short (Robbins & Wilner, 2001; Robbins, 2004).

We often hear the lament from quarterlife students in our classrooms, offices, and residence halls, as well as in our consultancies throughout the country, that they are restless and unfulfilled, or that life seems empty and/or boring, or that they never seem able to find a lasting satisfaction even in their most worthy accomplishments. Some students complain about being caught up in the academic or career rat race. Others admit openly that they are suffering from the incurable disease of "affluenza," an illness characterized by conspicuous and obsessive consumption (de Graaf, Wann, & Naylor, 2001). Some openly admit that they just do not want to grow up yet, but what they dread even more is having to return to the domestic nest to live with their parents after they graduate.

As debilitating as the quarterlifer's lament of meaninglessness is, many quarterlifers are surprisingly articulate about the conditions that are disturbing their equilibrium. Unfortunately, they do not seem to recognize that these conditions are the source of their malaise. In a follow-up to the Pew Research Center (2007) poll, Jayson (2007) asked young people in their twenties about their top goals in life. To a person, they said they wanted to be rich and famous, replicating the Pew findings that 81 percent of young people list being rich as their top goal, while 51 percent list being famous.

One young woman reported to Jayson, "When you open a celebrity magazine, it's all about the money and being rich and famous. The TV shows we watch—anything from *The Apprentice*...to *Us Weekly* magazine...We see reality TV shows with Jessica [Simpson] and Nick [Lachey] living the life. We see Britney [Spears] and Paris [Hilton]. The people we relate to outside our friends are those people." This young woman's comments speak volumes about who and what influences quarterlifers today, and they give helpful clues about the rise of meaning questions that deal with intimacy, success, and relationships.

Most quarterlifers we know wonder out loud why, increasingly, they experience so many of their successes as failures (there is really no ceiling on success for quarterlifers, because the self-induced pressure to achieve more and more can be so intense), and why their failures, as well as their hopes and dreams for the future, have to be so immobilizing to them. For these particular students—who tend to live their daily lives at perfectionist, career-driven, achievement-obsessed extremes—normal fears can often lead to crushing anxiety or debilitating depression. Although medication and talk therapy can help to allay these more severe psychological symptoms, a sense of meaninglessness lingers among many quarterlifers—often throughout their lifetimes.

The Meaning of Meaning

Here is how we, the authors, understand the term *meaning* that we will be using throughout this book. First, it is important to distinguish between the terms *meaning* and *purpose*. At times we will use these words interchangeably, but we also recognize that they differ in some fundamental ways. Here is Marinoff's (Marinoff, 1999) distinction: "Purpose is an ultimate object or end to be attained. It is a goal. Meaning has to do with how you understand your life on an ongoing basis" (p. 210). We think of meaning along these lines as well. For us, *meaning* is all about those interpretations, narrative frameworks, philosophical rationales and perspectives, and faith or belief systems that each of us brings to the various worlds in which we live, love, learn, work, and worship. *Purpose* has to do with pursuing certain goals, reaching resolutions, seeking results, and realizing particular objectives and ends in those worlds.

Thus what makes our purposes worthwhile or justifiable (or both) depends on those meanings that we attach to them and that drive our behaviors. Unfortunately, too often in the academy, we insist that our students pursue and achieve a whole host of academic and career purposes without first helping them to formulate systems of meanings to inform these purposes. To paraphrase Kant, purpose without meaning is empty, yet meaning without purpose goes nowhere. Finding the balance is the key to melding meaning and purpose, but, for us, it all starts with meaning-making. Without our meanings, our purposes are, sadly, meaningless.

We believe that meaning is, in the words of Yalom (1980), an "anxiety emollient." Sometimes it can have a soothing effect. At other times, meaning can be the midwife that helps all of us to give birth (at times, a difficult birth) to our core values—connections, commitments, joys, and loves. For Yalom, core values such as these prepare us to face, and overcome, our deepest anxieties regarding the challenges of death, freedom, isolation, and meaninglessness. We agree also with Sharon Daloz Parks (Parks, 2000) who says that meaning involves the "search for a sense of connection, pattern, order, and significance . . . it is a way to understand our experience that makes sense of both the expected and unexpected . . ." (p. 14) (See also Parks, 1991, for an earlier take on meaning-making.) Meaning therefore helps us to make cosmos out of chaos; it gives us choice in place of chance. Most of all, it gets us out of bed in the morning and off to face life's inevitable daily mixtures of pleasure and pain.

For us, a sense of meaning is what sustains us during those hard, perplexing times when everything seems to be up in the air and there are no certain answers anywhere to the most confounding questions that perplex us throughout our lives. Moreover, we agree with the psychologist Baumeister (1991), who claims that all of us, without exception, strive to make sense of our lives in four basic ways: purpose, value, efficacy, and self-worth. These are what he calls the "four needs for meaning—an existential shopping list" (p. 29). Unless all four of these needs get met, human beings are doomed to experience a serious, often irrevocable, loss of meaning.

For Baumeister, a sense of *purpose* acts as a major meaning-incentive. Human beings experience two types of purpose: "goal orientations" and "fulfillment." Goals are usually extrinsic, whereas fulfillment is intrinsic. We experience a sense of meaning whenever our goals are clearly understood and actively pursued and our fulfillments are genuine. And, following the example of Frankl (1963), Baumeister posits that all of us need *values*, because we are strongly motivated to draw upon morally defensible notions of right and wrong in our actions. Having a value base justifies our behavior; even more, it provides us with a guideline for making ethical judgments.

Baumeister also believes that we each have a need for *efficacy*. It is essential that we feel in charge of our lives, and that we can, at least to some extent, exert control over the events that befall us. Whether we are actually able to exert the power necessary to give us a feeling of control or it is simply the illusion of control that we experience—either way, our needs for efficacy can be met. Regardless, we need a sense of our own agency—that we are actors in charge of our own lives, and that life is not just an endless series of freak happenstances that render us helpless victims. Finally, each of us has an indefatigable need for *self-worth*. It is important to all of us that others respect, value, and trust us. Without a feeling of self-worth, Baumeister believes, human beings will experience a pervasive insecurity and self-doubt, and meaninglessness will be the tragic result. Self-worth goes beyond external sources of evaluation; rather, an internal sense of "what I do matters and has meaning" is key to a genuine sense of self-value.

Moreover, to paraphrase Nietzsche in talking about meaning from a philosophical perspective, we believe that those people who have a *why* to live can bear almost any *how*. This is the aphorism that enabled Viktor Frankl to survive several nightmarish years in the Nazi death camps during the Holocaust (1963). In our work with a variety of constituencies on college campuses, we realize that without our *whys for living,* the *hows* can often be deceiving. Admittedly, among some students there appears to be a growing interest in volunteerism, service learning projects, the Peace Corps, semesters abroad and at sea, campus ministry programs, and environmental and social justice initiatives on campuses throughout the United States. But without developing sound and enduring *whys*—philosophical compasses that result in an integration of lived values—students often find their well-intended *hows* to be short-lived and directionless. Some eventually lose their enthusiasm for service to others because the real-world, career payoffs seem incommensurate with their volunteer efforts. In the long run, it is the *whys* that will help students to experience the genuine satisfactions of making a palpable difference in the lives of real people residing in the larger communities that exist outside their campuses.

We fully recognize that the *whys for living* are virtually infinite in number. There is no bottom line or final word on the meaning of existence in general or of one's personal existence in particular. Some students will look to religion and spirituality for transcendent meaning; others will look to politics or human service careers for secular meaning. Still others will look to friendships and intimate relationships for intrinsic meaning, or to the creative arts, science, and the natural environment for extrinsic meaning. And still others will commit themselves to a variety of social justice issues in order to create activistic forms of meaning. Although we are more than willing to acknowledge that certain existential questions about meaning that come up throughout people's lives are universal in nature, we are also realists in contending that the answers regarding *how* we are to live are endlessly subjective—and they are many.

Scope and Structure

We wanted this book on meaning to be succinct, accessible, and, most of all, engaging and informative. Our intention was to make our chapters easy to read, with an ideal blend of both explanation and example. We include some personal narrative writing along the way, while still paying scrupulous attention to the relevant scholarship and appropriate resources on the topic of meaning (Nash, 2004). This book attempts to accomplish the following:

- Develop a powerful rationale for challenging and encouraging faculty and administrators to see themselves as mentors of meaning-making to all campus constituencies

- Equip all members of the campus community with the background knowledge and the tools necessary to create communities of meaning-making

- Provide a series of concrete steps for applying the theory and practice of meaning-making to teaching, leading, administering, and advising

- Use a number of student vignettes to point out the centrality of meaning-making on college campuses

We begin each chapter with a preview of its goals, purposes, and procedures, and in some cases a relevant scenario or case study. We end each chapter with a series of concrete recommendations for faculty, administrators, and students regarding the theory and practice of meaning-making. Some of our chapters are, of necessity, more conceptual than practical, and some more practical than conceptual. The first half of the book, in addition to including a number of real-life scenarios, spells out our philosophy of meaning-making. The second half of the book offers a number of real-world strategies that faculty, administrators, and staff can use to foster what we are calling "deep-meaning learning" on the topic of meaning-making.

Here is a brief overview of how we frame the book. In Part I, Making Meaning in the Quarterlife, we begin with a chapter on the quarterlife generation and its special challenges in making meaning. We follow this with a chapter delineating the existential and postmodern sources of meaning-making. We end this part with a chapter on the role of religion and spirituality in making meaning.

In Part II, Putting Meaning-Making to Work: Tools of the Trade, we apply the pedagogy of constructivism to meaning-making in college classrooms, alternative campus-wide learning settings, and off-campus sites. We include a series of practical, meaning-making tips for use inside and outside the classroom—for teachers, administrators, and staff throughout the campus. In this part, we feature chapters on the ethics of meaning-making and how to use meaning-making maxims throughout the campus.

In Part III, Our Own Attempts to Make Meaning, we, the authors, talk very honestly—in the form of two personal reflections addressed directly to our readers—about the ups and downs of meaning-making in our own work, and about what gives our own lives meaning.

We have also included a Resources section, Resources for Meaning-Making Educators. The first, Resource A: Four Therapeutic Approaches to Meaning-Making, examines four contemporary ways of thinking about, and educating for, meaning-making: logotherapy, narrative therapy, philosophical counseling, and positive psychology. All four frameworks—which, for us, are the conceptual heart and soul of meaning-making education—are united in the sense that their overall goal is to promote healthy, self-determining, first-person, here-and-now meaning-construction. Resource B: Crossover Pedagogy, develops a rationale, as well as recommendations for implementation, for what we call "crossover pedagogy." Crossover pedagogy is our attempt to spell out in greater detail the various ways that faculty and student affairs professionals can work together to advance the meaning-making agenda for higher education.

We are grateful to the works that have preceded ours and influenced our thinking about teaching for meaning. We recognize five volumes in particular. Sharon Daloz Parks's (Parks, 2000) *Big Questions, Worthy Dreams*, addresses mentoring communities that foster faith development and meaning-making for young adults. In their empirical work, Braskamp, Trautvetter, and Ward (2006) make a case for "putting students first," based on a concept they call "holistic student development." These authors discuss the changes that will be necessary in the classroom, in the larger campus, and in the external community in order to foster, and deliver, a holistic education—one centered in faith development. Fink's (Fink, 2003) latest work presents us with a "taxonomy of significant learning" as well as a model of "integrated course design," which includes a compendium of charts, graphs, and figures designed to get students fully engaged in their learning. We also appreciate Sullivan, Rosin, Shulman, and Fenstermacher's (2008) *A New Agenda for Higher Education*, a work that originated in the Life of the Mind for Practice seminars. They outline a rationale, and a plan, for teaching "practical reasoning and responsible judgment."

Finally, we have turned to an old standby in the literature for characterizing student development, particularly the ethical and intellectual growth of college students. In many ways, Perry's (1970/1999) nine-stage model of cognitive development holds up well today, forty years after it first appeared. We have been informed again and again by Perry's research whenever we tried to frame the moral, philosophical, and epistemological cycles of quarterlife choice-making. Quarterlifers today still grapple with dualistic, relativistic, and universalistic-committed ways of thinking about the meaning of their lives. We are grateful to Perry for the term *transition* to explain the developmental passages that students in the quarterlife need to negotiate before they can build a sustainable set of meanings to guide their life's purpose. Transitions and cycles best explain our own approach to quarterlife choice-making rather than the language of linear or chronological stages.

These previous works have helped shape our thoughts about meaning-making as a cross-campus venture. We have created *our* book to speak to university faculty and administrators as *educators*, *meaning-makers*, and *mentors* of students' meaning-making.

Although it is true that higher education writings dealing with the topic of spirituality have been appearing in the student services literature increasingly in recent years, few, if any, treat the subject of meaning-making on as many levels as we do. (One exception is Chickering, Dalton, and Stamm, 2006.) Our specific goal is to provide a theory-into-practice model of meaning-making for the entire college campus—one that will enable all constituencies to engage in this important process.

Caveats

A spate of recent literature on current millennial/quarterlife students criticizes them because they are anti-intellectual, addicted to the Internet, suffering from incurable attention deficit problems because the Google culture has made them "stoopid [*sic*]"—that is, unable to concentrate, and distracted. What is more, critics accuse students today of being relativistic, politically correct, suffering from excessive doses of positive self-esteem, mesmerized by reality television shows, and celebrity-obsessed (see Baron, 2008, Carr, 2008, and Bauerlein, 2008).

Although some of these concerns are undoubtedly important, most are predictably hyperbolic. Every younger generation for hundreds, even thousands, of years has provoked handwringing from its cultural elders. In contrast to the latest round of critics, however, we respect and admire this new generation of "digital natives." In truth, they are far better adapted to contemporary cultural currents than are most of us who come from earlier generations. They will be the future high-tech "cosmopolites" that the new global order will need in order to function effectively (see National Leadership Council, 2008). Most of all, though, we experience every day the enormous potential of our millennial students to be intelligent, ethical, humanitarian, and productive persons (for a similar take, see Benton, 2008). In fact, the majority of them are there already.

We are often asked by skeptical faculty and administrators throughout the country if we think college students are mature enough to engage in serious thinking about meaning-making. They question whether college students have sufficient life experiences to have anything worth questioning, examining, or contributing.

After all, their reasoning goes, college students have a lot more on their minds than thinking about unanswerable philosophical questions. Besides, these critics argue, the primary function of higher education in the early years of the third millennium ought to be about preparing young adults for graduate school training and professional careers. For these critics, meaning-making feels too much like what ought to go on in the counseling center, or with campus ministry, or in a career services workshop. It has no justifiable place in the formal academic curriculum (see Walvoord, 2008).

These critics frequently charge that nobody really knows what meaning is about. Furthermore, they ask, to what disciplines does the subject matter belong? The humanities? The social sciences? The natural sciences? The arts? Or the professional schools? They also raise the question that if the concept of meaning requires an interdisciplinary approach, then where are the genuine interdisciplinary programs, and scholars, on the college campus to examine it? Too often, faculty believe that the concept of meaning is just too impractical, vague, subjective, and "soft." This last word is one that we hear over and over again from more hard-line administrators, scientists, and social scientists who believe that unless we can measure, count, weigh, interview, and test knowledge, it has no value.

What really seems to bother most critics, however, is whether meaning-work even belongs on a college campus, except possibly in a school of divinity (Walvoord, 2008). Who would know how to teach about meaning without reducing it to an exercise in abstract philosophical analysis or without smuggling rigid religious and political biases into the conversation? Also, if it is true that students differ in their intellectual abilities and learning styles, then how would we teach about meaning in such a way that all learners would get something out of it? Finally, some educators claim that because the concept of meaning seems to be so tied into a particular kind of maturity level, any education grounded in meaning-making is sure to go over everyone's heads. Most college students, some campus educators observe, are not noted for either their maturity or their intellectual acuity.

Our response to all of these charges—in addition to listening to and learning from them—is to make the following three points (see also three recent works that take a tack similar to ours: De la Chaumiere, 2004; Kronman, 2007; and Walker and others, 2006, especially Chapters Six and Twelve).

First, in our several decades of experience in higher education, we have heard the meaning questions coming from students of all socioeconomic, racial, and ethnic groups, in all major and minor concentrations of study, in all campus locations, and at all ages and stages of development. Moreover, we are convinced that every student we have ever met is a philosopher (someone who, when encouraged, asks the deeper questions of meaning and purpose, and who, with the aid of gifted educators, can learn to appreciate the *questions* as much as the answers) in careerist disguise. We have yet to meet a student who is not eager to engage in creating a personal meaning framework. It takes longer for some students to come around, of course, but with support from faculty and student affairs administrators, everyone eventually does. Why? Because meaning-making confers benefits on the human species. It is an evolutionary adaptation that has improved our species' chances of survival through the millennia. We hope to demonstrate this fact in the chapters to follow. For now, however, let us say that quarterlife students we have encountered everywhere ask, in their own ways, the philosophical and existential questions that human beings have asked for thousands of years.

Second, let us grant that the kind of interdisciplinary study we urge for meaning-making is difficult to create in higher education. But it does exist in pockets throughout the country. In fact, it has been the academic goal in a number of honors colleges' curricula (Nash & Scott, 2009). Moreover, we believe that interdisciplinary inquiry is a necessary tool for problem solving in such professional schools as business, education, and the health sciences. What could be more practical than this type of education? Social problems cannot be addressed by only one field of study; they require the resources of a number of disciplines to solve them.

Some of the outcomes of this problem-solving will be measurable, and some will be more a matter of self-report; some will be concrete, and some will be attitudinal. If this observation of ours is accurate, then training in meaning-making is one of the essential tools of interdisciplinary problem-solving. The basic questions that we ought always to be asking of ourselves and our students are these: Why and how does the type of career you are preparing for give your life meaning? How will it contribute to the needs of others to make meaning in their own lives? These kinds of questions are calculated to keep us, and our students, honest about our motivations and purposes.

Third, the intellectual argument for structuring a curriculum around meaning-making is very similar to the rationale for a general distribution requirement, a general education minor, a liberal studies degree, or a liberal arts component for all major areas of study. After all, if the poet is right in saying that "nothing human is alien to me," then it is imperative that students investigate just what it is that is human to all of us—beyond the fact that we are infinitely diverse. Even the validity of the poet's assertion itself calls for interdisciplinary examination. If we have nothing in common with our fellow human beings, then how is it possible for us to justify helping them solve their problems without imposing our parochial beliefs and techniques on them? Could it be, therefore, that what is human to all of us is our universal quest for meaning and purpose? We think so—and that's what this book is all about. Come join us on this quest.

About the Authors

Robert J. Nash is an Official University Scholar in the Social Sciences and Humanities at the University of Vermont. He is also the 2009 recipient of the Joseph A. Abruscato Award for Excellence in Research & Scholarship in the College of Education and Social Services. He has published ten books as well as more than one hundred articles, book chapters, monographs, and book reviews in many of the leading journals in education at all levels. His previous book for Jossey-Bass, co-authored with DeMethra L. Bradley and Arthur W. Chickering, was *How To Talk About Hot Topics on Campus: From Polarization to Moral Conversation*, published in 2008. Professor Nash is a nationally acclaimed speaker on a variety of topics.

Michele C. Murray is an experienced university educator and administrator and has developed expertise in Jesuit higher education. She is a frequent presenter at national conferences and is a graduate of the Harvard Institute for Management and Leadership in Education. She currently serves as associate vice president of student development at Seattle University.

Part I

Making Meaning in the Quarterlife

1

Is the Quarterlife Generation Ready for Meaning-Making?

The following questions come up again and again during our many off-campus consultancies on the topic of meaning-making:

- Can college students handle the intellectual complexities of meaning-making?

- Are they mature enough?

- Have they had enough life experience?

- Is the concept of meaning of equal interest to all students?

- Does meaning-making require a particular level of emotional and social intelligence?

In response to these questions, we start off this chapter by describing the mindset of the *quarterlife generation*. We emphasize the big and little meaning questions that the quarterlife generation is asking these days. Following this, we introduce a five-cycle sequence of quarterlife challenges around the issue of choice. Then we introduce one young woman who has wrestled with some of the archetypal quarterlife questions to develop a path of meaning and purpose. We close the chapter with a practical section on how to take advantage of a meaning-making moment in a particular educational setting. (Parts of this chapter appeared in slightly altered form in Nash's article "Crossover Pedagogy," appearing in *About Campus*, 2009, pp. 2–9. Reprinted with permission.)

Quarterlife Challenges

Two of the leading writers on the quarterlife generation (Robbins & Wilner, 2001; Robbins, 2004) believe that this period of life spans the ages from twenty to thirty-five, with significant developmental overlaps for both late teens and pre-midlifers. Thus the quarterlife generation includes most undergraduates as well as most graduate students. Robbins and Wilner think of this period in the adult life narrative as a challenge for the following reasons:

- It is threatening for quarterlifers to face the world on their own, many for the first time, away from the securities of families of origin, earlier schooling, and, for older quarterlifers, familiar jobs, marriages, and surroundings.

- Unprecedented competition for highly specialized jobs in the twenty-first-century world is fierce, and the resultant emotional stress can be devastating.

- The pressure to select the right colleges and universities, the right preprofessional major and minor fields of study, and the right graduate schools, professions, and occupations, in order to succeed later in the work world, can be nerve-racking.

- Friendships are, at best, tentative, and committed, intimate relationships are often put on hold, because so much of one's future is up in the air.

- Quarterlife concerns about success and failure in a changing economy and in an increasingly specialized, technological job market induce intense anxiety, depression, eating disorders, drug abuse, and, in extreme cases, violence and suicide.

- "Do what you love, and love what you do" seems for many quarterlifers to be a near-impossibility, either in college or in the job market, because the expectations are so high to secure future jobs that will confer security, status, wealth, and power benefits.

- Credit card debt, school loans, and personal bankruptcies are out of control.

We prefer not to think of the quarterlife experience as a *crisis* but rather as a series of exciting, real-life possibilities for students to make meaning. Although it is true that some students do live their quarterlife years in a narrative of panic, stress, and insecurity, others live in very different narratives of meaning. Here are some big and little meaning questions (some of the questions, which we have reworded, come from Robbins, 2004) that all quarterlifers are asking, in one way or another, on our campuses, regardless of the particular narratives they may inhabit (note the similarities between these quarterlife questions and some of the existential questions about meaning typically associated with midlife):

- *Hopes and Dreams*—How do I find my passion? When do I let go of my dream? What if I don't get what I want by a certain age? How do I start over, if I find I need to?

When is the right time to make a commitment? Is it possible to have a fulfilling relationship and a fulfilling job at the same time? What if I make the wrong choice on either side? Am I stuck forever?

- *Educational Challenges*—Am I studying what is right for me? Why do I have to be so preoccupied with gearing up for graduate school and a career when I'd just like to enjoy exploring the arts and humanities? How well am I handling the freedom of college and being away from home for the first time? Why does my college experience neglect all the really important questions that come up for me regarding my hopes and dreams for the future?

- *Religion and Spirituality*—What is the right religion for me? Why am I so critical of my childhood religion? Why is it that a noninstitutional spirituality seems, at times, to be so powerful for me? Will my parents be disappointed if I don't remain loyal to the religion of our family? Why does God seem so far away from me on some days and so close at other times? Can any good come from doubting? Do I need a religious faith to be a moral person? Can I be good without God? Is there any other way to make a meaning that is enduring without religion or spirituality? Why is it that so many of my college friends think of religion in such negative terms? Will I be able to make it in the world without experiencing the consolations of organized religion along with its supportive communities? In what religion will I bring up my children, if I have any?

- *Work Life*—Will I always have to choose between doing what I love or making lots of money? Will I ever really look forward to going off to work every day? Is it true that I'll change careers many times before I retire? If, yes, then what's the point of taking all this time to prepare for a particular career? Will I ever find work where I won't feel such stress to produce all the time? Does my work always have to be so competitive and bottom-line? Is it possible to find a career that is congruent with my personal values? Will I eventually have to settle for a career driven by my obligation to pay off the tens of thousands of dollars that I will owe in student loans? What does "balance" look like when work and stress build up? Why is it that I feel I have so much potential, but I am afraid to actualize it? Why am I so haunted by self-doubt?

• *Home, Friends, Lovers, and Family*—Why is it so hard to live alone but also so hard to sustain a relationship? Is there really such a person as a "soul mate"? How will I know when I fall in love with "The One"? Am I loveable? How do I avoid feeling stuck in my relationships? Why can't I find close, enduring friends who stay the course without drifting away? Is there something about me that causes this? Why is the thought of moving back in with my parents so terrible? Now that I've moved away, how do I make friends? Who will be my true friends, will I ever fit in, and how will I know who I can trust?

• *Identity*—Why is adulthood, at one and the same time, so threatening to me yet also so attractive? Why is it that I alternate between thinking that my life is either exciting or boring? How can I stop feeling overwhelmed about everything? Why do I worry so much about how I look? Why can't I like who I am? Will I ever be truly happy with myself? Why do I feel so guilty when others claim I am privileged? Why is everyone so hung up on identity politics? Aren't we all human beings underneath our skin color, sexual orientation, neighborhoods, and private parts?

Many of these questions are part and parcel of life's journey, no matter the journey-taker's age or stage. Still, quarterlifers seem to be experiencing a deluge of doubt and possibility that is unique to that place between adolescence and adulthood. Books and internet resources (Robbins & Wilner, 2001; Robbins, 2004; Steinle, 2005) have been popping up to fill the void. Each of these resources affirms the questions of quarterlife and offers a most welcome comfort to the intended audience: "Quarterlifer, you are not alone!"

Notably, Robbins and Wilner (2001) and Steinle (2005) chose to populate their guides to the quarterlife with the voices and circumstances of real quarterlifers. The young adults featured in these books discard the mask of self-assuredness to reveal the confusion and pain they sometimes experience in trying to find their way. They wonder how to lead a more fulfilling, less "empty" life than the one they know; they express their dismay at the realization that life is not always fair; and contrary to the Pew Research Center findings discussed in the preface, they want to know how to pursue a career that means something to them personally and will make a positive difference in their communities.

Regardless of gender, race, or social class, the respondents for each text underscore how universal many of these questions of meaning are. Although their social identities may frame the context in which they seek clarity, these quarterlifers express the same basic frustrations, excitements, worries, and questions (and even the same answers), regardless of the part their social identities suggest they play in life. Each of them wonders, through their interviews and written responses, whether they will discover a meaning and purpose worth living (and even dying) for.

Cycles of Quarterlife Meaning-Making

The students we have encountered are no different from the quarterlifers represented in print. We find that not only do our quarterlife students ask the same powerful questions, but they also pass through recognizable meaning-making *cycles*. Different from stages or other linear and sequential developmental steps, the cycles of meaning-making in the quarterlife tend to appear and reappear with each new meaning challenge. Some of us are more ready than others to undertake the meaning-making project. Being aware of these cycles helps us to find the best ways to time, fine-tune, and present meaning-making opportunities to the right audiences, at the most appropriate time, and in the most effective manner. However, we are always very cautious in the use of our developmental cycles, because we do not believe that any kind of sequencing should be the last word on who, how, when, and why to teach meaning-making.

If carried to an extreme, developmental ages and stages can often become tight little boxes that slot and plot students throughout their college experience—and, sadly, long afterward. In some ways, we prefer Robert Havinghurst's phrase "developmental tasks." *Cycle* is a metaphor for describing particular sequences of quarterlife development, and, in some senses, the metaphor works very well. But mastery of all the earlier tasks of childhood and early adult development is necessary before quarterlifers can move on to the next sequence (Havinghurst, 1972). The term *cycle* also indicates the somewhat repetitive nature of meaning-making. Meaning develops in spiraling layers over time, and we want to allow for the likelihood that quarterlifers will find themselves revisiting one or another cycle on their way to becoming more fully themselves.

We offer what follows as suggestive and not definitive, as observations based on our informal experiences with quarterlife students over the last several years. (We are indebted to David L. Norton, 1976, for inspiring us to think about the ongoing interplay between seeking self-fulfillment and working for the fulfillment of others. He calls this developing a "philosophy of ethical individualism," and he believes that reconciling these two sometimes conflicting ideals is the challenge of a lifetime for all of us.) The existential theme for each stage is *choice*, with its different configurations, as students travel through the quarterlife cycle of meaning.

Cycle One: *I choose myself.* Quarterlifers realize at some point that they must start to take responsibility for their own lives. This moment of existential awareness may happen suddenly or gradually, over a brief or long period of time, at any age. This narrative of self-awareness and self-construction takes this form: "Only I can live my life for myself. Nobody else can tell me who I am and what I must live for. From this moment on, I'm the one who has to make sense of my life. And I've got almost forever to do it, because I'm young and healthy, and I feel immortal. Even though this independence is challenging, I'm looking forward to being on my own, without anyone telling me what to do."

Cycle Two: *Choosing myself is scary.* Quarterlifers begin to develop a sense of their own finitude. Their self-awareness takes this shape: "I like choosing who I am and who I want to become, but I'm afraid choice carries with it certain risks. I can do anything that I want, it is true, but what is it I really want to do? The people whose advice I respect sometimes want different goals for me than I do. At times I'm afraid of letting down people whom I respect and love. I don't want to disappoint anyone, but I also want to be independent and happy with my own choices about how to live, love, and work. But what is it I can do that is worthwhile? Who should I love? When should I make lifelong commitments, if at all? What should I believe? I need mentors and guides I trust and respect, but who should these people be? I know that others are depending on me to fulfill my promise as an adult, but just what are my duties to myself and my duties to others? What should I do when these duties are in conflict? Is it really possible for me to live a life of personal integrity when every choice I make stands to harm or to help others, and I've got to decide whose side I'm on?"

Cycle Three: *I'm not really as free to choose as I thought I was.* In the third cycle, quarterlifers become far more aware of their own boundedness. They realize that their choices are limited by their external circumstances, their individual temperaments, and other conditions over which they have little control. They still relish the idea of being autonomous agents who are able to construct their own meanings, but now the whole experience takes on a sharper, existential edge. It is more tuned in to the limitations of finite existence and bounded choice-making, as well as to what the Greeks called *fortuna* ("chance" or "luck"). No longer is the quarterlifer a superman or superwoman.

Happiness is, at best, a fleeting thing, and the months and years are as passing seasons. Now these questions arise: "Is there any enduring meaning in my life? When I've done everything I'm supposed to do, will this guarantee that I'll be in a satisfying relationship and a good job, and enjoying my life? If I've worked hard to achieve my goals, will this mean that I'll finally be happy and fulfilled? I know so many people who, to the outside world, appear to be incredible successes. But they often tell me they feel so unsettled and so restless. Some of them are even doing self-destructive things. If all goes well when I graduate, I will still have more than two-thirds of my life to live. But I don't ever want to be in a state of depression about opportunities lost. Where do I go from here? Will I be able to settle for less than I want, knowing that there are limits on my ambitions?"

Cycle Four: *I'm becoming more, not less, cautious in my choices.* During this cycle of meaning-making, quarterlifers start to realize that age, events, and added responsibilities are taking hold of them . . . almost by surprise. Often, when we listen to quarterlifers at this time of meaning-making, we are reminded of a Woody Allen line: "I'm not afraid of death. I just don't want to be there when it happens." Their self-talk covers more than just death, of course; it usually takes the following form: "Life is happening to me almost when I'm not even looking, and, lo and behold, I'm getting older. Who I see in the mirror every morning is not who I used to see. Now what? I've still got so much left that I want to do, but I'm realizing that what I want to do might actually take more time than I will actually have. How can I avoid slipping into despair, frustration, and just plain exhaustion?

"Will people still love and respect me, even though I probably won't be as active a risk-taker as I want to be? In my later years, what in the world will I have in common with people who are younger and more creative and vital than I am? Will I look too eccentric and settled to them, completely out of touch—the way that my parents and teachers look to me now? It won't be long before I'm out in the world, hustling like everyone else, and I'm really afraid of losing my passion for life. I never want to compromise my integrity, or lose my sense of humor, or give up on my faith that there is some force greater than me in the universe."

Cycle Five: *I will choose my meanings to the best of my ability, and I will try not to live a life of regret or bitterness.* In the fifth cycle, meaning-making becomes less concerned with the navel-gazing questions of self and more concerned with developing a genera-tive, outward-facing philosophy. This cycle is less about resignation for quarterlifers than it is about authentic realization both in and out of community. *Authenticity* is the realization that we are the *auth*ors (each word has the same Greek word root—*authentes*—meaning "one who makes or originates something") of our own lives. In some ways, this cycle is a restatement of Cycle One, only now it is grounded in a narrative of existential responsibility (*response-ability*—the ability to respond) to others as well as to self:

"Yes, it is true that I am the author of my own life, but there are limits. There is around me a circle beyond which I cannot pass, but within that circle I have tremendous freedom to make choices; choices that can be as satisfying, exhilarating, and life-expanding as any I've ever made. Only now I need to proceed more carefully, not thinking only of myself but also being willing to respond to the needs of others. I am not a completely free agent, and I recognize now that there is a balance between freedom and responsibility. I live in a complex social network that imposes certain duties and obligations on me. Having said this, however, I also realize that this social network also confers a wonderful sense of freedom. I am not completely alone. I have others on whom I can rely to help me make wise and good choices."

Introducing Maigret Lisee Fay: The Life and Times of a Cycle-Five Quarterlifer

Inspired by a presentation of the quarterlife cycles of meaning that we made, Maigret wrote to us about her take on her quarterlife experiences. We were astounded by the insights she shared and asked her permission to include her story in our book. Much to our delight, Maigret agreed. Unlike some of the other quarterlife portraits and vignettes we will share throughout, we do not filter Maigret through our own lenses as mentors for meaning-making. Instead, we want Maigret to speak for herself in this piece, with her own chosen title.

Twenty-Seven: Exactly Where I Am Supposed to Be

I'm sitting here thinking about what life is *supposed* to be. Then there's what it *is*. Where do they meet? Nobody has room for both. So we conform to the *supposed* to, or accept the *is*. Or, we balance in the middle. I AM the middle at 27. I am not settled, but not restless either. I'm not among the newlyweds with baby on the way, but I am also not feeling that my life is missing anything right now. I am exactly where I am supposed to be.

I offer my thoughts on acceptance, perfectionism, career, and reflection and how these play a role in, and contribute to, my quest for meaning as a quarterlifer. I need each of these components in order to create meaning in my life. My approaches to these allow me to maintain a feeling of contentment and centeredness, which ward off the pressures and uncertainties that plague many quarterlifers. In sharing this reflection, I hope to provide a different perspective for others in their quarterlife phase, and I hope to better understand myself.

Acceptance

I believe Paul Tillich's words that "He who risks and fails can be forgiven. He who never risks and never fails is a failure in his whole being." This is why recently, I embraced the "control my own destiny" mentality over the "let go so things can fall into place" mentality.

(Continued)

Long story short: I risked; I am forgiven; I am back to letting go. Accepting myself and forgiving myself for mistakes made has been a great source of meaning-making in my life. I like the person that I am, and I want to be present to my life. Before we speak of getting along with others, first we must get along with ourselves. I love what has come before by respecting my past. I love what is ahead by not obsessing over it. In being happy within myself, I can enjoy life and not be constantly searching for something else. To me, that is truly being open. The moments when I stop trying to figure it all out or come up with all of the answers are the times that I discover the most meaning and acceptance of my current place in life.

Perfectionism

The danger in giving in too much to perfectionism in my quarterlife, when everything seems to be "up in the air" already, is that I will miss out on living life and celebrating my successes. I think perfection-ism could also cause me to miss out on learning lessons from my mistakes. If I am too caught up in trying to "avoid messes" then I lose time for appreciating the moment. In his *Confession*, Leo Tolstoy describes his battle with perfectionism. He says, "The starting point of it all was, of course, moral perfection, but this was soon replaced by a belief in overall perfection . . . a desire to be better in the eyes of other people. And this effort . . . was very quickly displaced by a long-ing to be . . . more renowned, more important, wealthier than others." Tolstoy became so consumed with being perfect and being seen as perfect by others, that his values shifted. His life was centered on an unattainable goal and dissatisfaction followed.

A little bit of perfectionism can be a good thing, but too much will stir up an already overflowing pot as a quarterlifer. I already have enough decisions to make about how I want to live my life and how I want to develop the meaning in my life; I do not need the added pressure of trying to make that fit some unattainable mold determined by a source outside of myself. I will continue to make messes as I navigate my life—a good life is full of many little messes, and sometimes in cleaning up the mess we find our meaning.

Career and Calling

I used to have this fork. It came from a set of utensils made for toddlers. This was back in the '80s though, so children's utensils were still made of metal, just like their adult counterparts. Not all that plastic, rubbery, safety stuff we have now. I remember we had four each of forks, spoons, and butter knives. The handles were white, porcelain animals wearing blue overalls. The spoons were cats, the knives were bunnies, and the forks were dogs. One of the forks had accidentally gone through the dishwasher at some point. The steam and heat proved too much for the little puppy and he cracked. After the accident, his ear was gone along with half of his face. He was broken, fragile. The break had exposed the smooth, white insides of the porcelain. I remember caressing the place where the dog's skull would have been, had he been a living thing; I was very attached to this damaged fork. As a little girl, I *had* to be the one using that fork at dinner. I believed I could protect it and prove to my parents that it did not need to be thrown out. To me, it was just as good as all the others. I remember all of this vividly.

Even at such a young age, I had a sense of caring that I think I was born with. I had to care for the fragile, broken fork that no one else wanted. I don't think anyone taught me to love the *broken* and neglected, I think this was the part of me I brought into the world. Of course, this value of mine was reinforced and strengthened by my upbringing, but I had a natural inclination towards helping.

Now I find myself teaching children with autism as an interventionist. Maybe it was chance that brought me here, but as I learn more about my work, I learn more about my own values. In reading my agency's code of ethics for a previous course I took, I came across one principle that struck a chord in me. Our "Societal Obligation"

(Continued)

states that "Employees ... shall, through their endeavors and community affiliations, advance the understanding of the nature of ... developmental disabilities. ... They will strive for the de-stigmatization of these conditions, and for the amelioration of human suffering. They will work to the best of their abilities to contribute to the welfare of the community as a whole, and to promoting the dignity, self-determination, and worth of the people they serve." This is what I do. When I read this to myself, I literally overflow with passion and drive. It is an incredible feeling that no words, no image I can conjure up could come close to portraying. You just have to trust me when I say *this means something to me*.

One of my keys to happiness and a meaningful life is doing a job that means something to me. The job I have found for myself really is a vocation. It is my "summons or strong inclination to a particular ... course of action." I feel compelled to do this work. If it is going to be what I spend the majority of my time doing, then I have to believe in it. I do this work to "become" more myself, not just to "acquire" a paycheck. That, combined with causing what I believe to be a positive impact on another person's life, is all I really need to feel successful.

Reflection

To truly create a meaning-filled life, I also make time for reflection. Knowing myself is necessary, especially when working intensively and directly with people, like individuals with autism where I will experience physically, emotionally and mentally draining days. Since this work matters to me, I don't want to crack under the pressure. I want to be able to provide therapeutic support for a child no matter how I am feeling internally, while still validating and accepting my internal feelings at some point. This is why I value my ability to write about my life up to this point. Some may see it as self-indulgent, or without much of a point. However, writing my story allows me to better myself by getting to know what really matters to me and why. I apply this every day in my one-on-one work with people who are outside of the "mainstream." I ask myself questions to make sure I am being thoughtful in my meaning making. Friedrich Nietzsche said, "We only hear questions that we are able to answer." I think it is necessary to open yourself up to the questions that don't have answers. You might just find all the answers you need. You might just find yourself.

Exactly Where I Am Supposed to Be

I believe we can lead several different lives within a lifetime, but only one life at a time. Whenever we choose to lead a certain life, we follow its particular path. This also means choosing *not* to lead other possible lives at that time. Being limited to one path at a time is really a great gift, because it allows us to fully enjoy the present moment. Some things I can plan, some are out of my hands, but I believe that I am exactly where I am supposed to be right now. Each day can bring a new struggle, or a new release. My definition and awareness of my own identity helps me to make the decisions of how I will walk each path I am presented with.

What sometimes makes these decisions challenging is the fact that quarterlifers today are in an unprecedented situation: we have all of the options in the world, but now there are *no* guidelines or rules for choosing the right path. Subsequently, I believe the need for trusted guidance and a support system are, in some ways, more important than at other transitional life stages. Those of us facing the transition from college life into the Real World need people to turn to who understand the plethora of options facing us. Having professors and professional mentors that are aware of the challenges facing quarterlifers and the common themes of people in this period of life, will help us to navigate our way to a more meaningful and fulfilling journey.

The problem, or "quarterlife crisis," really emerges when you cling too tightly to where your life is *supposed* to be or allow the negative thoughts about where your life *is* run rampant. Compassionate educators and mentors have the opportunity to help their quarterlife students be fulfilled by the *middle*.

What Cycle-Five Quarterlifers Can Teach Other Quarterlifers

Maigret's reflection offers the following lessons for quarterlifers:

- It is possible to live one's life whole. Integration and wholeness (the meaning of integrity) are achievable, if one is willing to work for it. At least for some quarterlifers, integrity need not be a pipe dream.

- It is possible for us to match our inner and outer lives, at least some of the time. For example, Maigret understands that her inner life always defines and shapes her outer life. Therefore she takes time out of her busy schedule to look for what we might call "inner" and "outer" narrative overlaps. For her, being in the world in a way that reflects her full humanity is more than just an abstract philosophical question. It is a very practical one.

- It is possible to find a close symmetry between our ideals and our realities. It is not necessary for ideals and realities always to be at war with one another. What we hold by way of our most praiseworthy convictions can be translated into actual commitments.

- Maigret demonstrates that one can live in a variety of sometimes conflicting roles and narratives without becoming schizophrenic or causing harm to others. She is working hard to achieve balance in her life.

- Maigret is finding a way to integrate both heart and head in her work without compromising either one—without putting blinders on her feelings or on her thinking. This is an ongoing struggle for all of us, because either our heads seem to want to control our hearts or vice versa. Maigret is seeking a wholeness of head and heart. She is rapidly becoming what we might call a "whole being."

Two Potential Meaning-Making Moments

Quarterlife students like Maigret, representing all ages and stages, frequently come to us in our roles as faculty and staff, directly seeking our advice about the meaning of their lives. We sometimes look at them with bewilderment and helplessness, but more often with empathy and solidarity. How many of us in higher education have really taken the time to examine the meaning of our own lives? Most of us know that we were born, we live, love, and learn, and then we will die. All human beings, no matter their educational level, wonder if there is anything more to life than this "eternal recurrence," the Hindu view that time repeats itself cyclically *ad infinitum.*

Approximately 120 billion human beings, since the beginning of human time, have lived this repetitive cycle (Dillard, 1999). Nobody escapes it. Few are remembered for long. One of the universal meaning questions that all of us ask in our own ways has to do with the inevitability of our eventual death and the short shelf life of others' memories of us: will we be remembered even months or years after our death, let alone decades or centuries? Or will we merely melt into one enormous statistic as tens of billions of others have before us? Does any of this really matter?

One of our recent quarterlife students recently spoke to us about a philosophy professor of his (let us call him Dr. So-What-Now-What), with whom he had a love-hate relationship. He told us that this man, steeped in Nietzsche, Schopenhauer, Buddhism, and Hinduism, always made the following comment over and over again to his classes, whenever students were arrogant enough to think that they had come up with a sensational new insight about the meaning of life: "Such as it always was. Such as it always is. And such as it always will be. So what? Now what?" Little did this student know that his philosophy professor was restating Schopenhauer: "The true philosophy of history lies in perceiving that, in all the endless changes and motley complexity of events, it is only the self-same unchangeable being which is before us." Perhaps his professor was even trying, in his own way, to provoke a thoughtful response from his students. Perhaps not. The student was never sure.

We believe this professor could help many of his Cycle-Two, Cycle-Three, and Cycle-Four quarterlife students to think in a different way about the meaning of history in their own lives by getting them to unpack, and discuss, Schopenhauer's short narrative passage on time, change, and changelessness. At the very least, and even though this professor's familiar riposte always manages to bring his students up short, he might be able to help quarterlife students to look deeper within themselves to accept their responsibility to make meaning of their lives, no matter how repetitive and predictable these lives might seem. If our developmental sequence of quarterlife questions is accurate, then all of our students, each in his or her own way, are ready to tackle this philosophy professor's take on the meaning of history.

Whether intentionally or not, this professor creates meaning-making moments in his classroom, and we commend him for this. But for quarterlife students his words should not be left hanging; they are potential stimulants that cry out for continuing conversation, clarification, and interpretation. For example, quarterlifers at all stages of the developmental cycle need the professor's help to think further about the following types of meaning-making questions: Is there a "true philosophy of history," as Schopenhauer says? Does history have a purpose? A fate? A design? Or is it all a matter of brute chance? Or is the "purpose" nothing more than some historian's pet theory imposed on it? Why does Schopenhauer choose the words "motley" and "complexity" to describe historical events? Also, in what sense is there "only the self-same unchangeable being" before us? Do quarterlifers believe this? Why did Schopenhauer believe this? In other words, the philosophy professor could become a philosophical counselor, a meaning-making educator, if only for a little while.

Schopenhauer's philosophy of history raises universal questions for all of us, whether we are quarterlifers or not. We all need to come to terms with the fact that tens of billions of people have been born, lived, and died since the beginning of human time. Some of these 120 billion people lived life better, of course, and some lived it worse. Some died living; some lived dying. Some lived for the next life; some lived for the now. Some lived without a concern for meaning; some found it impossible to live without meaning.

The meaning of life's ceaseless ebb and flow is not for Dr. So-What-Now-What to assert for his students, of course. Nor is it for any of us to declare. This is each quarterlifer's task to discover for him- or herself. Therefore, as meaning-making educators, we must ask ourselves: how can we help each of our quarterlifers to understand and respond to such a large question, given where each might reside in their unique narratives of meaning? How can we cut it down to size? We think quarterlifers are more than ready to consider questions like these. In fact, we believe that this entire generation is capable of responding to such questions, at all points throughout their years of meaning-making. It is our responsibility to know which quarterlife sequence each of our students is living in and then be ready to ask them the appropriate questions, just as we have with Maigret, whose responses we read in an earlier section.

One more example will suffice. Another of our quarterlifers, a junior English major, remarked that he was more and more becoming a creature of rituals and routines. In the words of Victor Hugo, one of his favorite authors, whom he quoted frequently, he was trying to "recover the ground beneath my feet." He went on to say, in Hugo's words, that he did not want to become a "rock that is massive, haughty, and immobile" as he got older, had a family, became successful in a career, and accumulated possessions. Instead, he wanted to strive for *gelassenheit*, or "letting be." As we talked, Robert asked him what advice he might give to other quarterlifers like himself. He said: "Live and let live. Practice some generosity toward others, especially toward those whose choices, ideas, and lifestyles you dislike. Let go, and let be. Enjoy. In the end, it's all a matter of taste and temperament anyway, right?" In many ways, Maigret in the previous section would agree, even though she might choose to live these responses in a different way—through service to others.

It was clear to us that this student's comments were an outgrowth of the quarterlife meaning-making cycle in which he lived. Hugo spoke directly to many of his Cycle-Three and Cycle-Four fears. Equally clear to us, his comments also confirmed the fact that we are all more alike than not, even though our individual stories, phases, and stages are singular. We all have a need to tell our stories in our own special ways and to have others tell theirs as well. What binds us all together is the universality of our questions, the overlaps in our stories of meaning, and the commonality of our psychobiological needs. What sometimes separates us, though, are the unique, age- and sequence-related stories we fashion in order to deal with our particular cries for meaning. But this separation need not resign us to a life of isolation and loneliness. We tell our stories of meaning, as do most other quarterlifers, to reach across the terrifying chasm of meaninglessness and separation to make contact with others like us.

Robert often says this to his classes at the beginning of a new semester:

> I make the assumption that each of us is all about discovering and making meanings that will sustain us in the days and years ahead. Let us, therefore, agree that your meanings may not work for me and vice versa. Therefore, please resist the temptation to foist your "successful" formula for finding the keys to your existence on me, and I will promise to return the favor. Meanwhile, whenever it is necessary during our time with one another, let us agree to huddle together within the protective cocoon of

our mutual humanity for the comfort and affirmation we need when things go dismally wrong, or for that matter, ecstatically right. Be willing to share your meanings with the rest of us, and we will do the same with you. Beyond this, we cannot, indeed, dare not, go.

Finally, here is what Dr. So-What-Now-What might have said to that student to draw out his thoughts regarding Schopenhauer's thesis of eternal recurrence. Granted that we are born. We live. We love. We learn. We get old. We die. Do you think there is anything more? Does anything really change? Or is *everything* change? Do we read the meaning of our lives from the past to the present, or from the present to the past, or from the present to the future? How do you read the meaning of your life up to the present time? Are we living in fast or slow motion? What speed are you living in? Is it all about "infinite recurrence"—Bill Murray's *Groundhog Day,* over and over, and then it's just beginning once more? Or is it only about the "eternal now," past and future beside the point, the present moment all there is—never duplicable, no facsimiles, be here in the moment a la Ram Dass, nothing more, nothing less? Finally, do you think Philo was right centuries ago when he said that the "true name of eternity is Today." What do you think he meant by that comment?

How One Quarterlifer Created Meaning in a Seminar

What follows is the personal statement of a quarterlife student, Meredith Long, after taking a semester-long course with Robert. We reproduce this personal reflection because it demonstrates well two points: first, most quarterlifers, if given a chance, are willing to pursue the meaning-making project with great intensity and enthusiasm; second, quarterlifers experience the meaning-making project in such different ways. This quarterlifer starts her reflection with a quote from one of the authors she read during the term.

The point of non-vocational higher education is, instead, to help students realize that they can reshape themselves—they can rework the self-image foisted on them by their past, the self image that makes them competent citizens, into a new self-image, one that they themselves have helped to create (Rorty, 1999, p. 118).

For me, this statement by Rorty more than adequately describes my experience in this course. I have been introduced to many new perspectives, and have questioned, refined, and redefined many of my own. It was refreshing to be able to converse so freely with fellow "philosophers." I have learned much about myself, my fellow class-mates, and my teacher through the sharing of our personal narratives. It seems amazing to me that twenty or so perfect strangers could grow so close in such a short amount of time. It just goes to show that we all have more in common than we might realize.

I would say that, according to Nel Noddings (1995), in a way, we are all existentialists in that "existentialists often choose stories rather than argumentation as their mode of communication. They do this because they believe that life is not the unfolding of a logical plan; one cannot argue from trustworthy premises what a life should be like or how it should be lived. Rather, meaning is created as we live our lives reflectively. Stories give us accounts of the human struggle for meaning. They inspire and frighten us. They tell us how we might be—for better or worse—if we choose to act this way or that" (p. 62).

I believe this proof-text from Noddings beautifully sums up what we have accomplished together this semester. In the beginning of the semester, we were introduced to the "art" of moral conversation and scholarly personal narrative writing. Both individually and collec-tively we reflected on readings, conversations, and personal stories, and then we attempted to create meaning on both a personal and communal level. Our classroom served as our own community, within which we were able to create a safe haven, where the free flow of ideas and sharing of personal experiences were encouraged and supported. We were able to share personal accounts of our own struggle for meaning, free from judgment. At times I was inspired, at others deeply saddened, and others still, surprised by how much my own narrative overlapped with those of some of my classmates.

I know I make meaning in my daily life by simply appreciating the fact that I am here. I am lucky because I have people around me whom I deeply love and who support me. I am passionate about the career I am pursuing. I am in touch with my spirituality most when I am outside, surfing, snowboarding, riding my bike, or hiking with my dog. The way in which my mind and body work together in harmony centers me. I feel at peace. I know that there is pain and suffering in the world. Sometimes things seem unfair and don't make sense to us. It is during these times I believe it is most important to connect with others and to live reflectively.

I am not sure I believe in God in the traditional sense or as an ultimate meaning of life, but I do believe in living the best way I know how. I believe in living with passion and authenticity, helping others when I can, enjoying the things I love to do, seeing the world, experiencing different cultures, being healthy in a way that exercises and enriches my mind, body, and soul. I believe in having the courage and honesty to take my life for what I believe it to be, and to make the most of it each day. I will continue to question myself and the world around me as well as share my experiences with others in hopes that they will, in turn, share theirs with me. I believe this process is necessary in order to continue to develop my own life-narrative. Thank you for everything.

From Quarterlife Questions to Meaning for a Lifetime

For Robbins and Wilner (2001), the quarterlife years, beginning around age twenty, are full of questions that poise emerging adults on the precipice of change. Responsibility. Relationships. Definitions of success. Careers. Values and beliefs. All of these seem to be up for grabs as adolescence begins to give way to adulthood. The old ways of thinking, sensing, feeling, and believing fall away, and college students attempt to cobble together new ways that will carry them into the next stage of their lives. The feeling of crisis, Robbins and Wilner point out, occurs when the old ways have crumbled, but nothing substantial has risen to take their place.

By the time traditional-aged college students receive their baccalaureate diplomas, they will have been in school for sixteen to eighteen consecutive years. For many of them, graduation day represents the tremendous pride of accomplishment alongside the crippling fear of the unknown. To the best of their recollection, they have never *not* been students. To the best of their recollection, September means a return to school, a return to a comfortable way of life. Whether they have firm post-graduation plans or not, many students panic at the thought of entering the world that lies vast and mysterious before them. The rules change after college, and they are not sure whether they know the new game.

In the next chapter, we examine two philosophical approaches to meaning and meaning-making—existentialism and postmodernism.

2

Exploring the Meaning of Meaning

Existentialism and Postmodernism

I n this chapter, we attempt to clarify the meaning of the *concept of meaning* within the framework of existentialism and post-modernism. (In our Resources section, at the end of the book, we present several other, related approaches.) In doing this, we provide a bit of philosophical, sociohistorical, and educational perspective on the existential meaning of meaning. Also, we introduce a series of down-to-earth, meaning-generating questions, with a strong existentialist/postmodern flavor, that can guide students in their ongoing examinations of what gives their lives meaning. To frame these questions, in the Resources we introduce the reader to the work of the existential logotherapist Viktor Frankl (Frankl, 1963, 1979, 2000). We show how Frankl's framework, and other psychotherapists' as well, can be useful to those of us who are directly engaged in the meaning-making process with students.

First, however, we begin with a real-life scenario of a particular student on one of our campuses who is experiencing a crisis of meaning, even though she is about to graduate summa cum laude in her double major of history and political science. She is also a member of one of the oldest Phi Beta Kappa chapters in the nation, an officer in her national sorority, and an innovative editor-in-chief of her college newspaper. On paper, her academic record is impeccable—indeed, enviable. She appears to be an outstanding candidate for graduate work in one or the other of her disciplines, or for admission into a professional school, if she so chooses. Although Amy does seem to be an extreme case, her struggles with making meaning are universal. Here is her story.

Amy's Meaning Dilemma

Although Amy has amassed a record of accomplishments that makes her the envy of her college friends, she is a modest person. She fills a room with her considerable charisma and power, even though her physical stature is slight. In spite of these gifts, however, Amy is also miserable and unhappy, more often than she wishes to admit. She is a restless soul who has experimented, at times, with a variety of drugs and at frequent intervals has engaged in indiscriminate sex and alcohol abuse. Moreover, she is someone who, to this day, battles with a serious eating disorder. Even though she was raised by two fairly devout Christian parents, Amy has chosen to live outside her parents' faith tradition, and her life seems to be bereft of any metaphysical meaning and purpose that might sustain her during her troubled times.

As a self-acknowledged skeptic, Amy has turned her back on organized religion. Moreover, she has refused to take the time to explore any possible benefits that an inner-directed spirituality might offer her. She asks too many questions of religious authorities and friends, and she gets too few answers to satisfy her. Dogmas and doctrines turn her off, as do her friends' well-meaning accounts of their semi-ecstatic spiritual experiences. She seems always to be the doubter, the outsider looking in, the person who, as she puts it, has no "feel" for either religious rituals or a sense of spiritual transcendence. Amy refuses to distinguish between being religious and being spiritual, because for her they are both the same. They require a leap into the unknown that she is unwilling to take.

Seemingly without warning, Amy can become melancholic and despairing. She sometimes succumbs to an anxiety so profound, and to migraine headaches so pounding, and to a personal confusion that is so impenetrable, that all anyone who loves her can do is to hold her, comfort her, and wait for the raging storm of turmoil within her to subside. She often lives her life in a precarious dance with fear, and she dreads the thought of losing her grip and falling into a hole with no bottom. She yearns for a certainty that she can build her life on, because everything seems to be so up in the air. She is tired of living her life immersed in one personal, existential challenge after another, one ethical dilemma after another, and never being able to reach a final solution that is satisfying.

But deep down, Amy is smart enough to know that certainty is an illusion. She understands that life is a crapshoot, and that accidents can happen anytime and anyplace and usually do. She realizes that no truth is guaranteed, especially the truths of those who claim to be in possession of an infallible revelation of one kind or another that will redeem her, and others, forever. Unfortunately, this existential awareness of uncertainty offers Amy little comfort over the long term. She is growing increasingly despairing about life's prospects. She is not ready to enter the job market, or to pursue a doctorate, or to enter law school. She is just not ready to get on with her life. She is not ready to make a serious relational commitment. In her own mind, Amy exists in a kind of surreal limbo totally devoid of either meaning or purpose.

Amy finds herself looking to the future with a combination of anxiety and dread. Her most common response to her condition lately is to express a series of loud, resigned sighs whenever she gets down on herself and others. Amy knows that this is no way to live a life that, on the surface, seems so full of promise. She is ashamed and frustrated, particularly when others tell her that she has everything to live for. She wonders increasingly what this "everything" might be. At present, she lives much of her life in a blank torpor going through the motions, and no amount of university counseling or antidepressant medications has been able to help dispel her malaise.

Existential Perspectives on Meaning

Like the vast majority of college students whom we have met during this first decade of the third millennium, Amy is on a troubled journey to make meaning of her life. Most of the time, there seems to be little that we can do for such students other than to be there with generous amounts of affirmation and encouragement and, of course, compassion. Like so many students today, Amy leads a fragmented life. She often experiences good and evil as interchangeable aspects of her daily existence, and much of the time she can't tell one from the other. The freedom to create her own life in her own way is good, to be sure, but it also carries with it the terror of failure, isolation, and hopelessness. Although it is easy to recommend cure-all antidotes for her terrible angst, there is no guarantee that any one of them will be helpful. If this is true, then what exactly are campus educators to do for the growing army of meaning-challenged students like Amy who arrive on our campuses?

Those of us who serve students throughout the campus also experience similar kinds of doubts, confusions, and fears. To deny this is simply disingenuous. Like Amy, we, too, need plausible—indeed, inspiring—reasons to rise to the constant challenges of our work every day. Psychological burnout has long been an issue for caregivers whose professional vocations seem, at times, to be nothing more than an endless cycle of crisis and response, crisis and response, over and over again. These amount, in the end, to what one of our students crudely and morbidly described as "continually pissing on fires that never get extinguished, until the time comes when we, ourselves, burn up." It is during these times that the perennial, existential questions of meaning surface for us and for all the Amys we see every day on our campuses.

Here is an abbreviated sample of some of these larger, meta-meaning questions that we hear more and more, both in and out of classrooms: Why? So what? What sense does it make? Who cares? Is there a larger purpose to any of this beyond brute luck and dumb circumstance? How much freedom do I really have to craft a life? Why should I even bother? What do I believe anyway? Do I have any purpose in my life that will make my life worth living and loving—especially during those terrible times when it looks like everything is falling apart? What is worth knowing? What do I stand for? What should I believe? What should I hope for? Whom should I love? What is the source of my joy? Why do I and others suffer? Why should I be moral? What is the difference between faith, spirituality, and religion, and which do I have? Does my life have a special purpose?

These types of questions are existential in nature. Thus they require an understanding of some of the basic premises of the philosophy of existentialism. What follows, then, is a brief account of existentialism, along with our own creative reconstruction of this philosophy of meaning—so its principles can then be adapted to the meaning-making initiatives that we advance in the chapters that follow.

Setting the Record Straight on Existentialism

Historically, the movement called *existentialism* (a word first coined by Viktor Frankl to point out that there is no predetermined, metaphysical essence; there is only being or existence, and it is up to us to create our own values and meanings in a world where all the older certainties have disappeared) was a reaction to the Renaissance and the Enlightenment modernist periods in Western Europe and the United States. These intellectual and political revolutions gave birth to freedom from the religious hegemony that had existed throughout the middle ages in the Western world. The dawn of science and technology ushered in a new modernist worldview—one grounded in the values of rationality, independence, individualism, and self-determination (see Tarnas, 1991, pp. 388–394).

However, the downside of these positive values (often taken to an extreme in the late nineteenth and early to mid-twentieth centuries) resulted in the formation of large collectivist societies and a reductionist approach to science and technology. *Scientism* became the new religion of the modern period, and large political and commercial bureaucracies grew more and more powerful, as individuals got swallowed up in the modern, state-controlled system. Communitarian societies gave way to huge collectivist (and communist) social orders. The glories associated with the phenomenon of technocratic, economic, and military modernization in the Western world were short-lived. Many of these modernistic innovations set the stage for the horrific conditions of world wars, nuclear arsenals, holocausts, gulags, fascism, and nazism. It was under these conditions that the philosophy of existentialism emerged.

Much has been written by critics about the *downside* of existentialism: its alleged nihilism, atheism, angst, spiritual vapidity, sense of the absurd, and terrible isolation and loneliness (see Johnson, 1988; Ford, 2007). Maslow once dismissed existentialism because it appealed mainly to "high I.Q. whiners." Indeed, existentialism itself, as it evolved in the writings of Heidegger, Sartre, and Camus, bears at least some degree of responsibility for this bad press. These philosophers and writers made it a point to focus their examination of the human condition on such themes as individual suffering, death, anxiety, uncertainty, dread, nausea, helplessness, pointlessness, and godlessness. For these writers, God had forever disappeared from the world, meaninglessness prevailed everywhere, there were no more universal values that could bind people together in enduring social relationships, and human beings were now "condemned to be free," in the words of Sartre. All of this gave rise to a widespread sense that meaning and purpose were at best ephemeral pursuits and at worst bound to end in failure. Thus existentialism created a mood that many considered to be one of gloom, doom, and despair.

The Upside of Existentialism

In contrast to the preceding description, we wish to emphasize the *upside* of existentialism, as elucidated by such thinkers as Frankl, Tillich, Jaspers, Buber, Marcel, Yalom, and Cupitt (see Schrader,

1967). This is the dimension of existentialism that is optimistic, responsible, authentic, life-affirming, inspiring, and creative. This is the invaluable meaning-making side of existentialism (a precursor to more optimistic forms of postmodernism), and we believe it has the potential to be one of the most functional tools in helping college students to create positive meaning for their lives. Therefore we ground our understanding of existentialism in the following reconstructed principles:

• Abstract categories and neat conceptual systems fail to grasp the fundamental mystery of human existence. There is always something more, something beyond human comprehension.

• Those of us in the academic world need to raise questions with students about the "human predicament," dealing with such issues as alienation, anxiety, inauthenticity, dread, sense of nothingness, transience, and anticipation of death. No matter how much we sugarcoat these issues, or ridicule them in the disdainful tone of Maslow, or deny them as irrelevant to the purposes of the academy, students still need to learn how to confront and deal with them. In fact, faculty and administrators need to do this as well. Why? Because these issues are the unavoidable, sometimes daily, reminders that everything around us is finite, temporal, and ephemeral. This includes fame, fortune, love, and pleasure, but also obscurity, poverty, hate, and pain.

• Oh, that all of us finite creatures—administrators, faculty, and students alike—could live our lives heeding the advice of the most famous existential therapist in the United States. Here is what Irvin D. Yalom (2008) says: "Keep in mind the advantage of remaining aware of death, of hugging its shadow to you. Such awareness can integrate the darkness with your spark of life and enhance your life while you still have it. *The way to value life, the way to feel compassion for others, the way to love anything with greatest depth is to be aware that these experiences are destined to be lost* [original italics]" (p. 147).

• Although the universe may seem to have no rational direction or creative scheme, and though it sometimes seems to be without intrinsic meaning and seems absurd, there is still more to life than meets the rational eye. William James called this the "More." St. Ignatius referred to it as "magis," that which brings greater glory to God. Carl Jung called it the "Inconceivable God." And Paul Tillich called it "Ultimate Concern." Our students wonder why they do not have the opportunity, both in their seminars and in places other than chapels on campus, to talk more about matters of faith, mystery, spirit, and transcendence. Recently, for example, one of Robert's students, while meeting with him over coffee, made the following unsolicited remark: "I just finished reading the most amazing book—*The Little Book of Atheist Spirituality* (Comte-Sponville, 2006)—that my girlfriend gave me for my birthday. She is an out-atheist, but she makes it a point to call herself a 'spiritual atheist.' She sees no contradiction here, and, now, after reading this book, neither do I. I have changed so many of my stereotypes about religion and spirituality. Reading this book, and discussing the ideas with her, was better than 90 percent of the courses I have taken at this university."

• In spite of Nietzsche's claim that "God is dead," and the postmodern pronouncement that there are no more "grand moral narratives" to anchor our values and ethics, people still need to be responsible for their actions. One of the reasons why many of our students turn away from the postmodern skepticism of so many humanities courses is that they have searched in vain there for some kind of moral ground on which to stand—ground that does not shake and wobble when they need a firm foundation for making ethical decisions. In hypotheses such as the death of all grand moral narratives, the humanities can create the space for the open-ended meaning conversations that students are so hungry to have.

• Death is inevitable and final, and, despite our denials and evasions, it awaits all of us. Our responsibility as higher educators is to help students cope with, and overcome, the anxiety and avoidance usually associated with this reality. Students must understand that they are not immortal, and they will not live forever; that aging and dying are necessary dimensions of being fully human; and that life truly begins when one's finitude is fully grasped. Therefore, the one question worth asking every single day is this: Given the fact that I will die—who knows when? possibly tomorrow, possibly in a thousand tomorrows, possibly in ten thousand tomorrows—how then do I choose to live my life right now (Yalom, 2008)? We find that a question like this focuses students' attention very quickly. The brute fact of death and impermanence hovers over them even at their young ages, because many of them have lost loved ones to illness, accident, or aging.

• How can we solve the dilemma of using our freedoms, hard-won from the older, dominating religious and political myths, to re-create ourselves and our world in the absence of those traditional gods and authority figures? If, as some existentialists claim, there are no final, unimpeachable answers to be found in the consoling metaphysical fictions of the past, where then do we go to learn how to be free and purposeful in our daily lives? Our students are hungry to craft narratives of responsible freedom that do not degenerate into narratives of license and irresponsibility.

• How do we avoid the despair of meaninglessness that, for some, leads to what Camus once called the "metaphysical revolt"? This is the choice of ways of coping with the loss of the older metaphysical certainties: either to commit suicide, or, in the case of so many of our students, to live an escapist life of nihilism, hedonism, or consumerism. Students of the twenty-first century are acutely aware (some firsthand) of campus suicides, mass shootings, self-destructive alcohol and drug abuse, sexual exploitation, and massive credit card debt. They want guidance in dealing with both the terror and temptation of Camus's "metaphysical revolt." They want our help in creating a rationale for living a narrative of meaning that can hold up even when life's prospects appear to be most bleak.

• Knowing that, in the end, each of us is called to make meaning, all of us on campus need to continually ask the following questions: how can we assist students to find the most effective ways to make the wisest choices in their own, and others', best interests? How can we help young people find their own best wisdom paths? How can we encourage them to use their personal freedoms to become interdependent agents in the world, acting always with prudence, compassion, and responsibility toward others?

• Given that one of the prices that must be paid for the personal freedom gained from the breakdown of the older authoritarianisms is the inevitable isolation and loneliness that form the unique destiny of each and every human being, how can we help students to deal with these conditions? Even more urgent, in the face of this unavoidable isolation and loneliness, how do we inspire students to reach out to others in order to form intimate, lasting, authentic relationships and community—the necessary preconditions for finding happiness and fulfillment in a self-constructed world? Some campus observers have made the argument that cell phones, texting, emailing, computer surfing, iPods, instant messaging, PlayStations, and electronic games have cut all of us off from one another—a situation that ends up only exacerbating our isolation and loneliness.

• Finally, existentialism confronts each of us with a double paradox. We need to create a meaning in a life that has no intrinsic meaning. We must also understand that, at times, meaning-making is more a by-product of living a life of activity and purpose than something consciously sought as a fixed object. If this double paradox is valid, how then do educators encourage meaning-making in the face of what some disillusioned students reared in traditional religions will see as ultimate meaninglessness? Obviously, this paradox may not exist for those students who believe that life is a divine gift, and by cultivating the human virtues, this gift becomes that much sweeter.

• Also, how do we convince students that the *finding* of meaning is often indistinguishable from the *process* of pursuing it? Meaning is not always an external goal to be pursued; it is frequently the aftermath or by-product of an activity to be enjoyed for its own sake. Why is it we put so much emphasis on accumulating career credentials on our campuses (career counseling centers are thriving, as well they should, in twenty-first-century America) while ignoring, or minimizing, the benefits of the intellectual and emotional learnings necessary to make sustainable meaning? These are the deep learnings that will stay with our students for a lifetime, even while they make a number of career changes—five to ten times on average, according to some commentators (Bronson, 2003; Palmer, 2000).

Returning to Amy

Amy, the meaning-challenged student we met at the beginning of this chapter, faces what we think is the ultimate, existential crisis of meaning. How can she wring meaning from the incessant demands of her day-to-day life? For Amy, a confounding combination of her life's quotidian nowness and ordinariness, its irritating ups and downs, its perplexing mixtures of joy and tragedy, its dizzying busyness that convention says should be worn like a badge of honor, its relentless pressures to succeed along with its seductive temptations to fail through a series of self-imposed abuses, overpowers any deeper sense of meaning and purpose that her life might have for her. Amy needs to understand that there are multiple ways to create meaning other than driving herself to succeed according to others' expectations. She does not have to continue to feel unfulfilled and miserable along the way.

There are alternative ways to live a life of meaning in the academy, and some of our students have found these. In contrast to Amy, we hear several students express, both in private and in public, their complete wonder over the incomprehensible miracle of their existence. We are touched by the transcendent sense of joy these students experience in their contacts with nature, pets, travel, and children. Some devote their time to the arts, the sciences, or scholarly pursuits in general. We are also inspired by the serious commitments many of our students make to public service and volunteerism, to creating enduring, loving relationships, and, increasingly, to finding religious communities where they might be able to discover the spiritual meaning that too often gets away from them in the day-to-day stresses of pursuing the "good life." Finally, a growing number of students on our campuses proudly self-identify as social justice activists, civil liberties advocates, or environmental activists, because these activities satisfy their desire to create significant sociopolitical meanings.

Despite the presence on our campuses of a growing number of meaning-fulfilled students like these, however, we still see a disproportionate number of students like Amy. These are the poor souls who are immersed in self-destructive angst. More commonly, though, we are struck by the existential plight of the majority of our students who come into our classes, offices, and residence halls just wanting to find something that they can believe in, something that they can give their hearts and heads to. Their dilemmas of meaninglessness are not nearly as severe as Amy's, but this does not make their existential struggles any less important to us.

We are haunted by the comment of one student who said to Robert during senior week: "I have had upwards of sixteen years of formal education, and only once in any classroom was I encouraged to talk honestly and openly about the sense of mystery and depth that I frequently experience in my own life. Ironically, this occurred in a course on sociobiology that I took during my sophomore year. Why can't we ever talk in higher education about what gives our lives real meaning? Why can't we talk about this everywhere on campus throughout the four years that we spend here? And I don't just mean in all-night bull sessions in the residence halls or in the downtown bars and cafes!"

We believe that, in the work we do on our college campuses, existentialism has the potential to give higher education a depth that it sorely needs. Higher education must find a way to speak with conviction and compassion to today's aimless, yet desperately searching, Gen-Xers, Millennials, and quarterlifers. The existential lesson for all of us in higher education is to encourage students to live courageously, purposely, and actively in the face of all of life's perplexities. Today, there are just too many students like Amy on college campuses throughout the United States who suffer from the ravages of anomie and burnout. There are too many students like Amy who just do not know how to transcend those crushing feelings of helplessness and hopelessness when thinking about their own, and the world's, futures. We propose that one way educators can begin the process of meaning-making with students is by applying the principles and practices of Viktor Frankl's logotherapy. Logotherapy is one of the upsides of existentialism, as many of its basic premises are rooted in the principles of this particular philosophy of meaning.

The Postmodern Worldview: We Made It All Up

In this section, we explain the postmodern worldview insofar as we see its direct relevance for meaning-making (for a comprehensive volume of essays on postmodernism, see Anderson, 1995). We devote this section to a brief overview of postmodernism, from both a philosophical and a literary-theory perspective. In Resources for Meaning-Makers at the back of the book, we examine four of the newer therapeutic approaches to meaning-making grounded in both existentialism and postmodern theory.

Note that we are not recommending that higher educators henceforth become either postmodernists or psychotherapists in order to do effective meaning-work with students. Far from it. What we are suggesting is that educators across campus have much to learn from postmodern philosophers and literary theorists, as well as from psychotherapists and counselors whose primary work with clients is to help them understand and reconstruct their broken, meaning-starved lives. Meaning-making is an interdisciplinary activity, and educators, like philosophers and psychotherapists, need all the help they can get. As in logotherapy, we believe that educators have much to learn about meaning-making from a variety of cross-disciplinary approaches. For example, in Chapter Three, we will look at several *religio-spiritual* approaches to meaning-making that we believe hold great promise for those whose intellects, temperaments, beliefs, and talents lean in this direction. We refer to religion and spirituality as *religio-spiritual*, because we do not know how it is intellectually feasible to separate out religion from spirituality and vice versa.

The Postmodern Worldview

The postmodern meaning of meaning, as well as meaning-making, is largely the work of philosophy. Generally, there are two types of philosophers: *realists* and *nominalists* (see Ford, 2007). Some philosophers refer to these two groups as *modernists* and *postmodernists*. In the language of education, the loosely constructed parallel might be *objectivist pedagogy* and *constructivist pedagogy*. The realist believes that there is an objective world out there and that the task of the educator is to discover it, examine it, and invest it with meaning by looking behind its appearances to find a set of permanent truths that might hold for all times and places. This is the *Platonic school of education*. The nominalist, however, believes that even more real than the world outside of us is the world inside of us. For the nominalist, the task of the educator is to name things, to invent and construct concepts and categories that give meaning to the phenomena we observe in the world. This is the *Kantian school of education*. Each of these schools has produced a number of diverse educational progeny through the centuries, each with its own twists, turns, and tugs.

In the field of philosophy, realists hold that the primary task of philosophers is to discover, adapt to, and understand the world as given. It is not possible to go through the day without hearing at least some version of this realist view of the world: "It is what it is." The natural sciences are one way for philosophers to grasp the objective reality, the "is-ness," of the world out there, and the social sciences are a way to apply the objective knowledge that the natural sciences provide.

Nominalists, however, believe that philosophy is more about creating, defining, and changing the world as it appears to us. For nominalists, there is no version of "It is what it is," but, rather, "It is what we name it to be; it is who we are and what we believe and perceive." The arts, humanities, literature, and religion are a few of the disciplines that nominalists use as resources to inform their work in making meaning.

Whether realist or nominalist, however, philosophers are always asking questions of meaning and purpose, each in their own fashion. Each philosophical type believes, as expressed in the words of William James, that "the greatest discovery of my generation is that human beings can alter their lives by altering their attitudes" (quoted in Marinoff, 2003, p. 12).

Historically, Epicurus (341–270 B.C.E.), the Greek Stoic, said that philosophy, even more than medicine, was the best remedy for what he called "diseases of the mind." Henry David Thoreau (1817–1862), a self-made philosopher of the New England Transcendentalism movement, claimed that to be a philosopher "is not merely to have subtle thoughts, nor even to found a school . . . It is to solve some of the problems of life, not theoretically, but practically" (quoted in Marinoff, 1999, p. 3). Both Epicurus and Thoreau are what might be called "applied philosophers." Epicurus was the original philosophical therapist, and Thoreau the prototypical philosophical pragmatist.

Despite their differences, however, what remains their commonality to this day is that neither of them wished to relegate philosophy
to the study of abstract ideas for their own sake. Although this
activity has a significant role to play in academic philosophy departments, it does not exhaust the "real-world" functional possibilities of
philosophy. For both these thinkers, philosophy is about meaning-
making. Moreover, in some significant ways, both Epicurus and
Thoreau, separated in time by more than two millennia, represent
earlier takes on twentieth-century, postmodern philosophy.

Postmodernism traces its intellectual origins back to Kantianism
and nominalism, as well as to existentialism. It reached its decon-
structionist heyday in the mid-twentieth century as the backdrop for
continental literary theory (DeMan, 1979; Derrida, 1978; Foucault,
1972). At present, postmodernism has moved into the psychotherapeutic realm. It serves as the major theory and practice framework
for the three therapeutic movements we describe in the following
chapters.

Philosophically, Nietzsche, the nineteenth-century precursor of
postmodernism, believed that truth was, at best, actually a "mobile
army of metaphors." For Nietzsche, truth was a matter of perspective, and all truth claims made sense only when understood vis-a-vis
a particular truth claimant's pet metaphors, socially constructed
stories, and the dominant language usage of a particular culture at
a particular moment in time. The twentieth-century philosopher
of postmodernism, Jean-Francois Lyotard (1984), defined postmodernism as "incredulity toward metanarratives." No longer would any
overarching story of truth—whether religious, political, historical,
or economic—rule the day, he stated, because all claims to transcendent truths of one kind or another are nothing more than mere
outgrowths of a particular time period's unique "language games,"
preferred supernatural stories, and influential power hierarchies.

Postmodern literary theorists think of truth as narratively constructed. An apt motto for them might be "We made it all up—
everything—lock, stock, and barrel." No single truth claimed by

an author is ever outside of that author's time, culture, or perspective. Everything is interpretation, and interpretation goes all the way down, even though, in one sense, there can never be any final or ultimate "down" down there (Fish, 1989; Rorty, 1999). All literary knowledge, truth, and values are filtered through a variety of interpretive stories; truth claims of one kind or another, textual meanings of one type or another, always end up reflecting the value systems of individual authors, and of readers as well (the latter is known as "reader-response" theory [Fish, 1989]). The upshot of this narrative relativism for postmodern literary theorists is that the meaning of a text is, at best, indeterminate: it can never be pinned down to one meaning or another, because it is subject to multiple interpretations. Every text, without exception, will always contain irreconcilable contradictions and incoherencies.

The four meaning-making therapies that we describe in our Resources section managed to rescue what is worthwhile from earlier, more pessimistic and self-contradictory forms of postmodernism. Regarding the latter, for example, if everything is up for grabs, including the claim that everything is up for grabs, then postmodernism collapses under the weight of its own logic. The postmodern claim to truth can be no more certain than any other claim to truth. It, too, is subject to multiple interpretations, perspectives, and special interests. So what is left?

Despite the logical contradictions, logotherapy-, narrative-, philosophical-, and positive-psychology therapists are able to lay claim to three central values in postmodernism. First, each one of us has the capability (some would say the responsibility), if only we are willing to make the choice, to craft our own stories of meaning, no matter how rebellious and heretical they may seem to others. Second, each of us is potentially a creative artist because, in the absence of any objective, context-independent truth, it is up to us to invent new ways of seeing, understanding, and transforming our worlds. We are not passive observers; we are active agents in the creation of our realities.

Finally, each of us is free to find meaning that is no longer grounded in a predetermined set of absolute metaphysical truths that are said to exist outside of us in some transcendent realm. Instead, each of us is on a journey, either individually or collectively, to create meaning. Ford describes one way to undertake the journey: "Now, the message is to thoroughly enjoy and submit to the spell of the moment—of love, beauty, or happiness—without going outside the moment to think about its meaning or how it relates to an all-encompassing myth, idea, or extrinsic purpose. In the arresting phrase of the American philosopher George Santayana: 'There is no cure for birth and death save to *enjoy the interval*'" (Ford, 2007, p. 139). There are other ways, of course, to experience the interval, and this depends on the meaning that individual seekers (who may be religious, for example) apply to a concept like "interval," as well as to "enjoy."

Summary of Pivotal Postmodern Themes

• Postmodern philosophers, literary theorists, and psychotherapists and counselors acknowledge that the trouble with trying to discover objective truths in our worlds is that we are constantly distorting them with our narrative truths. It is just too easy for objectivists in the academy to make the following assumption: there is simply one truth criterion, and this is based exclusively on a value-free weighing, interviewing, measuring, and counting of data. Postmodernists claim that this is but one story of truth. As valuable as it may be, there are other stories of truth to be told, many of which are equally valuable.

Does this mean that all truths are equivalent in value? Is postmodernism just another excuse for a wishy-washy relativism? Postmodernists assert that it all depends on our truth criteria. A writer who is sure that his lord and savior Jesus Christ is the "way, the truth, and the life" possesses a truth that he is willing to fight and maybe even die for. An atheistic writer might be equally sure that unless such a conviction can stand up under the test of rigorous experiment, it must be discarded or allowed to fall by the wayside. He, also, possesses a truth that he is willing to fight and maybe even die for. Whose truth, therefore, counts as more valid? Which truth should carry the day in academia, or in the lived world outside that all of us, including academicians, inhabit?

Here is the postmodernists' answer, bound to be unsatisfying to both objectivists and naive realists: it all depends on our story, because it is always the story that frames, explains, and justifies any claim to an exclusive truth. There is just no way around this, claims the postmodernist. No matter how convinced, brilliant, or enlightened the scholar is, students will still be asking these types of questions (if not out loud, then silently): "Says who? Where are you coming from? Why? So what? Why should it matter to me?"

• Our individual quests for meaning and purpose are, in large part, a product of our peculiar tastes, temperaments, talents, timing, tribes, and training (our six postmodern Ts). Although we do experience great freedom to make choices in our lives, particularly in the ways that we choose to recompose our personal and professional stories of meaning, we will always be bounded by the impact on us of our particular genetics, psychologies, histories, sociologies, and nests and hives of influence. Each of us will live out our stories until our dying days within the universal plot line of contingency, choice, and chance (our three postmodern Cs).

Postmodern educators spend much of their time trying to ferret out the particular six postmodern Ts in their students' lives. To do this effectively, though, they need to know their stories. Good postmodern educators, like good ethnographic interviewers, are fine story seekers as well as engaging story tellers. The work they do with students is most vital whenever it is based on narrating. Working with students in a variety of locations on a college campus is always more than simply telling, training, or shaping them. It is also knowing how to evoke students' stories in order to make personal connections with them. Postmodern educators recognize again and again the significance of Socrates' dictum: "Know thyself." Thus they try to never miss an opportunity to draw out the stories in which their students choose to live, study, work, and play, on and off campus, every day of their lives.

• The postmodern educator understands that *all truth perspectives are simultaneously true and false, whole and partial, strong and weak,* each in their own ways. Often, the postmodern educator will make a distinction between upper- and lower-case truths, between "Truth" and "truth." Upper-case Truths are seen to be context-independent; lower-case truths are seen to be context-dependent. The important point for the postmodern educator, however, is that we need contending truth narratives and perspectives to bump up against one another, so that our own narratives can be kept honest. Unfortunately, there are few educators in the academy, in spite of their disclaimers, who consistently practice this perspective. We claim that we are pluralists, yet we spend entire careers putting down opposing truth perspectives—sometimes snidely, other times self-righteously, and at still other times, sad to say, cruelly. This includes some postmodern philosophers and literary theorists as well. Not many educators escape the "gotcha!" socialization of the academic culture. We call this intellectual "rigor." Sadly, for many of our students, it instead comes off as intellectual "rigidity."

For example, at times we have urged our students to attend an academic conference. What they find, and report back to us, is that many faculty can be mean-spirited in their academic presentations. There is little or no perspective sharing going on in many of these sessions; just endless showing off, self-promotion, advocacy, guilting, scolding, jousting, and ridiculing (see Karabell, 1997). This is one reason why some faculty who have achieved tenure and promotion do not even bother to attend their professional conferences. And if they do, they spend most of their time sight-seeing, networking, and socializing—away from their conference hotels and scholarly sessions (see Phelps, 2008). Only a small percentage of tenured faculty actually choose to make presentations.

Several decades ago, Jacques Barzun (1968) called scholarly conferences "the waxworks of the intellectual world." His solution was simple: "[P]apers should be read by machine in some empty ballroom, to permit the absent listeners to stay at home and work" (p. 250). And Damrosch (1995) observes: "Again and again in conference panel sessions, the introductions and the speakers' presentations take up almost all of the time, with at most only a few minutes for questions at the end" (p. 197).

• Postmodernists hold that there is no putative truth that goes all the way down to some bottom line, or to some basic foundation, or to some final answer. In matters of narrative truth, there are only interpretations, perspectives, points of view, and personal preferences. There is no "down" down there, no unimpeachable ground upon which to rest, once and for all. Interpretation and perspective are what go all the way down. Truth and reality are infinitely interpretable. So too is the notion of validity. Everything is up for grabs. There is no final word on anything—including, in particular, the types of assertions that postmodernists make (a few postmodernists will acknowledge this logical entailment).

• Given all of the preceding points, postmodern truth criteria therefore include these qualities, among others: *open-endedness, plausibility, vulnerability, narrative creativity, interpretive ingenuity, coherence, generalizability, trustworthiness, caution,* and *personal honesty.* The four therapies that we examine in the concluding Resources section of our book emphasize these qualities, each in their own ways.

Conclusion

We close this chapter with a series of questions (with a strong postmodern flavor) that we often ask our students. We ask these questions to get them to dig a little more deeply into their back-ground beliefs—their taken-for-granted assumptions about what constitutes knowledge, truth, and values. We find that questions such as these very quickly get to the heart of the matter: the extent to which there may be contradictions between what students pro-fess to believe by way of what gives their lives meaning and how they actually live their meanings every single day (Nash, Bradley, & Chickering, 2008, pp. 59–60):

- Do you think of your truth as something "out there"? Or as something "in here"? What are some of these background truths that keep you afloat when you think that everyone else seems to be sinking?

- Why do you think of your truth as an "it"? Or as a process? A personal preference? A negotiated compromise? An absolute? Or a myth?

- Is it possible for you to possess multiple truths, some of which may even be contradictory? If so—if everything is always up for grabs—then how is it possible for you ever to stand for something without wavering?

- How do you arrive at your truths in the first place? What makes a truth *true* for you?

- Is it ever possible for you to separate your truths from the way you were raised, trained, and socialized, or is this impossible?

- On what grounds do you privilege some of your truths over others, especially when these might be in conflict?

- In the event that your individual liberty were ever to be in irreconcilable conflict with your community responsibility, or vice versa, what side would you come down on, and why?

- When was the last time you made a compromise regarding one of your basic truths that might have been in conflict with someone else's basic truth? Can basic truths be compromised and still be basic truths?

- How is it possible to emphasize respect, tolerance, and maybe even compromise in conversations about what gives life meaning, and yet still hold fast to personal beliefs and perspectives that may be critically different?

3

Finding Meaning in Religion
and Spirituality
Why Can't My Faith Be Cool?

I n this chapter we try to explain the inseparability, for many of our students, of religion and spirituality from the meaning-making project. It is at this point where postmodern philosophy, as well as its offspring—the three secular psychotherapies that we discuss in the Resources section—begin to diverge from religion and spirituality on the path to meaning-making. We do not say that, on principle, these secular divergences rule out any convergence with nonsecular meaning-making, because clearly they do not. There is lots of room for meaning overlap, as we saw in Chapter One, in which we presented an original developmental sequence of meaning-making stages.

But in a general sense we are describing a very different meaning system in this chapter, one that is more faith-based, metaphysical, and transcendent than what we have discussed earlier. Having said this, however, we also recognize that there is a great deal of diversity in this meaning system, so we make our generalizations with extreme caution. We try to be very respectful of the differences that exist within nonsecular realms of meaning.

For example, for some people, what psychologists call *mood-elevation* can occur well outside the conventional boundaries of sacred buildings and formal religious rituals. Feelings of awe and transcendence can occur during an outing in the woods, or in the midst of a flow experience at an A.A. meeting, or during childbirth, or while listening to a symphony orchestra, or when totally immersed in a hobby like gardening or painting. Even hallucinogenic drugs have been known to produce alternate states of consciousness. There have been times when we, the authors, have experienced this mood-elevation in our seminars, or one-on-one in a getaway retreat with a group of our students. We have also heard many of our students talk about experiencing an indescribable sense of joy and peace at daily mass, or while meditating in a Buddhist ashram, or during a labyrinth walk, or when present at temple while the Torah is read.

In this chapter, we draw on Robert's experiences in teaching a yearly course on religious pluralism, and on Michele's presence with students at a number of cross-campus religious gatherings (see Nash, 2001; Nash & Bradley, 2007; Nash & Bradley, 2008; Nash & Baskette, 2008; Nash & Scott, 2009). We begin with a short scenario. Then we present a series of assumptions we make about why we think educating students about the religious and spiritual sources of meaning-making are important. From there, we describe several types of religious and spiritual seekers who come into our respective academic and student affairs venues, including the portrait of one quarterlifer, Lara, who calls herself a "spiritual pragmatist." Lara has blended her religio-spirituality with her quest to develop meaning and purpose. Finally, we make some concrete recommendations regarding how to engage students in conversations about this very controversial subject on both sectarian and secular campuses.

Why Is Faith So Threatening to Academia?

This section heading is a question that one of Robert's students, Harold, raised during a difficult one-on-one meeting when he was trying to decide whether to transfer to a religiously affiliated college in the Midwest. Here is the gist of what he said:

I am very comfortable with my religious background. Yet I don't have many opportunities to discuss this with professors, student affairs folks, or even my friends. Whenever I bring up my faith in casual conversation, people look at me as if I'm brainwashed. The two religious studies courses I've taken here have been much too abstract for me. The professors obviously had no passion for the subject matter. Both professors are self-described agnostics, and, even though they tried to be fair, at times their antireligious prejudices came out. I really find higher education to be elitist and dismissive when it comes to matters of religious faith.

I was raised in a Christian home, and I am very faithful to what I learned in church every Sunday. My church community back home is wonderful. The people are so grounded. They know what life means. They don't ask deep questions about their faith. Most are really spiritual people, who take for granted that there is a God, that God is merciful, loving, and just, and that we are all responsible for helping one another in this life. My community believes that there are absolute moral principles that hold for all people in all times and places. The Golden Rule is one of these. Loving our neighbor is another.

Why does this university have to make everything so complicated? Why does my faith have to be so threatening to folks around here? Everything else seems to be accepted. Skepticism is cool. Hooking up is cool. Smoking pot is cool. Getting drunk is cool. Habitat for Humanity is cool. The ropes course is cool. Being green is cool. Social justice is cool. A semester abroad is cool. Why can't religious faith be cool? Why can't my Christian spirituality be cool?

The Cry for Spiritual Meaning Is Everywhere

Whether Christian, Muslim, Jewish, Buddhist, or Hindu, or whether theist, agnostic, atheist, or polytheist, students come to college with all shapes and sizes of spirituality. By spirituality, we mean the following: a penchant, probably hard-wired into all humans, to ponder the imponderable, to ask the unanswerable questions about the meaning of life, especially its omnipresent, unavoidable pain, suffering, and death—conditions that paradoxically coexist with life's unalloyed joys, pleasures, and satisfactions. More succinctly, spirituality begins with the question raised time and time again by such philosophers as Leibniz, Schelling, Schopenhauer, and Heidegger: "Why is there something rather than nothing?"

Among our students, the spiritual questions that surface most frequently include these:

- Does my life really matter to anyone but myself?

- Why am I plagued at the most inopportune times by a longing for something more, even when it seems that I have it all?

- Why am I so restless? Is there really some purpose or rationale to life that can produce stability or a sense of permanence?

- Why, in spite of all the corruption and selfishness in the world, do I still cling to the possibility that I, and others, can live our lives with dignity and integrity?

- Is there any larger reason why I am alive—beyond satisfying my basic physical and psychological needs?

- Why do my pleasures and joys seem so fleeting?

- Why do people have to make war, oppress the have-nots, and impose their intransigent beliefs on unwilling others when a live-and-let-live philosophy of life seems so intuitively right?

Some of our students answer these questions by constructing narratives of meaning that are quite private and personal. Others are much more public about their spirituality, sometimes locating themselves within the frameworks of conventional religious traditions. Some students are grounded in doctrinal certainty, like Harold in the preceding scenario; others are nagged by incessant doubt. The spirituality of our students manifests itself in many ways. All our students, however, need some sense of personal identity, a semblance of a community life in which they can participate, a reasonable way to discern what is right and wrong conduct, and a starting point for explaining those aspects of life that seem either enigmatic or ultimately unknowable.

Stanley Hauerwas (Hauerwas, 1977) says that "the true stories we learn of God are those that help us best to know what story we are and should be, what gives us the courage to go on" (p. 80). Neil Postman (Postman, 1996) believes that "each of us uses the word *story* as a synonym for *god*, with a small *g* . . . god is the name of a great narrative, one that has sufficient credibility, complexity, and symbolic power to organize our lives around it" (p. 5). And Anne Lamott (Lamott, 1994) is convinced that "spiritual stories are the way to truth . . . the only way we can get to the bottom of our own anger and damage and grief" (pp. 30, 201). In our work with students on a number of college campuses, we find a near-exponential growth in interest in spiritual and religious meaning-making.

Harold represents a great many students. According to the study of Spirituality in Higher Education (2003), over two-thirds of students reported having great interest in spiritual matters, and a similar number expressed a commitment to a particular religious expression. These students are hungry for discussion about what matters to them, yet over half reported that their faculty never engage them in discussions about religion, spirituality, or the meaning of life. In an alternative search for answers, some young people turn to the Internet seeking explanations for all things religious and spiritual, others turn to more conservative interpretations of their religious rituals, and still others seek community with like-minded peers (Hayes, 2007). In light of these developments, Astin, Astin, Chopp, Delbanco, and Speers (2007) advocate that educators match students' desire to explore the big questions of life with an enthusiasm for engaging these questions inside and outside the classroom.

These students want to know how religion fits into their evolving stories of meaning. Theirs is an urgent question: what is there about religion and spirituality that might help them shape their destinies, understand their histories, and develop a moral imagination, and might give them something worth living and dying for? Students like Harold—who wants his faith to be thought of as cool, or at least not thought of as freakish—want desperately to live in what Wuthnow (1998) calls a "spirituality of dwelling." Their spirituality is rooted in a community of belonging, and they are happy to have found the sacred space that best enhances their sense of well-being. It is here in this religious dwelling place where they can best experience the seasons of their lives with all of the requisite rites of passage and coming-of-age ceremonies and affirmations.

Students like Harold appear to have found what many of our students seek, although they cannot quite put words to it: a refuge of consolation and comfort to which they can retreat during the hard, desolate times. Even those students who, unlike Harold, may be content to live a more individualistic life of spiritual seeking and exploring, or who may be worldly skeptics, nevertheless appreciate what Harold is: a person of quiet faith who wants only to be left alone (or, better still, accepted) by others. Later on in this chapter, we describe a number of different types of believers and nonbelievers who come into our classrooms, residence halls, offices, and student centers. For now, suffice to say that what they all have in common is the need for something to believe in, something to hold onto, something to get them out of themselves when they are too full of themselves.

The lure of all the world's religions and spiritualities is universal: which stories of meaning best speak to our special human needs and longings today? For example, does the story of Jesus, Buddha, Confucius, Solomon, or Muhammad continue to help us understand who we are, whom we belong to, how we should behave, and how we might come to terms with the overwhelming mystery of our existence? For students like Harold, the unequivocal answer to this second question is "Yes." As Fowler (2004) observed:

> Faith is deeply related to the human need to find and make meaning, and to do so in a trusting relation to the divine Being and Spirit from whom creation issues. Faith orients one to life and its purposes, and to creation, with its origins, its ordering, its enormity, its hospitality to life in its myriad forms and expressions, and its mystery. (p. 412)

To engage Harold and his like-minded peers in conversations of meaning is to engage their faith traditions, the source of their meaning. To engage faith is first to respect and appreciate it.

One further observation in this section is important. In contrast to the overflow of angry critiques of religion and spirituality that have made the best-seller lists in recent years (Dawkins, 2006; Harris, 2004; Hitchens, 2007), a number of scientifically trained commentators are making the case for what we might call a "spiritual gene." These thinkers (see, for example, Collins, 2006; Comfort, 2008; Vaillant, 2008) argue that human beings are inherently spiritual people. Our spiritual tendencies, located in our unique brain design, confer survival benefits on us. Many of our spiritual emotions such as love, faith, hope, forgiveness, and compassion are selected by evolution. They are a positive force for happiness. Haidt (2006), for example, makes the statement that ". . . religious people are happier, on average, than nonreligious people . . . an effect that arises from the social ties that come with participation in a religious community, as well as from feeling connected to something beyond the self" (p. 88).

Thus, even though to some of us on college campuses it may appear to be counterintuitive, religious people always manage to score the highest in happiness and well-being tests (Seligman, 2006). Religion and spirituality, for better or worse, and for whatever reasons, are more highly correlated with such emotional states as joy, optimism, and hope than any other human belief system. Some neurobiologists (see Vaillant, 2008, for an extensive bibliography) have done much empirical and laboratory research confirming that the "spiritual emotions" produce strong evolutionary benefits that help those who experience them to survive.

Perhaps James and Maslow, nonscientists from earlier generations, were onto something: religion makes people feel whole, good, transformed, self-actualized, and full of awe, love, and wonder. Life now has meaning. People are motivated and happy. The lesson for all of us—whether believer, agnostic, or nonbeliever—on college campuses everywhere, is that religion and spirituality deserve to be taken seriously. When religion is working well, for example—when it tries to reconcile rather than divide—then it becomes a powerful force for meaning-making; for a sense of community, self-transcendence, service to others, and compassion.

Religious and Spiritual Illiteracy on Our Campuses

We are convinced that most of our students, and many faculty, know very little about religion and spirituality, even though they may have lots of uninformed opinions that they present as fact (see Prothero, 2007). This type of ignorance is unacceptable in a twenty-first-century, multifaith, multireligious, global community. Clearly, in our experience, there is an unmistakable secular bias on college campuses. Worse, on many nonsectarian campuses, there is outright disdain for those students who make and find meaning in their faith experiences.

Therefore we believe that, whether teacher or administrator, counselor or lay person, believer, explorer/seeker, or nonbeliever, it is crucial for campus educators to think about the role that the study of religion and spirituality plays in the meaning-making of students of all ages, at all levels in higher education, in public and private, secular and parochial venues. As campus educators, we must think seriously and systematically about the risks and benefits, the disadvantages and advantages, of dealing with such sensitive material. However, to ignore issues of religion and spirituality in the twenty-first-century is to miss what is vitally important to so many of us in the task of meaning-making. For these reasons, we make the following recommendations:

• All of us on campus need to reexamine our own latent biases both for and against organized religion and private spirituality. This self-examination process, although difficult and time-consuming, is key to working with and understanding our students. Its importance cannot be underestimated.

We believe that this very popular dichotomy among our students represents an unstated bias against organized religion and a bias in favor of private spirituality. We hear the following all the time: "I'm spiritual, not religious"—as if the former is intrinsically superior to the latter. Although we recognize very clearly that there are significant conceptual, historical, and emotional differences between the two terms, we try to help students who are predisposed to this kind of meaning-making to see the benefits in each approach. We do not want them to miss the forest for the trees. We do not want them to be binary thinkers in the area of religio-spirituality (see Nash, 2007).

• It is important for campus educators in every venue to learn how to talk respectfully and compassionately with one another, and with their students, about a topic that throughout history has caused as much pain, suffering, and division as it has comfort, joy, and reconciliation.

• If campus educators truly want to diversify their formal and informal curricula, and if they truly want to develop educational and clinical offerings that respect all kinds of differences, including religious and spiritual differences, then they need to radically revise the nature and content of diversity and social justice education. *Multiculturalism, diversity,* and *pluralism* are empty catchwords unless they include religious and spiritual diversity, and nonbelief diversity as well. Too often social justice education favors particular types of differences and rules out others. In the twenty-first century, religio-spiritual identity is the core identity of billions of people on this planet. It is also the primary way to make meaning for at least two-thirds of the world's inhabitants.

The Universal Quest for Religio-Spiritual Meaning

Religio-spirituality represents, for us, the quest for meaning that lies at the heart of all cultures, people, and professions. We believe strongly that the quest for meaning in life is what a genuine liberal education should be about. We think of a general education as not being owned by any one academic discipline or particular degree program. General education encompasses a series of interdisciplinary offerings that cut across several of the humanities, natural, and social sciences, and professional preparation programs—including pre-medicine, pre-law, psychology, biology, business, philosophy, religious studies, history, literature, art, music, theatre, and others.

For us, all degree programs need to deal with the universal as well as the particular; with the religio-spiritual as well as the material needs of human beings. Most important, in those programs that provide professional preparation, campus educators must put as much emphasis on the quest for meaning in life as they do on the shaping of particular techniques and skill sets. "Know thyself," the great Socratic dictum, is as important to us in professional training as the imperative "Know how to use the tools of thy trade."

Thus we try to encourage our students to engage in what we think of as true liberal learning. We want them to explore their biases both for and against the religio-spiritual content in the courses that they take and in the experiences they have outside their classrooms. We want them to understand as much as possible what the world's major religions hold to be true and why. We want them to engage in some deep, personal meaning-making. We want them to explore what they believe or disbelieve about religio-spirituality and why. We want them to draw out of their diverse campus experiences what is intensely personal as well as what may be content-rich. Evidently, students throughout the United States want exactly this type of educational experience as well, as a number of studies show (see the survey research being done at The Higher Education Research Institute at UCLA, www.spirituality.ucla.edu; see also the Pew Forum on Religion and Public Life at pewforum.org).

One approach to dealing with religious and spiritual meaning-making consistent with what we have written in previous chapters borrows from the perspective of narrative therapy. At some level, all teaching and learning are autobiographical. Like religion, teaching for meaning comes out of highly personal narratives that campus educators create in order to elicit, and to answer, the most confounding existential questions—the ones that defy easy scientific, political, or technological answers. For example, the most captivating religious narratives—Buddhism, Hinduism, Christianity, and Islam, among others—feature unforgettable characters, momentous events, and luminous ideals. And their languages are often sonorous and seductive. At its best, religion as a narrative, as a powerful storytelling device, reaches out and captures our imaginations, because the vitality of its message and the vividness of its language are potentially life-transforming. We are moved to fresher understandings of the deeper, previously concealed meanings of our lives.

The lesson here for campus educators is surely not an original one, but it is of the utmost importance nevertheless. Educating for religio-spiritual meaning-making ought to recognize that good teaching, like the most powerful religio-spiritualities, is all about storytelling, and that the best meaning-making aims first at the heart and soul before it can ever find its way to the mind and hand.

In Neil Postman's words, "[D]o the stories provide [students] with a sense of personal identity, a sense of community life, a basis for moral conduct, explanations of that which cannot be known?" (1996, p. 7). Postman aptly captures the meaning-making content and process of teaching about faith, spirituality, and religion on a college campus.

We have discovered that we are more likely to get students from a variety of religio-spiritual backgrounds to open up publicly about their guiding beliefs and leaps of faith whenever we de-emphasize the revelational, doctrinal, and corporate elements of religion in favor of the aesthetic and the poetic, the philosophical and the literary. Although we do teach this very important, defining religio-spiritual scaffolding of the faith and wisdom traditions, we also work very hard to approach discussions of religion as a series of compelling and useful narratives that people have constructed for thousands of years in order to explain life's tragic anomalies as well as its unexpected gifts of grace. We know of no better way to mine the richness of an expanding religious and spiritual pluralism on secular college campuses throughout the United States than to get our students to exchange their religio-spiritual stories of faith with each other in a nondoctrinal, mutually respectful manner. And they will do this, especially if we are scrupulous about exemplifying what we want them to do.

For us, education has a deeply spiritual component, as does most cocurricular work with students. We have come to realize that education is as much about helping students to name their doubts about themselves, their studies, and their work, with honesty and integrity, as it is about testing, grading, credentialing, and professionalizing. At the same time, education ought to encourage students to create and nurture a faith (trust) in themselves, and in others, that is honest and integral. Whether we are talking about religion or spirituality, we strive to help our students create personal narratives that combine the qualities of faith, doubt, honesty, and integrity in such a way as to deepen their understandings of themselves and others. We try to create a sense of *vocation* in our various campus sites—getting students to think of their careers as more of a calling, as a commitment of faith without guarantee, as a risky response to the summons deep within them to minister to others wisely and compassionately.

The Types of Students Who Come into Our Campus Venues

Several religio-spiritual types of students make their way into our lives each semester (Nash & Baskette, 2008; Nash & Bradley, 2008). The majority of our students have been raised in the mainline Christian and Jewish religions. We also get our share of Muslims, Buddhists, and Hindus. Occasionally a few pagans and Wiccans show up. Moreover, we notice that a growing number of self-acknowledged atheists and agnostics manage to find their way to our course on religious pluralism. Although the latter publicly eschew any overt interest in theology or theism, ironically, of all our students they are often the most excited to explore the meaning of meaning-making. Within each of these formal denominational and religious identifications, however, it seems that certain types of believers and nonbelievers always show up in our various campus settings.

Orthodox Believers

Some of these students are *orthodox* believers, like Harold in our opening scenario; they come in all religious and philosophical stripes. Their confident, sometimes gentle sense of certainty attracts, more than repels, many of us throughout the semester. Many orthodox Christian believers self-identify as fundamentalists, born-again, nondenominational Christians, evangelicals, charismatics, and Pentecostals. As well, there are orthodox believers in other faith traditions such as Islam, Judaism, Hinduism, and Buddhism, among other religions. In response to these orthodox believers, however, a small coterie of outspoken anti-orthodox skeptics always manages to remain unconvinced, and they often have great difficulty concealing their disdain for any expression of unquestioning, orthodox belief. The anti-orthodox skeptics are the students and faculty who discourage students like Harold from going public with their strongest orthodox convictions. They end up making the Harolds on college campuses feel "uncool" because they still embrace the church communities and teachings of their families; because they do not question, but instead accept.

Our educational challenges are great with both this particular group and its detractors. Each side manages to rankle the other with equal fervor. We believe, however, that, without knowing it, each group needs the other in order to more clearly define what they stand for and what they oppose. In a sense, this represents a complementarity between two oppositional groups that strengthens, rather than weakens, their respective belief systems. We see this type of oppositional complementarity being played out on the world scene in such locales as Iraq, Palestine, Israel, India, Pakistan, and, yes, even here in the United States. We can better understand the dynamics of this belief/nonbelief complementarity on a macrocosmic scale, because we see it duplicated all too often in our microcosmic campus settings. We make it a point to share this global insight with our students.

Mainline Believers

Some of our students are *mainline believers* who are neither excessively conservative or avant-garde. They dislike authoritarianism in religion as much as they dislike faddism. They prefer a life of traditional worship that balances traditions, standards, self-discipline, and moral conscience with a degree of personal freedom, biblical latitude, and the *joie de vivre* of close community life. Often, they remain in the Catholic and Protestant churches and Jewish temples of their parents and grandparents. We have frequently found that mainline believers are as uninformed about the details and complexities of their own religions as they are about the world's major and minor religions.

Our major challenge with this group of mainline believers is, first, to encourage them to become informed about their own faith systems. Then we need to help them understand that their need for religious stability and spiritual rootedness does not necessarily have to rule out important compromises and changes that any belief system requires in order to remain vital, responsive, and pastoral. The key, of course, is for our mainline believers to learn how to make reasoned compromises without falling prey to an array of co-optations and dilutions of the original sacred messages in their own faith narratives.

Some of our students are *wounded believers* who define their religious experience mainly as a reaction to the physical and mental abuse (often perpetuated in the *name* of religion) that they have suffered at the hands of hypocritical, over-zealous clergy, lovers, parents, relatives, and friends. Their self-disclosing narratives of guilt, suffering, denial, reconciliation—in some cases—and eventual healing always win our attention, believer and nonbeliever alike. We often hear stories of pain and bitterness from those wounded students who self-identify as "recovering" Catholics, Jews, or disgruntled members of any number of Protestant Christian denominations.

It is quite difficult, at times, for us to help our wounded students to avoid overgeneralizing and projecting onto all religious institutions their own personal turmoil with religion. We try to listen compassionately to wounded believers, and we refer those who are in acute distress to the appropriate mental health professionals. We also remind them of Viktor E. Frankl's comment: "Suffering ceases to be suffering in some way the moment it finds meaning." Although religion has certainly wounded some people, it has also healed others. Reading dramatic, personal accounts of healing, reconciliation, and redemption in a variety of religio-spiritualities frequently helps these students to put the problem of good and evil (what theologians call the problem of *theodicy*) into perspective (see, for example, C. S. Lewis, 1962).

Mystics

Some of our students are religio-spiritual *mystics* who remind us continually that more often than not a genuine faith requires a discerning silence on the part of the believer rather than a learned, theological disquisition. Some turn to the East; some to alternative American religions; some to folk religions and Native American spirituality; some to private forms of spirituality; and some are mystical followers of conventional faith traditions. Most express a love for mystery, stillness, and attunement that eludes those of us who too easily fit the stereotype of the fitful, ambitious, hard-driving Westerner. Mystics are a popular group of students in our class, and many are comfortable calling themselves *seekers* who are on a *journey* to find (some prefer the word *create*) larger meaning.

On the mystical meaning of spirituality, Bede Griffiths (1990) sheds light on the transcendent power of everyday experiences:

> Something breaks suddenly into our lives and upsets their normal pattern, and we have to begin to adjust ourselves to a new kind of existence. The experience may come through nature or poetry, or through art and music; or it may come through the adventure of flying or mountaineering, or of war; or it may come simply through falling in love, or through some apparent accident, an illness, the death of a friend, a sudden loss of fortune. Anything which breaks through the routine of daily life may be the bearer of this message to the soul. (p. 114)

What Griffiths is saying to us is that, at times, spirituality, as separate from the formal teachings and practices of organized religion, can lift a veil and help us to see our lives as if for the first time. We become aware that there is a deeper level of meaning to existence. During these moments, we no longer exist only as solitary, existential individuals. Now we experience the universal oneness of the human condition that binds us all together. We are hit in both our hearts and heads with the sudden realization that no matter what church we may belong to, what sacred book we revere, or even whether we are theists, agnostics, or atheists, in the end life is pretty much an unfathomable mystery. And each of us is a finite creature struggling in our own ways to experience all that our existence has to offer.

Most students (including even atheists and agnostics) with whom we talk about religio-spirituality have had at least one inexplicable mystical experience in their lives that upsets their usual religio-spiritual routines or secular protocols. Whether it's a numinous awareness that comes through a transformative encounter with the magnificence of nature, or a loving relationship, or a vividly inspiring piece of writing, or a terrible accident, or an unbearable loss of some kind, most students see, if only dimly, what Peter Berger (1970) has called "fleeting signals of transcendence," or what we think of as quick glimpses of the extraordinary in the ordinary.

We remind our students that these mysterious moments can pull us all together at times, because at the very least they remind us that life is pretty much an unfathomable mystery, even to nonbelievers and true believers. We just cannot explain all of life's enigmas, no matter how scientific or rational we may think ourselves to be. At some level of our existence, we are all stymied about how life works at those most difficult moments in time. Just when we think we have it all figured out, something breaks into our lives and upsets our comfortable philosophies of life.

Secular Humanists

Some students whom we know self-identify as *secular humanists*. They are convinced that, all too often, self-described believers turn to the supernatural in order to escape from the difficult responsibilities of individual freedom. For secular humanists, a humanistic, "self-centered" ethic can stand on its own as a defensible way of a person's being in the world and living an authentic human life. What is necessary is that all of us need to confront the inescapable fact of our human finitude, and make a conscious choice to create ourselves through our daily projects—that is, through our courageous strivings to make meaning in an absurd universe. We have had some humanists in our classes who are spiritual, and who even refer to themselves as *secular theists*, or *spiritual atheists*, but these types are rare (Nash, 2003).

Most of our secular humanists are skeptics, agnostics, and atheists who are deeply suspicious of any and all religious claims to absolute truth. Some are social justice activists who are on a mission to eradicate discrimination and oppression. Others are environmental advocates who proudly color themselves "green." And still others are civil libertarians for whom the First Amendment is a kind of holy scripture. As committed moral relativists, all of these types are dedicated to the use of science and reason to solve human problems. They also openly challenge all religious and moral certitudes, ethical universals, and what the postmodernists among them refer to as *grand spiritual narratives*.

They frequently encourage the rest of us to put our faith not in church doctrines or dogmas but in the awareness that we are all social constructors of our own religio-spiritual realities. Some of these nonbelievers are proselytizers; some are strictly scientific; some are inveterate questioners like Socrates; and some are militantly dogmatic and aggressive in their disdain for religio-spirituality. Some of the more temperate secular humanists in our classes agree wholeheartedly with Tennyson that "there is more truth in honest doubt than in all the creeds of the world."

A Quarterlife Portrait of a Spiritual Pragmatist

In this section we sketch a portrait of a quarterlifer, Lara Scott, whom Robert has known for half a dozen years. Lara has moved back and forth through the five cycles of meaning-making we developed in the first chapter. At this particular point in her life, however, she has arrived at a good place, a place we call *Cycle Five*. In many ways she represents many of the quarterlife students who come in and out of our lives each year. She is in the trenches each and every day trying to grow in the virtue of integrity and trying to create a meaning in her present-day life that will sustain her throughout her entire life.

Because Lara possesses an integrity that is both spiritual and down-to-earth, she calls herself a *spiritual pragmatist*. Her spirituality is thoroughly practical. Although she lives in full awareness and acceptance of the unfathomable mystery that surrounds her life, she is not a contemplative. Nor is she a regular churchgoer, although she was raised in a Lebanese-Orthodox and Christian Science family. She is more of a doer. Using the terms we apply to particular religio-spiritual types of students, we would describe Lara's quarterlife religio-spirituality as humanistic, secular, and mystical. Lara embodies the following three qualities, in her own signature fashion.

Humility

Lara practices humility in everything she does. There is not an ounce of arrogance or pretentiousness in her. She knows her limits. She has learned equally from both her failures and her successes. She always tries to give others the benefit of the doubt, even though at times she can be a bit of a skeptic. Although she is no pushover in a seminar discussion, she knows from experience that there is always a better idea, a sharper insight, another perspective to consider.

She reminds us of Comte-Sponville's (2001) observation that humility keeps us honest, because in the end we realize that "all knowledge is a narcissistic wound, a blow to our self-esteem." As much as we know, there is so much more to know, and therefore we know that we really do not know much at all. This was what the Oracle at Delphi said to Socrates, whom he called the "wisest man in Athens," because Socrates alone knew that he did not really know anything.

Thus Lara gives even the most controversial authors she reads in her courses the benefit of the doubt, at least initially. She may disagree with their thinking, but she is open to the possibilities. She asks wonderfully probing questions, coming out of many different perspectives, and then she makes up her own mind about the answers. But she is always willing, in Schwehn's (1993) words, "to surrender [herself] for the sake of the better opinion." This, in our experience as educators, is the epitome of intellectual humility.

The conversations that Lara has with others outside of class about many of the classic existential questions are open-ended and generous. She is always fascinated by these questions, and she never enters a conversation with the agenda of foreclosing on any of them. She knows that these questions will always remain ambiguous and indeterminate. Her wide-eyed enthusiasm for these unanswerable questions never abates. Questions lead to further questions, and in her conversations she refuses to settle for easy answers.

She has talked about many quarterlife issues with her family, friends, classmates, campus administrators, and professors. She approaches all of these with generosity and enthusiasm, two of her finest spiritual qualities. During the time that Robert has known Lara, she has helped him to formulate this trenchant insight—there can be no genuine humility without generosity and enthusiasm toward others. She has also convinced him that humility must be a key virtue in the meaning-making pantheon, not just for quarterlifers like herself but for all of us who are trying to fashion lives of integrity and purpose.

Faith

Lara's faith is not strictly religious. It is, instead, what she is: both spiritual and pragmatic. In some senses, it is also very secular. It is pragmatic in that it has a strong service component. It is a tool to help others. It is secular in that it is connected to no specific church or sacred text. Her take on faith is always down-to-earth and thoughtful. It is also very much a faith in process. Raised a Christian, Lara spent the beginning of her post-secondary experience in a Christian college, before transferring to a public institution when her religious college closed its doors. During her junior year, she volunteered to live for a year in a southern city, working with a religious order to serve the inner city poor. This year was a watershed period for her, in the sense that she learned to put her faith into action by ministering directly to others.

Direct service is the outward expression of faith for Lara. She makes us think of Dorothy Day, the Catholic activist, who founded the Catholic Worker movement in the 1930s. Day believed that service was a religious obligation, so she set up a series of clinics in New York City to tend to the needs of the poor. Her work established the precedent, today, for what is known as "community service." This is the work done by young college volunteers, like Lara, in schools, hospitals, soup kitchens, nursing homes, and prisons, among other sites. Perhaps the most wonderful quality of Lara's service is the humbleness of her heart. She expects no rewards or praise. She gives out of her own profound need to help others less fortunate.

Lara's faith is more about trust than blind belief. She has faith in the sense that she has an ingrained confidence about how her life will unfold. She trusts that good will eventually come from everything that happens in her life, if not sooner, then later; and, if not later, then somehow she has missed it in the present. She believes that this is her fault and not the fault of the universe. She has reached a point in her young life where she is able to believe what she questions and question what she believes. She realizes what Goethe understood: "In matters of faith and belief, everything is both simpler than we can imagine, and more entangled than we can conceive."

Lara also refuses to position herself as an all-or-nothing God-denier or a God-affirmer. Her spirituality is both noble and open-ended. There is not an inch of religious woundedness, or bitterness, or self-righteousness in her, and this makes it a pleasure for most everyone to engage in religio-spiritual discussions with her. She brings few antireligious or anti-nonbelief agendas to the conversation, and she seems authentically open to all the possibilities. For us, this is the truest expression of integrity, and also very rare in a quarterlifer.

Love

Lara's love refuses to call attention to itself. It is not grandiose. Her calling has been to work with young people of all ages, including elementary school children, whom she tutored for awhile, and for whom she has a special fascination and affection. During her current studies, she gives all she has to the students she administers to in her residence hall. As a residence director, she is on call, either officially or unofficially, twenty-four hours a day. There are times when she must choose between making time for her friends and making time for her charges in the residence hall.

When emergencies occur on campus, Lara understands that her first duty is to her residents, so they take priority. But she has worked hard to prime her loved ones for those moments when she must be away from them, particularly when they may need her as much as her residents do. This conflict is never easy to resolve, and it is a work still in progress. She knows that it will always be a struggle for her to arrive at an appropriate balance between the demands of her work and the demands of her loved ones.

Lara's love, as an educator and as a friend, is a combination of compassion, generosity, and a gentle sense of humor. Her compassion undergirds her service to the needy as well as her work in the residence halls. She knows that suffering makes all of us fellow creatures. It confers meaning. It is what each of us has in common, as Viktor Frankl well knew. Her generosity is about giving to others unselfishly, because she understands that there can be no love without giving. Robert has seen Lara change her plans at the last minute in order to drive a friend many miles away to another city in an emergency. Recently she has also stood behind another friend, a fellow resident advisor, who she believed was seriously wronged by residential-life administrators. She supported this person at great cost to her own preprofessional well-being. She has often gone above and beyond what is required of her for students in her residence hall. She lives Spinoza's insight: "Love is the goal, generosity the road to it."

Finally, Lara knows that a sense of humor is a sign that we ought not to take ourselves so seriously all the time. Humorless living, loving, and working are signs of deficiencies in meaning. In our many years in higher education, we have discovered that, in general, humorless people lack humility. Those who are devoid of joy and mirth often also lack a calm, gentle, and generous spirit. Think of the chronic complainers and cruelest gossipers in the academy; chances are they are the ones without humor, or without any sense of irony, paradox, or absurdity.

Lara, however, can be both funny and kind. Her humor is never at someone else's expense. She is good at poking fun at herself. Her humor is a function of her humility. When people are with her, they laugh heartily because they recognize the implications of her self-deprecating humor for their own lives. Good humor, as Woody Allen has demonstrated time and time again, laughs at oneself and not at others. It plays upon its own neuroses. Here is a typical Woody Allen line (all references are taken from Allen, 2008): "Is it better for me to be the lover or the beloved? Neither, because my cholesterol is over 600." Here's another: "I don't know what's worse, no God or no plumber on weekends." Good humor ferrets out the delicious ironies in life. Good humor lightens our touch and adds a note of levity to our gravitas. Good humor reminds us that there can be truth in laughter and joy in sorrow. Lara is a practitioner of good humor, and most of us need this kind of kind of meaning to balance the seriousness in our lives.

Like Maigret in Chapter One, Lara is at home with herself. She is sensitive to the importance of her approach to religio-spirituality in fostering a narrative of meaning. She helps everyone around her to understand that it is possible to possess a spirituality that is neither strictly rational nor strictly nonrational. It is more of a secular, pragmatic spirituality, and it features such qualities as generosity, faith, humility, love, and compassion. She demonstrates that it may be possible for even a devout secular humanist like Robert to be a spiritual pragmatist.

The Art of Mixed-Belief Capaciousness in Making Meaning

We try to encourage theists and secular humanists throughout our respective campuses to avoid the trap of demonizing one another. We urge both groups to learn what we call the *art of mixed-belief capaciousness* (Nash & Baskette, 2008). We ask, for example, if there is any way that they might be able to embrace, or see the contiguousness of, even the smallest kernel of truth in the opposing narratives. Are their worldviews capacious enough to include even a fraction of a truth from a different religio-spiritual story? If not, then we urge each group to at least make a commitment to try to understand (not agree with) what is so precious and life-sustaining in the faith system of the other for the other. What are the positive implications for meaning-making of all the different belief systems?

We believe that what Ninian Smart calls the practice of "structured empathy" is more than possible between believers and nonbelievers (Smart, 2000). For Smart, "structured empathy" means getting at the "feel" of what is inside the belief system of another person by doing everything we can to get a genuine sense of the way the other person structures particular worldviews of belief and meaning. We let it be known that each of us has a right to tell our stories of meaning with as much passion and conviction as we wish. However, we all must learn to honor, not critique, those beliefs that give people's lives a special meaning, no matter how absurd or wrong they may sound. We insist on the virtue of *respect* for one another when telling our religio-spiritual stories. The Latin root of the word *respect* (*respicere*) means to look back, again and again, in order to find value in what one may have initially opposed or dismissed.

To respect another's religio-spiritual story is to express a willingness to look carefully at what gives each of us meaning, what helps us to meet each new day, over and over again. To do this with a genuine spirit of openness and generosity, we need to show respect to one another by the way we listen, ask questions, and interpret information, no matter how discordant our differences may at first appear. Or, to say it another way: we refrain from *professing*; instead, we engage in *processing*. We are together to help one another *process* a wide range of religio-spiritual phenomena in order to enrich and deepen our own faith understandings. What better way to converse about a controversial topic like religio-spirituality than to be fully open to its possibilities as well as to its liabilities?

One of the major advantages in identifying a number of religio-spiritual types like the ones just described is becoming aware that there is as much diversity *within* particular religions and spiritualities (and nonbelief systems) as there is *among* them. The presence of each of these religio-spiritualities in every individual and group we meet on campus is proof that the search for meaning is multifaceted, never-ending, and complex—even though at times it may exist out of sight, just below the surface.

Variety can, indeed, be the spice of life, as the old cliché goes. But it can also represent a grave threat to true believers of all kinds. Variety is an enemy to exclusivity. Thus it is our double intention as campus educators to try to maintain the wonderful distinctiveness of each of our students' religio-spiritual views and, by extension, to encourage them to recognize the uniqueness in the religious views of others. At the same time, however, we want to provide our students with accurate and helpful narrative classifications like the ones we have listed in this section. How better to understand the rich variety of religious experiences among a number of Americans today?

How to Avoid Giving Offense

There are times when we think we may be failing, when we wonder if it is possible to deal openly with religio-spirituality on college campuses without offending a variety of people. *Is offense inevitable, given the low boiling point of the topic?* This question comes up for us time and time again in our work both inside and outside the classroom. Thus we often introduce this question as a conversation starter whenever we work with groups of students on the topic of religio-spirituality as one way to create meaning. We put our own hopes and fears out there for students to examine, and talk about, publicly.

At first, most students shy away from this topic. They are concerned that going public with their own versions of religio-spirituality will stereotype them as "God-freaks"—a label that one of our students sometimes hears when he is with his fraternity brothers who put down believers. As we spend more time getting to know students who are religio-spiritual, however, they come to feel more empowered to raise faith issues with us and with one another, because they know they will not be uniformly labeled and dismissed.

Related to this issue of giving offense in discussing matters of religio-spirituality is the question of whether it is ever possible to talk about any type of value-loaded meaning-systems in a relatively value-free way. Some of our students wonder why they should stir up the hornets' nests of religion and spirituality in their on- and off-campus settings when so much could be at stake for them, including possible loss of friends, public censure, and charges of what one student called "preaching and screeching" about his Christian faith. Why not just leave well enough alone? these students ask. Many academicians we know on college campuses believe that religio-spiritual beliefs are so deeply personal and private that it is simply beyond their jurisdiction to discuss these in public forums of any kind. And even if they tried to carry out such a discussion, they would not know how.

We have found that it is sometimes necessary to separate out the *cognitive* from the *emotional* dimensions of religio-spiritual conversation whenever we talk about making meaning. At other times we try to recognize, and validate, the powerful emotional content of our students' religio-spiritual convictions. To this end, we encourage our students to freely express the intensity of their beliefs, but always in a mutually respectful and sensitive manner. One way we try to maintain a balance between the cognitive and the emotional in our conversations with students is to rule out of order the favoring of one perspective or another. Rational and emotional approaches to making meaning have equal worth as learning styles in our interactions with students.

Also, we try to avoid raising questions about the validity of the truth claims of various religio-spiritual points of views. What criteria could we ever identify that would meet the unanimous approval of all the various believers and nonbelievers throughout our campuses? Even more fundamentally, what exactly does *validity* mean when religio-spiritual content comes up? Our main agenda, therefore, is always to focus on the central question of why the religio-spiritual approach is the best way for particular individuals to make meaning. We see our professional roles always to inform, clarify, and respond. We do not intend to reform or perform. We strive to establish a communication process that promotes no hidden agendas, only the goal of fostering a pluralistic philosophy of religio-spirituality in stress-free settings throughout our campuses.

Religio-Spiritual Starter Questions for Use Throughout the Campus

We have been successful with students in a variety of campus settings asking the questions that end this chapter (Nash & Scott, 2009). We strive always to do this with *humility*, *faith*, and *charity*—the qualities often associated with a religio-spiritual way of being in the world with others. *Humility* requires mutual vulnerability, intellectual generosity, and a realization that the questioner is always a modest "guide on the side" rather than the privileged "sage on the stage." *Faith* calls for the establishment of a trust between the questioner and the student that there will be no preestablished agendas imposed on conversations about religio-spirituality. All conversation will be open-ended, confidential, and intimidation-free. *Charity* is all about affirmation, respect, and gratitude. It is the willingness to attribute the best motives to another, and to express affection, care, and support, even when the "hot buttons" get pushed.

Here are some conversation-starters, responses, and sustainers that work for us:

- Your words made me think about . . .

- I respect that you . . .

- I relate to what you just said in that . . .

- Let me tell you where I'm coming from, and I'd love to hear your response.

- Please tell me why you feel so strongly about . . .

- Thank you so much for what you've just said; perhaps we can talk further about this sometime?

- Do you know how important your voice has been in our one-on-one conversation [*or* in our group]?

And here is a representative sample of our questions to students, regardless of their spiritual types, that eventually get us more deeply into religio-spiritual issues:

- What gives your life meaning? What makes life worth living for you?

- Have you read any books (fiction or nonfiction) in the last several years that you can honestly say have changed the way you think about (or live) your life? Which ones? How so?

- What beliefs, morals, or ideals are most important in guiding your life at this time? Which ones would you pass on to your children

- Do you believe your life should have a purpose? If yes, what is your purpose, and how did you discover it? If not, why not?

- Can you give some specific examples of how your important beliefs, morals, or ideals have found actual expression in your personal and/or professional life? If you can't, why not?

- Whenever you must make an important personal or professional decision, what pivotal moral beliefs or ideals do you sometimes fall back on?

- Do you think there is a plan for human lives? Is there one for your life? If yes, where does the plan come from?

- When your personal or professional life appears most discouraging, hopeless, or defeating, what holds you up or renews your hope?

- What does death mean to you? What does failure mean? What about success? Happiness? Justice? Morality? Evil? Good?

- Why do you suppose some persons and groups suffer more than others? Why do some persons and groups experience more success and happiness?

- Will human life go on indefinitely, do you think, or will it ultimately end? If you don't care for the question, why not?

- Do you consider yourself a religious or spiritual person? If yes, how and why? Do you consider yourself a nonreligious, nonspiritual person? If yes, how and why?

- Some people believe that without religion morality breaks down. Do you agree or disagree? Why?

- Do you make a distinction between religion and spirituality? If yes, what is the difference for you?

- Is there a master plan to your life, do you think? Or is it all about blind chance?

- Do you think your actions make any real difference to anyone or anything in the larger scheme of things? If yes, why? If no, why not?

- When is the last time you had a conversation about religion or spirituality with a family member, a student, a supervisor, or a faculty member (choose one)? How would you describe the conversation? If you haven't had this kind of conversation, why do you suppose you haven't? Why doesn't it ever come up, do you suppose?

- Were you raised in a particular religion? If so, what was it? If not, why not, do you suppose? If you were, do you still practice that particular religion? If yes, why? If no, why not?

- If you were ever asked, how long do you think you would be able to talk intelligently about the particulars of their faiths with students who may represent such backgrounds as Islam, Christianity, Buddhism, Hinduism, atheism, Judaism, or Taoism?

- Do you remember ever getting any formal training about how to understand, and deal with, religious differences in your professional work with students? Why did this happen or why didn't it, do you suppose?

- How would you characterize the general religious or spiritual leanings of the people in the place where you work, hang out, or study?

A Final Thought: Religio-Spirituality in the Wake of 9/11

One important personal insight we gained right after the tragedy of 9/11 was that there were few, if any, absolute atheists, or nonspiritual students, on our campuses (Nash, 2002b). Even the most staunch nonbelievers were unwilling to declare openly that life was utterly without depth, mystery, or otherness, that acts of terrorism fully and finally invalidated a belief in any kind of transcendence. Few of our students were bold or stark enough to announce to anyone who was willing to listen that their lives, in the end, were shallow, without meaning, lived entirely on the surface, totally devoid of a single truth that they were able to take seriously and without reservation. Many postmodern skeptics whom we met on our campuses in the early months after 9/11 were unwilling to deny the infinite and inexhaustible depth that somehow gives shape and substance to human lives.

In some as yet inscrutable way, the vast majority of our students ended up standing with that troubled nineteenth-century genius, Friedrich Nietzsche, who said: "The world is deep, and deeper than the day could read. Deep is woe. Joy deeper still than grief can be. Woe says: Hence, go! But joys want all eternity, want deep, profound eternity . . ." (cited in Tillich, 1948). All of the types of believers and nonbelievers we have described earlier in this chapter, each in their own way, needed that "deep, profound eternity that makes all the world's grief and woe endurable."

During those terrible days immediately following the attacks on the Twin Towers and the Pentagon, many of our students found themselves poised precariously somewhere between the paradox of both embracing *and* demystifying the unknowable. Could any of them (could any of *us*) really know for sure why a group of extremist

Islamists, in the name of Almighty Allah and holy jihad, hijacked four jumbo jetliners with a plan to fly them into buildings? Or why would they sacrifice their own lives and kill almost three thousand others? Actually, it is this type of confounding mystery that ignites a passion for the presence of religion and spirituality in so many people's lives. At the nadir of such puzzling, often tormenting problems as 9/11 (and natural disasters like Hurricane Katrina and destructive tsunamis) comes the phenomenon of religio-spirituality. This is just one more example of how so many of our students are able to create meaning out of apparent meaninglessness.

In one way or another, colleges and universities claim to "educate the whole student." As students flock to campuses across the nation, they bring with them intellectual and personal capacities—capacities their educators will help unlock, expand, and perfect. Students also bring with them their religio-spiritual ways of seeing the world and making meaning of it. To engage whole-student education is also to engage the religio-spiritual dimension as well as the intellectual and the social. As we have discussed in this chapter, the religio-spiritual realm is often uncomfortable and unfamiliar territory with seemingly impenetrable borders. Students and educators alike can be ignorant of the basic tenets of the world's religions. Also, because students represent a multitude of spiritual types, people all over campus are worried about offending others who believe differently. But if educators are truly to meet students at the point of meaning and educate holistically, these borders must be crossed and this territory must be explored.

Quarterlife students are wading in the chest-deep waters of meaning, attempting to reconcile their deepest-held beliefs with their often surprising or heartbreaking observations of the world. They are measuring their ways of knowing against those of their peers, their teachers, and the great thinkers who have passed before them. During the four to six years of an undergraduate education, they hold all of these comparisons in tension and mix them with their families' expectations and their own hopes for the future.

The next part of the book presents a number of concrete suggestions for putting meaning-making to work. Based on our own experiences on college campuses, we share several practical approaches for faculty and student affairs professionals to assist students along their journey. Although college educators cannot consult a crystal ball to give students the certainty they desire, through the deep learning pedagogies we introduce in Part II they can help lay the foundation for students to create patterns of lifelong meaning. The challenges of the quarterlife may not be completely averted, but surely its extent and effects can be lessened. At the very least, the meaning that students learn to make while in college will set the stage for how they are able to tackle the multitude of changes they will meet in their post-college lives.

Part II

Putting Meaning-Making to Work: Tools of the Trade

4

A Pedagogy of Constructivism
Deep-Meaning Learning

In this chapter, we briefly develop an overall rationale for deep-meaning learning in working with students at all levels and in all venues of higher education. We explain how the search for meaning is most likely to be successful on college campuses whenever educators can help students see the deep connections between subject matter, marketable skills, their personal values, and their interests in contributing to the common good—whether by performing community service to others, dedicating themselves to a social cause that results in self-transcendence, or creating something artistic. We frame all of this in what we call a "pedagogy of constructivism." In subsequent chapters in this part of the book, we offer concrete examples of how a pedagogy of constructivism can be an excellent delivery system for guiding students in their efforts to make meaning.

One important reason we are writing this book is to help faculty, administrators, and student service leaders throughout the campus to create a series of formal and informal educational experiences grounded in an approach that we call "deep-meaning learning." Deep-meaning learning is the essential precondition for responding to all the meaning questions students commonly ask. Deep-meaning learning gets beneath the surface of taken-for-granted assumptions about what constitutes a good education, which in today's terms usually means preparing students for careers or professional graduate training.

Deep-meaning learning responds to students' quests to learn who they are in relation to the world around them. Deep-meaning learning goes beyond simple knowledge retention and the cultivation of specific skill sets. Deep-meaning learning is interdisciplinary. It is integrative. It is heart-, head-, and hand-based. It encourages honest self-examination and a continual reexamination of what is important and what is not in the ongoing search for meaning. Deep-meaning learning is both emotional and cognitive, speculative and practical, spiritual and material, religious and secular, theoretical and experiential.

Deep-meaning learning requires both service to the self and service to others—in equal proportion. Deep-meaning learning entails a series of interdisciplinary offerings, featuring the common theme of meaning-making, that cut across several of the humanities— including psychology, philosophy, religious studies, history, literature, art, music, and theatre, as well as the social sciences and natural sciences. In short, the great Socratic dictum "Know thyself" is the necessary fulcrum for deep-meaning learning.

Rachel's Deep-Meaning Learning

Rachel, a student in one of Robert's recent philosophy classes, made the following comments in a final reflective paper about her meaning-making experience throughout the semester (the words that follow are inspired by Michelle Demers, MFA, a gifted writing instructor and former student of Robert's). Rachel's insights represent a vintage example of deep-meaning learning. Here is what she said about her learning as a result of reading, writing, and talking with others during the semester. It is important for the reader to realize that Rachel did much of her meaning-making outside the classroom and even beyond the campus. Robert's course gave her the opportunity to expand her "classroom" into a number of different communities.

I am at my best when I am able to *bypass the logic* in my thinking about deeper things. I was taken by the comment that you attributed to St. Anselm: "God does not save the world by logic alone." I now realize that while logic is an important tool for me to use in preparing to be a health care professional, as important for me is to learn how to lead from my heart as well as from my head. I'm not sure I've found the perfect formula to do this, but I'm more conscious of it. What I am relying on more and more in my studies and internships, however, is to trust my intuitions and my feelings. This past semester, for example, I've done so many things in the community outside the university that I've wanted to do ever since I came here. I went with my gut. I decided not to be so logical and calculating. I tried out for a role in the community theatre. I got involved with a project downtown at the peace-and-justice center. I visited an ashram every two weeks.

I am also learning to *go within for answers* to my deepest questions. The answers, I've found, lie more inside than outside of myself. I still love to read, study, and analyze, and I do hang out in the lab at times, but I now realize that I'm doing all of this through my own integrating filters, or what you call my "constructivist lens." Why should I continue to spit back information in my classes that I've dredged up on Wikipedia or in a Google search? This isn't real education. Meaning lives within me, not on the Internet, and I can often find out what's really important to me if I'm comfortable being with my own silence. I've even started to do some serious meditation. This always makes my parents chuckle because they think of me as an "activity junkie." Meditation now fills the spaces between my frenetic activities, and what's happening is that I find I don't need the distractions of all the noise I use to make in my life. All of that seemed so peripheral when I started to really get into meditation. I still have fun, but now I'm much more centered and less driven. I am the one having the fun; the fun doesn't have me.

(Continued)

The most exciting discovery for me is to learn how much I *love the arts*. Literature, music, and the performing and visual arts now form the core of my life. These are gifts to me from the universe with no strings attached. The essence of life can be gleaned through the arts. I now do pottery, a little acting, even some painting. Most of all, I'm writing poetry. I'm a pretty damned good poet, I believe, and I don't need the endorsement from some English professor that I've passed tests on how to analyze poems. Instead, I actually do poetry for me. It's become my special way to record my meaning-making journey. Poetry is my process of self-discovery. I have to admit, though, it was a hoot to get one of my poems published in the campus newspaper.

You have talked about deep-meaning learning in this class, Robert. Here's what the process has produced for me. I have learned how to *develop my own consciousness*. As Stephen R. Covey says, we all need to "sharpen the saw." In order for me to be effective for others, I must first nourish myself. If I don't, I will soon burn out. It happens all the time in nursing. I am learning how to sharpen my own saw by going inside myself in order to put my everyday stresses into some kind of perspective.

I honestly believe that it is not the *words* of my instructors that make the deepest impact on me. It is the *consciousness* of my instructors. I can now spot a healthy consciousness a mile away. I suppose, Robert, that you would say some instructors have a clearer sense of what gives their lives meaning than others. Some instructors live in a narrative that is positive, loving, hopeful, and trusting, and this narrative of consciousness speaks volumes to students even before they open their mouths. I guess this is what I mean by developing my own consciousness. Thank you for all your help this semester, and, if I may say so, I hope you continue to find a way to keep developing your own consciousness.

A Constructivist Approach to Educating for Meaning

Rachel, in the preceding narrative, took full advantage of the constructivist model of teaching and learning that she experienced in her semester-long seminar of philosophy of meaning-making. We believe that educating for meaning entails a genuine *constructivist* approach to education. *Learning Reconsidered: A Campus-Wide Focus on the Student Experience* (Keeling, 2004) notes that "the degree of [classroom/personal development/societal disconnection on college campuses today] is profound and has serious implications for both teaching processes and the structures institutions use to help students learn. Today's growing emphasis on integrated learning structures, such as cluster courses and living-learning communities, may in some cases be an acknowledgment of the need to restore the missing holism" (p. 8).

A constructivist approach to teaching, advising, and leading throughout the college campus is one significant way to repair decades of damage that has resulted from part-whole, inside-outside, thinking-doing, teaching-learning disconnections and dichotomies in higher education. Rachel found ways to reconcile many of the dichotomies of the academy for the sake of her own best learning.

One of the advantages of engaging students, professors, and administrators in cross-campus meaning-making activities is to restore means-ends continuity to the educational process. The fact is that, in addition to living our lives in campus community settings such as classrooms, residence halls, faculty offices, and in a variety of cocurricular campus sites, each of us, like Rachel, also lives in our own evolving stories of personal meaning. Each of us must, at various times during our life cycles, remake ourselves and our relationships. Educating for meaning, both inside and outside the conventional academic structures, will effectively teach all of us how to integrate site, selves, and subject matter into a complete learning experience.

Noddings (1995) points out that constructivist ideas started with Jean Piaget, who in turn was influenced by Immanuel Kant, an eighteenth-century philosopher. Both thinkers believed that we can never know the world in and of itself, because our minds and external environments are always in constant interaction with one another. The "epistemological subject"—the individual learner—ends up actively constructing, rather than passively receiving, the outside world. John Dewey (1933) took the concept of constructivist learning one step further. He advocated that educators lecture less and engage students more. He urged them to think of education as reflection *and* action, intellectual inquiry *and* dialectical process, whose ultimate purpose is to enable learners to create meaning through direct experiential activity.

Most important, however, Dewey, and later Jerome Bruner (1990), set the stage for a generation of educators to understand that students bring a wealth of prior knowledge and experience to their learning. Education, therefore, is as much about helping students to make meaning of those prior experiences as it is about filling empty buckets or writing on blank slates. Rachel went from being the "epistemological object" in her scientifically based studies to becoming the "epistemological subject" in all the rest of her life. She gave herself permission to dig deeply into her own evolving consciousness, and this in turn influenced the type of health care professional she wished to become. In the next section, we spell out more concretely some core constructivist teaching-learning strategies for helping students to make meaning. We believe that approaches like the ones that follow liberated Rachel to get the most out of her studies, particularly during her final year.

Creating Constructivist Settings for Deep-Meaning Learning

Here are several recommendations for establishing a climate for deep-meaning learning that have worked for us. We are grateful especially to Brooks and Brooks, 1993, for their work with public school teachers on behalf of constructivist teaching and learning. We are also in the debt of Kessler, 2000; Kronman, 2007; Phillips, 2001; Rhode, 2006; and Tompkins, 1996, for informing some of the following propositions:

Encourage students to take the primary initiative for their own deep-meaning learnings.

Allow us to introduce "Denise," a student who took her education very seriously. A speech-pathology major, Denise was meticulous about her studies. Young as she was, she recognized the gravity of the potential effect that her training would have on her future clients. She wanted to ensure that she was in the best position possible to give them the care they deserved. In addition to her student leadership roles, Denise was a student assistant in Michele's office; like other students, she worked to help ease the burden of tuition at a private university. Unlike many of her peers, Denise was more "adult" and less "late-stage-adolescent" in her cares, concerns, and composure.

Interested in the origins of Denise's maturity and sense of self-responsibility, Michele asked her about the secrets to her academic and personal success. Without missing a beat, Denise asserted that although she observed so many of her peers waiting for instructions from others, she believed that she, and she alone, had to be "in the driver's seat" of her education and her life. Denise experienced her own self-determination—her own agency—and she knew it.

Not every student is like Denise. To encourage students to be the primary initiators of their own deep learning means that we need to recognize and respect the existential autonomy of each and every learner who comes into our learning spaces. In some cases the invitation to learn deeply and for meaning will be a student's first awakening to self—not as a passive receptor of information supplied by another but as the primary agent in the learning process.

Suddenly the educational process becomes dynamic, with lasting effects.

A much beloved chemist, Dr. Jennifer Sorensen of Seattle University, begins the first day of her classes by announcing to her students, "Welcome. I am your captain on this journey, your guide. You are not tourists; you are the crew, and you will do the heavy lifting." The students in Dr. Sorensen's class know from day one what to expect. They will not be passive bystanders waiting for their professor to hand down knowledge from on high. Instead, they will be active participants in the lessons they construct per their teacher's instructions. Dr. Sorensen's classes are dynamic, indeed, and her students are the better for it.

Karabell (1997) observes that "as the power balance shifts away from professors and toward students, the emphasis on process-learning is becoming more pronounced" (p. 18). Process teaching, as opposed to content-teaching, puts the student's questions and concerns at the center of the teaching-learning experience, because it is calculated to engage students in more active, personal ways. Power is more equally distributed in a process seminar, as is the case in a give-and-take, problem-solving session between students and administrators. No longer is there any justification that makes sense to students for the traditional tug-of-war between them and so-called "educational authorities."

Students resist buying into the traditional, often elitist divisions in the academy between the expert and the novice. They are becoming a formidable force in higher education, because they fully understand that they possess the power of the consumer. More and more, they express their refusal to do business as usual by walking away from authoritarian educators. They insist that their point of view regarding what is important in their own lives be considered valuable and that, at the very least, they deserve to be heard and respected, before they are challenged or dismissed outright. Whenever learning is geared toward meaning-making, students will remind us over and over again that they, and they alone, are the ultimate experts in creating purpose, point, and rationale in their own lives.

The trick for us as educators is to frame our work with students in such a way that the content and professional experience we have to offer them can actually inform the real-life choices that our students make both within and beyond the campus. Asking students the hard questions is an important function of educators—but more and more students are wondering, *to what functional end?* A vast amount of current research shows that when students are directly involved with their own learning; when they are given the freedom to design activities that complement what they are learning in the classroom; when they have educators in their lives who are willing to make personal connections with them, and who express a genuine interest in their developing efforts to make meaning; and when they see the connections between subject matter, personal development, and career choices—then and only then does education matter (see Light, 2001, for extensive documentation for the claims we make here).

Throughout the first half of this book, we laid the foundation for meaning making, and in the second half we offer many suggestions for drawing students personally into the learning experience. None of these techniques will work, however, unless educators are willing to get to know their students firsthand on a personal level. Our students have rich personal histories, and they are struggling with existential issues that go way beyond their designated roles as test-takers, knowledge absorbers, and anonymous course attendees whose names just happen to appear on our class lists.

Remember always that there are many valid ways to teach and learn.

In fact, it can be said that the now-confirmed scientific theory of multiple intelligences requires a corresponding theory of multiple pedagogical techniques, strategies, and interdisciplinary content.

The sad fact is that the majority of faculty and administrators have little or no knowledge (or understanding) of multiple intelligences. There are many reasons for this, of course, but most can be reduced to one explanation: the academy rewards, and selects for, those who possess one particular type of intelligence over all the others—what Gardner (2006b) calls "linguistic and logical-mathematical" intelligence.

This is the type of intelligence that reaps the most benefits in the academy, as our reward systems are grounded in this particular type of intelligence. If faculty and staff can present evidence that they are skilled speakers, writers, logical thinkers, grant writers, and problem-solvers, then they are duly rewarded with promotions, salary increases, and, in the case of faculty, tenure, and released time from teaching in order to do research. Increasingly, however, many students today come to our campuses manifesting other types of intelligences. Higher education needs to know how to educate a multiply-intelligent student body. This requires, of course, that the academy be far more willing to employ and support professional educators who themselves manifest multiple intelligences.

Certainly linguistic and logical-mathematical intelligence is important in today's high-tech, results-driven, problem-plagued world. But there are other intelligences that confer survival benefits on all of us as well. These other intelligences are particularly suited for effective meaning-making. These alternative intelligences, according to Gardner, are musical, spatial, kinesthetic, naturalistic, inter- and intrapersonal, and Gardner's most recently described intelligence, existential. We contend that meaning-making requires, at the very least, an acknowledgment by educators that students learn in different ways, and that one type of intelligence is not necessarily superior or inferior to another. The implication for all of us in higher education is that we need to look for ways to link more effectively *what* we do to *how* students learn.

In the realm of meaning-making, it is obvious to us that inter- and intrapersonal, as well as existential, intelligences are key.

Meaning-making educators who are skilled interpersonally in working with people, who can communicate well across differences, and who have mastered the arts of evocation, inspiration, and clarification, are naturals for working in meaning-making settings with students. So, too, educators who are adept intrapersonally, who are enthusiastic about the inner life, who are empathic and intuitive, and who are not put off by the outward expression of personal feelings work well in a variety of meaning-making venues on college campuses (Gardner, 2006b).

It should be obvious by now that existential intelligence is especially important to deep-meaning educators. Logotherapists, narrative therapists, philosophical counselors, positive psychologists (see our *Resources* section at the end of the book), and constructivist educators are the professionals who demonstrate perhaps the greatest propensity for the existential approach to meaning-making. Some of these people have a well-developed spiritual sense. All, however, have, in Gardner's words "a human capacity to pose and ponder the biggest questions . . . all of which have to do with the broader issues of existence, identity, faith, and spirit" (p. 41).

One implication of the multiple-intelligences approach for future research is the extent to which the following proposition holds: the most effective deep-meaning educator needs to be someone whose dominant learning style is inter- and intrapersonal and existential. Likewise, another proposition holds that a meaning-making pedagogy is more likely to have an effect on learners whose multiple intelligences are predominantly inter- and intrapersonal and existential. The results of such research hold important implications for teaching for meaning. One of these is the question of whether educators should be concerned about matching teachers with learners who reflect their own dominant intelligences.

**Realize that students are interpreting, as well as observing,
the "outside world" they are attempting
to analyze, explain, and change.**

All of us, educator and learner alike, *perceive* as well as *receive*. There is no such thing as an immaculate perception (or reception) when it comes to learning about and making meaning. We have written in previous chapters about the epistemological subject, the constructivist consciousness, and postmodern epistemology. Thus, when it comes to making deep meaning, we come down primarily (but not exclusively) on the side of constructivist interpretation rather than the objectivist observation. Obviously, one cannot construct what one cannot observe, and so *inside* and *outside* are inextricably linked in some ways. The dilemma for deep-meaning educators, however, is to help students to differentiate between what is given to their consciousness and the role that their interpretive narratives play in making sense of what is given. This dilemma is a shorthand way of explaining meaning-making. What is out there makes sense only insofar as we impose a narrative of meaning on it.

Obviously, there is no final word regarding which side of the interpretation-observation equation possesses the whole truth. We can only say what we have said before in so many words—*it all depends*. At minimum, deep-meaning educators need to understand that students have the ability to construct, deconstruct, and reconstruct everything that they see, hear, and feel. The extent to which students do the interpretive work is directly proportional to the extent to which they will make meaning of the material before them. Interpretation of some kind, to some degree, is simply unavoidable. This is the way that the human mind functions both biologically and psychologically (Gazzaniga, 2008; Edelman, 2006). For those of us who are interested in doing deep-meaning work with students, the implications appear to be obvious: we need to honor the right—indeed, the necessity—of students to create their own narratives of meaning in their own unique ways.

We also need to help them discover whatever deep connections there may be between what exists inside of them and what exists outside.

There are two poignant proof-texts that Robert has sometimes used in his teaching to elicit responses from students about the inside-outside, constructivist-objectivist dilemma of meaning-making. The first is written by Don Cupitt (2005), the famous "atheist priest": "We don't need any absolutes, or any external support; a world in which everything is relative can hang together surprisingly well, just as liberal democracy, although often believed to be 'soft,' turns out in fact to be a much stronger form of society than absolute monarchy" (p. 76).

For Cupitt, the epistemological constructivist, *inside* almost always precedes *outside* in the sense that we see what we believe, as in the popular song some years ago "every little breeze seems to whisper Louise." *Who* we love shapes *how* and *what* we experience in the world. "Absolutes," for Cupitt, have nothing to do with the world of values, faith, and morals, because there are no scientific certainties in these realms of knowing. They all require a "leap" of intuitive trust—compatible with some people's temperaments, but incompatible with others'. Of course, in politics, Cupitt is talking about "democracy" in the ideal. Realistically, he would wholeheartedly agree with the countercontention that for many countries and peoples, democracy is contraindicated as an absolute good—for a variety of critical contextual reasons.

The second proof-text is written by Norman L. Geisler (1984): "Few of us can ever live a life totally devoid of all absolutes . . . without an absolute center we would lack an integrating point for our lives . . . it is easy to say there are no absolutes, but it is much more difficult to really live as if there are none . . . one can only move the earth [make constructive social changes] if one has a firm place for a fulcrum . . . without such a fulcrum we are living on the shadow of a shadow . . . claiming absolutely that there are no absolutes" (pp. 146, 147, 148, 149).

For Geisler, the epistemological objectivist, *outside* almost always precedes *inside* because without absolute moral and faith pivots, everything would wobble. The center would not hold. Even when we deny the existence of absolutes in the faith-values realm, few of us actually live our lives as if we believe this statement. If the axiological or ontological center is only a matter of cultural conditioning, taste, and perspective, then on what grounds can we actually change anything? What ground(s) do we stand on, and on what authority? Geisler, by implication, asks constructivists a compelling political question: if you say that democracy is the best sociopolitical arrangement in the sense that it confers the greatest amount of autonomy on its citizens, why should your principle of autonomy count for everything, or even anything? Your moral ground is too shaky to support this absolute assertion.

Any kind of teaching, but especially teaching for meaning, demands that the student receive continual encouragement to be an active participant in the entire learning experience—both inside and outside the classroom, both on campus and beyond.

The core of a meaning-centered pedagogy, whatever its emphasis and wherever its location, is the student's right and responsibility to construct a meaning that is unique to the learner. At best, meaning-making educators are mediators of content and practice as these occur in the learner's lived experiences. We are talking here about the irrefutable fact that there is as much learning going on for students *outside* the classroom as there is *inside*. Deep-meaning educators never miss an opportunity to get students actively involved outside the classroom walls. Moreover, they are always on the alert to help students process their extramural learning experiences— whether this processing takes place in an office, classroom, conference room, cafe, residence hall, or downtown restaurant. Deep-meaning learning has the potential of occurring anywhere and everywhere. It is bounded only by the limits of our imaginations.

Anne Colby and her coauthors Ehrlich, Beaumont, and Stephens (2003) make a strong case that when educating students for "lives of moral and civic responsibility," getting them outside the classroom is the key. They summarize well the research that demonstrates the effectiveness of "cross-fertilizing," "extracurricular activities." These activities start with lively, meaning-relevant "cross-campus conversations" (see also Nash, Bradley, & Chickering, 2008). Deep-meaning educators must learn how to foster these types of conversations in smaller units such as residential life complexes. They will need to encourage students to participate in community service programs, as well as get directly involved in political clubs and in a variety of other civic organizations. The latter include, of course, religio-spiritual and secular-humanist groups (Colby et al., 2003, pp. 218–257).

Educators will need to know how to assist students in connecting theory and practice, analysis and action. If an education for meaning is all action, then it quickly degenerates into what Robert calls "action stupefaction." On the other hand, if it is all analysis, then it becomes "analysis paralysis." Either way, the result is a tragic loss of genuine, deep-meaning making. Having encouraged a generous dose of experiential, out-of-classroom activities, therefore, we are acutely mindful of the following axiom: if it is true that experience teaches best, then it is equally if not more true that reflective experience teaches the best of all.

In this respect, we appreciate the findings of the National Survey of Student Engagement, sponsored by the Carnegie Foundation and the Pew Charitable Trusts (Kuh, Kinzie, Schuh, Whitt, & Associates, 2005). The Survey provides an excellent index for helping students reflect on their experiences. Here are its recommendations:

- Encourage students to ask questions at all times about the possible connections between in-class learnings of subject matter and out-of-class activities.

- Allow students to work with classmates in small groups outside as well as inside of class to achieve a productive, mutual sharing of extracurricular learning activities.

- Build into the syllabus the requirement of a community-based project, and specify that ongoing, reflective, written analyses of the student's participation in the project are a necessary adjunct of the activity.

- Make yourself available as often as possible outside of class to help students make connections between their experiential learning and their reading, writing, and content-learning.

- Give prompt feedback to students, about not only their academic performance but also their ability to make the connections between theory and practice.

Finally, we advocate strongly that all of us on college campuses encourage students to write their theory-practice reflections in the *first-person singular* voice. *I* speaks far more forcefully, and personally, than *he, she, it,* or *they* (see Nash, 2004; see also the section in the next chapter on encouraging students to write personal narratives).

Constructivist educators understand that meaning-making is all about the student; we are there mainly to evoke, respond, inform, and clarify.

Students take center stage on the meaning-making college campus. At best, we educators are located somewhere backstage or in the orchestra pit. Only secondarily, if at all, are we there to direct or choreograph. Neither is our classroom function primarily to provoke, expound, propound, and complexify. These latter pedagogical functions—the conventional practices of most higher educators—can only blunt and defeat students' pursuit of meaning-making. This contention of ours raises the issue of just how qualified most higher education faculty—as well as administrators—are to be constructivist educators.

Critiques of professors who dislike teaching and would rather spend most of their time researching, writing grants, and producing original scholarship are rampant in the higher education literature, as well as in the popular media (Getman, 1992; Smith, 1990). But like most sweeping caricatures, this one just is not true. Proportionally speaking, very few professors actually engage in serious research and scholarship, and of those who do, the majority teach in perhaps one hundred of the most elite colleges and universities in the country. Furthermore, of this privileged group, a large percentage stops doing original research and creative scholarship upon getting tenure. (See the *Faculty Scholarly Productivity Index* for full documentation and analysis at http://chronicle.com/stats/productivity/page. php?primary=10&bycat=Go&secondary=91). Therefore, most professors in the majority of the 3,500 institutions of higher education in the United States get paid primarily to teach, advise, and do committee work. Certainly this holds true for those who work in the nation's hundreds of community colleges and proprietary schools. Our point is that the academic culture in more than 90 percent of higher education is built on the teaching function of its workers (see Getman, 1992, and Chace, 2006 for two different types of critiques regarding the conflicts between faculty publishing and teaching).

In many of these so-called teaching institutions, however, faculty are still driven by the myth of tenure-track terror, fueled by the unrealistic desire of second- and third-tier institutions to enter the first-tier ranks. Even though this rarely if ever happens (why this goal is important in the first place is a question we ought to be asking throughout higher education), the publish-or-perish imperative in these institutions keeps junior faculty constantly on edge. It reduces the time and effort they can put into their teaching. This is a shame, because one of the major functions of higher education faculty everywhere is to teach.

Although it may be true that grants and scholarly publications put some institutions on the prestige map, it is effective, responsive, and passionate teaching that attracts and retains students—without whom there would be no colleges and universities. Moreover, teaching for meaning opens up all kinds of creative research opportunities for those faculty who are indeed rewarded more for publishing and grantsmanship than anything else they do. Teaching for meaning-making is a promising field for new scholarship on pedagogy, interdisciplinary studies, and applied research.

Having made the preceding points, we believe that the realistic, everyday question for most of us in the academy ought to be how to make our teaching better. How can we get our students actively and passionately involved in their own learning? What excites them besides cell-phone texting, surfing the Internet, and Facebooking? How can we convey to them that, when push comes to shove, we want to teach *students* first and *subject matter* second? Better still, how can we find that special pedagogical flow in our classrooms that does not even promote such a dichotomy; a flow that makes process and content, and teaching and research inseparable? Whether one publishes a hundred articles or none, these questions ought to be central to the academic experience.

For our particular purposes in this chapter, the central question is, what does it take to be an effective constructivist educator, particularly when it comes to teaching about meaning and meaning-making? How can we put the student at the vital center of the teaching-learning transaction? We urge meaning-making educators to become familiar with research that reinforces over and over again the value of constructivist teaching (for example, Bain, 2004). This research points the way to what students will need in order to be fully engaged in their own learning.

Richard Light's (2001) findings confirm that when educating for meaning is working well, the following learning patterns are evident both inside and outside college classrooms:

- Students engage actively in their learning, with a vibrant sense of expectancy and excitement.

- Open-ended, evocative, problem-based questions in lively conversation are far more prominent than close-ended, test-based answers.

- Learning is interdisciplinary, unbounded, and wide-ranging.

- Teaching and learning are frequently story-based, personally vulnerable, and honest.

- A variety of pedagogical techniques fill the learning space, including lectures, genuine small and large group conversations, colloquia sessions, service learning, and a number of internet chat rooms, discussion groups, and blogs, among others.

Rachel, introduced earlier in this chapter, is proof positive that all of these teaching-learning patterns can help a student immensely in the personal quest for meaning.

So, too, the latest research on brain-based learning by neuroscientists such as Gerald Edelman (2006) and Michael Gazzaniga (2005, 2008) demonstrates that students learn best when they are given the opportunity to personalize their learning by looking for its practical implications in their everyday lives. Rachel, in her written reflection, noted that she began to thrive in her studies at the same time she was developing her own consciousness. She deliberately sought out courses and teachers that avoided the all-too-common disconnects among self, content, and persons.

When students can see the organic connections between subject matter and their interests in performing service to others, or dedicating themselves to a social cause that results in self-transcendence, or creating something artistic, then their learning becomes intense, focused, integrated, and full of passion. Dichotomies disappear. During this time, students' neurons are at optimal firing capacity, and their cognitive patternings are rich and complex. Also, according to this brain-based research, although students highly appreciate some type of evaluative feedback from educators, nearly always the imposition of grades acts as a serious deterrent to their relaxed alertness and complex cognitive processing.

Constructivist education is predicated on an approach to knowledge that views teaching, leading, and learning as experiential, conversational, narrativistic, conditional, developmental, socially and culturally created—as much heart- and hand-based as it is head-based—and always profoundly personal in nature (see Nash, 2008). Rachel had mastered head- and hand-learning throughout her formal schooling. She got the most out of the conventional "chalk and talk" lecture approach to teaching. What was missing in her undergraduate, preprofessional education, however, was heart-learning. In those years she had the *precision* but not the *passion*. By the time she graduated, she was both precise *and* passionate, competent *and* compassionate—an unbeatable combination for her vocation as a health-care professional.

Finally, according to the research of noted constructivist learning theorists Brooks and Martin (1999), the best teachers and leaders are full of enthusiasm about their work and the potential of their students to learn how to shape productive philosophies of life. They are also the ones who know how to tell, and to draw out, engaging, meaning-relevant stories (see the section on storytelling in the next chapter). They have outstanding evocative skills. And they are unusually adept at involving students in genuine, nonhierarchical, mutually vulnerable, give-and-take conversations about making meaning and constructing purpose-driven lives (Nash, Bradley, & Chickering, 2008).

Conversation is the key element in all types of meaning-making.

In fact, there can be no genuine constructivist pedagogy, or deep-meaning learning, without continual conversation between and among educators, learners, and others within the ever-expanding circles of students' relationships. We are not necessarily talking about Socratic dialogue—which, to at least one observer (Rhode, 2006), too often "becomes a shell game in which the teacher first invites the student to 'guess what I'm thinking,' and then finds the response inevitably lacking. The result is a climate in which 'never is heard an encouraging word, and thoughts remain cloudy all day'" (p. 79).

In contrast, we are convinced that the best conversation—from the Latin word *conversare*, to live together (in order to learn about oneself and others)—happens when students and educators spend much of their time in learning spaces connecting with one another on deeper levels. This means drawing one another out and educating through honest give-and-take inquiry about what is really important in the search for meaning in the lessons and events of the day, both inside and outside the classroom and lecture hall. This is not "shell-game discourse"; rather, it is "mutual-vulnerability conversation."

In the real world, each of us lives in conversation with others because we enjoy it. Our students enjoy it, even if they limit conversation to elliptical text-messaging and hastily written emails. We caress each other with the words we choose. We also hurt each other with the words we use. We can open spaces, or we can restrict them, in our conversations both in and out of the classroom, the residence hall, and the office. We can make our learning spaces safe and comfortable, or we can make them threatening and coercive. We can spend all our time pontificating and telling, or we can spend much of our time in our learning spaces connecting with one another, drawing each other out, and educating through honest give-and-take conversation about what's really important in the search for meaning in the lessons and events of the day.

We have found, in our own interactions with students throughout the campus, that our work sparkles most during those times when we are really conversing with one another. There is an honest, deeply respectful interchange about the things we agree and disagree on. In this sense, when conversation is working well, we are all teachers for one another. We talk together. We learn from each other. We make meaning together. It never gets tired or old. We exist in solidarity with one another, both in the classroom and in the workplace. No matter how high-pressured or technical our work, conversation is possible, even necessary. We have had neighbors who work in diverse fields—high school teachers, emergency room doctors, firefighters on the job, even busy kitchen chefs—tell us that conversation with their colleagues and clients, even when truncated, is the best way to get something done or to make sense of their lives.

Here are a few brief recommendations for engaging students in deep conversation about meaning:

- Create a welcoming conversational space with students, one that features maximum psychological safety and invites maximum participation.

- Encourage conversation at all times by asking probing, open-ended questions.

- Spend time one-on-one with students whenever possible—hanging out is the favorite activity of quarterlife students, and it is the best way to initiate candid moral conversation about meaning, because it underplays status and power differentials.

- When talking with students about issues of meaning and purpose, attribute the best motive and assume the best intentions.

- Show some humility and open-mindedness by first looking for the truth in what you oppose and the error in what you espouse.

Finally, we should never forget the principle that asking good questions of one another about the meaning of meaning, and the meaning of our own meaning-making, is the *sine qua non* for open-ended conversations with one another. The poet Rainer Maria Rilke asks us to "love the questions . . . I want to beg you, as much as I can, to be patient toward all that is unsolved. Try to love the questions themselves. Do not now seek the answers which cannot be given you because you would not be able to live them. Live the questions now. Perhaps you will then gradually, without noticing it, live along some distant day into the answer" (quoted in Christensen, Garvin, & Sweet, 1991, p. 163).

There is as much learning about meaning taking place in the silent spaces of the student's life as there is in formal and informal educational settings.

What is there about silence, both in and out of the classroom space, that scares educators and students (see the section on silence in the next chapter)? Why do we think that verbal noise is the only sign of learning? Do our students always have to be actively doing and saying something in order to be learning? Some research shows that a wait time of at least five to ten seconds after each question elicits a far more thoughtful response from students than an immediate reaction (Jensen, 1998).

Zen Buddhists know well that the most significant meaning-making moments in our lives take place in our silent spaces—in the stillness of our hearts, heads, and souls. Mindfulness is all about attending to what is outside of us, by being fully present in the moment, and by being *quiet*. Ask our students where they do their deepest thinking; it is usually when they are alone, away from tele-visions, radios, cell phones, and electronic games. Ask them where they do their deepest feeling, and it is usually with others, especially with people they trust. Push the question a bit further, and students will say that it is always during the quiet times when they are best able to understand *why* they feel the way they do.

We make deep meaning in our silent spaces. Robert some-times asks students these questions: What is your favorite physical space for just being alone with yourself? Do you make a distinction between being alone and being lonely? Do you have a special place you consider a sanctuary? If I were to ask the entire class to sit in silence for the first (or the last) fifteen minutes of every class, how would you feel? When and where have you most recently felt most calm, most at peace, most in flow? Is it easy or hard for you to build in some time during your day to just be by yourself, to quiet the "chattering monkeys" in your head, and to reflect on what truly matters to you at the present time in your life? Where do you seek rest and renewal?

Many students in Robert's classes have never been asked to think about such questions. But when they do, they generally tend to be very grateful. A graduate student in a counseling program once said,

> I realize, after thinking about your questions, that I can't stand silence. I tend to rush people into saying something, even my clients. I take sleep medication all the time, because I seem to have thousands of your "chattering monkeys" going off every second of my life, especially when I'm trying to fall asleep. I'm not doing very well in my counseling practicum because I'm blabbing all the time, particularly when I feel incompetent, which is most of the time. I know now that I need to create the silent spaces in my life that will provide me with the opportunities to reflect on why I want to be a counselor in the first place. Isn't this question a meaning question?

Yes, it is a meaning question. And one book that we would strongly recommend to this counselor-in-training, as well as to every single educator in the academy, is a book written for public school teachers and students—Rachael Kessler's *The Soul of Education* (2000). What Kessler calls the "soul," we are calling "meaning." Kessler posits "Seven Gateways to the Soul in Education" and we maintain that these gateways are applicable to students at *all* levels of education.

Six of Kessler's seven gateways are the yearning for deep connection, the search for meaning and purpose, the hunger for joy
and delight, the creative drive, the urge for transcendence, and the
need for initiation. We are concerned here mainly with the seventh
gateway: the longing for silence and solitude. She says, "[T]his is an
ambivalent domain, and is fraught with both fear and urgent need.
As a respite from the tyranny of 'busyness' and noise, silence may be
a realm of reflection, of calm or fertile chaos, an avenue of stillness
and rest for some, prayer or contemplation for others" (p. 17).

Here are a few tips that Kessler offers to educators for "opening
the gates" to our silent spaces:

- Allow some quiet time in all our personal interactions
  with students.

- Remember that many students who tend to be feelers
  can use the quiet spaces to restore an equilibrium
  between their emotions and their thoughts.

- Build in a series of reflective time-outs during a
  teaching-learning experience.

- At times, ask students to free-write what went on for
  them during the reflective time-outs.

- Before a faculty or an administrative meeting, take the
  time to sit in silence with colleagues before the meeting
  begins (this will probably bring about the most
  resistance of all our tips).

- Get students to journal in silence for at least five to ten
  minutes a day—in their favorite, quiet hangout spaces.

Kessler recommends journaling in response to these questions (and dozens of others in her book) about silence and
stillness:

"What, of all I feel and believe, is truly my own?"

"How can I change feeling lonely?"

"How does one learn to trust oneself, to believe in oneself?"

"Who or what do I really want to connect to?"

"What is it that I did really well today?"

"What is it I wish I had done differently?"

"How do I find balance between the demands of the world and my inner needs for rest, rejuvenation, and simply being?"

"How can I create a peace within me that will radiate outward to others?"

"How can I slow down when everyone around me is speeding?"

All these strategies are calculated to help students go inward before they go outward and upward—the inevitable directions where meaning-making takes all of us. Without the silence, however, we run the risk of only going *backward*. Without the time for quiet reflection, it is unlikely that meaning-makers would ever reach their ultimate destinations.

Deep connections to others can supplement the work of meaning-making that is very difficult to achieve in formal educational settings.

Some religions believe that the way to the self is through others. Some believe that the way to others is through the self. What most religions have in common, however, is the pivotal role that caring relationships play in making meaning. In fact, most religio-spiritualities are predicated on the importance of making deep connections with others—God, family, friends, lovers, even strangers. One psychotherapist (Yalom, 2002) has even gone so far as to say that the most effective therapeutic relationship is one based on mutual engagement, reciprocal openness, vulnerability, and egalitarianism. His basic premise is that all of us are "fellow-travelers," in that none of us is ever absolved from the responsibility we have to make the most of our freedom to create meaning.

Like the great religious teachers—and like Yalom—we too believe that building different types of relationships between and among educators and students is the necessary (but not sufficient) condition for successful meaning-making. A growing body of research supports this assertion. We believe that Light's findings stemming from his decades-long research (2001) on the Harvard Assessment Project can be extended universally to all teaching-learning locations. Through the years, hundreds of his student-interviewees reiterated the point that their best classes—the ones that were most memorable, useful, and intellectually challenging—involved being able to make connections with others.

Students mentioned getting involved outside of class with the arts, special-interest clubs and groups, and a variety of content-linked, experiential activities. While the hands-on experiences were important to them, even more important were the interactions they had with others in order to achieve a common goal. Through these interactions, not only did students get things accomplished, but, equally important, they learned how to work, converse, and play together. Thus they learned the invaluable human skills of how to initiate, sustain, and deepen relationships.

In the classroom, students especially appreciated small classes. In this setting students were best able to get to know the professor, both in and out of the classroom. Students also enjoyed classes that emphasized writing assignments. They particularly appreciated classes with a lot of writing, because over 90 percent of them felt that being able to write clearly and creatively was the most important single skill they hoped to develop during their undergraduate years. Moreover, it was through their writing that students were able to get the professor's attention in order to develop an out-of-class relationship based on personal mentoring. Also, students learned best about how to write when they were able to share their writing with small groups and, in the process, receive valuable feedback from their peers.

The warning flag that predicted future academic frustration and failure, however, was when a student felt a sense of isolation from others. Light's research showed that initial feelings of being isolated only served to intensify the state of isolation, because the student, motivated by feelings of embarrassment and loneliness, tended to dig in, withdraw even more, and work alone. Isolation led to increasing feelings of desolation. But when faculty and staff reached out to put students in touch with like-minded others, as well as with counselors, their grades and attitudes drastically improved. Another finding of Light's is that when the residence halls include a great deal of ethnic, racial, social class, and religious diversity, particularly during the first year, friendships multiply almost exponentially during the next three years on campus. Often, it takes awhile for friendships to develop in first-year living arrangements, and the road can get bumpy along the way. But it is essential to keep in mind that friendships emerging from those initial living groups "can and do shape all future social interactions, especially inter-ethnic social interactions" (p. 44).

Most qualitative and quantitative researchers who study the best ways to educate students just do not talk much about fostering "deep connections" in the teaching-learning experience. These relationships are very difficult to measure, and there is not a lot of precedent in higher education for how to create and deliver this type of pedagogy. Regardless, John Henry Newman's (1854/1990) comments about the university in the mid-nineteenth century still retain a cogency for us today: "The personal influence of the teacher is able in some sort to dispense with an academic system, but that system cannot in any sort dispense with personal influence. With influence there is life, without it there is none. If influence is deprived of its due position, it will not by those means be got rid of it; it will only break out irregularly, dangerously. An academic system without the personal influence of teachers upon pupils is an arctic winter; it will create an ice-bound, petrified, cast-iron university and nothing else" (p. 311).

We hold that without these "deep connections"—and this includes the "personal influence" of the educator—students are unlikely to take the meaning-making project seriously. They will be reluctant to take the personal risks necessary to make significant changes in their lives. Deep connections with others, both in and out of classes, enable learners to avoid the anguish of loneliness and isolation. To touch and be touched by other persons is life-affirming. In our experiences with college students, they frequently talk about making deep connections, not just with students and educators, but also with nature, animals, and a transcendent power, as well as with a variety of nurturing communities. It is the close, trusting connections with other people, however, that students cherish most of all.

We are not talking about sexual intimacy or lifelong partner commitments. Rather, we are talking about forming connections with communities where a deep sense of belonging is present. In our own teaching, whenever students feel that our classrooms are experienced as communities of belonging, where genuine communion between educators and students is possible, then the activity of meaning-making gets pushed to deeper levels of intensity. Students take the process more seriously because they feel safe, supported, and respected. And when this happens, as Tompkins (1996) has written, the classroom becomes a "hallowed space."

Tompkins notes that the way students are taught to talk with one another in and out of the classroom on their campuses is the way they will interact with people throughout their lives. They will perform, compete, and strive to win in the outside world, if inside the academic space they are rewarded based exclusively on their ability to give educators what they want. According to Tompkins, what educators want most of all is for students to be individualistic, competitive, efficient information processors, followers of rules, and excellent test-takers, who know how to defer to those in authority.

Tompkins calls for a radical transformation of higher education. She wants academic preparation to include "qualities besides critical thinking." She advocates developing virtues for the academy, among them "generosity, steadfastness, determination, practical competence, humor, ingenuity, and information" (p. 219). But more important, she also wants an academy that prizes "mercy and compassion . . . [and encourages] quiet reflection, self-observation, and meditative awareness" (p. 220). Above all, Tompkins wants higher education to have both "a center and a soul." It is with these words that we end this section on the need for educators to forge "deep connections" among themselves, students, subject matter, the outside world, and significant communities of belonging. In the next section, we offer some concrete suggestions about how to create deeply connected communities of learning through the art and craft of story-telling.

Effective educators understand that helping students to make meaning is directly related to the ability to tell their own personal stories of meaning-making.

Even better, good educators are not afraid to evoke such personal stories from their students (Nash, 2008). Tell a story of personal meaning, and you have captured your students' attention. Draw out your students' personal stories of meaning, and you have won them over for life. Here are the words of Sara Lawrence-Lightfoot (2000) on stories:

> Teaching is storytelling. It is the place where lives can meet. . . . Stories create intimate conversations across boundaries. Stories disturb and challenge. . . . They are able to incite humor or passion or even irrationality. . . . I use stories to create deeper connections with my students, to reveal the universal human themes that we share, and to bridge the realms of thinking and

> feeling. . . . In those moments of personal revelation students experience my vulnerability, my trust, and my respect. . . . As their teacher, I offer them my "dreams," and I ask them to "tread softly." (pp. 111, 112)

Stories actually confer survival benefits on all of us. (The Latin root of *narrative* means "to know, to tell, to construct new knowledge.") Stories make us human. They give our lives focus. They get us up in the morning and off to work. They help us to solve problems and to survive with dignity, style, and grace. In our stories, we live what we narrate to be the "real world." For some of us, our story of life is a win-lose athletic contest. For others, life is a love affair, or a cosmic or spiritual quest, or a business venture, or one long, unmitigated catastrophe. For many of us, the stories we live in are religious, or political, or philosophical, or occupational, or recreational. And these stories color how we see and experience the world we live and work in. However they differ from each other, each of us inhabits a particular narrative at all times. And this narrative understanding affects others, just as their narratives affect us.

All of us on college campuses create the stories that we live in, but we also live in the stories that we create. This is the central pedagogical meaning of constructivism: students make meaning in so far as they introduce, digest, and incorporate what they learn into their own stories. Therefore, as an educational philosophy, constructivism confers power on each of us. The stories we—educators and students alike—love, and the stories we hate, provide deep insight into what we value and what we do not; into who we are striving to become both personally and professionally, and who we are not.

The lesson here for all of us who teach and administer in higher education is that we are more than disembodied, unstoried, meaning-deficient experts in the work we do with students. We are not invincible, bionic professionals who are without feelings or histories or philosophies of life. We have personal stories to tell about the multifaceted human beings that we are. Likewise, our students have their own personal stories to tell. We need to learn how to tell our stories in such a way as to make an impact on our students. This is when students really start to listen. It is even more important, however, that we take the time to draw out our students' stories, whenever we think this might be appropriate to the lessons we are trying to convey to them. Evoking and invoking stories should always be done with nonexploitative sensitivity and generosity.

With this in mind, we try very hard to listen to students' stories. How, for example, can we truly understand how a student will respond to a challenging reading or writing assignment, a piece of difficult advice, or a well-intentioned criticism or recommendation, without first understanding the story that a student might be living in at any given time? Although it is safe to say that every student wants competent educators who are knowledgeable, respectful, and personally accessible, they also want something more. They want to be understood as real human beings. They want to know that their stories matter to us. They want us to understand how they make sense of the chaos in their lives. They want us to respect them as meaning-makers.

Here are a few tangible suggestions for evoking students' stories:

- Talk about your own life as a series of stories. These are what students remember the most, because storytelling humanizes us—in addition to enchanting others.

- Help students to frame their experiences as stories of *survival* whenever possible. This helps them to realize that rather than being passive victims of one external force or another, they are indeed resilient, active creators of meaning.

- Evoke deeper stories of meaning from students whenever possible. This includes encouraging them to develop further those personal stories that are religious, political, social, cultural, and educational. Doing this enables students to see that they are actually complex meaning makers with multiple identities.

• Point out commonalities and universal themes in students' stories wherever these might emerge. These commonalities will connect students to one another in powerful ways.

• Share your dreams, and ask students to share theirs. As Lawrence-Lightfoot reminds us, we should tread softly, because it is in the dreams that meaning begins.

• Teach students how to evoke stories of meaning from one another whenever the occasion arises. They, like you, can be story evokers.

Deep-meaning educators encourage students to do a great deal of personal narrative writing in order to convey their stories of meaning. Making meaning is largely a function of being able to "me-search" subjectively as well as to research objectively.

The denial of the value of the self's stories in an academic setting is born in the command all of us have heard in school at some time: never use the "I" in formal writing. The "I," we have been told, is incapable of discovering and dispensing wisdom without the support of the "them," the certified experts. Messages like these leach the fascinating, storied self out of the budding writer, leaving only the clichéd, and often pinched, stories of experts to recirculate over and over again. Robert's first order of business in encouraging personal narrative writing is to let his students know that the search for meaning is very difficult unless they can write personally about their quests. We need to let our students know that their personal stories count.

Vivian Gornick (2001) says, "A serious life, by definition, is a life one reflects on, a life one tries to make sense of and bear witness to. The age is characterized by a need to testify. Everywhere in the world women and men are rising up to write their personal stories out of the now commonly held belief that one's own life signifies" (p. 91). For Gornick, personal narrative writing starts with the *writer's* life rather than with the lives, thoughts, and activities of others. Robert Nash (Nash, 2004) calls this genre of self-creation "scholarly personal narrative" (SPN) writing. This type of SPN writing encourages students to make sense of the raw material of meaning-making first from the inside out before going from the outside in. What matters most in personal narrative writing is the conviction that the writer's own life actually testifies. It matters. In the end, what truly matters is the sense of meaning that the writer is able to create, and then to convey, both to self and to others.

Many students in our classes are confident that they can write a term paper, a research paper, or a literature review with, as some say, their "eyes closed." They know the templates for these conventional types of manuscripts by heart, because they have done so many of them throughout their years in formal education. They know from practice that it is mostly just a matter of understanding how to fit some new pieces of the knowledge puzzle into the old research templates. But telling a personal story in a classroom setting, with the professor present, is hard for most students. Writing one's personal story in a creative way is even more difficult.

To prepare his students for personal narrative writing about meaning, Robert challenges them to dare to stand for something in their writing. He asks them to try to take a position on something with strong conviction and by displaying palpable affect in their language. He gives them permission to allow their authorial voices to be clear, distinct, and strong, and, above all, personal. He tells them to resist the conventional academic temptation to be "objective": stoical, qualified, subdued, abstract, and distant. He acknowledges that at times it is okay, even desirable, to try to be detached or dispassionate, and at other times to be scientific and objective. But it is also okay, particularly when writing about meaning, to be fully engaged and excitable, to be transparent and vulnerable.

An undergraduate student we'll call "Sarah" came to Robert's office one day to report the following:

You know, all this stuff about postmodernism and existentialism that you've been talking about lately. Well, I tried a little bit of it with my own writing. I was getting stuck in writing my honors thesis for another professor, and I couldn't understand why—that is until I listened to you talk about personal narrative writing and its rightful place in the scholarship of higher education.

My original intention was to write a kind of literary reflection for my thesis by telling a powerful story of loss and survival, with my extended Jewish family as the central protagonists. I wanted this reflection to focus especially on my grandparents who were prisoners at Auschwitz during the Holocaust, and who I consider to be courageous, noble survivors. Moreover, I wanted to write this kind of reflection in order to understand why I identify so readily with being a "cultural" Jew but balk at being called a "religious" Jew. In the most important sense, then, I wanted the study of my grandparents to really be a study of myself.

In contrast, my honors thesis advisor wanted me to conduct formal interviews with my grandparents, leave myself out of the study as much as I could, and then test for validity by doing proof checks of inconsistencies when I analyzed the data coming out of the interviews. I could only react, "huh"? This all seemed so bloodless and contrived to me. After all, I love my grandparents, and I have listened to their stories for years. I also know what I need from these interviews, and what I would like others to learn from them about their own ethnic heritages. Whether or not my grandparents' stories are inconsistent, or even exaggerated, is irrelevant to me. I only know that they have suffered beyond my worst nightmares.

(Continued)

So, I decided to write my thesis as a scholarly personal narrative manuscript, and I placed myself at the center of my writing. I started with something that my grandfather once said to me and I've never forgotten: "If there is a God, then he is a butcher. He is the Gestapo officer who burned my brothers and sisters. He is the camp commander who spit on my mother's grave. This cowardly God stood idly by, as the smoke from the ovens, baking all those innocent children and adults, curled to his damned heavens. I lost my faith in God once and for all in those death camps, but I found something better there: a more enduring faith in the people I love, like you, Sarah. When I saw how fragile life is, and how it can be so easily destroyed by a handful of monsters, I realized that cherishing one another is all there is. There is nothing more than this, and it's up to each one of us to love intensely and compassionately. Everything else is a pathetic fairytale."

I decided to write about how my grandfather's account of his terrible death-camp experiences really frames everything that I believe today about life's purpose and meaning. His account has helped me to create a meaning in my life that gets me through my own periodic bouts with depression, hopelessness, and angst. Like him, I believe that there is nothing more to be achieved in life than living genuinely, loving passionately, connecting frequently with others, and doing my best at all times to make my world a more humane and caring place. In my thesis, I tell lots of stories about my relatives, and I pull no punches. And, guess what? My advisor loved my stories. In fact, she told me that she, herself, was a Jew, and the relative of two concentration camp victims, but she never got to know them because they died at Auschwitz. She and I would have never known this about one another if I hadn't taken the risk to write personally from my heart and soul.

Oh, and just one more thing: like Eli Weisel after writing *Night*, I reclaimed my own religious faith after writing about my grandfather's loss of his faith. I realized that, in my case, I need a God, especially during those times that are bleakest and most horrible for me. Although I've never been in a death camp, I have "died" lots of small deaths, particularly when I lost my dearest friend who committed suicide two years ago. Without a God to believe in during those worst of times, my life would be totally without meaning. Thank you for inspiring me to write so personally, and, along the way, to discover what's really important to me.

Life, as every writer knows, is incongruous, complex, and paradoxical. It can bore us, soothe us, upset us, confound us, sadden us, inspire us, and anger us, sometimes all at once. Therefore, Robert's writing instruction to students like Sarah is to try always to be honest. He asks them to say what they mean and believe what they say. He reminds them to leave room in their meaning-making writing for the ellipsis dots that, in theory, can always end every sentence they write, and every story they tell, and every truth they proclaim. Why? Because personal narrative writing never ends; it only stops, for the time being. There will always be something else to add. All meaning evolves—given the passage of time, the changing of life's conditions, and the natural growth of each and every meaning-maker. What gives our lives meaning in the here-and-now will inevitably change in the who-knows-where-and-when.

Here are some guidelines that Robert gives his students as they begin the adventure of writing about their quests for meaning in a personal narrative style:

- Start with the "I" before you proceed outward to the "you" and the "they."

- Make your voice distinct, candid, and uniquely your own.

- Make sure that you convey a clear sense of the meaning-theme running throughout your writing. Playwrights call this a "through-line."

- Don't forget to tell some good personal stories.

- Remember, at all times, that *me*-search writing about meaning is the indispensable source of *re*-search writing; when done well, it can even lead to *we*-search writing as others read and respond to it.

- It is okay to cite other authors' works and ideas, as long as these citations come from your heart and soul rather than as ritual padding from your head. In other words, be passionate about, and cite, the ideas of others only insofar as they fuel your own drive to make meaning.

- Take some risks; depart from the usual research writing formulas, rubrics, and templates.

- Keep telling yourself that you have a personal story worth telling and a point about meaning-making worth sharing.

- Remind yourself over and over again that scholarly writing can be fun, engaging, and pleasing to write . . . not only for the writer but also for your readers.

- Strive for an academic *rigor* in your personal narrative writing that is closer to academic *vigor* than it is to academic rigor *mortis*.

Rethink conventional assessment strategies and homework assignments. Educating for meaning requires bold, creative, risk-taking evaluation initiatives.

The key is to remember that the most important part of the word *evaluation* is *value*. The best way to evaluate the outcomes of meaning-making learning is to ask students themselves what the *value* of their experience has been. According to Bain's (2004) research on effective teaching, the best evaluation stresses learning rather than performance. Performance means living up to others' expectations and requirements. Learning means that students take full responsibility for their own intellectual, emotional, kinesthetic, and personal development. Performance is mainly about acquisition, storing information, and taking tests. Learning is developmental and an end in itself. Meaning-making educators are as interested in knowing *who* the student is as *what* the student knows.

A meaning-making approach to learning teaches to the *person* rather than to the *test*. It recognizes that any kind of assessment process is flawed at best, because in some sense it always represents the personal judgment, and intellectual biases, of the assessor. Furthermore, as most of us know intuitively, no evaluative judgment ever originates from a completely "objective" sense of what represents failure or success. Robert sometimes says to his students: "Tell me how *you* were judged in school, and I'll tell you how you will judge *others*. Better still, tell me how you *felt* about being judged throughout your education, and I'll tell you what you purposely *include*, and *exclude*, in your assessment of others."

Some of Bain's best teachers asked their students to evaluate themselves, while still requiring them to provide various types of hands-on evidence that learning did, indeed, occur. Often, these students presented this evidence in face-to-face conversation with their teachers, in addition to writing extensive narrative self-evaluations, complete with such "evidence" as learning portfolios, time logs, daily or weekly written reports, and a variety of independently designed work projects. The upshot for the successful assessment of learning in meaning-making is to encourage students to set their own goals and to take full responsibility for determining whether or not they were able to meet those goals.

Responsible Construction

A constructivist approach to deep-meaning learning engages students beyond their intellects. Deep-meaning learning connects head to heart to hand, underscoring that what students think about influences how they act and feel and who they become. The reverse holds true, too. Who students are (and who they are becoming) shapes what they think about. A pedagogy of constructivism respects this symbiotic relationship between subject (learner) and object (lesson) and leverages students' head-heart collateral to bring the lesson to life. What each student contributes from his or her interpretation and experiences adds to the education of all, including the teacher.

Make no mistake, we are not advocating free-wheeling curricula with no content parameters. On the contrary, we are recommending that educators think anew about the learning arena. For students, that arena stretches far beyond the classroom, the residence hall, and even the campus. With some advance preparation, educators inside and outside the classroom can put this expanded learning arena to work, and they can use it to guide students to dive more deeply into what they could just as easily skim across.

To help educators envision how this deep-meaning learning might work, the next chapter offers several practical tips for incorporating constructivist pedagogy. In the pages that immediately follow, we discuss easy-to-use methods for connecting heart and hand to what the head is already doing.

5

Make Room for Meaning
Practical Advice

In this chapter, we use the frameworks presented in the first sections of this book to outline practical tips and suggestions for all educators in order to set the stage for meaning-making. Because each of the practical sections that follow is grounded in the four therapeutic frameworks we examine in the Resources section "Approaches to Meaning-Making," we urge readers to consult that final section of the book (either before or after reading this chapter) for further explanation of some of the more technical concepts we occasionally mention here.

For example, the very process of meaning-making is grounded in logotherapy and the need for all of us, no matter our unique backgrounds, to create, in Nietzsche's words, "whys to live for." This is what Viktor Frankl's logotherapy is all about. So too, the use of storytelling and story construction, as a way for students to seize control of and author their lives, is the major construct of narrative therapy. Asking philosophical questions in the classroom (regardless of the subject matter) for students to ponder, and planning moments of reflective silence for students to pause and to process the relationship of philosophy to their own meaning-making, is directly linked to philosophical counseling. Finally, helping students to build on their strengths, not concentrate on their weaknesses, and to assist them in the universal quest for personal happiness, is the province of positive psychology.

In the sections that follow, we present five pedagogically sound and practical themes, and we discuss how each might be applied in the classroom, in out-of-classroom venues, and in one-on-one meetings with students. Whether these pedagogical tools are applied in the seminar room, the lecture hall, the community service site, the residence hall, or the advising meeting, we are confident that they will help quarterlife students make sense of the world and their place in it. Please keep in mind, however, that these are *tools*, not *rules*. They may or may not work for everyone. They may need modification. They may need to be replaced by other tools that work more effectively. We offer these tools as suggestions, not doctrines.

Tell Stories

Stories have their entertainment value, absolutely. A long lecture peppered with a few good stories keeps everyone alert and engaged. But stories also create the capacity to move students from the abstract to the concrete and back again. As we discussed in the first part of the book, stories provide a powerful gateway to meaning. They are a window onto what or whom we value, how we view ourselves, and how we interpret the world around us. The stories we tell ourselves and share with students create a rich, multidimensional context from which they can readily access meaning regardless of expertise. For the same reason that we might choose to use a relief map to demonstrate why Denver is known as the "Mile-High City," we also tell stories to illustrate perspective and relationship. The story, like the relief map, gives the subject matter concrete context and dimension which a nonexpert can easily grab hold of and use to create meaning.

Inside the Classroom

Try to be a storyteller as much as an information dispenser. Help students to understand that all perspectives on subject matter are up for grabs, in the sense that they are other people's informed or uninformed interpretations. Help them to know the difference. Show that there are many sides to any particular disciplinary narrative. For example, the history of westward expansion in the United States has multiple narrative perspectives, which vary widely depending on the primary storytellers: white men or women, native peoples or freed slaves, the wealthy or the poor, believers or nonbelievers. Together, the perspectives of these groups weave a certain complexity that enriches understanding. Present content from the perspectives of many narratives of meaning, including your own—*especially* your own interpretive, intellectual slant. Ask students to ferret out additional perspectives, and challenge them to discover their own.

Point out how some disciplines are *thin* and some are *thick*. Some are based on unambiguous stories of meaning that leave less room for multiple interpretations, complications, and complexity; some are based on more ambiguous stories of meaning that are deeper and more expansive. In the former, greater emphasis might be put on the facts; for example, the more empirical disciplines such as science, math, and some of the social sciences such as physical and cultural anthropology; in the latter, there will be more room for creative interpretation; for example, the arts and humanities.

However, recognize that no discipline is ever exclusively thin or thick. Sometimes the empirical disciplines can be thick and the humanities thin. It all depends—on the particular narrative context of the discipline and the narrative perspective of the scholar or practitioner. As in narrative therapy, whenever clients are encouraged to dig beneath the surface to create a "rich, thick description" of their lives, so, too, in the disciplines, we should encourage students to look deeply into the meaning of subject matter. One way they can start to do this is by reading between the lines of the scholar or practitioner's unique presentation of the discipline.

Select, from the sciences, literature, arts, and other subject matter, examples of how individuals have somehow risen above their stories of origin, particularly when these actions may have taken great courage. *Externalize* these stories for students by identifying their adaptive strengths and maladaptive weaknesses. Show the results of both adaptation and maladaptation on the lives of these exemplary individuals. Whenever appropriate, share a few of your own stories of success and failure, of those times when you took some warranted risks and those when you did not. At the very least, students may learn how to become more adaptive, and less maladaptive, in their own personal struggles.

Point out that it is possible for anyone to *deconstruct* the conventional ways of understanding a discipline, whether this be in the humanities, social sciences, or sciences. Deconstruction begins by taking apart the guiding beliefs, ideas, and practices of the various practitioners or scholars of the disciplines. Knowledge is narrative, and, as narrative therapists teach their clients, we made it all up; we narrativized everything, including all the knowledge systems that students study and that professors research and teach. The "taken-for-granteds" in any discipline are a function of the various stories of truth that govern the disciplines.

Help students to understand the background assumptions and main ideas of the various knowledge systems by deliberately asking *deconstructive* questions such as these:

- What do you suppose is the main agenda of the author?

- What story of good or bad, right or wrong, valid or invalid, truth or error, is the practitioner or scholar telling?

- What unique outcomes do the authoritative figures in the discipline hope to achieve by the way they think, write, and validate their "truths"?

- What is the storied history of the discipline, and how do its unique events over time correspond to today's realities?

- Have there been recent efforts to create a new story of the discipline, a new way of looking at ideas, data, people, events, and so on?

- What conflicts arose within the discipline as a result?

- What alternative stories of your discipline's approach to truth would you suggest?

Encourage students to tell their own stories through either reflection assignments or in-class discussions. Ask them to relate their personal or family histories to the course content, and observe how the material begins to take new shape for them as they apply their own perspectives to it. Teach them to evaluate multiple perspectives, their own included, so that they may begin to connect personal values to class concepts and draw meaning from these connections. As students begin to attach meaning to the subject, they become increasingly invested in their own learning.

Case in point: Laurie, a student in Michele's class, was grappling with her understanding and opinion of affirmative action as a remedy for social inequities. At first Laurie played it safe, giving pat responses and parroting an ideology she had siphoned from someone or somewhere else. Although she knew facts about the subject, Laurie was personally divorced from it; the material held no meaning for her. When prompted to consider the effects of disparate high school curricula on a student's preparation and readiness for college, Laurie's eyes suddenly grew wide as she began to make her own personal connection to the discussion.

Her older sister, it turned out, had attended a school without a college prep curriculum. While Laurie was tackling a full load at a private four-year college, Laurie's sister, who according to Laurie had more academic talent, was struggling to accumulate transferable credits at the local community college. That she and her sister had two different experiences and therefore two different perspectives created new possibilities for Laurie. She began to see how the perspectives of authors, classmates, and teachers were born of their narratives and did not necessarily speak for all. Rather than limit herself to others' interpretations of events, concepts, and ideas, she learned the power of her own meaning-making ability. In this scenario, Laurie—or more accurately, Laurie's story—was her own best teacher.

Outside the Classroom

Do not miss the opportunity to show students that there are many possible ways of interpreting a particular state of mind, a policy, an incident, a crisis, an interpersonal success or failure. One person's terrible crisis might be another person's incredible opportunity. Students need to understand that there is both risk and benefit in all undertakings. Narrative therapists use such terms as "re-authoring" or "re-storying" for the process we undertake in making meaning of our lives. Narrative threads make our lives understandable, to both ourselves and others, because disparate events and themes get woven together to form a story. Whether we do this consciously or not, we always re-author and re-story our experiences in our work settings, because this is the best way for us to make sense of what is happening around us. It also gives us control of our external circumstances.

One student with whom Michele worked closely re-storied his narrative as a first-generation student. We will call him "Sam." During the summer between high school and college, Sam felt his excitement and pride about being the first in his family to attend college give way to fear. He worried he would not fit in with a student body he imagined to have tonier upbringings than his own. Sam became embarrassed by his working-class background, and once he arrived on campus he did everything he could to hide his family circumstances from his peers. Sam's desperation to present what he thought would be a more acceptable image pushed him to choose less-than-legal methods for making the money his adopted lifestyle demanded. Sam self-medicated with alcohol and marijuana to ease the pain of his double life, a life he created for fear of being discovered as a fraud.

Over the course of his second year of college, Sam began to unburden himself. Michele remembers the day Sam shared that his parents were manual laborers as a tearful one, indeed. With the help of professional counseling, Sam reframed his narrative as a first-generation student. He released the shame he felt and replaced it with a renewed sense of pride for all he and his parents had accomplished. Freed from the weight of his own negative interpretation of his background, Sam was able to negotiate a healthier, more successful college experience. By his third year, Sam was on the dean's list, involved in campus leadership, and enrolled in an internship program in his chosen field. Sam had shifted the meaning of his own story, and in the shifting he found the freedom to be who he is rather than who he thought others expected him to be.

Help students to understand that what gives their personal lives meaning has both its thin and its thick dimensions. Also, create group opportunities for members to share stories to help them discover commonalities in their own narratives of meaning—insofar as these might overlap with other people's stories. Looking for meaning-overlap in one another's stories—even though on the surface they may appear to be so different—can strengthen the virtues of empathy and compassion for all parties. Sharing thick stories of meaning has the potential to draw people together by allowing them to be more vulnerable to one another. Sharing thin stories of meaning is a good initial strategy for breaking the ice with others. These thin types of stories require little risk on the part of the storyteller and could set the stage for later sharing thick stories of meaning that emanate as much from the heart as from the head.

Ask students to identify the four or five most significant moments of their lives—those moments that have shaped who they are, what they believe, how they think, and what they value. Then ask them to name how they see themselves currently—as a friend, a community citizen, a leader, a scholar—and who they hope to be in a future at least five years hence. What results is one depiction of the story they have lived. Ask them to discuss why they chose to highlight those four or five scenes from their lives. They will begin to understand that who they are now and who they hope to become is, at least in part, a function of how they interpret where they have been and what they have experienced.

Equally revealing is the discussion about which scenes from their lives they chose not to include. Ask them to consider the story that the excluded scenes would tell about who they are. As they follow the exercise, students experience the ways in which they interpret their own narratives and begin to see themselves as author, or storyteller, with the power to confer meaning on the events of their lives. This approach works especially well with intact student groups, such as leadership organizations, student staffs, and residential communities. As they share their narratives with one another and describe the meaning they are making of their lives, they implicitly invite their peers to hold them accountable to the values that give shape to that meaning.

Remember the basic principle of narrative therapists: vulnerability begets vulnerability—and let this begin with the educator. So we have found in our work with students: exchanging our own thick personal narratives, at the appropriate time and place, encourages students to do the same with us and with one another. There is no better way to build trust and foster a genuine sense of community than for us to start the process. One significant benefit that comes from this kind of community building is an improved sense of collegiality and teamwork.

One-on-One with Students

Prolonged advising or mentoring relationships have the potential to be immensely consequential in the lives of students. The safety of the one-on-one relationship affords students the mental and emotional space to tell their stories, to see themselves as the authors of their own stories, and to re-author them as needed. Over coffee or lunch, or in the unexpected office visits, student and mentor learn together the student's narrative. What are her goals? What is his family like? How did he choose this major over that one? With a few well-placed questions, and perhaps a few examples from his or her own life, the mentor in essence hands over the keys for the student to unlock the meaning of his or her story.

Help students to understand that they are capable of separating themselves from one or another of the various identities imposed on them by well-meaning others. Identity is a narrative construction. So, too, students are not co-identical with the personal or interpersonal problems they are experiencing. By externalizing their conflicts with others, they can better name their problems and feelings, get outside of these, and resolve these conflicts. Encourage students to understand the meaning of stereotyping and labeling by externalizing these. This will help them to examine the many ways they tend to stereotype and label *themselves*. They need to know that it is possible to create newer, more creative, and more fluid identity stories.

In a real sense, we are all multi-identitied, not mono-identitied. If students can understand how easily they box and limit their own identity stories, then they can encourage others to enlarge and enrich their stories as well. (Little known by most students is the Latin etymology of the word "identity." It means "the same; being identical with.") Being nonjudgmental, with both themselves and others, and refusing to limit themselves to a narrative of sameness, forms a good foundation from which students can start re-authoring such stories as racism, sexism, homophobia, anxiety, anorexia nervosa, and self-doubt, among others.

Students need to understand that they can *re-member* (to add or subtract key figures in their world) their pasts in healthier, more productive ways. They can reconstruct or deconstruct them. They can focus on the positive attributes of key individuals and groups from their own histories instead of the negative ones. In revisiting the old stories of meaning-making, students can identify the positive traits of significant others who figured in their earlier lives and name the beneficial influences of these individuals. By the same token, students can decide to exclude certain persons from their troubled history of meaning-making. Re-membering does not always have to result in inclusion, however. At times, exclusion is the outcome of re-membering people who may have adversely affected the construction of stories of meaning. Whether re-membering the past results in reconstruction or deconstruction, the overall impact is the same: students begin to experience themselves as active agents in the construction of their own meanings. (For more about re-membering, with an example, see Resources A.)

Ask Philosophical Questions

Whether the content is thin or thick, whatever the discipline, educators can think philosophically and also try to get students to think as philosophers do. Philosophy is asking the large—and the small—questions and then following all leads to answers, wherever these questions and leads might take the questioners. In a sense, all knowledge systems are philosophical. They begin and end with questions—about causes, effects, events, people, right, wrong, value, truth, error, passion, beauty, faith, and so on. More concretely, the types of questions that college students of all ages are asking share these common themes: relationships; family life; work, careers, vocations; developmental crises; moral and ethical issues; and dealing with finitude, loss, loneliness, and angst. All of these themes relate directly and indirectly to the larger need to create meaning and purpose in order to make sense of all that confounds us throughout our lives.

Inside the Classroom

Students who are asking these types of questions could benefit greatly from reading, and talking about, such philosophers as Plato, Aristotle, Marcus Aurelius, Martin Buber, Camus, Confucius,

Descartes, Dewey, Epicurus, Hobbes, Hume, William James, Kant, Jung, Kierkegaard, Lao Tzu, Mill, Nietzsche, Ayn Rand, Rousseau, Sartre, Spinoza, Thoreau, Mary Wollstonecraft, Cornel West, and Kwame A. Appiah, among a whole host of others. What all of these disparate thinkers through the ages have in common is that they are lovers of wisdom, and they are wonderers. Each, in their own way, has sought to answer the timeless philosophical questions that students still ask today—with even greater urgency, it seems.

Late-night college "bull sessions" are a common venue for students to air their meaning-questions about life, suffering, love, peace, and war. The classroom can be just as common a venue as any residence hall or coffeehouse in which to engage the questions, both large and small, that haunt meaning seekers of all types. The added benefit of the classroom is the guaranteed presence of a teacher, who is not the all-knowing "sage on the stage" but the equally curious "guide-on-the-side." Engaging philosophical questions as they relate to course content encourages students to dive deeply into the ocean of wonder rather than skate easily across the ice of the obvious; grappling with the philosophical questions curbs their immediate need to "know what's on the test" and begin learning for learning's sake.

Inquisitiveness is the precondition for knowing anything. So, too, learning begins and ends in wonder, according to Aristotle. Learning is about asking questions, being curious, inquiring, analyzing, and solving problems. Philosophy is the starting point for all the disciplines in the sense that particular knowledge systems are always a function of the particular epistemological (knowledge), ontological (reality), and axiological (values) presuppositions of the researcher, writer, and scholar. A few basic philosophical questions that all students ought to be asking before, during, and after they embark on the voyage into understanding subject matter are these: What is the belief or meaning system of the major figures in the discipline we are studying? How did these thinkers come to believe this? Why was this important to them? How do these beliefs play out in practice? And what are the positive and negative conse-quences of these beliefs—to the discipline, to the researcher, writer, and scholar, and to the world at large?

Philosophers are trained to construct and dismantle arguments of all types. One underlying assumption philosophers make is that all knowledge systems are fallible, each in its own way. We agree with Karl Popper (1968) that all scientific knowledge is falsifiable in the sense that it rarely, if ever, reaches the point at which it cannot be questioned or challenged. No scientific finding is immune to further testing, refinement, or interpretation. For Popper, as for most philosophical counselors, falsification is the royal road to scientific truth.

Students ought to have the cognitive skills to ferret out the intellectual strengths and errors in the disciplines they study. Just as important, students need to know, in the words of Marcus Aure-lius, that "the happiness of your life depends on the quality of your thoughts." Thus good philosophical thinking has the potential to produce good meaning-making. And good meaning-making is more likely to lead to enduring happiness. Educators, along with their students, have the opportunity to assess the value of their subject matter by asking the extent to which a particular discipline might lead others to find happiness in the world outside the classroom.

Outside the Classroom

What constitutes the good life? This venerable question—the basic tenet of Aristotelian ethics—is the backbone of many cocurricu-lar programs, especially judicial programs, leadership development, athletics, and residential living. In these venues, students prac-tice the virtues of good living they discuss in class. What does it mean to belong to a community? How am I accountable to the peers I lead? What are my responsibilities to my leaders? What are the characteristics of true friendship? Am I being a true friend? What is the balance between my rights as an individual and my responsibilities to the community in which I live? These questions, and others like them, have the power to transform cocurricular activities from resume padding and institutional formalities to hands-on, practical experiences of shaping a working definition of the good life.

Students' cocurricular involvement affords them the opportunity to encounter their consistencies, as well as their inconsistencies, between thought and deed. With the guidance of student affairs professionals, students can strive for congruence and integrity. In the residence halls, students have an opportunity to reconcile their hopes for community—mutual respect and aid, appropriate social connections, and shared interests and benefits—and their personal behaviors. For example, are they able to defer to residential community agreements and resist the temptation to play their music loudly, out of respect for neighbors who may be studying or may have vastly different musical tastes? In student leadership organizations, professionals and advisors can ask the questions that help students appraise the alignment between their views on ethical and proper use of power and the ways in which they wield the privileges of their positional leadership.

Nowhere is the formation of a philosophy of life more potent and necessary than in the dreaded conduct or judicial hearing. Students facing the possibility of suspension or expulsion on the basis of their poor behavioral choices stand precariously on the brink of personal disaster. In addition to sorting out the facts of the case to determine level of responsibility, the judicial officer's role is an educational one. Every conduct officer we have known has been as interested in helping students explore the whys of their negative behavior as they have been in identifying and assigning responsibility for the whats. Students who have had to face the consequences of their actions in this way may not characterize their hearings as philosophical moments, but the results indicate that they often are. Regardless of the outcome of the hearing, students often refer to their meeting with the conduct officer or judicial board as a turning point, a pivotal moment of choosing between what was and what could be.

Students' lives outside the classroom are veritable laboratories of philosophical meaning-making. Through their cocurricular involvements, they test their hypotheses of the good life and measure the behavior they display externally with the ideals they hold internally. It is perhaps more accurate to acknowledge the meaning-making potential of the cocurricular environment. For students to actually reap the benefits of wrestling with philosophical questions, they have to be in the ring with those questions. Student affairs professionals and faculty who serve as advisors to student organizations have a clear role in identifying those breakthrough questions and accompanying students as they learn to answer them in the everyday occurrences of life beyond the classroom.

One-on-One with Students

No matter the educational venue, students need to know that they have the cognitive capacity to solve most of their own problems. But before they can do this, they need to be aware of their philosophy of life, what gives meaning to their lives, and who they might turn to in order to construct beneficial systems of meaning. Mentors and advisors with whom a student has a particularly trusting and open relationship can help that student develop his or her system of meaning. With a few well-placed questions to guide the process, meaning mentors can help students scaffold a philosophy of life that can carry them through the dark hours, as well as the triumphant ones.

Students need to ask this basic question: "Will a therapist or counselor be the first person I turn to in order to solve my personal problems?" Here are some other likely questions: "What have some of the greatest minds in history said about the existential dilemmas that have come into my life lately—problems that do not require a strictly medical or psychological response?" "How does my worldview influence my attempts to create meaning in my life, and what exactly is my worldview?" "How do I go about understanding and, when necessary, changing my worldview?"

Students will benefit greatly from knowing how to distinguish between questions that are psychological and require intensive therapy, and questions that are philosophical and require reflective conversation. Philosophical conversation grows out of such basic questions as these:

- How do I know the difference between right and wrong in this particular situation?

- Why is it that I allow my passion to override my reason when certain situations arise in my life?

- Why do I sometimes end up harming someone, particularly when I am trying to benefit that someone?

- Why do I, and others, have to suffer?

- What is love, and how will I know when it happens to me?

- Why is it easier to be loved than to love?

- Why does there have to be so much conflict in the world?

- Why does there have to be so much conflict in my own personal life?

- Are there essential differences between the sexes?

- Why can't I understand what motivates the opposite sex?

- How is religion different from spirituality, and why do so many people my age claim to be spiritual and not religious?

Create Purposeful Silence

The sometimes frenetic pace of twenty-first-century living is not kind to silence. Students (and faculty) today are connected at all times—to friends and family, to entertainment, to all sorts of information—through their multitasking, multifunctional, personal digital assistants and laptop computers. The digital age brings new meaning to the phrase Timothy Leary coined to capture 1960s psychedelic culture: "Turn on, tune in, drop out." Students have turned on and tuned in for sure. They are plugged-in, hard-wired, and virtually networked. But they have not so much dropped out as they have zoomed forward, collecting experience after experience with nary a minute to seek respite and refuge in silence and discover what any of it may mean to them. For many students, moments of silence are rare and unwelcome. So unfamiliar with silence are they that for many students the idea of being alone with their thoughts and feelings creates stress, agitation, and even anxiety. Thirty minutes of unstructured silence may leave many students ready to climb the walls, but five minutes of quiet to ponder a question or two is just enough of an introduction to be productive without becoming overwhelming.

The relentless distractions of daily living seduce many people into long, protracted periods of moving from one thing to the next. The result is habitual compartmentalization, a seemingly unrelated collection of to-dos, thoughts, activities, and relationships jammed into the limited container we know as life. Silence is an antidote. Habitual silence creates the space to draw connections between, and make sense of, ourselves in this world. Pico Iyer (1993) suggested:

> We have to earn silence, then, to work for it: to make it not an absence but a presence; not an emptiness but repletion. Silence is something more than just a pause; it is that enchanted place where space is cleared and time is stayed and the horizon itself expands. In silence, we

often say, we can hear ourselves think; but what is truer to say is that in silence we can hear ourselves *not* think, and so sink below our selves into a place far deeper than mere thought allows. (p. 74)

As Iyer has profoundly observed, silence affords a rare opportunity to simply *be* and perhaps to know ourselves in a more meaningful way. If students are to reap these benefits, they need to learn how to seek out this elusive silence, how to approach it, and what to do with it once they find it.

Inside the Classroom

Five minutes of silence once or twice a week at the beginning or end of class can create just enough mental space for students to grab hold of their course material and make it their own. Give students open-ended prompts that require them to stretch. If they are able to stretch far enough, the product of silence is a deeper learning through a new insight or perspective. Here are some common questions for a five-minute reflection:

- What is your reaction to this?

- What questions still linger for you?

- How is this related to other coursework you have done?

- How is this different from (or similar to) your experience of the world?

- What surprised you?

- How does this challenge your perspective?

- How does this align with your perspective?

- What one question would you ask the author or researcher and why?

Productive silence allows students time to collect their thoughts and prepare to contribute to the learning environment. Michele is fond of opening potentially heated class discussions with a five-minute free write on a provocative prompt. Whether she immediately follows the silence with group discussion or asks students to exchange thoughts with a neighbor, the result is a more robust, complex, and engaged class period. Students who are otherwise reluctant to speak somehow muster the courage to present their thoughts to the group. One student, she remembers, especially appreciated the time set aside for her to collect her thoughts: "Our discussions always move so quickly that by the time I know what I want to say, we've passed the point and gone on to another topic. When I have time to free write, I can think through what is most important to me and I am ready to offer my contributions."

For students who are better prepared to handle longer stretches of silence, regular journaling is a useful tool. Robert asks his students to compose one journal entry per assigned reading. Journal components range from summarizing the key points and providing a reaction to discussing the author's backstory and the subtextual perspective it creates. The journal establishes a space for students to be in conversation with each and every author, idea, and concept. Through journaling, students enter into a more active relationship with course material that leads to deeper learning and quicker pathways to meaning.

For the educator, the journal is a privileged view into how each student is making meaning in the course. They write about what is important to them and why, often connecting concepts to their personal narratives and to the deeper meaning-questions they happen to be pondering. The weekly journals Michele requires of her students give her insight about how to teach each student: What makes this one tick? What makes that one ticked-off? What breaks his heart? What makes her leap for joy? Students teach Michele through their journals, giving her fresh perspectives to consider and the opportunity to check her own biases. Through their journals, Michele's students teach her about the subject anew.

Silence bestows its benefits of meaning-making on student and teacher alike. It is a clever pedagogical tool in that it gives the appearance that nothing is happening, when in fact silence is where it all happens. The sound of silence, although initially deafening, is the sound of head-to-heart deep-meaning learning; it is the sound of meaning in the making.

Outside the Classroom

Students may benefit even more from purposeful silence outside the classroom. Their cocurricular world mimics, in many ways, the lives they will lead once they graduate and leave our institutions for the world of work, family, and home. Slowing down is a luxury, and although many students may desire silence in their busy lives, they often do not know what to do with it. Offer techniques to recollect and incorporate them into residential communities and leadership groups. This allows students to experience how well-placed silence fits into their busy schedules and helps them to develop a commitment to carving out quiet time on their own.

St. Ignatius of Loyola, founder of the Society of Jesus (Jesuits), required his priestly companions to pause in silent prayer several times a day, or at least once. In praying, the *Examen* of Consciousness Jesuits place themselves in the presence of God and review their day. The *Examen* asks about the blessings and the challenges of the day and ends with a concrete commitment for improvement. (See *The Examen Prayer: Ignatian Wisdom for Our Lives Today* by Timothy Gallagher, OMV, 2006.) This simple, personal review takes five minutes, and over time it helps to reveal patterns in a person's life and is an instructive tool for meaning-making. Whether or not students are particularly religious, the *Examen* helps them tap into their spiritual dimension.

Introduce the *Examen* at the beginning or end of weekly student group meetings. The guiding questions are easily amended to fit a wide range of spiritual types. For students who are more religious or who have active faith lives, the questions might be along the lines of (1) Where did I find God today? (2) Where did I lose God today? and (3) How can I improve my relationship with God tomorrow? For nonbelievers or students for whom God is an abstract concept, the questions might become (1) For what am I grateful today? (2) What do I regret? and (3) What can I change tomorrow so I increase my gratitude and decrease my regret?

Over the course of an academic quarter, semester, or year, students will astound themselves with the patterns they see emerging in their own lives. They begin to see the complete story created by events and interactions they previously considered to be discrete and distinct from one another; they become aware of the consequences, both positive and negative, of behaviors, thoughts, and attitudes; they develop a desire for conscious and meaningful living. We are aware of students who have altered their approach to college as a result of regularly entering this guided silent reflection. After a semester of practicing a weekly *Examen*, one student exclaimed,

> Wow! I hadn't realized that my partying was interfering so much with my relationships, not to mention my schoolwork. Each time I went out I thought I was having a good time, and I was. But I wasn't connecting the drinking and socializing to the feelings of guilt and regret I felt every week at not completing my assignments to the best of my ability and at not following through on commitments I had made to family and friends. In the moment, I guess I just thought, "Who cares? I'm having a good time." But the reality is so much different. I mean, I care.

Five minutes of silence once a week to ponder a few reflection questions gave this student an opportunity to take stock of his actions and decisions. Before he needed anyone else to intervene, he confronted himself with the evidence of his own life, and he made the changes necessary to begin living in a way that more closely mirrored the life he had imagined for himself.

One-on-One with Students

If silence feels like an awkward tool to wield in group situations, it can feel even more so in one-on-one situations. In the United States, we are socialized to make small talk—no matter how small—whenever we find ourselves alone with another person. To be conversational is to be welcoming and friendly. Silence between two people—intimate relationships notwithstanding—is, on the other hand, plain uncomfortable. People feel self-conscious, wondering whether they should look the other in the eye or direct their gaze elsewhere. They fidget and clear their throats to break up the tension that silence between two people sometimes creates.

Silence is a sign of standoffishness at best and a sign of anger at worst. Silence is seen as somewhat of a punishment or an attention-calling form of control, as in "Why are you giving me the silent treatment?" This brings to mind a student we once knew who would come into the student government office and park herself near the front door without saying a word. For weeks this behavior continued, until one day another student said, "You know, you suck all the fun out of the room when you do that." Situation resolved. The "silent" student still visited the office daily, but with a different energy. Her peer's clever admonition snapped her out of whatever funk she was in.

Notwithstanding the downside of silence, when purposefully placed, silence between two people can be instructive and even liberating. Use silence to punctuate probing questions. Invite students to sit in quiet consideration before offering a response. This use of silence almost always yields more thoughtful responses, and sometimes opens doors to the unexpected.

Michele recalls a conversation with a student who was earning a poor participation grade in her class. The two made an appointment to discuss, ironically, the student's silence. Over steaming cups of tea, Michele asked the student what was happening for her that she was so reluctant to participate even when called on—and she immediately followed the question with a request that the student sit in silence for a while before answering.

A few minutes passed, and then tears rolled down the student's cheeks. The truth came out: her mother's hospitalization for a psychotic break; the pressures of working nearly full-time to pay for college; embarrassment at not understanding all of the course material. The student's anxiety surfaced, and a different discussion ensued than the one the student had planned. (The student later confided that she was ready to tell Michele that her lack of classroom participation was due to Michele's poor classroom management. Inaccurate as this portrayal would have been, in her mind it was a much safer, albeit roundabout, route to take.)

A few minutes of silence allowed this student to access the murky depths of her experiences rather than skim the surface. Neither she nor Michele was prepared to have that particular conversation, but in retrospect, that was the conversation the student needed to have. Silence between two people need not bring awkward discomforts; it can instead be the precursor to the most meaning-filled conversation possible.

Silence acts both as a pause and as a process. As a pause, silence is a temporary break in the noisy static of daily life, a coveted place of calm and refuge. As a process, silence is an act of abstinence, a refraining from doing and decision making. The process of silence is a handy tool for the meaning mentor's toolbox.

Students seek out their advisors and mentors at times of great deliberation: Which law school should I attend? Am I too young to get married? Should I study abroad or stay on campus and try for a major leadership position? Which job should I accept? How do I tell my parents that I'm switching majors and may be in school for an extra semester? These questions and others like them have been on the minds of students we have known, and these questions respond favorably to silence as part of the decision-making process.

In the face of these types of questions, suggest that students make the best decision they can, given the information they have, and then shelve it for a few days. Sequestering the mock decision in silence for a short period of time allows the student to feel the gravity of the decision and all of its potential consequences. At the end of the two-or-three-day "silence," students have a much better sense of which decision is most congruent with their deepest needs. Without much intervention, they know how they should actually answer their own questions.

Tackle Tough Topics

Opportunities for deep learning often take us by surprise. We find ourselves unprepared for the off-hand comment that derails our plans; we find ourselves paralyzed by the unexpected off-color joke that denigrates this or that group; we find ourselves panicked and disoriented when news of massive tragedy strikes. These are the toughest meaning-making moments. They are tough because the issues themselves are tangled, sticky, and complicated; they are tough because we sometimes feel inadequate to bring order out of unbelievable chaos; they are tough because they pluck our personal passions. And these moments are made tougher still by the pressure of our roles as educators—responsible for leading students to create meaning out of mess.

Inside the Classroom

Imagine this scene: The faculty member (let's call him Dr. Know) distributes a case study about a Christian mega-church. Several students grumble that faith and religion, however tangential to the lesson, are out of bounds in classroom discussion. It is Dr. Know's intention to focus the class on the church's innovative business plan and how its unconventional methods reached out to an entire population of people who had previously rejected traditional forms of worship and organized religion. Despite Dr. Know's best efforts, the class bypasses the lesson plan. Instead of analyzing the strengths and weaknesses of the business plan, the class begins a contentious discussion about the validity and appropriateness of Mega-church's form of worship.

One student finds the facts of the case irreverent and disturbing to her sense of "right relationship with God." Others observe that the church's atmosphere is more like a rock concert than a religious experience and question how much faith formation can actually occur. Another student defensively admits to his membership in a similar mega-church community and takes offense at the ignorant assumptions his classmates are making. Frustration, resentment, and irritation are palpable in the room. Dr. Know frequently and nervously checks his watch. He knows that time is ticking away, but mostly he fears the direction of class discussion. Aside from eschewing the lesson for the day, the class had veered vigorously into religion and faith, a territory that was unknown and uncomfortable for Dr. Know.

What is happening in this scene? What should Dr. Know do? What would happen if he steered the class away from their faith-and-worship debate and toward the lesson of innovation? What if he scrapped his lesson plan and opened the floor to the topic that has caught everyone's attention? What if he ignored the direction of students' comments and moved on? What would happen if he did nothing? Perhaps none of these possibilities seems appealing. What would happen if Dr. Know recognized this moment as one of potentially valuable meaning-making and created space, however small, to tackle the tough topic of faith in the classroom?

This semifictional scene repeats itself regularly on college campuses across the nation. Faith. Race. Politics. Poverty. War.

Religion. Gender. All of these topics, and others like them, are fraught with differences of perspective. They are volatile and have the potential to disturb the equilibrium of a well-managed class. They are also the stuff of great meaning and deserve attention. Students are hungry for some guidance, particularly around the hottest issues, to sort through their own opinions and beliefs. They are anxious to weigh their experiences, to make sense of the grounds that seem to shift endlessly beneath them.

In the days following September 11, 2001, we were surprised by the number of students who reported that they did not discuss the horrific event in any way as a part of their classes. They perceived an absolute silence on the part of their faculty, and they were sorely disappointed by it. Several students said their faculty acknowledged the tragedy but then quickly moved on to the day's lesson. This same phenomenon happened in the wake of Hurricanes Katrina and Rita and their devastating effects on coastal Louisiana, Mississippi, and Texas. It happened again following the heart-wrenching destruction caused by the tsunami in Southeast Asia and the more recent earthquakes in Pakistan and China, and it happened after a college student, someone like them in many ways, went on a murderous rampage at Virginia Polytechnic Institute.

Each of these tragedies raised the deep questions that plague people of all ages: the meaning of life, the disparities experienced by the human family, fanaticism, poverty, privilege, hatred, religious and ideological differences, illness. We asked some of our colleagues about what looked like a pattern of nonresponse by some faculty. Many said that to spend time on unpredictable news events would throw off course progress. Some worried that they were not qualified to lead such a discussion and deferred to the events planned by campus student affairs professionals or to the prayer services sponsored by university ministry offices. Several brave souls admitted that they did not know how to raise the issue for meaningful discussion when they were so bewildered themselves. Like Dr. Know in the preceding semifictional portrayal, the faculty in our nonscientific poll allowed a potentially powerful meaning-making moment to slip away. Perhaps some were conscious of not wanting to editorialize and give away their own personal positions. Perhaps some were uncomfortable venturing into waters outside their professional expertise. Perhaps some were caught off guard and felt underprepared to dive into the deep. Perhaps some realized their syllabi could not absorb any detours. Whatever the reason, the opportunity passed by without much notice except by the students, who received the unintended message that the ability to compartmentalize is a necessary survival skill.

To these faculty, and to Dr. Know, we say, "Dive in!" One needs no particular expertise, save that which comes from experience as a human being, to begin tackling tough topics in the classroom. Remember that vulnerability is okay. The vulnerability that comes of admitting that some topics are beyond one's area of expertise can create enough space for students to rely on their own meaning-making mechanisms to make sense of tough topics rather than always relying on a teacher to make sense of it all for them. The classroom instinct is to exercise a distancing intellectualism. In the face of tragic circumstances or confounding human conditions, meaning is more likely to be found in an examination of deep-seated personal philosophies. One cautionary note, however: Choose a level of engagement that is commensurate with your skill and comfort. Low-risk interventions, such as the use of silence, are suitable in nearly all situations, whereas higher-risk interventions, such as "moral conversation" (see Nash, Bradley, & Chickering, 2008), require thoughtful application and possibly more planning and skill.

Outside the Classroom

Challenging, tough topics are not limited to the world outside the college campus. Some of the toughest topics educators have to tackle arise from student behavior. One of the inexplicable trends in college student culture today is the ubiquitous "theme party."

With derogatory names like "South of the Border," "Pimps and Ho's," "White Trash," and "GI Joes and Army Ho's," invitations to these parties encourage students to dress and behave as hyperbolic stereotypes. Far beyond classic toga parties like the one famously depicted in *Animal House*, these parties combine excessive recreational drinking with the outward expression of harmful prejudices. The foolish-looking bedsheet toga has now given way to any number of costumes degrading to women, working class and poor folks, people of color, and religious minorities. For obvious reasons, these parties often spark conflict, and some institutions have experienced a crisis of campus climate in the aftermath of parties with particularly oppressive and cruel themes.

Faculty and student-affairs administrators have crucial roles to play in moving students from the madness of these offensive parties to meaning. Through community meetings, speak-outs, open forums, and featured speakers, staff and faculty can raise the questions that ask students to consider their behavior within a wider social context. Commonly, members of the student body are the chief organizers of these events, and they rely on advice and guidance from educators about desired learning objectives and the different approaches that help achieve those objectives. Advisors suggest frameworks, common readings, and ground rules to follow, so students have a better chance of working together to resolve issues facing their community and avoiding the trap of demonizing one another. We have witnessed several of these student gatherings, and although heated with anger and emotion, students generally walk away with greater insight, having, for the first time, drawn a connection between their actions and the impact on the community.

One-on-One with Students

A student once asked Michele to approve "Jell-O Wrestling on the Quad" as a fundraiser for his club. His vision was one of female students in bathing suits wrestling each other in a plastic kiddy pool filled with flavored gelatin. He and the members of his club had thought of just about every detail. They imagined a tournament-style event in which student groups or groups of students would pay $20 to sponsor a particular wrestler. The money would go to the club and bragging rights would go to the young woman who emerged victorious at the end of the day. True story.

Sex. Alcohol. Drugs. Personal hygiene. Ethical treatment of others. Eating disorders. Violence. Dysfunctional relationships. Death. Illness. Tragedy. In addition to race, gender, class, and religion, these are tough topics educators regularly address in a multitude of campus venues. Of the many students who talk with us about their meaning-making journeys, all have experienced at least one personal crisis of meaning, whether major or minor, involving one or more of these tough topics. Most of them felt as though they were making up solutions as they went along. Some of them were fortunate to have the help of a professional counselor or some other educator who accompanied them as they fought to find their way. As these students graduate and return to visit, they tell us that the courage, patience, and honesty with which their educators approached them continue to influence their actions and interactions. What may have passed as barely a blip on the radar of the educator has made a lifelong impact as the student-cum-alumnus negotiates the uncharted territory of adulthood.

In the Jell-O wrestling situation, it would have been easy to tell the student "No" and call it a day without even batting an eyelash. Instead, what ensued was a lengthy discussion. Michele presented several concerns—safety and liability among them—and then asked the student how he and his club members planned to protect the dignity of the women who agreed to wrestle. Surprisingly, he had thought about safety issues in depth: the club would purchase an inflatable kiddy pool, which provided more cushioning for the wrestlers; the event would take place on the grassy lawn, which would minimize serious injury in the event someone slipped and fell; wrestlers would sign some sort of release of liability form; and the club was willing to contract emergency personnel to be on hand.

The question of women's dignity, however, staggered him. He had not considered the idea of personal dignity or whether his proposed event would violate his peers in any way. He asked thoughtful questions about gender relations and about the forms of entertainment and the depictions of overly sexualized women extolled in popular media. He was uncommonly honest about what he and his buddies hoped to see at the event—women covered in goo, entangled in titillating competition, and the occasional "peek-a-boob" exposure of his classmates' body parts.

He wondered if the event would be degrading if the women agreed to participate, and then he thought of his younger sister. Michele asked him what recommendation he would give his little sister if she had been approached to wrestle in an event like this for "fun." He was adamant in his opinion, and he surprised himself with his quick reaction. He decided he would not want his little sister to agree to participate, because he would not want young men ogling her the way he and his pals planned to ogle their fellow students.

This student had not expected to have this frank conversation. He thought he was there just to get a signature on his event request form, a meaningless formality. Instead, his views were challenged, but he did not seem to resent it. He was genuinely engaged in conversation and allowed himself to be affected by it. The result? He left Michele's office renarrativizing his perspective on women, and he convinced his club to find another way to raise the money they needed.

Connect Content and Context

Thirty years after he was supposed to graduate from Harvard University, Bill Gates, founder of Microsoft, finally received his (honorary) degree. In his commencement address, Mr. Gates shared with Harvard's class of 2007 what it had taken him several decades to discover: the meaning of their college education. In short, Mr. Gates exhorted the graduates to consider that the privilege and honor of studying at and graduating from Harvard created for them a responsibility to leverage their talents, access, and power to alleviate the awful inequities suffered by disenfranchised people of the world. Mr. Gates lamented having left Harvard without a context for the intellectual lessons he learned; in his address he expressed an expectation that today's graduates would follow a different path. His address was a call to action for the Class of 2007, and it was a "call to meaning" for Harvard University and with it all other institutions of higher learning. (For Gates's complete remarks, see www.hno.harvard.edu/gazette/2007/06.14/99-gates.html.)

Whether it is the meaning of social justice as Bill Gates described it or meaning of some other kind beyond that of self interest, the making of that meaning is not likely to come about through coincidental happenstance. Instead, students need guidance and some structure to connect educational content to a context greater than the limited scope of the college classroom or residence hall.

Inside the Classroom

Context brings learning to life; it involves the senses. Context creates learning that students can hear, touch, smell, see, taste, and sometimes feel with their hearts. The result is students with a greater understanding of how the abstract lessons of their college courses fit into the concrete world they observe and experience on a daily basis.

The increasing popularity of service-learning is one method for bringing context to the classroom. Experiential education is not to be confused with experimental education. Practitioners cite Kolb's (1984) model of experiential learning for creating the framework for service learning. The cycle of activity, reflection, conceptualization, and experimentation is a powerful learning tool.

At Michele's Jesuit university, many faculty are quite skilled at creating meaningful contexts for the academic content they present. The chemist involves students in troubleshooting formulas for a fair trade coffee consortium in Nicaragua; the writer dispatches students to hold writing clinics at local schools; the engineer challenges students to create water delivery systems for sub-Saharan Africa; the accountant sends students to tax preparation clinics for low-income families and individuals; the sociologist and the psychologist arrange for their students to volunteer at local shelters; the photographer assigns projects for local nonprofits—the examples go on. Service-learning increases the chance that students will see their academic work in action, which reinforces what they learn by making it "real." Students experience the consequences of their actions, whether positive or negative, in the field, often leading to greater insights than they could have achieved by studying alone.

In the absence of service-learning opportunities, well-written case studies can provide substantial context as well. In picking through a case, students wrestle with real-life complexity and have the advantage of working through the ramifications of key decision points from a bird's-eye view. Good cases abound in the social and natural sciences as well as in business, and they allow students to play with the pieces of real-life puzzles. In some senses, working through a case study is like playing with lit matches without the fear of getting burned.

Outside the Classroom

From the look and feel of campus grounds to the dining halls, from the residence halls to student services, and from the offices of staff and faculty to the student recreation facilities, the entire campus provides a context for meaning-making. A college or university campus is not unlike a small town, and the students who inhabit the space lead full lives there. Everywhere they travel on campus presents an opportunity to connect the content of institutional values and learning objectives to the context.

University mission statements, from east to west, proclaim that they will educate tomorrow's leaders. What percentage of students

on these campuses is exposed to some type of leadership involvement, either on campus or in the surrounding community, and what
is the quality of their leadership involvement? Many institutions
claim to value diversity. How diverse is the student body? Staff and
faculty? If visitors spent significant time on campus, would they see
artwork representing different cultures or have the opportunity to
attend a worship service in their faith traditions? Some programs
say they promote ethical decision making. Do they maintain deadlines and help students manage the consequences of not meeting
them? Do they cultivate the "student" in their star student-athletes?
Do they have and uphold codes of conduct and academic honesty?
Few institutions would say they are degree factories, churning out
four-year credentials just so students can obtain any job as long as it
is well-paying. If this is true, how do they guide students to appraise
their skills, values, and talents so that they may direct themselves
to opportunities that fit? In nearly every on-campus venue is a
profound opportunity to promote congruence between what the
institution says is the education it offers and how students actually
experience that education.

One-on-One with Students

Connecting content to context is a simplified process in one-on-one
meetings with students when compared to the process within other
educational venues across campus. The content is whatever lesson
is at hand: ethics, history, politics, accounting, self-responsibility.
The context, however, is always the same: that particular student
in face-to-face contact with the educator.

Deep-meaning learning is amplified in the one-on-one setting.
The abstractions of the classroom or student group meeting are
suddenly made concrete and personal. In the one-on-one setting,
the educator and the student can linger over the ways in which the
student connects to the material, thereby deepening its meaning
to him or her. Ask questions that draw the student more closely

into the material: What about the lesson—be it biochemistry, philosophy, or managing emotions—excites or confuses? In what ways do the student's personal or family experiences relate? How does the lesson fit or disrupt the student's previous notions about the world?

Harnessing the intensity of a private tutorial with the ease of a casual social conversation, one-on-one meetings with students are a powerful gateway to meaning. These meetings give students an opportunity to digest content material as it relates to them, and they give educators a glimpse into students as unique individuals. The message to students is one of caring and personal attention; the message to educators is one of immediate effect; the message to both students and educators is one of mattering.

Expanding the Educator's Toolbox

The preceding pages offer a smattering of suggested methods for creating learning environments in which deep-meaning learning can flourish. Some methods may work for some educators, while different methods work for others. These are not one-size-fits-all, but a wide array of strategies and tools that educators can try to see which ones fit, which ones will fit with personal alterations, and which ones do not fit at all.

Each of us has our favorite, most reliable tool that we keep handy and ready to use at any meaning moment. We know how to wield these tools, and they feel comfortable enough in our hands that students do not feel manipulated or worked over by meaning. We also have tools we are trying to develop, to make them our own. There are, we are sure, plenty of tools that did not make it onto our list but also have the potential to elicit powerful meaning-making from students. The point is to have as many tools ready and accessible as possible to enhance our work as educators as well as students' experiences as learners and meaning makers.

Over the years we have found that preparing the tools is one thing, and preparing the educator is something else all together. The methods we described in this chapter will certainly help, but the full magnitude of their potential will be realized only when the faculty and staff who use them have carefully considered their roles as meaning mentors. In the next two chapters, we address some of the inner work of educators for meaning.

6

The Ethics of
Meaning-Making

We must never forget that in a group or person-to-person setting, constructivist conversations about meaning must first be ethical conversations. In meaning-making education, there is much room for moral mishap. Temptations abound for both educators and students to violate confidentiality, to practice beyond their competence, to indoctrinate, to favor or disfavor particular meaning narratives, and to be overzealous in pushing new pedagogical techniques on students. Inevitably, mistakes in pedagogical judgment will occur.

The seductions of manipulation, adulation, exploitation, and exaggeration are powerful. Because the academy has done little to encourage active meaning-making on college campuses, we have no precedent on how to proceed in this process without causing harm to ourselves and our students. For better or worse, we will be making up our interactive ethic as we go along. So much of how we ought to treat one another in the meaning-making project will be a product of trial and error. For this reason, and because there is so much at stake, we want to take time to explore the implications of what we are calling the "ethics of meaning-making."

Ethics has become an important topic in the helping professions today. When Robert (1996) first wrote his book on applied ethics for the human services and education, there were fewer than ten such works in these fields. Now there are hundreds, perhaps thousands.

Ethics has to do with moral standards, codes of conduct, doing the right things for the right reasons, being able to defend decisions and actions when other people's interests are at stake, cultivating qualities of moral character, and constructing belief systems that lead to behaviors that are right and good. The threat of litigation that hangs over all the helping professions has made ethicists of us all. There is no longer any escape from the responsibility we bear: to do unto others as we would have them do unto us, and then to be able to explain and defend our actions to others. No longer can human service professionals, on or off campus, avoid the responsibilities that come with being trustworthy trustees for the common good.

In this chapter, we will offer a tentative and evolving code of ethics for meaning-makers. We will do this with caution and humility, because in matters of ethics, so much depends on personal moral judgment. Whether or not one completely agrees with Nietzsche that "there is no morality, there is only interpretation," it is clear that at least some degree of subjective interpretation is always present in the ethics arena. There are no money-back, guaranteed formulas for being ethical. There will always be counterprinciples, counterrules, countercommandments, and counterarguments to those courses of ethical action that we think are irrefutably right. The miracle of being human, however, is that despite our many moral failures and self-deceptions, our frequent falls from grace, we are basically decent and kind. No matter how often we fail to live up to our highest moral ideals, most of us come back to try again.

Thus it is up to each one of us to determine how much we ought to do, and how far we ought to go, during those intense conversations (either in or out of the classroom) about what gives students' lives meaning. In what follows, we will point out some of the moral dangers that lurk in the midst of all meaning-making encounters. We begin with a distillation of a conversation about meaning-making that took place recently in one of Robert's classes. We start with this classroom interaction, because we think it illustrates some of the ethical potholes that appear whenever we find ourselves navigating the uncharted roads of meaning-making education.

Different Takes on Meaning

Ariel: I'm tired of talking about meaning. What meaning was there when my father died a long, drawn-out death from lung cancer? He was forty. We begged him to stop smoking. He didn't. I'd flush his cigarettes down the toilet, and he would yell at me. One day he even smacked me across the face and told me to mind my own business and get out of his life. I did. So did my mother, who eventually took off and left me and my brother high and dry. I spent most of my teenage years being my brother's mother. Life is cruel, there is no meaning, and the most we can ever do is clean up the shit after it happens and move on. Our readings and conversations are fairy tales. I signed up for this course expecting to do philosophy, and instead I got group therapy.

Marissa: I lost my taste for religious meaning when my parents told me never to come home again, because I am planning to marry my girlfriend, Bess. Why did they say this to me? Because they believe that God will send them to hell for raising a lesbian daughter like me. They want their God to know that they will not tolerate such sinful behavior on the part of any of their children. It's funny but, in spite of this religious nonsense which caused my parents to disown me, to this day I still feel tremendous guilt about dropping out of my Christian church community. Having read Tolstoy in class this semester, I found some comfort in his words: "I have no doubt that there is some truth in religious doctrine, but there can also be doubt that harbors a lie; and I must find the truth and the lies so I can tell them apart."

Vincent: You know what gives my life meaning? Relationships and connections, that's what! I thrive on personal relationships. I need human connections. Here is my meaning—I am my own truth, my own meaning, but without being able to share my meanings with others, what would my meanings ever really mean? I learned in our class a few

(Continued)

weeks ago that my Myers-Briggs type is ENFJ (extroverted, intuitive, feeling, and judgmental). This is so me. I can't stand the thought of being alone, of living a life of isolation. So I constantly seek out the company of others. I know there's a downside to this, and it's the danger of being emotionally dependent on people for my meaning. The lengths to which I will go to be in relationships with others worries me. I realize now why I hate the college fraternity I belong to—with all their horsing around, their partying, and their sexism. I need them so I don't feel lonely, but I am miserable when I'm with them. Will I ever get this contradiction in my life worked out?

Claude: At this stage in my life, my meaning is simple. I want to live my life truthfully. I want to see the world as it really is, and not how someone wants me to see it. I want to be in charge of my own life. I want all my achievements and successes to be the result of my genuine efforts. I don't want anyone to give me false praise or reassurance. I want to be what the existentialists we read this semester call "authentic." Even if this means that I must give up all my inauthentic relationships—including even my close friends if necessary—I and I alone must take responsibility for my happiness, my choices, my very life. Yep, this is how I want to live.

Emily: Whenever I try to talk about meaning in this class, my heart pounds, I get anxious, and, frankly, there are times when I want to throw up, because I'm so scared that I'm going to make a fool out of myself. I've decided that I have a love-hate relationship with meaning. I wake up in the middle of the night thinking about connections I'm making to the readings and conversations we're having in class. I'm working on coming to terms with my performance anxiety and fear of going public with personal stuff. I just want to thank all of you for bearing with me throughout the semester. I've valued all your contributions. I've learned so much from you. I can listen with an open heart and open mind to all of you, and this has taught me to listen to myself the same way. I am secure in my unanswered questions, because I've learned that the most significant meaning-questions are the ones that don't have easy answers. But, and I hope you all understand, I still feel embarrassed, confused, overwhelmed, and intimidated by so many of you. I can't wait for the course to end, but, at the same time, I can't bear the thought of not being a part of this group every week. Am I totally weird?

Deborah: I love my God, I love my family, and I love my friends. I even love my country. I know all of this sounds too simplistic to be true. I know that some of you think I'm the token, Bible-thumping, conservative, moralistic Republican in the class. But I don't agonize over meaning like all of you do. I know what the meaning of my life is. I know where to find my truth. I feel so out of place here, because I don't have a need to dig as deeply into the meaning of my life like so many of you do. I've learned how to let go and let God, family, and friends fill my life. I love something that Reinhold Niebuhr said in one of our books: "Meaning is all about self-transcendence . . . the problem of meaning transcends ordinary rationality, sense experience, and scientific explanation. Self-transcendence leads inevitably to the search for a God, a Supreme Power, who transcends the world." This is where I'm at, and it's more than enough for me.

Phil: Okay, I have sad stories to tell too. I love my mom when I see her, but she is clinically depressed. I have no idea who my biological father is. My mom tries to crack jokes to cheer up her six kids, but the bags under her eyes, and her constant shaking after another night of heavy drinking, betray her true feelings. She is sad and lonely. I wonder if any of this would be different if we had been white, rich, and lived in the suburbs. But, you know what? I don't dwell on this stuff. I don't question my situation anymore, because these questions take time away from opportunities to re-create my life. When I read the *Tao Te Ching* in another course this semester I had a breakthrough in my thinking. Instead of whining about all the drama in my life, from now on I'm going with the flow—no more doubting or agonizing over my miserable life—now it's going to be all about living, being happy, choosing well, and allowing the Tao to enter my life wherever, however, and whenever.

(Continued)

Jackie: I've loved the readings this semester—authors like Niebuhr, Nietzsche, Malcolm X, Viktor Frankl, even some of the post-modern philosophers that I didn't completely understand. You know what I did this term? I created a file of all the quotes that really spoke to me during the semester. I was shocked to learn that I have over five hundred of them. They have enriched my life. Two stand out. One is by Viktor Frankl: "Live as if you were living a second time, and as though you had lived without meaning the first time, even though you might have had everything material that you ever wanted. How would you be changed?" The other one is much simpler but just as important to me. It's from Monty Python: "The meaning of life is this: try to be nice to people, avoid eating fat, read a good book every now and then, have regular bowel movements, have people in your life you can love, get some walking in, but, most of all, try to live in harmony with folks of all creeds and nations. Oh, and it doesn't hurt to have a cuddly pet."

A Code of Ethics for Meaning-Makers

At the very first class meeting, Robert talks about the need for all participants to agree on a meaning-making code of ethics—a set of mutual rights and obligations that will govern the conversational process. Class discussions like the example just presented can be intense and personal. A safe conversational space is a critical prerequisite for getting students to open up about their past and present experiences with family, relationships, religion, traumas, and personal failures as well as successes. Students need to do more than show up and show off in a mutual, give-and-take discussion. Meaning-making education is not about memorization, test-taking, name-dropping, listening passively to lectures, doing last-minute cramming, or trying to figure out what the professor wants to hear in a one-way monologue disguised as a seminar dialogue. If we set the right tone, our students will feel free, perhaps for the first time in a college classroom or campus office space, to be candid and forthright in their self-disclosures. They will learn very quickly not to waste time on impression management.

When meaning-making conversation is real, all of us will be entering uncharted ethical territory in our educational spaces. Thus we will need to proceed with caution. David A. Garvin (in Christensen, Garvin, & Sweet, 1991) is the first scholar we know who has attempted to develop a rationale for a code of ethics that educators can use in classroom conversations about very sensitive and personal topics. Robert has created a conversational code of ethics that embodies some of Garvin's principles, in addition to his own. Some of these ethical principles can also be shared directly with students to help them interact respectfully with one another when talking about meaning:

- Treat each person fairly, impartially, and equitably.

- Whenever in doubt, always remember the principle of *primum non nocere*—first, do no harm.

- Treat each person in the group always as an end, and never as a means.

- Abstain from *ad hominem* attacks and ganging up on individuals with unpopular views.

- Respect, do not violate, students' rights to privacy.

- Keep confidences; what goes on in the seminar stays in the seminar.

- Do not foist personal beliefs on others.

- Seek informed consent in everything you do.

- Understand that not everyone is ready to be a vulnerable meaning-maker; avoid imposing vulnerability on others.

- Know when students might need professional therapy in addition to (or in place of) philosophical counseling and narrative therapy (see Resource A).

No matter how "pure" our motives and reasons, we must avoid the imposition of a preferred set of beliefs and values on students. No unorthodox angle on meaning ought ever to be suppressed simply because it appears to go against what educators think is philosophically, psychologically, or spiritually "correct." Marissa and Deborah, in the preceding class conversation, have an irrefutable right to express their religious views, particularly when these might go against the prevailing secular trends in class and throughout the campus. Robert believes that one of the virtues of a postmodern, constructivist approach to meaning-making is its basic assumption that, after all is said and done, each of us makes it all up—to suit our tastes and temperaments, our philosophies and belief systems, the ways we were raised and trained, and our visions of who we want to become. Who, therefore, is qualified to rule any meaning system out of order on a campus—if, in effect, we made it all up to suit our personal needs?

To insist on meaning-making correctness, like political correctness, is a conversation stopper. It is a sure-fire prescription for sabotaging, and terminating, an open-ended search for meaning. Marissa and Deborah have much to contribute to conversations about meaning and purpose, as do Claude and Phil with their Taoistic and existential worldviews, respectively. Robert took Ariel, Marissa, and Phil aside at separate times during the term and suggested that they might benefit from visiting the counseling center to help them deal with their particular family situations. Ariel and Phil took him up on the offer and courageously sought the professional counseling they needed to work through their issues.

At no time, however, did Robert intervene publicly in the classroom conversation to silence, patronize, or counsel them. He was able to decouple students' basic meaning-messages from the emotional content in their contributions to the class discussion. He did this by helping students to look for explicit connections between their own, often troubled, construction of meanings and what they were reading, writing about, and discussing in the seminar. Self-disclosures became relevant only to the extent that they were grounded in the insights of the various authors and connected to previous points raised in class. Students constantly referred to specific proof-texts in the assigned readings, and these served as takeoff and landing points in the seminar conversations.

As one way to frame his feedback and connect it to the content of the course, Robert focused on each student's character strengths, according to the principles of positive psychology. He identified the salient places in each of their meaning narratives where they accepted responsibility to be the authors of their own lives, according to the principles of narrative therapy. Finally, he connected relevant content in the course readings to important thematic insights in their individual stories, and he referred the class to appropriate philosophical-psychological ideas, according to the principles of philosophical counseling. Whenever relevant, Robert called attention to the fundamental wisdom contained in Frankl's logotherapy: no matter how extreme our suffering, there is always a meaning to extract from those times when each of us is pushed to our limits.

Also, we need to trust the process in conversations about meaning. In addition to introducing a code of ethics for conducting conversations about meaning, educators will need to exercise prudent leadership throughout the conversation by gently and persistently keeping people on track. Yet we must also be ready to get out of the way whenever possible. We need to avoid pushing students beyond their comfort levels. We need to be careful not to make overt judgments of approval or disapproval of what students have to say. We must beware of practicing beyond our competence (this is especially important if we choose to use some of the strategies of the various postmodern psychotherapies and pedagogies we discuss in Resource A), and covering up our *preaching* by calling it *teaching*.

Resisting Temptations to Take Over

It is important to resist the well-intended professorial temptation to rescue students prematurely whenever they stray into uncharted meaning-making territory. This is an indirect violation of students' autonomy. All too frequently, educators' well-intentioned rescue actions deliver the message that students are too brittle and unable to handle serious self-exploration and candid self-disclosure. We have found, however, that if left to themselves, college students are very skilled at protecting their privacy. Most know just how far they can go during meaning-making conversations before they begin to feel uncomfortable. They are keen self-censors. Most of the time students can be their own best rescuers. They have the potential to be incredibly resilient, self-correcting, and kind—not only with themselves but also with others. It just takes a little time.

The students in the seminar conversation presented here learned, over the course of a semester, how to support one another. They discovered that their peers' moral qualities of compassion and generosity were enough to help them get over the rough spots. Much of the time, these students drew one another out by asking clarifying questions, by withholding initial negative opinions, and by always trying to attribute the best motive to one another. They applied the "golden empathy rule" of ethical conversation: listen as you would be listened to, question as you would be questioned, and disclose only as much as you would have others disclose to you.

On those rare occasions when students do tend to cross the line between discreet, topic-relevant self-disclosure and indiscreet self-disclosure for its own sake, educators will need to make a prudent intervention. Robert finds that one question he asks is very helpful in this regard: "How does what you have so honestly shared with us relate to some of the larger questions from the texts that we have been discussing?" Such a return-to-the-topic question reminds everyone that meaning-making has the potential of being universalizable, at least for some people. Robert calls this "moving from *me*-search to *we*-search" in meaning-making conversations with students.

Perhaps the most difficult challenge for educators in meaning-making sessions, however, is to be less preoccupied with teaching and telling and more concerned with listening and learning. This is the best way to show respect for those we serve. Michele remembers vividly a conversation with a student, Victoria, who was troubled with some difficult life decisions. Victoria allowed the source of her confusion to spill out, and Michele, almost as if on autopilot, launched directly into interpreting meaning and offering possible solutions. Victoria stopped her with a plea: "I just need you to listen right now." Victoria did not want or need help in the form of quick fixes. She did not need a teacher, an advisor, or a counselor. Victoria needed only a compassionate ear, so she could *hear herself* make meaning out of her situation.

As group facilitators, we need to be attentive to how students are interpreting what is going on. No matter how messy the potential consequences, we need to ask for feedback on the conversational process at strategic intervals. We need to continually make a concerted effort to see the meaning-making process through the conversationalists' eyes. We have to be a lot less reluctant, or afraid, to hand over leadership of the meaning-making conversation to various members of the group. This is one way to empower others. Often, students are well-equipped (at times, more so than the educator) to deal with those classmates who are cynics, attention-seekers, hypersensitive, and, in the worst cases, so wounded that they may have become traumatized.

Finally, Kessler (2000) effectively identifies two other important ethical concerns. She maintains that educators need to be hyper-vigilant about the "dangerous border between caring and attraction when discovering the beauty [and vulnerability] in each student"

(p. 164). It is even more destructive, according to Kessler, when some meaning-making educators become "inflated with the fantasy of being a 'spiritual guide,' or 'healer.' In contrast, our real power comes in asking what will *empower* our students and in cultivating our humility and humanity, not our own charisma or indispensability" (p. 164).

To Kessler's ethical cautions and recommendations, we can only say "Amen!" and offer our vigorous endorsement. We can never become our students' parents, spiritual gurus, or romantic interests, and any attempt to assume these roles is bound to fail—either in the short term or over the long term. Moreover, whenever we practice beyond our competence, or impose our egos and wills on others, we transgress serious ethical boundaries. This warning holds, of course, for *all* educators on college campuses, especially the professoriate. An attitude of intellectual superiority can easily lead to a sense of messianic fervor on the part of some faculty, or to a sense of social justice self-righteousness on the part of some student affairs administrators. What too often gets lost in the lust to save the intellectually and politically deficient souls in our midst is the principle that our primary moral responsibility with students is to help them to find their own answers, not to parrot back ours. No matter how "incredible" our own charisma, indispensability, and genius, we are in higher education mainly to serve students. They do not come to our campuses to serve us.

Final Ethical Tips

We will wrap up this short chapter by applying several of Yalom's breakthrough therapeutic insights to our own work in conducting conversations about meaning. The ethical implications we identify in Yalom's approach for our meaning-making purposes are entirely our own. In fact, Yalom's wonderful book, *The Gift of Therapy* (2002), has nothing to do with ethics, at least on the surface. Below the surface, however, it has everything to do with the moral obligation each of us bears to treat one another with the most profound respect and kindness. This is especially obligatory whenever we are engaging in face-to-face, high-stakes, meaning-making communication.

At the heart of each of the eighty-five short chapters that Yalom's book comprises is one recurring axiom: "*[T]herapy should not be theory-driven but relationship-driven* [author's italics]" (p. xviii). At the core of all our own work with students is a similar postulate: *in the end, theory matters little—if care, concern, and connection are missing in the meaning-making interactions we have with our students.* Here are our ethical tips for all meaning-making encounters:

- Avoid becoming a diagnostician. Unless you are a certified counselor or therapist, leave clinical diagnosis to the professionally competent.

- On matters of meaning, all of us are fellow travelers. *Ipso facto*, no traveler has the upper hand. We are all unique individuals. To believe otherwise is to claim an omniscience that is spurious. At the very least, claiming to know what is good for others is a dangerous self-deception—and very likely harmful to them.

- Check in with students as frequently as possible, particularly when the conversational process gets heated and threatens to veer out of control. Solicit process feedback at all times. This honors our ethical duty to prevent harm to others. Go light on product feedback at all times. This honors our ethical duty to respect the autonomy of each and every individual we encounter in the meaning-making process.

- Remember always the responsibilities inherent in the power of position that you possess. Even though you cannot be the expert on making meaning for everyone else, you *can* be the expert on helping and supporting students on their individual, meaning-making journeys.

- Be empathic at all times. There is very little about meaning-making that doesn't stir up deep-seated feelings. Be there for students always. This is what they will remember long after they have heard all your learned interpretations, translations, and explications. Each of us has a moral responsibility to feel *for*, if not *with*, others, when discussing sensitive issues concerning what gives lives purpose and meaning.

- Let your students know they matter. The best way to do this is to *listen* to them before you *profess* to them; to *support* them, not *fix* them. Treat each of your students as an individual whose personal story of meaning is unique and significant. This honors the ethical principle of respect for autonomy.

- Do not be intimidated by open expressions of feelings. Thinking without feeling is abstract and lifeless. Feeling without thinking is uninformed and directionless. Be aware, however, that behind most thinking about important topics are strong feelings that we educators have traditionally learned how to suppress in others as well as in ourselves. We have been steeped in opinions like those of Immanuel Kant, who once referred to feelings as "illnesses" of the mind. Good meaning-making education alternates among outward expressions of affect, cognition, and effect. What do we feel? What do we know? To what end—so what, now what?

- Self-disclosure and transparency in meaning-making work best when students, not faculty or administrators, are at the center of the stage. Whenever you are tempted to expose your own feelings, ask yourself this question:

"How does my self-disclosure benefit my students?"
Find the balance between being opaque and being
translucent in your self-disclosures. To do otherwise
is to use students as means to satisfy your own ego needs.
Instead, treat students as ends in themselves, at all times.

- Know the difference between being *authoritative* and
  authoritarian. The former represents your professional
  responsibility to share the knowledge, wisdom, and experience you possess by virtue of your training and official
  position. This is one way to act on your duty to provide
  benefits for students. The latter represents the temptation
  to exploit these very same privileges by imposing
  your will on students—on the grounds that you are
  more powerful, older, and more "degreed-up" than they.
  This type of authoritarian behavior—"teacher knows
  best"—is a frontal assault on the dignity and autonomy
  of students. Cherish your privilege to be a facilitator,
  not a dictator, of meaning-making on a college campus.

- Help students to understand the full implications of a key
  existential maxim: "Everything fades, and alternatives
  exclude." Meaning-making takes time, and meanings
  change over time. Only our students can choose
  how to live their lives, and it is they who must realize
  that each of their choices will, of necessity, preclude
  other choices. Who among us wants to bear the heavy
  burden of determining which alternatives students
  ought to include, or exclude, in their lives? Not only is
  this ethically irresponsible, but it is also a no-win game.

- Safety first, middle, and last! This should be one of the
  primary ethical maxims for all teaching and learning. It is
  important to remember, however, that safety in a group,
  or in a one-on-one encounter, does not have to preclude

a prudent amount of interpersonal excitement, creative tension, careful intellectual examination and analysis, and sensitive feedback. On the one hand, without a genuine sense of safety, how is it possible for students to discuss openly such hot-button issues as values, ethics, faith, doubt, work, relationships, responsibility, freedom, choice-making, death, community, connection, love, hate, and a number of other meaning-related topics? On the other hand, how is it possible for students to discuss these serious topics without stirring up a certain amount of tension and anxiety? The trick is to establish a mutually respectful conversational environment that prepares students for both the expected and the unexpected.

- Know well how the interpersonal dynamics of projection, displacement, and transference affect both you and your students. Each of us has a natural tendency to see our best and worst selves in others; to displace onto others our own personal issues that actually have nothing to do with them; and to equate students' admiration for our *role* with adoration for our presumed *charm* and *expertise*. Knowing how each of us misuses these defense mechanisms will help us to avoid exploiting our students. It will also help us immeasurably in resisting the temptation to buy into all of their transferences. Both Freud and Yalom have called this phenomenon *counter-transference*, and it is always, and everywhere, lethal for meaning-making educators, and for our students as well.

- Remember always that there are places deep within the human spirit where visitors are not allowed. In the work of meaning-making, it can be tempting to "help" students draw connections by probing deeply into their inner sources of confusion, sadness, anger, or even bliss. This is not helping; it is *trespassing*. Educators cannot force students into meaning; they can, however, issue the invitation. Students themselves have to decide whether or not to follow the lighted path, and indeed to decide which path to follow. Know the difference between knocking on the door of their meaning and storming the castle.

7

Meaning Maxims for Both
Inside and Outside the
Classroom

In this chapter, our tips for educators will take a somewhat different form than in previous chapters. We will present these tips in a
brief list of maxims that we think succinctly capture the basic beliefs
and unique helping style of meaning-making education. Maxims
(sometimes we refer to these as aphorisms) are short, pithy sayings
that condense centuries of wisdom, or years of personal experience,
or electric moments of "Aha!" insight, into a few ingenious, kinetic
lines. They are at once brief yet deep. At their best, these sayings are
full of energy and purpose. They can be inspiring and generative.
They can motivate students to do some of their best thinking about
meaning-making, because they are open-ended and always open to
fresh interpretations.

We have discovered in our meaning-making discussions with
students that frequently a well-chosen maxim, uttered (by them
or by us) at just the right time, can highlight and summarize a
conversation, or draw out an original insight, in a way no lengthy,
jargon-ridden, scholarly discourse can. A maxim can be as enticing
for students as a catchy song lyric or a signature sign-off line at the
end of an email. We often ask our students to compose their own
meaning maxims, and then we encourage them to further develop
these maxims in a series of reflective writings. Composing maxims

stirs the meaning-making juices; unpacking them is even better, in that it generates valuable afterthoughts and applications.

First the maxim, then the commentary—this is a teaching-learning formula that, in our experience, is nearly foolproof in stimulating the imagination of millennial students. Maxims speak to this generation because they are short, sweet, and easily communicable. They simulate texting and instant messaging—without the cell phone or BlackBerry. When we encourage students to do the follow-up commentaries on their maxim-messages, we find that they are more than eager to think beyond their initial constructions in order to make better sense of these for themselves and others.

There is an art to effective maxim-making, and our students relish the creative possibilities. Nietzsche, perhaps the greatest maxim/aphorism coiner of them all, said this about the promise of his own short constructions: maxims are like "cold baths . . . quick in, quick out." Some truths about life, according to Nietzsche, can be "seized hold of only suddenly—which one must surprise or leave alone . . ." Nietzsche urged us to go one giant step further, however. He claimed that we will never understand just how serious a maxim can be until it has been "deciphered." The true meaning of a maxim lies in its "exegesis" (Hollingdale, 1977, pp. 18–20). Exegesis is about explaining further the meaning of a word or passage. Exegesis is what biblical scholars do with various scriptural passages. It is also what literary theorists do with the writings they study closely.

For example, Robert sometimes assigns his students a particular set of maxims written by Antonio Porchia (1886–1968) (as well as a number of others composed by different authors), as an introduction to this art form. He also encourages them to do some initial exegetical unpacking before they read other maxims or construct their own.

Porchia was an uneducated gardener, born in Italy and raised in Argentina. He wrote all his aphorisms while gardening. He was a loner, who saw the whole world in his garden each day. He found his greatest wisdom and joy while nurturing his garden, distilling all of life down to its three major events—birth, growth, and death. He wrote only one short book's worth of aphorisms in his entire life (translated in a 2003 collection). We include here eight of Porchia's maxims that Robert uses, from a total of forty-five:

- When you and the truth speak to me, I do not listen to the truth. I listen to you.

- One learns not to need by having needed too much.

- If we could escape from our sufferings altogether, and did so, where would we go outside them?

- Would there be this eternal seeking if the found existed?

- Suffering does not follow us. It goes before us.

- The person who has seen everything empty itself is close to knowing what everything is filled with.

- The little things are what is eternal, and the rest, all the rest, is brevity, extreme brevity.

- The fear of separation is all that unites.

Because Porchia's maxims are both provocative and evocative, and written in a simple, down-to-earth way, Robert's students devour the opportunity to make sense of them for their own meaning-narratives. Robert's instructions to his students are direct:

1. There are no right or wrong interpretations of maxims. There are only creative commentaries. Think of these eight maxims as expressions of Porchia's philosophy of life. Therefore, what do you think is this philosophy?

2. What do you think each of the maxims means, if anything, regarding your own search for meaning?

3. What maxim(s) would you create as a response to Porchia?

Maxims like Porchia's enable students to become both skilled maximists and reflective exegetes. These maxims get students thinking below surface meanings. They stimulate their narrative imaginations. They offer dollops of insight in simple declarative statements that cry out for further elaboration. It does not take long for students to get hooked. Soon students learn how to capture our attention (while focusing theirs) with spontaneous encapsulations of their meaning-learnings; but more important, they learn how to keep our attention with their thoughtful analyses.

What follows is a brief series of maxims that we have used, in addition to Porchia's just introduced, in our meaning-making interactions with students. These are but a few samples of hundreds, perhaps thousands, that we have come up with over the years. We unpack the following maxims for our readers in the same spirit that we do with students. We address these maxims to both classroom teachers and student-affairs educators simultaneously.

> *If you want comfort, go to the priests. If you want truth, go to the philosophers. If you want courage, go to neither; look first to the self.*

This maxim is Arthur Schopenhauer's (1970). In one of Robert's undergraduate classes, a student made the claim that living with courage is the best way to create meaning. Robert asked the group, as a thought experiment, to share some immediate, uncensored impressions of what they thought courage might look like. The images they shared were active rather than passive; of someone taking a serious physical risk rather than prudently staying out of harm's way. One student gave the example of a firefighter dutifully rushing into the burning World Trade Center on 9/11 to rescue the victims of the terrorist attack. Another told the story of someone diving into deep and treacherous waters to save a struggling child from drowning. Still another talked about a soldier standing alone against the rifle fire of radical Iraqi insurgents in order to protect a convoy of civilians. One student mentioned a neighbor who took a great risk to save a kitten in a tree from the fallen, live power lines following a hurricane.

Robert pointed out that these images were all well and good, even laudable. But they were mainly masculine images of courage. Historically, courage has meant a male warrior's strength and daring, overcoming the enemy, persisting, and emerging victorious from battle. The saying "It took balls" is a vulgar, yet direct, reference to the supposed manliness of courageous acts. The yin/yang stereotype of passive women and active men bespeaks the bias toward seeing courage as a masculine virtue, a testosterone-driven quality of moral character.

It was at this point that Robert decided to share Schopenhauer's maxim on courage with the group. He asked the group to become meaning-exegetes and to unpack the maxim's relevance for how courage might be helpful in their own lives. One student suggested that physical or martial courage is just not that impressive or desirable for her. She said that there were many "courageous" yet obnoxious historical figures who robbed banks, blew up buildings and themselves in the service of some cause, put many lives other than the enemies' at mortal risk in wartime, assassinated national leaders, destroyed the environment in order to build one more oil well, and killed, raped, and plundered in the name of ethnic cleansing or a final solution.

Another student said that he saw a film many years ago that lionized as heroes the pilots (one of whom won the Congressional Medal of Honor as someone who went above and beyond the call of duty) who dropped nuclear bombs on Hiroshima and Nagasaki in Japan during World War II, obliterating a quarter of a million civilians in a flash. How many hundreds of thousands of survivors, and descendants of those survivors had their lives shortened, or are still alive today trying to cope with the physical consequences of disabling genetic mutations, remains a mystery.

The conversation began to focus on the following questions: To what glorious ends do even the more praiseworthy valorous actions lead? How do they increase the quality of meaning in a person's life? What meaning-system motivates an act of bravery? In response to these questions, students came up with the following reasons for acts of courage: Some heroes do what they do in order to achieve the adrenalin rush that comes from putting themselves, and others, in grave danger. This is like jumping out of an airplane, or scaling an apparently impassable, icy mountain, or shooting dangerous rapids in a canoe. Or maybe they are just following orders as good patriots, employees, citizens, or religious believers are expected to do. Or maybe they do it out of a need to win medals, or find their names in the next day's newspaper headlines, or to win favor with God or Allah or some general or politician. Or perhaps these courageous figures have given up all hope and use their exploits as a way to commit a socially acceptable suicide, going down with all flags flying and guns blazing, so to speak.

Toward the end of the discussion, Robert once again brought up Schopenhauer's maxim on courage. Finally, one student said, "I read somewhere that courage is all about taking heart." (This is what the French and Latin roots of the word *courage* mean—*heart* or *spirit*.) "During those trying times when we are stuck in the valley of meaninglessness, the temptation will be great to turn to the priests and to the philosophers for answers. This will not always be satisfying, though, because all too often the answers lie in the self."

Another student said this: "When I'm stuck in that terrible place between feeling that my life is totally without meaning but wanting meaning to come into my life in the worst way, I remind myself to listen to my heart, to check my breathing and my pulse, to trust what my stomach, bladder, and bowels are trying to tell me. It is only when I am able to take heart, to have courage, to lead with my spirit as well as my intellect, to trust myself, that I inch a little closer to some type of worthwhile meaning."

Finally, one student's comment brought the conversation about the relationship of courage and meaning-making full circle. Her self-disclosure was powerful:

I may never lead a division of soldiers into battle, or defeat several oversized bullies on my little brother's middle-school playground with a dazzling display of karate chops, or defuse a live bomb, or rush into a burning automobile to pull its unconscious occupants to safety. No, Schopenhauer is right. I need to look first to myself. Whenever I do, I find that my kind of courage is even better than the conventional stuff of which legends are made. You see—my greatest act of courage in the last few years has also been the source of my most important meaning-making. *It goes by the name of overcoming my need to be perfect in order to be loved.*

Who taught me this? Not my parents, or my minister, or my teachers, or my siblings. I'm proud to say that I taught myself this truth about meaning-making. It came during one of the most trying times in my life. I realized that I had become an unhappy, almost desperate perfectionist because I felt this was the only way that people could ever love me. What was happening, though, was that I didn't love myself. Pursuing perfection was just another excuse to avoid doing the real work of making myself worth loving. Now, I find that my life has meaning, because I am able to accept my imperfections. More than this, now I work on my strengths, not my weaknesses. I am more concerned with loving than being loved. And you know what? I'm becoming a pretty loveable person! In fact, I realize that I've always been loveable.

To different minds, the same world is a hell . . . and a heaven.

These words are Ralph Waldo Emerson's (1803–1882), and they are his way of saying that good and evil do not exist outside of each person's particular narrative about them (1990). Naive realism is based on the assumption that we are able to see the world directly—as it is "objectively"—without filters of any kind. For naive realists, good and evil are objective realities. They are what they are. In contrast, as we suggested earlier, life is not always accurately understood as "it is what it is." Educators can do students a great service by helping them to distinguish between what it is we can see directly and what it is we see only indirectly. "It is what it is" is good advice when it cautions us to let go of what we cannot control, or change, and to move on. Alcoholics Anonymous says it well in Reinhold Niebuhr's "The Serenity Prayer": "God, grant me serenity to accept the things I cannot change, courage to change the things I can, and wisdom to know the difference."

Sometimes, "it is what it is," as in Niebuhr's prayer, is a remarkable exercise in acceptance of a given reality—that which we cannot change. But in any objectively real situation, like Frankl's concentration camps, the power one has lies in choosing a particular attitude toward that reality. It takes a stout heart to face certain pain or displeasure and then choose to narrow the parameters of its effect. In one sense, an unexpected diagnosis of a critical illness, for example, is what it is. The disease exists, but the patient has an opportunity to choose how to live through it. This is the appeal of Kris Carr's *Crazy Sexy Cancer* film and book. "Why, when we are challenged to survive, do we give ourselves permission to truly live?" she asks on her website (www.crazysexycancer.com). In Carr's inspirational example, "it is what it is" reflects the serenity of acceptance without the resignation of defeat.

However, too often "it is what it is" is meant by millennial students to be a conversation stopper. Not used to playing with ideas for their own sake or dealing with the strong feelings often surfaced by a clash of strongly held belief systems, millennial students in Robert's classes sometimes choose to opt out of a difficult, charged conversation. One way they do this is by bringing it to an abrupt close with a "bottom-line" assertion. Such an assertion sometimes signals what postmodernists and existentialists might call an unwitting confession of moral cowardice. This is the attempt to escape any personal responsibility for making changes by looking outside of ourselves for those authorities who might be able to give us unconditional answers to conditional questions.

In contrast, we believe that students must, first and foremost, understand that meaning-making is an individual activity. Moreover, meaning-making is rarely, if ever, a matter of "it is what it is." Rather, meaning-making is a combination of "it is who I was, who I am, and who I want to become." Happiness and meaning do not exist *outside of* our beliefs about them. Whenever we hear students resorting to this bottom-line retort, we respond in this way: "Your 'what it is' may not be my 'what it is.' Please unpack your 'what it is' for me, so that I can understand what has meaning for you—and vice versa." Robert often says to his students: "Why is your bottom line 'bottomer' than my bottom line? On what grounds, and whose truths shall win the day? If I don't accept your bottom line, then what? Do we go to war over our difference? Do we resort to 'might makes right?'"

Things won are done; joy's soul lies in the doing.

Pleasure comes more from making progress toward goals than from achieving them. Shakespeare captured it perfectly in the maxim that leads off this section (quoted in Haidt, 2006, p. 84). There are times when process is as important as product, particularly when the product sought is personal happiness. Mihaly Csikszentmihalyi is known as the "father of flow psychology," and his work serves as the philosophical cornerstone for positive psychologists. For Csikszentmihalyi (1990), happiness is an *autotelic* (self-goal) experience: it is a self-contained activity. It is doing something for its own sake, instead of doing it in expectation of some future benefit. Although there are times when *exotelic* (outside-goal) activity is expected of us in our work and study—and it is indeed praiseworthy when we do this well—nevertheless, our greatest happiness and meaning come from autotelic activity.

Optimal well-being, or happiness, is most likely to occur during those moments in our lives when we do not seek these directly. Rather, intense, focused involvement in the process or activity itself (such as art, music, sports, play, writing, conversing, dancing, running, skydiving) is the ultimate reward. We are lost in the activity. Self-consciousness all but disappears. It is not *we* who do the activity; it is the activity that does *us*. On occasion, we have had a few autotelic students say: "The written assignment wrote me, not the other way around. Before I was aware of it, hours had passed, the paper was done, and I was both exhilarated and exhilarated— at the same time." Oh that we might meet more of these students inside *and* outside our classrooms!

We think that one of the main reasons why so many students on our campuses get bored, burnt out, driven, angry, and alienated, and then look to drugs, sex, junk food, alcohol, violence, or internet addiction to fill their free time is because they have become excessively exotelic. Unfortunately, higher education today is all about producing exotelic graduates—careerists who are, in Freud's telling sexual metaphor, "married to their jobs." They cathect their work with all their libidinal (sexual) energy, with nothing left over to share with an intimate partner. Too many students who attend our campuses today do so mainly to earn the credentials that will admit them to all-consuming careers. Sadly, such students are out of flow. They work for extrinsic rewards, and when these rewards lose their meaning, they look elsewhere for satisfaction. Too frequently, however, the "elsewhere" is not the best place for them to search for meaning.

One of the ways that we try to counter the hegemony of exotelic activity in the academy, whenever we see it in our students, is to ask them about the quality of their autotelic lives. What is going on in their personal lives that makes them happy, that gives them surcease from the student rat race, that thoroughly consumes them in a healthy, joyful way? When in their lives do they feel less driven, less addicted, and less self-destructive? When, how, and where do they experience the flow, and why does this happen less than they would like? When is the last time they said "I would do this, even if I did not have to." To use a word becoming more and more clichéd on our campuses, we will ask our students: what is really "sweet" about the quality of your life in this place?

> *The secret of happiness is good love and good work . . . in this order.*

It was Sigmund Freud who allegedly uttered this maxim on his deathbed. Haidt explains: "love and work are crucial for human happiness because, when done well, they draw us out of ourselves and into connection with people and projects beyond ourselves . . . happiness comes from getting these connections right" (2006, p. 223). This is what positive psychologists call "vital engagement." Perhaps some philosophical counselors, in the spirit of the Ancients' emphasis on balance and harmony, might add "good health and good play" to Freud's comment. Whatever one's preferences for the happy life, however, it goes without saying that we all need external connections and projects to make the kind of meaning that gets us outside of ourselves. Relationships satisfy our human needs for attachment and intimacy. Without some kind of social bonding, as a number of studies have shown, people become passive and despairing (Goleman, 2006). Whenever children, for example, are deprived of a set of stable caregivers, they often become "aloof loners or hopeless clingers" (Haidt, 2006, p. 114).

This pattern also holds true for adults because, according to the research, childhood attachment styles tend to persist throughout the life-cycle (Vaillant, 2002). When the earlier stages of child development are positive, then the later stages of passionate and companionate relationships are healthy. It is almost impossible for any of us, even though we may enjoy our solitude and independence for a time, to be happy without lovers, friends, or confidantes in our lives. Secure personal attachments are a necessary prerequisite for making meaning.

The Hindu philosopher Krishnamurti poignantly captures the importance of personal attachments and love for living the full life:

> If you have no love—do what you will, go after all the
> gods on earth, do all the social activities, try to reform
> the poor, enter politics and education, write books, write
> poems, accumulate wealth, enhance your power and
> influence, become famous—but you are a dead human
> being. Without love, you will be lonely, your problems
> will increase, and multiply endlessly, you will be isolated.
> But with love, you have everything. With love, you are
> whole. With love you have meaning. (1993, p. v)

Work that is satisfying also makes us happy. It confers meaning
on our lives. The work that is especially significant, according to
the research (Seligman, 2006), is work that is complex and spontaneous, and that allows for some autonomy and creativity—all
the while generating commitment to the project. In the jargon of
psychologists, such work satisfies our "effectance needs." Those of
us who see our work as *jobs* do it for the money, with little or no
personal investment of meaning. Those of us who see our work as
careers do it for prestige, power, and promotion; but after awhile,
the career seems like a race to be won rather than a process to be
enjoyed for its own sake. (Ironically, the Latin root of the word
"career" means *racetrack*.)

However, those of us who see our work as a *vocation* seem to be
genuinely happier than those of us who experience our work as jobs
or careers only. It is important, however, to understand that how we
experience work is a matter of perspective and interpretation.
We are the ones who invest the work we do with meaning or meaninglessness. Thus it is possible for blue-collar workers to think of
their work as vocations and for professional people to think of their
work as jobs. It all depends. The secret is to experience our work as
"love made visible," in Kahlil Gibran's words (Haidt, 2006, p. 222).
The implication of Gibran's insight for our students is for us to help
them draw on their strengths, and on what they love, as they go about
creating vocations for themselves. Positive psychology's definition

of *passion* could very well be this: *what we want to do because we can do it, and because we love to do it.* No matter the level or type of work, the meaning of it is what counts. Students need to find a way to make the most of their unique strengths, passions, and interests if they are to discover happiness and satisfaction in the workplace.

Not then . . . not when . . . Zen.

This is a pivotal maxim of Robert's. It is his shorthand way of stating a general goal of meaning-making conversation: be here in this single hour, living now, right now, right away—with ourselves and with our students. Robert often says this to his students before he begins a seminar session: there is no past, no future, during our time together; there is only "now," or "this," which is the Chinese and Japanese meaning of the word *zen*. Robert's maxim encourages his students to be attentive, open, and mindful of all that is happening in the Zen. There is no better preparation, or setting, for talking about such an evocative topic as meaning.

Moreover, a Zen presence is the main staple of effectively facilitating meaning-making conversations. Zen presence establishes or undermines the legitimacy of the process from the very first minute of the conversation. Presence is about projecting a sense of ease, unflappability, poise, and self-assurance. Effective meaning-making educational leaders have a special kind of personal bearing. They are dignified, informed, enthusiastic, and professional, without being intimidating. They are compelling without being controlling. They are superbly prepared on the issues to be discussed, but they can also be spontaneous, even serendipitous, when new twists and turns emerge. They are conspicuously in charge without being arrogant. The Zen of effective conversational leadership is just being present with others. It is also balancing self-confidence with humility, and rationality with intuition.

Robert remembers a meaning-making session in his seminar that soon grew into an exercise in angry contestation and name-calling (Nash, 2008). The subject was the role of religion in making meaning, and one student, a fervent Christian, made the comment that meaning was impossible without the presence of God. Another student, a fervent nonbeliever, countered by asserting that meaning was impossible within any kind of a religious framework. From that point on, the seminar fell apart. One of the quieter, older students asked for a time-out. He was obviously upset. He suggested that the class take an immediate fifteen-minute break to get a snack, visit the bathroom, and cool off. When the group returned, he then asked that everyone take the time to "revisit Zen." He counseled the class to "breathe deeply," "be quiet," and respond in writing to the following question: "What do we all need to do to exemplify the best qualities of compassionate conversation in the time that we have left in this course?"

Here are the meaning-making guides for Zen conversation that the class came up with during a lively hour-long, post-incident interchange:

- Explain, clarify, question, rephrase, respect, and affirm.

- Evoke, don't invoke or provoke.

- Support without retort.

- Flow, glow, and let it go—don't fight or flee.

- Be generous at all times, without exception.

- Attribute the best motive.

- Speak always for yourself and not for some group.

- Help others to shine, while concealing your own brilliant light under the proverbial bushel.

> *Do not ask me to list my mistakes. Ask me, instead, what I have learned from my mistakes. Only then will you truly know me.*

matter, anyone who errs grievously may well do the same). Inwardly, they experience wild disbelief that they have disappointed those whose opinions mean the most—parents, mentors, teachers, close friends. By harping on the mistake, we reinforce their need for self-defense. But if, instead, we point toward the opportunity for them to demonstrate character, we communicate a belief in the students' basic integrity and an expectation that they will rise to the moral challenges they face.

> The mass of men lead lives of quiet desperation
> . . . and go to the grave with the song still in them.

Henry David Thoreau is the author of the first part of this maxim but not the second. Although Thoreau definitely penned the first clause, in *Walden*, the second, anonymously written clause captures the imagination as if Thoreau, himself, authored it. Taken together, these two thoughts, regardless of who expressed them, sum up why the quest for meaning is so important to so many. Few people we have known would choose to lead desperate lives, and fewer still would hope to discover, at the end of their days, that they had not fulfilled their purpose in life.

As we discussed earlier, "vocation" equals work plus love, and perhaps even great love. But to have a sense of vocation, from the Latin *vocare* (to call), is also to have a sense of living out a personal calling. Not to be confused with vocation to religious life or vocational training associated with skilled manual labor, personal vocation speaks to one's singular, or most noble, purpose in life. Vocation is the confluence of natural talents, learned skill, and deep passion that creates a unique contribution to a community or a profession. As Buechner (1992) explained, it "is the place where your deep gladness and the world's deep hunger meet" (p. 95). The personal vocation is the "song" one must find the courage to sing.

In one of Michele's class discussions of Parker Palmer's (2000) *Let Your Life Speak*, a student named Kirby asked, "What happens if you don't know your song, or if you find out you're singing the wrong

These words were written by Jules Renard in 1898. Of all the maxims we have listed, this may be the one that is most important to share with students in the wake of their personal mistakes and failures. (We should take care to remind ourselves of this maxim during our own moments of obsessive self-indictment.) This is not a statement dripping with false sentimentality, nor is it an escape hatch from the reality of the situation they have created for themselves. Rather, it is a statement of fact that, sincerely offered, can rescue a student from the self-destructive downward spiral of shame. The focus is not on the mistake, but on the opportunity for character-building in the wake of that mistake—the opportunity to take responsibility, accept consequences, make reparations, and commit to a different way of being in the future.

Imagine the student who is caught cheating on a test or plagiarizing a paper, the student who is documented by campus officials for marijuana possession, or the student government leader who is confronted with misusing positional power for personal gain. Of the students we have known who have found themselves in the midst of these or worse controversies, every one of them, to a person, has said that admitting their actions to those in authority with whom they have close relationships was the most trying personal test they had experienced in their young lives. They were concerned with the consequences they may face, and that frightened them. But more than that, they were preoccupied with the possibility that their mentors and role-models will write them off as cheats, addicts, or unethical lowlifes.

The power of a conversation focused on character and integrity is in its ability to disarm the defensive posture of the one accused. To concentrate on the character-building potential of the situation is to stay in the present, with an eye toward a better future, rather than lament decisions of the past. This opens the door to a continued relationship, despite the disappointment of poor choices. Often, students who make grievous mistakes expect to be shunned, and they prepare themselves by hardening their exteriors (for that one? What happens when you don't know what your life is telling you?" Kirby's question was profoundly wise and spoke to the anxiety so many students face. In our experience, students believe, or at least want to believe, that their lives have meaning and purpose, but they are often stopped short in trying to discern what that purpose might be. Their paths are clouded by others' expectations about what they should do with their lives, or they mistake others' paths for their own. In Kirby's question was deep desire—the desire to feel called to a purpose, the desire to learn his own song, the desire to sing it out loud.

As mentors for meaning, those educators who are faculty and student affairs professionals have the awesome opportunity to help students learn their songs and find the courage to sing them. Whether by the example of living out one's own passion or by guiding students to uncover and pursue their passions, the meaning mentor's role can be indispensable to their discovery of purpose. And it is in the place of purpose, the place of meaning, that the true joy in life can be found.

> There are many who seek knowledge for the sake of knowledge: that is curiosity. There are others who desire to know in order that they may themselves be known: that is vanity. Others seek knowledge in order to sell it: that is dishonorable. But there are some who seek knowledge in order to edify and love: that is teaching.

This somewhat long maxim is St. Bernard of Clairvaux's (1090–1153), and we believe that, despite its judgmental tone, it carries much truth for meaning-making educators. Seeking knowledge for its own sake is a noble endeavor, and teachers who do this can be both inspiring and wise. But it is not enough. Seeking knowledge in order to be a productive scholar who is well-known, even renowned, is understandable, even justifiable, for those of us who have trained many years for the academic life. But it is not enough. Finding ways to make a living, or to supplement a salary, by becoming a paid consultant, national speaker, or famous, best-selling author is, in itself, neither dishonorable or exploitative. But it is not enough. What is necessary, beyond the pursuit of knowledge, fame, or financial enrichment, is a passionate commitment to teach as an act of love and generosity. This act is meant to inspire and support students in their individual searches for meaning. This kind of committed teaching often becomes its own reward, both for educators and students.

Meaning-making educators are *philia* teachers. They are Aristotle's "virtue friends," who make students better human beings as a result of their special relationships with them. They are willing and able to draw out their students' personal stories, particularly when they are relevant to the content being studied. Philia teachers sometimes discover that students' personal stories are far more important than the content being taught. Why? Because when all goes well, students' stories add resonance and life to their studies. Students *are* their stories, and it is through their stories that we will come to know them—on their own terms, not on ours. Students' stories give us a way to understand how they frame and negotiate their worlds. Whenever we take the time to evoke their stories, we send students the message that we are more than willing to meet them amidst the briars and thickets of the personal narratives they inhabit.

Each of our students is a precious question to which there is no final answer. Like Socrates, meaning-making educators respect and love the questions more than they do any answers. There is no question, no student, that is unimportant. In principle, no expert has anything more to teach them about forging meaning in their lives than any single one of them has to teach themselves. Every piece of wisdom is an hypothesis waiting to be tested. There are just no guarantees that one great thinker's key to the meaning of life will open all the doors to meaning for anyone else. In this sense, both students and educators are equals. We are each our own meaning makers. Each of us is a question waiting to be asked, seeking its own intellectual reference points, and moral compasses, in order to be answered. As philia teachers, committed to edification and clarification, we educators are here to affirm the multiple questions, and to love and accept each of our students on their own terms, even while we attempt, as best we can, to inform, clarify, and enrich their quests for meaning.

Philia educators are not seeking erotic favors from their students. That is a love that is ethically unacceptable. Instead, educators and students come together in friendship and love for reasons that are far more urgent, and exciting, than sexual or political favors. You see, all of us on a college campus come together to make mutual meaning. We come together, in Cardinal Newman's nineteenth-century words, because "without personal influence in a university there is neither life nor learning" there (Newman, 1990). We come together to delight in each other's company; to experience joy and illumination in our mutual conversations and explorations; to flourish in the sense that we get the opportunity to become all that we can become with special people who make us feel safe and significant. Therefore, in the senses mentioned here, it is far more ennobling, and satisfying, for us to experience a large philia love (a companionship love best shared among friends) than a small erotic passion.

What follows are a meaning-making professor's inspiring words as she describes the type of relationship she attempts to build with her students. She is a friend of Robert's, a teacher-educator who has a long history of working with teachers-in-training, and she is one of the most popular professors in her college. For us, her relationship with students represents what we are calling a "large philia love." Sadly, though, we know too many seasoned, professorial colleagues who would tend to dismiss as supererogatory—above and beyond the call of duty—what she describes in her inspiring words. In contrast to some of her colleagues, we consider her to be a personification of Bernard of Clairvaux's edifying lover: a warm and compassionate friend and guide for her students. Here is how she tries to promote meaning-making both in her teaching and out-of-classroom interactions with her students:

In my classes I work hard to make sure my students feel known. I take the time to get to know them as whole people and to reflect this through my questions, my concerns for all aspects of their well being, and my humor with them in class. Outside of class, I try to go to the games of my student-athletes, the productions of my theater students, the recitals of my musicians and singers. I hold evening pizza-and-advising sessions, not really to advise but just to have some relaxed time where we can simply be together in conversation and laughter. When laughter turns to tears, as it has many times in my office, I have worked hard to listen fully, and to base my reaction on the precious individual nature of the person in front of me. Sometimes this has meant simply listening and passing the tissues. Other times it has meant helping to brainstorm solutions or actions. And twice, it has meant actually walking students to the counseling center to schedule appointments.

I also work hard to make sure my students feel they know me. I attempt this by using personal anecdotes often to illustrate my points or simply to share something of myself—joyful or sorrowful. I bring my sons to class from time to time, so that my students are able to see me in a larger sense. My office is filled with photographs of my family, and drawings by my sons. In class, I talk about my successes and failures when I was a teacher in the public schools. In advising sessions, I am quick to share my own challenges when I was an undergraduate.

My hope is to build bonds across the learners in my classroom. My goal is to build a true and trusting community of learners—one where it is safe to take risks and make intellectual leaps, and even to fall on our faces sometimes. So, yes, it is important for me to build relationships with students that are caring, heartfelt, honest, profound, and authentic. How else, I ask, could I help them to be meaning-makers?

Through the years, our colleague has listened, and responded, to countless impromptu tales of students' successes and failures, sadness and joys, hopes fulfilled and hopes dashed, love and hate, faith and faithlessness, dreams and nightmares, wisdom and ignorance, and optimism and pessimism about their futures. She has come to understand that in America today we are in the midst of a paradox: we live lives of poverty amidst our abundance. The loss of meaning among so many young people is what the worm has nibbled away deep within the apple of heightened American expectations. Our quarterlife students are caught between pulls of independence and interdependence, isolation and community, passion and apathy, and, perhaps most seriously, between pulls of spirituality and materialism.

Underlying all the conversations that she has with students are feelings of intense self-doubt, endless self-questioning, and a gnawing regret over opportunities lost and relational roads not taken. Almost every student she meets with suffers from an ongoing restlessness that has its roots in a crisis of meaning and purpose. Her students talk about whether all the sacrifices they are making to ensure that their futures are, in the long run, worth what they think they are losing. Some are in varying states of despair over the prospect of ever finding a stable and secure meaning to their lives. Everything is so up in the air to them. Some are unwilling to give themselves over to a single, avocational passion for fear of being sidetracked from their career goals.

Others, however, get animated only when they talk about their avocational enthusiasms, and they spend much of their free time engaging in these activities, often to the detriment of their studies and career preparation. They choose to foster relationships in their residence halls and in off-campus housing, instead of in their classrooms. They pursue hobbies and other personal activities as a way to escape from peer- and parent-driven pressures to build magna cum laude transcripts, resumes, and careers. These students are the secessionists from the career rat race, and they want our colleague's affirmation that this is okay. Like our colleague, we find that the quarterlife challenges that we are privileged to hear about each and every day of the week in our classes and other campus locations—whenever our students are most willing to let their guards down—are riveting and instructive.

We have taken to heart the advice of Saint Ignatius of Loyola, the founder of the Society of Jesus. He said at the beginning of the *Spiritual Exercises*: "Let it be presupposed that every good Christian is more ready to save his neighbor's proposition than to condemn it." Robert, who is not a Christian, and Michele, who is, both make it a point, in everything we do, to affirm our students' propositions about what gives their lives meaning, and never to condemn them. When necessary, of course, we gently question them, particularly when these propositions may be self- or other-destructive. We always try to get students to clarify their propositions. We make it a point to shut our mouths and open our ears. We look for generalizable lessons for our, and others', life-narratives. We are careful never to advance our pet political, educational, philosophical, or religious agendas during give-and-take conversations about meaning. And, believe it or not, in our interactions with students, teaching gets done, and learning gets accomplished—but mainly in the subtexts of our mutually open and warm human encounters.

> *Listening is an act of love.*

This powerful statement is the motto of the *Storycorps Project*, Dave Isay's brilliant and compassionate love affair with creating an oral history of twentieth- and twenty-first-century life in the United States. Inside the Storycorps booth, the lives of ordinary people are recorded for posterity. Grandmothers, doctors, bus drivers, veterans, fathers, daughters, prisoners, rescue workers, siblings, and teachers—all interviewed by someone who cares enough to ask the questions—share the moments of their lives, from the marvelous and the mundane to the tragic and the joy-filled (Isay, 2007).

The miracle of Storycorps is not in the telling of the story but in the hearing of the story or, more important, in the storyteller's feeling heard. In the intimacy of the booth, the generosity of the storyteller is matched, and perhaps surpassed, by the generosity of the interviewer. The one who listens, who asks the questions and patiently awaits the answers, is silently honoring the other: "I want to know you. Tell me who you are; you can be yourself with me. I value you." To hear one interview (www.storycorps.net) is to know that the telling of the story is an act of liberation and that the listening, as they say in Storycorps, is truly an act of love.

In higher education, as with most professional arenas, we tip-toe around the word "love." Sure, it is acceptable to toss the word around when speaking of ideas or inanimate objects, such as, "I love medieval literature." Or "I love pepperoni pizza with onions and green peppers." But when dealing with people, to utter the word "love," even when only referring to the *philia* friendship we described earlier, is to put oneself in a perilous and compromising position. To suggest that educators should love—that is, *listen to*—their students more feels somewhat like a daring flirtation with taboo. Nevertheless, the loving is in the listening, and students, like the Storycorps interviewees, want to be heard.

How many students—or even colleagues, for that matter—have walked into our offices wanting to be known, to be heard? Countless numbers, no doubt. Happily, the act of listening does not require a high-tech recording booth. No. A low-tech face-to-face meeting of the minds and hearts will suffice. More than anything else, listening requires time, a spirit generous enough to withhold judgment, and an attitude attentive enough to know when to ask the next question and which question to ask. This is all the storyteller needs to unravel the questions and the moments that beg for deeper understanding. When the storyteller is done, a brave listener might even turn the tables and, in true Storycorps fashion, ask, "Is there anything you wanted to know about me that will be helpful to you?"

Part III

Our Own Attempts to
Make Meaning

8

Two Personal Reflections for
Our Readers

Dear Readers,

We hope it has occurred to you by now that becoming a meaning mentor—a guide for quarterlifers as they seek paths to meaning—is nearly impossible without some carefully conceived system of personal meaning-making. To accompany or lead students on their own quest for a philosophy of life seems somehow inauthentic unless the mentor has experienced entertaining similar deep questions. In the same way, it felt inauthentic for us to write about meaning without acknowledging our own abilities, and sometimes inabilities, to make meaning.

In the two personal reflections that make up this final chapter, we reflect on our individual attempts to make meaning. We include our own personal narratives at this particular juncture of the book to illustrate two points. First, the quest for meaning is a lifelong activity for all of us. Nobody ever escapes it; nobody is ever immune to its lures. At no time in our life cycles do we ever gain permanent closure in the pursuit of meaning. And this holds for us as well as for our students.

Second, we believe that you, the reader, will find it useful to observe how we, the authors, actually apply some of the theories and practices we write about in the previous pages to our own personal and professional lives. In other words, in our personal letters we want to exemplify what we explicate. Too many books in the field of higher education tend to be packed with learned explication—at the expense of personal exemplification. We do not want that to happen here.

We ask that you read our narratives with generosity. We wanted to write this book to begin the conversation about purpose and meaning—not because we believe we are experts in making meaning or have somehow mastered the art of writing about it. If nothing else, we hope that our personal reflections in this section will tell you a little more about us, as well as about the *whys* and the *ways* we work with students in order to explore meaning. Our greater hope in this particular chapter is to share our personal stories as candidly as we can, so that they may draw you into a deeper intimacy with the ways in which you, yourself, make sense of the world and your place in it.

With great respect,
Michele C. Murray and Robert J. Nash

Swimming Lessons

Michele C. Murray

"Why are you here?" This is a loaded question. Loaded with the metaphysical and the existential. Loaded with wonder and meaning. Loaded with inquisition and probing.

"Why are you here?" This is the question my colleague and I ask every year on the first day of the undergraduate class we teach. Beyond "This class is required for my major," we want to know what these students, juniors and seniors, want to learn. We want to know why they have come. In part I ask this question because I wish someone had asked me, "Why are you here?" when I was in college.

Like many students I have known throughout my career, I spent a good part of my college years floating on the surface. Contrary to a popular clichéd admonition, sinking and swimming are not the only options; one can also choose to float, to be generally aimless, to be without much meaning. For at least part of my college career, I was a very good floater. I had constructed a very small world for myself without much awareness of how truly small (and, I admit, self-absorbed) it really was. As with one who actually floats on the water's surface, I saw and experienced little other than what was directly in front of me. The floater has limited context for where she is, much less where she is headed. I was a good floater. Mindless at times about who or what was around me, about who I was or where I was going.

There were days, I am sure, when I was doing little more than taking up space. I was involved in a few student organizations, and with the exception of one miserable bump in the road, I earned decent grades. Still, I was just floating on the surface. If the seventeen-year-old version of me were here, she would say that she wanted to do more than float through the first few semesters of college. She would say that she was just waiting for someone to ask her to swim.

The Invitation

As a teenager I thought Martha Quinn had the world's best job. As a video jockey (VJ), Martha introduced the latest music videos and chatted with the hottest pop and rock music stars on what was fast becoming a cultural icon and teen bellwether, MTV. In my own mind, I had all the skills one needed to be a VJ: I loved music, I could talk to just about anyone, and I studied popular culture. So although I considered multiple career possibilities in those first few college years—including forensic psychology, child psychology, and public relations—it seemed completely reasonable for me to announce to my parents that I had settled on moving to Manhattan and joining some of my favorite VJ personalities, like Kennedy and "Downtown" Julie Brown.

I do not recall my father's reaction, which means either he took the news in stride, believing that it was a passing fancy not worthy of response, or I did not have the courage to tell him the whole reason for my wanting to move to New York. For sure, I tested my idea on my mother. With a characteristically feigned confidence, I told her I had all the skills. After all, in eighth grade I had accurately predicted Madonna would be a huge hit before any of my friends had even heard of her or listened to her music.

My mother, for her part, did not directly oppose my choice. Characteristic of her temperament and her experience mothering a headstrong daughter, she instead expressed enough disapproval and concern to make me think twice. She also opened the door of possibility. I believe she said something to the effect of, "You can do so much more with your life. You do have the skills and probably some of the talent to be a VJ if you want, but those skills and talents deserve more from you."

Because I was not expecting her to jump for joy at the thought of her daughter becoming an MTV VJ (in fact, I was not even sure she would know what that was), I was not crestfallen by my mother's apparent lack of enthusiasm for my choice of work. Rather, her words left me contemplative and feeling a bit confused, and this response of mine is what caught me off guard. What did she mean that I could do more with my life? As far as I was concerned at the time, becoming a VJ was doing "more." From my naive, uninformed perspective, being a VJ meant doing and having a lot more—more money, more fun, more glamour. In Frankl's words, I was focused on "the means to live" and not on "the meaning to live for." My young college-aged mind could not conceive of what else "more" was out there for me. What more did my mother want for me that I did not know enough to want for myself? Without my knowing it or even perceiving the importance of this conversation, my mother had extended the invitation for me to swim.

Float ... Sink ... Swim

As with many floaters who are abruptly startled from blissful reverie, I had a moment of panic. My mother's words had the effect of splashing cold water on my face and calling me to action. "You can do more," I heard her voice telling me. And the voice of self-doubt responded immediately, "What is 'more'? What more can I do?"

Like many students I have known, I attended college because the baccalaureate degree was the key to landing a secure future, and, truth be told, because in my family college was the expected next step after high school. But once I arrived in the hallowed halls of academe, I had no idea what to do or where to go. I am neither proud nor ashamed of my early dreams of life as an MTV show host. Those dreams were merely a reflection of where I was at that time in my life—a place of disconnection. I had not yet learned that the true passions of my heart could shape how I should apply the knowledge I was gaining from my coursework and my out-of-class involvement. The influences of popular culture and media had more sway over how I envisioned a successful life than my own values. Perhaps I had not yet learned to trust my internal compass. Perhaps the dial on that compass was not yet calibrated to "true north." Whatever the reason, the result was that in some senses, I was a young woman who was full of promise and yet somehow woefully lost to herself.

If I wanted the "more" my mother beckoned me to find, I had to first find out, "Who am I?" "Why am I here?" These are the questions of the "quarterlife crisis," as identified by Alexandra Robbins and Abby Wilner (2001), the questions of the emerging adult, the questions of meaning-making. Transitioning from floater to swimmer is not easy, as Robbins and Wilner point out in their many interviews with countless twenty-somethings who are befuddled, overwhelmed, and sometimes panicked by making their way in the "real world." Somewhere between the idyllic ignorance of floating and the meaningful agency of swimming lies the real possibility of sinking under the weight of so many questions with so few answers.

Like so many traditional-aged college students and young graduates, I was using floating as a way to avoid growing up—not because I did not want to but because I did not know how. And now that I look back on those years, I realize that floating also had become somewhat of a defense mechanism, particularly around matters of race and racism. Discovering who I was in relation to the world around me meant, at least in part, coming to grips with my experiences of growing up black in 1970s Northern Virginia.

By no means do I share in the terrible and terrifying collective memory of my fellow African-Americans who lived through the dehumanizing days of Jim Crow and worse. Instead, I lived a strange half-life. With the exception of one interracial family around the corner, mine was the only black family in the overwhelmingly white neighborhood, and throughout my school years, it was common for me to be the only person of color in class. My parents had moved us to the Washington, D.C., suburb because the county was known for its excellent public education. But as a family we did not talk about what it was like to be "different," and I certainly did not talk about the comments I heard from my peers and even a teacher or two. Instead, I learned to float.

I floated above the current, pretending to ignore it. I set aside the politics of race; I attempted to avoid the curse of racism and the particularly cruel demon of internalized racism. I felt bad about being black; I felt worse about not being "black enough." I remember trying to find the delicate balance between being too smart and not smart enough. If I pulled out the stops and let the mental pistons rev up to full power, I was somehow "acting white." If I dumbed it down to ease the discomfort of those detractors, I was suddenly under suspicion of being an "affirmative action case." Either way, the message was clear to me: it is far better to escape notice, to float above the fray. Floating became a way of coping with painful realizations and questions I was too timid to share.

Floating. It is a way to preserve some sense of self, a way to reach some sort of equilibrium, in the midst of chaos. The first thing any beginning swimmer learns is how to float. The patient teachers assure their aquatic students, "If you get nervous, turn on your back and float. You'll be just fine." Robert Kegan and Lisa Laskow Lahey (2001) indicate that self-preservation behaviors like floating (metaphorically speaking, of course) are a perfectly natural psychological response to protect ourselves from our underlying fears and self-doubts. Whether they are guarding against feelings of inadequacy related to race, gender, social class, or sexual orientation, I have met many a student who, like me, chose to float rather than sink from battling the self-doubt that hangs over them.

The chaos that comes with emerging adulthood is not limited to the realm of identity development. It seeps into relationships, as students wonder whether and when they might find someone special or as they find out the hard way that "loving the one you're with" in the meantime can lead to shallow intimacies and regret. It seeps into questions of worthiness as they face academic challenge, sometimes for the first time, and wonder if they belong in college at all. It seeps into questions of the future as they wonder what they should do with their lives and begin to dread graduation as they realize they do not know—or worse, it seeps in once they have graduated and realize that what they thought they wanted to do is all wrong.

Every student—to a person—I have known throughout my professional career has undergone some sort of personal trial as he or she has struggled through the chaos of growing up. The temptation to float above it all, to practice the art of avoidance, is very alluring. It is, I am sure, part of the reason why I had flirted with the idea of joining MTV rather than really digging deep into who I wanted to become. I can empathize with the college students I know today. I certainly had my share of battles with the turmoil of becoming my adult self. And at times I felt as if the confusion would sink me.

Still, by the middle of my college years, the challenge was clear: stop floating. Floating, it seemed, was getting me nowhere. And since sinking was not an option, I had to learn to swim.

Every Would-Be Swimmer Needs a Flotation Device

The decision to stop floating through life was gradual, and it was as daunting as it was liberating. In so many ways, the first few tentative steps toward the "more" were not unlike my experience of learning to swim as a young child. At age five, I liked the safety and ease of the flotation ring, but I also wanted my independence in the water. I floated easily. (Hmmm. A pattern I was destined to repeat, I suppose.) My swimming instructor, a cheerful teenager, who was so patient, kind, and wise, said I was ready. I learned to blow bubbles first, getting used to the feel of the water around my face. I learned to kick. I practiced moving my arms. But when it was time to actually swim, I remember flailing about. Learning to swim was not easy, nor was it difficult; it was just new. My instructor held me up and kept me from drowning in my own wasted energy. She taught me the rhythm of finding my way, and then . . . I swam. By myself! I was free. I no longer needed the plastic ring unless, of course, I *wanted* to take a break and float for a while. If I floated again, it would be on my terms; I was a swimmer.

In less than two weeks one summer, I learned to swim in the neighborhood pool. It would take me several years, beginning in college and stretching beyond graduation, for me to start "swimming," instead of floating, through life.

Discovering what mattered to me, learning who I was, and opening myself to who I was meant to become—this was the process of coming fully alive. In those first few months of daring to ask the questions I had suppressed for so long, I found myself flailing. Much like those early days in my neighborhood pool, I needed assistance. Unlike those early days, though, the help I needed would not come from an older, wiser instructor. In fact, my help would not come from a person at all. The stability I needed I found in my faith—a faith I rediscovered through the process of learning about myself.

A cradle Catholic, I received the first holy sacraments of baptism, Holy Communion, and reconciliation at my parents' behest. As a teenager, I was confirmed a Catholic without much thought or meaningful preparation because . . . well, because that was what was expected.

By the time I entered college, I had all but rejected the faith of my family. I did not understand the rules, why they were there, who made them, or why I had to follow them. Mass, to my mind at the time, was a boring, formulaic ritual with no relevance to me or my life. This period of my faith life, if one can call it that, was marked not so much by unbelief as it was by rebellion against a perceived, self-righteous rigidity, against an old-fashioned dogma that, truth be told, I did not actually know. Sadly, at the time, I did not have even the slightest inkling of curiosity to learn what I did not know. Instead, I walked away.

As far as I was concerned, the world had become unpredictable and people unreliable, and sorting it out seemed to invite more trouble. Rather than dive into the mystery of life, I took the easy way out and decided it was far better to float on the surface. In terms of Fowler's (1981) faith development theory, I had taken a sharp detour between stages three and four. I had shrugged off the convention of my Catholic upbringing but had not yet replaced it with the critical reflection that marks the beginning of an adult faith life.

But lo and behold, the quest to understand myself and my place in the world that began with my mother's encouragement to find the "more" led to something else too. There is no claim of causality here, but the journey to answer the question "Who am I?" led me to wonder, "*Whose* am I?" I began to desire a relationship with the God who created me. For me, the journey toward meaning began on the road to faith; I was beginning to grow into my adult self.

Having long before given up my childish fantasy of introducing music videos and interviewing my favorite artists, I graduated from college determined to break into public relations. After some trials and tribulations I accepted a position at a small Catholic girls' school, where, if I wanted, I could explore Catholicism while holding a respectable job and collecting a paycheck. I had hit the proverbial jackpot, and the unexpected bonus: this job became the gateway to discovering a calling to education. I poured myself into learning the ins and outs, the whats and whys, of the Catholic faith. If I was going to reject it, I had better know why. I read, participated in the sacraments, and asked questions of anyone who would enter-tain the conversation. What I found profoundly changed my mind and heart. Instead of rejecting the faith, I fell in love with it. My faith helped me make sense of the world. The lives of the saints became a source of inspiration. I turned to these spiritual heroes to learn how they reconciled the heartbreaks of the human condition and the realities of an imperfect world with the perfection of God's love. They taught me to pray and to trust.

Mine was a conversion experience, a turning of the soul toward the eternal. The more I learned, the more at peace I felt. As I came to terms with God and his love for me, the self-doubt that had plagued me for so long began to melt away. I, too, was created in God's image, and I began to understand that aspects of my identity, my race particularly, had no bearing on my self-worth. I was finding that, like the swimming instructor who had supported me when I was flailing in the pool, God and the Catholic faith I was beginning to call my own were sure and gentle buoys. I would not sink.

The Buoy and the Diamond

Faith is a funny thing. To believe in that which you cannot confirm except by what you know in your heart is not logical in any way. To order your life according to what you cannot prove seems even less so. Faith is also tricky to negotiate. Taken too far in one direction, it becomes the stuff of fanaticism and violent conflict. And yet when people leave themselves open to recognize and appreciate the beauty of faith traditions other than their own, they also run the risk of falling prey to relativism. It is only by grace that my faith in the Lord balances between dogmatic rigidity and extremism on the one hand and the despair of crumbling absolutes.

When I was still new to my adult faith, I clung to the "rules" as one would cling to a buoy in uncertain waters. The surety of definite boundaries and resolute ideology was somehow comforting. I was an objectivist. Until, that is, I had an influential conversation that I will never forget. A friend, a very conservative Catholic, and I were discussing the merits of the faith. He sighed with relief when he said how lucky we were to be Catholic, children of the "true faith." With good work, participation in the Sacraments, and adherence to the Catholic faith, Heaven was promised to us; he was confident of that. What about the many, many non-Catholics of the world, I questioned. Was Heaven closed to them? "Yes," he replied.

Always one for an argument, I persisted: "But God created all people in His image; all of us are his children, isn't that right? So let's take folks in rural China or Tibet, who not only will have no chance of being exposed to Catholicism but are faithful adherents to Buddhism. They're good people, but they're condemned?" I continued, "That doesn't make sense to me. Why would God create a person, a beautiful soul, knowing that he or she has no chance to enter Heaven?" I reminded him that people of other faith traditions, Jews, Baptists, and Muslims, for example, made similar claims of truth exclusivity and that to outsiders these claims seem naïve and insular. I am not a theologian and have no special authority on truth claims. I was just arguing for the sake of it, at least in part (my father is a litigator; logical argument is a virtue in my family), but I was also intrigued.

I had come to believe that unless something is a matter of capital "T" Truth—that is, absolute, objective truth—it was simply a matter of opinion. In the case of this argument, where did Truth end and opinion begin? I wondered. Perhaps clinging to the buoy was not always the best strategy for me. As a result of that friendly debate, I let myself slightly loosen my grip on that life-saving buoy. Perhaps Truth, with all its resolute objectivity, is not fully accessible to us earthbound mortals. After all, God is infinite and all-knowing; who are we to assume we can know the mind of God?

Some might accuse me of starting down the slippery slope of relativism. But I am convinced that Truth is out there; it exists. I now like to think of Truth as a multifaceted diamond—beautiful, precious, and rare—of which none of us has a complete 360-degree view. Whatever vantage point each of us has of this Truth-diamond is influenced by the experiences we have had and the identities we hold that shape our interpretation of those experiences. I suppose, then, that I am somewhere between being an absolute objectivist and a relativistic constructivist. I rather think of myself as a complex combination of both terms—objectivist and constructivist. Some might charge that this is a classic case of fence-sitting. I do not think so. Instead, it joins the courage to reject the postmodernist claim that "we made it all up" with the humility to admit that we made up at least some of it. The combination of the two words, constructivism and objectivism, is my way of knowing. It is my way of making sense of the world. It allows me to ask questions without losing sight of certainty. It creates space for others' ways of knowing without threatening mine. I need them both.

Finally, a Swimmer

I do not have an adequate vocabulary to explain or to convey what my faith now means to me. The faith I grew to love was my road to meaning, my way of answering the question, "Why are you here?" If my mother's words of so long ago sparked a desire to do something other than float through life, it was the gift of faith in a gracious and loving God that taught me to swim.

The same freedom I felt as a new swimmer in my neighborhood pool is mine again, but the "swimming lessons" are not over. I learned as a child that there are different levels of swimming and different strokes to master. Dog-paddle is not the same thing as freestyle, and backstroke is one thing while the butterfly is quite another. The same is true of my faith journey. I am no Olympic swimmer, and I am no saint. As with all relationships worth having, I work at mine with my God—some days harder than others, I will admit. I am the one who is inconsistent, not God. But over time, I have felt His continued and steadfast holy presence. I have been gifted with several moments so holy—including and especially the day I married my soulmate, a man who believes in no god and follows no religion—that, even today, I am brought to tears by the memories.

Instructing Others

I am still learning to swim. I am still sorting out what I learn and observe of the world and trying to understand my place in it. I am still reaching for new plateaus of meaning. In most disciplines, academic or otherwise, one does not begin instructing others until a level of expertise is reached. This is not so with meaning-making. Instead, to be a meaning mentor one needs only life experience, self-knowledge, and an interest in others and their journeys. In fact, I think those who continue to search are self-possessed enough to share what they know in head and heart, and those who have humility enough to admit to their lingering questions are the ones who are the most authentic meaning mentors. And quarterlifers need these people in their lives.

As I work with college students, it helps me to remember that mentoring others into meaning does not require the possession of an extraordinary technical expertise. It also helps to remember that I floated for a long time before I answered the challenge to do more. I see college students every day who are struggling, mostly silently, to learn who they are. I ask them the questions I wish someone had asked me when I was their age. I urge them toward the "more" in the way my mother urged me. It is nothing less than a privilege to accompany young people as they learn to find their way, as they learn to swim.

The Joy in My Teaching Is the Meaning in My Teaching

Robert J. Nash

Two long maxims from thinkers who have influenced me greatly are the inspiration for the reflection that follows. The first is from Kierkegaard: "If I were to wish for anything I should not wish for wealth and power, but for the passionate sense of what can be, for the eye, which, ever young and ardent, sees the possible. Pleasure disappoints. Possibility never. And what wine is so sparkling, what so fragrant, what so intoxicating as possibility. Is there any greater joy?" The second maxim is from Kurtz and Ketcham: "We can experience both joy and sorrow, even at the same time, for joy and sorrow are not opposites. It is not joy and sorrow, but *their opposites* that cause damage; for the opposite of joy is cynicism and the opposite of sorrow is callousness." You will see in the paragraphs that follow how each maxim has been an important source for the joy and meaning that I find in my teaching . . . even now after more than four decades.

I want to introduce you to seven students, the types who find their way to my personal narrative writing seminars, as well as to all the other meaning-making courses I teach each year. These seminars enroll graduate students who are currently employed as human service professionals, as well as traditional and nontraditional undergraduates. What I appreciate about students like these is that, despite their unique quarterlife challenges—and for many these are considerable and dramatic—each has found a way to live a life of joy. I think it is instructive that in the last quarter of a century, less than 10 percent of the major research in psychiatry focuses on how to be joyful (Barber, 2008). All of the nonmedicating psychotherapies that we feature in our *Resources* section make a case, in their own distinctive ways, that joy is within everyone's reach, with or without the 230 million antidepressant prescriptions that physicians dispense every year. All of the seven persons whose profiles I sketch here see the "possible" in their lives. They choose to drink Kierkegaard's "sparkling wine of possibility" rather than live their lives, in Kurtz's and Ketcham's terms, trapped in the "dark despair" of "callousness, sorrow, and cynicism."

Seven Profiles of Joy

First, meet Joan, an early-thirty-something special educator, who is battling a rapidly metastasizing stomach cancer. Her long-term prognosis is not good, but she refuses to crawl into her bed and feel sorry for herself, after meeting daily with her oncologist for the energy-sapping chemotherapy and radiation treatments she must undergo. Instead, she goes to school every day to work with special-needs children, enthusiastically attends evening classes at the university, and is in the process of writing a book about her life as an educator and union organizer. Here is something that she recently wrote to me:

> Since I was diagnosed with advanced cancer, I have been writing a personal narrative that I want to get published. Two months ago I began an online update for family and friends, but my audience has changed from a group of people who all know me personally to a readership that is over eighty-percent people I don't know. They say that they are all helped by my writing. It gives my life a sense of meaning and purpose, and, strange to say, even joy, to be able to help others living with advanced cancer. When I write, I am so often reminded of what a caring and invigorating atmosphere I found in your meaning-making courses. I miss that.

At times, Joan arrives in my seminar pale and shaken. Her eyes are bloodshot, and her wig is disheveled. She wears her perpetual nausea on her face. She can be eerily quiet. Occasionally, during the term, she'll get up and leave in the middle of the class, and we won't see her again for a few weeks. But she always returns, sometimes, in an act of defiance, without her wig, and with a big sigh of relief that she has once more met the chemotherapy beast and overcome it. Now she can write her story for yet one more day.

Over here is Marilyn, a student in a graduate program in public administration. Marilyn is an evangelical Christian, a person who believes with all her heart and soul that Jesus Christ is the answer to the most unsettling questions about the meaning of life, including why bad things always seem to happen to good people. Regarding the latter, Marilyn's mom suffers from a long-standing, crushing depression, and during her worst times, she secludes herself away from everyone who loves her, including Marilyn. She locks herself in her bedroom for hours at a time, mumbling incoherently, often crying, until she is ready to emerge to try to live her life anew one more time. Marilyn has never felt so helpless as during these up-and-down cycles. She turns to the scriptures to find the solace and strength she needs to endure, and she is convinced that the answers are there.

At her "public ivy" university, Marilyn is a fish swimming in strange waters in her graduate program, because most of her peers are secular, skeptical, and politically progressive. Many in her seminar cohort are also religious cynics, who present themselves as spiritual agnostics, but who are actually wounded ex-believers, angry and often bitter. Because Marilyn is an out-of-the-closet evangelical Christian, she rarely misses an opportunity to witness—to talk openly in a seminar about her religious beliefs, and the comfort and wisdom they bring her. She works very hard, though, to not be haughty, judgmental, or proselytizing because she knows that many of her peers disdain her conservative Christian principles. She often feels alone and isolated, like her mom in a way, in a very secular, liberal, university environment. But she tries always to be joyful and enthusiastic in her relationships with others, no matter how secular they might be. She looks for the presence of God's love in everyone she meets and greets, even though their beliefs may be different from hers.

Over there is Kathy, a diabetic since her early teen years, whose diabetes has progressively worsened over the last few years. She lives from one blood sugar test to the next, hoping that she won't go into insulin shock and coma. She also lives constantly with the overriding fear that she may very well die an early death from diabetes complications the way that her mother did at age forty. Kathy herself has just celebrated her twentieth birthday, and the bitter irony is not lost on her. Her mother's physical condition began to deteriorate at about the same age, to the point where she eventually had to undergo amputations and suffered from blindness and a host of other degenerative disorders, before death mercifully took her.

himself as "stupid," compared to his "brilliant" "preppie" buddies. He cringes whenever he reads course syllabi that expect him to participate actively in seminars. Even though he is a frequent visitor to the university's disabilities center and has received much help there with his attention deficit disorder, he still tries to avoid seminar-type learning environments. However, it is almost impossible for an English major to spend an entire undergraduate experience sitting anonymously in a lecture hall.

Bruce fears that whenever he starts talking in a seminar he will expose himself, once and for all, for the academic fraud that he thinks he is. He seriously considers taking my course as an Independent Study, because he suffers from something he calls "presentation jitters." For the present, though, Bruce is determined to remain in the seminar as a full-fledged member of the class. He resolves to speak up, if not in the large group, at least in the small group sessions, and at least once during each meeting. Most of all, though, each session he forces himself to read sections of his personal narrative writing to the group. And when he does this, he beams from ear to ear, and, not surprisingly, his classmates beam with him, knowing that he has taken a risk and emerged victorious.

That African-American woman getting herself settled in her seat is Shelly. The small child with her is her daughter, Niki, five years old, and nicely behaved while sitting next to her mom during a three-hour seminar every week. Shelly is a single mom and caretaker, a full-time graduate student, who also holds a permanent leadership position in residential life at the university. Shelly has been on her own since her middle teens. She refused to heed the well-meaning advice of her friends and parents to have an abortion when she was pregnant with Niki. As a result, everyone near and dear to her abandoned her because they thought she was being selfish and foolish and would have to go on the public dole called welfare.

So Shelly went to live for a year in a homeless shelter at the tender age of sixteen. She gave birth as a teenager, went on to successfully complete high school and college, and is now in her

Kathy has not let the nightmare of this insidious illness slow h down, however. She plunges ahead, and she has become a high successful leader at her university. She is currently preparing for t LSATs so that she can enter law school in the coming year. S will graduate summa cum laude, even though her eyesight is faili because of her diabetes. It seems that Kathy has become everyon friend and safety net. Because she has suffered both physically a mentally in learning how to cope with her diabetes, she make compassionate sounding board for friends in crisis in her soror and in student government. Like all the rest of us, they often ne a little encouragement to help them hold up under the stresses their busy lives. Kathy is always available to listen and to suppor

Just now, next to me, sitting down at his usual spot in the semir circle is Fred, an undergraduate, who must work forty-eight hour week as an emergency medical technician (EMT) in the local h pital emergency room to make ends meet. His parents and siblir live in a trailer park in the poorest community in his small, ru state. This is a community with the highest incidences of uner ployment, domestic and drug abuse, and alcoholism in the sta Fred receives very little financial aid from the university, and wh he does get goes exclusively to defray high tuition costs.

Fred earns little more than a bare subsistence wage by workii all night in a hospital crisis center. He has seen patients in all kin of terrible disrepair, due to catastrophic accidents, and he has he several automobile crash victims in his arms while they died. The are times when he is so tired after working a grueling night sh that he can barely keep his eyes open during class, but he do Fred wants an education more than anything, and he never fails show up for class wearing his hospital scrubs along with a broa enthusiastic smile.

Sitting on the side, slightly back from the circle, is Bruce, a firs generation undergraduate college student who always feels out place in an academic setting. While in high school, Bruce was diag nosed with a "learning disorder," and he carried this burdensom label with him throughout his high school years. Bruce thinks final semester of a very prestigious master's degree program in higher education administration. She has already been accepted to a well-respected doctoral program in another state. As a recent winner of the very competitive Gates Millennial Fellowship, her dreams of becoming a college professor are starting to take shape. At this point in her life, Shelly is content beyond her wildest dreams, because not only is she a success in the academy's eyes, but she also has a young child whom she loves with all her heart. In fact, Shelly believes that she has it all.

Matthew, that person rushing into class a little late, the young man with a determined but sleepy look on his face, is a very talented varsity athlete. He is also a brilliant student, a political science major, carrying a 3.8 academic average into his senior year. As a two-sport elite athlete at the university, Matthew spends all his free time studying and practicing. He wants to attend business school to study for an MBA. He also wants to become an All-American in hockey, the university's most acclaimed varsity sport.

Matthew once said in class that he averages three hours of sleep a night, and that he regularly pulls all-nighters to "ace" his exams. So far, he has withstood the terrible temptations that many workaholics and overachievers in academics and sports face—to overcaffeinate and overmedicate his constant state of fatigue. He once fell asleep halfway through class on a late afternoon, and only his own loud snoring woke him up. He then spent many weeks apologizing to all of us for this misbegotten slumber and promised that it would never happen again. It didn't. In spite of his exhausting schedule, however, Matthew cannot think of living his life any other way. He loves his classes, he loves playing hockey, and, most of all, he is proud of his self-discipline. He is even prouder of the fact that he finds the time to coach a youth hockey team on the weekends. Whenever he sees the joy in the faces of his preteen players after a hard game, he remembers why he pushes himself so much. For Matthew, it's all about the sense of well-being he gets from doing and giving his best.

Before the semester ends, students like these, whatever their ages or stages, social class or race, will have exemplified the meaning of joy as I think of it. Every person who comes into my seminars is waging a personal battle, and most enter the fray seeking to build a meaning for their lives that includes joy as well as courage, love, integrity, and perseverance. Most manage to stand up to their fears, stare them down, and work hard to overcome them. Some will show their joy in their sheer tenacity to persevere, despite all the odds. Some find a hope, religious or philosophical, to hold onto in order to deal with their present suffering, so that they can avoid falling into despair. Some choose, by a sheer act of will, to remain optimistic about their prospects, even when life appears to be bleak and even hopeless. Some, because of their day-to-day struggles to endure the hardships imposed on them by events over which they have no control, become more generous and merciful toward others.

But, as in every single case that I've just described, my students manage to bear up under life's *sturm und drang* without losing heart or their exuberance for life. They do this by living their ordinary lives in an extraordinary way. Few, if any, of them ever call undue attention to themselves—either to their sacrifices or to their well-deserved victories. Instead, they re-create themselves as joyful human beings via a daily display of "little victory" narratives. It is unlikely that any of these students will ever be idealized in the national or even the local media. Each of these seven students resembles so many other students who have been in my seminars on meaning-making over the last several years. I will never forget a single one. Each teaches me much about how to look myself in the eye, and to take heart, in the most profound sense of what it means to be joyful.

Joy and Happiness

All of this is to say that I, too, want the joy in my life that is a by-product of how each of the seven students I describe have chosen to live their lives. I find that I am a more effective teacher when I am joyful. In fact, I am a better human being, because then I am able to bring joy into the lives of all those people I love. What exactly is this joy that I am trying to wrap my words around in this section? For me, it is the disposition to rejoice. It is being able, and willing, to live a life of delight. It is an approach to living that is open to the surprises in the mundane; it looks always to affirm the extraordinary in the ordinary. This is how I've chosen to create meaning in my life during the most recent years of my four decades in the academy.

Joy for me is lighting up the world, if only for a little while, both for myself and for those who are in my company. It is a feeling of exultation that says to others: "My life is good, and I am glad to be living it. Please join me if you can. I will do everything possible to help you to become joyful as well, if this is what you wish." It is being aware of life's bountiful gifts, even when life's bountiful pains are all around me. It is being in awe at the remarkable displays of love and courage I find everywhere around me every day, as manifested in the lives of people like those I've described. It is marveling at the resilience of my students, and my loved ones, to make meaning, especially when life seems most meaningless.

Joy, for me, is different from happiness. Joy is a state of being, while happiness is a state of mind. Joy is a process, what Zen Buddhists call *karuna*, an unencumbered, untargeted love that spreads itself everywhere at all times; happiness is a specific outcome issuing from a specific action. Joy is being good; happiness is doing good. Joy is a lasting attitude and a presence. Happiness is more fleeting, dependent on good fortune and success. Joy is projecting an aura of well-being. Happiness is about achieving pleasure and contentment.

Joy is ontological; happiness is utilitarian. It is no coincidence that the root meaning of "happiness" is the same as "happenstance": occurring as a result of chance and circumstance, whereas the root meaning of "joy" is the same as "rejoice": choosing consciously to celebrate life, over and over again—re-joying, so to speak; bringing joy to others, always and forever, world without end, amen.

Both happiness and joy are necessary for living a full and meaningful life, of course, and there is nothing intrinsically wrong with happiness or intrinsically right with joy. But it is important to understand that happiness functions mainly on the pleasure principle. The more pleasures we experience, ergo, the happier we are said to be. However, as Aristotle pointed out, pleasures are, at best, momentary and ultimately unsatisfying, because there is no ceiling on just how many of them we might need in order to be permanently happy. Pleasure begets pleasure and, left unchecked, leads to hedonism. This, unfortunately, is the antithesis of happiness.

The danger of happiness taken to an extreme, according to the positive psychologists we examine in the final part of our book, is that when it is our sole end, it can devolve into the endless pursuit of pleasure for its own sake. And this can become selfish and obsessive. Epicurus's dictum "Eat, drink, and be merry, for tomorrow we die" is actually a prescription for dying to oneself, to others, and to the joy and delight of life in general. In philosophy, there is a concept accurately called the "hedonistic paradox": the more deliberately one consciously seeks happiness, the less likely one is ever to attain it. Think of striving after the once-and-for-all incredible orgasm, the ideal romance, the perfect job, the best vacation, and the permanent weight loss program.

The paradox is that happiness occurs mainly as a side-effect, or aftermath, of being fully and un-self-consciously immersed in the process of doing what one likes; of being fully caught up in the ebb and flow of all that life has to offer. The positive psychologists call the downside of happiness "hedonic adaptation" and the upside "flow." It doesn't take long for us to adapt to whatever fleeting happiness we find in our lives, and then we need more. The trick is to learn how to avoid this adaptation, and "kiss your joys as they fly," to use Goethe's phrase; or in the words of the founder of positive psychology, Mihalyi Csikszentmihalyi, to learn how to experience "total immersion" or "being in the zone" while doing a task that fully engages one's attention.

This rings true to me. I have found that when I'm least conscious of needing to be happy, but allow myself, instead, to bask
in the afterglow of other people's happiness, it's at that moment
that I am actually the happiest. Hence the paradox. Whenever, as
a teacher, lover, friend, and parent, I clutch at happiness, trying to
make it happen once and for all, it disappears. I am left with anguish.
But when I become more tuned in to what is going on around me
right here, right now, then, I, and all those in my orbit, are happier.
We are living in the fullness of a timeless present. Even better, we
are joyful—not all the time, of course, but at least more often than
not. The positive psychologists, whom we discuss in the next section, would agree strongly with me. For them, positive psychology
is synonymous with joy.

Most important to me, though, is living my whole life knowing that I alone have invented it, every last detail, and I alone am
responsible for it. And what's equally essential is knowing that others have invented what's important to them as well. None of us has
the permanent, inside track on truth, but each one of us has the
right to look for an inside track on what gives *our own* lives meaning, and nobody else's. This is one of the illuminating teachings of
postmodernism and narrative therapy. What brings joy to my life is
the knowledge that I can create and re-create my world based on
how I choose to perceive and frame; how I choose to narrativize it.
And so can all my students. I, and they, can re-joice (re-joy) each
and every day, each and every way, if this is what we choose to do.
I am convinced that I've made everything up, every last bit of it,
as have all my students; as have all those who preceded them, and
all those who, in turn, preceded them, back to the beginning of
human time.

We made up all the philosophies, all the religions, all the politics,
all the arts, and all the sciences, every single last one of them.
This is our glory as a human species. We create what we need, and
we see what we believe. Only I can choose from these bodies of
knowledge what makes sense to me and what doesn't, and the same

is true for all my students. There is no escape from the responsibility each of us has to create what Nietzsche called a "usable fiction" to get us through our days in our own best ways. There is no way to evade our responsibility to create a framework of understanding that allows us to treat ourselves, and others, with the utmost integrity and care. Sartre's basic theme running throughout all his work is this: we are condemned to be free. Even though we did not make the choice to be born, from the moment we reach our age of reason we are responsible for everything we do. We are responsible for our passions, our joys, and our ways of living with others. We are responsible for our very being. Nothing escapes the existential net of personal responsibility.

In the end, it's all about my story. It's also about my students' stories. And there is no unstoried place outside of ourselves, no narrative-independent view from above or below, where we can go for the final word on which story gives us the most ultimate meaning, or which one ought to dominate all the others, including, and especially, the one I am narrating here. Every story of truth is context-dependent, and hence local, not universal or transcendent.

And every story of truth, no matter how inspiring and consoling, is situated in a reality wherein nothing is permanent, and everything is subject to change, including a particular story of truth. All is transitory, and no investment in a particular belief or a way of life need be fixed forever. Everything becomes something else over time, even its opposite. The Buddhists call this *anitya*, impermanence, or the recognition that every circumstance offers a possibility for something new to take shape, and it usually does. Everything changes into something else.

For me, a belief in the unending process of story-making confers the greatest freedom on all of us to choose our own best joys, and it, also, prevents us from imposing these impermanent joys on others. This process ought to keep us humble, compassionate, and loving. It ought, also, to keep us light-hearted and artistic. But of course this is only my story about the story of story-making. Coincidentally, it's also Elie Wiesel's:

> There are a thousand and one gates leading into the orchard of mystical truth. Every human being has his own gate. We must never make the mistake of wanting to enter the orchard by any gate but *our* own. Or of wanting others to enter any gateway to mystical truth but *their* own. (1958, p. 5)

The Joy in My Teaching Is the Tao in My Teaching

Where does my own narrative of joy come from these days? The answer is Taoism, which holds an abundance of meaning for me as a peaceful way of being in the world. I am speaking here of philosophical, not religious, Taoism. In my quest to become a more joyful teacher and a more serene human being, I have found few wisdom texts as helpful to me as Lao Tzu's *Tao Te Ching* (*The Way and Its Power*). The Tao is extraordinarily consistent with my post-modern, existential, philosophical bent, and with my free-thinking, broad-ranging spirituality. Taoism has saved my soul because it has redirected my intellectual restlessness and existential rootlessness toward something wise and humble. It has helped to reduce the friction in my personal life and in my teaching. I am not fully there yet, of course, and probably never will be, but I'm well on the way to locating the Tao in my life. You see, for me, the Tao is just another name for meaning—a meaning that is full of a sense of irony, paradox, trust, flow, compassion, and love.

I am striving to achieve an "effortless effort" in my teaching, what Taoists call *wu wei*. No longer do I experience the need to force my degreed-up brilliance on my students. The irony is that I impress at precisely the moment that I am not trying to impress. No longer do I wish to dominate my students' learning space by filling it with my sage injunctions. I now understand that, in the spirit of the *Tao*, I am at my best when my students barely know that I exist, at least some of the time. I know that when my work is over each semester, the best evaluation I can ever receive from my students is when "they will say, 'we did this ourselves'"(17) (this verse number and all that follow are taken from the *Tao Te Ching*).

I find that I am most effective when I am least assertive. I am most powerful when I have little need to impose my big fat ego on my students. I am an effective mediator of conflict in my classroom when I look for the complementarity, rather than the polarization, in opposing points of view. In other words, I flow and I glow. I do not fight. I absorb the blows. I do not resist them. I try to transform the blows into something constructive by yielding to their force. I remember always the Chinese insight: "Never push a river. It moves by itself."

The ongoing process of conversation in the classroom features its own mysterious logic. I have learned through the years that most of the time, unless I fight it, everything in the classroom conversation is as it needs to be, or as *we* need it to be. And my best pedagogical move is to find the natural trajectory of the yin and yang of conversation, and the conflict that often accompanies it, and go with it. With faith and endless patience, I find that opposites tend to reconcile themselves, but this happens only when I detach my interests from the interests of my students. Listen to the words of the Tao that guide my teaching:

> Be like the Way, and practice non-interference. Wait for others to seek a remedy rather than forcing it upon them, and offer assistance only when the solution has been spontaneously developed by circumstances. Allow everything to slip into the spontaneous flow of things. (37)

Now, when I walk into a classroom for the first time, I am at peace. I am strong in my convictions, but I am also soft, because I believe, with Lao Tzu, that "the softest things in the world overcome the hardest things in the world." (43) There are times when I can teach best without words, and I can do the most without doing anything. I have learned how to be active by being passive. When I let go of myself in the classroom, I allow my students to be themselves in my classroom. I try to talk as little as I can, so that my students might talk as much as they can. But I also know when my students need to hear my words as well. There is great opportunity for all of us to learn, including the teacher, in the emptiness and silences of a classroom space. But there is also a time when our words need to fill those spaces so that we all might share our insights together.

I am relaxed, not always, but much of the time. I can still be a bit of a stress case, particularly when things seem to be falling apart in my groups. But my stress eases whenever I listen carefully for the words that aren't being spoken. It's when I relax that I'm able to hear what isn't being said. My intuition and mind's eye click in, and I can begin to discern meaning in the simple mystery of our being together. It is then that we can play and be spontaneous, and at that point, miraculously, the learning turns serious. It is in play that our ideas come to life, our wonder gives birth to creativity, and our chaos produces order. Learning runs its course, and surprise is the order of the day.

In retrospect, I find that my pride has always cometh before my falls. Self-promotion has only served to increase my anxieties as a teacher. While my ego is still sizeable, it no longer fills my classroom. Now I am able to let live and let go in my seminars. As a result, I have grown in insight, and so have my students. I have stopped arguing, and my students have become more generous toward themselves and one another. In the words of the *Tao Te Ching*, I no longer "stand on my toes" in my teaching spaces. (24) Instead, I try to make it possible for my students to stand on their own toes, in their own best ways, without standing over others.

I try not to "leave tracks by demanding recognition." (27) Neither do I want to "bind anyone through the imposition of dogma." (27) Thus my students become more intuitive in their learning, more willing to trust their own excellent intellectual instincts, and more able to establish their own learning goals. My practice is one of pedagogical noninterference, as much as I am capable. I am learning how to cede professorial control. I am learning how to yield my authority to the natural authority of all the learners who make their way to my courses each semester.

My intention is to teach far more by example than by fiat. Without that self-conscious "scholar" striving to cover all the bases in my classroom, I find that now everything is possible. Resistance has disappeared, and my students are joyful. Hence I am joyful. Because I have discovered my "light touch," my students respond to me without the slightest fear of my "heavy touch," without fear of reprisal or repression. (32) Through the Tao of teaching, I have learned the two most joyful lessons of all in the classroom: gentleness is strength; and example, not experience or expertise, teaches best. Knowing this, I am full of joy beyond my wildest dreams, at least on most days.

Returning to My Seven Profiles in Joy

I still manage to stay in touch with the seven students I portrayed at the beginning of this essay. Each is prospering in the sense that each understands the complementarity of joy and sorrow. Each has mastered the quality of resilience, the ability to bounce back time after time in order to glean fresh insights from the obstacles and challenges they face in their lives.

Here is a wonderful personal insight that one of my seven joy exemplars recently sent to me. This former student, now a social worker in a large urban area, has found great joy in the personal writing that she is doing about ministering to parentless inner-city youth who must live in homeless shelters. She hopes eventually to get published. Here are her words:

> Robert, whenever I sit composing ideas in front of
> my computer, I discover a conscious mind working

somewhere in my brain. I know beyond a shadow of a doubt that there is really a "me" in there. I've proven that I actually exist in the world. How do I know this for sure? Because my jumbled thoughts flow out of my brain and down through my arms and hands onto my keyboard. I punch the letter keys, and then, don't ask me how, I see my thinking take the shape of words on my computer screen. Now I'm real. My mind is made concrete in neat block lettering a few feet from my eyes. Whenever this happens, I feel an indescribable joy, because I've released into the world all the chaotic shapes and forms that have been bottled up inside my brain. *Scribo, ergo sum.* I write, therefore I am.

Compare this to what I hear when I ask some of my former doctoral students why they didn't finish their dissertations. There is no fresh revision of the Cartesian *Cogito* like my social worker's anywhere to be found. The response usually features one or more of these twists:

It wasn't fun or joyful anymore. I was researching, and writing, what my advisor and my committee wanted, not what interested me. I grew tired of my topic. I was living out my advisor's dream for me and not my own. I lost my passion. I found my joy elsewhere: in my job, or in an intimate relationship, or in teaching at lower grade levels that does not require a terminal degree. I simply fell out of love with learning. The whole thing became a chore instead of a pleasure, a downer rather than an upper. I was never able to get into a flow.

Each of the students I described earlier has taught me about the joy in my meaning and the meaning in my joy. I've known educators who could make analyzing a telephone directory or a rock an exciting learning adventure. But I've also known teachers who are so dead to themselves, and to the world, that everything they touch in a classroom turns to tedium and dust. During the last several years, I've been working diligently on visibly expressing an enthusiasm and excitement for everything I do as an educator, no matter how many times I've taught the same content or dealt with the same advising issues. I've learned from decades of experience that joy teaches best, joy advises best, joy loves best, and joy reaps the most rewards.

Cynicism and disengagement, the opposite of joy, are the killers of a learner's dream, and a professor's too. It is surely true that economic conditions are tough in the academy today for a variety of reasons beyond anyone's individual control. But when people ask me, "How are you?" I always say, "I've never been better." This is not an honorific, disaster-denying, happy-face, reflex response. For me, it's the whole truth. I have never been more joyful, because I'm doing what I believe is the best job in the world *for me*—reading, writing, teaching, and being a philia friend to colleagues and students whom I respect and love, especially those seven students whose profiles of courage I described in the opening of my letter.

I close my letter to all my readers by sharing a few simple "rules of joy" by which I try to live my teacher's life:

- Dare to experience the world as a child does. Or, better, as a college student does who is grappling with the complexities and mysteries of the academic disciplines for the first time.

- Look for the miracle of joy in the classroom first, before looking for the joylessness. Often the miracle can be found in the most unexpected places: in unconventional, sometimes zany, questions; in candid and impromptu reactions to routine reading and writing assignments; and in the generosity and support that students and instructors are more than willing to give to one another, if it is the norm to do so.

- Do all of these things in the name of saving, not condemning, students' propositions. And look always for the personal story that lies behind the student's academic persona. Find that story and, eureka! you've found the student as a person.

- Stay in the present in the classroom. It is here that genuine innocence, vulnerability, passion, and compassion live. And the *opposites* of these qualities—guilt, insensitivity, apathy, and aggression—often arise when we dwell on the past and brood over the future.

- Don't give in to the periodic brokenness that comes out of teaching: boredom, self-criticism, uncertainty, physical and mental fatigue, unrealistic expectations, restlessness, and self-doubt. In this brokenness, true joy and freedom are waiting to be born. All it takes is shouting a courageous "yes" to live, to love, and to learn; and a determination to resist the suicidal lure of the "no." Is there really any other alternative, short of giving in and giving up?

And now we come to Resources for Meaning-Making Educators. The four meaning-making psychotherapies that we describe in the Resource A section are joy-filled therapies in the sense that they start with students' strengths and build from there. There is no determinism, psychopathology, blame, helplessness, or meaninglessness in any of these therapies; rather, they all offer hope, agency, and meaning. In Resource B, we explain a new collaborative model of meaning-making across campus, which we call "crossover pedagogy."

Resources for
Meaning-Making Educators

Resource A: Four Therapeutic Approaches to Meaning-Making

T he approaches to meaning-making that we explain in this closing section are based on four overlapping types of psychotherapy. In no way are we encouraging our readers to become practicing therapists without a license. Not only is this unethical, it is also unwise and unnecessary. We think of psychotherapy in broad, humanistic terms: psychotherapy is the art and science of counseling, teaching, advising, exemplifying, and leading. It emphasizes a balance between individual freedom and social responsibility; autonomy, self-determination, self-transformation, and informed decision making. It also features a number of ways of thinking and talking about, as well as engaging in, the activity we call *meaning-making*.

In one sense, then, our take on psychotherapy is actually a window onto the best practices of what good educators could do with, and for, their students. At our best, we instruct, inform, and support students as they engage in the process of developing adaptable philosophies of life—systems of meaning that will sustain them during both the good and the bad times. In this final section, we present several student examples. We offer these real-life examples to invite further discussion from our readers; thus they are meant to be suggestive and provisional, not exhaustive or definitive. Our hope is that readers, in their own wisdom, will see the possible educational applications of these newer meaning-making approaches in psychotherapy. This is why we think of them as tentative in nature.

We choose to feature four of the newest types of meaning-making psychotherapy—logotherapy, narrative therapy, philosophical counseling, and positive psychology—because they are rooted in sound philosophical principles, they are sources of innovative pedagogy and leadership, and they represent a radical departure from the disease-dysfunction medical models of the mind in classical schools of psychology. In contrast, they build on students' strengths, not their weaknesses, and they advocate strategies for constructing lives of meaning and purpose that are both practical and achievable.

Logotherapy: An Antidote to Meaninglessness

Viktor Frankl is the creator of logotherapy. Here are the bare facts of Viktor Frankl's tragic yet transcendent life. Born in Vienna, Austria, in 1905, Frankl was something of a prodigy. At sixteen, he gave a public lecture on the meaning of life. In high school, he wrote an essay on psychology and philosophy as important tools for making meaning, and he corresponded with Sigmund Freud, who inspired him to publish his first article in the *International Journal of Psychoanalysis*. In 1924 he began his medical studies and worked with Alfred Adler. It was during this time that he first used the term "logotherapy." In 1930, upon receiving his medical degree, Frankl broke with Adler's group of disciples because his work as a logotherapist took him in a very different, philosophical direction.

In the fall of 1942, Frankl, a Jew, and his family were arrested by the Nazis and deported to the Theresienstadt concentration camp near Prague. He spent three agonizing years there, where his wife, Tilly, both parents, and his brother were gassed to death and then incinerated. He was later incarcerated at Auschwitz-Birkenau, Dachau, and Turkheim. He almost died several times in these death camps. What kept him going was trying to write his first book, *The Doctor and the Soul*, by committing it to memory and then hurriedly writing it on confiscated bits of paper when the guards were not looking. Frankl survived the horrors of four death camps before he was liberated by the Allied forces when the war ended. He went on to write thirty-two books, including *Man's Search for Meaning* (originally titled *From Death Camp to Existentialism*)—considered by the Library of Congress to be one of the ten most influential books of the twentieth century. Frankl's long academic career took him to the University of Vienna and Harvard, among a number of other institutions. He died on September 2, 1997.

All of Frankl's scholarship and therapeutic work were inspired, and fueled, by his own terrible suffering and human loss. Frankl frequently wrote about the torture and murder of his fellow prisoners that he witnessed every single day of his years of incarceration. He woke up each morning thinking that this could very well be the day his captors would herd him, along with others, into the gas chambers. His "will to meaning" is a direct outgrowth of his personal struggles to survive the worst agonies imaginable. Here is how Frankl (1979) articulates his belief in self-transcendence: "I can see beyond the misery of the situation the potential for discovering a meaning behind it, and thus to turn an apparently meaningless suffering into a genuine human achievement. I am convinced that, in the final analysis, there is no situation that does not contain within it the seed of a meaning" (p. 53). In the section that follows, we think of existentialism as the theory and logotherapy as the practice.

Logotherapy Explained

Here, in a nutshell, are the basic concepts of logotherapy, as created by Frankl over a period in excess of fifty years:

• *Logos is a Greek term that denotes "meaning."* Logotherapy is a therapy of meaning-making. Logotherapists believe that finding and creating meaning in one's life is the primary motivational force. The "will to meaning" represents a hard-wired, psychobiological drive to "find values for the sake of which to live." These might include a political cause, service to others, righting injustices, a commitment to a religious faith, or a loving relationship.

• *Existential frustration is a term that represents our basic need to find micro-meaning in our day-to-day lives, as well as macro-meaning to explain the cosmic enigmas of human existence.* Frustration sets in when our work, relationships, and commitments turn sour, or when they totally preoccupy our daily existence; when these troubling distractions keep us from undertaking the personal reflection, and action, necessary to make meaning.

• *The existential vacuum describes the state of mind that people experience when they feel that life is meaningless, when they find themselves asking more and more frequently questions like "Is this all there is?"* People then become bored and flat. Unfortunately, antidepressants do not improve this condition. In Frankl's words (1963), people suffer from "Sunday neurosis, a kind of depression which afflicts people who become aware of the lack of content in their lives when the rush of the busy week is over and the void within themselves becomes manifest" (p. 169).

• *The meaning of life is personal.* Each person's way of making meaning is concrete, not abstract, and unique, not commonplace. Each of us deals with the existential universals of finitude, suffering, joy, and hope in our own signature fashion, according to our own perspectives, tastes, temperaments, talents, and training. Logotherapists refuse to impose value judgments on their clients, because they understand that values are not simply given; rather, they are either chosen or created anew.

• *There are four primary ways to make meaning.* As logotherapists, we create meaning through our deeds, values, love, and suffering. Concrete *deeds* based on a strong humanitarian commitment can help us to find purpose in the world. The *values* of compassion, concern, and caring can steer us in the right direction. *Love* is spiritual, and it brings out the best in others. *Suffering*, the core of logotherapy, provides the most fertile ground for making meaning, because without love and compassion we would not be able to make sense of our suffering, nor would we be able to transcend or reconfigure it. Logotherapy teaches us how to reshape our attitudes toward not only our physical suffering, but, just as important, our psychological suffering. This includes our inevitable disappointments, frustrations, confusions, and dissatisfactions. The practical question for us then becomes *not* "Why this suffering?" but "How can I give my suffering a meaning that will enlarge and enrich my way of being in the world, and enable me to get on with my life?"

• *Individual freedom is a key postulate in logotherapy as it is in existentialism*. Human beings are more than the automatic byproducts of their races, ethnicities, social classes, biologies, genders, sexual orientations, life circumstances, sufferings, fates, destinies, religions, or politics. For logotherapists, it is undoubtedly true that all of these factors, either individually or collectively, exert great influence on the choices we make to become who we are at any given time in our lives. But they are not everything. Here are Frankl's words (1963): "No person is ever fully conditioned or determined; we determine ourselves whether to give in to conditions or to stand up to them. We do not simply exist, but we always decide what our existence will be, what we will become in the next moment. We have the freedom to change at any instant" (pp. 206–207). Thus the meaning that we learn to create for our lives provides the framework for the decisions we make about our existence.

Seven Core Principles of Logotherapy

What follows are the *Seven Core Principles of Logotherapy* (Pattakos, 2008, p. vi). These principles have the advantage of bringing the sometimes abstract ideas of existentialism down to earth where each of us lives. In the context of logotherapy, they provide students with a handy values agenda that is both accessible and inspirational. They are a reminder that meaning-making is the responsibility of every one of us. Nobody can do it for us. Nobody gets out of this life without doing it—even when the results might be disastrous. All of us who serve students on campus need to devise a number of creative strategies and opportunities to keep these core meaning-making principles front and center throughout the college experience. Here, in a nutshell, and articulated in our own words, are these seven core principles of logotherapy:

- All of us have the freedom to choose our attitudes and perspectives on life.

- All of us have the need to commit ourselves to purposes, values, and goals that are within our capacity to actualize.

- All of us have the power, and the responsibility, to impose meaning on any given moment during the course of our lives.

- All of us need to learn to avoid working against ourselves in the sense that sometimes we unwittingly sabotage our own best efforts to find satisfaction, joy, and meaning.

- All of us need to learn how to look at ourselves from a distance in order to achieve perspective—especially when this might encourage us to laugh at ourselves and our self-defeating follies.

- All of us need to know how to shift the focus of attention from ourselves, and our most nagging personal issues and problems, to build the coping strategies we will need in order to face, and overcome, conflict and stress.

• All of us need to learn how to extend beyond ourselves by investing our time, energy, and resources in something more than ourselves, something outside of ourselves.

Logotherapy Questions for Amy

In our work with students, we find that asking them certain types of questions, detailed shortly, frequently gets them thinking more deeply and expansively about meaning-making. These questions tend to activate their "will to meaning," to use Frankl's phrase. Most of our students have had no systematic experience in digging deeply into what it is that gives, or might give, a sense of purpose and meaning to their lives. Even fewer have been offered the opportunity to do this in their classrooms or elsewhere on campus.

These are our starter questions with meaning-challenged students, and they are existential in nature. (The content of our questions is inspired by Pattakos, 2008, a logotherapist and founder of the National Center for Meaning. Pattakos works primarily with corporations, businesses, and human service organizations. However, we put our own existential twists on the questions that follow, based on our extensive experience with college students of all ages and stages, cycles and transitions of development.)

Again we meet Amy—the student in our opening scenario in Chapter Two, who is struggling with the problem of meaninglessness in her life without really knowing why. We present her with a series of questions rooted in the principles of logotherapy. We want these questions to help her access what we call her "zero-level" beliefs about meaning. Logotherapy-inspired questions like these have the potential of helping students like Amy to identify what really matters to them—which sets of ideals and values keep them going when things look most grim, or when their lives seem pointless and devoid of satisfaction and happiness.

Here, following directly from these core principles of logotherapy, are the meaning-making questions that we often ask students like Amy in a variety of venues on college campuses:

• What might you do to make your life more satisfying at this very moment? Pretend that there are no restrictions on the satisfactions you would like to experience in your life right now. What is preventing you from realizing these satisfactions?

• What is it you could do when you feel trapped or confined by your studies, or by your frenzied, unfulfilling extracurricular activities or vacuous friendships, or by your destructive relationships? What is your escape plan for spirit-restoring, just-plain-fun, get-away time?

• What is your vision of the best way to live your life right now? Is there anything you might be able to do to make this happen sooner rather than later?

• Can you think of any time in your life when you felt good about helping others? What, if anything, has prevented you from being involved in a number of service projects in the community outside your campus?

• Can you think of some good outcomes that might result if you decided not to live up to other people's expectations of you?

• What is it you would miss most if you decided to drop out of school, or resign from a particular extracurricular activity, or move out of your current residence, or dump someone you value or maybe even love?

• How would you respond to a dear friend who considers you a trusted confidante and who came to you with these general questions: "Why am I so sad? Why do I feel so stressed? Why do I get so bored? Why can't I really love someone? Why is it I don't feel really loved by anyone?"

• Can you think of a time when you refused to compromise a core value in your life, even if compromising this value might have satisfied other needs you had?

• If you knew for sure that you would live seventy-five more years, how would you choose to live your life right now? Would this foreknowledge make any difference to you? Why or why not? What if you knew that you had twelve months to live? Would anything change for you?

• What do you think your loved ones might say about you in a eulogy to be read at your funeral, in the event of an untimely death during this, the prime of your life? Also, if you were to prepare a eulogy for yourself right now, what would you say? How would the two eulogies be different or similar?

• If you were to outline a memoir of your life's trajectory from birth right up to the present time, what would be the highlights, the lowlights, the regrets, the hopes realized and the dreams deferred, and the climax? How would you expand the memoir to include the future years of your life, the years yet to be lived, the highs and lows yet to be experienced, the hopes and dreams to be realized?

• What people in your life make you laugh? Who are the happiest people in your life? When does your own sense of humor tend to get activated? When does it get suppressed? When is it easiest for you to laugh at yourself? When is it most difficult? Why?

• What pleasant activities, or fantasies, do you think about when your life seems most grim? What are your real-life strategies for warding off a grinding sense of failure, or despair, or disappointment? What can you do to forget yourself during those times when you seem most self-absorbed and self-punishing?

Narrative Therapy: Making Meaning by Telling Our Stories

For narrative therapists, what remains useful from postmodern philosophy and literary theory is the hypothesis that human beings live in stories about reality as much as they live in reality itself. Here is the way that Peter Brooks (2005) explains it: "Our definition as human beings is very much bound up with the stories we tell about our own lives and the world in which we live. We cannot, in our dreams, our daydreams, our ambitious fantasies, avoid the imaginative imposition of form on life" (p. 123).

Moreover, Jerome Bruner, a twentieth-century cognitive psychologist and a convert to postmodern thinking, has gone so far as to say that in the humanities and social sciences "the truth that matters is not empirical truth but the narrative truth" (1990, p. 19). Thus the best way to understand the self is to think of the self as a storyteller, a "constructor of narratives about a life." In fact, for Bruner, as for many narrative therapists, the construct of self is actually a multiple telling of stories. The self is a "distributed self, enmeshed in a net of others" whose primary task is to make meanings through narration (2002, 111–112).

What narrative therapists (see Freedman & Combs, 1996; Morgan, 2000; White & Epston, 1990) tend to agree on is that each of us is both constructivist and constructed. The stories we construct then turn around and construct us, and we them—for as long as we live. This is what we call the "constructivist circle," and any work on meaning-making with clients and students needs to begin with this premise: locate the meaning story of the meaning-maker, and you will go a long way toward locating what the meaning-maker really means by "meaning." Moreover, teach students how to create more transformative stories of meaning, and they will have the power to change their lives.

Basic Assumptions of Narrative Therapy

In this section, we describe a series of assumptions that narrative therapists make about the meaning-work they do with clients.

- Our lives are *multistoried*. There is no single, dominant story that defines us once and for all. There is always the possibility of a variety of interpretations, by both ourselves and others, of the stories we live in. At any given time, one of these alternative interpretations could provide us with the resources we need to renarrativize a story of meaning that might be dysfunctional, harmful, or self-destructive. We are responsible for our construction of stories of meaning—both those that are *dominant* as well as those that are *alternative*.

- We live in stories of meaning that have two sides: *thin* and *thick* description. *Thin* stories lack depth, understanding, and complexity. They stem from living in unexamined narratives of meanings. It is not unusual for others to create thin stories of meaning for us, in either childhood or early adulthood— particularly others who have the power and influence to create these stories, such as parents, clergy, educators, peer groups, media pundits, and bosses. It is in the thin stories that so many of our students live, and these students are frequently the most frantic meaning searchers.

    Thick, rich stories of meaning, however, are often *alternative* stories. These enable us to see more than one side of the meanings that we have created. We have the potential to experience what could be called "meaning overlap" with other people's stories. We are given the chance to complicate and deepen our meaning narratives whenever key people, events, and new insights occur. We are encouraged to find the will to refuse to cling to the older, thin narratives of meaning (these might include religio-spiritual, relational, success, educational, political, or personal identity stories) that no longer define or benefit us or others.

• *We are not reducible to the meaning stories we live in.* Rather, we are responsible for creating and re-creating those stories of meaning that guide us at any point in our lives. No matter how self-destructive or self-empowering these stories of meaning have been, we have the ability to *externalize* and identify (bring to the conversational process) those nagging underlying problems that continue to plague us in our efforts to make meaning. We have the intelligence and will to separate ourselves from the issues that upset us. We are not co-identical with our issues. We do not have to engage in self-labeling, self-pathologizing, or self-diagnosing. We are not the problems we describe; rather, we are the potential authors of solutions to these problems.

We can learn that there is potential meaning in everything, even suffering, as Frankl noted. It is up to us to externalize our failures (put them outside us) in order to create healthy and responsible solutions to our nagging personal problems. It is possible for us to renarrativize our identities and circumstances by investing them with a new sense of meaning and purpose. Likewise, we possess more than one identity. We are not creatures who are reducible to only one particular nationality, political party, race, class, ethnicity, sexual orientation, or gender. We are able to self-narrativize complex, intersecting descriptions of many self-identities, and these diverse differences hold the key to the creation of new stories of meaning for us.

• We are able to *deconstruct* those stories of meaning that cause us such problems as guilt, anxiety, defeatism, perfectionism, addiction, boredom, depression, and alienation. *Deconstruction* begins with examining those *background assumptions* that make our meaning narratives dysfunctional and self-destructive. This entails that we bring to the surface those *taken-for-granted* explanations and behaviors that keep us fearful, disempowered, and obsessive. Deconstruction of old narratives of meaning is the precondition for naming, thickening, and implementing alternative stories of meaning. The ultimate objective of narrative therapy is to move from deconstruction to reconstruction of the meanings that we impress on ourselves and others.

• Deconstruction leads to re-membering conversations. As noted in Chapter Five, to *re-member* our lives (to add or subtract key figures in our world), it is necessary for us to visualize those people in our world who bring out the best in us; who see us in a different light from the self-defeating, negative ways we sometimes see ourselves. Re-membering *histories of connection* that have been good for us is one way for us to shake up our static lives.

Changing our communities of significant others is a powerful way to recreate those narratives of meaning that worked for us in the past and will continue to benefit us in the future. *Re-membering* relationships in the past that were once beneficial to us can sometimes help us to re-member our present and future lives by filling these with people who can be positive influences on us. Such re-membering can also lead to a deliberate decision to exclude particular people from our lives, as we go about the work of constructing narratives of meaning that will bring out the best, not the worst, in ourselves and others.

Reconstructing a Narrative of Suffering

Here is a narrative vignette of a student in one of Robert's classes a few years ago. We will call him "Jacob." In telling Jacob's tale, it is our intention to show briefly how some of the principles of narrative therapy worked in this particular case to help a student create a new sense of purpose.

Robert's Chapter Eight reflection for readers began with Kierkegaard's declaration that he knows of no wine so sparkling, fragrant, or intoxicating, no joy so great, as possibility. This is how people experience Jacob today, but it is not the narrative he used to inhabit. He has suffered greatly in the past, and when he first came into Robert's life as a college senior, he was depressed, negative, and despairing—so much so that Robert sent him to the counseling center. At the time, Jacob's beloved younger brother, an uncontrolled alcoholic, was putting his life at serious risk because of bad choices. Every unexpected phone call from his West Coast home made Jacob's heart pound with apprehension. His alcoholic brother had recently tried to take his own life after dropping out of college.

In addition, Jacob's best friend had recently been killed in a terrible automobile accident, and this event caused Jacob to fall into the darkness of depression for many months. To make matters even worse, at one point during Jacob's final semester, there was a scare as he thought he might have testicular cancer. Although he eventually learned that he did not, he underwent several days of incredible personal torment waiting for the test results. Given the magnitude of Jacob's personal misfortunes, it seemed clear both to him and to others who knew him that he needed help to overcome his crushing sense of despair.

Professional counseling helped greatly. Informal conversations with friends and faculty helped as well. So, too, did Jacob's decision, spurred by the encouragement of a student affairs professional, to get involved with a meditation group on campus. At the deepest level of his consciousness, Jacob knew that he needed to re-vision his life. For example, he had to find a way to get in touch with his long-neglected spirituality. He relished the challenge of becoming a kind of mystical adventurer, at one and the same time a Buddhist, a humanist, a Taoist, and a naturalist. He took up hiking, skiing, and even snowboarding. For the first time in his life, Jacob started to jog and do yoga. He taught himself to meditate, hung out with students who were interested in alternative spiritualities, and occasionally even went on labyrinth walks and visited ashrams. He created a spirituality that was neither institutional nor doctrinal. Nor was it monotheistic or polytheistic. Jacob worked hard to create a spiritual way of being in the world that was just right for him.

His newfound spirituality was not one for the saints, priests, ascetics, or gods. Rather, it was a continually flowing stream of asking gentle questions about life's vicissitudes and being on the lookout always to find the sacred, healing spot that resides in the center of all human and natural fracturedness. William James, the great American philosopher, called this the ability to find the joy amidst the suffering of "life's torn-to-pieces-hood." Jacob's spirituality was rooted in his desire to discover a meaning to live that was larger than himself. His spirituality took on the form of a reverence for life in all of its diversity. It was a reverence rooted in the virtues of humility, forgiveness, gratitude, and mindfulness. It expressed itself as a profound thank-you for life's unsolicited, and unearned, gifts.

Today, Jacob's face wears a perpetual smile, although he is no Pollyanna. He rarely frowns. He does very little complaining. He attributes the best, and not the worst, motive to intimates, friends, and acquaintances alike. Jacob tries to give his life freely to others whenever they need him, with no strings attached. He laughs readily. He radiates kindness, caring, and compassion. His is the kind of spirituality that attracts rather than repels—a spirituality that expresses itself as a gentle, Buddhist way of being in the world. It is a form of Zen Buddhism that knows the complementarity of joy and sorrow, and of passion and compassion.

What makes Jacob's joy most wonderful at this time in his life, however, is that, in spite of the many ups and downs he has experienced, he has overcome the temptation to give in to a bitter cynicism or a mean-spirited callousness. Such temptations still enter his life more than he would like. After all, he is human, and during those painful moments when he is aware of his finitude, he is subject to dark moods. In spite of this, however, Jacob is committed to experiencing his life as a miracle and to treating others as miracles. He is understanding more and more each day the truth of the poet Blake's insight that there is great possibility, especially in sorrow, to give birth to his better self.

How, then, did Jacob get from despair to joy? Consciously, with the help of others, he transformed his narrative way of being in the world. Jacob decided that he was capable of residing in many narratives at once. His life was multistoried. While it was true that much tragedy had befallen him in a relatively short time, it was equally true that there was joy and love in his life as well. Jacob consciously chose to experience as much as possible the joys of living in other narratives. The despair narrative just seemed too thin for him. It resembled the story of meaning that his pessimistic parents inhabited nearly every day of his life when he was young. They saw themselves as helpless pawns of a cruel fate. He remembers his father constantly saying: "There is no hell in the afterlife, because hell is already on earth."

During his worst times, Jacob chose to thicken his life by adding an alternative story he had long neglected—he added a spiritual chapter. Jacob purposely sought to deepen and enlarge the meaning of his life. No longer would he cling to the old, negative stories that he had allowed to define him. Jacob became an active change-agent on his own behalf. He identified and externalized his issues, thanks to the interventions of others, and refused to be beaten down by them. Jacob made the decision to seek alternative solutions to the miseries that formed such a large part of his life.

Jacob intentionally deconstructed his old meaning story by reexamining some of his background beliefs about pain, suffering, and self-destructiveness. He began the long process of adding several new chapters to his life's narrative. He re-membered his life by adding key people who would enrich and enliven his spiritual story. Jacob sought out individuals and groups that helped him to examine, and understand, his life in new ways. This re-membering led him to discover many different communities of belonging. He deliberately chose to shake up his sad and sorrowful life. From that point on, he would make it a point to surround himself with people who themselves resided in a variety of alternative spiritual narratives. Jacob, in his early twenties, had reached a time in his life when he was ready to reclaim that part of himself that was optimistic, joyful, and hopeful.

Philosophical Counseling: Getting In Touch with Our Inner Philosopher

Philosophy, in Greek (*philosophia*), means "love of wisdom." Philosophers are lovers of wisdom, and, what is more, lovers of those who seek wisdom. Sometimes philosophers ask technical questions that deal with problems of epistemology (knowledge), ontology (being), and axiology (values). Sometimes philosophers ask big meaning-questions—like the ones we asked in our two previous chapters—knowing that these questions may or may not bring definitive answers. For a newly emergent group that calls itself "philosophical counselors," however, philosophy is both down-to-earth and practical (see Marinoff, 1999, 2003; Raabe, 2000; Schuster, 1999).

Philosophical counselors see their concrete role as helping clients to deal effectively with difficult ethical dilemmas, to understand and express feelings, to resolve tangible and intangible crises of meaning and value, and to come to terms with personal identity issues. They also help clients to make wise career decisions, confront and ameliorate relationship problems; achieve short- and long-term life purposes and goals; learn more about developmental, age- and stage-related changes; and face the challenges of sickness, illness, and death, among a number of other day-to-day issues and concerns (Marinoff, 1999).

Whether realist or nominalist, members of this group are less interested in engaging in abstract, self-referential analysis than they are in helping people to solve the real-life problems of making meaning. They tend to take to heart this aphorism of Socrates: "The unexamined life is not worth living." So, too, they are likely to support the assertion of Marcus Aurelius: "The happiness of your life depends upon the quality of your thoughts." In the work that philosophical counselors are doing in community agencies and private offices, and in some counseling centers at colleges and universities, they would most likely add to Socrates's words one of Robert's aphorisms: "The unlived life is not worth examining."

Viktor Frankl, the logotherapist whose work we examined in the previous section, could be called a philosophical counselor, even though he never used this title. He, like most philosophical counselors, would be in full support of the following assumption by Lou Marinoff, the founding president of the American Philosophical Practitioners Association and the creator of philosophical counseling. Marinoff is fond of saying that while medicine can cure *disease*, philosophy, well used, can cure *dis-ease*. Regarding the dis-ease of meaninglessness, he says: "[in conventional psychotherapy] our deepest questions of meaning remain unanswered. Worse, our beliefs go unexamined. The alternative is the practice of philosophy . . ." (Marinoff, 1999, p. 15).

It is important to understand up front that philosophical counseling, a nascent movement experiencing the usual growing pains, is very controversial among some conventionally trained psychotherapists (see Duane, 2004). Among the criticisms leveled at philosophical counseling by its opponents are these: inadequate mental health training for philosophical counselors; overly abbreviated clinical training for licensure; unresolved conflicts between philosophical counselors and those fully licensed clinicians who practice Albert Ellis's rational-emotive based therapy; and an overly simplistic five-step "problem, emotions, analysis, contemplation, equilibrium" (PEACE) process created by Marinoff (which we will briefly introduce later in this chapter); in addition, they voice sharp skepticism that a rational, philosophical approach to emotionally we live—that is, how thoughtfully, how nobly, how virtuously, how joyously, how lovingly—depends both on our philosophy and on the way we apply it to all else. The examined life is a better life, and it is within our reach. Try Plato, not Prozac!" (Marinoff, 1999, p. 271).

• Many of our problems in creating sustainable meanings in our lives require philosophical practitioners to clarify them. These are professionals who are qualified to offer insight from the world's great wisdom traditions. Why should all our personal issues be reduced to psychological ones requiring extensive (and expensive) treatments of psychotherapy, drugs, and other medical interventions? Sometimes our problems grow out of troubled philosophies of life, patterns of illogical thinking, and slap-dash moral and ethical decision making.

• Some of the greatest philosophical minds in history have weighed in on all the meta-questions of meaning that we raise in earlier chapters of this book. Thus we have thousands of years of thinking to draw on in trying to resolve some of these questions for ourselves. No single discipline, expert, or worldview possesses exclusive ownership of meaning-making.

• Philosophical counseling has the potential to offer an additional (or alternative) perspective on meaning-making: it helps students to think about their problems as philosophical in origin and nature; as resulting from faulty thinking, unexamined living, and thin frameworks of meaning. Philosophical counseling helps to sharpen students' thinking. It develops their analytical skills. It encourages them to look to their heads as well as to their hearts and guts as they try to work through some of their deepest meaning issues. Philosophy looks to all the disciplines—including science, psychology, and religious studies—in addition to its own specialized body of knowledge. Exposure to philosophy can help students learn how to handle love relationships, live morally, plan fulfilling careers, create sound narratives of

based problems is clinically useful. Marinoff's response to
criticism is to the point: "We have never, not ever, h
gle case in which philosophical counseling caused psycl
harm ... Even sane, functional people need principles to li
we are offering what Socrates called the examined life, the
to sit with a philosopher and ask what you really believe ar
sure it's working for you" (Duane, 2004, p. 1).

Basic Assumptions of Philosophical Counseling

What follows are several key sets of assumptions that underlie
sophical counseling. It is important to understand that we
want to turn all educators into professional philosophers. T
neither possible nor desirable. Not everyone in the academ
the background, temperament, or disposition to do the tecl
work of philosophy. But all of us can cultivate what Phillips (
calls a "fresh taste for philosophy."

Phillips is the creator of hundreds of what he calls "Soc
Cafes" throughout the United States. He has brought philos
down to earth, and he has taught people of all ages and all v
of life to emulate his hero, Socrates, in asking open-ended q
tions. Phillips believes there is a philosopher in every one of us.
task has been to awaken this "love of wisdom" in people, and
has done this in cafes, coffee shops, senior centers, assisted-liv
complexes, prisons, libraries, day-care centers, public schools,
churches. If Phillips can do this, so can we. We believe that,
Phillips, meaning-minded educators can find the following ba
ground beliefs to be helpful in working with students:

• Marinoff offers an excellent distillation of the critical role
that philosophy is able to play in the making of meaning: "How
freely we live depends both on our political system and on our
vigilance in defending our liberties. How *long* we live depends
both on our genes and on the quality of our health care. How *wel*

meaning, and cope with the nitty-gritty existential challenges that face them every day of their lives, among a host of other concerns.

• Following in the 2,500-year-old tradition of Socratic dialogue, philosophical counselors ask open-ended questions. They draw out the hidden assumptions and unconscious agendas underlying students' thinking. When relevant, they refer to the ideas of great thinkers. They try to keep students' actions consistent with their declared beliefs. In the absence of the latter, they help students to construct rich, informed, and responsible worldviews. They operate from the premise that often it is the dialogue itself between counselor and student that is most clarifying.

• Philosophical counselors urge us to remember that *therapy* has more to do with curing and healing illnesses, but *counseling* is mostly about people consulting, conversing, deliberating, and thinking together about everyday issues and problems. In this sense, philosophy is closer to counseling than it is to psychotherapy. Neither approach is wrong, of course, and both approaches have their strengths as well as their weaknesses. The trick is to know which approach to use in a given situation with students. Some problems call for a therapeutic response, others for a counseling response. Some problems are a result of a mental illness, others a result of a thinking illness. The latter problem requires a philosophical intervention, and because at some level we are all philosophers (even though we may lack a Ph.D. in philosophy), all of us in higher education have the ability to heal a student's "thinking illness."

The Peace Process

One way for campus educators, both inside and outside the classroom, to deal with students about everyday issues and problems is to use the PEACE (an acronym for the following stages) process developed by Marinoff (1999). Here is his framework, which is designed for educators as well as for counselors. It is a problem-solving approach best suited for resolving thinking illnesses.

Stage One

Help the student to identify the specific *problem* that seems to be so bothersome, and that seems to arise so frequently and insistently. Ask the student to state the dilemma in the proverbial nutshell, to get some clarity and to cut it down to workable size.

Stage Two

Get the student to put a name to each of the *emotions* that may be swirling around inside. Personal problems ignite emotions, and it is important that the student not ignore the latter because of the immediate need to solve the former.

Stage Three

Help the student to *analyze* (that is, talk openly, honestly, and reasonably about) the connections between the first two stages. Also, stimulate some early problem-solving with questions like these: Is your strong emotional reaction to the problem helping or hurting you as you think about your issue? What might be some initial steps you could take to resolve your problem? Why do you suppose you are so upset about this issue, person, or situation?

Stage Four

Teach the student how to *think philosophically* about the problem; how to cultivate a philosophical disposition (gaining some contemplative distance) toward the problem instead of indulging in endless self-blame, perseveration about the problem, or self-destruction. Here are some starter questions to work with: What is universalizable in the problem? What is personal in it? What might some important thinkers have to say about it? What might the student be able to learn from how philosophers have grappled with the problem through the centuries? What in the dilemma is psychological, philosophical, political, religious or spiritual, ethical, and so on?

Stage Five

This is where you can actively help the student to resolve the problem—at least enough so that some steady state is reached, some *equilibrium* restored. In this stage, personal anxieties are lessened, sadness and anger are diminished, counterproductive defenses are down, and a return to normal, productive functioning is achieved.

Amy Redux, Once Again

Here is Amy once more—our quarterlife poster child for what represents success in higher education, at least on the surface. She is a remarkably high achiever in almost all areas of her college life, including—and especially—the academic. But she battles personal demons that at times seem overwhelming to her. She is restless, despairing, dissatisfied, and self-destructive. She appears to have little meaning or purpose in her life, other than to fulfill what she perceives to be others' unrealistic expectations for her success. On the brink of graduation, with everything to look forward to, Amy feels both helpless and hopeless. She asks the perennial quarterlife question: "Is this all there is?"

Marinoff's PEACE process is an excellent guide to making meaning because it can happen in one session or in several; in formal, professional settings or in more relaxed hangout areas, either on or off campus. With Amy, the process actually unfolded in the following way.

Stage One

Amy identified her *problem* without making judgments about it. As much as she succeeded in her life, it never seemed to be enough.

She had purpose without meaning. She knew how to achieve her objectives, but she had no way of understanding her life on an ongoing basis. She won awards and honors, but she believed in nothing—no ideals, loyalties, or the power of love. She had unwittingly become a nihilist.

Stage Two

Amy identified, and owned, the *feelings* that her problem of meaninglessness provoked. She took full responsibility for feeling unsatisfied, uninspired, bored, frightened, despairing, depressed, and joyless. Medications helped, but only so far. They dulled her edge, but they also made her feel lethargic. Moreover, whenever she stopped taking her meds, her problems only intensified.

Stage Three

Amy *analyzed* the problem; that is, she acknowledged, accepted, and separated the problem from the feelings associated with it. She realized that her problem was existential. It was a philosophical illness. She had the intellectual means to achieve her goals, but she had no meaning to live for. She read Sartre and Camus, and realized that she had been living in the world as a *being-for-others* instead of living as a *being-for-herself*. She was acting unauthentically, in that she was allowing others to author her life for her. She read Aristotle and understood that there is no ceiling on success; success creates pressure to be even more successful, *ad infinitum*. Her feelings were a consequence of existential angst and meaninglessness. She understood that she needed to work on her existential issues before she could come to terms with her feelings. She loved reading Nietzsche's hundreds of aphorisms. They were so down-to-earth, some were wonderfully witty, and all were profoundly helpful to get her to think about her issues more deeply and from many angles. Most of all, however, these aphorisms had considerable shock value. Everything, for Nietzsche, is up for grabs. Nothing is sacred. Although Amy would like a "guardian angel" who is a philosophical life-coach, someone who would give her all the answers to her problems, she knows that this is an impossibility. At some level she is grateful. Because she owns her life, she also owns her feelings and her thoughts.

Stage Four

Amy tried to restore some balance to her life by *stepping back and looking at* the whole situation in order to move on. She undertook an extensive reading program based in existential philosophy and psychology. She learned about such concepts as the existential moment of awareness; existential ennui; finitude; authenticity; escape from freedom; no exit; and so on. She also read about eastern and western religious forms of meaning-making. She learned to think about purpose and meaning in a variety of ways, and she came to the conclusion that there is no definitive Final Solution to the problem of meaninglessness. Rather, there is only the here-and-now will to survive, the will to make meaning, the will to transcend. Final Solutions must give way to Ongoing Questions. She started the long, liberating process of asking herself: "Success for whom, according to whose criteria—and why?"

Stage Five

Finally, Amy was able to reach a welcome state of *equilibrium* in her life. Her "Aha!" moments of existential awareness led her to take action. She no longer engaged in addictive, self-destructive behaviors as an anodyne for her nagging feelings of despair. She worked very hard to please herself before pleasing others. She explored a variety of ways to create a meaning worth living for—a meaning to guide and inform her purposes. She learned how to appreciate and enjoy the process as much as the product. She was delighted that, at least for awhile, she had achieved an improved state of being. Amy is hopeful, indeed optimistic, that she will be able to follow the same PEACE steps in solving her future problems. At present, all seems well. But she wants to look more deeply into a therapy called *positive psychology* (see the next section). She wonders if Shakespeare's

Hamlet was right when he said "there is nothing either good or bad, but thinking makes it so." Or if Doris Day, in Alfred Hitchcock's 1956 remake of *The Man Who Knew Too Much*, was more on the mark when she sang, "*Que sera, sera*. Whatever will be, will be. The future's not ours to see. *Que sera, sera*." Is seeing believing, or is believing seeing?

Positive Psychology: If I'm So Successful, Why Aren't I Happy?

Jonathan Haidt (2006) says that "helping people find happiness and meaning is precisely the goal of the new field of positive psychology" (p. x). For Haidt and other positive psychologists, happiness is all about relatedness; it is both a state of mind and a state of union with others. It comes from both within and without. The positive psychologists are emphatic that finding meaning, purpose, and fulfillment are difficult, if not impossible, unless people first believe they possess the virtues and strengths to achieve some kind of human flourishing. Their empirical research shows that the virtues necessary for achieving the "happiness state," the ones that show up time and time again across most religions, cultures, and a variety of ethical and moral systems, are wisdom, courage, humanity, justice, temperance, and transcendence.

A Brief History of Happiness

Actually, the nature of happiness—why it is important; what its virtues and vices are; how to experience it; how it relates to love; how, from an evolutionary perspective, it confers survival benefits on us; how it fits with the reality of human suffering; how it has been defined by the world's religions; and how it might help us to find love, vocation, peace, harmony, health, and connection to others—has been an interest of philosophers for millennia. Aristotle's classical explanation of happiness emphasizes what he calls *eudaimonia* (well-being). For Aristotle, as for several of the ancients, happiness is an all-encompassing term. It has to do with the quality of an entire life. To the extent that human beings are able to fulfill all of their potentialities—particularly in the exercise of reason, prudence, harmony, and justice—then they are fulfilled. To use a modern, Maslovian (Maslow, 1968) term, they have achieved *self-actualization*. Aristotle went so far as to claim that the happy life is a morally good life. Thus health, wealth, and happiness are a product of living morally. But Aristotle was also a realist and a pragmatist: he knew that it was almost impossible for genuine human flourishing to occur in conditions of neglect, poverty, or oppression. He knew well that there is always a political dimension to happiness, as do many social philosophers today (see, for example, Rawls, 1971).

From the philosophers' perspective, then, what follows are a few representative answers to the question, what does it mean to be happy? Socrates believed that happiness is internal, not external. It is based on knowing oneself and living a life that is consistent with the best that human reason has to offer. For Epicurus, Zeno, and other Greek Stoics, happiness was getting beyond a belief in divine retribution and the fear of death. Happiness, they believed, can best be achieved by withdrawing from the fray of petty politics, refusing to promote narrow self-interests, and not getting caught up in the pursuit of transient pleasures. Instead, Stoics like the Roman Emperor, Marcus Aurelius, believed that keeping all of life's ups and downs in quiet perspective, in the company of wise and simple friends, was the way to reach the ultimate state of happiness.

In contrast, for the early Christians, happiness consisted in the realization that human beings could be reborn through the grace of Jesus Christ's suffering, death, and resurrection. The ultimate happiness resided, not in the depraved human world of sin, but in the salvation of the soul in an afterworld. To "live right" in Christ on earth would grant human beings the right to live happily in paradise with their Lord and Savior after death. Happiness for Christians from the Middle Ages onward has been to bask in the magnificence of the Beatific Vision of God in heaven forever. All worldly happiness pales in comparison.

Bentham and Mill, the nineteenth-century utilitarian philosophers, contended—in reaction to this radical, other-worldly, Christian individualism—that actions are good only when they produce the greatest happiness for the greatest number of individuals on this earth. To seek individual salvation as one's exclusive goal is selfish, they thought, and the pursuit of otherworldly salvation is a distraction from our mutual obligation to produce happiness in the here and now for as many people as we can. What both Bentham and Mill also recognized, however, is that the Golden Rule of Confucius, Hillel, and Jesus urges people to get outside of themselves in order to love others. This is not only the key to living right; it is also the key to living happily.

What is morally praiseworthy for utilitarians is what advances the worldly interests of all of us, not just some of us. Mill went further than Bentham, however, to include worldly pleasures in his calculus. His was a hedonistic perspective on happiness, the pursuit of what he called the "higher pleasures"—goals that are artistic, philosophical, or moral. He also refused to issue the usual Victorian injunctions against the happiness provided by sexual and other carnal pleasures. Ironically, Mill, always the dignified, Victorian gentleman and rationalist, was also a sensualist—but never a libertine.

In the early twentieth century, social scientists began to enlarge the happiness worldview. Their take on happiness as an integral dimension of meaning-making is both descriptive (based on empirical research) and prescriptive. We will mention just two of these earlier twentieth-century social scientists—Maslow and Rogers—who served as important precursors to the positive psychology movement that got under way in the 1990s. (We are grateful to Dr. C. George Boeree at www.ship.edu/~cgboeree/may.html for his wonderful overview of the two psychologists we cover in the following paragraphs.) Abraham Maslow (1968) was one of the first humanistic psychologists and is sometimes referred to as the creator of the *Third Force* in psychology—the other two forces being Freudian and behavioral. He created a hierarchy of "being needs (or B-values)" that include physiological, safety, belonging, esteem, and self-actualization needs.

Maslow's self-actualization needs are the harbinger of a basic premise of positive psychology: once the lower, survival needs are met, human beings have other needs—what we call "meaning-needs" or "happiness-needs." We are then able to seek autonomy, solitude, spontaneity and simplicity, humility and respect, creativity and humor. According to humanistic (and transpersonal) psychologists, all of these self-actualization states of being are a precondition to the fullest experience of happiness. Maslow's lifelong study of self-actualized persons revealed that the top B-values were a sense of unity or wholeness, aliveness, playfulness, self-sufficiency, and a strong sense of meaningfulness. According to Maslow, when human beings are unable to get their B-needs met, they respond with *metapathologies*. These include depression, despair, disgust, alienation, and cynicism—the byproducts of extreme, nihilistic forms of existentialism that we described in the previous chapter.

Carl Rogers (1902–1987) is one of the more hopeful twentieth-century humanistic psychologists. For him, all human beings know inherently what is good for them (he calls this *organismic valuing*). Among these organismic values are positive regard (self-esteem and self-worth), congruity (closing the gap between the "real self" and the "ideal self"), and absence of anxiety. For Rogers (1995), the "fully-functioning" person, one who has attained happiness and is living a life of meaning, is someone who is open to new experiences; who lives existentially in the here and now; who trusts feelings, intuitions, and instincts; who does not fear the freedom of making choices—even risky ones with no guarantees—and who is willing to be creative in all aspects of daily living, including in work, play, and love.

For therapists who work face-to-face with clients to help them achieve happiness, Rogers advocated four central qualities: congruence (being real and honest with the client), empathy, unconditional respect, and positive regard. He went so far as to say that regardless of the particular therapeutic intervention, these four relational qualities would always be the pivotal variables in helping clients to be happy. Rogers' contributions to humanistic psychology—in particular the nonjudgmental and fully accepting approach of the counselor, along with the faith that the client in each case knows deep down what is necessary for being happy—laid the groundwork for the central premises and practices of positive psychology in the late twentieth century. Rogers and the positive psychologists would be in full agreement that happiness consists in being true to oneself, being fully immersed in the ebb and flow of each day's activities, and leading a life that is balanced, joyful, compassionate, and relational. For Rogers, as for all positive psychologists, the absence of these qualities is a sure prescription, sooner or later, for personal unhappiness and meaninglessness.

Basic Assumptions of Positive Psychology

Note: We have gone directly to the website of the Positive Psychology Center at the University of Pennsylvania [http://www.ppc.sas.upenn.edu/faqs.htm] for some of the following information. We also summarize other key concepts from the following direct sources: Csikszentmihalyi, 1990; Haidt, 2006; Seligman, 1990, 1993, 2006. This bulleted passage is our own complete rewording and reconceptualizing of their work.

• Positive psychology, although still a fairly nascent psychotherapeutic movement, is rooted deeply in humanistic psychology, philosophy, literature, religion, the arts, and the natural sciences. What it does differently from a number of conventional systems of therapy is to put the emphasis on such "elevating" qualities as well-being, optimism and hope, human goodness and excellence, and intimacy and commitment. Positive psychologists are concerned with helping clients to build those skills and strengths that will keep them healthy, happy, and optimistic about their present and future lives (Haidt, 2006).

• Positive psychology is a descriptive, rather than a prescriptive, system of meaning. It does not preach or prescribe, because it understands that happiness comes in many sizes and shapes. There is no one size or shape that fits everyone. It does presume to teach, however, and what it teaches is that there are buffers that can protect people from the ravages of mental illness that often take the form of despair, pessimism, and sadness. For positive psychologists, prevention, not cure, is the goal of their work with clients. Healing suffering and pain is important, but preventing these from happening in the first place is more important. The best preventative is for the client to develop the inner life by building on personal strengths and qualities that result in resilience, joy, and self-confidence.

• Positive psychology is an empirical, interdisciplinary field of study that has produced a wealth of data related to the causes and best treatments of such physical problems as alcoholism, dieting, eating disorders, and sexual dysfunction. It is also a field of study that draws a valid set of conclusions from its data about how best to treat clients who suffer from such psychological problems as anxiety, panic, phobias, obsessions, depression, anger issues, and post-traumatic stress disorders. Positive psychologists understand that each client will respond to particular interventions in different ways, but all clients have a right to make informed choices based on the outcomes of sound empirical studies—even when these studies might depart radically from the conventional wisdom of the helping professions (Lyubomirsky, 2007; Snyder & Lopez, 2006).

- Meaning-making in positive psychology focuses on such virtues as the capacity for love, courage, compassion, resilience, strength, integrity, self-understanding, self-transcendence, self-control, and wisdom. It is these strengths that contribute to improved psychological and physical health, that foster better personal and professional relationships, and that result in more productive and fulfilling communities. These virtues make it more likely that meaning-making will take a healthy direction.

Another Quarterlife Take on Happiness

What follows are excerpts from a letter to Robert that one of his quarterlife students, the aforementioned Maigret, wrote after spending a semester studying meaning-making within the context of positive psychology. She well exemplifies several of the basic assumptions we have just presented. Keep in mind, however, that this is but one person's take on what she needs to be happy. She has chosen, in her own best way, her own path to mental well-being and positive meaning. She has chosen to respond to a crisis of meaning within the context of her own particular narrative perspective on the world. She has found a way to deal with her beloved grand-father's death that makes sense for her. For this student, what she calls "independent happiness" is a meaning-perspective that works well. Here is what she said in her letter:

I have feared this moment my entire life. At twenty-six, it was my first experience with death. I have had all my grandparents in my life for my whole life. I have considered myself lucky for this. Now, I have three grandparents living. I can recall telling my first-grade teacher that I never knew my great-grandmother and thinking that was a really sad thing. I wonder how it must change a child's concept of life to experience death early on and how I might be different if I had.

In *The Question of God* (2002), Dr Armand Nicholi Jr. says "... Freud reveals that his awareness of death began as a young child. When he was about two years of age, his young brother Julius died" (p. 217). As a young child I had no concept of the loss that many had already experienced. For Freud, he became consumed with a fear of death. He over-examined his thoughts of mortality, and he certainly had a close relationship with loss and death pretty consistently throughout his life. Would he have been a different man, a happier man, had he not been obsessed with these dark thoughts as a child? I tend to think that had he not experienced death until he was older and more emotionally stable, he might have had a very different mindset. I can't ever be sure, but maybe I can attribute some of my own overall happiness to my lack of experience with death.

I consider myself a very happy person. I know this may seem a strange thing to say when I have just gone through my first loss of a loved one. I have to admit that after getting over the initial shock of losing my grandfather, Popi, I wondered how I could be handling it so well. I kept thinking it was going to hit me at any moment, and I would fall apart. However, that never really happened the way that I always feared it would. After spending the last week contemplating my own emotional reaction to this loss, I feel I can attribute it to two things: my relief at the end of his suffering and my personal foundation in happiness. My experience seems similar to Freud's experience of the loss of his mother. In *The Question of God* Freud talks about feeling "no pain, no grief" at her loss due to "the great age and the end of pity we had felt at her helplessness. With that a feeling of liberation, of release..." (Nicholi, p. 225). When I got the phone call from my mother during class two weeks ago saying that they were gathered around his bed waiting, I found myself praying that he would be able to let go. This made me aware that I was still praying to some energy, or spirit, or God, even though intellectually I say I am questioning the God that my Catholic upbringing taught me to believe in.

(Continued)

I think that my current stance about God, or a higher power of some sort, plays a large role in my overall happiness. My happiness comes from within; it is not artificial and manufactured. I do not rely on a thing or a person for it. Some people are "independently wealthy." I consider myself "independently happy." Lately, within the past year and half, I have been on a journey to discover my happiness and claim it. As I was reading one of our texts, *Eat, Pray, Love*, Elizabeth Gilbert (2006) said something that spoke to me and put words to where my internal happiness may come from. Gilbert explains that the yogic view is based on this assumption: "We're miserable because we think that we are mere individuals, alone with our fears and flaws and resentments and mortality . . . We have failed to recognize our deeper divine character. We don't realize that somewhere within us all, there does exist a supreme Self who is eternally at peace. That supreme Self is our true identity, universal and divine" (p. 122). Maybe the general contentment that I feel comes from within because I finally took the time to examine and get to know myself. Just maybe, dedicating this time to myself allowed me to begin to recognize my internal "supreme Self."

Meeting this part of my character helps me to have faith in myself and my integrity in all areas of my life: with friends, with work, with family, and with strangers. I also know that this is just part of the journey, and that as time goes on I can only learn more and come to know my "supreme Self" better. I am young, but I am my whole self for right now. I will change and grow with time, of course, but I do not need to feel like anything is missing, because I am exactly who and where I should be at this point in time.

As long as I come back to this awareness, I believe I can maintain a happy mindset. Gilbert also said "The hub of calmness—that's your heart. That's where God lives within you. So stop looking for answers in the world. Just keep coming back to that center and you'll always find peace" (p. 207). The notion that God was in me, not only in some unattainable higher being, explained to me where my internal peace could come from at the loss of my grandfather. Before reading *Eat, Pray, Love*, I wouldn't have known how to explain it. But now I can say that what I have been doing for the past year and a half is returning to my center when things got overwhelming. It makes me feel that I don't really need answers to the big questions, as long as I continue to examine them. I know that people have to die. And, you know what? I'm okay with this. I'm actually happy. I'm finding my "hub of calmness," maybe for the first time in my life.

A Journey Through the Wilderness

Maigret's comments remind us of something that Marcel Proust said: "We do not receive wisdom, we must discover it for ourselves, after a journey through the wilderness which no one else can make for us, which no one can spare us, for our wisdom is the point of view from which we come at last to regard the world'" (quoted in Haidt, 2006, p. 152). Happiness, like meaning, does not come easily. There are no magic bullets, simple self-help formulas, or quick fixes. Csikszentmihalyi (1990), despite all his emphasis on happiness as an unintentional spinoff of the flow experience, nevertheless acknowledges that the way to happiness will always be a challenge.

So it was for Maigret. She knows that it will take hard work, a kind of *metanoia* (Greek for a profound change of heart and mind), and infinite patience, if she is going to continue finding meaning whenever tragedy and heartbreak strike. Happiness is a byproduct of Proust's "journey through the wilderness" that each of us must make on our own in our own unique ways. Wisdom is often born out of Nietzsche's famous aphorism—"that which does not kill me makes me stronger" (1886/1977). This is also the aphorism that was so much a part of Viktor Frankl's philosophy of suffering as the necessary precondition to make meaning. This student is learning how to be stronger when events in her life threaten to break her.

We often remind our students that nothing they experience— and this includes their personal failures as well as their successes—is ever wasted. Experience teaches best, and, potentially, what it teaches best of all is wisdom. Wisdom is knowing how to make meaning, and all of our experiences add up to a "point of view," a "way of seeing" (the Latin etymology—*videre*—of the word "wise") the world either tall or small. It is up to all of us to make meaning out of the "wilderness" of our lives. Perhaps this is why real, off-campus "wilderness experiences" are increasing in popularity among college students. They give students a chance to make meaning while dealing with the very real challenges of the wild. It is no coincidence that increasingly some of our students yearn to become ropes-course instructors and are avid hikers and climbers.

A painful, sometimes fatal "journey through the wilderness," whether metaphorical or real, in order to find oneself has been the perennial theme of inspirational works of fiction and nonfiction through the ages. Even today, these writings are best-sellers among college students. For example, as we write in 2008, Randy Pausch's *The Last Lecture* (2008) is the best-selling nonfiction book among college students. When he wrote it, Pausch, a forty-seven-year-old computer science professor with three young children, was suffering from terminal pancreatic cancer (see www.thelastlecture.com). Pausch was asked to deliver his university's "last lecture." He talked, not about his fatal prognosis, or the pain he was experiencing from radiation and chemotherapy treatments, or the "death terror" of having to face his mortality at such a young age. Instead, he talked about his journey to discover love, faith, hope, seizing every moment of the day and living fully in the present, because none of us can ever be completely sure that we will have a chance to live in a tomorrow. (Randy Pausch died on July 24, 2008.)

Also, Jon Krakauer's *Into the Wild*, first published in 1997 and made into a film of the same title in 2007, subsequently stayed on the college best-seller list for over a year. Krakauer's narrative chronicles the four-month experience of a young man from a wealthy East Coast family, who walked alone into the Mt. McKinley wilderness to invent a new life for himself. Sixteen weeks later, his decomposed body was found by a party of moose hunters in Alaska.

Christopher Johnson McCandless, an elite athlete and an honors graduate of Emory University, had given up everything "wandering across North America in search of raw, transcendent experience." He lived the challenging life of a young nomad: ascetic, intense, idealistic, and extremely high-risk. He made the decision very early in his life to forsake a future of wealth and privilege to search for meaning in the Alaska bush country. Tragically, it was in the bush that, while seeking enlightenment, McCandless died from starvation.

We have often recommended films and books to our students that exemplify Proust's insight that none of us can ever be spared from experiencing the long, difficult journey through what St. John of the Cross called the "darkest nights of our souls." What is more, it is unlikely that we will ever be truly wise or happy unless we go into the metaphorical "wilderness." For example, Sanders, in his 1998 book *Hunting for Hope*, writes about how he used a hiking trip into the Rockies with his teenage son, Jesse, to dig deeply into how a father's despair can darken a son's world. Sanders rediscovers a sense of hope during his father-son trip into the wilderness, after Jesse openly challenges his pessimistic view of a planet ravaged by pollution and what today we call "global warming." Sanders must make a choice between his ongoing, debilitating sense of despair over the future of the planet and building an optimistic and loving relationship with his son. He decides to make it his priority to find the beauty that exists in precious human relationships while still working for environmental reform.

Finally, Maigret exemplifies the wisdom of Haidt's aphorism: "Work on your strengths, not your weaknesses" (p. 169). This is one of those maxims that is so easily expressed but so quickly repressed. Yet for positive psychologists, it is such virtues and strengths as wisdom, courage, humanity, love, justice, temperance, and transcendence that produce happiness. In this sense, virtue can be its own reward. Getting students like the letter-writer to practice the strengths that come easiest to them, rather than obsessing over their weaknesses, produces success. We have never met a student who does not possess at least a few signature strengths.

Maigret's strengths are many. This is what is genuinely positive about positive psychology. Find your particular strengths (curiosity? creativity? perseverance? resilience? kindness? leadership? humility? hope? humor? zest?), and draw on these whenever life gets you down. It is even possible to draw on a strength in order to circle around a weakness—not always, of course, because weaknesses need to be confronted at some time. Robert's student letter writer was wise enough to draw on her strengths in order to circle around her sorrow over the death of her beloved Popi. In the end, however, she emerged stronger, more at peace, and, yes, happier.

Resource B: Crossover Pedagogy

The basic assumption inherent in crossover pedagogy is that all of us in the university are meaning-mentors. In a project as broad, deep, and challenging as preparing our students for the confoundingly complex, hyperpluralistic world of the twenty-first century, educators on a college campus—administrators, faculty, and staff members—are *co-owners* of the intellectual life and rightful heirs of the liberal learning ideal. We fully endorse collaboration among faculty and student-affairs educators to help students face the overwhelming personal, professional, and global challenges (many of which we have yet to even conceive) of the coming decades. We believe that helping students to do all of this constitutes intellectual excellence.

Crossing Sacrosanct Boundaries

Student learning spans the artificial in- and out-of-class boundaries their educators create as a function of their particular on-campus roles. Scholars who study student learning and engagement (Kuh, Kinzie, Schuh, Whitt, & Associates, 2005) argue that students are more engaged and successful in the learning process when their campus environments support more permeable boundaries between classroom, cocurriculum, and community. Furthermore, on campuses that foster very high student engagement, faculty and student affairs see themselves as partners, rather than adversaries, in the effort to promote student learning (Kuh et al., 2005).

When Kuh et al. (2005) analyzed the data from the National Survey of Student Engagement (NSSE), they noticed that some institutions had higher-than-predicted levels of student engagement. The team studied twenty of these colleges and universities in their Documenting Effective Educational Practice (DEEP) project. Among expected curricular factors of student engagement, such as academic rigor and student involvement with faculty research, the team identified some factors that may surprise some. The team's investigations revealed that institutions with consistently high marks for student engagement had a spirit of "shared responsibility for educational quality and student success" between academic and student affairs. DEEP institutions had "a high degree of respect and collaboration . . . so faculty, academic administrators, and student affairs staff work together effectively. Cocurricular programs are designed to complement, and not compete with or undercut, student achievement" (pp. 164–165). DEEP institutions, then, are able to focus on student learning without the distractions of destructive turf wars.

Manning, Kinzie, and Schuh (2006) followed the DEEP study with insights of their own. Regular collaboration between academic and student affairs yielded the most robust learning for students. Years of student feedback indicates that these observations are true—at least in our experiences. Egos aside, faculty and student affairs professionals who are able to work in partnership with one another create a dynamic campus environment. The two complement and enhance one another's roles, and students reap the benefits. Manning, Kinzie, and Schuh stress the increase in a holistic, coherent learning process for students, in which one learning experience, whether in- or out-of-class, builds on another. Again, the evidence suggests that engaging students in deep learning and learning for meaning requires the talents and skills of faculty and student affairs professionals together.

Shades of Meaning-Making

The evidence from NSSE and DEEP suggests unequivocally that the most effective institutions are those that emphasize student learning as the responsibility of both faculty and student affairs professionals. Once again, the research shows that student learning extends well beyond the classroom and the faculty reach. When they are able and willing to work together, faculty and student affairs professionals can create dynamic campus environments that inspire learning on all fronts. On college campuses, student growth knows no boundaries; learning takes place everywhere. The classroom stimulates intellectual growth, but is not the exclusive domain of such growth. Likewise, cocurricular programs may inspire self-reflection and meaning-making, but these are not the only places where students learn deeply about themselves and the world around them. The "Eureka!" moments, whether small or monumental, occur when the mind and heart are engaged in critical reflection, and faculty are not the only ones who can create conditions for students to lessen the distance between head and heart.

Entertaining students' questions of meaning and accompanying them as they seek answers requires any educator—faculty or student affairs professional—to stretch beyond a subject-level expertise. The challenge of working with students as they ponder life's puzzles may draw on an educator's academic training (Connor, 2007)—whether that training is in ancient civilizations, mathematics, student learning and development, or economics—but more often than not it relies on the educator's humanity and willingness to mentor students as they wander down the road of meaning. Whole-person life lessons are what made Randy Pausch's (2008) *The Last Lecture* so popular. Yes, his personal story, including his valiant battle with terminal cancer, is tragic, but this is not what has made his book a bestseller or what sends people daily to his website or to videos of his lecture on YouTube. Pausch gave his last lecture on "Really Achieving Your Childhood Dreams," and with his words he has shed light on the paths of so many others. Pausch, a computer scientist by training and calling, is eminently qualified to educate the whole person. There is widespread recognition of his wisdom among quarterlifers and midlifers alike, which explains in part the runaway best-seller status of his book.

As Pausch's lecture attests, meaning-making occurs in all the nooks and crannies of campus life, and its sources of inspiration can be found all over campus. Connor (2007) points out that the cocurriculum presents multiple opportunities for students to explore their course-related concepts and apply them to their life experiences. In the comfort of the residence, or in the challenge of a leadership role, students test their new knowledge and work it into their lives, proving that they are more than mere receptacles for new information.

Likewise, Koth (2008) has developed a method for students to deeply consider their questions of meaning within the context of the classroom. Koth's "moments of meaning" encourage students to personalize the sometimes difficult leap between the intellectual content of the course and their heartfelt, even spiritual, reactions to it. Although some may criticize "moments of meaning" as "soft" pedagogy, Koth's methods have inspired his students, and they have been aware enough of the power in his classroom that they have sought him out in gratitude.

Meaning-making happens when students connect the dots between what they learn in their courses, what they observe of the world, what they discover about others, and what they know about themselves. Their educators, whether faculty or student affairs professionals, act as guides in the process, but students are the ones who have to make the meaning connections. For students, the process of making meaning of self, others, and the world they inhabit is not an either/or proposition. As whole people who engage in the educational process called college, students find that the process of making meaning is a both/and proposition. They are not interested in the petty jockeying for position between faculty and student affairs professionals.

No educator, whether faculty or student affairs administrator, should be blinded by self-interest or a particular way of seeing the world. Academic myopia and leadership arrogance do nothing but inflame all the traditional internecine hostilities and shift attention away from students and their processes of learning and meaning-making. To see the campus as bifurcated is to miss the miracle of meaning-making that happens somewhere in between. All educators need an appreciation for the myriad ways in which students learn and all the people and experiences involved in that learning. For them, today's most meaningful learning experience may happen in a philosophy class during the study of compassion and the good life, but tomorrow's lesson may come from the compassionate interaction with the librarian, foodservice worker, physics professor, or resident director. In every on- and off-campus venue, students are adopting tools and making mental, emotional, and spiritual connections that will help them pursue meaningful lives of their own. Working together, faculty and student affairs professionals reach the greatest number of students and help them find their own passions in life.

Howard Thurman, an influential Baptist minister and Morehouse valedictorian, noted: "Don't ask what the world needs. Ask what makes you come alive, and go do it. Because what the world needs is people who have come alive." Keeping in mind Thurman's words, helping students become more fully alive—is there any better *raison d'être* for an educator, whether faculty or student affairs professional? Educating the whole person is an honor and a privilege. However, none of us can do it alone. The work needs all of us—faculty and student affairs administrators—and we cannot think of a more noble partnership than this one.

Our Attempts to Do Crossover Pedagogy

Both authors of this book have tried to introduce alternative types of scholarship as well as fresh ways of teaching and learning in higher education. We have increasingly chosen to do more coteaching, coconsulting, and coauthoring. For example, Robert recently coauthored a book with a student affairs administrator, DeMethra L. Bradley, and a national leader in higher education, Arthur W. Chickering (Nash, Bradley, & Chickering, 2008). The authors wrote about a way to talk across disciplines and administrative venues about red-hot topics on campus. They referred to this kind of dialogue as "moral conversation." Robert refers to these collaborative ventures as "crossover pedagogy." In music, the term "crossover" means combining different musical genres to appeal to a wider audience. In pedagogy, the term "crossover" describes an approach to subject matter, teaching, learning, and alternative educational settings that is based in quarterlife developmental theory, interdisciplinary scholarship, constructivist philosophy, multiple intelligences theory, positive psychology, moral conversation, and story-telling.

We have already described our take on developmental theory. It follows that of Alexandra Robbins and Abby Wilner (2001), who trace the various quarterlife transitions (roughly from late adolescence to the early thirties), and the life-cycle tasks germane to each of those periods, that students pass through on their way to reaching middle and late adulthood. Interdisciplinary scholarship describes the recent efforts of educators like Daniel Goleman (2006) and Jonathan Haidt (2006) to solve concrete personal and social problems by drawing on a number of related academic and applied disciplines.

Constructivist philosophy, as articulated by a number of postmodern philosophers and literary theorists, is the theoretical background for all our meaning-making work in higher education. It assumes that each of us *constructs* knowledge in addition to simply *receiving* it. We are active participants, as well as passive observers, in the various worlds we inhabit. For constructivists, there is no such thing as a context-independent approach to understanding and resolving personal and social problems. Without exception, we filter the world through our individual and collective matrices of understanding. The world is less like a scientific laboratory and more like a Rorschach ink blot; it is not described so much as it is interpreted.

Multiple intelligences theory is the work of Howard Gardner (2006a, 2006b), and when it was first introduced, it was a revolutionary addition to the cognitive-competence literature. In a nutshell, the theory holds that intelligence is a complex set of abilities, talents, and mental skills, the majority of which cannot be tested by standard I.Q. measures. These intelligences include other ways of knowing, in addition to the more conventional logical-mathematical, linguistic, and spatial intelligences so highly revered and rewarded in academia. Gardner refers to these other ways of knowing as "musical," "bodily-kinesthetic," "interpersonal," "intrapersonal," "naturalist," and "existential" intelligences. By implication, Gardner raises this pedagogical question: Why should we privilege one or two intelligences over all the others in higher education if it is true that each of us learns in different ways?

Positive psychology—as explained in the previous section, this was first introduced in the latter years of the twentieth century by Martin E. P. Seligman (1990)—is an interdisciplinary corrective to the dominant focus on pathology, victimology, and mental illness so prevalent among the psychotherapeutic sciences. It emphasizes the positive emotions (such as kindness, compassion, humor, optimism, joy, and generosity) and shows how we can live happily by cultivating traits such as these as well as several others.

Moral conversation (Nash, Bradley, & Chickering, 2008) is a way for people to communicate peacefully and empathically with one another across an array of competing and, at times, conflicting worldviews. Its ultimate objective is not guilt-mongering, conversion, argumentation, or ridicule. Rather, this communication process posits as its primary ideal the need to arrive at a compassionate understanding of the differences that exist among diverse belief systems and contending groups before moving to critique and challenge.

Finally, story-telling, or a narrative approach to both teaching and learning, helps us to understand our lives as a series of stories, each of which includes significant events, groups, and individuals, and all of which are linked loosely in some kind of sequence across time, according to a number of dominant and recessive plots, themes, and conflicts. Narrativists like Sara Lawrence-Lightfoot help us to make sense of our multiple experiences by creating stories that weave the disparate ups and downs and ins and outs of our lives into some type of cohesive framework of understanding.

Creating Meaning Together

Robert has found that crossover pedagogy works best when he teams up with student affairs educators who meet and work with students in a variety of out-of-classroom settings. He and they have cotaught such courses as religious and cultural pluralism, scholarly personal narrative writing, applied ethics, and philosophy of higher education. For example, what follows is an account of an actual incident that recently occurred in one of Robert's crossover, coteaching seminars that illustrates the benefits of a cross-pedagogy approach.

The coteachers were helping students to learn the importance of having moral conversations as a way to understand, rather than to attack, what often comes across to us as irreconcilable differences in one another's worldviews. Robert, a philosopher, went about his usual task of framing, conceptualizing, and analyzing the principles of moral conversation for students. One of them, however, responded with this provocative question: "What if what we are hearing from someone is so obviously hateful, mean, and wrongheaded that the only response worth giving is a negative one, like fighting fire with fire?" Robert's coteacher, a student affairs administrator, responded to the student in such a way as to evoke a variety of perspectives on the question. She asked: "How, for example, would you have responded to that fundamentalist Christian man who was preaching in front of the chapel on our campus yesterday? He was shouting at passersby that unless we all accept his lord and savior Jesus Christ, then we will burn in hell forever."

This question—asked in a noncombative, timely, and savvy way, by an administrator-educator who, in response to a number of student and faculty complaints, happened to be on the scene investigating the preacher's presence on campus—completely turned the conversation around in the seminar. Now the discussion took on a real-world, more evocative flavor. Students began to talk about substantive issues related to freedom of speech, how to put themselves in the stories of others in order to understand them better—particularly when these stories might be harmful or off-putting—and how to converse with others whose views are radically different in such a way that educators can draw them out rather than shut them down. Robert and his coteacher also posed this question to the class: how, in principle, does the fundamentalist preacher's diatribe differ from the social justice activist's attack on "homophobes, sexists, and racists" (which had happened a month earlier, in almost the same spot)?

Although the class did not reach a final resolution over such a knotty real-world example of how to deal most effectively with fundamentalist conversation-stoppers of all stripes—whether radically conservative or radically liberal, or religious, political, educational, or philosophical—Robert and his coteacher did find a way to apply the theoretical principles of moral conversation to an actual campus incident. She was able to show how she handled the situation by engaging the young fundamentalist in a moral conversation about the most effective ways to get his message across. Because he was also the recipient of some unwanted vitriol (including some choice vulgarities) from his angry, secular student audiences, he was grateful for a chance to talk with an administrator about how he could best reach students who might be interested in "hearing the word of the Lord."

The central thrust of crossover pedagogy is to engage in meaning-making education with students, whenever, wherever, and however this comes up on a college campus. Crossover pedagogy assumes that all of us in the academy, whatever our official designations and functions, have the potential to become *crossover educators*. We train, develop, rear, teach, instruct, inspire, inform, exemplify, model, mentor, supervise, prepare, and edify, each in our own ways. Moreover, education occurs in multiple settings, at times simultaneously, occasionally by design, but most of the time randomly. Crossover pedagogy entails that all of us on our campuses think of ourselves as equal members of an educational jazz ensemble—a pluralistic metaphor inspired by Sharon Welch's (1999) work.

As equal members of an educational jazz ensemble, we each retain our signature melodic variations, improvisations, and dissonances, yet we also agree on a central theme. Our individual riffs are to be judged mainly on how effectively they mesh and, as Welch would say, create "compassion, energy, creativity, and a delight in the surprise and unexpected gifts of life" (1999, p. 25) in order to respond to each student's quest for meaning and purpose. Crossover pedagogy undoubtedly will be messy, but ultimately it will be effective. Zachary Karabell says it well: "So let the university be a place with multiple owners . . . the result may not be neat; it may be unwieldy. But it will serve an American society that has since the beginning been messy, contradictory, and at its best, incredibly vibrant and astonishingly creative" (1997, p. 246).

Millennial Students and the Search For Meaning

Faculty and student affairs educators will need one another if we are going to be successful with a new breed of student—the millennial generation. Born around 1980, millennial students, according to the latest research by Spencer, are optimistic, self-confident, collaborative and team-oriented, technologically literate, and interested in improving their communities. They are eager to learn in nontraditional ways. They value process as much as content, emotional as much as analytic learning, and meaning-making as much as money-making. They want opportunities to exercise all their multiple intelligences.

Also, according to Richard Light's long-term work on the Harvard Assessment Seminars, millennial students are drawn to a particular type of educator. These are professionals who understand the social and cultural factors that shape millennials' special twenty-first-century learning preferences. For example, having been exposed to cooperative learning experiments in high school, as well as to service-learning projects in their local communities, millennial students look for opportunities to translate their classroom learning into on-site assistantships, practice, and field experiences outside the campus, including travel abroad. This will require faculty and student affairs educators to work together, given our different types of expertise.

As George E. Walker et al. (2006) have pointed out, traditionally sacrosanct boundaries in the academy are beginning to overlap. Interdisciplinary and cross-disciplinary studies are gaining in popularity, especially in university honors colleges as well as in small liberal arts colleges. For example, at Robert's nationally known, environmentally conscious university, faculty from a number of social science, natural science, and humanities disciplines get together to coteach and coresearch in order to examine all the angles and aspects of creating sustainable and efficient educational ecosystems. So, too, in the graduate program in Higher Education and Student Affairs Administration (HESA) where Robert has one of his academic appointments, a number of faculty and graduate students collaborate across their respective disciplinary specializations (philosophy, anthropology, leadership theory, educational theory, diversity studies, communication theory, and so on) to coteach, coauthor, copresent, and coconsult throughout the country.

Crossover Pedagogy in Action

In the last decade, Robert has chosen to coteach several of his courses with student affairs professionals because these leaders meet millennial students every day in the world outside the classroom. This is the chaotic real world where students also learn what are perhaps their most important lessons, because it is here that they actually live, love, and laugh, as well as lament, languish, and lapse. Student affairs professionals who collaborate with Robert in his seminars represent a broad spectrum of administrative venues—campus ministry, student activities, judicial affairs, career services, residential life, cultural pluralism and multicultural affairs, continuing education, service-learning, and international education. It is in these various locations that students must come to terms with *both* micro *and* macro meaning-making questions.

In truth, crossover pedagogy is not just a luxury; it is a necessity. Student affairs collaborators are closer to the everyday robust life of the campus beyond the seminar room and lecture hall. They bring a certain type of real-world credibility to their collaborations with faculty. They know about leadership theory and practice. Also, because they are so well-versed in developmental theory, student affairs professionals understand well where, in the unfolding developmental sequence, the meaning-based questions in the next section are coming from. They are also acutely aware of the specific life-cycle tasks that students must work on to answer these difficult questions of meaning and purpose for themselves.

Faculty must learn not to give in to the temptation to separate theory from practice. Student affairs colleagues—scholars and meaning-makers in their own right—are instrumental in helping students transform theory into practice and also translate practice back to theory. They are students of Paulo Freire (whom many have read) in the sense that they strive for genuine praxis in their work. One plausible reason why student-affairs professionals, like some faculty, are effectively able to feature praxis in their work is that it is based on the "five-minds" research of Howard Gardner (2006b).

According to Gardner, all educators on a college campus must learn to cultivate the "creating" and "respectful" minds of effective leaders. *Creating* minds break new ground, pose new questions, and find innovative ways to get things done. *Respectful* minds welcome pluralism, empathize with the plight of others, and look for ways to interlink diverse groups. So, too, we all need to cultivate the "disciplined" and "synthesizing" minds of respected scholars. *Disciplined* minds master a specific body of knowledge and then contribute to it. *Synthesizing* minds evaluate information objectively in order to put ostensibly disparate bodies of knowledge together. Finally, we need to develop an ethical mind. *Ethical* minds, according to Gardner, are altruistic in that they try to motivate others to move beyond narrow self-interests to enhance benefits for everyone.

No group of educators has a right to lay exclusive claim to one or another of Gardner's minds. Faculty *and* student affairs educators each possess, and express, all five minds in their own special ways.

Dealing with Difficult Issues

Recall from Chapter One the meaning-making themes and tasks that quarterlifers must confront during their late teens to their early thirties. Let's consider each of them in turn for the purposes of our crossover pedagogy discussion.

Hopes and Dreams

Crossover teaching enables educators to address the question of hopes and dreams both theoretically *and* experientially, both rationally and emotionally. Collaborators must remember at all times to demonstrate respectful minds, in the sense that we need to show empathy. We also must express our creating minds, because we need to know how to ask the questions that will help our students to break new ground in their thinking.

During meaning-making conversations about the challenges and opportunities of adulthood, we must share our own unique experiences of becoming adults. We must talk honestly about our own personal, ongoing efforts to deal with the challenging issues of commitment, work, stuckness, and growing up and assuming responsibility. We need to openly share our views on how we face the inevitable presence of excitement *and* boredom in our own everyday lives. Faculty and student affairs administrators must learn to switch roles at strategic times during the conversation, to avoid being stereotyped by our students. We need to show sides of ourselves (a different "mind," if you will) that tend to demolish the stereotypes that some of our students associate with each of us because of our official titles.

Religion and Spirituality

We must always take religio-spiritual questions very seriously whenever they arise in our classrooms. Because of our different roles, we bear firsthand witness to how students deal with these issues both inside and outside the classroom. We have seen these types of questions take shape in the residence hall and the chapel as well as in the seminar room; in the student center and the multicultural conference room as well as in the lecture hall. Crossover colleagues must consciously withhold personal judgments whenever such questions come up, because we understand well that such existential questions are a necessary function of the millennial or quarterlife developmental process.

Moreover, because there is no particular humanities or science agenda that crossover colleagues yearn to push (as so many strict academicians do), each of us is better able to bring C. P. Snow's two opposing, academic cultures closer together. We need to look for significant intersections between supernaturalism, naturalism, and humanism. We both must exercise our synthesizing minds in this regard. We become *processors*, not *professors*, on matters of faith, religion, and spirituality. We need to exercise our "synthesizing minds" to point out common themes in our students' religio-spiritual journeys. We must also introduce some relevant background literature for our students to consider.

Work Life

We find that crossover pedagogy speaks especially well to work/nonwork life issues. According to the research, the majority of academicians tend to spend most of their lives in the professoriate, unless they fail to get tenure. A faculty career is a lengthy, one-way track from kindergarten to graduate school to the faculty. In contrast, student affairs professionals have had to deal with a diversity of work situations, activities, and job changes over the course of their lifetimes. Their career track is less linear, and they move from location to location and position to position more frequently.

Thus, as coteachers, we can respond to work/nonwork life questions raised (and implied) by a variety of students, both from a faculty member's perspective and from the perspective of a student affairs professional. Although the performance pressures and challenges may be similar in intensity for both of us, the meanings associated with such terms as *vocation, work, career,* and *job* can be very different. This dual perspective on the work that we do can only be very good for our students.

When Freud, on his deathbed, uttered the words "Good love and good work" to someone who asked him the meaning of life, he put love first. This was no accident. But he also singled out work as a close second. It is important that crossover colleagues point this out to students. In a recent post-course group assessment, Robert's students reported that they thoroughly enjoyed the way he and his coteacher came at love and work from their different (as well as their similar) angles.

Home, Friends, Lovers, and Family

Because these themes come up time and time again in meaning-making seminars, crossover educators need to make it a point to express their respectful and ethical minds in trying to help our students to (1) think beyond their own self-interests and (2) expand their circles of belonging to include others beyond their groups of origin.

We must purposely not avoid discussing the importance of loving relationships in creating meaning. Throughout the semester, Robert's students tend to raise universal questions that touch the heart of what gives their lives the most satisfying sense of meaning and purpose. Crossover teaching during the term helps students develop several different perspectives on the universal questions of community, love, and significant relationships. At the end of a semester, most students in a meaning-making seminar begin to see themselves as implicated in a communal reality beyond themselves. Robert finds that all five of Gardner's minds are active in responding to these powerful relational questions. And, thanks to the collaboration with his student-affairs coteachers, he is able to examine these types of issues from the perspectives of a number of developmental frameworks.

Identity

During a typical semester, identity issues come up often. At some point, we need to confront the ubiquity of the influence of identity development on each of us. We must examine social class, gender, race, religion, sexual orientation, and a number of other lesser explored identities without fear, without self-righteousness, and without inducing guilt. We need to be vigilant in the use of our disciplined and synthesizing minds, to point out both the strengths *and* the weaknesses of identity politics. In the third-millennium evolution of the academy, identity is currently the hot issue in the social sciences and humanities, no matter the particular subject matter.

One of the upsides of examining the concept of identity is that our students become aware of the powerful influences that their particular communities of belonging have had on them. One of the downsides, however, is that some students persist in limiting their total identification to one particular group. They tend to meld themselves into a single, overarching collective identity. As a result, they also begin to lose interest in discovering whether they might have anything in common with other students in the seminar whom they designate as out-groupers. They lose the chance to reclaim themselves as multi-identitied, not mono-identitied human beings.

Identity development is an important step in the process of becoming a proud, confident adult and of making meaning that can change the course of one's life in several positive ways. But taken to the extreme, we have found that mono-identity development can confine and divide rather than liberate and conjoin. As a result of teaching courses dealing with issues of pluralism for several years, Robert believes strongly that faculty and student affairs professionals need one another's ethical and respectful minds when students talk about their identity issues. A cross-pedagogical approach that includes coteachers from a variety of educational venues on campus can help students achieve some reasonable balance between the lures of an extreme individualism and the seductions of an extreme tribalism.

Given the powerful potential for crossover pedagogy to unite all educators in the aim to prepare students for the complexities of the twenty-first century, we encourage all campus constituents to think imaginatively about constructing new teaching-learning configurations throughout the campus. With these bold innovations, teaching for meaning will become a reality. And with luck and effort, the academy will produce more active meaning-making graduates.

Recommendations for a Crossover Pedagogy

We are not naive. The type of crossover pedagogy we are advocating will not be easy to achieve. But we think the following recommendations, based on our experience in this area, will increase your chances of successfully launching a crossover venture between faculty and student affairs administrators.

Be prepared for conflict among individuals and among units with competing vested interests.

An administrator or a faculty member who is trained in conflict resolution and mediation would be a good addition to the educational alliance we are advocating. A professor of philosophy once remarked to Robert that to think deeply about anything worthwhile will result in growing angry. Anger is inevitable, he said, whenever people get below the surface of thoughts and feelings, and nothing penetrates the surface of everyday life like honest and probing conversation about worldview differences. We can recall very little in our experience that ignites conflict more than an uncensored disclosure about one's personal philosophy of life, particularly when the disclosure might contain a direct or implied critique of somebody else's beliefs.

Misunderstandings are bound to arise on controversial topics because narratives and languages are so diverse and frameworks of interpretation (what Charles Taylor, 1991, calls "backgrounds of intelligibility" or "horizons") so many and varied. Feelings will get hurt, people will be miffed, and some students, faculty, and administrators will intentionally or unintentionally lob a sabotage bomb or two into the middle of a conversation. Instead of panicking or downplaying conflict, we must learn to trust the process whenever we meet with students in any campus venue. Things may go wrong before they go right. We must have faith that conflict will eventually correct itself if we know how to deal effectively with it and are willing to turn it into opportunity for understanding and growth on everybody's part.

Build alliances that encourage all the major campus constituents to work together.

For crossover pedagogy to work well on a college campus, all the major constituents will need to cooperate with one another.

This means that faculty, staff, student affairs administrators, and, of course, students will need to stop seeing each other as adversaries and stop setting up the usual and customary authority hierarchies.

One powerful thematic focus for creating genuine living-learning communities (particular types of educational spaces that currently represent a high priority for many student affairs administrators) on college campuses is the problem that currently plagues the entire globe, and this, of course, includes all of higher education. *How do we live peacefully and constructively in a pluralistic world?*

What do we do when worldviews collide? We have had some practice in higher education over the last decade in learning how to handle racial, ethnic, sexual orientation, and gender differences, but what about worldview differences? How can all of us on college campuses work together to build, and learn to live together in, a genuine pluralist polity? Is this even possible, given the almost sacred status of identity politics on some college campuses wherein groups practice a kind of multicultural endogamy rather than a pluralistic exogamy? Or when many endogamous groups think of exogamy merely as a way of compromising, or selling out, their deepest, most sacrosanct, convictions?

We make the following *a priori*, general assumption about joint interdisciplinary activities in the academy. All of us—faculty, staff, students, and administrators alike—will initially be threatened by the blurring of conventional borders. There is comfort and safety in predictable norms and traditions. Some faculty members, for example, are disciplinary purists, or intellectual loners; some administrators fear facing the inevitable hazards of any kind of innovation that can't be measured and defended objectively, or that might require financial resources that are already thinly distributed across campus.

Some faculty and administrators do not know how to reach out to (or be reached by) colleagues; others zero in on only what they need to do in order to win scholarly and administrative acclaim, pay raises, tenure and promotion, and institutional leadership advancement. A few from each group are just plain lazy. Interdisciplinarians and innovators on college campuses are risk-taking border-dwellers and border-crossers, by definition. They live at the margins of organized bodies of knowledge and top-down administrative arrangements. They are in the dangerous territory of straddling intellectual and leadership frontiers.

We fully understand that not everyone on a college campus—and this includes students—is temperamentally or intellectually comfortable with the type of teamwork and moral conversation that we are advocating. Having said this, however, we need to add that we have met many enthusiastic border-dwellers and border-crossers in the academy, and we have worked closely with them. We have collaborated with student affairs professionals who were highly knowledgeable about academic subject matter and also adhered to high academic standards. We have also talked at length with faculty who cared greatly about their students' various quests for personal and social meaning.

The truth is, when it comes to helping one another deal with a multiplicity of personal meanings and perspectives on the world, we are all rank amateurs, learning as we go along. Moreover, it remains a challenge for all of us in higher education how we might talk to one another with confidence and comfort about explosive issues that have the potential to tear apart a community and a society, even if we are veritable strangers to one another. Sadly, we are still learning how to have free-flowing, unfinished, and unabashedly candid, personal conversations in the academy, but we have learned all too well how to start, finish, and win academic and administrative debates and arguments.

It will be difficult to shift our perspectives on how to facilitate fruitful conversations about the hard and troubling issues around meaning-making. Each person's journey is different and is to be honored. When it comes to the most complex existential questions—what the French refer to as *les profondeurs*—there are no certified experts. Consequently, we in the academy need to cultivate a profound sense of patience, humility, love, faith, and trust, and a natural taste for adventure. It also helps to be intensely interested in people's unique meaning-stories and quest narratives. Mastery of academic content and achievement of social justice, although admirable goals, can happen on college campuses only when they go hand-in-hand with the aforementioned traits.

Create new configurations of teaching and learning based on the concept of diffusion.

Professors have a natural fondness for the classroom. This is where they first learned; this is where they practice their craft year after year. But we are suggesting that wonderful learnings occur in other sites as well. Therefore, all of us must emphasize the concept of diffusion in our educational efforts as we come together to help our students to create meaning.

Diffusion entails dispersing teaching and learning through-out the academy. This requires a belief that liberal learning can occur *outside as well as inside* the officially recognized academic structures—classrooms, credit hours, research papers, semester-long courses, lectures, and exams. Changing these centuries-old ped-agogical structures will be the most difficult challenge of all for those of us in higher education. Robert Hutchins (1995), the for-mer president of the University of Chicago, once said that it is easier to move a graveyard than it is to move faculty to change their thinking about academic matters. To be fair, this probably holds true for many student affairs professionals as well. There-fore we encourage all campus constituents to think imaginatively about constructing new teaching-learning configurations through-out the campus; for example, on the Internet, and in coffee houses, cafeterias, residence halls, chapels, cultural pluralism centers, and student activities rooms.

Finally, look for examples of successful crossover pedagogy both inside and outside your institution.

We need to take the time to research what has worked on other college campuses. Successful crossover pedagogical initiatives have been present on many college campuses for years. We often hear the stories of where they went wrong, but we seldom hear the stories of where they were successful. It's worth taking the time to seek out our peers elsewhere who have made successful attempts in the area of crossover pedagogy.

References

Allen, W. (2008). *The insanity defense: The complete prose*. New York: Random House.

Anderson, W. T. (Ed.). (1995.) *The truth about the truth: De-confusing and re-constructing the postmodern world*. New York: Tarcher.

Astin, A. W., Astin, H. S., Chopp, R., Delbanco, A., & Speers, S. (2007). "A forum on helping students engage the 'Big Questions.'" *Liberal Education*, 93(2), 28.

Baggini, J. B. (2005). *What's it all about? Philosophy and the meaning of life*. New York: Oxford University Press.

Bain, K. (2004). *What the best college teachers do*. Cambridge, MA: Harvard University Press.

Barber, C. (2008). *Comfortably numb: How psychiatry is medicating a nation*. New York: Vintage.

Baron, N. S. (2008). *Always on: Language in an online and mobile world*. New York: Oxford University Press.

Barzun, J. (1968). *The American university: How it runs, where it is going*. Chicago: The University of Chicago Press.

Bauerlein, M. (2008). *The dumbest generation: How the digital age stupefies young Americans and jeopardizes our future*. New York: Tarcher.

Baumeister, R. F. (1991). *Meanings of life*. New York: Guilford Press.

Benton, T. H. (2008, August 1). "On stupidity." *Chronicle of Higher Education*, A27, 30.

Berger, P. (1970). *A rumor of angels: Modern society and the rediscovery of the supernatural*. New York: Anchor.

Braskamp, L. A., Trautvetter, L. C., & Ward, K. (2006). *Putting students first: How colleges develop students purposefully*. San Francisco: Jossey-Bass.

Bronson, P. (2003). *What should I do with my life? The true story of people who answered the ultimate question.* New York: Random House.

Brooks, J. G., & Brooks, M. G. (1993). *The case for constructivist classrooms: In search of understanding.* Alexandria, VA: Association for Supervision and Curriculum Development.

Brooks, J. G., & Martin, G. (1999). *In search of understanding: The case for constructivist classrooms.* Alexandria, VA: Association for Supervision and Curriculum Development.

Brooks, P. (2005). *Realist vision.* New Haven, CT: Yale University Press.

Bruner, J. (1990). *Acts of meaning.* Cambridge, MA: Harvard University Press.

Bruner, J. (2002). *Making stories: Law, literature, life.* New York: Farrar, Straus & Giroux.

Buechner, F. (1992). *Listening to your life: Daily meditations with Frederick Buechner.* New York: Harper.

Carr, N. (2008). *The big switch: Rewiring the world, from Edison to Google.* New York: Norton.

Chace, W. M. (2006). *One hundred semesters: My adventures as student, professor, and university president, and what I learned along the way.* Princeton, NJ: Princeton University Press.

Chickering, A. W., Dalton, J. C., & Stamm, L. (2006). *Encouraging authenticity and spirituality in higher education.* San Francisco: Jossey-Bass.

Christensen, C. R., Garvin, D. A., & Sweet, A. (Eds.). (1991). *Education for judgment: The artistry of discussion leadership.* Cambridge, MA: Harvard Business School Press.

Colby, A., Ehrlich, T., Beaumont, E., & Stephens, J. (2003). *Educating citizens: Preparing America's undergraduates for lives of moral and civic responsibility.* San Francisco, CA: Jossey-Bass.

Collins, F. S. (2006). *The language of God: A scientist presents evidence for belief.* New York: Free Press.

Comfort, R. (2008). *How to know God exists.* Alachua, FL: Bridge-Logos.

Comte-Sponville, A. (2001). *A small treatise on the great virtues: The uses of philosophy of everyday life.* New York: Henry Holt and Company.

Comte-Sponville, A. (2006). *The little book of atheist spirituality* (N. Huston, Trans.). New York: Penguin.

Connor, W. R. (2007). "Watching Charlotte climb: Little steps toward big questions." *Liberal Education, 93*(2), 6.

Csikszentmihalyi, M. (1990). *Flow: The psychology of optimal experience.* New York: Harper Perennial.

Cupitt, D. (2005). *The great questions of life*. Santa Rosa, CA: Polebridge Press.

Damrosch, D. (1995). *We scholars: Changing the culture of the university*. Cambridge, MA: Harvard University Press.

Dawkins, R. (2006). *The god delusion*. New York: Houghton Mifflin.

de Graaf, J., Wann, D., & Naylor, T. H. (2001). *Affluenza: The all-consuming epidemic*. New York: Berrett-Koehler.

De la Chaumiere, R. (2004). *What's it all about? A guide to life's basic questions and answers*. Sonoma, CA: Wisdom House Press.

DeMan, P. (1979). *Allegories of reading: Figural language in Rousseau, Nietzsche, Rilke, and Proust*. New Haven: Yale University Press.

Derrida, J. (1978). *Margins of philosophy* (A. Bass, Trans.). Chicago: University of Chicago Press.

Dewey, J. (1933). *How we think*. Chicago: Regnery.

Dillard, A. (1999). *For the time being*. New York: Knopf.

Duane, D. (2004, September 14). "The Socratic shrink." http://query.nytimes .com/gst/fullpage.html?res=9505E5DA1731F932A15750C0A9629C8B63 &sec=health&spon=&pagewanted=al.

Edelman, G. M. (2006). *Second nature: Brain science and human knowledge*. New Haven, CT: Yale University Press.

Emerson, R. W. (1990). *Ralph Waldo Emerson: Selected essays, lectures and poems*. New York: Bantam.

Fink, L. D. (2003). *Creating significant learning experiences: An integrated approach to designing college courses*. San Francisco: Jossey-Bass.

Fish, S. (1989). *Doing what comes naturally: Change, rhetoric, and the practice of theory in literary and legal studies*. Durham, NC: Duke University Press.

Ford, D. (2007). *The search for meaning: A short history*. Berkeley, CA: University of California Press.

Foucault, M. (1972). *The archaeology of knowledge* (A. M. Sheridan Smith, Trans.). London: Tavistock.

Fowler, J. W. (1981). *Stages of faith. The psychology of human development and the quest for meaning*. San Francisco: Harper & Row.

Fowler, J. W. (2004). "Faith development at 30: Naming the challenges of faith in a new millennium." *Religious Education*, 99(4), 405–421.

Frankl, V. (1963). *Man's search for meaning: An introduction to logotherapy*. New York: Simon & Schuster.

Frankl, V. (1979). *The unheard cry for meaning: Psychotherapy and humanism*. New York: Touchstone.

Frankl, V. (2000). *Man's search for ultimate meaning*. Cambridge, MA: Perseus.

Freedman, J., & Combs, G. (1996). *Narrative therapy: The social construction of preferred realities*. New York: Norton.

Gallagher, T., OMV. (2006). *The examen prayer: Ignatian wisdom for our lives today*. New York: Crossroad.

Gardner, H. (2006a). *Multiple intelligences: New horizons*. New York: Basic Books.

Gardner, H. (2006b). *Five minds for the future*. Boston, MA: Harvard Business School Press.

Gazzaniga, M. S. (2005). *The ethical brain: The science of our moral dilemmas*. New York: HarperCollins.

Gazzaniga, M. S. (2008). *Human: The science behind what makes us unique*. New York: HarperCollins.

Geisler, N. L. (1984). "The collapse of modern atheism." In R. A. Varghese (Ed.), *The intellectuals speak out about God: A handbook for the Christian student in a secular society*. Chicago: Regnery Gateway.

Getman, J. (1992). *In the company of scholars: The struggle for the soul of higher education*. Austin: University of Texas Press.

Gilbert, E. (2006). *Eat, pray, love: One woman's search for everything across Italy, India, and Indonesia*. New York: Penguin.

Goleman, D. (2006). *Social intelligence: The new science of human relationships*. New York: Bantam Dell.

Gornick, V. (2001). *The situation and the story: The art of personal narrative*. New York: Farrar, Straus & Giroux.

Griffiths, B. (1990). *A new vision of reality: Western science, Eastern mysticism, and Christian faith*. Springfield, IL: Templegate Publishers.

Haidt, J. (2006). *The happiness hypothesis: Finding modern truth in ancient wisdom*. New York: Basic Books.

Harris, S. (2004). *The end of faith: Religion, terror, and the future of reason*. New York: Norton.

Hauerwas, S. (1977). *Truthfulness and tragedy: Further investigations into Christian ethics*. Notre Dame, IN: University of Notre Dame Press.

Havinghurst, R. (1972). *Developmental tasks and education*. New York: David McKay.

Hayes, M. (2007). *Googling God: The religious landscape of people in their 20s and 30s*. New York: Paulist Press.

Hitchens, C. (2007). *God is not great: How religion poisons everything*. New York: Twelve.

Hollingdale, R. J. (Ed. and Trans.). (1977). *A Nietzsche reader*. New York: Penguin.

Hutchins, R. M. (1995). *The higher learning in America*. New York: Transaction.

Isay, D. (2007). *Listening is an act of love: A celebration of American life from the Storycorps Project*. New York: The Penguin Press.

Iyer, P. (1993). *Falling off the map: Some lonely places of the world*. New York: Vintage.

Jayson, S. (2007, January 9). "Generation Y's goal? Wealth and fame." http://www.usatoday.com/news/nation/2007-01-09-gen-y-cover_x.htm

Jensen, A. R. (1998). *The g factor: The science of mental ability*. Westport, CT: Praeger.

Johnson, P. (1988). *Intellectuals*. New York: Harper & Row.

Karabell, Z. (1997). *What's college for? The struggle to define American higher education*. New York: Basic Books.

Keeling, R. P. (Ed.). (2004). *Learning reconsidered: A campus-wide focus on the student experience*. Washington, DC: National Association of Student Personnel Administrators & American College Personnel Association.

Kegan, R., & Laskow Lahey, L. (2001). *How the way we talk can change the way we work: Seven languages for transformation*. San Francisco: Jossey-Bass.

Kessler, R. (2000). *The soul of education: Helping students find connection, compassion, and character at school*. Alexandria, VA: Association for Supervision and Curriculum Development.

Kolb, D. A. (1984). *Experiential learning: Experience as the source of learning and development*. Englewood Cliffs, NJ: Prentice-Hall.

Koth, K. (2008). "Exploring religion and spirituality through academic service learning about religious and spiritual pluralism in a professional education course." In M. R. Diamond (Ed.), *Encountering faith in the classroom: Turning difficult discussions into constructive engagement*. Sterling, VA: Stylus.

Krakauer, J. (1997). *Into the wild*. New York: Random House.

Krishnamurti, J. (1993). *On love and loneliness*. New York: HarperCollins.

Kronman, A. T. (2007). *Education's end: Why our colleges and universities have given up on the meaning of life*. New Haven, CT: Yale University Press.

Kuh, G., Kinzie, J., Schuh, J., Whitt, E., & Associates. (2005). *Student success in college: Creating conditions that matter*. San Francisco: Jossey-Bass.

Lamott, A. (1994). *Bird by bird: Some instructions on writing and life*. New York: Pantheon.

Lawrence-Lightfoot, S. (2000). *Respect: An exploration*. New York: Perseus.

Lewis, C. S. (1962). *The problem of pain*. New York: Collier Books.

Light, R. J. (2001). *Making the most of college: Students speak their minds*. Cambridge, MA: Harvard University Press.

Lyotard, J. F. (1984). *The postmodern condition: A report on knowledge.* Manchester, UK: Manchester University Press.

Lyubomirsky, S. (2007). *The how of happiness: A scientific approach to getting the life you want.* New York: Penguin Press.

Manning, K., Kinzie, J., & Schuh, J. (2006). *One size does not fit all: Traditional and innovative models of student affairs practice.* New York: Routledge.

Marinoff, L. (1999). *Plato not Prozac: Applying eternal wisdom to everyday problems.* New York: HarperCollins.

Marinoff, L. (2003). *The big questions: How philosophy can change your life.* New York: Bloomsbury.

Maslow, A. (1968). *Toward a psychology of being.* New York: D. Van Nostrand.

Morgan, A. (2000). *What is narrative therapy? An easy-to-read introduction.* Adelaide, South Australia: Dulwich Centre Publications.

Nash, R. J. (1996). *"Real world" ethics: Frameworks for educators and human service professionals.* New York: Teachers College Press.

Nash, R. J. (2001). *Religious pluralism in the academy: Opening the dialogue.* New York: Peter Lang Publishing.

Nash, R. J. (2002a). "How September 11, 2001 transformed my course on religious pluralism, spirituality, and education." *Religion & Education,* 29(1), 1–22.

Nash, R. J. (2002b). *"Real world" ethics: Frameworks for educators and human service professionals* (2nd ed.). New York: Teachers College Press.

Nash, R. J. (2003). "Inviting atheists to the table: A modest proposal for higher education." *Religion & Education,* 30(1), 1–23.

Nash, R. J. (2004). *Liberating scholarly writing: The power of personal narrative.* New York: Teachers College Press.

Nash, R. J. (2007). "Understanding and promoting religious pluralism on college campuses." *Spirituality in Higher Education Newsletter,* 3(4), 1–9.

Nash, R. J. (2008). "A personal reflection on educating for meaning." *About Campus,* 13(2), 17–24.

Nash, R. J. (2009). "Crossover pedagogy: The collaborative search for meaning." *About Campus,* March-April, 2–9.

Nash, R. J., & Baskette, S. M. (2008). "Teaching about religious and spiritual pluralism in a professional education course." In M. R. Diamond (Ed.), *Encountering faith in the classroom: Turning difficult discussions into constructive engagement.* Sterling, VA: Stylus.

Nash, R. J., & Bradley, D. L. (2007). "Moral conversation: A theoretical framework for talking about spirituality on college campuses." In B. W.

Speck & S. L. Hoppe (Eds.), *Searching for spirituality in higher education.* New York: Peter Lang.

Nash, R. J., & Bradley, D. L. (2008). "The different spiritualities of the students we teach." In D. Jacobsen & R. H. Jacobsen (Eds.), *The American university in a postsecular age.* New York: Oxford University Press.

Nash, R. J., Bradley, D. L., & Chickering, A. W. (2008). *How to talk about hot topics on campus: From polarization to moral conversation.* San Francisco: Jossey-Bass.

Nash, R. J., & Scott, L. (2009). "Spirituality, religious pluralism, and higher education leadership development." In A. Kezar (Ed.), *New horizons for leadership development of faculty and administrators in higher education.* Sterling, VA: Stylus.

National Leadership Council. (2008). *College learning for the new global century: A report from the National Leadership Council for Liberal Education & America's Promise.* Washington, DC: Association of American Colleges and Universities.

Newman, J. H. (1990). *The idea of a university.* South Bend, IN: University of Notre Dame Press. (Original work published 1854).

Nicholi, A. M. Jr. (2002). *The question of God: C. S. Lewis and Sigmund Freud debate God, love, sex, and the meaning of life.* New York: Free Press.

Nietzsche, F. (1886/1977). *Twilight of the idols* (Walter Kaufmann, Trans.). New York: Penguin Books.

Noddings, N. (1995). *Philosophy of education.* Boulder, CO: Westview Press.

Norton, D. L. (1976). *Personal destinies: A philosophy of ethical individualism.* Princeton, NJ: Princeton University Press.

Palmer, P. J. (2000). *Let your life speak: Listening to the voice of vocation.* San Francisco: Jossey-Bass.

Parks, S. D. (1991). *The critical years: Young adults and the search for meaning, faith, and commitment.* New York: HarperCollins.

Parks, S. D. (2000). *Big questions, worthy dreams: Mentoring young adults in their search for meaning, purpose, and faith.* San Francisco: Jossey-Bass.

Pattakos, A. (2008). *Prisoners of our thoughts: Viktor Frankl's principles for discovering meaning in life and work.* San Francisco: Berret-Koehler.

Pausch, R. (2008). *The last lecture.* New York: Hyperion.

Perry, W. G. (1970/1999). *Forms of ethical and intellectual development in the college years: A scheme.* San Francisco: Jossey-Bass.

Pew Research Center. (2007, January 9). "A portrait of 'Generation Next': How young people view their lives, futures and politics."

Phelps, C. (2008, June 13). "Presenting abroad." *Chronicle of Higher Education*, C1, 4.

Phillips, C. (2001). *Socrates cafe: A fresh taste of philosophy*. New York: Norton.

Popper, K. R. (1968). *Conjectures and refutations: The growth of scientific knowledge*. New York: Harper Torchbook.

Porchia, A. (2003). *Voices* (W. S. Merwin, Trans.). Port Townsend, WA: Grand Canyon Press.

Postman, N. (1996). *The end of education: Redefining the value of school*. New York: Vintage.

Prothero, S. (2007). *Religious literacy: What every American needs to know—and doesn't*. New York: HarperOne.

Raabe, R. B. (2000). *Philosophical counseling: Theory and practice*. New York: Praeger.

Rawls, J. (1971). *A theory of justice*. Cambridge, MA: Harvard University Press.

Rhode, D. L. (2006). *In pursuit of knowledge: Scholars, status, and academic culture*. Stanford, CA: Stanford University Press.

Robbins, A. (2004). *Conquering your quarterlife crisis: Advice from twentysomethings who have been there and survived*. New York: Penguin.

Robbins, A., & Wilner, A. (2001). *Quarterlife crisis: The unique challenges of life in your twenties*. New York: Jeremy Tarcher/Putnam.

Rogers, C. R. (1995). *On becoming a person: A therapist's view of psychotherapy*. New York: Mariner Books.

Rorty, R. (1999). *Philosophy and social hope*. New York: Penguin.

Sanders, S. R. (1998). *Hunting for hope: A father's journeys*. Boston: Beacon Press.

Schopenhauer, A. (1970). *Essays and aphorisms*. (R. J. Hollingdale, Trans.). New York: Penguin.

Schrader, G. A. (Ed). (1967). *Existential philosophers: Kierkegaard to Merleau-Ponty*. New York: McGraw-Hill.

Schuster, S. C. (1999). *Philosophy practice: An alternative to counseling and psychotherapy*. New York: Praeger.

Schwehn, M. R. (1993). *Exiles from Eden: Religion and the academic vocation in America*. New York: Oxford University Press.

Seligman, M.E.P. (1990). *Learned optimism: How to change your mind and your life*. New York: Vintage Books.

Seligman, M.E.P. (1993). *What you can change and what you can't*. New York: Ballantine Books.

Seligman, M.E.P. (2006). *Authentic happiness: Using the new positive psychology to realize your potential for lasting fulfillment*. New York: Free Press.

Smart, N. (2000). *Worldviews: Crosscultural explorations of human beliefs* (3rd ed.) Upper Saddle River, NJ: Prentice Hall.

Smith, B. (1997). *Belief and resistance: Dynamics of contemporary intellectual controversy.* Cambridge, MA: Harvard University Press.

Smith, P. (1990). *Killing the spirit.* New York: Viking.

Snyder, C. R., & Lopez, S. J. (2006). *Positive psychology: The scientific and practical explorations of human strengths.* New York: Sage Publications.

Spirituality in Higher Education. (2003). "The spiritual life of college students: A national study of college students' search for meaning and purpose." Los Angeles: University of California-Los Angeles Higher Education Research Institute. http://www.spirituality.ucla.edu/spirituality/reports/FINAL_REPORT.pdf.

Steinle, J. (2005). *Upload experience: Quarterlife solutions for teens and twentysomethings.* Evergreen, CO: Nasoj Publications.

Sullivan, W. M., Rosin, M. S., Shulman, L. S., & Fenstermacher, G. D. (2008). *A new agenda for higher education: Shaping a life of the mind for practice.* San Francisco: Jossey-Bass.

Tarnas, R. (1991). *The passion of the western mind: Understanding the ideas that have shaped our world view.* New York: Harmony Books.

Taylor, C. (1991). *The ethics of authenticity.* Cambridge, MA: Harvard University Press.

Tillich, P. (1948). *The shaking of the foundations.* New York: Scribner.

Tompkins, J. (1996). *A life in school: What the teacher learned.* Reading, MA: Addison-Wesley.

Vaillant, G. E. (2002). *Aging well: Surprising guideposts to a happier life from the landmark Harvard study of adult development.* New York: Little, Brown, and Company.

Vaillant, G. E. (2008). *Spiritual evolution: A scientific defense of faith.* New York: Broadway Books.

Walker, G. E., & others. (2006). *The formation of scholars: Rethinking doctoral education for the twenty-first century.* San Francisco: Jossey-Bass.

Walvoord, B. E. (2008). *Teaching and learning in college introductory religion courses.* Hoboken, NJ: Blackwell Wiley.

Welch, S. (1999). *Sweet dreams in America: Making ethics and spirituality work.* New York: Routledge.

White, M., & Epston, D. (1990). *Narrative means to therapeutic ends.* New York: Norton.

Wiesel, E. (1958/2006). *Night* (Marion Wiesel, Trans.). New York: Hill and Wang.

Wuthnow, R. (1998). *After heaven: Spirituality in America since the 1950s.* Berkeley: University of California Press.

Yalom, I. D. (1980). *Existential psychotherapy.* New York: Basic Books.

Yalom, I. D. (2002). *The gift of therapy: An open letter to a new generation of therapists and their patients.* New York: Perennial.

Yalom, I. D. (2008). *Staring at the sun: Overcoming the terror of death.* New York: Jossey-Bass.

Index

THE STORM

What Went Wrong and Why During Hurricane Katrina—

the Inside Story from One Louisiana Scientist

IVOR VAN HEERDEN

and

MIKE BRYAN

With Field Sketches
by the Author

VIKING

VIKING

Published by the Penguin Group

Penguin Group (USA) Inc., 375 Hudson Street, New York, New York 10014, U.S.A.
Penguin Group (Canada), 90 Eglinton Avenue East, Suite 700, Toronto, Ontario, Canada
M4P 2Y3 (a division of Pearson Penguin Canada Inc.)
Penguin Books Ltd, 80 Strand, London WC2R 0RL, England
Penguin Ireland, 25 St. Stephen's Green, Dublin 2, Ireland (a division of Penguin Books Ltd)
Penguin Books Australia Ltd, 250 Camberwell Road, Camberwell, Victoria 3124, Australia
(a division of Pearson Australia Group Pty Ltd)
Penguin Books India Pvt Ltd, 11 Community Centre, Panchsheel Park,
New Delhi – 110 017, India
Penguin Group (NZ), Cnr Airborne and Rosedale Roads, Albany, Auckland 1310,
New Zealand (a division of Pearson New Zealand Ltd)
Penguin Books (South Africa) (Pty) Ltd, 24 Sturdee Avenue, Rosebank,
Johannesburg 2196, South Africa

Penguin Books Ltd, Registered Offices: 80 Strand, London WC2R 0RL, England

First published in 2006 by Viking Penguin, a member of Penguin Group (USA) Inc.

1   2   3   4   5   6   7   8   9   10

Copyright © Ivor van Heerden and Mike Bryan, 2006
All rights reserved

Maps on pages 70–71, 74–75, and 270–71 by Adrian Kitzinger

ISBN 0-670-03781-8

Printed in the United States of America

Designed by Nancy Resnick

*This book is dedicated to those who lost their lives during
Hurricane Katrina and to their families.*

*The book is also for the first responders, who unselfishly
did their best against the odds to save lives.*

*I also dedicate this book to disaster science researchers everywhere, who
follow their passion even under duress and never lose sight of the ball.*

*And finally, I dedicate this book to my mother, Ivy Phyllis Bebb,
who taught me to always stand by one's principles. She also taught me
the power of prayer.*

CONTENTS

Religion that God our Father accepts as
pure and faultless is this:
To look after orphans and widows in their distress
And to keep oneself from being polluted by the world.

James 1:27

THE STORM

DISASTER, TRAGEDY, FAILURE— AND HOPE

By eight o'clock Monday night, August 29—almost fourteen hours after the landfall of Hurricane Katrina—even I was tempted to join in the back slapping at the state's Emergency Operations Center (EOC) in Baton Rouge. Using every available megaphone, I'd been warning for years about the inevitable catastrophe that would befall New Orleans and southeastern Louisiana: a total drowning. So had all of my colleagues and many other scientists who had studied the lay of the land. It was bound to happen, sooner or later. It could have happened with Katrina, if she had tracked just twenty miles to the west and on a northwesterly course. Earlier studies using our now famous storm-surge computer model at LSU had showed that hypothetical catastrophe clearly. On Katrina's actual course, our model still predicted the flooding in New Orleans and in the parishes to the east and south, but most of these areas had flooded before, never disastrously. They could be drained quickly, with minimal permanent damage. On Monday night, this is what we thought.

Communications were suspect. After the National Weather Service office in Slidell, across Lake Pontchartrain from New Orleans, issued its warning at 8:14 A.M. Monday morning of a breach in the levee along the Industrial Canal, that office lost power. The office in Mobile, Alabama, then took over, but apparently the warning got lost. At the EOC, we knew that the Mississippi coastline to the east would have been essentially wiped out, but here's the blunt truth: Our attention was focused on New Orleans, and not simply because we lived and worked in Louisiana. Most—I would hope *all*—of the professionals in the center were aware of New Orleans's particular peril, and some had devoted a fair portion of their careers to studying the city's vulnerability, partly because it is a fascinating subject with life-and-death consequences. And now the Crescent City had apparently managed to keep its head above water once again; it would live to sweat out the next big storm. So it seemed at eight o' clock Monday night, and I was packing up to leave when a young staffer walked into our cubicle at the EOC and said he'd just picked up a call from a nursing home that had taken in two feet of water, and it had risen half a foot in just the last hour.

Fresh or saline? That was my first thought, because it's always the question about unwanted water in New Orleans. If it's fresh, it's rainwater—a normal flood; if salty, Lake Pontchartrain (which is actually brackish), and this might mean a serious breach of the lake-front levee system on the northern side of the city. We didn't have the results of the taste test in the nursing home, we didn't even know where that home was, but surely the Army Corps of Engineers, which had built the levees and whose cubicle in the EOC was right next to ours, would have known about a lakeside breach and somehow been able to spread the word. On the other hand, Katrina and the heavy rain were long gone. Why the rapidly rising water *now?* The tiniest little chill ran up my spine. But I had nothing to pin it on and no good way to find out much more, so at 9:30 P.M. I hit the road to join my family at our home twenty miles east of Baton Rouge. I had no idea what had happened out there in New Orleans.

But then, I *did* know. Driving home. Thinking again about that suddenly rising water. How could rainfall runoff possibly cause that flooding? It couldn't. There must have been a new breach in a levee. But surely the Corps would know about it! Surely their people and the local levee boards were monitoring every foot of the 350 miles of levees that protected the city from the Mississippi River and Lake Pontchartrain. But then, why had the Corps's staffers said nothing?

When the worst had been expected in New Orleans over the weekend, numerous officials had warned people who weren't leaving town to be sure they had an ax handy, because they were going to need it to chop their way out of the attic. They were trying to scare folks. Now their warning scared me. If there had been a major levee breach anywhere, thousands and thousands of people were going to bed in the dark, thinking the worst was over, and they would wake up in the middle of the night to a horrible discovery and be forced into those attics.

At my home, all was relatively secure—a few trees down, one close call, but no roof damage. With no electricity, land phone, cable, or Internet, with only spotty cell coverage, the isolation was almost complete—and welcome. I'd finally be able to sleep. But I couldn't sleep. I was thinking about those people scrambling out of the rising water—if they could scramble. The call had come from a nursing home. How were those folks going to *scramble* anywhere? Did the able-bodied have axes? Could they wield them? And would the attic be high enough? Would the *roof* be high enough? In the Lower Ninth Ward and parts of St. Bernard Parish, maybe not. Lying in bed, I envisioned the deaths of thousands.

I did finally fall asleep, and it was almost noon when I got in the trusty Xterra to drive back to the EOC. The sun was shining, the air was calm. Maybe I was wrong. Maybe the nursing home report was some kind of fluke. I turned on the radio for the latest—and my heart sank for good. Something terrible *had* happened with the levees on Monday, and no one had told us. Water was pouring into the city. Should I have turned around the night before and returned to the EOC? I'll ask myself that question for the rest of my life and reconcile my failure to do so with the knowledge that Monday night was much too late to spread the alarm—because there was no way to spread the alarm. Battery-powered radios could pick up a few channels, including locally famous WWL, but otherwise the city had been in the dark. With no electricity, everyone would have gone to bed.

As I drove to Baton Rouge, I began getting angry. As the days advanced, I got angrier. New Orleans had not even been the bull's-eye for this storm, which also had turned out to be less powerful than expected. Nevertheless, much of the city was going under, with the whole world watching in disbelief. How could the United States of America have left one of its crown jewel cities so vulnerable to a *pre-*

ventable disaster that I and many others had been warning about for years? How could this nation have been so unprepared for the aftermath? Hurricane Katrina was both a natural disaster and a systemic failure on the part of our society. Together, they produced tragedy.

This book is about both the storm and the failure—and the tragedy. I am a disaster science specialist and hurricane researcher who tends to wear his heart on his sleeve. I rarely hold my tongue. I rarely see any good reason to, and certainly not in this case. As a scientist, I champion a reality-based view of the world, old-fashioned as that may be, and marshy, swampy coastal Louisiana is the very definition of an inherently vulnerable landscape. It has always been susceptible to the ravages of hurricane winds, storm surges, and the invasive activities of a certain species of mammal (and I don't mean nutria). Large neighborhoods in New Orleans had flooded during Hurricane Betsy in 1965, and eighty-one folks had drowned. But then the Army Corps of Engineers beefed up the levees and there had been no other major flooding from storm surges in forty years—just the fairly regular flooding from the torrential rain the city expects several times a year. People had let down their guard. After all, New Orleans is—or was—the city that care had forgotten anyway. On the other hand, some of the local geographers and oceanographers and engineers and the like—you know, the pocket-protector crowd, as we were known before computers—started to suspect that Louisiana was not only more vulnerable to devastation than its citizens wanted to admit, but far more vulnerable *than it had been*, because the wetlands that buffer the inland zones, including New Orleans, were disappearing at an alarming rate. Restoring these coastal wetlands was one key to long-term alleviation of surge flooding, but could the state pull off such a complex endeavor requiring billions of dollars and the total commitment of the citizens.

In 1994, when I took over as head of the state's coastal restoration program, I decided to find out. My abiding faith was simple (and it still is): The catalyst to compromise is a thorough understanding of the science. Within eighteen months, however, I was gone and our new, comprehensive initiative was dead—details forthcoming, but which I can summarize here as the petty politics of junior bureaucrats who had the ear of the official decision makers and of politicians bearing grudges. Our plans for the vital coastal restoration fell apart, but we had to keep trying.

In 1998, Hurricane Mitch hit Honduras with the torrential rains and flooding that killed more than ten thousand people, left one million homeless, and caused massive damage to that country's fragile infrastructure. As it happens, then-president Carlos Flores is an alumnus of LSU; his wife a native of Louisiana. Prompted by some Honduran expatriates and Bruce Sharkey of LSU's landscape architecture department, Dr. Lynn Jelinski, the university's vice chancellor for research at the time, asked an ad hoc group of researchers to fly down to assess the situation. I was on that team, working for the Louisiana Geological Survey. Also on the trip was Marc Levitan, professor of civil engineering, premier "dynamic wind" expert, and a complete prince of a fellow. The Hondurans had great ideas but lacked the governmental support structure to make things happen. Traveling around the country, we found many ways that LSU could help, but we also found out, then and subsequently, that the "Beltway Bandits" with the good connections to the U.S. Agency for International Development were going to get all the work. Once again, a lot of American aid would mainly help certain corporations get on their feet, rather than help sort out some of the real issues in Honduras, where the poorest people of necessity live in the most flood-prone areas.

Marc Levitan and I had never met before this trip, but it turned out that we had a lot in common besides hurricanes. We are both turned on by applied research, stuff that's applicable to real-world problems. We both enjoy working with local and state governments as well as the chase for funding from some of the more "serious" sources. It also turned out that each of us had recently approached Lynn Jelinski with different but related ideas, Marc for a center to research hurricanes, me for one for applied sciences that would cover hurricanes, coastal restoration, and environmental issues. Over beers one night in Honduras, we decided to join forces. Jelinski represented a wonderful window of opportunity in the upper administration at LSU. Very early in her tenure, Jelinski, who had come to Louisiana from Cornell, could tell that the state had many challenging problems. She had great vision, and she understood the potential of applied science—an exception to the rule on campus. (In its quixotic attempt to become the Harvard of the Bayous, LSU does not give much respect to "applied" research. And there is almost a disdain for working with and for local agencies and governments.)

One year later the LSU Hurricane Center was a reality, with Marc the director and myself the deputy director. Marc has always stood by me when I've had my tiffs with LSU. He has never lost sight of the goals we set for our work. During every emergency he has always been a barrel of energy and an inspiration.

Shortly before the original hurricane center got rolling, Louisiana's Board of Regents was given tobacco settlement monies to set up a public health research trust fund. Along with many other suitors, of course, I and a multidisciplinary team of scientists from three different universities applied for funding to set up a sister institution to the Hurricane Center, one that would focus on public health issues related to the big storms. We were passed over in the first round because, we were told, our scope was too broad. I refined our proposal, focusing just on New Orleans, and the following year we received $3.65 million for five years. The Center for the Study of Public Health Impact, commonly known as the Hurricane Public Health Center, opened in 2002.

Each center is a "virtual" organization. We don't have a building. We don't even have a coherent suite of offices. We have only a group of dedicated scientists from many fields working to understand all aspects of a major hurricane strike on southeast Louisiana. What, exactly, would be the effects? What could we do to prepare for and mitigate them? For all of the alarms raised over the preceding years about the dire vulnerability of New Orleans, no group had analyzed the threat in all its complexity. This became our job. We are now known for the computer models that predict with astonishing accuracy the storm surge that can be expected from a hurricane of a given strength approaching any section of the Gulf Coast, but we have also studied problems with evacuation, public information, contamination (air, water, and soil), housing, stray animals, infectious diseases, the famous levees, and much more. We set out to demonstrate the incredible challenge of both preparing for the most dangerous storms and dealing with their aftermath. We always believed that both tasks would be exponentially more difficult than the emergency management establishment seemed to grasp. Our research supported this belief. Then Katrina proved the point.

As our work continued and our research was published and disseminated by all possible means, some people and organizations were willing to listen, some weren't. Among the latter was FEMA, the Federal Emergency Management Agency. In July 2004, the agency paid in excess of five hundred thousand dollars for an exercise in which numerous agencies at all levels of government worked for eight days on their response to a hypothetical hurricane that had catastrophically flooded New Orleans. The sorry story of "Hurricane Pam" has received some press coverage already, and it will receive more—in this book, if nowhere else. As much as we at LSU tried to get the latest and best science into the picture during this exercise, we were never really given an opening. I, specifically, was the foreign geek, the guy from South Africa with the odd first name and the odd last name and the odd accent. Such was my impression, fixed forever by the woman from FEMA I was trying to convince of the need to plan for short-term housing for hundreds of thousands of evacuees—tent cities, I called them. She sarcastically answered, "Americans don't live in tents." Okay, then, *McMansions,* but these people are going to need a roof over their heads! And so they did.

Immediately after the storm, I received permission to shift some of our funding from research about catastrophic hurricanes to an operational response to this particular one. Our new job was to provide services and expertise for the recovery effort. Our Geographic Information Systems (GIS) database—seventy categories of information, any combination of which can be layered on a map—was used by FEMA and other agencies as they scrambled to accomplish what they should have been well prepared to accomplish years earlier.

Landfall for Katrina was Monday morning. As the flooding in New Orleans spread on Tuesday and the pathetically inadequate response became more evident by the hour, my mood lowered. Along with some of my colleagues, I wanted to scream in frustration and, yes, in a bit of self-vindication, "We told you so!" On one of my first tours of the submerged neighborhoods I waded past a house in the Lower Ninth Ward in which the only possessions still above water level were the family photographs on a high mantelpiece. The water was fetid, the air was rancid, I had seen a floating body not a block away, and there, right in the middle of this apocalyptic disaster, was a surreal vision through the open window of gowned graduates, smiling brides and grooms, proud parents and grandparents, happy babies. For some reason, this was the scene in the stricken city that put me over the edge and broke my heart. Where were these people now? If even alive, what future did they have? How had they been served by their government? I felt I could and should speak for them, and I did.

As the director of the Hurricane Public Health Center and, more to the point, as one of the more notorious Cassandras of recent years, I was a pretty obvious target for the hundreds of reporters soon on the scene—print, radio, television, local, regional, national, international—who were also asking these questions on behalf of their audiences. In retrospect, I think I became a popular interview because I was (and remain) a straight-ahead guy who calls it the way I see it, and in this instance my call coincided with the conclusions the reporters were rapidly drawing for themselves. As the "natural disaster" story evolved into the "national disgrace" story, the reporters lost patience with the politicians and bureaucrats who spent the first five minutes of each press conference thanking all the other politicians and bureaucrats arrayed left and right for their great work. The reporters welcomed me as someone willing to state bluntly that some of those officials had failed in their responsibilities, that assorted government agencies had ignored years of excellent science, failed to heed warning after warning, failed to plan for the disaster, failed to act when it did happen, and, if the past is indeed prologue, would probably now fail to rebuild New Orleans properly and assure its safety from another catastrophe.

Suddenly I found myself on television all the time. On *Larry King Live* the first Friday night after the storm—my third night in a row on the show—I answered Larry's question about the failed response so far and then said, "We in Louisiana can only trust that our governor, and especially the president, are putting all the resources of the federal government and our *mighty military* to bear on this problem." I laid on the sarcasm in that final phrase, and, naturally, I like to believe that the arrival of the first large contingent of military helicopters the following morning was not coincidental. When I watched the scenes of white cops confronting at gunpoint groups of mostly black residents, I flashed back to startlingly similar scenes of apartheid South Africa, where I grew up and went to school. Don't get me wrong. I'm not drawing a straight analogy between apartheid in the 1980s and racial attitudes in my adopted state of Louisiana in 2005. I say only that some of the ugly scenes in New Orleans had undeniably racial overtones, and I got angry, and the anger helped me find fresh energy to press ahead and continue communicating the whole story.

Subsequently, as producers and reporters started to investigate the specific causes of the levee breaches that were responsible for *87 percent* of the flooding, by volume, in New Orleans proper, I didn't hesitate to point their efforts in what I was pretty sure was the right direction—that is, *not* the direction in which the Army Corps of Engineers was trying to lead everyone. Various Corps officials insisted for weeks that the storm surge from Katrina had overtopped and overwhelmed their Grade-A levees. Our team thought the levees had failed, plain and simple— *buckled*—for reasons we had to determine. Over the following months five groups conducted research into the issue: the University of California—Berkeley team funded by the National Science Foundation; the American Society of Civil Engineers (ASCE); the Senate Homeland Security and Governmental Affairs Committee; the Corps; and the state of Louisiana (led by our team at the LSU Hurricane Center). A consensus developed. Our team was correct. The truth did get out. I honestly didn't care whether making sure that it did cost me my job, and for a while it looked as if it might.

Over thirteen hundred citizens in Louisiana and Mississippi died due to Hurricane Katrina—the number as of February 2006, and certain to go up, perhaps dramatically, as the missing are reclassified. Six months after the storm, one hundred thousand families were still homeless. Some of those deaths and some of those dislocations were inevitable, because Katrina was a natural disaster. Others—the majority—were man-made. I don't see how we can avoid that conclusion. The levee systems failed inexcusably. We now thoroughly understand the need for coastal restoration as a buffer against the big storms, but land loss continues at an alarming rate. So what next? Should we clean up and rebuild New Orleans—to the extent even possible—if we then repeat the mistakes of the past? No, because the point overlooked in much of the Katrina media coverage is the fact that this hurricane was *not* the big one. I've learned that people don't want to hear this, because it makes them angry. But there it is. As Katrina *should have* affected New Orleans proper, she was decidedly a medium hurricane. Sometime in the foreseeable future a bigger storm will not take that last-minute jog to the east and every square foot of New Orleans—all of it, not just 80 percent—will be underwater, and deeper underwater than this time. Unless, that is, the right measures are authorized and funded immediately, then executed promptly and properly.

I don't like to see good science pushed to the sidelines just because it conflicts with narrow interests pushing their self-serving agendas. Such politics as usual helped to inundate New Orleans in 2005. If science and engineering had been allowed to play their proper role in the development of policies for the wetlands and the levees, we wouldn't be in this situation today. If nothing changes in the future, one fifth of the state of Louisiana—everything south of Interstate 10, including the city of New Orleans in its entirety—will disappear beneath the waves, gone for good, and we will have no one to blame but ourselves. Future historians will be writing books about the "Cajun Atlantis."

Hard as it is to believe, nature has actually given us a bit of a second chance. There's something left to work with in New Orleans. We must put aside the politics, egos, turf wars, and profit agendas if we're going to reconstruct this city effectively, engineer proper levees, and restore the buffering coastline.

This wedge of the continent has been changed forever, physically, economically, culturally. What will the new city be like? Will it become Nuevo Orleans (undocumented Mexican laborers are already the dominant cleanup force throughout the city, living ten to a room, conceivably to stay around and replace blacks as the dominant "minority"), or Six Flags Over New Orleans, or something else? And the former residents who can't afford a ticket to the new city, or just don't want one—where do they end up, and in what circumstances? These questions I can't answer. From my vantage pretty near the center of the story, I'll stick to those I can.

I am not a reporter. In this context, I am not even objective. What follows is not a diary or a recapitulation of events during the Katrina emergency. It is my assessment of how we got to this truly tragic moment—the story I have come to think of as the nearly perfect folly—and how we must proceed from here.

ONE

STORM CLOUDS

Despite their incredible power—Katrina generated energy equivalent to one hundred thousand atomic bombs on her journey across the Gulf of Mexico—hurricanes are actually quite fragile. For that matter, so are the bombs. The design and machining tolerances required to produce a blast instead of a squib are minuscule. Both the storm and the bomb are therefore living proof of the main tenet of chaos theory: Small changes in a system may have large consequences down the line. (Did a butterfly just flutter past my window?) We expect about ninety or so tropical storms to develop worldwide every year. In 2005, the Atlantic Basin alone produced a record twenty-seven tropical storms, with a record fifteen developing into hurricanes. The public asks why so many. Researchers wonder why so few.

Each system begins as a thunderstorm or group of thunderstorms, which are more or less ubiquitous in the tropical summer and common enough in what passes for winter. The reason is simple: The warm air rises, and as it rises it cools, and as it cools it can hold less water vapor, which therefore condenses into droplets of water, which then fall as rain. The condensation releases latent energy in the form of heat, which then reinforces the dynamics of the storm. The visible evidence is the cumulus and cumulonimbus clouds that presage or confirm the presence of thunderstorms. They are a daily affair—but then they're gone, because the storm has a built-in limiting factor: Downdrafts of cool, dry air from the heights block the system from drawing in enough warm, moist air from the surface to sustain the action. Thus the "heat engine" utilizes most of the available resources of heat and humidity within half an hour, perhaps an hour, and quickly fades into unwritten history, with the tourists immediately returning to the beach or the homeowner to the porch to enjoy the sunset. All of us who live along the Gulf or Atlantic coasts can loll away many a pleasant summer afternoon watching this physics lesson unfold (but not those who live on the West Coast, where summer is the dry season, because this region is dominated by cool maritime polar air masses that suppress the necessary convectional uplift over land).

In the late summer of 1989 I also lolled away some of those afternoons in the U.S. Virgin Islands, where I was studying the suffering coral reefs of the Buck Island National Reef Monument off the northeast coast of St. Croix, an environment about as tropical as tropical can get, as I learned on the very day I sailed into the port at Christenstead after the six thousand–mile voyage from South Africa. I'd left home with my sailing partner, Nan, six months before, and that's exactly how long I had—six months—to get the official U.S. port of entry stamp that would activate my green card, that wonderful document that is the initial step to acquiring U.S. citizenship. So the whole trip east across the South Atlantic and then north across the equator was a slow race against time (remember, a sailboat averages maybe 8 mph to 10 mph; a bicycle is faster—except on water). On September 19, 1989, a few days before we arrived in Christenstead and a few more days before I had to obtain my documents, St. Croix was hit hard by Hurricane Hugo, a Cat 4 storm (lingo for Category 4 on the famous Saffir-Simpson scale, on which Cat 5 is the strongest storm). I had no idea. South Africans rarely experience cyclones, as tropical storms that form over the Indian Ocean are called. (The exception was Cyclone Demoina, which struck the Zululand coast in October 1984. The winds were minimal but the rains were not; forty inches in twenty-four hours cost four hundred people their lives.) At Christenstead on St. Croix, what an unbelievable sight as we sailed in, with boats tossed everywhere and buildings destroyed. The *Maggie* seemed to be the only sailboat afloat in the whole harbor. Welcome to the United States!

Destruction or no destruction, I had my paperwork problem and had to find the immigration lady. I eventually did, and she was very helpful after I dragged a couple of chairs from the wrecked office and set them up on the wharf on a bright sunny day—as they usually are in the wake of a storm. The necessary forms were water-stained, but they worked. I was home free. The next day I took up temporary residence at the St. Croix Yacht Club, or what was left of it, which was very little besides lots and lots of stunned snowbirds. Soon I was living aboard the *Maggie*, a couple of hundred yards off the pier of the West Indies Marine Lab. I dived all day with some great folks, did good work, I believe, sipped Cruzan rum cocktails in the evenings, and shared potluck dinners with other cruisers. I had loved growing up in South Africa, but this life in the tropics was an unexpected dream come true. Still, all of us always had an eye on the weather and had checked out the available hurricane holes in which to stash our boats.

In order for a group of thunderstorms to organize into an official low-pressure zone—a "tropical depression"—some trigger must serve to alleviate the drying influence of the downdrafts. One such trigger can be an easterly wave floating westward across the Atlantic from the hot waters off the African coast. As many as one hundred of these can form every season, each a freestanding aberration in barometric pressure, a disturbance that can induce a group of thunderstorms to, in effect, wrap around themselves and thereby get something bigger going. The odds that any given cluster of thunderstorms will get organized are very low, but with two thousand clusters breaking out around the world every single day, why only ninety tropical storms in an entire year worldwide? As I said, these things are fragile.

The easterly wave floats along . . . still floating . . . one thousand miles . . . nothing happening, smooth sailing . . . but then, when conditions are just right—when the chaos is just right—this wave or maybe the tip end of a low-pressure trough or some other mechanism we don't fully understand (there are numerous candidates) gently pulls the trigger on the rapidly rising column of air at the center of the disturbance, which has a lower pressure than the surrounding air, and this low-pressure action sucks in more air, and this rapidly moving air evaporates seawater from the ocean, bringing still more moisture and heat into the system—the heat as a result of friction, both from the action of the wind on the water and from the molecules in the atmosphere rubbing against each other—and the planet below spinning toward the east induces a cyclonic, counter-clockwise rotation to the whole thing.

That's when the National Hurricane Center (NHC) in Miami takes official notice, and thus was a certain disturbance over the eastern Bahamas christened as the twelfth tropical depression of the 2005 Atlantic season, on Tuesday, August 23, 2005. Advisory #1 pinpointed the center near latitude 23.2 north, longitude 75.5 west—about 175 miles southeast of Nassau in the Bahamas. The depression was moving toward the northwest, with some strengthening likely. All interests in the Bahamas and southern Florida were advised to pay close attention, because further watches and warnings would probably be posted soon.

The NHC forecasters had very little doubt about the general direction this new depression would take. What a change from one hundred years ago—1900, specifically, when a hurricane with no name (these were not utilized until 1950) entered the Gulf of Mexico headed toward the northwest. The renowned Cuban hurricane researchers, whose tradition of excellence had been fostered in the local Jesuit community, had tracked this hurricane as it stormed along the length of their island and had predicted its track into the Gulf, but the American forecasters insisted it was 150 miles northeast of Key West and threatening the Atlantic Seaboard. Four days after these forecasters warned fishermen in New Jersey to stay in port, the storm struck Galveston 1,500 miles to the southwest, flattening that Texas beach resort and port, killing at least eight thousand people—the deadliest storm tragedy in U.S. history, and the subject of *Isaac's Storm*, by Eric Larsen, the most popular hurricane book ever published.

We can fault the American forecasters for their xenophobia about the Cuban team (even before Castro), but otherwise their ignorance just reflected the state of the art at the time. If a storm didn't leave a trail of firsthand reports as well as actual destruction while crossing the islands of the Caribbean or the Bahamas, forecasters had no way of even knowing where it was, or even *if* it was. This shortage of reliable information improved dramatically in 1909, with the introduction of the maritime radio, which allowed ship captains to alert forecasters to deteriorating local conditions. Given enough of these reports, forecasters might get a good idea about present location but still have no clue about destination. In 1944, the first reconnaissance aircraft flew into storms to take measurements, and at about the same time, radar, newly invented by the British in World War II, was able to pick up storms as they approached the coastline. In the 1960s, satellite images revealed storms in remote areas of the tropics, storms whose very existence might have escaped detection otherwise, and by the midseventies the geostationary satellites were beaming back tropical images every thirty minutes. Today satellites and reconnaissance aircraft measure (or estimate, in some cases) air pressure, temperature, humidity, and wind speed throughout a storm and the surrounding atmosphere. Forecasters do have a clue about a storm's destination—a very good clue.

Benjamin Franklin, of all people, may have been the first of us weather watchers to figure out that the big storms are independent phenomena with somewhere to go. I read the story in *Hurricane Watch*, by Bob Sheets, a former director of the National Hurricane Center, and Jack Williams, founding editor of the famous *USA Today* weather page, which single-handedly changed the way weather is reported in the United States. On October 22, 1743, stormy skies over Philadelphia blocked Franklin's disappointed view of a lunar eclipse. Weeks later, he was quite surprised to read in the newspapers that Bostonians had enjoyed a fine view of the phenomenon *before* that city had been socked in by the storm. How strange, Franklin thought, because the wind in Philadelphia on the fateful night had been from the northeast—the direction of Boston. How could the storm *from* the direction of Boston have hit that city *later* than it had hit Philadelphia? As Sheets and Williams tell us, it was seven years before this wise man revealed, in a letter, his theory of independent movement. He called it right. The storms do move independently, but they are embedded in the atmosphere and track in conjunction with the overall movement of that atmosphere, which in turn is often guided by powerful steering currents.

A key controlling factor for storms is the jet stream, a current of fast-moving air in the upper level of the atmosphere, usually between six and nine miles above the surface. It is typically thousands of miles long and a few hundred miles wide, but only a few miles thick, and as it shifts now to the south, now back to the north, it denotes the strongest contrast in temperatures at the surface—a cold front, classically. In the northern hemisphere, another major steering force is the overall east-to-west flow *at the surface* in the tropical latitudes, over both the Atlantic and the Pacific oceans. We know

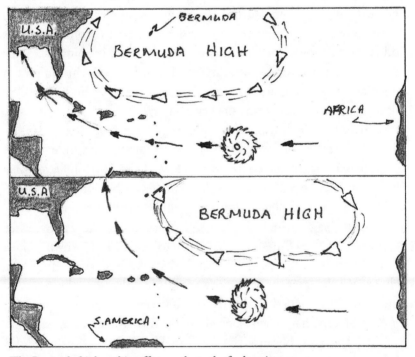

The Bermuda high and its effect on the path of a hurricane.

this flow as the trade winds, which sweep from the east and northeast across all of the islands of the Bahamas and the Caribbean.

Therefore it is essentially impossible for an Atlantic storm in the lower latitudes to move from west to east for any considerable distance or period of time.

The most important single steering factor in the North Atlantic is often the notorious Bermuda High, a zone or ridge of high pressure often parked—that's always the verb—over Bermuda, about seven hundred miles east of North Carolina. This midlevel subtropical ridge can shift east or west, north or south, and it can be larger or smaller than normal, stronger or weaker, but a high pressure of some sort is almost always parked somewhere off the Eastern Seaboard. By definition, such a high-pressure zone repels any low-pressure zone. Tropical storms forming off the coast of Africa may move almost directly north, passing harmlessly to the east of the Bermuda High, or they may head toward the west below it. What they will not and cannot do is plow right into that high-pressure zone. Often enough they track to the west, strike the U.S. coastline, then swing north and east in the higher latitudes and out over the North Atlantic. Or they may execute this sweeping loop around the high before reaching the seaboard. Or, if the high is situated relatively close to the U.S. mainland, the storm might be shoved into the Gulf of Mexico.

As it happened in 2005, three British friends of mine had started out in late June to cross the North Atlantic from Florida to the Azores in their thirty-five-foot sloop. I pitched in with remote weather routing. Using a marine Internet service that connects to ships via marine high-frequency radio signals, they e-mailed me each day with their latitude, longitude, and course. Each morning, I gathered all the relevant maps and satellite imagery and plotted a suggested course to maximize wind conditions. I also sent them a short weather summary and forecast. Specifically, they wanted to stay out of the Bermuda High, because there is very little wind in the center of that high, which is not much fun on a sailboat. Nor did they want to sail too far north and get caught in one of the low-pressure systems that spin off the Canadian landmass every week or so—definitely not much fun on a sailboat.

It's amazing how great communications at sea have become in recent years. On my cruise across the South Atlantic in '89, there was no Internet, and I couldn't afford any of the rather expensive and bulky marine shortwave radio systems, much less the satellite gear. So all we had was marine VHF radios, and even though the antenna was fifty feet high its effective range was about thirty miles, occasionally fifty miles. One day, however, that was good enough, as a massive supertanker heading for the LOOP oil facility just off the Louisiana coast overtook the little sailboat at 10 degrees west, 10 degrees south, as I recall. The skipper called us up on the VHF, wanting to know how we were doing and if we needed anything. He even offered us some steaks, but we'd just caught a nice mahimahi and said no thanks. He also offered to make some calls on his satellite telephone. What a surprise for our families to get this call from a rather British-sounding Captain Robertson of the SS *Leonia*, assuring them that the *Maggie* was within sight and all two aboard were doing well. This good captain took some photographs as his supertanker plowed past and kindly forwarded them months later. I still prize the picture of my well-trimmed little honey sailing along in the middle of the Atlantic Ocean.

As the Hurricane Katrina emergency unfolded, due in good measure to the lack of interoperability across the communications net— simply put, the first responders couldn't talk to each other—I thought about the ease with which I'd routed my friends across the North Atlantic, the ease with which Captain Robertson had made those satellite calls sixteen years earlier. But in 2005, in Louisiana and Mississippi, in the United States of America . . .

My friends' safe crossing to the Azores in June took about six weeks. For those same six weeks I watched the Bermuda High and everything else going on in the North Atlantic. The weather was great for the sailors, generally speaking, but what I saw was alarming as it related to hurricanes. The year before, four had hit Florida in a matter of weeks. The Bermuda High was pretty stable during that period—a big reason all of these storms tracked up and over the Florida Peninsula. Now, in 2005, the high seemed to be mostly west of its parking space the year before, suggesting that storms taking the southern route around this high would not—could not—start the turn to the north until they were deeper into the Gulf of Mexico. And so it had happened. On July 4, Hurricane Dennis formed up in the eastern Caribbean, tracked to the northwest, hit Cuba as a powerful Cat 4 storm, weakened but then reintensified shortly after entering the Gulf on July 6, then hit the Florida panhandle as a Cat 3. On the day that Dennis entered the Gulf, Hurricane Cindy hit southeastern Louisiana with 70 mph winds and a lot of rain. This storm had popped up in the northwestern Caribbean, crossed the Yucatán peninsula, and then moved straight north. (Initially categorized as a tropical storm at landfall, Cindy was upgraded to a minimal Cat 1 six months later. Ironically, Michael Brown, the soon-to-be-infamous head of FEMA, chose August 23, the day tropical depression 12 was born, to announce southeastern Louisiana's eligibility for federal disaster funds arising out of Cindy's floods.) And then came Arlene, Bret, Emily, Gert, and Jose—storms that had already crossed the Gulf of Mexico that summer, heading one way or another.

The NHC forecasters expected the new depression to move slowly northwestward toward a weakness in the Bermuda High. However, all of the computer models forecast that the high would fill the weakness and repair itself, in effect, within thirty-six to forty-eight hours. This action should drive the new depression westward across southern Florida and then into the eastern Gulf of Mexico within ninety-six hours—four days. It was a relatively easy call, and even with the first bulletin I thought, here we go again. The summer of '05 seemed to be our turn along the Gulf Coast. Hurricane activity tends to be cyclical anyway. The 1950s and 1960s were relatively active in the Atlantic Basin; the 1970s and 1980s a little less active; then business began to pick up again in 1995. Since that year, forty-two major hurricanes (Cat 3 or stronger) have developed over the Atlantic Ocean. To find a period remotely as active we have to go back almost fifty years, and there are reasons to believe this current active era could last awhile longer.

On Wednesday, depression number 12 could boast of sustained

surface winds of 39 mph, and it had therefore earned official tropical storm status. The previous one had been Jose, so this name would begin with K. That's all I knew (the lists are posted years in advance, but I don't study them) until 11:00 A.M., when advisory # 4 christened her Katrina. I know a French TV documentary producer (also a sailor) with that name, and she's pretty feisty. This was the image that came to mind when I saw the new name—a storm with lots of wild spirit. But I guess that's always the case with a storm. South Florida could expect landfall on Thursday, with an almost certain track across the state and then into the Gulf of Mexico.

At home, this nervous sailor started to check out the anchors, rodes, and shackles stored in the attic. I warned my wife, Lorie, that the track of this new one looked ominous. Let's start to get ready. Our well-rehearsed plan calls for loading the emergency gear on our small motorboat, then taking it and the *Maggie* from the marina just off Lake Pontchartrain up to my chosen hurricane hole on the Tchefuncte River, close to a cypress swamp. This plan also requires trips to the gas station, because we'd need lots of fuel for the cars, the motorboat, and the generator. (In Livingston Parish, with its wealth of forests—I say "wealth," although the urban sprawl is quickly decimating these wonderful stands of trees—we lose power with any kind of wind storm. The small generator has been a good investment.)

As an outdoors-type person who isn't outdoors often enough, I don't need much of an excuse to check out the weather and the weather maps, and during hurricane season, none at all. After putting a cup of English tea in the microwave, the first thing I do every dawn is to open any e-mail alerts from the National Hurricane Center. Then I go to the NHC Web page and review the five-day track forecast and the discussion paragraphs. I'm not a meteorologist, but I follow their technical talk easily. Next I go to HurricaneAlley.net, a private-subscription provider with excellent graphics, including the "spaghetti plot," which shows all of the predictions of the dozen different computer models, including some from overseas, superimposed on one map. This graphic can give me or anyone else an idea of how much confidence to place in the official five-day track forecast.

General agreement among the models gives me some confidence in the forecast track, but if the spaghetti plot lives up to its name, with the various forecasts showing a lot of spread, I may go to other Web pages, especially a site supplied by the Navy, and to the marine weather charts that are transmitted through the marine WeatherFax service from Coast Guard stations, also available on the Web.

In this way I formulate my own opinion about a storm, because I like to give our storm-surge modeling team at the Hurricane Public Health Center a few days lead time before we go operational. There are six of us on this team: a computer modeler, an oceanographer, a GIS expert, myself, and two graduate students. The computer whizzes needed two years to set up our computer model specifically for Louisiana and to adapt it to the requirements of LSU's Super-Mike supercomputer (named after either LSU's mascot Bengal tiger or former governor Mike Foster, who got the funding for the blazingly fast machine). I wouldn't want to say these storm-surge models are the most important work we do, but they are certainly the most visible to the public. They have put us on the map, that's for sure. In the case of Katrina, on Wednesday I advised the team and some people with various agencies that we would probably go fully operational either late Sunday or early Monday. This would be the signal to the handlers who groom SuperMike to alert other users they could be bumped from the queue. Our models need a lot of computing horsepower.

Katrina was expected to strengthen modestly, and that's just what happened. She was a Cat 1 storm with sustained winds of 80 mph when she hit Florida between Miami and Ft. Lauderdale at 6:30 P.M. Thursday and swept quickly across the peninsula. That same afternoon I had been on a conference call with EPA officials and some folks from the state concerning the bill introduced in Congress by Louisiana senator David Vitter that would allow—no, *encourage*—the mining of cypress trees. These cypress resources have been logged one time—the early 1900s—with predictably bad results. But cypress mulch is in great demand these days—for gardens—so the squeeze is on from folks who know—every one of them—that the cypress swamps are some of the best defense against storm surge we have in Louisiana. At the state level we wanted to make sure the EPA understood this value and therefore why this bill was so patently ridiculous. I couldn't believe we were even discussing this plan for desecrating the cypress swamps just as another hurricane was apparently on its way into the Gulf of Mexico, and I said so during that conference call.

But what now for Katrina? Thursday night is when it got really interesting for the forecasters and the rest of us, because the meteorological certainties that had propelled the storm across Florida fell apart; the Bermuda High now had competition for influence. At all times across the entire globe, areas of high and low pressure are scattered throughout the atmosphere, and all of them within hundreds of miles will play some role in the track of a hurricane—the butterfly effect, the chaos effect. Nor are these pressures and steering winds uniform at every altitude. Experience and computer simulations have taught us that the strongest steering currents of all, in most cases, are those between thirteen thousand and sixteen thousand feet, but others have an impact as well. Nor are the large storms entirely passive regarding the influences from the surrounding atmosphere. They influence the air mass in which they're embedded. Sometimes parsing the net effect of the numerous influences is pretty straightforward, and most or all of the computer models are in general agreement. Sometimes, though, they disagree wildly and the spaghetti plot is just that. Just one particularly large and powerful cluster of thunderstorms on one edge of the storm can apparently cause significant jogs in the track. How can any computer program account for such uncertainty? It can't.

Steering currents can also be so weak overall, or in such well-balanced conflict, that the storm dawdles, loops this way and that, doubles back, meanders. This was the case in 1960, with the very powerful Hurricane Carla in the Gulf of Mexico before she finally came ashore with ferocity in South Texas. (Carla is well known in broadcasting circles as the storm that gave us Dan Rather, who made his name on the national scene while reporting live from the seawall in Galveston for the local CBS affiliate.) In June 2001, the track of tropical storm Allison provided devastating evidence of what can happen with even a modest storm when no single steering influence dominates. Some researchers argue that Allison wasn't even a tropical storm, technically speaking. Regardless, this rainmaker caused many billions of dollars in damage from flooding—by far the most costly tropical storm in this nation's history—as it made landfall on the Texas coastline south of Houston, floated northward for about two hundred miles, stalled, floated back to the Southwest and returned to the Gulf at almost exactly the same spot it had come ashore four nights before. Then it made a hard left, hugged the coast toward the east before coming ashore again in central Louisiana, proceeded east-northeast directly across Lake Pontchartrain, across the southern states and up the East Coast—with bad flooding all along the way. By and large, the forecasters saw the problem shaping up, because the storm was tugged this way and that by competing subtropical ridges, one east of Florida, one west of Texas.

In Allison, a measuring station northwest of Houston recorded twenty-six inches of rain in ten hours; the Bayou City's bayous filled to record levels, then overflowed. One small section of the Louisiana coast received over twenty inches of rain. These are monsoon-type numbers. My neighborhood in Livingston Parish took on twenty inches of rain, and all the local creeks flooded—predictably, I should add, because the urban sprawl swallows the cheaper parcels of land—the upland wetlands—and the "concrete effect" becomes more pronounced. This term, I believe, is almost self-explanatory. As the sponge and water-soaking values of wetlands are replaced by the 100 percent runoff, antivalue of concrete, the flooding impact of any amount of rain necessarily gets worse. In some parts of Louisiana, the hundred-year flood level has been redefined more than once and is now more than two feet higher than it was just twenty years ago. My home is on a mountain, relatively speaking—forty-one feet above sea level—and it was almost flooded by Allison's rains. Without four-wheel-drive we would have been utterly marooned for three days. I have tried my best to inform the local drainage board about these perils, but it is obvious to me that developers have a stronger voice in these matters. Now that the Katrina tragedy may get the government to rethink its coastal wetland options in Louisiana, why not also take a lesson from Allison and rethink the destruction of *upland* and river basin wetlands? But I doubt this will happen. The mighty greenback drives a lot of bad decisions. (Here's a tip to all prospective home buyers in Louisiana: If the road on which you drive to reach the subdivision is elevated on its own seemingly innocuous little earthen levee above the surrounding terrain, the highway department may know something you need to know. Ask the developer some hard questions about the flood plain in this vicinity. Regardless of what you're told, you might think about building your house on stilts.)

On Thursday night some of the NHC computer models had Katrina turning quickly to the north and hitting the Florida panhandle with a tolerable blow, but others were scarier. They had it proceeding west into the Gulf, strengthening, and only then swinging to the northwest and threatening the coastlines of Alabama . . . Mississippi . . . perhaps even Louisiana. The main source of their disagreement was a low-pressure center over the Midwest, which would try to pull this powerful low pressure in the Gulf of Mexico toward itself. But pull how hard and how fast? Those were the questions, and I had more than a hunch about the answers. Earlier in the year weak Cindy had moved over New Orleans, Dennis off to the east, Emily to the west, Franklin, Harvey, and Irene north into the Atlantic, and Gert and Jose into southern Mexico with little punch. But now the Bermuda High looked strong and the Gulf looked weak, and I decided Katrina was coming our way. Plus, the Gulf was so warm fishermen had been joking that there was no need to cook the catch, even if you didn't like sushi. They were pulling the fish out of the water prebaked. After a meeting Thursday at the Louisiana Department of Natural Resources to share some ideas about mining offshore sands to restore our barrier islands, I had told the assembled group, "This one could have our name on it."

By Friday morning, the computers were providing corroboration. The Bermuda High was pushing Katrina well into the Gulf.

The spaghetti plot was sorting itself out. This lady was headed west and then, presumably, northwest, and then, presumably, north. Some strengthening was expected. So it was on Friday morning that the e-mails and phone calls started flying in the offices of the LSU Hurricane Center and the Hurricane Public Health Center. "Looks like we might be busy the next few days," Marc Levitan, the director of the hurricane center, wrote the team by way of classic understatement. Marc asked if we were ready to start running the storm-surge models. Without a drastic change of course, we'd start the new modeling on Saturday morning, with the first publication on our Web site that afternoon. I chimed in with a reminder to the users of that site not to broadcast the Web address to the public, because the ensuing demand would surely overwhelm our underpowered server and down we would go, slowly but surely. This had happened during Hurricane Ivan the previous year, when downloading just one of the animated movies of the surge models had required one hour or more instead of the usual three minutes. There were complaints. So just paraphrase the results this time, I begged. (My appeal actually worked. Our computer was able to keep up with the demand.)

The National Hurricane Center's official advisory for 11:00 A.M. Friday stated that the hurricane, still Cat 1, could become a Cat 2 by the following day. Wrong! It was a Cat 2 within hours, and the 5:00 P.M. advisory stated that now Cat 3 strength was possible by Saturday. As difficult as forecasting the storm track may be, forecasting intensity is manifestly and inherently more complex and fraught with the possibility of error. A notorious example among forecasters was Hurricane Kenna, which formed off the Baja peninsula of Mexico in late October 2002. Kenna was supposed to make landfall as a moderate storm. In fact, it became a Cat 5 storm and then hit the central Mexican coast as a Cat 4. This forecasting gaffe was the subject of much discussion at the national hurricane conference held in New Orleans the following April. As researcher James Franklin said, with a bit of exaggeration, perhaps, "We were only off by 110 mph. It would be hard to miss by more than that."

Kerry Emanuel, a researcher at MIT and the author of *Divine Wind*, a terrific coffee-table book about hurricanes, has laboriously compared the actual wind speeds of several hundred hurricanes and typhoons over the past forty years with the theoretical wind speed for that storm as determined by the theory of heat engines. Surprisingly, only 10 percent of the storms generated winds approaching 90 percent of the theoretical maximum. A majority did not generate winds even half as strong as they were theoretically capable of. In short, very few storms get the most out of themselves.

It's hard to become a storm, and apparently it's hard to reach maximum potential as a storm. "Something is holding them back," Emanuel writes. "Meteorologists suspect two main culprits." The most important of these is believed to be wind shear, which I'll define in simplest terms as any conflict between the direction of air flowing into the center of the storm at different altitudes. A wind coming from the east at five thousand feet and one from the west at ten thousand feet creates a lot of shear, which will probably have a weakening impact on the storm. Such conflicting winds may disrupt the symmetry of the counterclockwise circulation. They may also import cooler or drier air. The wrong strong winds aloft—thirty thousand feet, say, five or six miles up—may shear off the tops of the highest thunderstorms, definitely disrupting the efficient functioning of the heat engine. Decapitation, we call it.

Shearing factors are deemed one key reason the South Atlantic is the only equatorial ocean that produces almost no tropical storms at all. Those prevailing westerlies are closer to the equator than they are over the North Atlantic, shearing apart impending storms with great efficiency. In addition, the cold Benguela ocean current sweeps up the west coast of Africa from the Antarctic, so the waters feeding into the equatorial current just south of the equator are colder than their northern counterparts. The only exception to the rule within memory developed off the coast of Brazil in 2004. The Brazilians didn't even want to call this storm a hurricane, but our NHC was certain and therefore gave it a name: Catarina. Some climate-change scientists believe its appearance is a reflection of global warming. In a world made warmer by increased greenhouse gasses, the South Atlantic could be in for more tropical storms.

The second factor that apparently saps hurricanes of strength is the fluctuating temperature of the water over which they pass. The warmer the better for strengthening, of course, but the surface temperature of large bodies of water—oceans and their gulfs—will vary by several degrees. This doesn't sound like much, but small variations can and will make a big difference. I said that Katrina, on her journey across the Gulf of Mexico, generated energy equivalent to one hundred thousand atomic bombs. That's amazing, but how about this one: A temperature increase of just 1 degree Fahrenheit in the Gulf could generate the energy equivalent of *one million* atomic bombs. So temperature matters. So does depth. The topmost, warmest layer of water can be quite shallow—in much of the Gulf of Mexico, less than fifty feet. A powerful storm that churns the water enough to bring cooler water to the surface is thereby choking off the heat that it requires to grow or sustain itself. A hurricane will sometimes leave a trail of cooler water in its wake, which can be discerned by satellite imagery. It is not at all coincidental that hurricanes often strengthen over the western Caribbean, where the warmest layer of water can be over three hundred feet deep. It was here that Hurricane Wilma metastasized from a Cat 1 to a Cat 5 hurricane overnight (October 19, 2005), recording the lowest barometric pressure ever in an Atlantic Basin storm. Wilma then predictably weakened but still pounded the resorts of Cozumel and Cancún on the Yucatán peninsula before turning sharply northeastward and hitting the southwestern coast of Florida—all according to the forecasters' plan.

Had Wilma proceeded straight north into the Gulf of Mexico, she might have found the warm waters of the Loop Current conducive to maintaining her record strength. This odd feature of the Gulf has presumably played a critical role in the development of many storms. The Loop is, in effect, an extension of the famous Gulf Stream, whose main current flows north through the Yucatán Straits from the Caribbean, then swings immediately to the east, past the Florida Keys and up the Eastern Seaboard. It is a closed eddy that sometimes extends farther north into the Gulf of Mexico. Like the Gulf Stream itself, it is about twelve hundred feet deep, deep enough to prevent cooler water below from rising to the surface as the winds churn the seas. Some researchers have surmised that Hurricane Camille, which struck Mississippi in 1969 with winds of almost 200 mph, the highest hurricane winds ever recorded on the continent, must have proceeded right up the spine of a perfectly positioned Loop, ingesting new energy every mile of the way. On the other hand, that can't be the whole story with Camille, because other storms have passed over the Loop and not strengthened at all. In 2005, Katrina certainly benefited from the Loop, which extended almost all the way to Louisiana in late August.

For the computer modelers, however, the basic problem with water temperature is that the specific number is simply not known for wide areas of the ocean at different depths, and it is financially and logistically infeasible to sow the thousands of bathythermographs necessary to collect this data. The utility of satellites is limited, because only the first few meters of the ocean reflect light or infrared waves. Coming on-line right now are exquisitely sensitive altimeters that can measure the level of the sea to within a few inches, thus providing information about the thermal structure beneath, but, by and large, the computer modelers have no choice but to use broad assumptions about temperature based on prior experience, time of year, and whatever measurements are at hand. Theoretically, a slower storm will churn up a given area of water more completely, therefore more likely bringing cooler water to the surface and hindering any strengthening, but can you reliably account for this factor in a computer model? It's tough. Researchers often resort to SWAG, or "scientific wild-ass guess." And even if completely accurate temperature data were available, no one can pin down with precision the exact impact of water temperatures on the overall system. Therefore the predictions are often fraught with error.

Like Kenna off the Baja peninsula in 2002, the puzzling case of Hurricane Lili the same year demonstrates just how tough predicting intensity can be. Twelve hours from landfall, NHC forecasters predicted a strike on the central Louisiana coast as a Cat 4 storm pushing a twenty-foot surge. Our LSU storm-surge models, which had just come on-line, predicted thirty feet of surge and, obviously, serious flooding west of the Atchafalaya Basin. But then Lili came ashore as a much weaker Cat 1, with a surge of only eleven feet. In the post-mortem, the forecasters studied a jet of drier air moving into the region—and therefore into the storm—from the west. They had believed this drier air would be entrained into the storm, but they underestimated its impact. A second factor was probably the passage of Hurricane Isidore across the same section of the Gulf just a week earlier. Isidore had seriously weakened over the Yucatán and was only a tropical storm at landfall near Grande Isle, Louisiana, but he left stirred up and presumably cooler waters in his wake. In addition, runoff from Isidore's inland rains would have still been pouring into the Gulf along the Louisiana coastline—water several degrees cooler than the main body of water. Only in retrospect did all become clear—or clearer.

As for Katrina, her strength exceeded expectations almost by the hour on Friday, and with each passing hour the excitement mounted for hurricane watchers all along the coast. This is an interesting aspect of human nature, of course: the bigger the storm the worse the damage, but the bigger the storm the greater the thrill. For professionals, the biggest storms get the juices flowing. That's a fact. You can see it with every weather forecaster on television. They want a monster, and they're disappointed every time the beast drops a notch in the category rating. It's human nature. In our various offices at LSU, calls poured in from around the state. What did we think? They always seem to veer away—what about this time? Is it really going to intensify? Could this be *it*?

Yes, this could be *it*. We could be in big trouble on Sunday night, maybe Monday morning. That was my (and everyone else's) conclusion by early Friday afternoon as I studied the spaghetti run on the HurricaneAlley Web site (not much spaghetti, lots of agreement), checked the various weather sites, and considered the National Hurricane Center's five-day forecast. I told the SuperMike team that starting the following morning we would need access to the full array of processors, and I told the investigators on a landfill matter with which I was involved, who were due in court for a hearing on

Monday, that they would be picking up bodies instead. Governors Kathleen Blanco of Louisiana and Haley Barbour of Mississippi declared states of emergency. The state Homeland Security officials in charge of the emergency operations center in Baton Rouge prepared to go operational. Late that night at home I loaded the motorboat with the anchors and the rodes. The next morning Lorie and I would roll out for the hurricane hole on the Tchefuncte River.

LEAVE, PLEASE!

A t 4:00 A.M. Saturday morning, the track for Katrina in the Gulf of Mexico still looked bad. Nothing good for New Orleans had happened over the previous five hours, and nothing good was expected to happen over the next five or ten. If this storm didn't hit the city dead on, it was probably going to come awfully close. I called Hassan Mashriqui, our storm-surge modeler. Was he ready? He was ready. Of course. Mashriqui (we always call him by his last name) knows full well the importance of these surge models.

In its simplest terms, the storm surge is the vast mound of water generated by the high winds of the storm (there are other factors, but the winds are the main one) and pushed across the open sea, and with most storms this surge accounts for the most catastrophic damage. (Andrew in Florida was the outstanding exception in recent years: that was all wind.) In tandem with the models used for forecasting hurricanes, the ones that predict the surge have revolutionized our understanding of storms and our ability to prepare for them.

From our perspective at the LSU Hurricane Center, the story of the surge models began in the early 1990s, when I worked with two excellent scientists and great guys, Paul Kemp and Joe Suhayda, on some early computer modeling designed to predict the synergistic benefits of rebuilding our barrier islands in tandem with our wetlands, all in order to save our state. Paul and I had been graduate students together in the since disbanded Department of Marine Sciences at LSU. That was in the late seventies and early eighties. Both of our projects—mine on the evolving Atchafalaya Delta southwest of New Orleans, his on the chenier coast to the west—were very field-time demanding. We spent thousands of hours out on the marshes, in the brutal, humid heat of the summer and on winter days that can be just as brutal on the other end of the scale. (This fact really surprised me, my first year on the scene. I would never have imagined that the Atchafalaya in winter is just above what we call "melt ice" temperature. It's cold water.) Paul is incredibly smart, both as a scientist and as someone who can read a situation. He also has a heart of gold and is willing to fight for the underdog—my kind of guy—and since we are both about the same size and stature and have fair, curly hair, we've been referred to as "the terrible twins." So be it. I'm proud to stand side by side with this comrade-in-arms.

Coastal engineer Joe Suhayda directed the Louisiana Water Resources Research Institute at LSU. A longtime faculty member, Joe was one of the very first of us to sound the alarm about the peril of New Orleans, and he had the great idea of taking film crews into the French Quarter, where he would hold up a long surveying rod to indicate how high the water would be in the worst flood—way past the wrought-iron railings of second-story balconies. (Joe has also put forth the idea of creating a "community haven" with a two-story wall that would seal off the French Quarter, downtown, government buildings, a hospital, and some housing. I have never been a fan of this approach, and I believe its drawbacks have been precisely illustrated in the events of August 2005. The sections of the city that would be protected by Joe's wall are, for the most part, the sections that stayed dry during Katrina. The exception is downtown, which had several feet of water during Katrina and would have been inside the haven. Yet look where New Orleans is at this writing: culturally and economically crippled. I think we have to protect the whole city.)

In the early nineties Joe, Paul, and I were having a problem convincing "the agencies" of the value of restoring the barrier islands. Some of those agency folks even argued that the barrier islands were not eligible for federal restoration dollars because they were not vegetated wetlands, an argument that incensed the three of us. They even invented some scheme to determine the wetlands benefit of proposed projects that totally ignored the reductions in wave impact provided by healthy barrier islands. They also ignored the reduction in storm surges and tides provided by healthy barrier islands. This was simply crazy. Not long before—August 1992—Hurricane Andrew, primarily remembered for the incredible wind damage inflicted on the towns south of Miami, with 125,000 homes seriously damaged or destroyed, had also ripped into Louisiana as a less dangerous but still potent Cat 3 storm. Fortunately it struck a relatively sparsely populated area on the central coast, where the wetlands are their healthiest, expanding even ("prograding," as we say). Damages in Louisiana amounted to $1 billion ($35 billion in Florida, second only to Katrina). This was serious damage, but it could have been much worse. Thanks to the healthy wetlands the storm surge was only eight feet. Eight hours after Andrew's landfall, I flew the coast with well-known Louisiana coastal oceanographer Shea Penland. The damage to wetland areas under stress from bad management was much worse than the damage to healthy marshes. Anyone could have seen the difference.

So-called wetlands scientists should have been able to understand that the barrier islands also help the wetlands, but they didn't. Joe, Paul, and I wanted a good computer model that could prove the benefits of the islands. Surge models had been around for a quarter century, when Chester Jelesnianski of the U.S. Weather Bureau (as it was still called at that time) developed SPLASH (Special Program to List Amplitudes of Surge from Hurricanes). This model scored an immediate triumph, predicting the devastating surge that accompanied Hurricane Camille in 1969. Jelesnianski then developed SLOSH (Sea, Lake, and Overland Surges from Hurricanes), which is still in use by the National Oceanographic and Atmospheric Administration (NOAA) and other agencies. Joe Suhayda had been working with a FEMA model that the agency used to calculate flood risk for insurance rates, and we rounded up thirty thousand dollars from the late Terrebonne Parish engineer Bob Jones, who believed as we did: the islands matter. The main town down there is Houma, and the marshes to the south are as ripped up as any in the state. Our idea was to use the computer to compare what the tides did to these marshes with and without the barrier islands offshore. If the models showed what we thought they would, we could really create on-the-ground value for restoration. And the models did show this value. Irrefutably. With happy faces we took the work to a meeting in Lafayette, where I, at least, was amazed to confront a group of agencies who were proudly armed with a long treatise about why computer modeling was no good, period. The U.S. Fish and Wildlife Service led the way in this obstructionism. I really thought I was in the Third World—no disrespect intended toward those nations. South Africa, for one, was light years ahead of us in terms of computer models. This attitude in Louisiana, in the United States, in light of SPLASH and SLOSH, was ridiculous. I got quite angry and frustrated, but Paul Kemp showed his mellow mettle yet again, stepped into the foray with his typically pleasant, disarming demeanor, and after an hour had convinced the agencies to take a fair look at our work.

That was the first use in Louisiana of surge models. Two years later, in 1994, then-governor Edwin Edwards appointed me to run the state's coastal restoration program, a story I'll relate later as part of the much larger story of the checkered history of wetlands protection in our state—an all-important subject if you want to understand how Katrina clobbered New Orleans. As was the case so often in those days, the team from the Environmental Protection Agency understood which projects made ecological sense, and restoring barrier islands definitely made the grade. Most of the academics also understood, but the U.S. Fish and Wildlife Service was still against us, and so was the Army Corps of Engineers, because we were the new guys with the new agenda. I wasn't going to let their obstruction stop me. I was going to make sure science got into the picture, and science, have you heard, *uses computers.*

The coastal restoration program could "sole source" contracts up to about fifty thousand dollars, so Paul Kemp got money to further develop a river basin model; Joe Suhayda got funding to get his first surge models operational; and a young Irish scientist at LSU, Gregory Stone, got some funding to set up a wave model for the Louisiana coastline. A decade later, modeling has become the rage, as well it should have. I like to believe that being a little hardheaded and at the same time resourceful paid dividends. I'll even argue that the funds I sole sourced to those three scientists may have been the best investment the state government has ever made. (Of course, some jaded observer of the local political scene will quip that the competition hasn't been very tough.)

In 2001, when I was trying to secure the funding for LSU's Hurricane Public Health Center, I cast around for what I thought would be the best surge model for both planning and operational support. I knew we needed this element in our package of features. Joe Suhayda was getting ready to leave LSU, and his low-budget model was neither the latest nor the best. I soon decided that the latest and the best was the ADCIRC model developed by Dutch-born Joannes Westerink, a professor of civil engineering at Notre Dame, and Rick Luettich, of the University of North Carolina. Both are geniuses at computational fluid dynamics, and their model is, for our purposes, without a peer. The acronym stands for "advanced circulation." The other widely used model, SLOSH, is excellent for its purposes, but somewhat limited when compared to ADCIRC, which works at a higher resolution, in effect—an almost infinitely fine resolution in theory, and much finer in fact. This is an important advantage when dealing with areas such as New Orleans, where small-scale features can have huge consequences, as we shall see. ADCIRC is also much more adept at simulating convoluted shorelines and incorporating features like highways and canals that can block—or accelerate— storm surge. ADCIRC can include tides (though it doesn't for our predictions right now); SLOSH cannot.

ADCIRC is a vastly complex mathematical and computation engine—just as complex as the programs for predicting a tropical storm's course and intensity. I am not a modeler, but I can appreciate the beautiful science. The equations in the model work their magic with data pertaining to the storm itself—position, track, wind speed at the surface (extrapolated, in most cases), and barometric pressure—and to the bathymetry of the seafloor and the topography of the floodplain (including bays, rivers, and significant obstacles). From a numerical standpoint, things get very sticky as the water front advances and retreats. The model must "wet" areas that start out dry, and vice versa. The water coming down rivers such as the

Mississippi and the Atchafalaya is a considerable factor. Vegetation is very important: Obviously, densely packed cypress trees offer more resistance to the surge movement than low-lying salt marsh grasses, and these grasses offer more protection than open water, which offers none.

Most of the model's data is organized in a grid that establishes the computation points. (An equivalent computation grid is set up for the models that forecast storm track and intensity.) In the surge model, the grid over the open ocean might be 25 kilometers (15.5 miles) on edge; that is, a computation point every 25 kilometers. On the continental shelf, the resolution gets finer as the grid tightens to 5 to 10 kilometers. In the most populated areas of the Louisiana floodplain, it tightens even more, getting as small as 100 meters, a level of detail that is critical for us, because we depend on both natural and artificial levees (including raised roads and railroads) for defense against the surges, and we can account for these with ADCIRC. By comparison, Joe Suhayda's old model worked with a grid only 1 kilometer (0.6 mile) on edge.

Our current model, ADCIRC S08, yields a grid with exactly 314,442 computation nodes. S10, under development, will have a finest resolution of 60 meters, for a total of 602,254 nodes. S20 will have a resolution of just 20 meters, or 2.7 million nodes—quite a number-crunching challenge. The modelers use hindcasting to perfect the program. Dozens of flood gauges are positioned throughout southern Louisiana, accurately monitoring the exact water height at each one. Location by location, ADCIRC compares the actual record with the computed, predicted level. Discrepancies are investigated and the explanations incorporated into the program. The programmers learn from the mistakes and improve the program.

How many lines of computer code run ADCIRC? I'm told that this common question can't really be answered with a single number, but when pressed to produce one that won't be totally misleading, just for the benefit of a colleague writing a book for the general public, our modeler, Hassan Mashriqui, answers—guesses—fifty thousand. This code takes an official advisory from the National Hurricane Center, unites it with the stored bathymetry and topography data, and produces a brilliantly colored graphic representing the expected surge for the particular advisory. That's the gist of it. The simulation takes two and a half hours on SuperMike, one of the world's fastest supercomputers, but the modeling team requires at least five hours to display the results on the Internet, because of all the pre- and postprocessing of data. (The potential for providing operational support during hurricane emergencies was one of the main reasons cited to legislators by Governor Mike Foster for building SuperMike.)

We send the ADCIRC outputs to a large listserve of emergency management officials at every level of government, nongovernmental organizations (NGOs), and the media. A version of the model is also used by the Corps for designing its levee system. (More to come on this subject, of course.) The Louisiana Department of Natural Resources uses it for studying coastal restoration projects.

As with all computer programs, the old adage "garbage in, garbage out" pertains to ADCIRC. Once we had the model, we needed the team to put it into effective action for Louisiana. I call these folks the "LSU surge warriors." First on-board was the main builder, Joannes Westerink (working long-distance from Notre Dame), then Paul Kemp, our oceanographer, and Mashriqui, whom I've known since he worked as a graduate student under Paul. I was immediately impressed by the polite fellow from Bangladesh with a very thorough understanding of computers, both software and operating systems, as well as hydrologic engineering, his academic background. Like Paul, Mashriqui has a heart of gold and is willing to fight for the underdog. Over the past decade, he, Paul, and I have worked on numerous projects together, including the saga of the Wax Lake weir, yet another aspect of the important wetlands question I'm holding for future discussion. The minute Mashriqui got his Ph.D. I hired him as an adjunct assistant research professor in the research center.

Then we have graduate student Young Souk Yang from South Korea; Ahmet Binselam from Turkey, an absolute whiz at geographical information systems; George Eldredge, a former student worker of mine, now a computer tech in the College of Engineering; and Kate Streva, a research associate who makes everything happen, and who was pregnant in her third trimester during Katrina. (Edan is the beautiful baby's name.) Early on, we also got great help from Jesse Feyen, one of Joannes's former students, now with NOAA. Tom Berg, whom I've never met in person, is also a fine friend. Tom runs the HurricaneAlley.net Web page. In return for free access to that subscription service we provide him with our surge-model outputs. In this way we get around the problem posed by our small server and can reach beyond the emergency management professionals who are our main "clients." In past years, when we needed more detail on model outputs and tracks, Tom always went out of his way to send those.

Notice that about half of the surge warriors are not American-born, and no surprise. This is where we're at in this country today. More and more of the faculty and the majority of graduate students in engineering and physical sciences are from foreign soil, and not just at LSU, everywhere in the United States. American kids are not that interested in long, demanding graduate programs that don't guarantee riches in the end. I think MBA programs may be sucking more than their fair share of the best students away from the sciences and engineering.

All of the surge warriors work on "soft money" (short- and long-term grants and the like), which makes us second-class citizens in the academic world, with no prospects for tenure. I'm jumping ahead here, but on day four of the Katrina emergency—Thursday—an important administrator at LSU told us that the operational support we were providing an array of agencies was okay, but what really turned him on was *federal dollars*, especially from the National Science Foundation. These make him really happy. I was flabbergasted at his timing. None of us in the room had had much sleep for a week (and would not get much sleep for many more weeks). No one was getting paid for providing this operational support. No one had been paid during the many previous emergencies. One of our many tasks was mapping 911 calls for the first responders, and on the next day, Friday, seventy-eight people were rescued from their attics based on our mapping. These were people who most likely would have died otherwise. And this guy was signaling that the university doesn't value what we were doing? There were some despondent and angry folks following that little pep talk. Marc Levitan and I had to go around and lift some spirits.

The man's general drift is also a sore point with me, as I've hinted earlier. Not that we don't need to study the umpteenth black hole a trillion trillion miles away. We do, but we also need the vision to see what society needs by way of practical science. A balanced view on research is lacking at many universities obsessed with competing for the big brownie points, where upper administrators' egos and boasting rights are more important than solving problems to the benefit of society at large. You would think that our work before, during, and after Katrina might have turned some heads at LSU, but not really. Witness the confession by the administrator. Witness the gag order placed on me by the school during the levee investigation a couple of months later (soon rescinded with apologies).

Before dawn on Saturday, August 27, I called Mashriqui. Were we certain that the university had cleared the way on SuperMike for the hurricane queue? Yes. The polite e-mail to that effect, addressed to all users, was time-stamped "2:32 A.M." (Someone else couldn't sleep, I guess.) Kevin Robbins, who runs the Southern Regional Climate Center and heads LSU's team at the emergency operations center in Baton Rouge, had e-mailed me minutes earlier asking that we run advisory #16, then #17. Kevin was as worried as I was about this storm; he wanted as much information as he could get. Mashriqui was worried. Everyone was—and everyone already seemed to be awake. The e-mails and phone calls were flying.

During the Hurricane Ivan emergency the year before, we had run two models at the same time, one using the track right down the middle of the National Hurricane Center's forecast cone of uncertainty, the other the track on the western edge of the cone. This was because the cone for Ivan kept sliding to the west as he churned across the Gulf, and we wanted to make sure that if the storm did take the most westerly track, we'd be ready with flood forecasts for New Orleans and vicinity. As it turned out, the models never showed flooding in the city, and there was never the fear in our offices that Katrina brought out. For Ivan, the city was evacuated based on the advisories coming from the NHC. In the end, after a long career of two-plus weeks in which it achieved Cat 5 status three different times—a record for an Atlantic storm—Ivan ended up hitting the Alabama shoreline as a Cat 3.

I felt that we would want to do the same thing for Katrina, running both the main track forecast and the western edge of the cone. We might also have more than one advisory running at the same time, so at 6:10 A.M. I sent another e-mail to the SuperMike folks: "This is an absolute emergency, we need all the nodes we can get, PLEASE." We got them. Katrina was starting to look like a monster; she had us in her sights. Even the computer geeks sensed this! Before long I e-mailed the NHC, because I had heard that they have a good draft of the advisory ready about an hour before it's released to the public. If they could e-mail that early draft to us, maybe we could save an hour. They didn't respond immediately—they were superbusy themselves, of course—and later I learned that they wouldn't have wanted to give us that draft anyway, because they make changes right up to the last minute.

Advisory #17, issued at 10:00 A.M. Saturday morning, put the center of Katrina 200 miles west of Key West, 405 miles southeast of the mouth of the Mississippi River. Movement was westerly, with an expected curve to the west-northwest. Sustained winds were approaching 115 mph—Cat 3—with strengthening anticipated. Cat 4 status was likely—that is, winds over 130 mph. At the office the e-mails and phone calls and media requests *poured* in. Who can catch AP? Who has time for NBC?! CNN wanted "people who can speak specifically to the issue of evacuation." Brian Kennedy, a producer for ABC, wrote, "I hope this note finds you well. We spoke last year around the time of Hurricane Ivan. . . . What may I ask will you and your team be doing in the next day? Are you available for an interview wherever you may be? We are in New Orleans." Okay, along with forty more that day, literally. The media had called us during Ivan, but now they really had our number. The drama was building, and maybe they could also sense the tragedy that was about to unfold. They asked, we answered.

When were the authorities in New Orleans going to evacuate the city?! The ADCIRC surge models were already scary. At 12:45 P.M. Mashriqui e-mailed the results of the first run, the one based on advisory #16, and added: "Note: Water gets in New Orleans from the Airport side. Very close and likely to overtop from every side." Ahmet Binselam immediately started to put the data on our Web page. Three minutes later I sent a note to Mark Schleifstein of the *New Orleans Times-Picayune*. There will be some flooding, I said. He was not surprised. In June 2002, the newspaper had published his and reporting partner John McQuaid's "Washing Away," a five-part series on the danger faced by New Orleans. The series won the Pulitzer Prize, and justly so. No one in any position of authority in the city of New Orleans or the state of Louisiana or the United States of America had any further excuse for underestimating what the city would someday face—and was now facing, in fact, barely three years later. (A decade earlier, the *Baton Rouge Morning Advocate*, as it was called before it dropped the *"Morning,"* had raised the same alarm with its series "Ill Winds," written by Bob Anderson and Mike Dunne, which covered hurricane preparedness along the entire Gulf Coast and won an award from the American Academy for the Advancement of Science.) I explained to Mark that he should ignore the flooding out west by the airport—in the model, a section of the levee in that area was lower than it actually is—but concentrate on the fact that the surge would be up to the tops of the levees, and there would be erosion and overtopping. Things were not looking good. Mark has a very matter-of-fact voice, but I could hear a slight rise in tone as he digested the news.

Shortly after three o'clock Saturday afternoon Mashriqui produced model #17, with the same upshot as the previous one. I immediately forwarded the results to every official at every level of government I could think of, and I added, "PLEASE NOTE. While the output does not show the city flooded our model assumes a uniform height for the levees around Lake Pontchartrain. . . . these surge heights will top the levees in some locations. In addition, we do not at present factor in the waves. . . . So please do not be swayed by the fact that the model does not show water in the city, it will get in. . . . PS the key is evacuate, evacuate." Landfall was about thirty-six hours away, maybe a little longer. I wondered why they hadn't ordered the mandatory evacuation of New Orleans. We were going to run out of time. Two hours later, in a note to Steve Lyons of the Weather Channel, I amended my assessment of model #17, pointing out that some levees assumed to be 14 feet above sea level are in fact only 11.5 feet. These will be overtopped, I told Steve. Pounding waves will induce erosion along the south shore of the lake—"a major factor." I concluded, "Basically, there will be a whole lot of flooding." When I'd met Steve earlier in the year I had asked him to always stress evacuation when reporting on any storm headed in the direction of New Orleans. In a new note to Mark Schleifstein of the *Times-Picayune* I wrote, "The bottom line is this is a worst-case scenario and everybody needs to recognize it. You can always rebuild your house, but you can never regain a life. And there's no point risking your life and the lives of your children."

Many days later we learned that Michael "Brownie" Brown, FEMA's head, wrote in an e-mail on Saturday, "This one has me worried." No kidding. Then Brownie expressed the wish that Jeb Bush were governor of Louisiana. What's really sad about this lame quip is that he may have been right, in a way. Just think. If someone with the clout of the president's brother had been the governor of Louisiana at some point over the past three decades, the levees protecting New Orleans and vicinity might be sound, and the swamps and marshes and barrier islands might have been restored with the thick grasses and plants and trees that serve as excellent storm buffering. That is to say, Louisiana might have seen something approaching the money that the federal government is pouring into the Everglades right this minute. The health of that famous river of grass is definitely important, but it's not life and death.

At 5:00 P.M. Saturday, Mayor Ray Nagin joined Governors Blanco and Barbour—and President Bush—by declaring a state of emergency. At the same time he issued a *voluntary* evacuation order, and added that it might become mandatory after his legal team determined the legality and wisdom of this act. One concern was the city's liability if they forced hotels and other businesses to close. I thought, Oh, come on, just do it! Nagin and everyone else in the business knew about the census number: 127,000 residents of New Orleans don't have cars. "This is not a test," the mayor said. "This is the real deal." He mused about the return of the swamp creatures, about a city underwater for two weeks, about a city that might never be the same again.

Mississippi county emergency managers, based on advice from the state, had already issued mandatory evacuation orders for their coastline, and parish emergency managers in Louisiana had done the same for the most vulnerable areas in Plaquemines, Jefferson, St. Bernard, St. Charles, and St. Tammany parishes. Residents had been leaving the imperiled lowlands farther south along the coast in moderate but steadily increasing numbers since Wednesday. They knew better than anyone that many of their communities were virtually certain to be underwater on Monday, no matter how Katrina might shift her track in the meantime. They didn't need storm-surge models to tell them this. The Mississippi River would become fifteen miles shorter. (It's true: Those last miles of the river's already ragged delta would be completely overrun by the surging Gulf of Mexico.)

Thirteen years earlier, on August 25, 1992, a mandatory evacuation had been ordered for the Morgan City region along the central Louisiana coastline only twelve hours before the arrival of Hurricane Andrew. The traffic jams were predictable; many people did not get out. Fortunately, they lived anyway. "It's a wake-up call!" emergency-preparedness officers proclaimed in the aftermath, and the following year the state legislature passed the Emergency Assistance and Disaster Act, setting up chains of command and coordination mechanisms for all levels of government. What happened? Six years later, in 1998, the evacuation of New Orleans for Hurricane Georges was a debacle. Six *more* years later, during the Ivan emergency, many of the half million residents fleeing the New Orleans area on Tuesday, September 14, needed ten hours for the eighty-mile run up to Baton Rouge.

I want to be fair to my state. Others have also had "colossal" traffic jams during hurricane evacuations—to borrow the adjective used in one of our LSU publications on the subject, referring to both Georges in '98 and Floyd the following year on the East Coast. During the Floyd emergency, evacuations were ordered for assorted coastal zones from Florida all the way north to Delaware, with as many as four million residents heeding those warnings and turning several interstates into parking lots. Colossal would also be the right word for the traffic jam in southeast Texas before the arrival of Rita, just three-plus weeks after Katrina. They brag about doing everything big in Texas, and they did this traffic jam big, too. The parked cars stretched from Houston to Dallas, 240 miles to the north. This may have been the worst tie-up in history. The photographs went around the world.

After Ivan, LSU transport engineers Brian Wolshon and Chester Wilmot, partially funded by our Public Health Center, used traffic computer models to develop a host of good suggestions to improve the contraflow mechanism. They worked closely with the state police and others to get it right. Maybe the most important advance was the realization that people in southern Louisiana need to be directed toward the *north*. During Ivan, the evacuations orders had started in Florida and rolled west with the storm. Floridians fled west and north, but most of the folks in Alabama and then Mississippi chose to head west, apparently. Near our house in Livingston Parish, Interstate 12 (an adjunct of I-10, in effect) was a parking lot, while the secondary roads had no traffic, as I learned when heading out and back from securing the *Maggie* in her hurricane hole on the Tchefuncte River.

Go north. That was the new idea, and it worked with Katrina. Contraflow provided nine lanes out of the greater New Orleans area. Folks leaving on Sunday did require sixteen hours to reach Houston three hundred miles to the west, but they had waited until the last moment, and the traffic was moving, if slowly. Computer models demonstrate that a good contraflow scheme increases outbound traffic by about 70 percent, but the models also confirm what all of us who drive cars already know: Any little bottleneck will screw things up, no matter how many lanes you have. This had been demonstrated clearly during the Ivan evacuation, when a work zone on Interstate 55, which intersects Interstate 10 about ten miles west of New Orleans, effectively negated the contraflow benefit on that escape route and contributed greatly to the problem. But what lengthy stretch of interstate anywhere does not have a work zone of some sort, on one side or the other? It's not practical to stop all work on the interstates in question during hurricane season. Automobile evacuation will never be easy, not when the forty-five million residents who now live in coastal regions from Texas to Maine are served by a highway system that is about as efficient as it was decades ago. The number of residents is projected to be almost seventy-five million by 2010, but the highway system will not expand correspondingly. Not even close.

There's another very major problem with evacuations: Most will prove to be unnecessary. Simply put, an effective evacuation takes time—at least forty-eight hours for a large metropolitan area confronting a major storm; in Louisiana, the preferred minimum evacuation time is seventy-two hours for a Cat 4 or Cat 5 storm—but the earlier the evacuation is ordered, the greater the likelihood for error in the forecast. Georges turned east, therefore New Orleans was spared. Ivan turned east, therefore New Orleans was spared again. Floyd eventually struck North Carolina, so South Carolina, Georgia, and Florida were spared. Rita turned east, therefore Houston and most of southeast Texas were spared. In each case hundreds of thousands, if not millions, of evacuated residents returned to undamaged homes and communities. In Texas, many thousands of evacuating cars were stuck in traffic just as forecasters were picking up Rita's turn toward the border with Louisiana. In fact, most of those who had evacuated on Thursday or Friday could have returned home on Saturday before the storm struck that border that night.

But it's not an easy call. The NHC's now famous "projection

cone" increases in width as the distance (and time) from the storm center increases. It is an excellent visual depiction of the range of error in the prediction. Introduced in the mid-1990s, the cone has become narrower and narrower, as the forecasters have become more accurate and confident, but the margin of error three days out is still 250 miles in each direction. One day out—twenty-four hours—it is 85 miles in each direction. Many people are surprised to learn—*I* was surprised to learn, from *Divine Wind*—that the best our science can ever achieve will be an error of 90 miles at three days, 30 miles at one day. The projection cone will never be a straight line.

This rude fact of life about chaos as it relates to weather was first demonstrated—by accident—in 1961, by Edward Lorenz, a professor of meteorology at MIT. The story has been told time and again, but its import is so integral to weather forecasting of any sort that I'll tell it again now, in the short form. Holding one set of answers to a problem in his hand, Lorenz decided to run the same calculations again and extend them further in time. In order to make this new job more manageable for the painfully slow vacuum tube computers of that era, he rounded off the variables to the thousandth place. That is, 2.378258 became 2.378, thus introducing an error of, at most, one in a thousand. This was not much, and in some systems such small differences in the initial state would yield small differences in the end state. In Lorenz's calculations, however, they yielded huge differences in the "prediction," so huge that he initially thought there must have been some mistake. But there was no mistake. He had stumbled across a bedrock principle of chaos theory. More broadly, the theory limits the most accurate imaginable weather predictions for a given locale to two weeks out. Better than that is now believed mathematically impossible.

Whatever the cost of narrowing the forecasting error for hurricanes to the theoretically achievable threshold, the expenditure will be worth it. Short distances mean everything with a hurricane. The truly devastating winds and surge zone of even the most dangerous storms is rarely more than one hundred miles across, and often much less than that. A shift in landfall of thirty miles will make a world of difference regarding not only the damage incurred, but the

evacuation necessary to flee that damage. The theoretically achievable accuracy of the computer models would have made most of the
evacuations for Georges, Floyd, Ivan, and Rita—to name just four
noteworthy examples—completely unnecessary.

Beyond the economic disruption, another problem with unnecessary evacuations is that some residents eventually get jaded and
don't leave the next time. Research shows that evacuating types usually do evacuate, but after two years of almost unending watches and
warnings and evacuations, the citizens of Key West, Florida, were
not in the mood with Hurricane Wilma in October 2005. Many ignored the mandatory evacuation order for the Florida Keys. Regarding Katrina, Governor Blanco would refer to the phenomenon
when testifying before the congressional committee investigating
the response: "You put your four kids in the car and you're sitting in
traffic and they're screaming and nothing happens and you go home
and say, 'I'm not doing this again. This is crazy.'" Overall, however,
the problem with Katrina and New Orleans is more complex than
for perhaps any other locale in this country. Our LSU surveys have
always showed that 30 percent of the residents of New Orleans will
not evacuate, the majority because they are "low mobility," in emergency preparedness jargon—that is, they have no ready access to a
car. Others shared the jaded view of the carriage driver in the
French Quarter who told a reporter, "They've been singing this
song for thirty years, and what? Nothing." And perhaps a number of
residents share the fatalism of the Druid priest John Martin, a resident of the French Quarter (naturally), owner of four snakes (including the giant Burmese python Eugene, somehow missing as
Katrina approached), who announced to any reporter who would
listen over the weekend, "I don't believe you're going to go until
God takes you. I've lived a good, full life and I'm not worried about
it. You've got to take life as it comes."

LSU sociologist Jeanne Hurlbert, who teamed with her husband,
professor of sociology Jack Beggs, to conduct our evacuation surveys in 2003 and 2004, quipped, "There's a reason New Orleans is
famous for the drink named the Hurricane. The culture here is 'We
don't evacuate.'" I think that attitude has softened somewhat in re-

cent years. The "Washing Away" series in the *Times-Picayune* had a powerful impact on many people. I like to believe the drumbeat of warnings issued by myself and many others has also had an impact. Certainly the compliance for Ivan in 2004 was much better than it had been for Georges six years earlier, when only one in three residents left town. Then in 2004 we had the three major storms in Florida, followed by the unbelievably catastrophic tsunami in Asia in December, which certainly had an impact on public attitudes. From that day on I often invoked the tsunami to dramatize the damage that could result from a major storm in New Orleans. I always invoked it in local TV interviews. When we were trying to get people to heed Mayor Nagin's plea for a mandatory evacuation (which finally came on Sunday morning), I said in a few interviews that "this could be our tsunami." An exaggeration, definitely, because well over two hundred thousand lives were lost in the tsunami, a number that would probably never be the case in New Orleans, but that's okay. The tsunami was a fresh image. I got a handful of e-mails criticizing the analogy, but they were water off this duck's back, because we needed to scare as many people as possible to get out of the city. Desperate times call for desperate measures. I wasn't the only talking head to invoke the tsunami, and I'll bet all of us combined received literally thousands of e-mails thanking us for doing our best to clear everyone out.

In the end, according to the calculations of the Department of Transportation and Development, 430,000 cars left metropolitan New Orleans and coastal areas to the south during the evacuation. Figuring (on the basis of previous research) 2.5 persons per car, the total is 1 million evacuees, 75 percent of the total population. Truly a remarkable achievement. Our conclusion that 30 percent would never leave, under any circumstances, was off by 5 percent. Thank God.

Still, more than three hundred thousand people remained in New Orleans and vicinity, for good reasons or bad reasons or no reason at all. What was the plan to deal with these folks? Time and time again over the following weeks, I would hear individuals say that everyone who remained behind had sufficient warning, could have found a way out, and therefore pretty much got what they deserved. I guess such hard-hearted observers thought of the people who didn't leave as something like heavy smokers: Okay, it's a free world (in some places), but don't come crying to me or my insurance company when you get lung cancer. Forget the mean-spiritedness. As a matter of public policy, such attitudes are irrelevant. So let's get such cheap thinking out of the way right now. No government—no nation—can sit by and watch tens or hundreds of thousands of people drown or otherwise die, even if it is the result of their own bad decision. As a matter of public policy, every official in the state of Louisiana knew that over three hundred thousand people would remain in the New Orleans metro area. Again, what was the plan to deal with them?

Years ago in South Africa I saw an old Charlton Heston movie, *The Omega Man*, some kind of doomsday apocalypse narrative featuring an empty city, and I distinctly remember wondering at the time, "How did they get everybody out?" This was before digital manipulation. It looked like a real city that really was empty. Over the following weeks in New Orleans I would think of that scene often and wonder how they got all of those people out. Maybe FEMA should have hired Hollywood.

At 9:58 P.M. Saturday ADCIRC produced the results of the surge model based on advisory #18, which had been issued five hours earlier. Run #16 in the early afternoon had looked ominous, #17 equally ominous, but here was the worst news in the vivid colors used for the models. New Orleans would flood. On Monday a large part of the city east of Industrial Canal would be under some water, as well as other sections to the west of it. All of this flooding would result from the overtopping of levees, *not* from any breaches or failures. Clearly, the models can't account for such failures, because we can't know where they would be. Correlate this latest prediction with the fact that the National Hurricane Center had issued a warning at 6:00 P.M. that the city had a 45 percent chance of receiving a direct strike from a Cat 4 or Cat 5 Katrina, and, well, this was bad. Evacuate now! Plus, the prediction could get even worse. The hurricane was still thirty-six hours away, and still strengthening. I said to Marc Levitan, "This is the one we've been working on. This is the big one. Let's hope it goes east, for New Orleans's sake." I think that's just about an exact quote.

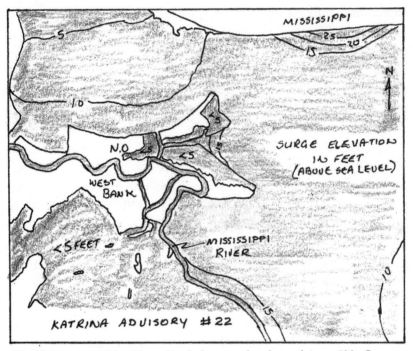

ADCIRC surge model with predicted elevations based on advisory #22. Contours every five feet; elevations above mean sea level.

It was a strange moment for all of us in the local "hurricane community." In Ivan the year before, the surge models had never predicted the flooding of New Orleans. For Georges in 1998 we didn't have nearly as good a product. Here, though, in real time, was a prediction we had confidence in. Most of us were jammed in Mashriqui's cubicle of an office when the pivotal graphic rolled out of the printer. We fell silent for a few moments. We'd been warning about this for years, but to actually "see" the flood in the ADCIRC graphic was truly shocking. Everything we had been talking about and studying for years was about to unfold before our eyes. I got a strong chill all over, and a real tightness of breath. (As an asthmatic, I'm always aware of this kind of thing.) Then we sprang into action. Someone may have said, "Let's get this out," but it wasn't really necessary. All of us knew what to do. I phoned Mark Schleifstein at the *Times-Picayune*. He was waiting for the outputs. We told everyone that the city would flood, and that the actual flooding would be even worse than our surge model had predicted, because some levees were believed to be below their announced heights and a wild wave field would develop on lakes Pontchartrain and Borgne.

Run #18 was projected onto the big screen at the state's EOC at 11:00 P.M. In our briefing we advised everyone present—FEMA, the National Guard, all state and local agencies—that the actual flooding would be worse. We reminded them that the levees along Industrial Canal had been breached during Betsy in 1965. (The reception was quite different than when Marc had presented the model based on advisory #16 earlier in the afternoon, that had showed ominously high surge levels. A senior Louisiana emergency official had seemed uninterested in that output. Subsequently, other LSU staffers complained that the new upper echelon of the state emergency agency was not utilizing the science, unlike the management the year before during Ivan.) If we had such flat-out failures this time, the flooding would be much, much worse. On a conference call from Miami, Max Mayfield, director of the National Hurricane Center, briefed Governors Blanco and Barbour and New Orleans Mayor Nagin. Get everyone out, he said.

Every media outlet was all hurricane, all the time, and they all had the news. No one paying the least bit of attention could have avoided it. No one. So when Michael Brown said days later that on Saturday it was "my belief . . . we had a standard hurricane coming in here, that we could move in immediately on Monday and start doing our kind of emergency response effort," I was livid, because we had called it right and called it early. Our warnings went out at least thirty-two hours before Katrina made landfall. That was ample time for FEMA to act. Get those buses rolling—no matter where you have to get them. This is the United States of America, not some desperately poor country with no resources. (The New Orleans firefighters deserve a word of praise at this time. Chief Gary Savelle gave his crews copies of the ADCIRC graphic I had e-mailed, and they started telling folks in the areas that would flood to *leave*. They acted in a responsible manner.)

Late Saturday night I worked with Mark Schleifstein on his story for the Sunday edition of the *Times-Picayune*. We both thought this was tremendously important, because Sunday would still give people enough time to leave—at least those with cars or access to cars. The following morning, the whole package was headlined KATRINA TAKES AIM, with three subheads above the fold on the front page: "An Extreme Storm," "Get On the Road," and "Wall of Water." The graphic showed in detail how the flooding would occur. As it turned out, many traditional nonevacuators did change their minds. They fled on Sunday, maybe with the naive notion that they'd get a motel in Baton Rouge, only to end up in Arkansas instead, but they did make it out. On the other hand, the parties on Bourbon Street were in full swing all night long. So I understand. But if just one person was saved by all our hard work—just one child—then it was worth it.

THREE

LAUGHED OUT OF THE ROOM

W hile the oblivious partied in the French Quarter on Saturday night, some of us tossed and turned. We were quite sure the fun was just about over, not to resume for quite awhile. In fact, Max Mayfield of the National Hurricane Center said on Sunday, "New Orleans is never going to be the same." Wow. I know Max to be a levelheaded guy and not prone to exaggeration. Then again, he can read a map and the data with the best of them, and he had stated on the air on Saturday that he'd never seen conditions so ripe for hurricane strengthening. It happened. On Saturday night Katrina exploded and officially reached Cat 4 status—sustained winds of 130 mph—at 1:00 A.M. Sunday morning. At 8:00 A.M., advisory #22 announced a Cat 5 storm headed for the Gulf Coast with sustained winds approaching 175 mph and higher gusts. The 10:00 A.M. advisory added "potentially catastrophic" to the description. Such a storm would flood New Orleans to the eaves *and* tear it to shreds. Likewise for all surrounding communities. An old saw in the disaster field holds that water damage starts from the bottom up, wind damage from the top down. If they meet in the middle, it's all over for that building. Based on these latest bulletins, such was the prospect with Katrina. Our LSU wind-modeling team estimated two hundred thousand severely damaged structures in a direct hit by such a storm. (This model correlates predicted winds with a modified FEMA database of all structures in given zip codes.) Wind engineer Marc Levitan said on Saturday, "If everyone doesn't get out, with the wind and the water, there is strong potential for mass casualties."

Over the weekend several factors played right into Katrina's hands. For starters, the Gulf of Mexico was even warmer than usual, 85 degrees or higher, mainly because of the insistently hot weather along the coast for weeks, perhaps also because we had had very little rain inland, therefore less relatively cool freshwater runoff. There were no big shearing factors on the horizon for Katrina, and a high-pressure ridge in the upper atmosphere was serving nicely to vent the heat from the highest reaches of the storm. (One of the incredible graphics put together by Kerry Emanuel for *Divine Wind* depicts the rising heat in a hurricane, with the hottest zone at the top of the eye—heat that is whipped away in a clockwise direction. In the strongest storms this venting process is achieved efficiently, thereby sucking up more heat from below: more wind—more strength.) Finally, on Saturday the storm had undergone an eye-wall replacement cycle, in which the innermost wall of high winds and clouds breaks down and is replaced by another wall. This cycle can lower the winds a bit—only to be followed, often enough, by an increase. Max Mayfield and his team knew that the replacement cycle during the day Saturday could be followed by strengthening that night and Sunday. So it was. The only good news was that the burst of energy that had taken the storm to devastating Cat 5 status would probably not hold up. Katrina could lose a little strength late Sunday while approaching the coast, but it probably wouldn't matter all that much. Whether she struck as a Cat 4 or 5, the flooding would be about the same, according to our surge models.

The big question was always the track, with the eventual landfall determined primarily by the influence of two high pressures and one low pressure. For the moment, a high pressure over the coast north of Katrina was steering the storm to the west, the same kind of action by which the Bermuda High steers many Atlantic storms to the west. But a turn more to the north was expected, due to the influence of, in the words of the NHC, "a weakness in the ridge associated with a large midlatitude low-pressure system over the northern United States and southern Canada." So our violent visitor would slowly and almost inexorably turn to the northwest, then the north. But how much? On Saturday morning the zone of uncertainty had stretched from the Louisiana/Texas border to Pensacola, Florida, with the main track right over New Orleans. That was quite a spread. By that afternoon the track had shifted slightly to the east, and the cone had narrowed slightly, but the storm could still go west of New Orleans. When we restarted our storm-surge modeling early Sunday morning with advisory #22 the storm was still on virtually the same track as with #18, the advisory from the night before that had first showed the flooding. The strengthening overnight offset the slight move to the east. The new flood forecast remained about the same. A slightly more definitive move to the east, however, would be very good news for New Orleans, just as a shift to the west would be very bad news. The absolute, 100 percent worst case would be for Katrina to make landfall at Grand Isle, almost due south of the city, and proceed to the north-northwest on a track taking her eye just west of the city. If this happened, the ADCIRC storm-surge output would look considerably different. We'd have something equivalent to the storm we developed for FEMA's Hurricane Pam exercise—a completely flooded city, with water over the tops of all the levees. Katrina certainly had the power to do this, but only if she tracked in the western part of the projection cone and slowed down just a touch. Forward speed is very important for the surge equations. The slower the storm, the longer the time for the surge to build and build. We always fear a slow-moving storm.

What did we know? What did we predict? What would happen?! Most of the reporters and TV producers were earnestly trying to get the best information they could. They were very polite and keenly interested in our data and opinions. We sent them to our various Web pages. A few requests were peremptory, as though they were doing us a favor. Some were ingratiating, a few pretty clueless. I—and I assume everyone else on the staff—got e-mail requests asking for thoughtful analyses of the long-term consequences of this storm as it would affect this or that specific issue. "Of course, I know you are busy today," would be the obligatory caveat. Well, yes. All of us ended up, over the next few weeks, with literally thousands of unanswered—unopened—e-mails and messages on our phones.

At 10:00 A.M. Sunday I joined a conference call with Dr. Jim Diaz of LSU's medical school and with Martin Kalis and a large team at the Centers for Disease Control in Atlanta. Within half an hour of our posting of surge-model #18 the previous evening, Martin had called to set up this meeting to discuss the public health problems that would follow hard on the heels of Katrina's imminent arrival. Then Martin sent us an e-mail (time-stamped 5:05 A.M.) with a revised list of the potential health impacts from the expected flooding, and it was a long list, all entries previously discussed, including everything from massive petrochemical spills during the storm to mildew issues for years to follow. Fire ants, too. Earlier in the week, knowing that I often mention these insects as a hazard during floods, Martin had forwarded a photograph of a fire ant colony floating on top of floodwater. I knew all about that, in part because a pasture rich with fire ants behind my home had flooded with the passage of tropical storm Alison. Donning my rubber boots, I searched for and found many clumps of ants about the size of tennis balls. Does the writhing, rotating action of the ball assure that a given ant will not be underwater long enough to drown? That's a pretty good hypothesis. Anyway, it was quite fascinating, but then I got into my scientist mode and experimented with several different insect killers. The winner was definitely the liquid jet-type hornet and wasp spray.

At some point during the Katrina emergency, a friend sent me a blog associated with the *Columbia Journalism Review* suggesting I must be some kind of nut for even mentioning the fire-ant hazard. I deny the accusation. The ants do interest me, but the problem is real regardless. The average yard in Louisiana has two fire-ant mounds, and during a flood these floating colonies will tend to end up where the humans do—on trees, for example. Any such encounter will turn out very badly for the people. In the South there have been instances in which an attack of fire ants caused people to release their holds on trees and drown in the flowing waters below. During Katrina, as it turned out, the number of fire-ant problems was minimal, probably because more people ended up on rooftops, not trees, for survival. However, LSU Agricultural Center entomology associate Patricia Beckley has documented that some people wading through the waters surrounding the Superdome encountered masses of floating fire ants. Elsewhere, pesticides and thin oil and gas sheens floating on the surface of the waters may have killed many of the colonies.

The CDC's two-page list of health impacts included West Nile virus, rabies, waterborne gastrointestinal diseases, burns, pulmonary irritations—the usual suspects, and more—and it was the job of both our center at LSU and the CDC to be prepared to provide relief officials and policymakers with the best information regarding all of them. The CDC provides medical support teams to any state requesting their help, and it also has rapid-assessment teams, a critical part of any response to a major disaster. They can assure that the correct medical supplies, health resources, and manpower are available as soon as possible. Because of our research we could give them a good heads-up on what to expect after Katrina.

I was not surprised by the CDC's prompt and efficient response to the telltale surge model. They're on the ball. Compared to some of the FEMA officials with whom we had dealt in the past few years, they are disciplined, scientific, fact-based, and results oriented. We had spent a day with them in Atlanta in October 2004, then later that year a group had come down to LSU, and we all went down to Charity Hospital in New Orleans. We would have liked to work more closely with them, but Bush administration cuts to their budget were so severe that Martin Kalis couldn't get the travel funds to come to our advisory board meeting in 2005.

Sunday morning, Mayor Nagin at City Hall finally ordered the mandatory evacuation, the first in the city's history, with Governor Blanco by his side. Finally. I know that "mandatory" is just a word, and it doesn't really mean that the cops are ordering everyone out at gunpoint, but it's a scarier word than "voluntary" and should have been invoked on Saturday, legalities be damned. We were now less than twenty-four hours before landfall. "We are facing the storm that most of us have feared," the mayor said. "This is a once-in-a-lifetime event. It most likely will topple our levee system." He had obviously seen our surge-model outputs. I assume he had seen that Sunday morning edition of the *Times-Picayune*. What a sad moment for this former businessman, who just the week before had been gloating about Donald Trump's impending visit to announce his new condo hotel on Poydras Street. Now the first-term mayor was likely to preside over an incredible catastrophe that would find most of Poydras Street under water. This was one of the announcements at which citizens were advised to have an ax handy if they refused to leave, because they would need it to chop their way out of the attic. I heard that some of the crews driving around town announcing the mandatory evacuation through bullhorns added dramatically, "Run for your lives." People did. Everyone had seen the tsunami footage. At one point on Sunday, eighteen thousand cars an hour were leaving the city. Slow going, but these last-minute leavers did get out.

Hotels become last-resort zones of "vertical evacuation." Although the hotel managements had always resisted any such official designation, they knew that they would fill up to the brim, and they did. I wonder how many of the people who stayed in the hotels know that the wind increases the higher one proceeds "up" the hurricane. Today's modern skyscrapers, including the hotels, are designed to withstand blasts of 120 mph, and I'm sure they would do so, but I can't imagine a more terrifying experience than huddling in the hallway on the tenth floor as the shrieking winds of a Cat 4 or Cat 5 hurricane shatter every window of my swaying hotel. I think I'd run for the hills instead. (Some high-rise buildings use pea-sized gravel as a roof covering. In a storm, this gravel becomes lethal window-smashing missiles. It is not rare to see, after a storm, skyscrapers with most of the windows on one side smashed, up to about 150 feet above the ground.) Most modern buildings have few strong, solid interior walls; office spaces are created with modular units or flimsy partitions. Once the windows have been blown out, these "walls" may be the next to go. Even if they don't blow away, the wind flow may create tunnels filled with blowing debris. Not a safe place with winds of even 60 mph. Imagine 120 mph, a couple of hundred feet in the air. Vertical evacuations are really a matter of absolute last resort.

The Superdome had been opened as a "special needs" shelter on Sunday at 8:00 A.M. for those residents with a good reason not to evacuate. Theoretically, people were even supposed to call a special number to see if they qualified for admission—a plan that never had a prayer. Colonel Terry Ebbert, the city's director of Homeland Security, explained that the infirm would be directed to one side of the building, where "we have some water." Those seeking shelter were advised to bring enough of their own food and water for a few days, but they should not plan on staying long. (And they should then proceed . . . where?) By noon Sunday, thousands of residents had lined up. Few had their own food and water; none had anywhere else to go or any way to get there. CNN reported that nine thousand men, women, children, and babies spent Sunday night at the Superdome. FEMA said fifteen thousand meals were on hand, but I also read that forty-one thousand meals were gone within the day. As with many of the numbers all of us read and heard over the coming days and weeks, I have no idea which ones are correct. I don't think anyone does. Contradictions abound. Someday, a group of academics or reporters, or both, with the time and resources will try to find out. This is going to be quite a challenge, and I'm not sure any such postmortem will clear up all of the questions. There was some food and water at the Superdome. We know this. But not enough. We also know this.

In their Sunday edition, *Times-Picayune* editors published a list of twelve locations from which people would be transported to the Superdome. The streetcars on St. Charles Street would also be operating for as long as they could. One terminus was less than a mile from the Superdome, and this system did bring a few thousand people to the big building. Others walked. Chester Wilmot, my colleague at LSU, reports that the city had 550 city buses and hundreds of other buses at its disposal, but no plans to use them in an evacuation. The goal should have been "transportation redundancies," in Wilmot's phrase. In 2001 the LSU Hurricane Center did a review of the effectiveness of buses, but pointed out that the 550 city buses plus "hundreds" of others, while it sounds like a lot, would not have been an effective means of getting the 127,000 persons without vehicles out of New Orleans. As it turned out, the buses sat in the various parking lots—flooded, many of them, as of the following day. To my knowledge, *not one group* of the infirm or elderly was evacuated by an "official bus" prior to the storm.

Two weeks after Katrina hit, on *Meet the Press* Tim Russert challenged Mayor Nagin about the flooded buses. The mayor said there had been no drivers. Moreover, he asked rhetorically, where would the buses have gone? This was a good excuse! Have a plan for the drivers. Have a plan to provide safe shelter for them after the work is done. Have a set of destinations prepared. On his show, Russert, like all of the reporters by that point, was in no mood for Nagin or anyone else's rope-a-dope. He quoted New Orleans's own emergency plan: "Conduct of an actual evacuation will be the responsibility of the mayor." Nagin replied that the overall plan was "getting people to higher ground, getting them to safety . . . and then depending upon our state and federal officials to move them out of harm's way after the storm has hit." The cavalry would come. That was the hope and expectation. At other times Nagin had referred to this strategy as Plan B: "The president, I'm sure, is going to send us what we need."

In short, the city's plan amounted to a "good samaritan" response, in the phrase of Brian Wolshon, transport engineer and a fellow researcher at our Hurricane Public Health Center. This was not good enough. In 2004, the American Red Cross had started looking into a program called Brother's Keeper, whereby religious organizations would ferry some of the immobile in New Orleans to safe church shelters outside of New Orleans. Not good enough. Some private citizens' group also had some plans. Not good enough. As wonderful as such gestures were, they were still just *gestures.* They could never evacuate more than mere thousands, when the problem was tens of thousands. The nursing home trade group for Louisiana concluded after the flood that at least two thirds of the city's fifty-three nursing homes were not evacuated, with tragic results.

In mid-February 2006, the Senate Homeland Security and Governmental Affairs Committee revealed that the State Department of

Transportation and Development had in April 2005 been tasked with developing plans and procedures to mobilize transportation to support emergency evacuations of at-risk populations. The state DOTD does not have buses or drivers, and so did not move on this responsibility. Secretary Johnny Bradberry was severely chastised by senators Susan Collins and Joe Lieberman, given the number of deaths during Katrina at hospitals and nursing homes. All reports are that Bradberry took his medicine without trying to pass the buck, something that seems to have been the hallmark of others this committee found fault with.

Tim Russert challenged Mayor Nagin on the public service announcement he had cut in July about evacuating the city. In Russert's phrase, the mayor had warned citizens that they were "on their own." An exaggeration, but several times the mayor had expressed doubt about a successful evacuation of his city. In July, he had said that a Cat 5 would be an "easy sell," in terms of evacuation. For anything less, he added, "The community says, 'We might ride this out.'" This belief about the Cat 5 factor was optimistic, of course. He surely knew of our widely disseminated conclusion that about 30 percent of the residents would not leave the city regardless. He must have believed it. As it turned out, as few as 25 percent stayed behind, which was great, but where was the plan for establishing safe higher ground for them? And what about the elderly and the disabled?

Russert informed Nagin that New Orleans had received $18 million since 2002 to plan for just such emergencies. Where had the money gone? "Levee protection and the coordination of getting people to safety," the mayor replied. What could he say? I actually felt sorry for the man. It's easy to criticize in hindsight, easy to criticize from the sidelines—and it seems to be easy for a good interviewer to make almost anyone look bad on television (as FEMA's Michael Brown would whine by way of self-defense during a remarkable interview on PBS's *Frontline* in November). However, the fact remains that the government does not have the luxury of the private citizen who dismisses those who stay behind as equivalent to smokers who get what they deserve. That's neither a practical nor a morally responsible public policy.

Testifying before Congress in December, both Governor Blanco and Mayor Nagin were accused of waiting too long to issue a mandatory evacuation order for New Orleans. The governor pointed to the extraordinarily successful evacuation: 92 percent of the residents of southeast Louisiana. (This is a very high number. Our best figure, as reported, is a still excellent 75 percent.) Nagin admitted that he should have handled the bus problem better. Indeed. The photographs of the flooded buses—the yellow roofs neatly lined up in the black water—will remain forever as one of the lasting images of Katrina in New Orleans, an iconic depiction of the horrible planning.

Over the following days and weeks we would hear a great deal about the legal responsibility for what happened in New Orleans. The simple truth is that under the Stafford Act (§401 and §501) of October 2000, once President Bush declared a national emergency on Saturday, August 27 (retroactive to the day before), the federal government was in charge. To my knowledge, the first reporter in the national media to get this right, postdebacle, was NPR's Ira Glass, on the September 9 edition of *This American Life*. Sure, Glass said, "there are plenty of things that state and local government did to screw things up," but the declaration of national emergency made all that moot, in terms of responsibility for what happened next. He was interviewing William Nicholson, author of the books *Emergency Response and Emergency Management Law*.

Of course, you have to plan ahead for such an eventuality, don't you? It would have been a daunting challenge, to say the least, for FEMA to have jumped in over the weekend to organize an extensive evacuation of the immobile without such prior planning. But FEMA knew the numbers. It knew the repercussions of heavy flooding. It knew what the city had and had not done to prepare. All of us in the disaster field did. The previous year city officials had been caught off guard and had opened up an unprepared Superdome just twelve hours before Hurricane Ivan made landfall to the east. Only a few thousand people showed up, and the city didn't flood (and was never expected to), but the absence of a workable plan was obvious. A year later it was already obvious again on Sunday.

It was FEMA's responsibility—by law—to serve as the cavalry—

and not just after the fact. I had walked away from the Hurricane Pam exercise one year earlier (to be discussed in some detail in Chapter 7) with the conviction that FEMA would assist in the evacuation of the city prior to any major storm. After Katrina struck and everything broke down, I asked Walter Maestri, the highly respected director of Emergency Preparedness for Jefferson Parish, whether this was also his understanding. "Absolutely," he replied.

Imagine. Almost all the suffering and displacement that followed Katrina could have been alleviated with just a few evacuee camps—tent cities—within fifty miles of New Orleans and an efficient system for getting people there. I had seen for myself how well and quickly these camps can be organized. In July 2003, my colleague Kate Streva and I had taken an intensive, ten-day course in refugee camps sponsored by Merlin, a nonprofit organization based in the United Kingdom. About thirty of us from many different countries, some with a wealth of experience, attended our classes in the peaceful English countryside of Sussex. The experience was quite an eyeopener for the two (and only two) Americans. Kate and I had known that a major hurricane strike on southeastern Louisiana would leave hundreds of thousands homeless and jobless, without transportation or schools, for months, if not years. Now we knew the best possible solution: evacuee camps, or whatever name you choose to call them. (Officially, a refugee refers to an individual displaced from another country. An individual displaced within his or her own country is an "internally displaced person," or IDP. During the Katrina emergency, I tried to use "IDP," but it never took. Instead, refugee was used for a few days before "evacuee" became the accepted description.) We may shrink in horror from the idea, FEMA may refuse to entertain it, but these tent cities are the easiest way to provide large numbers of evacuees with the required number of medical clinics (one per five thousand), latrines, cooking tents, and so on. They can be erected very quickly—within hours.

The FEMA folks not only refused to entertain the idea. They basically laughed me out of the room when I broached the subject during the Hurricane Pam exercise. They didn't want to hear about the army's proficiency in erecting such cities. (Just look at our efforts in

Bosnia and Herzegovina. And Iraq. Everyone has seen footage of
our troops and has a mental image of these tent setups, with wooden
floors and electric lights and cooling fans and privacy.) I suggested
prepositioning tents and supplies, as well as signing leases with major landowners north of Lake Pontchartrain, in St. Tammany and
Tangipahoa parishes. The laughter got louder. The woman said,
"Americans don't live in tents!"

Undeterred, I tried to push this concept during the Katrina
tragedy, in interview after interview. It was too late, I realize, but I
wanted people to understand the alternative to what was going on.
We could have had comfortable facilities ready to go, complete with
large tents serving as cafeterias, and as halls for entertainment and
lectures on dealing with all the paperwork problems that would follow. We would have had a ready workforce of residents, once the
cleanup started. Instead, we ended up with the local workforce scattered in one thousand different cities across the country, some still
in hotels four months after the storm, some still in the makeshift
tents they chose over the other options presented. Evacuees were
arriving in Baton Rouge without any medical support. Diabetics,
heart patients, and asthmatics were on their own, initially. After the
flooding began, many had severe staph infections from being in the
water so long. Others waited and waited, some for seven days, before they were bused all over the country with no real medical sur-
veillance until they arrived at their destination. The Astrodome in
Houston, where most from the Superdome were taken, filled to
overflowing and had to close its doors. Some evacuees were put on
planes and not told where they were going. (I wonder if the pilots
knew when they took off. I wouldn't bet on it.)

All because "Americans don't live in tents." FEMA refused to
even think about the most obvious option for dealing with the inevitable numbers of evacuees following the event that the agency itself had long recognized as one of the three most likely and dangerous
disasters for the country, along with a terrorist attack in New York
and another major earthquake on the West Coast. Americans need
to understand that their government is totally unprepared for major
natural disasters, let alone the terrorist's dirty bomb or biological/

chemical attack. Don't kid yourself. Very little, if anything, has changed since September 11, 2001. Domestically, that is. On the West Coast, in New York City, in Washington, D.C., in Chicago, pay heed.

On Sunday in Baton Rouge I didn't know all the details about the unused buses or the brewing travesty at the Superdome, but the networks were already carrying footage of families lining up outside the building as every public official in Louisiana, Mississippi, and Alabama issued new warnings and orders. In Texas, President Bush held a special press conference vowing that the federal government "would do everything in our power to help the people and communities affected by" Katrina. Max Mayfield briefed him by videoconference. FEMA spokesman David Passey said, "This looks like it could be worse than any natural disaster in the U.S.—ever." At LSU our phones were ringing off the wall, and Marc Levitan, Paul Kemp, and all of us took every opportunity to invoke keywords like "worst-case scenario" and "catastrophe" and "thousands possibly dead" and "EVACUATE." Someone quipped that the Big Easy was now the Big Queasy.

At 10:11 A.M. Sunday the National Weather Service office in Slidell released a remarkable warning. At the time, I didn't recall another like it, and I've since learned that nothing like it had ever been issued. "Most of the area will be uninhabitable for weeks . . . perhaps longer," this bulletin stated. "At least one-half of well-constructed homes will have roof and wall failure. The majority of industrial buildings will become non-functional. Airborne debris will be widespread. Power outages will last for weeks. Water shortages will make human suffering incredible by modern standards."

At 2:56 P.M. the surge warriors released ADCIRC model run #22, which showed a little more flooding than the previous ones, but in the same areas. The cone of uncertainty was getting tighter and tighter, and the track had not changed. The eye would probably move right over the east side of New Orleans. "Will the levees fail?" That was always on our minds. From much experience, I knew there would be a wicked wave field on all the surrounding lakes, and especially on Lake Borgne and Lake Pontchartrain. These waves could well erode the earthen levee systems (which proved so true in St. Bernard Parish).

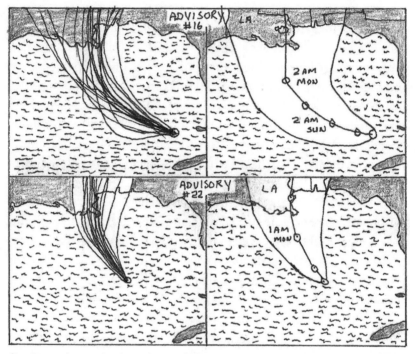

Spaghetti plots and cones of uncertainty for Hurricane Katrina advisories #16 (August 27, 2005) and #22 (August 28, 2005).

Since the latest model showed no significant change in the flooding advisory, I told every one to take a quick break, get their homes and families sorted out, and reassemble around 10:00 P.M. I suddenly caught the fear bug and decided I'd better beef up the defenses on the *Maggie*, so Lorie and I raced out and added two more anchors and stern lines. As we departed the anchorage I told her we might well lose the boat this time. In a couple of days we might be looking at the mast alone, a heartbreaking prospect. In December 1999, we had hauled the *Maggie* and for the next two years spent every other weekend on a stem-to-stern refurbishment at the boatyard in

Madisonville. That was a family project; our two daughters, then quite young, helped out with the odd small painting job and making sandwiches for lunch. Now I tend to relate such wonderful memories to those of the flooded families in New Orleans.

At 10:00 P.M. Sunday, Mashriqui sent out an e-mail stating that run #25 showed *less* flooding in New Orleans. Katrina's predicted track had moved a bit east and her winds were down slightly. Very important but also very dicey news. Would people lower their defenses just a little, even though the potential for flooding in the greater New Orleans area remained the same? I e-mailed the latest prediction to Mark Schleifstein at the *Times-Picayune*, and I immediately phoned Luigi Romolo, who was running the LSU briefings at the EOC, and told him *not* to lower any of his warnings. We definitely did not need to be undermining people's vigilance or changing a very last minute decision to leave. In an e-mail to Luigi I added a note—for the first time—that this more optimistic latest prediction from the surge model assumed that the levees held. I reiterated that a breached levee on the Industrial Canal caused much of the worst flooding during Hurricane Betsy in '65. At about this time, on CNN Paul Kemp answered a suggestion that the reduced wind speed was good by saying, "Well, that's not going to be a lot of solace for people in New Orleans, because that storm will also flood New Orleans. And what we're concerned about is getting people out of there." Referring to wind speeds, Paul said, "Ten miles an hour one way or the other is not going to make a big difference. This is a killer track." That became the new mantra. Marc Levitan showed me the latest results from the wind-damage model, which did not look good. In some areas south and east of New Orleans, 80 percent of homes would be badly damaged.

As dawn broke through the windy, rainy skies on Monday morning, with the eye of Hurricane Katrina just reaching the farthest marshes of St. Plaquemines Parish 125 miles away, I found the CNN truck outside the LSU dormitory where I had lived as a first-year graduate student in 1977. Twenty-eight years later, there I was talking with Miles O'Brien about the major hurricane barreling down on us—the "product," in a way, of my life's work. (Somehow

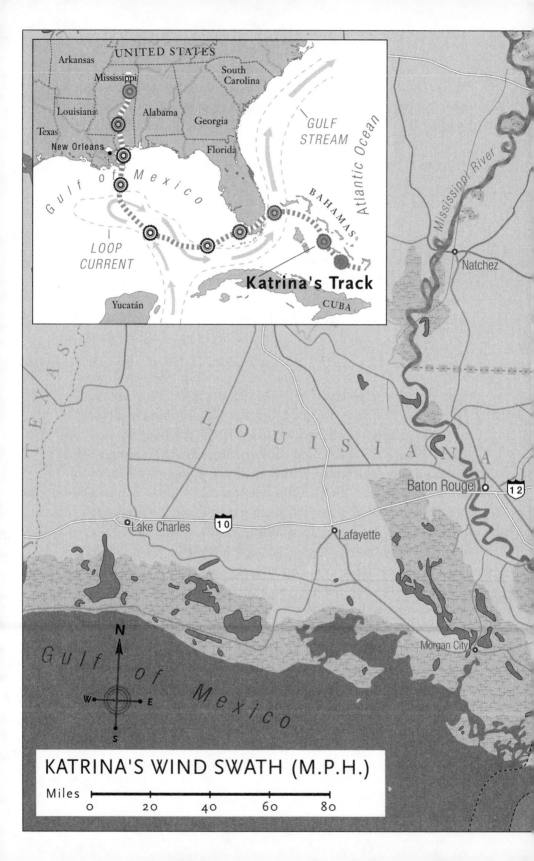

UNITED STATES

Arkansas

Mississippi

Louisiana   Alabama

Texas   Georgia

New Orleans   Florida

Gulf   o f   M e x i c o

LOOP
CURRENT

Yucatán

GULF
STREAM

Atlantic Ocean

BAHAMAS

Katrina's Track

CUBA

Natchez

Mississippi River

T E X A S

L   O   U   I   S   I   A   N   A

Baton Rouge   12

Lake Charles   10   Lafayette

Morgan City

Gulf   o f   M e x i c o

N

W   E

S

KATRINA'S WIND SWATH (M.P.H.)

Miles

0   20   40   60   80

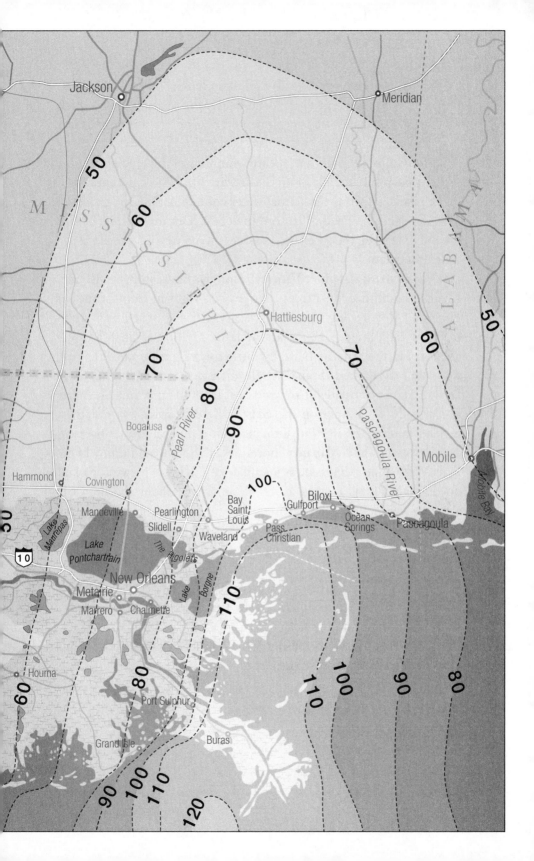

CNN had worked out a deal with the chancellor of LSU, Sean O'Keefe, who asked all of us to be handy for that network, which was fine. The request was accompanied by a note reminding us not to make landfall predictions. This was also fine. We never did that.) That four-minute interview at the beginning of day one gave me a great opportunity to talk about the extent of the flood, potential size of the rescue effort, the potential water contamination, the expected damage—and the need to restore the coast. Get the science before the public. Given the screwups that were to come, this proved especially important.

Driving to my daughter Vanessa's mother's house in Baton Rouge, I had to climb over two trees that crashed right in front of me on Highland Road. This was getting scary. I flashed back to a scene from my childhood, when a jacaranda tree fell on a car in a thunderstorm in Pietermaritzburg, the little town I grew up in. That car was totally squashed. Some people died. I was four at the time. Downed trees translate into a wind of at least 40 mph. Imagine what was already happening on the coast, where Katrina was just then making landfall, or in New Orleans eighty miles away, or over on the Mississippi and Alabama shorelines. People would die, I knew that. Meanwhile, Vanessa was sound asleep. Kids. The wind picked up dramatically as I drove east—alone (I was about the only car around)—with the idea of getting some quick sleep at home, but this proved nearly impossible. The wind was pretty loud, and I finally got up to take a look. It's amazing to see a 160-foot pine bend 40 feet or 50 feet, but our house is protected by quite a few acres of big trees—a healthy windbreak, so I thought we'd be fine. Then I heard a loud crack, and a cherry tree crashed onto a fence. Soon, a large oak missed the house by 6 feet, a magnificent magnolia by 8 feet. Again I needed the four-wheel drive to climb out the driveway and head back to work. It was time.

FOUR

LEVEES LITE

Everyone has seen the dramatic pictures: freighters on the Mississippi River towering above tourists enjoying their chicory coffee and beignets at Café du Monde in the French Quarter and, closer to Lake Pontchartrain, expensive homes hunkered in the shadow of what looks like an elevated canal of some sort across the street, protected by a very ordinary-looking concrete wall. The whole world must know now that 95 percent of New Orleans proper is below sea level, at an average depth of five feet. Most people don't know that the famous "bowl" is actually five independent bowls in the metropolitan area, each encased by its own set of levees.

One bowl includes the easternmost areas of the city and the outlying communities of Orleans Parish between Lake Pontchartrain and the Intracoastal Waterway: the Orleans East bowl, the deepest of them all. A second includes the easternmost areas of the city directly south of the first bowl, tucked between the waterway and the Mississippi River, and including the Lower Ninth Ward in Orleans Parish and a part of St. Bernard Parish that also harbors a large swatch of damaged marshlands: the St. Bernard Bowl. The western boundary of both of these bowls is the Industrial Canal that connects the lake and the river.

The third bowl extends from that large canal west to the 17th Street Canal, and from the lake to the river: the Orleans Metro Bowl, in my vernacular, the heart of the city. The fourth one reaches from the 17th Street Canal to the airport farther west, also from the lake to the river: the West Jefferson Bowl. (South and west of the 17th Street Canal the separation between these two bowls is the

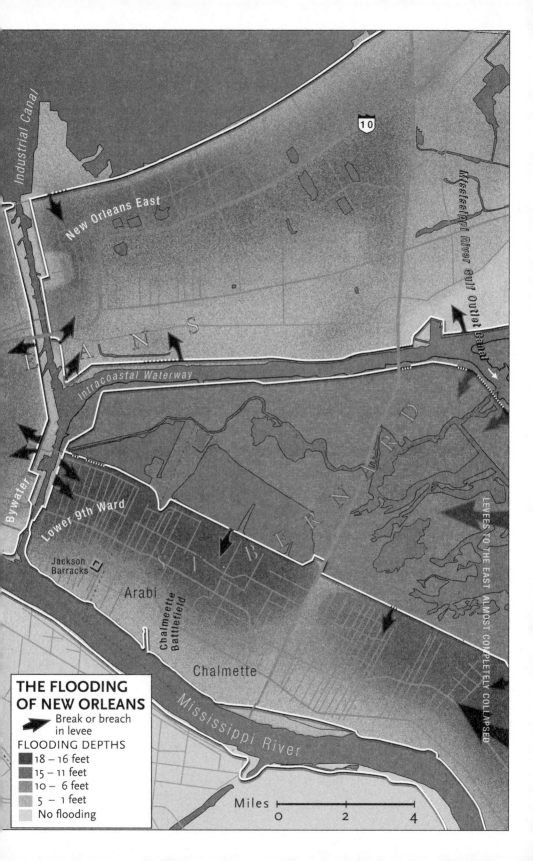

Industrial Canal

Mississippi River Gulf Outlet Canal

10

New Orleans East

E A N S

Intracoastal Waterway

B E R N A R D

Bywater

Lower 9th Ward

Jackson
Barracks

Arabi

Chalmette
Battlefield

Chalmette

S E

Mississippi River

LEVEES TO THE EAST ALMOST COMPLETELY COLLAPSED

THE FLOODING
OF NEW ORLEANS

Break or breach
in levee

FLOODING DEPTHS

18 – 16 feet

15 – 11 feet

10 – 6 feet

5 – 1 feet

No flooding

Miles

0   2   4

Metairie Ridge, which is actually the levees of an old distributary of the Mississippi). The fifth bowl is on the other side of the Mississippi River, the south side but called the West Bank because it *is* the west bank farther upriver. These outlying communities in Orleans and Jefferson parishes are somewhat protected by another set of levees ("somewhat" because the system is not completed, and won't be for years—and should not be, as I'll explain in the final chapter).

Those are the five main bowls. In addition, a long, narrow wedge of communities in Plaquemines Parish about forty miles southeast of New Orleans is protected by levees on the east side of the Mississippi. Downriver from there is another protected wedge on the west side of the river. Thirty miles directly south of New Orleans, another large area of dense development around Bayou Lafourche is encircled by levees. The grand total is about 500 miles of levee protection in southeast Louisiana (350 of them in Greater New Orleans). Prior to Katrina, the Army Corps of Engineers was working

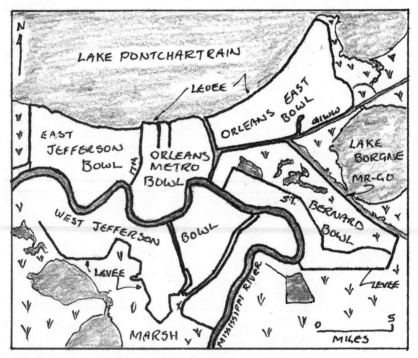

The five main bowls of Greater New Orleans.

on four major projects. One was the levees around Lake Pontchartrain; another was the Morganza-to-the-Gulf levee, designed to protect Morganza, Houma, and four other towns at a cost of well over $1 billion. Still in the design stage, this structure would be seventy-two miles long, nine to fifteen feet high, and state-of-the-art, a complex "leaky levee" whose floodgates and culverts would allow water to flow back and forth and replenish the marshes. That was the idea, and three years ago Terrebonne Parish levied, with popular approval, a quarter-cent sales tax to handle its share of the cost. Those taxpayers now have something over $10 million set aside. Not quite enough. In any event, all such plans are now up in the air, obviously.

Rainfall aside, the specific sources of flooding water that necessitate all of these levees are the Mississippi River, Lake Pontchartrain, and storm surge rolling in from the Gulf of Mexico to the east and south. Today, the operative problem is the last two—the lake and the Gulf—because the mighty river is now effectively held in check. It has not seriously flooded New Orleans or anywhere else in Louisiana since 1927, and it is not likely to again. Upstream from the city four different spillway systems, beginning with the Old River Control structure that diverts water into the Atchafalaya River one hundred miles to the northwest and ending with the Bonnet Carré Spillway just west of the city, can, in an emergency, dump fully half of the river's flow, as much as 1 million cubic feet per second. The levees along the river are 300 feet wide at the base and 100 feet at the top. They aren't going anywhere. They are built to an elevation of 25 feet above sea level, while the average annual high-water mark for the river is 14 feet. An unbelievable amount of water would be required to fill up those last 11 feet of volume in the channel, which is 600 yards wide as it flows through the city at an average depth of 90 feet. There is a tremendous margin for error designed into these levees. The Army Corps of Engineers, which is solely responsible for them, calculates that they'll protect New Orleans from anything less than an eight-hundred-year flood. That could be about right.

Local provocateurs do enjoy speculating that a tipsy captain could miss the hairpin right-hand downstream turn at the French

Quarter and smash his ship through the levee, but it would take a hell of a bash. On a Saturday afternoon in 1996—December 14, 2:30 P.M.—the *Bright Field*, a 763-foot freighter registered in Liberia (where many are, for legal purposes) and loaded with 56,000 tons of corn bound for Kashima, Japan, via the Panama Canal, rammed into the dock with the RiverWalk mall and hotel complex, not far upstream from the hairpin turn. No deaths, but 116 people were injured, with millions of dollars of property damage. At that location, a dock protected the levee, but the crash did make people wonder about the worst case. Really, though, the scarier scene for engineers is the collection of pressure-release wells on the west side of the Mississippi not far north of Baton Rouge. When the river is low, nothing is happening, but when it's up, these wells are bubbling with river water seeping under the levee, which right here happens to sit on a sandy base, which is highly permeable. When the river is high the pressure will push water through this sand and out the other side. We call these little eruptions sand boils, and without these wells to relieve that pressure, the levee here could fail, with a serious flood fight to follow. There's another collection of sand boils on the east side of the river not far from the LSU campus. Pumps move this unwanted water back into the river. Elsewhere, the Corps has laid down concrete mats, in an attempt to control erosion, but some deep holes have developed nevertheless.

The river levees do bear watching, and they are watched, but, all in all, the river is not the problem. The danger to New Orleans and vicinity, proved time and again and most catastrophically by Hurricane Katrina, has been the much less substantial hurricane levees along Lake Pontchartrain, the Industrial Canal, the Intracoastal Waterway, the Mississippi River–Gulf Outlet, the Harvey Canal in the West Bank, and elsewhere. None of these levees—none—are (or were) anywhere near as high or intimidating as those along the Mississippi River. The levees along Lake Pontchartrain range in height from 13 feet to 18.5 feet. (The difference principally reflects the designers' fear of wave "run-up"; that is, lots of waves pounding the shoreline and thereby significantly raising the effective level of the surge.) The other levees around the region range in height from a mere 5 feet to 17 feet. Extensive history and our storm-surge models produced long before Katrina show insufficiencies in many different areas, each a disaster waiting to happen, even without actual failures such as occurred during Katrina. With every levee holding intact and doing its job as built, parts or essentially all of New Orleans will still go under when a slow-moving major hurricane following any one of numerous scenarios hits the region. The details of the surge flooding disaster would depend only on the strength, forward speed, and direction of approach of the storm. With Katrina, the ADCIRC surge models pinpointed the primary problem as the levees along the Intracoastal Waterway and the Industrial Canal, which would be overtopped by the storm surge rolling in from the Breton and Chandeleur sounds and pushed up the Funnel, a feature shaped by the waterway and another shipping channel, the Mississippi River–Gulf Outlet (MR-GO).

MR-GO, as it is always labeled (sarcastically pronounced "Mister Go"), was built by the Corps to provide shipping with a straight shot into the Gulf of Mexico, a 76-mile route that cuts 40 miles off the trip down the winding channel of the Mississippi River. This route was originally authorized to be 650 feet wide at the surface, 500 feet at the bottom, 36 feet deep. It required removing more dirt than did the Panama Canal—hard to believe—and from the earliest planning stages in the late 1950s it was challenged by a host of opponents— including the Corps, because it did not remotely satisfy any of its cost-benefit analyses. Keep trying, Congress replied. The Department of the Interior stated that "excavation could result in major ecological change with widespread and severe ecological consequences." That's exactly what has happened. As a result of erosion, the channel in some stretches is now three or four times as wide as the design specification. Contiguous marshlands have been severely damaged, if not ruined. The canal feeds saltwater directly from the Gulf of Mexico into freshwater marshes and swamps and has effectively killed thousands of acres of wetlands, which are now just open water marked by the trunks of the odd dead cypress trees.

As I'll discuss in detail later, levees protected by healthy marshes are much less likely to fail. Simply put, MR-GO has devastated the

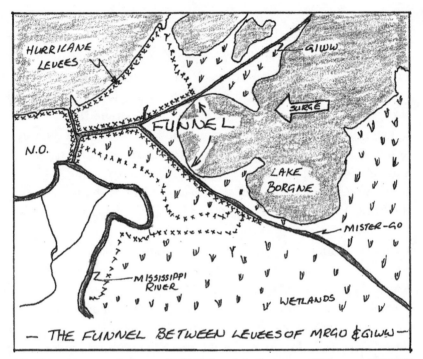

The Funnel between the levees of MR-GO and the Intracoastal Waterway [GIWW].

protective marsh structures immediately east of New Orleans, and by ruining these adjacent marshes it has made its own levees that much more susceptible to erosion and failure. In 1998, the St. Bernard Parish Council unanimously called for closing the channel. The following year Sherwood "Woody" Gagliano, an independent consulting coastal expert, presented a paper at a meeting organized by the University of New Orleans to consider the MR-GO question. Woody concluded, "The Mississippi River–Gulf Outlet, since its construction in 1965 as an alternative route for oceangoing vessels into the Port of New Orleans, has caused increased storm-surge vulnerability to developed areas of St. Bernard and Orleans parishes and extensive environmental damage to a vast region. Greatest impacts occur in St. Bernard, Orleans, and Plaquemines parishes, in that order. The channel is a serious threat to public safety and an environmental threat to the region."

No wonder it's also called Storm Surge Alley, or Hurricane Alley. Shut it down! Rebuild those marshes! Almost everyone agrees, but it still hasn't happened, even though only five ships a day, maximum, use the thing. Following Hurricane Ivan in 2004 the Corps even spent $17 million dredging it for the sole benefit of those lonely ships. Generally, annual maintenance costs vary from $13 million to $37 million.

The impact on the marshes is one problem with MR-GO. The second, more immediate problem, is its levees, because storm surge pushing across shallow Lake Borgne from the east is constrained by these MR-GO levees to the south and, to the north, by the long-standing levees of the Intracoastal Waterway. Initially ten or more miles apart, these two channels meet, and when they do the water building between their levees is squeezed into a single channel—the Funnel—only 260 yards wide, constrained by levees 14 feet to 16 feet high. Surge warrior Hassan Mashriqui has studied this phenomenon with zealous attention. His series of surge hydrographs and other velocity plots demonstrate without a doubt just how bad the "funnel effect" is right here. In concert with the denuded marshes, it could increase the local storm surge hitting the Intracoastal Waterway by 20 percent to 40 percent—a "critical and fundamental flaw" in the system, in Mashriqui's phrase. I remember the scene when he and Paul Kemp asked me to look at this data. They knew it was critically important, and so did I, because the levee designs and heights out here did *not* take this funnel effect into account. They weren't high or strong enough.

We have to get this news out, I said. Mashriqui and Paul started with a poster at a conference, and then we sought every other possible venue to warn people about this inherent weakness in the levee system. In January 2005, Walter Brooks, executive director of the Regional Planning Commission of the New Orleans Metropolitan Area, asked me to give a talk about hurricane surges and vulnerabilities at their offices in New Orleans. The surge amplification caused by the Funnel was a featured point, and during the ensuing discussions I was asked if we at LSU could come up with a conceptual plan to build a structure to protect the area. I said yes, of course. Jefferson Parish president Aaron Broussard said they couldn't wait for the

Corps, that the parishes would have to fund this effort themselves. The two Corps officials who were there said the Corps could also develop plans, but I got the impression that these parish presidents meant business. Walter Brooks asked me to return and give a longer talk that would be taped and aired on local cable TV. I was going to be overseas, so I suggested that Mashriqui give the talk. The Funnel was really his baby, anyway. He did a great job, and right before Katrina struck we were getting ready to draw up a proposal for the conceptual planning study.

The Funnel is six miles long. To the west, it—and the water in it—"T" into the Industrial Canal. It's hard to believe, if we step back to think about it. The federal powers that be had inadvertently designed an excellent *storm-surge delivery system*—nothing less—to bring this mass of water with a simply tremendous load—potential energy—right into the middle of New Orleans. If during any given storm the levees along the Intracoastal Waterway and MR-GO have not already been overtopped—or even if they have been, in a big storm like Katrina—something has to give at this critical intersection, and if the levees are anything less than optimal, it's not going to be the water.

That's what happened on the Monday morning when Katrina struck. At 6:10 A.M. the hurricane made landfall at the small town of Buras in the farthest reach of the Mississippi Delta. Katrina had weakened considerably overnight. By dawn, she was a minimal Cat 3 storm, with highest winds of 112 mph. Buras and vicinity were nevertheless devastated, of course. Forty miles to the north, where the winds were still a mere 60 mph, the first flooding of residential areas in the greater New Orleans area had already begun. The storm surge building on Lake Borgne east of New Orleans would peak at 18 feet at about 7:00 A.M., but several hours earlier the huge waves on top of the surge, driven by the winds from the east, made fairly quick work of certain stretches of the MR-GO levees, which were overwhelmed and in some cases destroyed. Water poured into the lower areas of the bowl between the Intracoastal Waterway and the Mississippi River, including Chalmette, Meraux, and Violet, with the Lower Ninth Ward farther to the west in serious jeopardy.

At about 6:30 A.M., the surge of fourteen feet to seventeen feet in the Funnel proper—the confluence of MR-GO and the Intracoastal Waterway—overtopped the levees on both sides. To the south this water poured into the communities that were already taking on water through the MR-GO breaches, now including the Lower Ninth Ward. To the north it poured into the neighborhoods in the adjacent bowl in Orleans Parish, between the Intracoastal Canal and Lake Pontchartrain. (Some of these neighborhoods had already been taking in some water from the earliest of all the breaches—between 4:30 A.M. and 5:00 A.M.—at the junction of the CSX Railroad and the northern arm of the Industrial Canal, right next to Interstate 10. The metal gates where the railroad tracks pass through the I wall of the levee were not working, apparently because of a prior derailment, and the pathetic sandbags in their stead gave way early on both sides of the canal. We know this because a nearby gauge measuring the water level recorded a rapid drop from nine feet to four to five feet above sea level. Water poured into the Orleans East bowl and the Gentilly section of the Orleans Metro Bowl to the west. While this breach was not a huge flood maker, it would have frightened local residents and, we can hope, alerted them to head for high ground—that is, the rooftops.)

At about 6:50 A.M., the surge coming through the Funnel hit the T at the Industrial Canal; some of this water was forced to the right, or north, and poured into Lake Pontchartrain, which was then ten feet lower than the surge. The rest was forced to the left, or south, where it was blocked by the closed locks that connect the waterway and the Mississippi River. (The locks were closed in order to separate the surge in the river from elsewhere.) As Mashriqui's model run had predicted, the levees along both sides of the Industrial Canal, from the river to the lake (a distance of five miles), were now overtopped. Water poured into the two bowls to the east, which were already taking on water, and now also into the bowl to the west—the Orleans Metro Bowl.

Alas, this overtopping did not relieve enough of the pressure on the flood walls. At 7:45 A.M., give or take not many minutes, two different sections of the levee along the eastern side of the southern end of the Industrial Canal—a total of about four hundred yards—

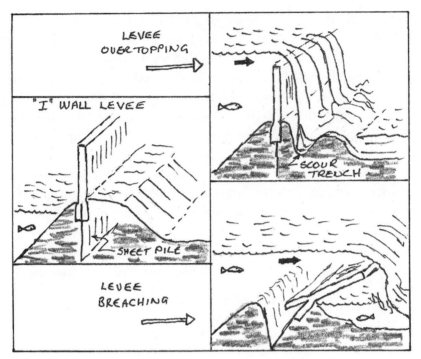

A breached levee versus an overtopped one.

abruptly collapsed. A wall of water, literally, exploded into the Lower Ninth Ward, with truly catastrophic results. Because these breaches occurred *before* the peak of the surge at 8:30 A.M., this neighborhood four feet *below* sea level was drowned by water as high as fourteen feet *above* sea level. That eighteen-foot head of water explains the total devastation of the homes within the three blocks of the breaches—devastation very like that on the Mississippi shoreline at just about the same time. Hundreds drowned in the space of about ninety minutes. Thousands were scrambling for their lives.

With overtopping, water is simply too high for the levee and flows over it. A breach is a rupture, a failure of some sort. A levee can be overtopped but never breached, or it can be breached even though it is never overtopped. The *breaches* along the Industrial Canal completely mooted our storm surge models for the St. Bernard Bowl, which of necessity assumed no such breaches and therefore predicted floods from overtopping alone, which would have ended shortly and been minor compared to what actually happened.

At about the same time, there were also breaches on the other side of the Industrial Canal—the west side, where a three hundred-foot section of an I wall failed at a railroad yard, and a seventy-foot section of levee comprised of a sandy "shell" fill was scoured and blew out. Yet another break, smaller than the others, occurred at the junction of a soil berm and a concrete wall. Thus the integrity of the Orleans Metro Bowl was now compromised, and surge water from the Industrial Canal started to flood the city.

Just about as the levees along the Industrial Canal failed, the eye of Katrina was passing to the east on its way to its second landfall on the Mississippi coast, now only as a Cat 2 storm with sustained winds of 98 mph. So the winds were way down, but the storm surge was not. Twenty-five feet to 28 feet above sea level, the surge obliterated almost everything within half a mile of the shore for 50 miles, with serious damage as far east as Mobile Bay, almost 100 miles to the east of the second landfall.

Extremely important question: Since Katrina was barely a Cat 3 storm at landfall on the Louisiana coastline and only a Cat 2 when the eye crossed the Mississippi coastline, why the record high surge? The answer is threefold. First, the momentum of the surge was established while Katrina was definitely a Cat 4 and a Cat 5 out in the Gulf of Mexico. As LSU's Elizabeth English put it, "There was essentially a lot more momentum in the water than there was in the wind." Second, the surge could maintain this momentum because the wetlands in its path are tattered, as are the Mississippi barrier islands. A third factor may have been the levee along the east bank of the Mississippi River. At landfall just after 6:00 A.M., a twenty-one-foot surge was building against this barrier from the east. Since the levee height is eighteen feet above sea level, it was soon overtopped. The surge immediately filled the river itself, in effect, then overtopped the levee on the west side and flooded the surprised residents who stayed behind over there. This surge was so powerful that even as it overtopped the Mississippi levees, therefore losing some of its head and volume, it *continued to build* to the north. Just an incredible

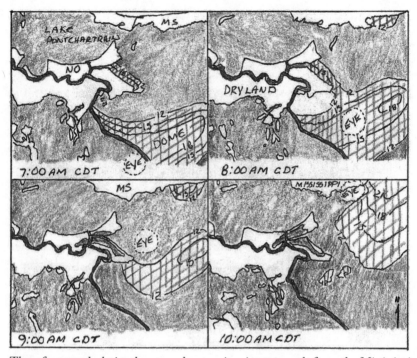

These four panels depict the surge dome as it migrates north from the Mississippi River levee to the Mississippi coast. Note how the surge dome forms ahead of the eye of the storm, is picked up by the eye, and then moves to the Mississippi coast.

surge, but hurricane guru Mark Schleifstein of the *Times-Picayune* has proposed a brilliant hypothesis by way of further explanation. Mark suggests that the levee on the east side of the river is so massive a barrier that it acted as a dam for that quadrant of the surge. As the eye of Katrina moved north, so did this dome of water. By 8:00 A.M., the eye had migrated over this dome, and the easterly winds on the backside of the eye then shoved the dome toward the east, away from the levee. The dome was then caught by the counterclockwise rotation, and at 10:00 A.M., as the eye made landfall on the Mississippi coast, so did the storm surge, augmented by this extra dome of water created by the levee along the Mississippi River. I wish I could say that this fascinating idea was mine, because it rings true to me as a partial explanation of the supersurge in Mississippi. We'll have to investigate further, of course. If Mark's theory proves correct, we have this terrible irony: The levees that protected adjacent areas from the Mississippi River exacerbated the storm surge on the Mississippi coastline to the north.

By 10:00 A.M. the eye of Katrina was well to the northwest of the New Orleans area, and the storm surge in the Funnel and the Industrial Canal was dropping as the now westerly winds pushed the water back to the east. Water quickly started draining out of the Lower Ninth. (It stabilized three days later at plus-five feet above mean sea level, then fell slowly to about plus three on Saturday.) In the bowl to the north, Orleans East, between the Intracoastal Waterway and Lake Pontchartrain, the floodwaters were also stabilizing until yet another pulse of water exacerbated this flooding, thanks to the fact that the concrete flood wall that extends for about one mile behind the Lakefront airport on Lake Pontchartrain is two feet lower than the earthen levee on either side. This aberration in levee height is quite bizarre. The earthen levee was not eroded or overtopped, even though the lake level was one foot from its crown, but the lower section with the concrete flood wall was overtopped for about three hours. What team of engineers designed the concrete levee two feet lower than the adjacent earthen counterpart? Did these engineers believe that water won't flow over a concrete wall?

The storm surge from Katrina that pushed the mass of water into the two easternmost bowls of New Orleans also pushed an exponentially larger volume of water to the north across Lake Borgne, across skimpy marshes, and through two tidal passes into Lake Pontchartrain. Here the water was trapped, and our surge warriors have modeled this basic scenario for about fifty storms. With these hypothetical storms, as the wind continues to push in the surge from the east, the lake rises, floods the low sections of Slidell on the north shore (which, for the most part, are unprotected by levees), and pounds the lakefront levees of New Orleans, twenty-five miles to the southwest. As the storm proceeds to the north, passing the lake on the east, the wind shifts to a more northerly direction, shoving even more water toward the southern rim of the lake and really challenging those levees, which rise to a height of fifteen feet to eighteen feet above sea level. At this moment, the life of New Or-

leans depends entirely on those barriers. What happens next depends on the details of the storm—mainly, the *exact* course and
speed of the storm prior to reaching the lake, and the strength and
direction of the winds on the lake. Several modeled scenarios produce a surge that simply overtops all of the levees protecting New
Orleans and drowns the city completely—no failures, no collapses,
just wholesale overtopping of levees that are not high enough.

That was *not* the scenario for Katrina. Mashriqui's last model
runs on Sunday predicted that the lakefront levees would suffice.
Those models were working with the prediction that Katrina was a
fast-moving Cat 4 storm that would lose a lot of steam after landfall
and track to the east of the city, leaving Lake Pontchartrain exposed
only to the left-hand side of the advancing storm, where the wind
speeds would only be that of a Cat 1 storm. That's what happened,
and those levees did suffice, with the exception of the section directly inland from the Lakefront Airport, as I just noted.

What did not suffice were three sections of the levees along two
long drainage canals that extend from Lake Pontchartrain deep into
New Orleans. These walls themselves were never overtopped by the
storm surge. They were high enough.

Were the walls as high as officially stated? Over the following
months, some observers would suggest that they weren't, thanks to
subsidence. The role of subsidence is definitely an important one
for the Katrina story, as we'll see, and accurate survey data on the
heights of the various levee systems in the greater New Orleans area
is scarce. Based on the best data we have, however, levee subsidence
had very little if any impact on the Katrina disaster. There is some
evidence of differential subsidence with some levees, where the soil
under a given section has compacted and subsided faster than adjacent areas, but none of these sections that we know about were overtopped. So subsidence is part of the levee landscape, but it does not
appear to have exacerbated the New Orleans flooding. Instead,
three sections of the levees on two of the drainage canals—a total
of about five hundred fatal yards—just collapsed, catastrophically,
drowning much of the Orleans Metro Bowl.

Drainage canals are required all over New Orleans for the simple reason that it rains here—a lot—and this water would collect in the bowls
if it weren't pumped up and out into Lake Pontchartrain by way of
these canals. On the other hand, some of these canals, with the pump
stations located deep within the city, could thereby also serve in a
storm to bring the lake into the city, so they must be equipped with
their own hurricane levees. For the most part, these walls are protected
from the violent wave action on the lake that batters the lakefront
levees—a key advantage, though not key enough, as it turned out.

Enter Louisiana politics. The levees along the drainage canals
(and throughout the region) are built by the Army Corps of Engineers, with the construction costs shared by the local levee districts,
which align with the parishes. These districts are then responsible
for maintenance and any other improvements they desire and are
willing to pay for. Greater New Orleans is one metropolis but two
parishes and two levee districts: Orleans Parish in the east, Jefferson
Parish in the west. The north-south dividing line is Seventeenth
Street, just as the 17th Street Canal is the dividing line between the
two westernmost bowls. This is a strange setup, and it can't possibly
be ideal. Complicating matters further, the levee districts are responsible only for the levees themselves. Parallel water and sewer-
age boards are responsible for the canals per se, and the pumping
stations. Assessing this scheme and the number of boards and authorities involved, one might suspect that political patronage has
played a role over the years, and might by now be deeply rooted.

In Jefferson Parish to the west the four state-of-the-art pumping stations are at the mouth of each canal, right by the lake, where
they function as part of the defense against storm surge, with well-
engineered and substantial concrete levee walls connecting the
pump stations to the earthen levees along the lakeshore. The water
in these drainage canals is not an unimpeded extension of the water
from the lake. In Orleans Parish, however, we have a very different
and more vulnerable system, on its face. The pump stations for the
London, Orleans, and 17th Street canals are at the foot of each

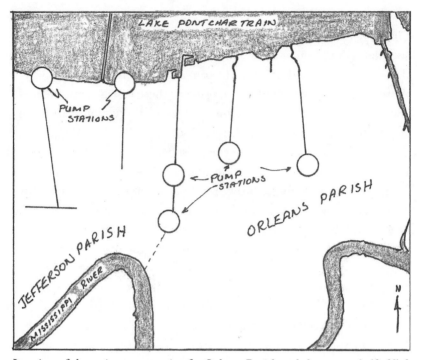

Locations of the major pump station for Orleans Parish and the eastern half of Jefferson Parish. Note the Jefferson pump station at shoreline, Orleans within the city, necessitating long parallel levees from pump station to lake.

canal, two or three miles inland. The water in these canals *is* simply an extension of the lake. The canal levees are therefore much more vulnerable to storm surge. A Dutch member of the postmortem team brought in by the American Society of Civil Engineers compared the two systems and asked about the one in Orleans Parish, "Why in the world would you invite the enemy deep inside your own camp?" Indeed.

Why the difference between the two parishes? I'll dig into this complicated issue further when I explain the investigation of the levee failures, but the difference partially reflects the simple fact that the Orleans pump stations were in the right place early in the twentieth century, when they were originally built at the edge of town. As the city expanded north toward the lake (which was possible only as pumping drained the swamps), the stations ended up deeper and deeper inside the burgeoning metropolis. In suburban Jefferson Parish, on the contrary, where residential and commercial development has been relatively recent, it was obvious that these neighborhoods would extend all the way to the lake, and that the lake is where the pumps belonged. In fact, it was the building of the lake levees and initial pump stations that allowed Jefferson Parish to develop and expand so rapidly in the 1960s and 1970s.

During Katrina, the difference became tragic. As the eye of the hurricane approached the entrances into Lake Pontchartrain from the east, the winds along the south shore swung to the northwest, pushing the violently turbulent surge, topped by ten-foot waves, against the lakeside levees. The surge itself was eleven feet in places, exactly what our ADCIRC storm-surge models had called for. The levees held. There was some wave splash over a few sections, but no overtopping. In Jefferson Parish, that is the end of the story, because these four main inland drainage canals are protected from the lake. In Orleans Parish, however—the heart of New Orleans—the surge pushed into the three main drainage canals—17th Street, Orleans, and London Avenue—impeded only by a bridge across each canal close to the lake. I say "impeded," but in fact the bridges had no negative effect on the surge heights at all, serving only to dampen waves that may have tried to propagate up the canal from the lake, as well as to slow down any water flowing in or out of the canal.

The storm surge in the lake peaked at 9:00 A.M. Monday. Less than half an hour later, when the water would have been at least four feet below the tops of the levees, a one-hundred-yard-wide section of the levee on the eastern side of the London Avenue Canal near the Mirabeau Bridge ruptured—failed catastrophically. How catastrophically? The home directly in front of the center of that breach was shoved ninety feet across the street. I managed to get some excellent home-video footage taken just after the breach occurred. It shows the water pouring in, over a mile and a half from Lake Pontchartrain and deep in the heart of the city. These waters coursing through this breach soon met the waters from the breaches and overtopping along the Industrial Canal levee a little over two miles to the east. The waters also served to lower the level in the canal, and the storm surge itself was also abating. So the head of pressure in that canal was now significantly less than it had been just half an hour earlier. Nevertheless, at about 10:30 A.M., when the surge was only seven feet above sea level, a second section of these London Avenue levees failed, this one on the west side and just south of the Robert E. Lee Bridge, less than a mile from the lake. An eight-to-ten-foot head of water poured into the neighborhoods of Lakeview to the west.

Not quite two miles to the west the levees of the Orleans Canal held, no doubt helped by the fact that the flood embankment fronting the pump station at the foot of the canal was overtopped for at least two hours. This embankment, about four hundred feet long, is six feet lower than the flood walls along the canal. The flood walls here are missing! This overtopping caused significant and early flooding at City Park, but it also lowered the pressure on the flood walls between the pumping station and the lake. In effect, Orleans Canal was a spillway for two hours, and the flood walls held. But another mile farther west, at the 17th Street Canal, one hundred yards inland from a new hurricane-proof concrete bridge at the Metairie Hammond Highway, the levee on the east side failed at approximately 9:45 A.M., a little earlier than the second breach on the London Avenue Canal. This breach flooded Lakeview, which was now taking on water from two sides.

Water would pour through the three breaches of the drainage canals in the New Orleans Metro Bowl for more than sixty hours, until early Thursday morning, when the water in this bowl equalized with the water in the lake at about three feet above sea level, and with the average home in the flooded sections standing in six to nine feet of water.

It all sounds so clinical, and it *was* clinical after the fact, as we set about laboriously putting together the narrative for all of the breaches around the city, collecting eyewitness reports, the rare time-stamped amateur video footage, professionally shot footage (almost all from helicopters), and even battery-powered and other clocks that were stopped by submersion in water. The idea was to correlate the reports and actual evidence with our hydrographic predictions, in order to establish the most complete possible forensics. What had caused these catastrophic levee breaches? This was the only way to find out. An important advantage of the ADCIRC program is that we can generate a flood hydrograph that depicts the water level at any given location over time. This graph generally has a bell-shaped curve—water stable, water rises, water recedes—with the slope and exact shape of the curve depending upon the location chosen. The hydrographs tell us when the surge peaked—vitally important to any good forensic study.

The following timetable summarizes the flooding of Greater New Orleans on Monday morning, August 29, with the arrival and passage of Hurricane Katrina:

4:30 A.M. or shortly before: The relatively minor breaches at the intersection of the CSX Railroad and the northern arm of the Industrial Canal send water into Orleans East and Orleans Metro bowls to the west. This flooding lasts about thirteen hours.

5:00 A.M. give or take: The MR-GO levees in St. Bernard Parish begin to erode and fail, with water pouring into the St. Bernard Bowl. Flooding was continuous for days, until the levees were sealed and pumping started.

6:10 A.M. Katrina makes landfall at Buras, on the west bank of the Mississippi River. Storm surge overtops the levees on the east bank of the river, crosses the river, overtops the levees on the west bank, and sends additional water into these neighborhoods in Plaquemines Parish.

6:30 A.M. The levees in the infamous Funnel are overtopped, flooding the Orleans East Bowl and adding to the flood in the St. Bernard Bowl.

6:50 A.M. The levees on both sides of the Industrial Canal are overtopped, with water pouring into the Orleans East, St. Bernard, and Orleans Metro bowls.

7:30 A.M. Sections of the levees on the west side of the Industrial Canal at the railroad yard are breached. This flooding lasts for twelve to fifteen hours.

7:45 A.M. The levee on the east side of the southern end of the Industrial Canal catastrophically breaches in two sections, sending a wall of water into the Lower Ninth Ward and other neighborhoods of the St. Bernard Bowl.

8:15 A.M. The embankment at the foot of the Orleans Canal is overtopped and floods City Park for about three hours.

8:30 A.M. The one-mile stretch of levee behind Lakefront Airport that is two feet lower than the adjacent earthen levee is overtopped by the surge from the lake. Floods for about three hours.

9:00 A.M. The storm surge from Lake Pontchartrain peaks in the three drainage canals in the Orleans Metro Bowl, with no overtopping of the levees.

9:30 A.M. Though never overtopped, one section of the levee on the east side of the London Avenue Canal near Mirabeau Bridge breaches catastrophically, flooding the Orleans Metro Bowl.

9:45 A.M. or thereabouts: Though never overtopped, one section of the levee on the east side of the 17th Street Canal breaches catastrophically, flooding the Orleans Metro Bowl.

10:30 A.M. Though never overtopped, one section of the levee on the west side of the London Avenue Canal breaches catastrophically, flooding the Orleans Metro Bowl.

It must be repeated: If the only sources of water in New Orleans had been the rainfall from Katrina (seven to ten inches), the predicted overtopping of the levees of the Intracoastal Waterway and the Industrial Canals, the overtopping of the Lakefront Airport levee, and the breach at the CSX railroad junction, the flooding in the Orleans East and St. Bernard bowls on the eastern side of Greater New Orleans would have been much less damaging, and the flooding in the Orleans Metro Bowl, the heart of the city to the west, would have been relatively insignificant. According to our latest calculations, 88 percent of the flooding in the Orleans Metro Bowl, by volume, was due to the breaches on the London Avenue and 17th Street canals. In Orleans East, 69 percent of the flood was due to breaches. In the St. Bernard Bowl, 92 percent. Thus, on average, *87 percent* of all the water that ended up flooding the greater New Orleans metro area was the result of levee failures that totaled less than 400 yards on the drainage canals and 650 yards on the Industrial Canal. It seems terribly unfair, and it is, but how large was the damaged area on the underside of the wing that doomed the space shuttle Columbia? One square foot.

By midmorning Monday these levee breaches had effectively sealed the fate of this uniquely vibrant American city. Not that most of us understood this at the time. In fact, few of us did, including me. As it would turn out, this lack of information and communication pretty well defines everything that went wrong in New Orleans over the following weeks, a systemwide breakdown that started immediately on Monday morning. Those of us stationed at the emergency operations center in Baton Rouge knew that Plaquemines and St. Bernard parishes to the east and southeast of New Orleans had to be decimated. Verification unnecessary, really. We knew that the Mississippi shoreline had to have suffered terrible damage. Verification also unnecessary. Archival work now tells us that the National Weather Service office in Slidell posted a flash flood warning at 8:14 A.M. for the Lower Ninth Ward, following breaches in the Industrial Canal levees. No one at the operations center got that message at the time, and then the Slidell office lost all contact with everyone as Katrina passed just to its east. At the center, feeds from the National Data Buoy Center, the U.S. Geological Survey, and both New Orleans airports were all down. We had no storm-surge, rainfall, or wind-speed information. Apparently Coast Guard people knew that there were residents stranded on roofs in the Upper Ninth, that there was a minimum of six feet of water in the Lower Ninth and ten feet in St. Bernard Parish. We had been predicting flooding in those neighborhoods, but nothing like that. Why didn't we know?

Everyone appears to have been working in a vacuum, totally reliant on information gleaned from the various briefings and, most important, word of mouth. The emergency operations center was still fully functional. We had power, Internet, you name it—but no communication out of the hurricane-damaged areas. Everyone everywhere appears to have been working in the same vacuum. Senator Mary Landrieu would admit soon that communications were "entirely dysfunctional." So much for the state's Smart Zone system, which had totally failed to cope. A lot of people are under the impression that cell phones are somehow above it all, but they're not. The system requires both electricity and functioning landlines. Any individual or group relying on them was in for a major surprise. Simply put, along with everything else during Hurricane Katrina, we had a ridiculous, tragic failure to communicate. Several times I thought about the ease with which I'd stayed in contact with my sailing friends crossing the North Atlantic earlier that summer.

By midafternoon Monday the storm was over, long gone, leaving behind partly cloudy skies and mildly gusty winds—a beautiful afternoon—but with water pouring into most of New Orleans through the multiple levee breaches. Why, then, did the phone call that night about the rising water in the nursing home puzzle me so much? (I related that fresh or salty story in the first paragraphs of the Introduction.) Governor Blanco did mention breaches to NBC early in the morning, but she could not have known about the canal breaches, which hadn't happened yet. Perhaps she was referring to those earliest breaches in St. Bernard Parish, or perhaps she was equating overtopping with breaching, as many would.

During hurricane emergencies we man our LSU booth around the clock, with each shift headed by a very competent individual from the Southern Regional Climate Center. From 2:00 A.M. through midafternoon Monday this was climatologist Barry Keim. He heard nothing about any breaches the whole time, and the LSU booth is

right opposite the Corps's booth. Look up from one of our computers and you look a Corps employee right in the eye. As I've related,
when the report of flooding at the nursing home came in to our
LSU cubicle Monday night, I am sure the Corps of Engineers employee heard it, along with me and others, and didn't say a word.

I arrived at the EOC just as Barry was leaving midafternoon, and
he expressed his belief that apparently things weren't as bad as they
could have been. Later I chatted with Marc Levitan, and someone
mentioned "dodging the bullet." All the while, some FEMA people
knew about the devastating flood under way. FEMA photographs
dated August 29 have since been posted on the Web. Marty Bahamonde, a twelve-year veteran and apparently the only FEMA staffer
to ride out the storm in New Orleans, told the Senate investigating
committee that he had informed one of Michael Brown's assistants
of the catastrophic flooding at 11:00 A.M. Monday. Brown in turn
told the same Senate committee that an e-mail went to Chertoff at
9:27 P.M. and that the White House was informed before midnight.
Yet Michael Chertoff told a House investigating committee that his
last report that night had been a thumbs-up. "It appeared that the
worst was over," he stated. Unbelievable.

People at the parish emergency operations center at city hall in
New Orleans (a smaller facility than the state EOC in Baton Rouge)
knew about the 17th Street Canal breach at 11:00 A.M. Colonel
Richard Wagenaar of the Army Corps of Engineers would tell PBS's
Nova that he knew by midday Monday about the inexplicably high
water in the middle of New Orleans, because he was blocked by it
on his first tour of the city. He said his group turned around and
went back to their bunker and would reassess the situation the next
day! Al Naomi, a project manager for the Corps, is quoted in *CNN
Reports—Katrina State of Emergency* to the effect that his people had
confirmed the 17th Street Canal breach by 2:00 P.M. Naomi said the
news "was disseminated. It went to our [EOC people] in Baton
Rouge, to the state, FEMA, and the Corps. The people in the field
knew it, the people here [Corps offices in Louisiana and Missis-
sippi]."

I read those statements with astonishment and can only conclude that something went very, very wrong in both FEMA's and the Corps's communications pipeline. Some of their people knew about the flooding, yet the word apparently failed to get out to the other agencies at the main emergency operations center. Or if the news did reach their people at the EOC in Baton Rouge, it wasn't passed around the room. This is the most devastating fact to me, because two thirds of the drowning deaths in New Orleans Metro bowl were due to the flooding from the three breaches on the drainage canals. That's the conclusion drawn from the most comprehensive mortality figures on the tragedy, data gathered by one of our hurricane center researchers as part of our GIS program. How many of those lives could have been saved if everyone who knew the facts had done everything in their power to make them known as widely as possible? Granted, spreading the word wouldn't have been easy on Monday. Power was down throughout the region. But both WWL-TV and WWL-AM never went off the air. Couldn't those who knew about the breaches have gotten immediate word to their counterparts at the operations center?

I'll put it this way: Knowledge of those breaches seems to have been tightly held, and the failure of the word to spread—whether due to incompetence or oversight or terrible communications—figured directly in the tragedy to come.

In February, House Republicans issued a blistering report about the delayed evacuation and the failure of the Bush administration to act on the early reports of levee failures. The day Katrina hit, between twelve and fourteen hours after most of the breaches occurred, Secretary Chertoff and the White House had been informed. This bold denunciation was titled "A Failure of Initiative." I rest my case!

FIVE

THE SECOND-WORST-CASE SCENARIO

On Monday morning Brigadier General Brod Veillon and Colonel Pat Santos were on duty at Jackson Barracks, the headquarters for the local detachment of the Louisiana National Guard. The barracks is in the Arabi neighborhood, in the St. Bernard Bowl on the eastern side of New Orleans. Santos had grown up at the barracks with his parents and had seen the major flooding from Hurricane Betsy in 1965, when the waters didn't even reach the bottom of the steps of the headquarters building. No surprise. This is relatively high ground near the Mississippi River. It doesn't flood. But early on this morning forty years later, Santos and Veillon and the other guards on duty watched in wonder as the water rose from nowhere to the first-floor windows in less than an hour. This building is two miles from the Industrial Canal breaches to the west. Such was the volume of water pouring through those gaping holes. I first heard the story of what happened next in November, when a group of us from LSU led a contingent of staffers from the House Committee on Homeland Security on a tour of the breaches across the city. I then received a note with the same story from a friend who used to work at LSU, whose husband is the commander of a National Guard unit that was stationed at Jackson Barracks on Monday.

In Louisiana the Department of Wildlife and Fisheries (DWF) has primary responsibility for search and rescue during floods, because they have the boats. On Sunday morning, six large boats and a dozen smaller ones were prepositioned at the barracks, because department officials had attended all of the surge-model briefings at the EOC and knew what was coming. On the other hand, they had no idea how high the water would reach, because the levee failures had not been anticipated. The boats were positioned on trailers, so as the water rose the boats did likewise. The DWF people and the guards had to use steel cutters on the tie-downs in order to release the craft. Two guards were assigned to each boat, and after the winds had died down they were on the water by 3:30 P.M. Monday. By that time the water was going down. (The water line clearly visible months later on these houses in the Lower Ninth, four feet up the front door, say, did not indicate the highest level the water had reached in the initial deluge Monday morning. Debris on the roof would tell us that the water was at least that high, an important factor in the forensics investigation. Another important determination was the highest storm surge, not counting waves. This water line could only be found in protected spaces such as closets.)

Overall, that completely unexpected and unprecedented flood at the barracks played hell with the first-response capability of the local National Guard units, but this remnant and their DWF counterparts were still the first rescuers on the water anywhere in the city, I believe (though I can't be absolutely certain of this). These men and women fanning out from Jackson Barracks could not believe what they confronted: In every direction, hundreds of bewildered, bereft people and their pets on porches, if they were lucky, or rooftops, more likely. The boaters set to work, ferrying the rescued to the courthouse of St. Bernard Parish, to the levees, to any high ground. Just before dark, Coast Guard and National Guard helicopters started to move those on high ground to the Superdome, therefore setting the stage, unwittingly, for the debacle that was to follow at that building over the subsequent few days. The boats had to cease operations with darkness, because the overhead power lines were now right at eye level for anyone on the water. (Some of the helicopters could operate at night with spotlights and infrared sensors.)

So there was a bit of rescue work already underway on Monday, but of course almost no one knew about this, either. By unofficial count, these small teams—many of whom had lived nearby and lost their own homes—pulled two thousand people from jeopardy in the days to come.

At 3:00 A.M. Tuesday morning a BBC producer called my cell phone, anxious for the latest. (In and around Baton Rouge we did enjoy spotty cell coverage.) My wife loved that, but she soon got used to it. Once your phone number gets into circulation, it's all over. Maybe if I had "slammed down the receiver" for those first calls in the middle of the night a different word would have begun to spread, but I didn't think that was part of my basic job description, which for four years had been to understand what such a storm would mean for this part of the country, aid in preparation, and spread the word. Now, when the worst was actually happening, was no time to back off.

As for the latest, well, early that morning—now twenty hours after the catastrophic flooding had begun in New Orleans—the world at large, including me, was *still* under the misimpression that the famed city had dodged the proverbial bullet. As I write this I'm looking at a congratulatory e-mail from a well-informed friend who works for a major oil and gas company in Maryland, time-stamped 6:22 A.M. Even CNN was confused: Later that morning it reported a "new" levee failure. Maybe that was a failure newly discovered by the network, but it was not a new failure. I couldn't help the BBC producer, who couldn't help me. Like a lot of people I learned the fate of New Orleans when I tuned in to WWL-AM driving to Baton Rouge that morning, as I described in the introduction. Then I knew what the reports about "new flooding" meant. They meant that the water in the nursing home had been salty. They meant that my worst fears were coming true. Yet at a press conference at four o'clock Tuesday afternoon Senator David Vitter said about the water, "In the metropolitan area in general, in the huge majority of areas, it's not rising at all. . . . I don't want to alarm anyone that New Orleans is filling up like a bowl."

At that moment the water was still rising in the Orleans Metro

Bowl, thanks to the levee breaches on the 17th Street and London Avenue canals, was stable in the East Orleans Bowl, and was falling in the St. Bernard Bowl (but still very high nevertheless). So I definitely wanted to alarm everyone that New Orleans either *was* filling up like a bowl or had *already* filled up like a bowl. We no longer needed to tell the flooded residents to run or swim or climb for their lives, because they now had no choice, but every official, bureaucrat, and functionary needed to understand what was happening and to get moving. Apparently the message wasn't getting through. A FEMA spokesperson agreed with Senator Vitter about the bowl not filling up, and added, "That's just not happening." His boss, Michael Brown, dispatched one thousand employees to the stricken area—and gave them two days to arrive. Brown also reminded all first responders to be sure to check in first with state and local officials. By all means, check in.

Most of us with the LSU Hurricane Center took a different approach with our interviews. If anything, we embellished the extent of the flooding. For one thing, we didn't yet know where it would end or at what depths. For another, all remaining residents needed to get out of New Orleans. (Mayor Nagin issued his bulletin to that effect the following morning.) In retrospect, it seems to me that it wasn't until midafternoon Tuesday that the terrible implications of the levee breaches became indisputable. We saw the pictures of people stranded on roofs, on overpasses, on levees. We saw the tsunamilike damage in southeastern Louisiana and the Mississippi coastline. We saw the early looting footage. We saw the rapidly deteriorating conditions at the Superdome, suddenly besieged with people flooded out of their homes and brought in by rescue helicopters, but with those same floodwaters now closing in on the big building itself. Staffs were evacuating patients from hospitals to the Causeway Cloverleaf overpass, where ambulances could then pick up these patients and drive them west on Interstate 10. So faint glimmers of the chaos to come were getting out, thanks almost entirely to our often maligned media, which did an absolutely amazing job during Katrina, in my view. On Monday they had been way ahead of everyone else. On Tuesday they kept their lead. For the next week the reporters and the cameras got to places that FEMA never reached, or so it seemed.

Invisible on Monday, the Army Corps of Engineers now surfaced on Tuesday to take a look at the problem. They arrived at the intersection of the Old Hammond Highway and the 17th Street Canal in tandem with officials from the state Department of Transportation and Development (DOTD), who were touring as much of the city as they could reach, trying to pinpoint the sources of the flooding and assess the status of the pump stations. Standing on the bridge over the canal, these stunned representatives looked at the gaping breach on the east side of the levee, a couple of hundred yards wide, a couple of hundred yards away. Twenty-four hours after the levee failure here water was still pouring into the city, with every home to the east deep underwater. To the west, just one hundred yards away on the unbroken side of the canal, the city was dry. For the most part, therefore, this canal marked the western edge of the major flooding. Soon officials from the Orleans Levee Board joined the group, but not by car. Their whole territory was flooding, so they had walked along the top of the flood wall from the district's storage yard behind the Lake Marina and Yacht Club, about half a mile away.

About 11:00 A.M., a few helicopters appeared overhead—a unit of the Texas Air National Guard. One of the choppers found a place to land, and the pilot conferred with DOTD's Mike Stack about hauling in sandbags from a nearby staging ground set up earlier by the levee board. Over the next couple of hours these choppers dropped maybe ten bags, then flew off across Lake Pontchartrain to refuel and never came back, no doubt rerouted to rescue efforts, because the dire straits of those remaining in the flooded neighborhoods was now known to all.

By the letter of the law the Corps was not responsible for responding to that breach at the 17th Street Canal—the Orleans Levee Board was—but that organization was effectively underwater and out of commission. The DOTD folks were operating under the general assumption that the Corps would take control of the situation. In fact, however, the Corps's personnel at the site were ordered to leave when the sandbag drop started on Tuesday. They did nothing at the site on Tuesday. The Corps would return the following day on a consulting basis, then arrive en masse and take over the job on Friday. Is it conspiratorial of me to imagine that their actions might have related in some way to the arrival Friday afternoon of President Bush to view the now world famous breach?

On Tuesday afternoon Mayor Nagin said that the city had dodged the worst-case scenario on Monday, when Katrina struck, but was now facing the second-worst-case scenario. Fairly phrased, I think. With a stricken sadness in his face and eyes, the mayor also acknowledged the harsh truth: The water would stop rising throughout the city only when it equalized with the water in the lake. From the air most of New Orleans looked like a houseboat community. Someone said, "We are *below* ground zero." For us at LSU the immediately pressing question was how far below? To figure that out we needed to know how high Lake Pontchartrain was, and the water level gauges at the midlake site were no longer transmitting data. So I headed out, with an ulterior motive as well. I wanted to check on my sailboat. I rushed home, picked up Lorie and the inflatable dinghy, and headed for Madisonville, talking to reporters via the cell phone until I lost coverage. Once off the highway we encountered lots of downed trees and power lines. At Madisonville the police had set up a checkpoint, but that's why I have my bright yellow LSU hurricane center sign on the dashboard. It always works, I'm proud to say. Once on the water we headed for a spot where I knew I could get the lake's water elevation, or at least a good estimate, and also determine if the Tchefuncte River was still rising, which was quite possible, because some of these river basins had taken in a foot of rain. Then, unbelievably, the cooling water pump on my dingy outboard engine quit. In eighteen years, this engine had never given me a problem. I paddled ashore, packed up the dinghy, and got across the bridge on the Tchefuncte to Marina Del Ray, where I had another rough water gauge. But I didn't really need it, because we had to wade in chest-deep water to get to the dock site. This water was about six feet above sea level, with the mean at that locale two feet. And the water was still rising. Not good for New Orleans.

Without the dinghy we now had no way to get to our hurricane hole, but just as we were about to leave in disappointment, the marina owner's son offered to take us up the river. Plenty of trepidation on the way, but to our joy the *Maggie* was fine, for the most part. But she was now awfully close to the bank, and when we pulled up on the anchor lines to move her, we couldn't. Something had rolled in over the lines, and all were stuck. Looking more closely at the anchorage, I could see what had happened. Sometime after I'd added anchors and lines on Sunday, a houseboat had pulled in and moved one of my main anchors. This just isn't done, not by real boaters. In my book, you respect other people's property. This refuge had lots of space; there had been no need to interfere with my carefully designed anchor spread. As it turned out, that houseboat owner cost me time and some tough conversations with my insurance company. On the other hand, it could have been worse. I had feared the worst for my boat.

On the river we saw a massive fish kill and schools of small minnows swimming close to the surface, apparently sucking air, a sure indication of low oxygen levels in the water. I wondered aloud what would happen to the whole lake system once the pumps in New Orleans started to empty the "witch's brew" out of the city and into this water. At the first chance I cell-phoned the information to the LSU desk at the state EOC. I also phoned surge warrior and GIS genius Ahmet Binselam and asked him to pull up the LiDAR data set for New Orleans. (LiDAR stands for light detection and ranging, a system for projecting laser beams from an aircraft and working with the beams reflected back to the source. [Radar is an equivalent tool using radio waves.] This technology has given us an extremely accurate elevation map for New Orleans—a dry New Orleans.) Combining this elevation map with the elevation of the floodwater gives us the depth of the water at any chosen location, and I asked Ahmet to generate three images for our Web page, one each to show the extent of the flooding if the water in the city stabilized at sea level plus five feet, plus four feet, and plus three feet. At the time, the lake was at plus six, maybe even more, but it had to start falling fairly soon. How far and how fast I didn't know, however, so it made sense to cover all bets in the likely range. This would give the emergency responders an idea of just how severe the flooding would ultimately be. We could also send all of the reporters to the page, all of whom wanted to know how deep the water would be. They also wanted to know how long before stabilization. I thought it would be a few days.

No sooner had I returned to my office at LSU than I got an e-mail from Mark Schleifstein, who was "holed up" in his "moat-surrounded newspaper building." While some of the other media were still reporting that the worst was over, with New Orleans spared, Mark knew better. He could see the waters rising at the *Times-Picayune* building about a mile north of the Superdome. He also heard about fellow staffers whose homes in nearby Lakeview were being flooded, primarily by water from the London Avenue breach. (A few hours later the editors of Mark's newspaper would have to order the evacuation of their building and head for Baton Rouge. From borrowed offices at LSU, they put out their newspaper through what became the vitally important Nola.com Web site.) I wasn't surprised that the coauthor of the "Washing Away" series instinctively understood that the critical issue regarding the flooding would be the level of the lake over the upcoming days. Could I give him any help? A few hours later, yes, as Ahmet posted the first map for flooding in New Orleans. What a wonderful person Ahmet is. He went many days with no sleep and was always pleasant. He had been severely beaten up the previous Halloween, possibly because he is a Muslim, and now he has a steel plate in his skull. The responsible parties are still unknown. Where are they now? I want them to know what a mild-mannered, peaceful person their victim is, and what a huge role he played in saving lives during Katrina.

That Tuesday night on CNN Larry King put out the number that crystallized the catastrophe for everyone: Eighty percent of New Orleans had flooded, with the waters still rising. Governor Barbour described the utter devastation along the Mississippi coastline, graphically confirmed by the footage. There were estimates of five thousand buildings destroyed in Biloxi, one fifth of the city. The storm had no respect for property values, that's for sure. On the opposite end of the economic scale from sections of the Lower Ninth Ward in New Orleans were the couple of hundred half-million-dollar homes in the South Diamondhead development on Bay St. Louis and the older homes on the water in Pass Christian, all swept away.

At the end of the program it was my turn, by telephone. Since I was the public health expert on the show, King wanted to know about West Nile virus. As it happened, I'd opened an e-mail on that subject that morning from a colleague at the University of Texas, Brownsville. I replied to King that "we're going to have a whole lot more folks gone down with West Nile." That prediction proved right. In December 2005, the Centers for Disease Control reported that the number of cases in Louisiana, Mississippi, Alabama, and Texas had increased by about 24 percent from 2004, all due to Katrina and Rita.

Our host asked me about toxic mold.

Definitely a problem for anyone wanting to restore a house that had stood in water for weeks.

"What's your read on the future?"

"It's very bleak." I then amplified on this assessment.

"How long is this going to take to rebuild?"

"Years. Years and years and years." I then amplified on this assessment.

King asked Governor Blanco if she wanted to comment on my list of issues. "They're all our worries," she said. "It's the very list of things I've been worrying about all day long . . . how to make sense of all this. A million people homeless is not something that happens just every day." The governor took some criticism in some quarters for looking, in those first few days after Katrina hit, like a deer caught in the headlights. I think that's unfair. To my mind she and Mayor Nagin have a much better defense for their responses immediately after the storm—set aside planning—because they were inside the story. It had happened to them. The situation in Louisiana and Mississippi now really was, as King replied to the governor,

"Unfathomable." The enormities of this disaster were just starting to settle in, and for many it was totally unbelievable. Everywhere you looked the wheels were coming off. Even a hardened professional such as Walter Maestri, head of emergency management for Jefferson Parish, burst into tears over the radio as he pleaded for help.

At home that night, with the water in much of the city still rising, I got a wonderful e-mail from a student in my DSM 2000 class the previous spring (an introductory disaster science and management course). John Tanory had a seventeen-foot boat with a 140-hp Evinrude motor in Houma near the coast, and he and his brother wanted to help. I suggested he contact the Jefferson Parish EOC, and wished him luck. I wonder whether John and his brother headed for New Orleans, early volunteers in our "Operation Dunkirk"—on the home front this time, and sixty years after the first one. The main staging ground for the freelance boaters working in the Orleans Metro Bowl became the corner of Poydras and Loyola streets, two blocks from the renamed Sewerdome. Rescuers could tow their boats right up to this intersection from the west, launch, and get to work saving lives. Over the following weeks, then months, I drove by this intersection often, and long after the city was completely dry there were still a couple of boats tilted on their sides here, looking exhausted.

SIX

INTO THE BREACH

E veryone finally knew the full extent of the flooding—Larry King and others had latched onto the "80 percent" estimate (I used 85 percent)—but on Wednesday morning, when we at LSU actually saw the first QuickBird satellite images supplied by Digital Globe, we were stunned. If anything, even my estimate seemed too low regarding the Orleans East, Orleans Metro, and St. Bernard bowls, almost all of which were forbiddingly dark and murky in these images. Altogether, 148 square miles of urban flooding. Had any large city anywhere ever been so devastated by water? The Dutch experienced massive flooding in 1953, but not in any of their very large cities. None of the Mississippi River floods had inundated major cities. Florence was famously flooded in 1966, but not to this extent. All I know for certain is that no such scene had ever been captured with such compelling images.

You have to understand. All of us at the hurricane center—and in other offices around the state and the country, for that matter— were almost as familiar with the basic scene on the table in front of us—New Orleans, uniquely defined by Lake Pontchartrain and the big river with the large crescent that gives the city its nickname—as we were with pictures of our own families. In a way, we were looking at our professional lives. It was quite strange, and these first pictures had a sobering impact on all of us. We could now see the enormity of the problem facing everyone still in the city and everyone trying to help everyone still in the city. Prone to worrying about worst-case scenarios anyway, I found this imagery really depressing— morbidly so. I felt a real sense of dread.

The first batch of ten pictures included three before and after comparisons, one each for the Industrial, 17th Street, and London Avenue canals. Looking at them again months later, I now realize that the one for London Avenue includes only the breach on the west side near Robert E. Lee Boulevard, not the one on the east side, near Mirabeau Bridge. Even though this breach was less than half a mile from the other one, no one had officially identified it! Not until Sunday—six days after the storm—when I joined a flight over the region, could I confirm to state officials the *two* breaches on the London Avenue Canal. That's how shaky everyone's information was that first week after Katrina swept through. It's unbelievable, considering all of the resources theoretically at hand.

Still, at the two hurricane centers we did have a tremendous amount of background data and information in the Geographical Information System (GIS) database, and during that first week, especially, we hustled to get it out there to everyone who asked for it—FEMA, the Centers for Disease Control, the Department of Health and Human Services, the state police, the Department of Wildlife and Fisheries, the state Department of Health and Hospitals, the emergency operations center—and some who didn't ask, because they didn't know we had what they needed. Even some of the state agencies were surprised by the cornucopia at our fingertips. Late Tuesday night, when it was already obvious that our computing power wouldn't be able to handle the demand for the GIS products and the maps, Kate Streva, Ahmet Binselam, and Hampton Peele, old friend and GIS wiz with the Louisiana Geological Survey, hauled all the machines from the offices at LSU to the cubicles at the EOC and set up a twenty-four-hour-a-day operation. Kate, third-trimester pregnant, organized the whole thing. When I was finally able to persuade her to take that baby home, John Pine of the geography department, and also a member of our team, took over with a flourish. On Wednesday afternoon I was at a briefing at which a state employee gave his update using a small-scale road map taped to the wall. This was the kind of map they hand out to tourists! Wait a minute, I thought. Given the national exposure of these briefings, given our incredible cartography resources, we can and will do better than this. I rushed back to LSU and called on John Snead, a good friend, head of the cartographic section of the Louisiana Geological Survey and part of our GIS team. John produces the official state map; I asked him to produce a large-scale version depicting southeastern Louisiana. The next day we taped this superior map to the wall in the press briefing room at the emergency center. Then everybody wanted one, which was fine. John's team ran off dozens of copies. Clearly, already, Katrina was shaping up as a major catastrophe, and in order to properly articulate what was happening where, everyone involved needed good maps. This is one of the unwritten laws of disaster management.

The Board of Regents authorized us to go to "full operational support"; that is, our researchers were authorized to participate in any support activity related to their expertise. On Wednesday night we had a big meeting to coordinate all this. Nor were the two hurricane centers the only disaster resources on the campus. Not at all. There are also researchers at Louisiana Geological Survey and in the geography, environmental studies, civil engineering, and other departments, and everyone wanted to share everything with everybody. That's the simplest way to summarize the response across the board in the Katrina emergency, and I don't exaggerate. GIS-savvy people I had never met suddenly stepped forth with their expertise and enthusiasm. In this respect, those first weeks were gratifying. I've already noted with emphasis that pure science is sexier than applied science for most universities. Even with all the visibility our LSU centers have received since they were founded in 2000 and 2001, respectively—and not just visibility, but with good, useful research—even though we bring in large sums of money, we have always been shortchanged when it comes to resources. Do I sound peevish? So be it. I think the blinders that upper administrators of many universities utilize in defining their institutions' role in society hurt everyone, and they don't endear the universities to legislators either, especially not in Louisiana. Anyway, given the second-class status of us soft-money scientists at LSU, there was some satisfaction during

Katrina when we could not only say "We told you so!" but also contribute to the immediate solutions as well.

Early on Thursday morning the water in the Orleans Metro Bowl finally achieved equilibrium with Lake Pontchartrain at three feet above mean sea level. In the St. Bernard Bowl to the east the water level dropped from its highest mark of plus-twelve until Saturday, when it was also stabilized at about plus-three, while in Orleans East the water level never got as high as sea level (though these neighborhoods flooded terribly, because some are minus-ten in elevation). I described in the previous chapter how GIS whiz Ahmet Binselam had combined our LiDAR-based elevation maps of New Orleans with three different hypothetical floodwater depths—three, four, and five feet above sea level—to show everyone where the waters would be after equilibrium. He posted those models on Tuesday. Over the next week all of the agencies engaged in search and rescue, including FEMA, the Coast Guard, the National Guard, Louisiana Wildlife and Fisheries, and the state police wanted the plus-three map to guide their efforts. Because resources were so limited, extremely jeopardized sites such as nursing homes were searched for survivors first, and those sites were prioritized according to water depth. Generally speaking, everyone except some of the freelancing rescuers tried to proceed from the deepest to the shallowest areas.

On Thursday we had a bit of a dustup with the French company that produces and owns the best high-resolution satellite imagery with which to determine flooding on the commercial market. LSU's Earth Scan Lab had received some of this SPOT imagery from the remote sensing laboratory at the University of Miami and immediately posted it on various LSU Web sites. The value of this imagery over the QuickBird photographs we had gotten on Wednesday morning is that it is very easy to discern flooded versus nonflooded areas with SPOT. Additionally, the resolution is good enough that I could use it to "inspect" the levee systems for the whole region to see just where and how bad the breaches had been. For example, at this still early stage of the disaster, we didn't have solid information

about conditions in the lower St. Bernard Parish east of New Orleans. Anecdotal reports were just about it, and they seemed almost
unbelievable. But by using the SPOT imagery to find all the levee
breaches we were able to see that the anecdotal was all too real.
About four miles of those levees had been completely destroyed.
Anyone who hadn't evacuated would have faced the almost unhin-
dered storm surge and water as high as fifteen feet above sea level! If
still alive, they would be in desperate straits now. So this SPOT imagery had proved its value almost immediately, but no sooner had
we started using it than the folks in Miami advised us to cease and
desist, to take it down from all LSU Web sites, and to advise anyone
who had already accessed the data—six hundred users, we quickly
counted—to also cease and desist. Our friends in Miami said the images were strictly NDA—No Distribution Allowed. So said the
French company that owns the SPOT imagery.

I quickly found out that this company already had a reputation in
Louisiana for aggressively defending its copyrights. Some time earlier the Department of Environmental Quality had purchased SPOT
panchromatic imagery for the whole state, fused it with Thematic
Mapper imagery, and released the beautiful package of images and
information to the public. The company immediately chastised the
agency and threatened a lawsuit. When it persisted with this threat,
the agency complied and has never done business with that outfit
again. On Thursday morning I e-mailed our contact in Miami the
following note: "As I write this e-mail people in New Orleans are
dying. The rescue squads as well as the public health and other
emergency medical personnel really need this data. This is a time of
national and international crisis. Tonight I will be a guest once again
on the Larry King show and I will make a point of telling the world
about this heartless approach to the New Orleans disaster, Ivor."

I was really angry. It was my pleasure to threaten that company
with what I sometimes get the impression is just about the only
thing any big company fears: bad publicity. (I don't know about in
France, but in the United States I understand that companies also
fear juries, which is why they pour so much money into the so-called

tort reform movement.) In any event, my little threat worked like a charm. In not much over an hour our colleagues in Miami told us that they had permission to set up a site to use the SPOT imagery of New Orleans for "humanitarian purposes."

Before the taping of my remarks for Larry King's show Thursday night, I ran into Senator Mary Landrieu, with whom I'd shared the King platform the night before and who was preparing for an interview with another network. I told the senator I was pretty distressed. I was pretty sure that King would ask my opinion about the response, whether "the wheels had come off" or something like that, and I felt the wheels of the emergency response *had* come off, and I would probably say so. She suggested a softer approach. Mindful of my status as a lowly soft-money scientist at LSU, and of the general wisdom of avoiding the overtly political, I was swayed by her advice. Holding back wasn't easy, but I did it. I told King, "The wheels haven't come off, but the wheel nuts have come off." Maybe that was a bit too technical for the broad audience, but I'll stand by the assessment now. Then I added (as I stated in the Introduction), "We in Louisiana can only trust that our governor, and especially the president, are putting all the resources of the federal government and our mighty military to bear on this problem."

Anderson Cooper was also on the show. Earlier that day he had famously come close to blowing his editorial objectivity while reporting from Biloxi, Mississippi, I think, although he'd already been all over the region. He was just tired of hearing politicians say they understood people's frustration. Had he heard Governor Haley Barbour's previous remark to that effect on this very show? I don't know, but he said, "It's not that people are *frustrated*. It's that they're *dying*." Anderson explained that some people on the streets could pick up news from satellite radio, and they heard the politicians congratulating each other about their great relief work, and it was driving them crazy. Actually, it was driving all of us crazy. As any disaster science specialist knows, the presence of politicians gladhanding and congratulating each other in the response phase of a disaster can only mean that things are going badly. All you had to do was watch the TV during the first days of the Katrina story to know the wheels had come off! I heard Anderson's interview while I was waiting my turn, and I really respected him for speaking out. A few days later I spent a few hours with him, and I told him that I admired him for saying what needed to be said. When he said in turn that he thought of me as one of the only honest, sane, and knowledgeable voices out there—well, that really put a lift in my step.

Also on Thursday—maybe Friday, I'm not sure, but right when the finger-pointing started—I found myself in a radio interview with someone who turned out to be a rabid reactionary on the West Coast who right off the bat started hassling me about all the corruption in Louisiana. So what? I said. There has been and is corruption in every state, and even though people down here enjoy talking about it as part of our political culture, I don't know if it's really worse than anywhere else. Chicago? Seems I've heard a few stories about the former Mayor Daley. New York? Boss Tweed. Boston? I understand the Irish had an iron grip in the old days. Los Angeles? The movie *Chinatown* was based on hard facts: The kingpins in Los Angeles stole that water. So how can you throw stones from one thousand miles away? What does any of this matter now, anyway? Any corruption in Louisiana isn't the reason FEMA, at the federal level, was totally unprepared for this catastrophe. This guy really pissed me off. Then I had another interview like that with some Canadian clown. A couple of people who stumbled across that show said I did a good job. I sure hope so. I had no patience for any of that, and I still don't. Where were the planning and the preparation for an event everyone in authority knew would happen eventually? And what are we going to do now?

The whole world saw the encampment beneath the I-10 overpass in Jefferson Parish, where there were no supplies or facilities of any sort, but where the helicopters were bringing in more people all the time. Also in Jefferson Parish was the large group of stranded folks who were directed to the bridge over the Mississippi River for impending evacuation and were turned away by armed cops. On the September 9 edition of NPR's *This American Life*, producer Alex Blumberg interviewed two paramedics from San Francisco who had been visiting New Orleans for a convention. After the storm they tried to escape the city in a number of ways. On foot they were told by police, at gunpoint, to turn back. What was going on out there?

Everyone heard about the woman who had used a door to float her husband's body to Charity Hospital, where the staff was hand-pumping ventilators for patients in intensive care, who were finally evacuated by boat to dry land, where helicopters picked them up. The makeshift morgue at Charity was now in one (or more) of the stairwells, because the actual morgue had been in the basement, which was now underwater, of course. All together there were about ten thousand patients and staff in the marooned hospitals of New Orleans, and these folks deserve—and will probably receive—a book about their remarkable stories.

As the reports piled up on Thursday, just about everyone lost it, I think. The ineptitude and the tragedy had become too much to overlook or explain away. Major General Harold Cross, the adjutant general of Mississippi, complained that he was communicating with his forces by courier, "like the War of 1812." That's truly embarrassing. In any ranking of the early snafus, the patchy communication should be high on the list. Number one, Governor Blanco said. "Interoperability" is the official lingo, and its absence had also been the problem on September 11, 2001, when New York City police officers and firefighters couldn't communicate with one another as they headed into the doomed Twin Towers. Their systems weren't compatible—that is, interoperable—and this failure almost certainly cost many lives. Chastened, disaster officials at every level of government in every state vowed improvement, but Terry Ebbert, the Homeland Security chief for New Orleans, said after Katrina, "From an interoperability perspective, we are worse today than we were before the storm."

How in the world could this be? The explanations are conflicting and complex and ridiculous—for example, the new federally funded 700-MHz radios in St. Bernard and Plaquemines parishes were deaf to the 800-MHz equipment in New Orleans and Jefferson parishes. In the city, a standoff between private-sector vendors vying to provide new equipment had stalled the interoperability initiative. And these are problems *everywhere*. A *Frontline* broadcast in November

2005 identified a grand total of three states that have installed effectively interoperable systems in all jurisdictions: Delaware, Michigan, and North Carolina. Speaking to the problem, Tom Ridge, former governor of Pennsylvania and former secretary of the Department of Homeland Security, blamed the states, because the federal government can't enforce standards. "Bull," replied Warren Rudman, former Republican senator from New Hampshire. The federal government imposes standards all the time, across the board, Rudman said.

The solution here is painfully obvious. We need one interoperable system covering every jurisdiction in this country, because disasters do not respect borders. New York City is on a border. Philadelphia. Portland. Washington, D.C.! If the fifty states and the federal government can't get it together to accomplish national interoperability, shame on them, shame on us.

In the preceding chapter I introduced the scene at the levee breach on the 17th Street Canal. The Corps had left the site on Tuesday—the rudimentary, woefully ineffective sandbag drop wasn't a Corps-authorized job—but the Corps then arrived en masse on Friday, as would the entourage of President Bush. I'm going to relate what happened in the interim in some detail, because the story has not been told before to my knowledge, and it illustrates in microcosm the heroic efforts and ingenuity of thousands of men and women in the weeks immediately following Katrina—and also the profound confusion and what sometimes seemed to be outright obstruction that also marked those days and nights.

The 17th Street Canal is the border between Orleans Parish to the east and Jefferson Parish to the west. Following Katrina it was also the western border of the flood. It was Orleans Parish that was flooding that week, and the Orleans Levee Board was legally responsible for the levee, and therefore for sealing the levee breach, which was on its side of this canal. But this entity had lost all of its equipment, and its employees were staged at the EOC or scattered far and wide. Jefferson Parish was mostly dry, but not entirely, because some of the flooding to its east in Orleans Parish was backing into adjacent neighborhoods to the west, where workers had their hands full throwing together a makeshift levee right about where Interstate 10 crosses the parish boundary. (Without this levee, just a few feet high, a large section of Metairie would have flooded to depths of perhaps five feet.) But there is also the West Jefferson Levee District, which is responsible for the areas of that parish across the Mississippi River. These were totally dry. Most of the "West Jeff" employees were living at the office, because their homes were without services, and in some cases roofs, but at least their homes were not underwater. All of these folks had long-standing experience with breaches in their incomplete flood-protection system—nothing like this breach, but holes and floods nevertheless. Also, levee boards around the state are always helping each other. It is the neighborly thing to do, not to mention the fact that this flooding in New Orleans was an unparalleled catastrophe for the entire region.

On Wednesday morning, therefore, West Jeff officials Harry Cahill and Giuseppe Miserendino, president and deputy director, respectively, arrived at the 17th Street Canal and volunteered their services and their crew to help. Over some kind of phone connection an official with the Orleans Levee Board officially asked the West Jeff team to do what it could. In conjunction with Mike Stack of the state Department of Transportation and Development and everyone else on hand that morning, a plan was devised to build a makeshift road, a working platform, from the bridge to the breach, using the earthen berm as a starting point, even though water was lapping up its side and it was too waterlogged for vehicles. With the right heavy equipment and dump trucks, the job was doable. Once at the breach the crews could either continue building the road all the way across or drive steel-sheet piling and create a dam. Time for that decision later. One point seemed certain: An aerial bombardment of sandbags would not be enough by itself. Someone's quick math guestimated that a squadron of choppers dropping one hundred bags an hour would require forty-eight hours to seal the breach, and even if these numbers were right, where were these helicopters?

How soon could they arrive? The prudent course was to forget the sandbag option, no matter how clean and simple it might seem.

Mike Stack called his department's personnel at the Emergency Operations Center—called them indirectly, that is. Using a landline at the nearby condo of a levee board official, Mike was somehow able to get through to his wife Linda's cell phone. (They had been flooded out of their nearby home and lost everything, and here he was, busting his ass to do this job.) Mike found Linda, she called the EOC, the EOC personnel presumably got in touch with DOTD secretary Johnny Bradberry's office, and in this roundabout way Mike was authorized to start the road-building job Wednesday morning. Corps officials were on hand that morning, listening, "consulting," whatever, but this was not their job. That was understood.

After clearing a ten-mile roundabout route to the breach site from their depot across the Mississippi River (trees, power lines, and debris were scattered everywhere, remember), the convoy of eight or nine pieces of equipment arrived at noon. Meanwhile, Giuseppe and Mike had located rip rap (broken concrete) and crushed asphalt at a couple of stockpiles coincidentally within blocks of the breach, and they "borrowed" some from the lakefront levee itself (which was now in no danger). They also commandeered an excavator from a nearby construction site. Someone could worry about the legal niceties later. The idea was to build a reasonably safe road to provide access to this breach as quickly as humanly possible.

West Jeff had brought along several small units of portable lights, and by 2:00 A.M. that first night the crew had hauled and filled and compacted five hundred feet of workable road along the embankment, with the floodwater right below them, with fewer than a dozen men. These guys knew what they were doing. Because of safety issues—total fatigue—they quit at that hour and returned Thursday morning to continue the job. By that afternoon, the crew had pushed the road close to the breach and were beginning work on a larger platform, a turnaround that could accommodate the equipment that would be needed for the much bigger job of closing the breach itself, by means soon to be determined. (A helicopter also dropped a few sandbags into the breach on Thursday—Giuseppe had brought them from the West Jeff yard—but it was not a very intensive effort.)

This is when everything started to get very complicated. On Wednesday the decision had been made to get a second job going at their work site, using steel-sheet pile in fifty-to-sixty-foot lengths to seal the canal at the Hammond Highway bridge and thereby prevent the lake water from even reaching the breach two hundred yards downstream. To this end, Mike coordinated with Boh Brothers Construction to bring a big crane from Baton Rouge and the steel from Houston. They should be able to start work the following day. When the crew from Boh Brothers arrived Thursday afternoon and began to assess the job of building the temporary dam, traffic congestion suddenly loomed as a potential problem, because the DOTD/West Jeff dump trucks had to cross that bridge with the fill material for the road job. Mike Stack assigned one lane to each crew.

Corps officials told Mike on Thursday that the Boh Brothers crew was now under contract to the Corps, not the state. They asked Mike about getting access to the canal for a Flexifloat barge from which another Corps-contracted crew could work to plug the breach from the water. They agreed that this contractor would get started on that job at 6:00 A.M. Friday morning. The new crew would need only an hour, and they would coordinate with the other crews. That was the plan, but when the DOTD/West Jeff team arrived at seven o'clock Friday, the bridge was totally blocked by the crew preparing to launch the barge. The Corps people told Mike they'd been ordered to do whatever was necessary to get this barge into the water. Mike replied that his crew had to have access to the bridge to build the roadway, and he said he would have people arrested, if necessary. (He now had state police escorts.) Soon enough, the DOTD/West Jeff crew got access to one lane of the bridge and continued building the road to the breach. The barge contractor then asked the Corps for permission to tear down a portion of the flood wall on the Jefferson Parish side of the canal. The levee district's chief of police said he would arrest anyone who damaged those walls without Mike's permission, which was not forthcoming.

Other complications followed. In the end, it was early evening before the barge was in the water.

Midmorning Friday, Corps officials pulled rank and announced to Mike that they had hired their own contractor to take over the road construction and seal the breach from the north end. Testifying before a Senate investigating committee months later, Colonel Richard Wagenaar referred to these events as a "turf war," and he said that an unnamed West Jeff employee "literally blocked our equipment. They would not let the Corps of Engineers operate." Wagenaar admitted that the Corps was not initially engaged, because it was up to the levee district to attempt a repair. So if the DOTD/West Jeff team was succeeding, why did the Corps feel the sudden need to get involved? Harry Cahill, the head of the West Jefferson Levee District, told the same committee that his crew had begun building the road because no other agency was doing anything. He described Wagenaar's depiction as "full of bull."

On Friday, therefore, confusion reigned—chaos, from what I gather—and DOTD secretary Johnny Bradberry huddled with General Don Riley of the Corps and officials from the Orleans Levee Board to get straight, once and for all, who was running this job site. Mike Stack entered the discussions. Giuseppe Miserendino entered the discussions and urged someone to do something about the danger posed to the workers by all the helicopters that had by now joined the action, flying directly overhead with their sandbags not one hundred feet above the ground. When the backwash from one chopper knocked Johnny Bradberry against the flood wall, he told Giuseppe that he'd take care of this, and he did. The choppers thereafter altered their flight paths, for the most part.

Literally hundreds of people were milling around the bridge area on Friday, suddenly including big guys carrying M-16s. This was a puzzle until word quickly spread that President Bush would pay a visit in the afternoon, boots on the ground this time, trying to make political amends for his pitiful flyover two days earlier. His entourage arrived at 3:00 P.M. Governor Blanco, when someone informed her of Mike's lost home, gave Mike a big hug, and then she told the president, and he gave Mike a big hug. (Telling the story, Mike smiles ruefully. The camera has disappeared. The Secret Service asked Mike for his address, for the forwarding of their pictures, but at this writing he hasn't yet received those pictures.)

Did the president's impending arrival have anything to do with the move by the Corps to take over the whole job Friday morning? I don't imagine it was irrelevant, but in any event the Army was now in charge. DOTD secretary Johnny Bradberry said so, and he ordered the DOTD/West Jeff team to work around the clock under the Corps's auspices. The overall idea now was for this crew to finish the road approaching the breach from the north, then work to fill the breach itself from that end, while the Corps used its barges to work on the middle and the southern end of the breach, while also dropping sandbags from helicopters. The dam at the bridge would not be closed off at this time, though it would be three weeks later as Hurricane Rita approached. With the equalization of Lake Pontchartrain and the floodwaters in the city on early Thursday morning, water was no longer flowing in from the lake, so the dam was no longer necessary.

With the Corps now running the operation, the road-building scheme changed. Work on the road actually suffered. It didn't speed up, that's for sure, because the eight trucks employed in the West Jeff system, enjoying ready access to nearby fill material, had maintained full capacity and managed a dump every few minutes. Now there were some long waits between dumps, because the dozens and dozens and *dozens* of trucks hired by the Corps were traveling in convoy to their distant supply source. Moreover, the West Jeff drivers were professionals at this kind of thing. Backing a loaded truck down a narrow, makeshift track above dangerous floodwater—they could handle the hazard, but some of the new drivers hired (for a reported seventy-five dollars an hour) by the Corps had trouble with the task. One of the West Jeff drivers was injured when a piece of debris broke the windshield of his truck. This guy refused medical treatment and finished the job without a windshield, and bleeding from the cuts on his face. These West Jeff levee pros were dedicated to the job.

Late Friday night—4:00 A.M. Saturday morning, actually—one of the subcontractors offered to drive a totally exhausted Giuseppe Miserendino home. On the way this man said he intended to make the new road "tighter." What did this mean exactly? Giuseppe wasn't sure, and he was too tired to find out. A few hours later Mike Stack told Giuseppe that Boh Brothers was taking over the entire operation *and* changing the deployment of equipment. The DOTD/West Jeff crew should stand down and leave just a skeleton crew at the site. Okay, Giuseppe said—he had no choice—but he was pretty certain that the Corps's plan would not work in the extremely confined space on that makeshift road. I'll skip the technical details here. Besides, the change lasted all of ten hours. Late Saturday afternoon the Corps realized that its new system wasn't working as well as the old one. Giuseppe got a phone call to immediately remobilize his men and resume work. With two crews working twelve-hour shifts, the breach was closed Tuesday afternoon. (When the Corps began work at the Robert E. Lee breach at the London Avenue Canal a week later, those crews used the road-building system employed by the West Jeff crew at 17th Street. I wonder whether the Corps completed those new roads as efficiently. I rather doubt it. The one at the 17th Street levee cost sixty thousand dollars, not counting whatever the Corps paid for the material hauled in by its trucks.)

On Saturday Mike Stack was ordered to take the day off and make some kind of living arrangements for himself and his wife. They ended up in a room with another couple at a Motel 6 in Baton Rouge, and they were lucky to have such relatively handy accommodations. Mike first learned about the changes at the 17th Street breach that afternoon from CNN, on which live shots of the work showed the new equipment! Puzzled, Mike was back at the site the following day, by which time the original program had been reinstituted.

Telling me this whole story months later, Mike and Giuseppe couldn't hide the emotions that bubbled up. They didn't try. As their crew had been building the road from the bridge to the breach, firemen and other rescuers were using the same bridge as a drop-off point for the stranded survivors they were plucking from rooftops. One day a fireman asked where he should take an eleven-year-old girl whose parents were gone. No one had any idea what to do with this girl. Where is she now? Mike shakes his head. One guy who had commandeered the second floor of a neighbor's house boated up to the bridge daily, trudged off in search of supplies, returned, and boated back to his new home. Food was scare. The levee district and local folks from the dry side of the canal brought some meals to the workers, and Mike brought what he could from his new home at the Motel 6. A cache of cookies held everyone in good stead.

Mike's main swamper at the job was Justin Guilbeau, whose nearby apartment was underwater but who nevertheless worked at the breach virtually nonstop for a week. He told me about the day he was in a boat with a fireman, who leaned over and pulled a cupcake in its plastic wrapping from the stinking green slimy water. After inspecting the package for leaks and finding none, he ripped it open and gulped the badly needed meal. He was that hungry.

According to the first bulletins that hit the airwaves, cops had just shot and killed four construction workers at the 17th Street breach. No, wait a minute, that wasn't right. Cops had shot and killed four *snipers* who'd been shooting *at* the construction workers at the 17th Street breach. That sounded more like it, but no, that wasn't right, either. Maybe the cops had shot and killed snipers over at the Danziger Bridge on the *Industrial* Canal. No, maybe that's not what happened either. In fact, it wasn't. Not even close, but to this day no one is sure what incident started this particular rumor. The same holds for thousands of others. I guess people as well as nature abhor a vacuum, because rumor ran amuck, instantly it seemed, much of it fed by photographs and video footage, which can be highly selective in their emphases, as we all know, and also highly misleading. The media did a great job the first few days, but certain elements sure got into rumor mongering. Looking back, I think the urban myths that took root during the Katrina emergency were just as damaging, in some ways, as the lack of information. Terrible misfortune and rolling incompetence were half of the story that first week. The other half was crime allegedly so pervasive and so violent that "chaos" seemed to be the operative description of the scene.

A visitor from Philadelphia said, "It's downtown Baghdad. I thought this was a sophisticated city. I guess not." Someone at Children's Hospital said that their worst problem was the *rumor* of looters storming the hospital, which was running pretty smoothly on generators. A doctor reported—or was reported to have reported, to be exact—witnessing patient evacuations coming under sniper fire. We read and heard about shots fired at ambulances, at helicopters, at cops, at utility workers, at the rescuers in the boats, at just about every moving human target. The state's DOTD broadcast a message over the airwaves on Wednesday to discourage freelancing boaters from hitting the waters of the city. Too dangerous for them. FEMA suspended boat rescue operations for the same reason. (Knowing FEMA, probably also because these folks weren't signing in and picking up their badges. Still, the boaters were pouring in, and it's a good thing. The *New York Times* ran a story about Guy Williams, president of the Gulf Coast Bank & Trust, paddling his canoe along the streets and finding 170 people stranded in one apartment.)

On Wednesday night Mayor Nagin ordered the fifteen hundred cops on duty to stop their search and rescue and concentrate on law enforcement. He said the looting "started with people running out of food, and you can't really argue with that too much. Then it escalated to this kind of mass chaos where people are taking electronic stuff." Now the bad guys "are starting to get closer to heavily populated areas, hotels, hospitals, and we're going to stop it right now." Later in the week he would blame the crime on drug addicts. Governor Blanco said the National Guard in the city were "locked and loaded." Both ordered mandatory evacuation of the city. "We have to," Nagin said. "It's not living conditions." True enough, but the evacuation never really happened. Joseph Matthews, director of New Orleans's Office of Emergency Preparedness, said, "The city is being run by thugs." Police superintendent Edwin Compass said, "The tourists are walking around there, and as soon as the individuals see them, they're being preyed upon. They are beating, they are raping them in the streets."

In Baton Rouge, no sooner had the city opened an emergency shelter at the River Center, a large convention-type facility, on Tuesday, than the rumors started flying, many of them apparently stemming from a routine dispute at a Chevron gas station. All of a sudden we, along with New Orleans, were surely going to be at the mercy of murderers and robbers. Our mayor, Kip Holden, complained that the state had dumped "New Orleans thugs" on his town and ordered a dawn-to-dusk curfew for all evacuees now in the shelters around the city. On Wednesday, a riot report brought SWAT teams to the River Center and precipitated the evacuation of the municipal building. In Slidell paramedics were prevented from going to work for hours because that town across Lake Pontchartrain from New Orleans was said to be overrun by gangs of thugs. On September 2, the *Army Times* gloated that "combat operations are now underway on the streets to take [New Orleans] back. 'This place is going to look like Little Somalia,' Brigadier General Gary Jones, commander of the Louisiana National Guard's Joint Task Force, told Army Times Friday as hundreds of armed troops under his charge prepared to launch a massive citywide security mission from a staging area outside the Louisiana Superdome. . . . While some fight the insurgency in the city, others carry on with rescue and evacuation operations."

I could cull the written and oral record for literally thousands of such stories and statements. But how much of all this was true? There was definitely looting and more serious crime, but was there an *insurgency*? Did looters force the doctors at Charity to hand over drugs? Did the "thugs" who had set up shop at the convention center really beat back eighty cops trying to restore order? Did pirates commandeer rescue boats for their own criminal purposes? What about the rapes reported at the convention center, at the Superdome, on the streets, everywhere? On the same edition of Larry King's show on which I referred to the wheel nuts coming off the recovery effort, Jesse Jackson suggested that these reports and rumors were probably exaggerated. Was he the only one who had noticed that it was the same five guys hustling out of the same Rite-Aid carrying the same loot, over and over and over, on channel after channel after channel? No, he wasn't, but such is the power of the image and the rumor.

LSU criminologist Ed Shihadeh, who was in demand for interviews, has studied the impact of crime rumors. They can actually be scarier than the real thing. Hearing about crime in the neighborhood creates a more generalized fear than being an actual victim. Writing for the Social Science Research Council, Russell R. Dynes and Havidán Rodríguez of the Disaster Research Center at the University of Delaware concluded, "[T]he images of chaos and anarchy portrayed by the mass media were primarily based on rumors and inaccurate assumptions. Some of these were supported by official statements by elected officials."

I certainly concur. For whatever reasons, government officials really exaggerated the "anarchy" issues. The many wonderful stories of selfless sacrifice seemed to have had a hard time competing. However, the truth did begin to catch up. Police superintendent Edwin Compass, who had made such incendiary remarks during the first week, more or less recanted a few weeks later, in an interview with the *New York Times*. (Compass soon resigned under fire.) It's our good luck that David Benelli, head of the sex crimes unit for the New Orleans police, actually lived at the Superdome for the entire week of its service as a refuge and, with his officers, followed up on every rumor that came along. So they were busy, that's for sure, and ended up making *two* arrests, for attempted sexual assault. Regarding everything else, Benelli told the *New York Times*, "I think it was urban myth." On September 26, the *Times-Picayune* provided a major critique of the crime rumors and quoted the Orleans Parish district attorney pointing out that the four murders in New Orleans in the week following Katrina made it a "typical" week in a city that expects two hundred homicides throughout the year.

In Baton Rouge, Mayor Kip Holden, who had complained on Tuesday about the "New Orleans thugs" dumped in his city, tried the next day to defuse the rumors of "looting, rioting or any similar situation." He said his first remarks applied only to actual thugs, not the many more law-abiding evacuees. By Thursday a grand total of one arrest had been reported among the evacuees. Nevertheless, the line at Jim's Firearms was over three hours long. The general perception of an entire populace in jeopardy led LSU and Arizona State officials to relocate the big football game to Tempe. (On the other hand, none of this kept property prices from skyrocketing. Wealthy evacuees from New Orleans bought homes sight unseen, then turned them for a profit when they did see them. Or were such stories just another sort of urban myth? Perhaps, but prices did go up, and within two weeks of the disaster there were essentially no homes on the market in Baton Rouge.)

The *Los Angeles Times* ran a story in November under the headline DOUBT NOW SURROUNDS ACCOUNT OF SNIPERS AMID NEW ORLEANS CHAOS. The many, many sniping stories had really caught my attention, and that of anyone who studies natural disasters, because sniping during such emergencies is almost unheard of. Write that down. Looting, yes; guys with guns, yes; homicides, a few; but random sniping? Highly, *highly* unlikely, and over the weeks and months that followed, more and more of those stories were determined to be something else, or nothing at all. The closest confirmed account was shots perhaps fired at a police station at the edge of the French Quarter. To my knowledge, that's it, and I have spoken with hundreds of sources, including evacuees, first responders (mainly law enforcement), government officials, reporters, and researchers.

New Orleans was never downtown Baghdad.

It helps a rumor to have something to work with, and in New Orleans, that was race. As early as Wednesday the racial aspect of this catastrophe had become impossible to avoid. Most of the people who had remained in New Orleans were black, and they were now either stranded in unimaginable misfortune or stealing everything in sight, or both. That's exactly what the pictures told us. For anyone with any knowledge of the city, surprise at this rather damning image could only have been feigned. Seventy percent of the population of the city is—or was—black. The Lower Ninth Ward, now completely underwater and its population now a diaspora, was 98 percent black. Of the one hundred thousand-plus residents without a car in the immediate family, 90 percent were black. It was not long before some black leaders in New Orleans and around the country began to cast the inept handling of the crisis in racial terms. Terry Ebbert complained bitterly about the lack of federal support, saying they should have arrived within twenty-four hours. Al Sharpton told Tucker Carlson on Fox, "If this had been Palm Beach, the Eighty-second Airborne would have been there Monday afternoon."

Let's face it. Hearing that remark, many if not most Americans immediately thought, "If this had been Palm Beach, there would have been no need for the Eighty-second Airborne because there would not have been any looters." Given the per capita income of such a community, I should hope not, but many Americans would be judging in terms of race, not wealth. The subject is a touchy one with me, as noted in the Introduction. Natal, where I grew up, was and is the most English (as opposed to Afrikaner), and therefore liberal (as opposed to reactionary), province in South Africa, but that didn't stop almost everyone in Natal from having black servants. We had one maid, Stephanie, a Xhosa, and from time to time my father would hire gardeners and day laborers. When I was thirteen or fourteen he bought an old house and rebuilt it over a number of years, hiring some Zulu fellows to help. After school, we, or sometimes just I, would check up on the work and give instructions. So a fact of life I can't deny is that under the apartheid system, and to some extent anywhere in Africa, where most white people have black servants, a white kid grows up instructing black adults how he (or she) wants everything done. I can sometimes be a little cocky, I'm told, and to the extent to which the allegation is true, I consider it a vestige of apartheid. At an early age I learned how to give orders, and it became kind of second nature.

At the same time I was completely aware of what was going on in my strange society. I knew the rest of the world was not organized in the South African fashion. I remember one day at the bus stop, waiting to go home from school. On the bench, certain seats were for whites, others for blacks. The same segregation held for the buses themselves. After this bad day at school, some black kids didn't get up to make room for me on the bench. A spoiled brat, I told them they had to move, and I saw a police car and waved at it. Those kids left. I wish I could find them and apologize. That was a turning point for me. I knew what I had done. I understood the injustice—and it was about time, because my parents, especially my mother, had always worked hard against apartheid. I didn't tell them what had happened.

As a student in Pietermaritzburg in the mid 1970s, a group of us tried to wage the good fight, but the combination of the security police and the government's equivalent of the Patriot Act was very effective in scaring us from acting too boldly. We were harassed at antiapartheid demonstrations. My sister, Gwyneth, who ran adult education programs for rural blacks in Johannesburg, had her office firebombed. But here in Louisiana it was different, wasn't it? I was in the land of the free, so I could do and say something. In New Orleans following Katrina I could hear the desperation in the people's voices—who could fail to?—and the preoccupation in some quarters on the crime question really angered me. The issue was totally overblown and hurt the reputation of New Orleans and Louisiana. There may have been a political agenda behind it as well, because it certainly serves to undercut public support for the relief effort.

Walter Maestri, the emergency manager of Jefferson Parish and one of the best such managers in the country, said many times to many reporters, "They told us they would be there in forty-eight hours. We just have to hang on for forty-eight hours." By my calendar, that meant that time was up on Wednesday. It was definitely up on Friday. Where the hell was the federal government? They were now in charge. Instead of effective action we were confronted by these Haiti-like scenes playing out in the United States. I saw the residue of latent racism. Or not so latent. Fear of looters and thugs, and recognition that their own scarce resources were spread pretty thin, seems to be the reason a crowd of several thousand people, including many elderly and children, were stopped by the police in Gretna, right across the Mississippi River from downtown New Orleans? I picture a different welcome if they had all been white. After those Gretna police officers were sued for that action, the city council voted unanimously to offer them the services of the in-house counsel. Councilman Chris Roberts sponsored a commendation and said that these officers had saved the area from being stormed by looters. He also said that a couple of thousand evacuees had been allowed to camp out until they could be bused to distant points. In a subsequent interview on national television, one of the Gretna officers explained that they had very scant resources of their own—water was short all around—and feared their supplies had run out already.

The worst of these provocations—for me, at least—may have been that *Army Times* piece about "taking the city back" and defeating the "insurgency." This really set me off. It was the ultimate insult to these people struggling to survive. There were some criminals in New Orleans; there are criminals everywhere. What are we teaching our young troops in today's army? Do they play too many violent computer games? Why say and print this crap?

How about Congressman Richard Baker from Louisiana, who was quoted in *The Wall Street Journal* as telling lobbyists, "We finally cleaned up public housing in New Orleans. We couldn't do it, but God did." Subsequently he stated he had been misquoted. But when I read such statements—there would be many equivalent ones to come—and I remembered that this man, specifically, professes to be a practicing Christian, but he obviously does not read the same Bible I do, definitely not the same passage in the Book of Matthew:

Then the King will say to those on his right, "Come, you who are blessed by my Father; take your inheritance, the kingdom prepared for you since the creation of the world. For I was hungry and you gave me something to eat, I was thirsty and you gave me something to drink, I was a stranger and you invited me in, I needed clothes and you clothed me, I was sick and you looked after me, I was in prison and you came to visit me." Then the righteous will answer him, "Lord, when did we see you hungry and feed you, or thirsty and give you something to drink? When did we see you a stranger and invite you in, or needing clothes and clothe you? When did we see you sick or in prison and go and visit you?"

> *The King will reply, "I tell you the truth, whatever you did
> for one of the least of these brothers of mine, you did for me."
> (25:34–40)*

I would like to point out that when the cavalry finally made it to New Orleans over the weekend, Lieutenant General Russell Honore issued a "guns down" order. "This is not Iraq," he said. "You are part of a humanitarian relief convoy."

I have a great deal of admiration for this man.

On Tuesday and Wednesday Mayor Nagin predicted that between 2,000 and 10,000 had died or would soon die in the city. He was criticized for this remark later, but the estimate was not a ridiculously wild guess. Before the storm many reporters had repeated the estimates from the American Red Cross that between 25,000 and 100,000 people might die because they could not or would not evacuate. Plus, Nagin was using his bully pulpit to attempt to speed the federal and state response to his flooded city. I can't hold that against him, and as Mark Schleifstein pointed out in the *Times-Picayune*, "Just think what the national media would be saying today if Nagin had said only 100 were feared dead—and it turned out there were more than 1,000." I think the mayor was also listening to some of our people at the hurricane center who, in the frenzy following the levee breaches, were attempting to estimate how many people may have been left behind by "backing out" the number from a variety of statistics. An estimate was needed in part to help guide the first responders who were combing New Orleans and other areas for survivors. (Our team was also able to plug all 911 calls into a GIS database that translated them into dots on maps. We could then correlate that information with Ahmet's flood-depth map, to help direct the rescuers.)

The fatality numbers I kept hearing behind the scenes—hundreds of deaths—just didn't add up for me. I've cited the public opinion surveys showing that about 70 percent of the 1.3 million residents of metropolitan New Orleans would evacuate under the threat of a storm such as Katrina. In fact, the citizens actually beat that figure, apparently, with 75 percent fleeing the area, as I've reported, but I didn't know this. Therefore we were calculating close to 400,000 people staying behind. If there were, at the very most, 50,000 people at the Convention Center and the Superdome combined—and there were probably nowhere near that number; more like 30,000— where were the remaining 350,000 people? Or assume that the city had achieved a world-record 90 percent evacuation rate, which might concievably have been the case, given the numbers of cars counted as they left town, and assume the highest possible number of refugees at the two makeshift shelters, there were still perhaps 80,000 people unaccounted for. Some of these would have been in the parts of Jefferson Parish that had not been flooded. Let's say they numbered 50,000. We still end up with at least 30,000 missing. With this analysis, our graduate student Ezra Boyd, who was developing a "flood fatalities model" funded by us for his Ph.D., thought the estimates of hundreds of deaths must surely be very low.

Ezra's model is the number of fatalities divided by the exposed population, and his hypothesis assumed a correlation between fatalities and water depth. His data from various floods around the world reveals this to be the case. Given the high water depths for Katrina, Ezra predicted a one-third fatality rate. With an estimated 30,000 people exposed to the flood—the lowest plausible number, pulling the calculation from the preceding paragraph—we could expect about 10,000 deaths. A more comprehensive but similar calculation that accounted for the range of estimated flood depths throughout the region lead to an estimate of perhaps 20,000 potential fatalities. That was the number initially provided to the state and local response agencies, and it was much too high. The *lower* number was even too high. Why?

Ezra's calculations did not account for two crucial factors: An evacuation far more successful than anyone had imagined and the effectiveness of the search and rescue operations. Indeed, it is clear that local first responders achieved remarkable success following

Katrina. The effort was not textbook, it was anything but coordinated, but it saved many, many lives. If it was not for these thousands of heroes, the number of fatalities could have been 10,000.

Six months later I'm still surprised at the quasi-official final figure of 1,300 deaths along the entire coastline, 1,100 in the New Orleans area. I hope it's right, but this is a really low number. The final answer may be considerably higher. Over 3,000 persons are still reported missing; of these almost 500 are believed to have drowned, based on a home address that was either totally destroyed or completely flooded. As of February 2006, we believe the upper limit for fatalities is 3,000. Let's hope we don't get there.

What about all the other numbers bombarding us that week, most of them enormous? While looking at the pictures of desperate and stranded people we heard about 13.4 million liters of water at the city limits, apparently, along with 10,000 tarps, 5.4 *million* ready-to-eat meals, 3.4 *million* pounds of ice, 135,000 blankets, and 144 generators. Tons of everything were ready to go. The Coast Guard, the National Guard, the Air National Guard, the Louisiana National Guard, the state police, the Army, Navy, Air Force, Marines—everyone was coming, but with the exception of the hundreds of rescue boats in the waters and a few helicopters in the air, there did seem to be an awful discrepancy between the resources in personnel and supplies allegedly available and those actually on hand and helping people. On Thursday night, just as I was suggesting to Larry King that the wheel nuts had come off, Mayor Nagin lost his cool on WWL radio and said about President Bush, "We [have] an incredible crisis here and his flying over in Air force One does not do it justice. Don't tell me forty thousand people are coming here. *They're not here.* It's too doggone late. Now get off your asses and let's do something and let's fix the biggest goddamn crisis in the history of this country. . . . Excuse my French, everybody in America, but I am pissed." Nagin later made clear that he meant no disrespect to the president, he was just at his wit's end. This was his "desperate SOS."

On Friday we did see signs of progress. The airport was functional again. A military convoy—the cavalry that the mayor had always been depending on—rolled into town with major fanfare from
the networks just about as another convoy rolled out of town—
buses with the folks who had been stranded at the Superdome who
were now on the way to the Astrodome in Houston. That nightmare
was coming to an end for twenty thousand or more people, and by
late Saturday evening the building was nearly empty.

What about the Convention Center three miles away, which was
never an official shelter but ended up with perhaps fifteen thousand
people by the end of the week? This was one of the biggest puzzles
of the whole first week. The *Times-Picayune*'s invaluable Nola.com
Web site may have been first outlet to reveal that several thousand
folks were stranded there, presumably refugees from the nearby
central city neighborhoods. This was on Wednesday morning. On
Thursday—over twenty-four hours later—Homeland Security chief
Michael Chertoff said on NPR's *All Things Considered*, "I have not
heard a report of thousands of people in the Convention Center
who don't have food and water." That same night—thirty-six hours
after the *Times-Picayune* revelation—FEMA chief Michael Brown
told Paula Zahn on CNN that he had heard about these people only
a few hours earlier. Zahn was incredulous, and said so. From that
moment, "Brownie," as President Bush called him, the man who
had been the stewards and judges commissioner of International
Arabian Horse Association for ten years before joining FEMA as
general counsel in 2001, was probably doomed. On *Frontline* two
months later Brownie claimed to have misspoken in that interview
with Zahn. When reporter Martin Smith noted that he had made
essentially the same remark on three separate occasions, Brownie
bristled and challenged Martin Smith to switch chairs with him and
see how he liked it. No matter. On the Thursday after Katrina
struck, his remark to Zahn fixed in a lot of minds, including my own,
the image of an agency, or at the very least a leadership, incompre-
hensibly and inexcusably out of the loop.

On Friday we read about the corpse in the wheelchair outside the
Convention Center, with the woman's name hand-printed on a card:

Ethel Freeman. The Reverend Isaac Clark said, "We are out here like pure animals. We have nothing. . . . Billions for Iraq, zilch for New Orleans." That day the first significant supplies of food and water finally reached these people. Some aid agencies said they had waited for three days, their vehicles packed with water and food, because FEMA had said not to go in unless they had the necessary paperwork from the state. The state knew nothing about this requirement, nor was there any such paperwork—and even if there had been, go anyway, for God's sake!

On Saturday the first buses rolled up to the Convention Center and the last of the big evacuations from New Orleans finally got under way.

SEVEN

IS ANYONE IN CHARGE HERE?

If I had been completely cut off from all news during that first week except for what I picked up from the media's questions, I could have followed the general course of events and had a pretty good idea of the evolving public perceptions and reactions. Over the prestorm weekend most of the questions had been of the "How bad will it be?" variety. But as early as Wednesday—two days after landfall—I was asked more and more about the warnings that I and many others had been delivering for years. I was asked about FEMA's Hurricane Pam exercise the preceding year, which had been designed to prepare everyone for a storm much worse than Katrina. With the flyover by the president on Wednesday and the assorted astounding remarks by FEMA's Michael Brown in the days to follow, I could tell where this whole story was headed: Where was the government? Where was FEMA? Where was the *plan* to handle this long-predicted emergency?

Part of the answer is conveyed by a brief history of FEMA—officially, the Federal Emergency Management Agency—which was created by President Carter in 1979 under pressure from the state governors, who had wanted better federal help with disasters such as Hurricanes Betsy in New Orleans in 1965 and Camille in Mississippi in 1969, the earthquake in northern California in 1971, and Hurricane Agnes in the mid-Atlantic states and New England in 1972. Carter's executive order folded into the new agency some of the one-hundred-odd agencies that were nominally involved with disaster relief. Everything I've read holds to the line that upper management positions at FEMA quickly gained the reputation of being a suitable reward for midlevel political hacks, sort of like an ambassadorship to some cold capital in central Asia, although this is unfair to the first chief, John Macy, former director of the Civil Service Commission, former president of the Corporation for Public Broadcasting, and then former president of the Council of Better Business Bureaus. Macy himself was not a hack by any means, but neither was he a professional disaster expert. Neither were Ronald Reagan's two appointed directors or George H. W. Bush's one.

In 1992, when Hurricane Andrew destroyed or severely damaged 125,000 homes in south Florida, FEMA was prepared to do essentially nothing, and that's what it did for days. Local outrage eventually stirred the first Bush White House into action, but it was too late to staunch the criticism, and the affair didn't help his reelection campaign against Bill Clinton. He carried Florida, but not by much, and the FEMA fiasco was partially blamed. (A quarter of a million people ended up living in FEMA's mobile homes in Florida for two years or longer.) Clinton won that presidential election and quickly took a tip from the big-city mayors in the Northeast, who know that the first thing they have to do to ensure reelection is to get the streets plowed after the snowstorms. Clinton brought in James Lee Witt as the new FEMA chief, the emergency response chief from Arkansas (and also his friend, to be sure). Witt was the first chief with extensive experience in the field. His top deputies had run regional FEMA offices. They were professionals. (Brownie's number-two man during Katrina was a promoted "advance man" for the 2000 presidential election. Next in line was a PR man for that campaign.) Clinton also elevated FEMA to cabinet-level status. Everyone acknowledges that Witt transformed the agency into a professional organization that did a credible job with the flooding of the Mississippi River in the Midwest in 1993, the Northridge earthquake in southern California in 1994, and Hurricane Floyd in North Carolina in 1999. The most innovative work of FEMA in those years was Project Impact, a nationwide mitigation initiative to help change the way this country deals with disasters. Instead of waiting for them to occur, Project Impact communities initiated "mentoring" relationships, private and public partnerships, public outreach and disaster mitigation projects that would preemptively reduce damage. They revised local building and land-use codes, and some even passed bond issues to pay for new measures that would help an entire community. FEMA calculated that the program saved three to five dollars for every dollar spent. From its inception in 1997, nearly 250 communities and 2,500 business partners embraced Project Impact.

In 2001, President George W. Bush appointed Joe Allbaugh to take over FEMA. Not a disaster man; instead, Bush's chief of staff while he was governor of Texas, then his campaign manager in the 2000 presidential election. Among Allbaugh's first moves was dropping Project Impact as an "oversized entitlement program." He said he intended to deemphasize the federal role in emergency preparedness, then he bizarrely told the *Times-Picayune*, in an interview for its 2002 award-winning Washing Away series, "Catastrophic disasters are best defined in that they totally outstrip local and state resources, which is why the federal government needs to play a role."

Read it and weep. The contradictions in those attitudes reveals a mentality that completely fails to understand that poor preparation for a predicted disaster exacerbates the problems of coping with the aftermath of that disaster exponentially. Yet how could anyone in authority in the disaster business miss this necessary correlation?

In the weeks following the September 11 terrorist attacks, FEMA got high marks across the board for coordinating the search-and-rescue operation. Its budget exceeded $6 billion. Then it was folded into the new Department of Homeland Security, where, as a small agency with a smaller budget of only $4.8 billion, it sank almost without a trace. Allbaugh himself told *Frontline* that the FEMA of 9/11 was not the FEMA that failed to handle the Katrina disaster. Even Brownie Brown, who had taken over the reins in 2003, complained that his little outfit had suffered from the "taxes" imposed on it under the new structure. Two months before Katrina he had circulated a memo complaining about the ever lower status of his agency and the lack of funding for any preparedness function whatsoever. (In October, after Katrina, Bush administered the coup de grace in this respect, removing any preparedness role from FEMA and giving it to the Preparedness Directive in the Department of Homeland Security. FEMA is now strictly a response organization. Again, are these people thinking about the relationship between preparedness before the fact and response after the fact?)

Worse for FEMA, terrorism became the main focus for the department. Homeland Security has handed out over $8 billion to the states to buy just about anything they want in the name of anti-terrorism. We all know the stories: bulletproof vests for the fire department dogs in Columbus, air-conditioned garbage trucks in Newark, self-improvement seminars for sanitation workers in the District of Columbia. States and localities far removed from any likely terrorist attack have received a much higher percentage of the funds than makes any sense whatsoever.

We call this pork, which is really just a polite word for corruption. Call it "soft" corruption.

What was FEMA's specific plan for rescuing New Orleans from the disaster that the agency itself had predicted for years? One day a group of academics or reporters, or both, is going to take it on themselves to try to penetrate the bureaucratic barriers and dissect it in painstaking detail. As I've said, that's going to be quite a book and quite a challenge to put together. The job will take years. For one thing, there is no there there: FEMA is really a coordinating agency. Prior to being moved into the Department of Homeland Security it tried to bring together the activities of at least sixteen different major programs in different departments of the federal government, plus all the state and local programs. Maybe the new organizational chart makes the coordination under DHS easier on paper, but the experience on the Gulf Coast in 2005 makes me wonder. Presumably, the agency itself will conduct such an investigation of its performance, but no bureaucracy investigating itself is likely to provide the answers we need.

Of course, Homeland Security officials defend FEMA's readiness, pointing, for example, to the five logistics centers around the country. Formerly, there were sixty-five. Is five necessarily better than sixty-five? Maybe, maybe not. By way of excuse for the absence of supplies on the ground immediately after Katrina struck, we heard time and again that FEMA couldn't preposition its forces directly in the path of a major hurricane. True, of course. So where were they prepositioned? We know that Wal-Mart activated its emergency command center in Bentonville, Arkansas, on Wednesday, August 24, five days before landfall. It was staffed the following day, and emergency supplies were shipping out on Sunday—the Sunday before landfall. Where, *exactly*, were all of FEMA's rescue teams, supply teams, supply caches, and all the rest on the Sunday before the storm? How about on the Thursday *after* the storm? What auxiliary communications systems were ready to go? (Brownie told *Frontline* that FEMA did have communications, "Just not enough.") What plans were in place to get the New Orleans airport up and running immediately? (What was one of the first facilities secured in Iraq? The Baghdad airport.) Where were the transport planes packed and waiting at airports out of harm's way. What facilities had been preselected for handling a million evacuees for a long period of time? (I know that answer. None.) Forget the published organizational charts, the flowcharts, the operational procedures documents. Where were the actual supplies and people, the wings and the wheels? How was everyone going to communicate? What were people *doing*?

I want to emphasize that I don't for a moment underestimate the enormity of the challenge FEMA faced with Hurricane Katrina. This was an immensely more complex job than the one the agency had faced in New York City following the 9/11 attacks, where the disaster area was tightly defined and immediately accessible, where every service was intact just two blocks away, with no vast diaspora of refugees. There's no comparison, really. More than two million evacuated during Katrina. One million were displaced from their homes for months, at minimum. Half a million were in shelters in the first two weeks of the disaster.

In fact, it would be easy to look at such numbers and think, well, no wonder FEMA and every other agency were overwhelmed. But that's an incomplete analysis, because this was not a catastrophe out of the blue—a tsunami, say. A hurricane like Katrina and the consequences were a given. The big numbers were not a big surprise, or any surprise at all. Plan for them, just as an army plans for a war (presumably), that is, with mind-numbing detail. Look at our huge effort in staging for the invasion of Iraq. Every contingency was thought through. (I'm talking about just the war here, not the ensuing occupation, many aspects of which might have been prepped by FEMA itself. In fact, it would be pretty easy to draw an analogy between the government's failed preparations for the predicted disaster of Katrina and the botched occupation of Iraq. War we're good at. The best. We stand alone. But then what? Of course, questions were raised in Louisiana about the fact that roughly 40 percent of the state's seven thousand National Guards were on duty in Iraq. No effect at all, we were told. Nonsense. Every guardsman I spoke to bemoaned the fact that their units were shorthanded and without enough people to do security, rescue, and logistics.)

Which brings us back to the Hurricane Pam exercise in July 2004, an intensive one-week war game, in effect, put together by a Baton Rouge consulting company on behalf of FEMA for the sole purpose of getting ready for the big one. Just the month before, William Carwile, FEMA's coordinating officer in Mississippi, had written Michael Brown an eleven-page memo stating that the agency's teams of national response managers were unprepared and receiving "zero funding for training, exercise, or team equipment . . . [and these responders] provide the only practical, expeditious option for the director to field a cohesive team of his best people to handle the next big one." AP reporters turned up this document in December 2005. It is full of other highly critical assessments. But maybe the Pam exercise would provide a way forward for FEMA. Marc Levitan was asked to sit on the committee setting up the exercise, and we were excited. FEMA itself—the agency that would be in charge of the disaster waiting to happen in New Orleans—had realized the necessity of planning and coordinating the work of all the other agencies involved. Apparently it understood the requirement of assessing the readiness of those agencies. Moreover, this was an opportunity to get our science out on the table. We had been officially studying the New Orleans peril for three years. We had looked at the hospitals' jeopardy and the problem of the shelters; we had conducted public opinion surveys; we had looked in great detail at the public health issues and had met more than once with the people at the Centers for Disease Control. All in all, we had an inventory, so to speak, of what would be at stake. Quite honestly, no one anywhere knows anything close to what we know about this subject. Nor could they be expected to. This has been our main job.

Naively, perhaps, we were primed to be real partners in the event. Marc had great hopes that we would be fully engaged in the exercise. But that was not to be. He is a very persuasive guy, very diplomatic, but as hard as he tried he could not convince the consulting firm FEMA had hired to broker the exercise that we had already developed with our GIS database much of what they needed. No, they replied, they would produce "all the necessary maps and such data." Our role was confined to producing a storm-surge animation for the fictional Hurricane Pam, a slow-moving Cat 3 that passed just west of New Orleans, flooded the city, and left sixty thousand dead. (The actual track was developed by the National Weather Service, with Marc designated as the LSU person liaising with them. The National Weather Service used its SLOSH surge model to get the flood just right; when they were satisfied, we did our ADCIRC animation.)

Colonel Mike Brown (no relationship), who was the assistant director of the state's Department of Homeland Security at the time, and who I'm sure was one of the prime movers in getting FEMA to stage this exercise, had always been one of the LSU Hurricane Center's strongest supporters. He had real-world experience that gave him an appreciation of the value of our research. At his bidding, our Hurricane Public Health Center was tasked with providing part of the introductory briefings for the exercise, which involved a couple of hundred people altogether from many different local, state, and federal agencies. Paul Kemp gave one briefing, I the other. We itemized everything we knew about the peril, right down to the fire ant issue. For the weeklong exercise itself I spent most of my time with the search-and-rescue planning team, made up mostly of state Department of Wildlife and Fisheries and Coast Guard officials. I felt at the time that these folks had a grip on the issues and got a lot done, and I think their performance during Katrina proves the point. As soon as the winds dropped Monday afternoon, they were out there—Wildlife and Fisheries, Coast Guard, Louisiana National Guard, and the various fire and police departments. Boats and supplies had been effectively prepositioned, including at the Jackson Barracks in Arabi, just outside the Lower Ninth, as I've described.

The search-and-rescue exercisers discussed how to deal with firearm-toting pirates who might commandeer a rescue boat to ensure their families got out of the flooded city first. Since this was Louisiana, where boat ownership is extremely high, they envisioned the large fleet of potential freelance rescuers (and some looters as well) who would probably stream out from the north shore of Lake Pontchartrain in something of an Operation Dunkirk. In the real one, British citizens had used their own craft to cross the twenty-three miles of the English Channel to rescue their soldiers trapped by the Germans on the French shore at Dunkirk—this at the beginning of World War II. For Hurricane Pam the exercisers set up predetermined pickup sites on the south shore of the lake—the city of New Orleans. Almost every boat in the state is equipped with a marine VHF radio, so we discussed the possibility of the Coast Guard's erecting a portable VHF tower if necessary. In the event, I don't know if this was necessary during Katrina, but certainly when I crossed the lake five days after landfall, the VHF communication system was alive and well. It turned out that the Katrina disaster, severe as it was, paled in comparison with what a storm like Hurricane Pam would do to New Orleans, so a full-fledged "Operation Dunkirk" was not set up. (Aaron Broussard, president of Jefferson Parish, did invoke the memory of the famous operation when he called for citizens with flat boats to help in the rescue.)

At one of the first meetings on the first day of the Pam exercise, I felt—*we* felt; the LSU group—that some of the maps weren't quite right. There were also some problems with the flood depths, as I recall. Anyway, I asked one of our mapmakers if we could generate a better map on short notice. It wasn't six hours before I got a call from someone with the state telling me to back off. The consulting company was very upset; allegedly, we were jeopardizing the whole exercise. So we backed off. Very frustrating, since we had all the information. But after a few days we ended up sharing a lot of our GIS data anyway. We produced flooding maps, we made posters. We were good scouts. We would see a need, rush back to LSU and generate the required map, and then bring it back to the exercise.

A day or two into the exercise, Colonel Brown asked me to put together a CD with the storm-surge models, examples of the GIS data, and background information. This request really helped our overall cause, I think, and we produced the disk overnight and handed out copies right and left. Then the colonel asked me to brief a White House representative (from the Office of Management and Budget, I think) who had just arrived. I outlined everything for him—evacuation, housing, contamination—but I don't think it had much impact. I got the sense that several federal officials were in attendance only because that's what was required. Perhaps not everyone at the exercise believed this catastrophe could actually happen. Perhaps the ideologues didn't think it was a federal responsibility. But such explanations don't account for the attitude of the FEMA people, who knew very well that this could happen and who, presumably, did understand it would and should be a federal responsibility. On numerous occasions, when we tried to interject some of our science, we were bypassed or even ignored by these knowledgeable people. As I said in the introduction, I just don't think some of them took us seriously. I, specifically, was the foreign geek who talked about tent cities or some such *organized*, short-term housing for the evacuees, and this was simply not in the cards—one of several critical blunders during the Katrina disaster response.

The success of the rescue efforts conducted by Wildlife and Fisheries, the Coast Guard, and the other first responders reflected the benefits of the Hurricane Pam exercise. I think it convinced *almost* everyone involved of the enormity of the challenge posed by a flooded New Orleans. However, in many other emergency response aspects, the exercise fell short. We know this for the simple reason that we know what happened—and didn't happen—during Katrina. During the Pam exercise there was discussion of the problem of evacuating the 127,000 people in New Orleans without access to vehicles. "To be determined at a later date" was the solution reached during the exercise, and I can only conclude that this same solution pertained to numerous other issues, because they never got determined at a later date, this despite the express intention to keep the "fairy dust" to a minimum. In fact, as I mentioned to Tim Russert, FEMA representatives had talked about a second Pam exercise to focus on the low-mobility groups. It didn't happen.

Now I want to amplify on the point I made while discussing the nonevacuation of the low-mobility groups over the weekend before Katrina: Once President Bush declared a national emergency on Saturday, August 27 (retroactive to the day before), the federal government was in charge, pursuant to the Stafford Act of October 2000. That act states (§401 and §501): "All requests for a declaration by the President that a major disaster or emergency exists shall be made by the Governor of the affected State. . . . As part of the request, the Governor must note that the State's emergency plan has been implemented and the situation is of such severity and magnitude that the response is beyond State and local capability and Stafford Act assistance is necessary."

Governor Blanco complied with this requirement on the Saturday before the storm. (Michael Brown would actually tell a House investigating committee in November 2005 that New Orleans was explicitly exempted from that request. Why would he say that? I'm looking at the official requests. There's no exemption for New Orleans.)

Once the governor's request is made through the regional FEMA office, state, local, and federal officials are enjoined to estimate the extent of the disaster and its impact on individuals and public facilities. This had definitely been done. I need only quote Michael Brown himself, who told CNN just days after landfall, "We actually started preparing for this two years ago. We had decided to start doing catastrophic-disaster planning, and the first place we picked to do that kind of planning was New Orleans, because we knew from experience, based back on the forties and even the late 1800s, if a Category 5 were to strike New Orleans just right, the flooding would be devastating. It could be catastrophic. So we did this planning two years ago. And, actually, there's a tabletop exercise with the Louisiana officials about a year ago. So the planning's been in place now. We're ready for the storm."

If the Stafford Act wasn't sufficient to establish federal hegemony—which it was—on Tuesday, the Department of Homeland Security declared Katrina an "incident of national significance," triggering the first use of the official National Response Plan put in place after September 11 and designed to bring all military and civilian units together in a seamless operation to confront a catastrophic event, be it natural or man-made or both (as in Katrina). In the earlier discussion of this subject I mentioned Ira Glass's interview with author William Nicholson on NPR's *This American Life*. I quote that interview again:

> NICHOLSON: Well, basically the way it works is, the Secretary of Homeland Security designates this as a catastrophic incident, and federal resources deploy to preset federal locations or staging areas, so they don't even have to have a local or state declaration to move forward with this.
>
> GLASS: And in other words, it doesn't matter what the governor says, it doesn't matter what the local people say, basically, once that happens, they can just go ahead and do what needs to be done to fix the problem.
>
> NICHOLSON: That's correct. It's utterly clear that they had the authority to preposition assets and to significantly accelerate the federal response.
>
> GLASS: And they didn't need to wait for the state?
>
> NICHOLSON: They did not need to wait for the state.

Secretary Michael Chertoff was now officially in charge of the largest domestic relief effort in this nation's history. As someone said, "It's exam time." Yet Chertoff would claim that America's "constitutional system" gave primary authority to each state. And Brownie would declare repeatedly that the states were always in control, that he didn't have the resources to take over, that FEMA's attitude was "'tell us what you need.'" In the remarkable *Frontline* interview he told correspondent Martin Smith that all along he had wanted to put the blame where it belonged, on Mayor Nagin and Governor Blanco, but he thought that wouldn't be appropriate or helpful. Brown was utterly unrepentant in that interview, although he did state that his worst mistake was not getting massive troop support instantly. In January 2006 he had become a tiny bit more willing to take responsibility. Speaking to a convocation of meteorologists, he acknowledged his failure to communicate the enormity of the disaster and to request assistance from the military sooner.

Hearing all this, I thought of an editorial in the *Biloxi Sun-Herald*, which I read about in a Paul Krugman Op-ed column in the *New York Times* titled 'CAN'T DO' AMERICA. The *Sun-Herald* editorial tells us that reporters were listening to the terrible stories of evacuees at a local junior high school shelter while looking across the street at Air Force personnel engaged in basketball and calisthenics. How dispiriting is that? As Knight-Ridder reporters revealed in an excellent article dated September 11, a 1993 report from the Government Accountability Office, the investigative arm of Congress, had concluded that the Department of Defense "is the only organization capable of providing, transporting and distributing sufficient quantities of items needed" in a major catastrophe. Yet the Pentagon remained aloof during this one in Louisiana. Secretary of Defense Donald Rumsfeld attended a baseball game in San Diego on Monday night. The boss of bosses was on vacation in Texas. No one in the Defense Department set up a Katrina task force until Wednesday.

In December 2005, however, FEMA officials still stuck to their guns, telling the Senate investigating committee that, yes, they had been overwhelmed, but local and state officials had failed to do their jobs with evacuations and shelters. At the Superdome state police had turned away two FEMA trucks loaded with food, water, and ice. That's what the FEMA folks told the senators, but I find any such story absolutely incredible. I would have to see the proof. What conceivable motivation could any state trooper have for such an action? FEMA wanted the state of Louisiana to tell it what was needed? Fine. The state forwarded a list forty-eight pages long—but the senators were told that FEMA got "hundreds and hundreds of requests in addition to valid requests. This is just a lack of understanding of what FEMA does."

Hold everything. If there was such a fundamental misunderstanding, whose fault was that? What agency is the overall coordinating agency in a national disaster? What federal agency was running the Pam exercise? Wasn't the major purpose of that exercise to understand exactly who would be doing what during an actual hurricane emergency? What agency's job is it to know and to plan for contingencies?

Michael Chertoff, the head of Homeland Security and Brownie's boss, referred to Katrina as an "ultra catastrophe" and a "combination of catastrophes that exceeded the foresight of the planners, and maybe anybody's foresight." This was two disasters in one, he said— the storm itself, then the flooding—and he blamed the flooding for the logistical problems. FEMA's Natalie Rule said the same thing: "It is not as simple as driving right up into the city of New Orleans and starting rescue as we might be able to do in other disasters, such as an earthquake."

Dissimulation or ignorance? Hard to say, but to those of us watching and listening, such statements were almost too much. On the Wednesday after the storm Brownie was honest enough to tell Larry King that the storm "caused the same kind of damage that we anticipated." Of course it did! The Hurricane Pam exercise theoretically planned for a catastrophe much worse! Brownie had returned from a tour of the tsunami damage in Asia and informed a major meeting that the most likely roughly equivalent catastrophe in the United States was . . . New Orleans. His agency had anticipated catastrophic flooding, staffed for catastrophic flooding, prepped for catastrophic flooding, war-gamed for catastrophic flooding—only to be completely overwhelmed by the real thing.

The *New York Times* reported that the federal government had foreseen the flood risk but not the levee failure. Fire whoever said this to the *Times*, because the distinction is absolutely ridiculous. As far as FEMA's planning was—or should have been—concerned, whether the standing water in New Orleans following any hurricane came from overtopping of the levees or failure of levees, the resulting catastrophe would present *exactly the same problems*. The Army Corps of Engineers would face a very different set of issues, but not FEMA. President Bush added to the confusion or obfuscation on Thursday when he said to Diane Sawyer on ABC's *Good Morning America*, "I don't think anybody anticipated the breach of the levees. They did anticipate a serious storm." A White House spokesperson explained later that the president meant that no one anticipated breaches *after* the storm had passed. In the first place, the breaches occurred just as, or even slightly before, the storm passed to the east of the city. In the second place, again, this distinction is utterly irrelevant. We at LSU had predicted the flooding; FEMA had brainstormed and war-gamed the flooding for years. We know for a fact that the news had penetrated the walls of the White House, thanks to Joby Warrick's reporting in the *Washington Post* in late January 2006. Forty-eight hours before Katrina struck, FEMA had laid out for White house officials a computer slide presentation comparing this storm's likely impact to that of Hurricane Pam—except that Katrina could be worse. At 1:47 A.M. on Monday, August 29, five hours before the storm hit, Homeland Security's National Infrastructure Simulation and Analysis Center e-mailed a forty-one-page assessment to the White House "situation room," repeating the dire warnings of breached levees, massive flooding, and major losses of life and property.

Tim Russert would challenge Secretary Chertoff on *Meet the Press* about how the president "could be so wrong, be so misinformed." The answer was not illuminating.

Then, on March 1, the AP published White House documents, including a video, showing that President Bush was in fact *not* so misinformed after all. In a briefing the day before Katrina hit, he had been clearly apprised of the imminent and possibly catastrophic danger in New Orleans. He didn't ask a single question, true, but he was told what was about to happen. The other major revelation from the documents is Michael Brown's apparent engagement with the crisis. He appears to be blunt, anxious, visibly concerned.

Senator Mary Landrieu, whose father, a former mayor of New Orleans, had evacuated the city for the first time, said at the Emergency Operation Center that she had difficulty convincing FEMA what just one breach in the levees could mean. She said Michael Brown "had a difficult time understanding the enormity of the task before us." Yet the video unearthed by AP shows a clearly focused Brown. He had told King that the damage was anticipated, as quoted above, and he had warned months earlier that the French Quarter could end up eighteen feet underwater (which it didn't).

It was all so bizarre and, yes, maddening. Then over the following weeks came the reports about Brownie's incredible e-mail exchanges throughout the period. On the Monday of the storm he wrote, "Can I quit now? Can I go home?" A couple of days later, "I'm trapped now, please rescue me." Should we interpret such remarks as facetious quips meant to relieve the pressure, as clueless jokes, or as unbelievably callous disregard? I don't know. Thirty minutes after he wrote an e-mail saying that no action had been taken on the use of airlines to evacuate people, his deputy director, Michael Lowder, wrote, "This is flat wrong. We have been flying planes all afternoon and evening." When FEMA's Marty Bahamonde wrote Brown that the situation was "past critical," his boss replied, "Thanks for the update. Anything specific I need to do or tweak?" Then there were the famous e-mails to and from one of his PR staffers concerning what clothes he should wear for the TV interviews. He was advised to roll up his sleeves—literally—and look busy.

But enough. Making sport of these people and their actions and inaction is too easy, and nothing about the Katrina catastrophe should be a laughing matter. People were dying.

It's possible for an organization with dazed and confused chiefs to nevertheless function well enough down the ladder, but this did not seem to be the case this time with this agency. According to Aaron Broussard, president of Jefferson Parish, Wal-Mart had tried to deliver three trailer truck loads of water to his people, only to be turned back by FEMA. Walter Maestri, the parish's superb director of emergency preparedness, said bluntly that FEMA reneged on its offer to relieve county emergency staffers forty-eight hours after landfall. In conference calls with FEMA on the Saturday before the storm, Jefferson Parish officials, including Maestri, went over detailed lists of equipment and manpower they would require immediately. Don't worry, the cavalry will be there within forty-eight hours: That was still Maestri's belief. According to Coast Guard officials, FEMA stopped the same parish from acquiring one thousand gallons of diesel at the Coast Guard station at Belle Chase, just down the road. FEMA's William Carwile wrote in an e-mail from Mississippi: "Biggest issue: resources are far exceeded by requirements. Getting less than 25 percent of what we have been requesting from HQ daily." On Friday, Bill Lackey, a FEMA coordinating officer in the disaster area, admitted bluntly, "It seems our planning was inadequate. We worked on it, we exercised for it, but the reality of it—we've been working as hard as we can."

The newspapers and the airwaves were crowded with such stories. And why did the TV crews seem to have such good access to most areas of New Orleans while FEMA didn't? The rest of us shook our collective head in wonder and dismay and anger. President Bush said to his FEMA chief, while touring Mississippi and the airport in New Orleans, "Brownie, you're doing a great job." (In Mississippi, he also lamented the loss of Trent Lott's shorefront estate and reminisced about all the great parties he had enjoyed on Bourbon Street, back in the day, when that's what he did.) The president's praise for Brownie on Friday morning followed by less than a day Brownie's admission to Larry King that he'd just learned about the thousands of people stranded at the Convention Center. Shortly after bestowing these kudos, the president tacked and said that the results of the federal effort were "not acceptable." That afternoon, on his way to the breach at the 17th Street Canal, he asked local emergency managers if they knew about the Hurricane Pam exercise. Of course they did.

"How did you use it?" the president asked Walter Maestri of Jefferson Parish.

"We used it as a bible."

"I'm sorry. Heads will roll."

EIGHT

WETLANDS FOREVER

Michael Brown, FEMA, evacuations, levees, floods, drownings, and death—we wouldn't be talking about any of this—I wouldn't be writing this book—the tragedy of Hurricane Katrina would never have happened were it not for the unique, precarious setting of New Orleans and southeastern Louisiana in this small wedge of the North American continent. For once, perhaps, a PR slogan is no exaggeration: Louisiana really is "America's Wetland." The state has 40 percent of the total coastal wetlands in the Lower 48. These four million acres of marshes and swamps and estuaries are one of the world's great ecosystems. For millennia the Mississippi River has supplied the immense resources of freshwater, nutrients, and sediment with which to build this vast expanse, which natural processes of erosion then break down. This dynamic interplay of land and water, where new lands are continuously built and old lands changed and lost, has produced an environment with an unsurpassed diversity in vegetation, wildlife, and fisheries, and an extraordinary biological productivity. On the other hand, it also poses problems for the society that chooses to live here. As the geographer Pierce Lewis put it so well, New Orleans is an "impossible but inevitable city": A port near the mouth of the Mississippi River is a given, but no land near this mouth is suited for the purpose.

The wetlands are absolutely vital for protecting this whole part of the state from any hurricane's storm surge. Along with the barrier islands, they are the best, most natural, least expensive buffer available. We can't understand why the Katrina tragedy happened, or the complexity of the rebuilding problem now facing us, without understanding this domain. It's time for a brief excursion into the local bush, where the real danger is not the alligators but the politics.

Of course, I knew almost nothing about the place when I first arrived at LSU as a graduate student from South Africa in January 1977. I saw the raw, unadulterated wetlands for the first time about a month later, when my supervisor, the wonderful teacher and mentor Harry Roberts, escorted me to the Atchafalaya Delta seventy miles south of Baton Rouge. Wow. I'd never seen such a landscape: bleak but exciting. It was a cold, gray day. The land smelled fresh—and it should have, because it was literally new land—land that was still growing. I immediately loved my new home away from home. For one thing, I've always been fascinated with water, any flowing water. As a boy I'd let a tap run over piles of sand and make little rivers and canals and, yes, levees, though I didn't think of them as such at the time. My mates and I made crude canoes out of corrugated, galvanized tin—the standard roofing material in southern Africa then and possibly now. We'd pound the corrugations and irregularities out of the tin until we had a flat sheet, wrap the metal on a kind of a frame made of wood, scrounge some leftover bitumen tar from construction sites on the roads, heat it up, pour it over the nail holes, and have a canoe. More than one. We put these rough-hewn craft on top of soapboxes made with old push pram (baby stroller) wheels and rolled them to the nearby ponds. When we were through canoeing for the day we'd sink the things, then bring them to the surface the next time, no mean task for small boys. Those canoes were totally unsafe; they had no floatation at all.

In apartheid South Africa in the sixties all young white men were conscripted into the army immediately after graduation from high school. I was luckier than most guys, in that I ended up in an engineering regiment and getting a land surveyor diploma, training that would serve me well. My parents wanted me to be an engineer, for some reason, so I studied engineering for two years at the University of Natal, but there was too much math. I called it quits and went to work at Lake St. Lucia in Zululand. That was in 1969, a time of exploration for me, living in a really wild swamp area in the bush, getting to know the Zulus much better, learning to speak some Zulu. They dubbed me "Ma'thatatini Nge en jeti," which means "someone who drives like a grasshopper," a comment about my method of driving a four-wheel-drive Land Rover along the muddy tracks in the swamps. Those were papyrus swamps, of which there are none in the United States. (By the same token, there are no cypress swamps like those of the southern United States in South Africa.) Lake St. Lucia is one of the last true African wildernesses, an incredibly diverse region, ecologically, geomorphologically, and geologically. You always have to be on the alert for large Nile crocodiles, fellows who see you as a meal. Over five hundred hippopotamus also make the Wetland Park their home, and they are also known to charge the odd boat.

The whole wetland complex was also an area undergoing enormous stress due to bad management practices in some of the river valleys feeding the system. Here I found my passion, one of them: understanding how natural systems function and how to correct the works of man when they interfere. I found that if I was quiet and looked carefully, I could get a feel for what was happening physically in the environment, what had happened, had changed, was natural, was not. At moments I would—and still do—get a funny, tingling feeling on my inner arms, especially in natural settings new to me. I feel like the natural environment is telling me how it functions. Strange, I know, but that's the way it feels. (Something must be going on with my family. My father, his brother, and my own brother were very good water diviners, using only a piece of wire. I didn't have that particular sixth sense, but I could balance a green stick on my hand and use its movement to guide me to the water. Dad talked to me about feeling the energy. It's amazing. You *can* feel the energy of the water below you.)

After two great years with the Zulus in that swampy bush, I returned to the University of Natal in my hometown of Pietermaritzburg and took a pure science degree in geology and botany. For the geology honors I studied two river mouths and a collection of beaches. Arguably, these were the first studies of the beaches on the eastern coast of South Africa. Occasionally, I'd get that feeling of electricity in my arms. I knew this is what I wanted to do—coastal work—and I soon touched down in Baton Rouge, my first trip ever to the United States. In fact, it was my first trip outside Africa, and I can thank David Hobday, whom I was extremely lucky to have as my senior lecturer. A tall, lanky geologist and extremely enthusiastic, Dave and I became friends. Once I decided to study overseas I sought his advice. He had done his Ph.D. at LSU and had some friends on the faculty who, as it happened, were coming out to South Africa for a conference. One of them was Harry Roberts of the Coastal Studies Institute; on the third day of our safari in the South African bush Harry invited me to work under him at LSU. Six months later, here I was, technically a "nonmatriculate" obliged to live in a dormitory for a year and obtain a 3.5 grade point average for a semester of senior-level undergraduate courses. If successful, I could then go forward with official graduate studies. At the time, LSU did not seem to recognize that other countries outside of Europe and North America have good education systems. In fact, those qualifying courses were a breeze for me, even a joke.

The Atchafalaya Delta was basically a wilderness and, for the most part, still is. It's rarely visited by anyone other than scientists, duck hunters, and bird watchers. In those days we had no radios and no safety flares, though I think we did carry some life preservers. It didn't matter to me. I'd spent so much time in the real bush, I had no qualms. (The alligators here don't come after you; compared with Nile crocodiles, they are truly pets. We did have to watch out for the bull sharks in the shallows.) My fieldwork called for a lot of heavy labor, literally hauling stuff around, and so did the work of my fellow grad students, so we usually helped each other out. One of these students was Paul Kemp, who would become my colleague at the hurricane center.

For six years I worked on deciphering the evolution and growth of the Atchafalaya Delta—a wild wetlands setting, yes, but in certain areas adversely affected by oyster shell mining activities (for roadbed material) and navigation channel dredging. Here I was drawn into my first environmental controversy in the United States. I and others felt that the shell dredging was eating up these exciting new Mississippi delta lobes. Louisiana was losing wetlands, and here the Army Corps of Engineers and the state were allowing this dredging company to just eat them up faster than they were being formed. I tried to fight these mining dredgers, working with a fellow from the U.S. Fish and Wildlife Service and a Sierra Club member. One morning I was called into a midlevel manager's office at LSU and told my "activities" were hurting my chances of getting my student visa renewed next time around. So I had to quit that campaign, but a month before returning to South Africa, with my Ph.D. firmly in hand, I got together with the folks fighting the shell mining and five months later received a newspaper clipping with the news that the shell mining had been stopped. There is always more than one way to cook a duck.

I probably spent three months out of every year in the wetlands. By the time I had my doctorate, I knew coastal Louisiana very well.

Just about the whole state of Louisiana south of Interstate 10 is new land, relatively speaking. Five thousand years ago the coastline was about thirty miles north of where it is today. The site of New Orleans was on a string of offshore barrier islands. *All* of this new land is sedimentation from the Mississippi River, laid down over the five millennia from the almost annual spring floods of the big river. The floods and the resulting sedimentation were not uniform through-out the vast floodplain, and the active delta of the river meandered back and forth, back and forth from Vermilion Bay in the west to St. Bernard Parish on the east, a stretch of coastline 180 miles across. We call these deltas "loci of deposition," and the switching from one to another is the process that has dominated this section of the coast—and, before that, a much larger section of the continent—for millions of years.

The river changes course in the wetlands because the sedimenta-tion in the active delta necessarily raises the elevation of that land as it extends seaward, until the slope of the river is so flat over such a distance that it finds a shorter, more efficient course to the sea.

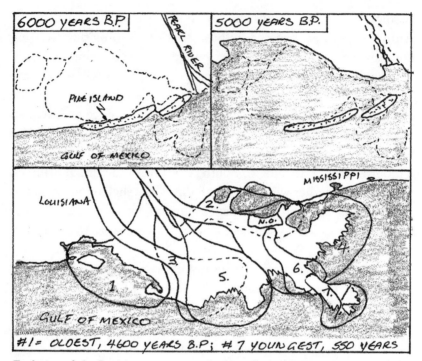

Evolution of the Louisiana coast over the last six thousand years (B.P. = Before Present). Note that New Orleans started off as a barrier island—Pine Island. This explains a lot of the beach sand that creates problems for levee builders.

Wonderfully adept science utilizing core samples and carbon-14 dating techniques has identified seven different deltas for the Mississippi in just the past seven thousand years. The geologists who specialize in this work have deciphered the layering for the whole coast.

The new Americans from lowland Europe who came to stay in this part of the continent brought with them a lot of experience with flooding and a good deal of know-how with levees. Most plantation owners built their own levee systems—with slave labor, of course. Founded after the floods of 1717 had subsided, New Orleans was built on the natural levee at the site, above the surrounding plain, and work immediately began on a mile-long, three-foot-high earthen levee on top of the natural one. This levee building continued for the next two centuries—and so did the floods. Following a terrible one in 1849, Congress passed the Swamp Land Act, and within a decade two thousand miles of levees confined long sections of the mighty Mississippi. In 1879, the Army Corps of Engineers, which had been created in 1802, got into levee building in a big way, but in support of navigation and channel training only, not flood protection—that was local government's role. Corps officials understood that the river and its levees would serve well as a jobs program that would never lose its mandate or its funding. And this work was going to feature brawn over brains.

In the long history of high water along this river, the tipping point was 1927. Before the awesome flood in that year, the federal government did not act under such emergency circumstances. The following year Congress directed the Army Corps of Engineers to build the system we have today. The whole story is the subject of a terrific best-selling book, *Rising Tide: The Great Mississippi Flood of 1927 and How It Changed America*. The author, my friend John Barry, also plays a significant role in following chapters about the investigation of the levee failures in New Orleans, and about planning for the future.

The latest generation of levees on the lower Mississippi River have done the job, virtually eliminating flooding in this stretch of the river. (The devastating flood of April to September 1993, one of the worst in U.S. history, was confined to the upper Mississippi.) They have entirely sealed off the river south of Baton Rouge. In fact, if it weren't for the determined efforts of the Corps, the Atchafalaya River, which breaks from the Mississippi two hundred miles upstream from the Gulf, would now be the main channel for the whole system, because it affords a significantly shorter course to the sea. But there was simply too much commercial infrastructure on the Mississippi below the junction with the Atchafalaya to allow that or any other distributary to take over the main flow and endanger navigation downstream. Also, the ensuing encroachment of saltwater up the channel of the Mississippi would endanger the freshwater supplies of many communities and industries. So the Corps harnessed the Atchafalaya at the Old River control structure, forty-five miles northwest of Baton Rouge, which opened in 1963 and now restricts the flow down this distributary to about one third of the total. (A big flood in 1973 almost washed away the original works at Old River. If it had, the Corps's best-laid plans would have been washed away as well, along with Morgan City and other communities downstream on the Atchafalaya, and that river would have taken over for good. Serious reinforcement was added to the original dam.)

The Mississippi River below Baton Rouge is a canal, really. It's a bit sad to think of it in those terms, but there you are. More to the point here—brutally to the point—this taming of the river is also the root of the problem for New Orleans and the rest of southeastern Louisiana. It is the main reason the entire region is so vulnerable to the catastrophic flooding caused by the storm surge of such hurricanes as Katrina.

To repeat, the entire Louisiana coastal zone is sediment from the Mississippi River deposited over millions of years. The sediments are usually highly organic, with lots of leaf litter and rootlets, and they have very high water content; as more and more sediment is added, any one particular layer gets squished from the new load overhead and therefore compresses and shrinks. That is, it sinks. Thus, marshland is just about the least stable of all soils. Imagine stiff yogurt, or soft playdough putty. It's not easy to walk across. Left absolutely alone, marshland will slowly compress under its own weight at the rate of a couple of feet per century. That's a lot, but there are locations in Louisiana where the soils are so mucky that subsidence becomes an issue within just a few decades—or, in some isolated cases, just a few years, or even faster in areas that have been drained for development. Yards in new subdivisions can sink within months of move-in, necessitating expensive yard soil replenishment.

The only way to compensate for the compression of the sediments is with ongoing, never-ending, inexorable sedimentation; otherwise, the wetlands will sink, and seawater will encroach and eventually kill the freshwater plants. The whole ecosystem will eventually collapse and sink even more. The whole process is more complex than this, of course, but this snapshot is a fair summation of what has been happening throughout southeast Louisiana for the past eighty years, simply because the levee system for the modern Mississippi River has prevented the flooding that yielded the natural accretion of sediment that created this soft land in the first place.

Or put it this way: Without new intervention, there won't be any land left to flood.

Local subsidence is not the only problem, however. Imagine the combined weight of all of the sediment that has been deposited by the Mississippi over all these millennia. The entire continental shelf sinks a little under this enormous load. Now match this wholesale systemwide subsidence with the fact that the seas are rising worldwide—six to eight inches in the last century, due mostly to long-term global climate changes, now due in turn mostly to our dependence on fossil fuels. Along the Eastern Seaboard, which has a small subsidence problem of its own, the local sea level has risen ten to twelve inches in the past century. In Louisiana the net effect is much worse, with the local sea level having risen on the order of thirty-six inches. And there is some good evidence that thanks to global climate change the sea level could rise at twice the current rate by 2100. This eventuality would doom much of the present shoreline around the globe and make the peril in Louisiana and New Orleans specifically even greater.

So the first point to know regarding the relationship of the disappearing wetlands and the peril in this part of the state is the irony that the flood-control measures necessary to create and then protect the infrastructure in this entire part of the state are contributing to the loss of the land on which this infrastructure sits. The second point is the impact of the oil and gas industry, without which the state of Louisiana would practically collapse, economically. Our wetlands are the nation's number-one source of crude oil (pumping more than the Alaska pipeline) and the second-leading source of natural gas, and in order to support and transport this production the companies have carved, by one calculation, eight thousand miles of cuts and canals throughout the wetlands. Since this entire network ties into the Gulf of Mexico, it provides opportunity for saltwater encroachment. It is subject to erosion and disrupts the natural flow of waters in the marshes. The whole artificial system works to the detriment of the wetlands. No one claims otherwise. The third undisputed factor is shoreline erosion, inevitable at all times but es-

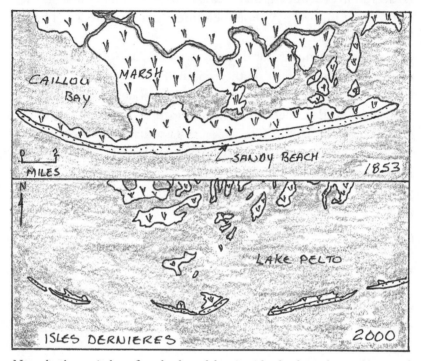

Note the dramatic loss of wetlands and barrier islands along the south coast of Louisiana, the Isles Dernieres chain. Loss of these wetlands means less surge protection; as a result some levee systems in the region are now too low.

pecially relevant when the natural sedimentation processes offer no compensation.

Just 150 years ago the ten miles between Isles Dernieres and the shoreline used to be a healthy marsh. It's all gone now, replaced by a shallow bay. In Cameron Parish on the western side of the state, Highway 82 has been moved back twice in the past 40 years, but it can't go back any farther, because it's on a ridge that protects a 30,000-acre marsh behind it. In the early 1990s the state set up 85 segmented breakwaters in a failed attempt to protect the stretch of coast between the beachfront communities of Holly Beach and

Constance Beach. Prior to Hurricane Rita sand had indeed built up on the eastern end of the stretch, but erosion has been serious to the west. Constance Beach used to have a two-hundred-foot beach and four east-west streets. Then it had almost no beach and just two streets. Following Rita, it is practically gone, as are most of the segmented breakwaters. Scientists had warned for years that the breakwaters would have no long-term positive impacts, would disrupt the local "alongshore" movement of sediment, and, when a hurricane struck, would all be wiped out anyway. All this proved true. Millions of taxpayers' dollars have been wasted.

The moral of this and many other stories in Louisiana: Know the science before you draw lines on a map and build hard structures. Serious consideration is now being given—and not just by bothersome scientists and officious bureaucrats, but also by the residents themselves—to deeding the lower coastal miles of Cameron Parish back to the Gulf of Mexico and moving everyone inland.

Many of the scientists who have studied the wetlands distribute responsibility for their disappearance more or less equally among the three factors: subsidence and the lack of river sediments, the oil and gas industry, and erosion. Without playing a numbers game, this seems to be fairly accurate. The infamous nutria, imported from South America for the fur market (reportedly, they escaped from their cages after a hurricane), are gluttons for marsh grasses and also blameworthy.

In the Crescent City, subsidence is both a natural and man-made phenomenon. The violent breaches of the 17th Street and London Avenue canals scoured deep holes in the soil and exposed the giant root masses of the cypress tress that thrived there up to three hundred years ago. The fact that these roots have not yet decomposed proves dramatically the resistance of cypress wood to water. When the engineer A. Baldwin Wood designed huge pumps powerful enough to drain the swamps between the Vieux Carre—the French Quarter—and Lake Pontchartrain, the city grew inexorably toward that lake until it reached the water itself. But the draining of the swamps also accelerated local subsidence dramatically. By definition, draining forcibly removes water from the soil, depleting its substance. The removal of the water also aerates the soil with oxygen, thus aiding the decomposition of the organic matter, depleting the substance of the sediment even more. Builders in the newly drained swampy areas understood the subsidence issues and knew that all homes had to be built on pilings, sunk seventy feet deep in some instances, so floors and walls would not crack as the soil sank unevenly beneath them. Of course, this sinking soil was the yard and many homeowners were dismayed to learn about the necessity of trucking in topsoil to make up for subsidence that could measure a foot a year. Moreover, the drainage canals dug to handle the floodwaters had to be (and still have to be) pumped regularly because they take in water from seepage. This water is from beneath the city. Thus the pumping also accelerates subsidence. The net effect is that the peat on which the city of New Orleans is built is compacting at a much higher rate than even the natural wetlands outside the city.

In recent years, two other, much disputed, theories have introduced new factors to be considered. In 2002, geologist par excellance Bob Morton, now with the U.S. Geological Survey, correlated the highest rate of wetland loss—thirty-eight square miles per year, in the 1970s—with the period of highest oil and gas production—those same seventies. Prior to Morton's work geologists had assumed that the oil and gas deposits were too far below the surface—eleven thousand feet to eighteen thousand feet—to have an impact on the rate of subsidence, but Morton hypothesizes that "regional depressurization" caused by the extraction of oil and gas is indeed a factor. Not surprisingly, the industry disputes his theory. If Morton is correct, there's nothing we can do about this part of the problem, because the oil and gas extraction is not going to stop. We'll be living in houseboats in Baton Rouge before that will happen. The other provocative theory is offered by consulting coastal scientist Woody Gagliano, who suggests that the large-scale subsidence of fault blocks—large sections of the earth's crust—is a major contributing factor, and there is growing evidence to support this idea.

The bottom line is clear: We are losing our wetlands in Louisiana,

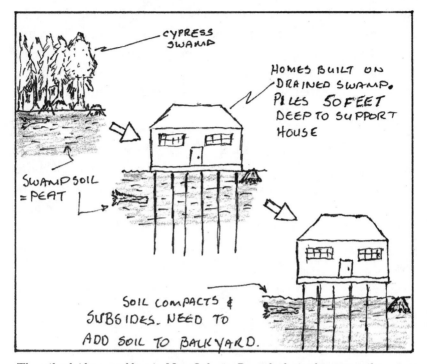

The soil subsidence problem in New Orleans. Recently drained swamp soils compact and subside rapidly, necessitating trucking in soil to maintain yards.

with dire consequences, of which the Katrina catastrophe is just the latest manifestation. Overhead photographs from half a century ago show many rich, healthy marshes and marshy prairies with small patches of water. Satellite photos of many of those same landscapes today show wide prairie lakes dotted with small patches of land. A fatal difference. If the marshes and swamps that comprise the wetlands are viewed as a sponge—and they often are in media stories—this one is in bad shape, ragged, with big holes and pieces hanging off. In the old days settlements out in the marshes were, for obvious reasons, built on the natural ridges and cheniers left behind as the whole sediment structure shifted over the decades and centuries. Those ridges might have had an elevation of eight feet to fifteen feet. Now three feet is more likely, because they're sinking. I think every major wetlands story in the press over the past decade has featured a colorful old-timer standing waist-deep in water where his home used to be, his face pensive and his mind "awash in memories," as *National Geographic* phrased it nicely. The old-timer's parents' house had been probably one hundred yards away, his grandparents' house five hundred yards away. Now those wetlands are totally wet—that is, underwater.

The average beach erodes at a rate of a few feet a year. At Port Fourchon, sixty miles due south of New Orleans and one of the main staging grounds for the vast oil and gas operations offshore, the beach loses forty feet a year. Highway 1 into Port Fourchon, on which tens of trucks roll up and down every day, floods all the time.

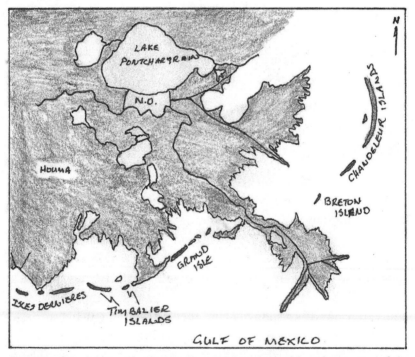

Location of the barrier islands that are crucial to the health and protection of the coastal region.

Any kind of southerly breeze sustained for a few days will do the trick. Throughout this part of the state, pipelines that were buried thirty years ago are now high and dry. The photographs are a staple of the magazines. It doesn't take a direct hit from a storm like Katrina to put the one-hundred-square-mile bird's foot delta (as we call it; there's a certain resemblance) in the very southeastern corner of the state—the mouth of the main shipping channel of the Mississippi—completely underwater. A tropical storm of any significance at all can accomplish this. (Ironically, the depth of the floodwaters caused by storm surge in some areas right on the coast is lower than in the past. Why? With less land to stop the water it just keeps flowing inland, inundating a greater area, some of it to less depth.)

We are also losing the protection of the aptly named barrier islands. Our activities have radically altered the natural sediment sources and pathways that maintained the barrier islands. Canals, breakwaters, segmented barriers, and other features of the new environment created by the oil and gas industry have all resulted in a rapid demise of these unique features of the Louisiana landscape. Unless something drastic is done, these islands and their many beneficial effects will disappear entirely in ten or fifteen years.

Thanks to subsiding land and rising oceans, the southern part of Louisiana is three feet lower than it was one hundred years ago, relative to mean sea level. The state loses twenty-five square miles of wetlands every year, over twenty times the rate recorded in the early part of the last century, when wetlands gain for the most part equaled wetlands loss. Since the 1930s, this has come to more than a million acres of lost land. In another one hundred years, if we don't get serious about rebuilding these wetlands, the land will be another three feet lower and, for all practical (and aesthetic) purposes, no longer land at all. Army Corps of Engineers project manager Al Naomi once took note of the subsidence problems around the world and then quipped, "We're not going to be only ones in the boat. We're just in the boat first." New Orleans will be, at best, a Venice, at worst, a new Atlantis—a Cajun Atlantis, as they say (ignoring or confusing the fact that New Orleans is a Creole, not a Cajun, culture).

This loss of the wetlands is not theoretical, not disputed, and not endorsed by even the wackiest observer. There are those who say, "Too bad—also too late," but no one says, "Hooray." This is because wetlands loss is not a zero-sum game. There are no winners. Every single interest in this part of the state—economic, environmental, and cultural—stands to lose. Alone among the economic interests in this part of the state, shrimpers, oystermen, and others who depend on brackish marshes to support the life cycle of their catch do benefit from the loss of freshwater sedimentation and the resulting encroachment of saltwater. But this benefit is for the short term only, because shrimp, for example, need marshes as their nursery, not open ocean. In the first phase of encroachment, the saltwater does create new brackish marshes, but the inevitable erosion that follows eventually destroys those same marshes and nurseries. These folks

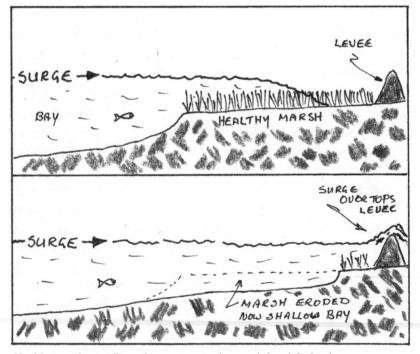

Healthy marshes swallow a lot more surge than eroded and depleted ones.

understand in their bones that the overall loss of the wetlands habitat is slowly, or not so slowly, eroding their way of life. They are often the men in the magazine photographs surveying the watery landscape that used to be the front yard.

Real estate developers hungry for terra firma are running out of acreage, so they dig canals to drain marshes and build ad hoc levees to protect the new sod from storm surge—until it doesn't. What companies would ever insure such homes? Louisiana and Texas traditionally rank one and two in flood insurance claims. Increasingly, insurers are not writing homeowner policies in the wetlands, or they attach an explicit rider excluding hurricane damage. I hate to vote with the insurance companies, but on this issue, who could blame them?

Most important for the subject of this book, the wetlands can protect us from storm surge. Along with the barrier islands, they are the best, most natural, least expensive buffer available. Restoring the islands and the marshes is restoring lost friction, which we desperately need. Now, some scientists dispute the protective value of the wetlands. Some imply that other scientists (including myself) use the storm-surge argument as politically correct cover for rebuilding the wetlands for their own sake. It's true that I believe we should rebuild the wetlands for a host of reasons, as I'll explain shortly, but even scientists from the Corps have calculated that every three to four miles of healthy marsh reduces storm surge by one foot. Camille was a vicious Cat 5 storm, one of the most powerful on record in the Atlantic Basin, but areas that did not flood in 1969 *did* flood during Georges, a smaller storm that followed a very similar track a quarter century later. A more modest than expected Katrina still shoved ashore a record storm surge partly because only battered marshes stood in her way. One of the most important research questions we hope to resolve post-Katrina is exactly how wetlands reduce surge under a range of hurricane conditions. Upcoming simulations by the LSU storm-surge warriors will compare the historical flooding of certain storms from the recent past, such as Betsy, with the flooding that would ensue from that same storm today. In every instance, I'm sure, vast new regions would be underwater. The reason? The missing marshes and barrier islands. Joe Suhayda has already published computer studies showing that the 9.3-foot surge at Cocodrie during Hurricane Andrew in 1992 would have been a foot higher without the barrier islands. Joe has calculated that a completely healthy marsh system could cut the storm surge in New Orleans *by half.* Joe has always done good applied science, so I won't be surprised if ADCIRC corroborates those findings. I'll be very surprised if it doesn't.

Of the one million acres of wetlands that have been lost over the past decades, more than one half lie directly seaward of New Orleans and the one million–plus residents of the greater metropolitan area. If nature had her way, these wetlands would be sapping the strength of the storm winds and quite literally swallowing the brunt of the storm surges. This is why, as we rebuild New Orleans from the moldy flooring of the flooded city, it is necessary to also get serious sixty miles away. Rebuilding and restoration have to go hand in hand. That's my battle cry.

But how do we accomplish this? I'll get into the specifics in the final chapter. In this one I need to lay out briefly how the political establishment in the state has failed over the past several decades to rebuild the wetlands, and thereby left southeastern Louisiana in the position of the sitting duck for big storm surges. As we now know.

The undisputed relationship between lost wetlands and increased vulnerability to storms isn't new. The first alarms were raised shortly after I arrived on these shores in 1979, and they've been raised continually and at ever higher decibels over the past quarter century—the daunting challenge has always overwhelmed the political system's ability to generate a meaningful response. Maybe the deaths of more than thirteen hundred Americans will change the political landscape. Maybe. Based on my experience within that system in the 1990s, I have my doubts. After I completed my six years of postgraduate work at LSU in 1983, I returned to South Africa, worked on environmental management and restoration projects around the coast, including the response to Cyclone Demoina in Zululand, and then took over an underwater diamond-mining operation off the west coast of South Africa and Namibia. That was a fascinating experience, but the operation was sold when the owner decided to liquidate assets. With the political climate in the country deteriorating rapidly, I decided to sail the oceans, and ended up studying the coral reefs off St. Croix. In 1990 I flew from the islands to New Orleans for Christmas and ran into my old swamp mate, Paul Kemp, who told me about the new coastal restoration program that was just getting going in Louisiana, officially titled the Coastal Wetlands Planning, Protection and Restoration Act, sometimes also known as the Breaux Act, for former senator John Breaux, but known in the trade by its acronym, CWPPRA (pronounced "Quipra"). Congress had passed this legislation the year before and funded it for a decade. Also, the first Bush administration had put in place a "no net loss of wetlands" rule. If you destroyed marshes in order to build another development, you had to set up some kind of mitigation elsewhere.

"You should come back to Louisiana," Paul said. "This is right up your alley." I agreed. Restoration was right up my alley, and I hadn't heard about the new initiative. As much as I'd loved the wetlands as a graduate student, I'd pretty much lost touch with the situation in Louisiana. But now I'd turned forty, and somewhere in magaritavilla an Aussie had warned that I'd lose my edge, sciencewise, if I continued sailing for five years before going back to my profession. (That was my plan; five years was the estimated time needed to circumnavigate the globe, with some time lost to stocking up the cash kitty with odd temporary jobs here and there.) The Aussie was right, and six months after my conversation with Paul I sailed the *Maggie* into her new home waters, Lake Pontchartrain. Quite a change from island life in the Caribbean. Soon I hooked up with the consulting company where Paul had worked for a while, pushed hard on restoration activities, then ran into another former graduate student pal working with the federal National Marine Fisheries Service, and I set to work designing projects with them. Shortly thereafter, I moved over to set up LSU's Natural System Management and Engineering Program, an applied research program. Through it all I got to know well the CWPPRA program for restoring the wetlands.

It is impossible to understand how CWPPRA—or anything else concerning the environment in Louisiana—works without appreciating how the New Orleans district of the Army Corps of Engineers works, because it manages the money and a large share of the projects. With an Army colonel at the top as commander and district engineer (some are not even engineers), the agency has a military-management veneer, but the real power lies in the civilian career managers. For one thing, every three years the Corps rotates the district engineer, so the learning curve at the top starts all over again, and three years might easily be required to move a project from a priority list to construction. Since I returned to Louisiana, there must have been half a dozen chiefs. I can't even recall all their names. Power necessarily devolves downward; the civilian managers really control both the short- and long-term agendas. Because they are long term and folks like Paul Kemp and myself are also long term, we give these managers fits. (The same folks in charge of the design and building of the levees that failed during Katrina are now fighting our Team Louisiana levee investigation, as we'll see, and have convinced their nominal superiors to spend a considerable amount of money on their own investigative teams.)

Across the whole country, most of the Corps's funding is for "earmarked" projects requested by specific members of Congress. Political interference, we call that. Pork. CWPPRA has the same problem in Louisiana. A task force bringing together five federal agencies and the governor's Office of Coastal Activities approves all projects—a total of 141 so far, including 62 completed and another 19 deauthorized. Some projects have been approved but not funded, others funded but then never begun. (The money comes from a user fee on small engines, boat fuel, and certain equipment.) In addition to the Corps, the federal agencies in the task force are the Fish and Wildlife Service, National Marine Fisheries Service, Natural Resource Conservation Service (formally Soil Conservation Service), and the Environmental Protection Agency. If each receives what it considers a fair share of the funded projects each year, it can maintain its workforce for the next year as well as keep its constituents happy. Each agency also has its special interests and expertise. Wildlife people tend to be concerned about habitat; soils people tend to be concerned about marsh management; and the EPA and

National Marine Fisheries are concerned about wetland creation. The oversight and funding mechanism was never an ideal mechanism, but what can we do? This is the nature of human beings and our bureaucracies.

There also seems to be an inherent suspicion between the Army Corps of Engineers and scientists, who in turn tend to believe that the Corps automatically advocates "hard" structures because these are what the Corps builds. For their part, Corps officials know that their concrete has saved the infrastructure in this entire part of the world from river flooding for the past half century. They understand the downside, of course, but they're not going to apologize for taming the Mississippi.

In the first decade of the CWPPRA program, Louisiana received about $40 million annually from the fund and added $5 million more from the Wetlands Trust Fund, which receives royalty money from the oil and gas industry, and the state also receives some in-kind payments. Several hundred million dollars are in the bank awaiting disbursement for projects funded but not yet begun or completed. The great majority of the projects are small, sometimes demonstration-level, and can be slotted into one of three categories: shoreline protection, wetlands creation, or hydrologic restoration. Shoreline protection is just that, usually accomplished by the placement of rocks. Wetlands creation is also just that. Sediment is mined and placed as new "proto" wetlands; dredge material from navigation channels is used beneficially, or river diversions bring in sediment-laden water from the Mississippi River. Hydrologic restoration generally involves manipulating water levels within marshes, including "marsh management" projects in which a levee or dike is built around a marsh to artificially lower the water level in order to sustain freshwater plants. Such management projects are not strongly supported by most coastal scientists. I could argue that they principally benefit ducks—and duck hunters, a major constituency in Louisiana. The very savvy Shea Penland, a fellow LSU graduate who runs the fine coastal research program at the University of New Orleans, has studied these projects carefully and concluded that more wetlands loss has occurred within marsh management areas than outside of them. *Ten times more*, if you can believe that—which I can. Wetlands creation is the way to go.

The CWPPRA program has been controversial from the beginning, often because this or that part of the state is allegedly getting more than its fair share of the money. (See "Coast in Peril," environmental reporter Mike Dunne's superb account of this issue and the whole wetlands history published by the *Baton Rouge Advocate* in 1999.) Sometimes the CWPPRA task force has found itself in competition with outside developers, most notably with its plan to restore over twenty-five hundred acres of marshland at Eden Isles in St. Tammany Parish, on the north shore of Lake Pontchartrain. Before it could restore this land the task force had to buy it, but it was outbid—twice—by housing developers. So this project was eventually deauthorized and defunded. We have instead today yet another major upscale housing development, with canals dredged to raise the elevations, and all canals connected to Lake Pontchartrain. Instead of better surge protection for Slidell, we have more infrastructure for the higher surge to damage. If these twenty-five hundred acres had been restored, the marshes would have helped during Katrina, cutting down the surge that hit the eastern part of Slidell.

Nevertheless, in the beginning, I was really excited about the opportunity to launch some first-class environmental restoration projects. Soon enough, however, reality set in, as it usually does, and not just with the little squabbles about the basin that got 7 percent too much money. I looked around the table and wondered, where is the thorough understanding of the science here? The CWPPRA legislation had been drawn up by scientists, environmentalists, and academics avowedly intent on bringing the science to bear, to provide checks and balances with the other interests. But at one of my first CWPPRA meetings, an important restoration official at the Department of Natural Resources (DNR), said we did not need any more science or any academics. I was astounded! *All* we needed was science—and money—and professional, apolitical management. Unite these three and step aside! That's what we needed to do, and do it with care, because when we change a complex physical environment, we change everything.

The analogy I sometimes used to make my point was a simple tank with some water and some fish. Start adding and subtracting water. Nothing much changes. But now fill one side of the tank with soil that forms a gentle bank sloping into the water. Now we have both water and land, and, in addition to the fish, a few plants and a little animal or two. Any audience can intuitively sense that the simple addition and subtraction of water and soil to this more complex environment may yield not so simple consequences for every element of the story, including the fish and the animals. In a dynamic environment like coastal Louisiana we have to understand these processes, because the details of the physical environment drive the system. With these audiences I was also subtly trying to sell the fact that we need sediment, sediment, and more sediment—correctly distributed—if we are to build wetlands and protect people.

On a related front, Paul Kemp and I were also battling the method used to evaluate potential CWPPRA projects, something called the Wetland Value Assessment, which was sans science and stank to high heaven. This scheme was devised by wildlife experts with no real understanding of the dynamics of the overall system. It was heavily weighted toward marsh management projects. A profound deficiency was its failure to give any credit whatsoever in the cost-benefit analysis for the value of wetlands as storm-surge buffers. What about Hurricane Andrew? Earlier I cited the important number: Thanks to the relatively healthy wetlands along the central part of the coastline where this Cat 3 came ashore in August 1992, the storm surge was only eight feet.

Another profound deficiency was the back-of-the-hand dismissal of the barrier islands, which got no credit for their contribution to surge buffering. They were not really considered as part of the wetlands "package." Other than the EPA and National Marine Fisheries—always the progressive groups—the other agencies were dead set against restoring the barrier islands. I was told a hundred times that the "W" in CWPPRA was for "Wetlands." Did I see a

"B" or an "I" in the acronym? So we could restore only *wetlands*, not barrier islands. Oh, my. For shortsighted bureaucratic thinking, I give that an "A."

In my earlier discussion of the ADCIRC storm-surge model I told the story of how Paul Kemp, Joe Suhayda, and I convinced Terrebonne Parish to give us thirty thousand dollars to do some early modeling to compare what the tides did to the marshes south of Houma, with and without the barrier islands offshore. The results were, as I said, irrefutable. Rebuilding the islands to their state one hundred years earlier would immediately stop the flooding of thirty thousand acres; "wetting times" would be much lower throughout the basin, very beneficial for wetlands trying their best not to drown. I've described the reactionary response that greeted this model in meetings. If I showed some of the CWPPRA folks what they wrote back then about the computer models, I'm sure they would be quite embarrassed.

The missing science was one problem that had to be addressed. Another, just as pressing, was the missing big picture. To my mind the most important part of the CWPPRA legislation was the long-term comprehensive planning effort, but, in fact, the larger and therefore probably more controversial projects lost out to smaller, straightforward, maybe even demonstration-level jobs that disbursed the available money without too many hassles. In November 1992 I organized a workshop in Baton Rouge, pulled in as many scientists as possible, supplied sandwiches, and explained the prototype version of our big-picture plan. We had to move away from the laundry list of small CWPPRA projects. These Band-Aids would never save the patient. No matter how many we used, we would, sooner or later, end up with a carcass. Of that I was sure, and so were many others. We had to turn things around with big, global thinking, with triage. In all of my classes I've always preached that we have to understand the evolutionary pathways of any given environment. How has man influenced it? How have we speeded up natural change, slowed it down, stopped it? For every movement there is a reaction. "Least interference" is the goal, but sometimes this goal requires major interference with the preceding interference in order to set things right. So it was and is with Louisiana's wetlands. Only large-scale diversions of the rivers and committed rebuilding of the barrier islands will do the job. Hurricane Andrew had grabbed my attention. I was surer than ever that we were sitting on a ticking time bomb. I wanted to organize these scientists into a united front, then take on the agencies.

We got the scientists on board—not difficult, the science is crystal clear—but had much less success pushing the comprehensive approach at the various meetings of the CWPPRA basin teams. (There were nine in all, each responsible for one basin in south Louisiana. I was the scientific adviser to the team in charge of the Atchafalaya and Mississippi River deltas. Such was my modest little platform.) Then, in mid-1993, Colonel Mike Diffley, district engineer for the Corps, called a meeting of all the teams. One after another the presenters laid out plans beholden to the usual approach. It was one small Band-Aid after the other. The colonel was uncomfortable with what he was hearing. I could see that and waited for my chance. (It's true that the real administrative power in the district seems to reside with the career civilians, but a boss who gets the big picture is still a tremendous asset, even though he'll be gone in three years, at most.) When Colonel Diffley called for a break and walked off to lean against the wall, away from everyone else, I approached him. As the old saying goes, "In for a penny, in for a pound." I told him that the academic/scientific community was going to shoot down these plans, loud and clear, because they showed no imagination and no grasp of the big picture. We had to change course in a fundamental way. As quickly as I could, I listed the four main bullet points of the big-picture approach. All the while he stared at the floor, then suddenly lifted his head and looked me right in the eyes. I assured him that we scientists would be more than willing to help. Just reach out to us at LSU and we would bring in the academic community and give him something he would be proud of. He knew how to find me, but I gave him my card anyway, and as he went back to his seat at the head table I said a quick prayer that I'd made a good case, and that he had heard me.

After the break the colonel stood up and graded the basin plans he had just heard D-, maybe only F+. The room was very silent. Everyone respected this man. What he said had impact. About a week later he came to LSU by himself, met with Paul Kemp, me, and one or two others, and asked us to write the introduction chapters for our plan, as well as the executive summary. He didn't have any money to give us, but he was accepting our offer of help. We had ten days. (Be careful what you pray for!) I don't know whether Colonel Diffley was just taking a what-the-hell long-shot gamble on a plan that might fall flat on its face, or whether he actually believed in us. Regardless, Paul and I tore into the task with twenty-two-hour days. In the end the job seemed worth it. Diffley was pleased and told us not to worry too much about the fact that the big-picture ideas were not yet fully developed. "All anyone will read will be the executive summary," he said, and I knew he was correct. Paul Kemp and I were elated, as were our supporters, but in the whole process we made some enemies in the Corps's civilian upper management, a fact of life that still haunts us to this day.

As one of the authors of the CWPPRA document, I decided to spice it up for a wider audience, add a great deal of detail, and publish it in 1994 as a white paper on the wetlands under the auspices of LSU's Center for Coastal, Energy and Environmental Resources (CCEER). The title was "A Long-Term, Comprehensive Management Plan for Coastal Louisiana to Ensure Sustainable Biological Productivity, Economic Growth, and the Continued Existence of Its Unique Culture and Heritage," but it became known (of necessity) as the CCEER report. The reference to "economic growth" was not a second thought, nor was the reference to culture and heritage. Along with my conviction that a big picture guiding big projects was the only salvation for the wetlands, I had developed a second one: that the politics could be put together only if restoring the wetlands and the barrier islands was primarily for the benefit of *people*, not of herons and alligators and marsh grasses. Well aware that public support would erode if restoring the wetlands was believed to be transgressing too much on property rights, I acknowledged economic dislocations but denied net economic losses. On the contrary, rebuilding the wetlands will yield major economic gains to the fisheries, protect the oil-and-gas infrastructure, and build ecotourism. (Before Katrina a relative handful of New Orleans's millions of visitors took an air boat out into the swamps and marshes. That market is a potential gold mine.)

The center received hundreds of requests for copies. The new publication was well reported in the media. I got congratulatory letters from far and wide, including from Senator Breaux. The agencies were a different story; some that are friendly now weren't so friendly then, but so what. I believe this paper remains an excellent guide post-Katrina—more than that, a mandatory element of the overall rebuilding effort, and I will lay it out in the final chapter.

In July 1994—about two thirds through his second term—Governor Edwin Edwards appointed a new head of the Department of Natural Resources, Jack McClanahan, an oil-and-gas man who immediately brought in another guy from the oil patch, Gene Spivey, to be his executive assistant. I knew I needed to meet the new chief of the most important of the state agencies associated with CWPPRA, and with the help of my friend Glenn Wood, a dredging operator, who was also a friend of McClanahan's, I got an interview with both him and Spivey. I give these two a lot of credit. They listened, they read the CCEER white paper, they endorsed the big picture. And to make the long story short, two weeks after meeting McClanahan he asked me to become the state's new restoration "czar." What an amazing change of fortunes for me. My predecessor, Dave Solieu, was the consummate insider. Here I was an academic with no political ties to the governor or anyone else whatsoever. How strange was that? I was about to get a whole different kind of education, one that has seriously colored how I now look at our long-term prospects in Louisiana.

The green forces in the state were confused and delighted by my appointment. Did Jack McClanahan, of all people, intend to cut the Gordian knot? No, I don't think so, but his stature as an oil man made it a whole lot easier to sell our "radical agenda"—that is, actually doing something big—as it would soon be labeled. A complicating factor was the ticking clock. I felt I had Edwards's support, and Jack McClanahan's, and I had the mandate to make changes, but Edwards was term-limited. He'd be out of office in January 1996, only fifteen months away. That might be the end for me as well, so we had to get something big in place; we had to convince everyone that we had a comprehensive, big-ticket plan, and we were going to see it through. In January 1995, we held a coastal summit and followed it with a white paper. We set out to reassess all projects so far authorized by the CWPPRA task force and to cut the smaller pork projects. The state wields something of a de facto veto over CWPPRA projects, because withholding our share of the cost effectively kills the job. So don't even bother putting up any bad ones for consideration. The word spread, and it really rang the bell hard.

The basic idea was to start rebuilding the barrier islands first, then to build the wetlands in the protected bays behind these. Immediately, we set to work on the project to mine the sand from Ship Shoal eleven miles offshore, using it to restore the islands. The science here was straightforward, but the politics were not. I spent a lot of time in Washington, working with the congressional staffs and the appropriations committee staffs. We got the Louisiana delegation to write letters of support. We got the very important congressman Billy Tauzin on our side. Tauzin told some folks from Houma that I was now "one of them." He took me to meet Congressman Bob Livingston, who in turn advised me to get every national environmental group on board. Along with Mark Davis, the new director of the Coalition to Restore Coastal Louisiana, I briefed as many of these groups as I could. I got $400,000 for the impact study from CWPPRA, with the Mineral Management Service "tasked" to do the job, which made sense, because this agency controlled, as a federal resource, the sands in question. By the fall of 1995, therefore, we thought we had all our ducks in a row. The Corps said they'd sign off on the project, given a proper feasibility study. Just about everyone at the state level was on board. We had the commitment to deauthorize a bunch of projects that had no value. We had the commitment to use one third of all CWPPRA money for big-ticket projects. We had letters of support from most of the congressional delegation. We had the national environmental groups on board, as long as we had the detailed impact study. Things looked good—so I quit my job as coastal restoration chief.

The timing seems odd? The explanation begins the previous year, 1994, when representatives Billy Tauzin and Jimmy Hayes had introduced the Private Property Owners' Bill of Rights. This legislation would have directed the government to compensate landowners when environmental regulations deprive them of 50 percent or more of the fair market value of their property. This one-sentence description of the bill sounds fair enough, but in reality it would have allowed you, a landowner, to claim that you would certainly have built a Wal-Mart on your one hundred acres of marshland if it weren't for these communistic environmental regulations, so you want full compensation for your lost fortune. The legislation also reclassified wetlands on an A, B, C, and D scale in terms of importance, and most would have been D—unimportant. The attorneys general from thirty-three states and territories wrote Congress to oppose this bill because it "would write into law the dubious principle that the government must pay polluters not to pollute." Simply put, this was narrow-minded, shortsighted, knee-jerk so-called property rights legislation. If every significant restoration initiative has to fight a horde of one-hundred-acre landowners blackmailing the federal government for maximum "Wal-Mart" compensation, forget saving south Louisiana for future generations. Such mind-boggling obstructionism would have killed coastal restoration, period, and guaranteed one Katrina catastrophe after another, until there was nothing left around here.

As this legislation made the rounds, we felt compelled to write letters to our congressional delegation making clear exactly what this legislation would mean for the long-term future of their state. The letters went out in July 1995. Contact us if you wish to discuss this further. We waited two weeks and heard nothing from any of them. Not one word, so Jack McClanahan, my boss, told me to release a copy. The media loved this letter, of course. Here was the oil man who headed the Louisiana Department of Natural Resources and his coastal restoration guy (me) saying that Billy Tauzin's legislation was wrong. There is no doubt that the letter did make Tauzin and Hayes look bad, but how else were we to oppose their incredible bill? We knew we had it right, and public opinion polls consistently showed public support for our work.

One day shortly after the letter was released, I was back in Baton Rouge enjoying a po' boy at a local establishment when I got a call from Tauzin himself, swearing, labeling me a "tree-hugger," etcetera etcetera. Then, at a CWPPRA meeting that Senator Breaux called in Washington one month later, Tauzin and Hayes launched into me. I was an "African dictator," and worse. Hayes said he would get me. Funny enough, one of Tauzin's staffers had told us a few months before that his boss was impressed with the progress we were making. That credit was totally irrelevant now. What should I do? The gubernatorial election was coming up in a few months, and Governor Edwards would be out of office a couple of months after that. I could see that folks were lining up for personal favors, and as the assistant secretary of the DNR, I was in charge of the coastal zone permitting division. I was wary of getting involved in the last-minute permitting deals that are almost a tradition in Louisiana and elsewhere, I'm sure. (Years later, an FBI agent who was part of the team that sent Governor Edwards to the penitentiary told me my instincts in that regard had been good.) Two powerful congressmen had put out a hit on me, politically speaking. Adding all of this up, taking into account my feeling that the big-picture initiative was in good shape and moving ahead, that I had accomplished what I had set out to do (Jack McClanahan had even received the EPA's Wetlands Award for 1995), I resigned.

This was a sad parting, definitely, but until McClanahan and Gene Spivey left when Mike Foster's new administration took over in January 1996, I was in constant contact with them and, in some ways, the acting restoration chief. I remained optimistic. Then everything suddenly collapsed. *Everything.* With Edwards out and Foster in as the new governor, with Jack Caldwell taking over from Jack McClanahan as the new secretary of the Department of Natural Resources, the prospects for responsible coastal restoration fell apart within two or three months. Caldwell's staffers sent letters to the state team working on the Ship Shoal feasibility study, questioning if there was any value in restoring the barrier islands. The dynamics of the feasibility study changed, and the funding for the Mineral Management Service part of the investigation was removed. Those folks were just "chased from the table," as one of them told me later.

Unbelievable—the wake-up call of a lifetime for me, and a blunt lesson about the vindictiveness of Louisiana politics. The Ship Shoal mining project was dead, along with the comprehensive, big-picture approach to solving the wetlands problem, all because of petty politics from the junior bureaucrats who were influencing the new man. The agencies that were used to getting their little share of CWPPRA funds every year wanted their little share every year, and they won out. I had no idea that these desk jockeys had the where-withal to sabotage us.

Such was my initial postmortem. In fact, though, the linchpin may well have been my falling out with Billy Tauzin and Jimmy Hayes over their ill-conceived takings legislation the previous summer that had died the ugly death it deserved. They had it in for me. When the administration in Baton Rouge changed, the two congressmen got their pound of flesh from me and more when they helped kill our comprehensive restoration initiative. Subsequently, a senior LSU employee told me that Tauzin's staff had also warned the university that if my name was on anything that needed funding—forget it. This whole episode proved to me that politics in Louisiana was getting in the way of restoration. I had seen how quickly the political system in the state, with just a change of governors, could totally derail a long-term restoration program that we had thought was cast in stone. (I guess I can be *very* naive.) The state therefore blew a golden opportunity to do something great. I saw immature, petty, childish, and pathetic tit-for-tat politics as the order of the day, and I saw that CWPPRA was not going to restore the wetlands, the coastline, the barrier islands—anything at all.

All in all, my tenure as the restoration czar was terribly disappointing regarding the big picture but gratifying regarding some smaller accomplishments. It was an incredible learning experience. Now, what would be the next best thing to do? I cast around for the new right focus for the long haul. As noted, I had always been impressed with Joe Suhayda's early storm-surge models. Now he had flood models for New Orleans. This was the future, I knew. Once we could really prove the importance of the wetlands in minimizing storm surges and protecting people, coastal restoration could live again. Hurricanes—storm-surge models—coastal restoration. They all had to come together. I also realized that we knew absolutely nothing about the actual impacts of hurricanes—specifically, about the impact of a major storm on southeast Louisiana and New Orleans. I started thinking in these terms, and this was the train of thought that would lead to the creation of the two hurricane centers at LSU, as I've related.

In 1998, right around the time of Hurricane Georges (how many wake-up calls did the people and their politicians need?), a new task force impaneled by Governor Foster estimated that current spending from all sources (mainly CWPPRA, of course) would mitigate only 14 percent of the projected land loss by the year 2050. Even given perfect results for every project, the state would still lose six hundred square miles of marsh and four hundred of swamp land. After dozens of meetings around the state, yet another new blueprint was produced, this one labeled "Coast 2050: Toward a Sustainable Coastal Louisiana." It called for spending $14 billion over the next twenty to thirty years, a threefold increase over what could have been expected from the CWPPRA schedule. But it was still mainly Band-Aids, and I failed to see how more of them would save this patient, who was in extremis. I was joined in my criticism by others. In our opinion, the only answer remained what it has always been: big, big projects.

I was excluded from the "Coast 2050" initiative. The plan referred to my previous planning efforts, but I was never asked to this new table. Maybe they knew I would be skeptical of Band-Aid approaches, but I imagine it was mostly just the dirty game of politics as it's played by so many in Louisiana. "Coast 2050" was then followed in rapid succession by a dizzying array of other, overlapping studies, plans, and funding schemes, none of them ever likely to produce the kind of money or vision required. To be frank, I lost track of the fate of some of them—in the particulars, that is. Overall, nothing much happened.

In 2000, Florida got $4 billion to restore the Everglades, matching it with $4 billion of its own funds. President Clinton officially launched a historic thirty-year restoration, supported by a broad coalition of national and local environmental, agricultural, business, and citizen groups. Someone quipped that our wetlands make the Everglades look like a petting zoo. That's correct. Why couldn't Louisiana coax that kind of money out of Washington? Pretty soon, Billy Tauzin, who had gotten so upset with me—and vindictive—for opposing his takings legislation, got religion of a sort and began exploring the possibility of funding the dust-gathering "Coast 2050" initiative from the Water Resources Development Act, under which the Everglades project was funded. As chairman of the House Energy and Commerce Committee, Tauzin was generally considered a point man for regulated industries, although oil and gas companies understand better than anyone the jeopardy of their inland infrastructure. They'd be delighted to see federal money rebuilding the wetlands that their own activities have been significantly responsible for tearing up. (Shell was a big backer of the state's America's Wetland public relations campaign kicked off in 2002. So was the maker of Tabasco sauce, headquartered at Avery Island.)

Quite a few people have started getting religion on the wetlands in recent years, at least for political purposes. We've been hearing less poppycock about "people first" and "people instead of wetlands." This is not and never has been an either-or issue. It is and always has been people *and* wetlands. Tauzin's new idea was not terrible, but the story was still not quite right. It needed the hurricane threat, the storm-surge threat, the imperiled people.

The environmental impact plan for Tauzin's idea has been submitted, but of course all bets are now off. The congressman himself has retired and taken a new job as head lobbyist for the pharmaceutical industry, over which his old House committee had jurisdiction. So it goes. Just before leaving office he made a heartfelt plea before the House Transportation and Infrastructure Committee. "Our paradise is about to be lost," he said. "Please let's don't have a commission where all of us, red-faced, say we saw it coming and didn't do anything. Please don't let that happen."

I now propose a moment of silence.

NINE

THE SCORE ON THE CORPS

On Saturday afternoon, September 3—five days after Katrina's landfall—our paradise—part of it—was indeed underwater, and surge warrior Hassan Mashriqui sent around a note asking about the total capacity of the 148 pumps at the 60 pumping stations in the metro New Orleans area. (Twenty-four of the stations are in the two western bowls. Orleans East has eight; St Bernard, eight; and Orleans and Jefferson parishes south of the Mississippi, twenty.) Mashriqui had pinned down the volume of water in the Orleans Metro Bowl at thirty billion gallons. Now all he needed was pumping capacity and we could get a reasonably accurate idea on how long the unwatering (a word coined by the Corps, I believe) would take, once the pumps could be powered up from the grid or generators and operate at some reasonable percentage of capacity. Of course, that "reasonable percentage" was the catch, but we needed to do better than the unwatering estimates thrown out over previous three days, which had been all over the place and were therefore not very helpful. The mayor said one to two weeks—not necessarily absurd, but highly unlikely. Colonel Richard Wagenaar, the commander and district engineer for the Corps in New Orleans (newly assigned in July, transferred from Korea) estimated three to six months. One FEMA official estimated six months to drain, three more to dry. God help us.

Somehow Newt Gingrich, the deposed Speaker of the House of Representatives, author of the Contract With America (or "On" America, depending on how you looked at it), now a fellow traveler with Senator Hillary Clinton on certain issues, got involved in a string of e-mails and suggested that there must be professionals in "drying things out" who could beat the current predictions. What about the Dutch? he asked. Someone else suggested contacting the dredging companies. Maybe they could position a long line of their barges along the Industrial Canal, say, and, instead of mud from the river bottoms and canals, pump out water from the bottom of the lake that was now New Orleans. I hope I didn't join in the wild numbers game—I don't believe so—but I did succumb to the pessimism when I told a reporter that the pumping issue was a "mission impossible" if they expected to achieve it within a couple of weeks. Looking back, I wonder whether the increasingly dire estimates for draining the water reflected not the best judgment but the deteriorating conditions in the city and the increasing sense that everything in this zone of devastation was going to hell. Pessimism sometimes seemed like the only reality.

The pumps for the 17th Street and London Avenue canals could not be turned on until the three breaches of those levees were patched effectively, because these pumps are deep inside the city. Engaging them with the breaches still open would simply pump the water back into the city by way of these breaches. Patching these breaches would be easier now that equalization between the lake and the water in the city had been reached, but the Corps was having a hard time finding contractors who could get their equipment into the city. Some of the pumping stations themselves were flooded and couldn't come on line until other pumps had lowered the water sufficiently. The debris problem, a given in a normal flood, would be exponentially worse in this one, because the water was so full of everything imaginable. Unless constantly cleared from the pump inlets, this debris will block the flow and place the pumps themselves at risk. Of course, the pumps require electrical power, of which there was almost none. Portable emergency generators were now on hand, but these required fuel, diesel or natural gas. Where were these replenishable supplies, and could the generators be positioned near a given pumping station? Someplace dry was required.

Another question was whether this water—this toxic stuff—

should be pumped directly into Lake Pontchartrain, from where it could spread into the marshes and swamps, or into the Mississippi River, thence into the Gulf of Mexico? The question was asked, but only two of the pumps for New Orleans discharge into the river. The priority had to be getting the water out of the city, no matter where it ended up or how toxic it turned out to be. The water would go into the lake.

At the LSU hurricane centers we had posited the pumping problem as a critical one in a flooded New Orleans, but we hadn't studied it "officially." It was our clear understanding from the Hurricane Pam exercise that, given an impending disastrous storm, the Corps would preposition barges loaded with pumps that would be ready to start the job. We had no reason as yet to second-guess the Corps, but on that first weekend after the storm, I was among the pessimists. Fortunately, some of the people charged with getting the pumps going were wonderfully ingenious. In a fine story on September 8, the *New York Times* would recount the saga at pumping station #6 located at City Park Avenue on the 17th Street Canal, the city's largest station, vitally important. In charge of the operation was Chief Warrant Officer Thomas Black, an engineer with Army's 249th Prime Power Battalion, recently returned from sixteen months in Iraq. A helicopter tour of the vicinity around the station had failed to pinpoint a suitable location for the emergency generator, but then someone noticed a stoplight working in adjacent Jefferson Parish. Could this team somehow link pumping station #6 to that electrical grid? Over two days they set up "a giant extension cord," and on Monday night, one week after Katrina hit, six of the fifteen pumps roared into action. (The others are so old they can't handle the standard 60-hertz current. They need their own 25-hertz generators.) The reporter noted that the racket could be heard from blocks away at night, since otherwise the city was dead quiet.

Mashriqui put everything together and concluded that the city could be empty in two to three weeks. That was quite an optimistic figure. In the end, the entire metro region—all of the bowls—would be declared officially dry on October 11, just over six weeks after landfall. This somewhat extended time frame reflects in part the re-flooding that followed levee failures along the Industrial Canal during Hurricane Rita in late September.

Exactly how bad was this witch's brew of water? We definitely needed to get going on this answer, and on the first Saturday after the storm I joined John Pardue, director of the Louisiana Water Resources Research Institute and a member of our LSU team, and headed off to get what early samples we could from the lake and the city. The marina on the north shore from which we set forth was a smelly place: dead fish and decaying biota. Once on the water I switched on the VHF and immediately heard that the lake was officially closed. The fine for approaching New Orleans by water was fifty thousand dollars and the risk of imprisonment. That punishment didn't seem likely, but I could envision being greeted by soldiers with rifles. We could probably talk our way past them—we had all kinds of useful identification—but the simpler course of action was to get permission, and after many tries, I managed to get through on the cell phone to Kevin Robbins, who directs the LSU team at the EOC, and he immediately arranged clearance for us with the Coast Guard.

The causeway across the lake was open to emergency vehicles, and there was a fairly steady stream going both ways. Above the city helicopters were buzzing everywhere in serious numbers, for the first time. Five days after the storm thousands of people were still stranded on rooftops, overpasses—just about any high ground. At the Industrial Canal, where we sampled the water flowing out, John and I heard at least one shot fired. At the London Avenue Canal we watched employees of the Orleans Levee Board adding mud and stones to the seal they had built at the bridge, near the entrance to the lake. One well-armed state policeman was standing there, all by himself, and not very friendly. (The two breaches at this canal were surrounded by floodwaters and inaccessible to vehicles, unlike the one at the 17th Street Canal, so serious work had to wait until the middle of the following week.)

The Environmental Protection Agency would be all over the water contamination question, partially in response to the criticism encountered four years earlier when it had refused to release the results of air quality samplings following 9/11. (We now know this air was much worse than the government first claimed.) In New Orleans the floodwater definitely wasn't potable—the *E. coli* was one hundred times safe swimming levels, and lead and arsenic levels were surprisingly high—but it was not as toxic as feared in terms of petrochemicals, mainly because the service stations in the city had run out of gas before Katrina hit, and the storage tanks and chemical plants south and east of city held up well enough, with the exception of a refinery in Meraux on the eastern edge of New Orleans and two partially filled storage tanks not far from Buras, which was landfall. These tanks have the diameter of a football field; the storm surge moved them the length of a football field. (This conclusion about the water seems to contradict the televised images of people wading through an iridescent sheen of oil or gasoline. The answer, as discussed at technical length in *Environmental Science and Technology*, is that such sheens can be—and were, in most of these instances—very, very thin.

Also on Saturday, Governor Blanco hired President Clinton's highly respected FEMA chief, James Lee Witt, as her adviser, and the Department of Homeland Security issued a document titled "Highlights of the United States Government Response to the Aftermath of Hurricane Katrina."

I didn't look at it. Still haven't. They had no time to send supplies where needed, but enough time to pat themselves on the back. That very night I was trying to scrounge up insulin for diabetic evacuees in Baton Rouge! The sister of an old friend from graduate student days at LSU had flown into New Orleans from New York on the Saturday before the storm to visit her parents in Baton Rouge and ended up volunteering at the triage site at the old Kmart that doctors from nearby Earl K. Long Hospital had set up to help with the evacuees pouring out of metropolitan New Orleans. Some of these folks were in dire straits, with no food or water for days, many lacking prescriptions and other medical needs, including insulin, which had been running low and was now running out. Calls to FEMA's medical hotlines had gone unanswered, the state's Department of Health and Hospitals couldn't help, all local pharmacies had to save their small supplies for regular customers. The situation at the triage center was getting quite desperate. That's when Anne Craig thought of me. She'd seen me on some interview or another, so maybe I could help. *Maybe*, I thought when she called me. I'd sure try. I called her brother Rob, who I didn't even know was a surgeon in Baton Rouge. We exchanged quick, amazed-you're-here greetings, and he drove over to the Emergency Operations Center. After an unsuccessful encounter with a woman from the Department of Health and Hospitals who was on duty that night—she was tired, she'd been up since 5:00 A.M., she had too much work to do, we weren't the only ones with problems—Rob found the secretary of DHH, who was friendly but just couldn't help us. Meanwhile, I called my man Marc Levitan, whose wife Lilian is a researcher at the Pennington Biomedical Research Center. Did they have any insulin? Better than that, we'd hit the jackpot. Pennington had just received a large supply, and we could have it. They even delivered the medicine to Rob at 1:00 A.M., and he carried it in the family van to the triage center. Mission accomplished—by freelancers stepping in when and where the official providers had failed. That was often the case those first two weeks.

While we were waiting for the insulin, Rob told me an amazing story, also indicative of the general confusion. Two days earlier—Thursday—he had treated a nurse who had evacuated from Baptist Memorial Hospital in New Orleans. This man had just recovered the year before from a relapse of multiple sclerosis, and he had stayed till the end evacuating patients, the last one a fellow who weighed about four hundred pounds. As this guy was being lifted out of his stretcher, he fell and pinned the nurse against the helicopter. The nurse passed out from the stress, and the helicopter crew brought *him* to Rob's hospital and Rob's care. He was not seriously hurt.

The next day, while on rounds, Rob was paged by his sister-in-law, Pam, who was trying to track down an in-law who had had open heart surgery at Baptist Memorial Hospital a few days before Katrina. The last information the family had received was that there had been complications, with their in-law taken to the intensive care ward. Now they had no idea where this man was, or his condition, and they were frantic. They had tried the state and FEMA, but no one had any list of where these patients had been evacuated to. Rob immediately asked the nurse he had treated the day before if he knew anything about a heart-surgery patient who'd been in intensive care. Well, this guy did know about this patient because he had taken him by helicopter to Thibodeaux General, and he even knew the bed number in the ICU unit there. Rob phoned Thibodeaux, confirmed everything, and spread welcome good news. Other stories didn't have such a good outcome.

The following morning, Sunday, I saw the whole Katrina tragedy for myself, end to end, from the air, flying with Mashriqui, a graduate student, and the world-renowned Louisiana wildlife photographer C. C. Lockwood. We flew from Baton Rouge in the west to east of Gulfport, Mississippi. It was an almost unbelievable sight. Miles and miles of New Orleans underwater, just the roofs of the homes visible in many neighborhoods; rescue boats still hard at it, along with the helicopters; at the 17th Street breach, Chinook helicopters dropping large sandbags; the infamous Superdome with its roof half peeled back; fires burning here and there; sailboats and motorboats strewn over car parking lots; two marinas empty except for the boats on the bottom; large stretches of the Interstates underwater; the interstate bridge over the Rigolets missing numerous spans. (In an interview with Mark Schleifstein of the *Times-Picayune* immediately after Hurricane Ivan in 2004, I stated that we would have lost that bridge if Ivan had come our way. Certain state officials later said I had overstated the problem. I guess not. The bridges need to be higher and of a different design, with the road sections tied down to the legs so they cannot "float off.") The Chandeleur barrier islands were missing the northern third of their mass, with no sign of the old lighthouse my family had fished from two months earlier. There were lots of life vests scattered over the water, and I wondered if a vessel had sunk. (There were no such reports.) The beach on Cat Island had been really hammered, and the island itself had been breached on its west side, with thousands of pine trees dead from salt burn—or perhaps not, because sometimes they come back. West Ship Island was almost half its former size, and a whole lot of East Ship Island was gone, but old Fort Massachusetts was still standing.

Of course, the Mississippi coastline was devastated beyond belief for about a mile inland. The Bert Jones Marina at Gulfport, where my family had always stayed for a summer holiday, was just a pile of debris—no boats, office, restaurant, or dolphinarium (my daughters love those animals). In Mississippi it was tempting to compare what we were seeing with the photographs of the tsunami damage, but that would be very unfair, since over two hundred thousand lives were lost in Asia. Still, this scene in America was incredible, and I have no good reason to challenge the claim that it was the worst coastal damage ever in the United States.

Passing over the Lower Ninth Ward in New Orleans, I lost it. I saw some bodies in the water but did not alert anyone. I knew there was nothing we could do, and I was having a hard time controlling my emotions. All of us were, because we were not prepared. I completely understood how Aaron Broussard, president of Jefferson Parish, could have wept that same day on *Meet the Press*. "It's not just Katrina caused all these deaths in New Orleans here," Broussard told the nation. "Bureaucracy has committed murder here in the greater New Orleans area, and bureaucracy has to stand trial before Congress now." The man would not be stopped on that program. (I was in the air at the time but read the transcript.) I've cited his reports about the supplies that FEMA wouldn't let through. He also revealed that FEMA had cut the antenna wires at the parish's communication tower on Saturday. Walter Maestri, the parish's director of emergency preparedness, confirmed the episode for me. With communications suddenly down, Walter immediately called the Motorola agent, who went to the antenna site, found the parish's antenna lying on the ground and a FEMA one in its place at the top of the tower. What should we make of this? Either unbelievable incompetence or—the darker explanation I try not to believe—someone with FEMA wanted to shut down the parish's local communications. In any event, parish officials took down the FEMA antenna and remounted their own, and the sheriff posted armed guards to protect it.

Five days after the storm—beautifully warm, clear days that were perfect for the rescue effort—no one yet had a grip on things. President Bush said there were twenty-one thousand National Guard troops in Mississippi and Louisiana, four thousand active-duty military on hand, seven thousand more active duty ordered in. Maybe so, but where were they? New Orleans Homeland Security director Terry Ebbert said there were only one thousand troops in New Orleans. What a time for Mayor Nagin and Police Chief Eddie Compass to pull off what must be one of the biggest PR blunders of all time when they offered five-day vacations—even trips to Las Vegas—to police, firefighters, and city emergency workers and their families. Cops had been accused of looting, and apparently several hundred were missing from duty entirely. Now this proffered holiday in Las Vegas? It was a terrible decision from any perspective, and editorialists around the country had a ball. I don't know how many workers accepted the offer. Very few, I imagine, but it seemed like the bizarre was becoming the everyday in New Orleans, even with the city now under much tighter control. On the following Tuesday we heard on CNN that the Superdome was likely to be torn down, per a "state official." Not happening. More after-the-fact stories related more lurid tales of heinous crimes at the Superdome and the other now notorious evacuee zone, the Convention Center, both now empty. As I've discussed, many of the stories about violent crime from the first week turned out to be urban myths, and the same would hold for these new tall tales, but there was plenty of real tragedy to fill the gap.

I joined CNN's Anderson Cooper in a two-hour helicopter tour and quickly concluded that his famous editorial anger the preceding week was not a ratings pose. I was glad to see that. Oprah Winfrey went so far as to demand a general apology from the country to the citizens of the devastated region. Has that been delivered? I don't think so. At the Astrodome in Houston, where most of the evacuees from the Superdome had been transferred, Barbara Bush issued her famously unfortunate remark that "so many of the people in the arena here, you know, were underprivileged anyway, so this is working very well for them." Colin Powell said that the root problem was one of economic class, not race, with "poverty disproportionately [affecting] African-Americans in this country." Oliver Thomas, president of the city council, said that "everything the tourists want to see are still in place. . . . We have a good foundation." The story broke about the two military pilots who rescued one hundred people the day after Katrina hit, only to be reprimanded for losing focus on their logistical mission. FEMA tried to forbid reporting on the recovery of the bodies, a bizarre action by an agency that, I would have thought, would have been too busy to worry about what the media was doing. (After all, the agency had just ordered twenty-five thousand body bags.) CNN went to court, and the attempt to censor the news was set aside, of course. I took this as still more evidence that important officials with FEMA and Homeland Security were as concerned about their image as about their work.

From my outpost at the LSU hurricane centers in Baton Rouge, I looked on and listened with amazement at how badly things had gone for a nation as powerful as ours. The city was stabilized by that first weekend, but rescue efforts were still required through the *following* week. The state Department of Wildlife and Fisheries said at one point that it was rescuing 650 people an hour. That adds up to a tremendous number. The Coast Guard said it had rescued 6,000, and that number actually sounds low, because they were as organized and equipped as any agency. All together an estimated 600 boats were working the streets of the city—one number I do accept at face value. This rescue effort was noble, but it was also the straightforward part of the job, in a way: Find the folks, take them someplace dry. Almost every other aspect of the emergency disintegrated in disarray, and I became more and more determined that the truth had to get out. We had to learn from these mistakes. Right about this time, a French TV crew came and stayed at my home. I'm a nice guy, plus I'd worked with them on a warning documentary two years earlier. Now here they were again, because it had happened. They were incredulous at everything they were seeing and hearing. Of course, they were preconditioned to hold this catastrophe against America in a fundamental way. Europeans—at least the friends who e-mailed me and almost every reporter and producer I dealt with, and that's quite a few from most of the Western European countries—now look on us as strange people in a strange land. A friend in England sent an e-mail outraged by the self-serving "no one could have foreseen" protestations of Michael Chertoff. After 9/11, we had heard the same whining protest that no one could have anticipated the use of jet aircraft as weapons of terror. In fact, plenty of thoughtful people had so anticipated, just not the right ones. Or had the right ones chosen not to listen?

A week after Aaron Broussard's appearance on *Meet the Press*, it was Mayor Nagin and my turn to press the case with Tim Russert that the failure we had seen over the previous two weeks was, with the exception of first responders, systemic. Nagin said that his biggest mistake was the assumption that the cavalry would be coming immediately. The federal cavalry had always been the city's ultimate and only hope, and this hope was profoundly misplaced. "To this day, Tim," the mayor said, "no one has dropped one piece of ice in the city of New Orleans to give some people relief." I said that despite the Hurricane Pam exercise and all the warnings and the prestaging of materials, the enormity of the challenge had never quite "sunk in" with FEMA and Homeland Security and the administration. Thirteen years after Hurricane Andrew—always the benchmark for preparedness people, the ultimate wake-up call—thirteen years later and—what?

The response at all levels was still "lacking," I said, by way of understatement. "Obviously, something is wrong with the system." I proposed a cabinet-level disaster czar empowered to get the military moving immediately. (I could have added that we also need a recovery-and-rebuilding czar.) Colin Powell had been mentioned as a great choice as a disaster czar, so had Rudy Giuliani, and at some point President Bush said that Karl Rove would be coordinating everything, but in November the job would go to Donald Powell, a Texan who had served as chairman of the Federal Deposit Insurance Corporation since August 2001. I wouldn't call him a czar, however, more like some kind of coordinator and point man. Whatever his capacity, over the following months I almost never read or heard his name.

John Kerry would soon blast the failed federal response to Katrina as the rotten fruit of a "right-wing ideological experiment." On the other side of the aisle, some Republicans said it was proof that government simply isn't capable of performing at that necessary level. Trust Wal-Mart instead. Trust yourself. And yet the Republican president requested and the Republican-controlled Congress approved $52 billion in aid for the region. Such intentions several decades earlier, at all levels of government, would have saved New Orleans and cost a whole lot less. If we are ever to deal with a dirty bomb, our nation must get a grip on dealing with large-scale natural disasters. We have to learn, and learn fast.

If "learning" is actually the problem, in some quarters. We also have to care.

That edition of *Meet the Press* two weeks after Katrina may have been the last major press conference for quite a while in which the word "levee" was not spoken. Right at this point in the saga, with conditions all along the coastline stabilizing to the extent that almost everyone now had a place of some sort, somewhere, to lay his or her head at night, with the waters beginning to go down slowly as the breaches were temporarily plugged and the main pumps came on line, augmented by mobile pumps, more of us were beginning to ask the hard questions about those levees and their failure. The truly horrible fact was beginning to sink in: The entire tragedy in New Orleans—not on the coastline and in Mississippi, but in New Orleans—was primarily due to five levee failures. I have repeated this fact a couple of times already, because I've learned that many people really don't understand. Some of New Orleans was going to flood regardless, but the city could have handled it. The pumps could have drained the flooded areas quickly. Instead, we had the dreadful flooding caused by these five failures, and I have to admit right now that I never trusted the Army Corps of Engineers to investigate itself and find out exactly what happened and why.

Immediately after the storm, on Tuesday, I told Terry Ryder, one of the governor's senior staffers, that we could not account for the amount of flooding reported in the media, given what we knew at the time. There had to be a catastrophic breach or breaches somewhere else. Terry, whom I have known for years as a no-nonsense person, told me to go find out. We did.

In an unguarded moment Al Naomi, a project manager for the Corps, told the Newhouse News Service on the following Friday, September 9, that he assumed a "catastrophic structural failure" of the 17th Street levee. Naomi had previously been quoted in a piece for *New Orleans City Business* complaining about budget cuts of $71 million for the Corps's New Orleans district. The fact sheet on this budget cut released by the Corps in May stated explicitly that the primary remaining job in the currently authorized improvements was "the parallel protection along the London Avenue and Orleans Avenue canals. Completion of this work is scheduled by 2010." In response to the circulation of this statement after Katrina, the Corps issued a news release stating that the levee failures had been in sections where the upgrading *had been completed*. Lieutenant General Carl Strock, who runs the Corps in Washington, D.C., said the same thing to reporters: "The levee projects that failed were at full project design and were not really going to be improved." (The embankments fronting the Orleans Canal pump station—the embankments that were overtopped because they were six feet lower than the adjacent flood walls—*were* still on the Corps's to-do list.)

Looking back now, I'm surprised at both Naomi and Strock's telltale uses of the words "failure" and "failed," because it quickly became apparent in September that the Corps would argue that the storm surge from Lake Pontchartrain had overtopped the levees and scoured dangerous trenches on the backside, necessarily weakening these otherwise solid structures to the point of collapse. Naomi and Strock had temporarily diverged from the party line, which was: "The levees were sound, but the event exceeded the design. Congress told us to design to a Cat 3, and that's what we did. Our hands were tied. Katrina was a Cat 4 storm."

Simply not so, and at the LSU hurricane centers we were immediately suspicious of this whole scenario. The lowest of the levees in question were supposed to be fourteen feet above mean sea level, and the ADCIRC surge models had predicted a surge in the lake topping out at ten feet, maybe eleven, because the lake was on the western, or weaker, side of Katrina, where sustained winds were 75 mph. That's a *Cat 1* storm, folks. The catastrophic storm surge had been to the east of New Orleans and, especially, on the Mississippi coast. For New Orleans and Lake Pontchartrain and the levees, Katrina was *not* a major hurricane. It's that simple, but as I mentioned in the introduction, I know from experience that people don't want to hear this. They want to have lived through this monster, and they want the catastrophe to have been caused by this monster. In the city itself, this just wasn't the case.

In October we got word from NOAA that, indeed, Katrina might have been just a Cat 3 at landfall, and then the National Hurricane Center confirmed the number in late December. Additionally, the forward speed was fast, 14 mph to 17 mph, so over the lake and the city Katrina was a fast-moving Cat 1 hurricane—nothing approaching the storm the Corps claimed the levees were designed to withstand. (Robert Howard, an atmospheric researcher at the University of Louisiana, Monroe, believes Katrina might have been only a borderline Cat 3 storm at landfall. His analysis is complex and, at this writing, incomplete, but he might be correct. Wind-speed numbers are not always hard and fast. A great deal of study is necessary to come up with the best ones, and the decisions can be changed years later. In the case of Hurricane Andrew, the official Cat 5 designation, an upgrade from Cat 4, wasn't announced until 2002, a full decade after the damage was done; Cindy was upgraded from tropical storm to Cat 1 status six months after the fact. With Katrina, we weren't surprised at the downgrading; the wind damage on the ground simply didn't reflect a major hurricane anywhere except right at the Buras landfall. Marc Levitan is a wind guy, one of the best. Touring the north shore of Lake Pontchartrain and parts of Mississippi, his team saw Cat 1 evidence—that is, roof damage to some, not even all, buildings, the odd tree down, but no catastrophic tree damage. Katrina had indeed weakened considerably in the overnight hours before landfall Monday morning.

Nevertheless, in the weeks following the storm, various voices from the Corps of Engineers kept emphasizing Cat 4 . . . Cat 4 . . . Cat 4. They wanted to fix in the public mind the myth that this very strong storm had overwhelmed the design to which they had responsibly built the levees. This myth is also reflected in an e-mail from Harley Winer, chief of the Corps's Coastal Engineering Section, to our own flood fatalities modeler, Ezra Boyd. It is dated August 2, 2005, just four weeks before Katrina. Ezra had asked whether "a major section of levee failing during a surge event is possible and . . . should be considered when looking at different disaster scenarios for New Orleans." Winer replied, "I don't think an engineered levee would fail during a storm." He added, "The federal levees are engineered and constructed to engineering standards. [T]he only levee failure is if the[y] are overtopped by a storm surge that exceeds the design." These statements pretty much sum up the Corps's attitude before Katrina and immediately afterward. Regarding the levee failures on the drainage canals, we just didn't believe it. Even at that early date, while we were still collecting data, we had a pretty good idea that our ADCIRC models had been essentially correct: no overtopping along the drainage canals in the Orleans Metro Bowl. The developers are constantly upgrading ADCIRC. They meet with a users group once a year to discuss recent developments and new ideas. Following Katrina, Jack Bevin, one of the lead forecasters at the National Hurricane Center, sent an e-mail saying that it looked like we had it right. We did, thanks to the excellence of ADCIRC and the highly accurate track and intensity predictions received from the National Hurricane Center. To get technical for a moment, one measure of model performance or accuracy is called the root-mean-square error (RMSE). If the model is perfect, with surge predictions exactly matching the actual event, the RMSE would be 0 percent. Paul Kemp has checked the Katrina models against fifty surge measurements throughout the area and came up with a RMSE of +/- 15 percent, which is extremely good. The levees on these canals were never overtopped. They failed of their own accord.

On the other hand, we couldn't really talk to the Corps directly about what we knew and what we doubted. If we had asked outright for the design and construction documents for the levees, they would never have provided them. Not then, not without pressure. Paul and I are not well-liked by some in the local district's upper management, although the more political and influential folks do like Paul. I've alluded to the combative atmosphere of the CWPPRA process in the 1990s. More pointedly, in 1993, Paul, Hassan Mashriqui, Joe Suhayda, and I had showed the Corps that they were in the wrong about the Wax Lake weir, a $36 million project that was supposed to reduce flooding in Morgan City, but did just the opposite. We got into this question because city officials and some local businesspeople asked us to. The Atchafalaya River, a major distributary of the Mississippi, of course, has two outlets at the Gulf, the Lower Atchafalaya and Wax Lake outlet. In the early nineties the Corps found itself dredging the Lower Atchafalaya River annually, because this river is the navigation route to Morgan City, an important port for shipbuilding, oil and gas, and fishing interests. The dredging cost about $4 million a year, and the Corps surmised that pushing more water down the Atchafalaya would reduce the amount of sedimentation and therefore also reduce the necessity for dredging. So it built a weir across the Wax Lake outlet, about a mile below its takeoff point from the Atchafalaya, eight miles upstream from Morgan City.

Almost immediately the local riverfront businesses, and especially the shipbuilders, were flooding more often. The Corps reminded them that it had bought the flood easements from the original landowners years before. Owning the flood easement means "we can drown you if we want to." So even if the weir was causing higher water and floods, the Corps was covered—legally. So it believed and so it said. Obviously, though, the business owners were upset that the flooding had gotten much worse immediately after the weir had been installed, and the city hired us at LSU to take up their case. We were happy to do so. The science was not all that complicated. While the Corp's idea had been to solve the sedimentation problem in the Atchafalaya by flushing more water down the channel, it was actually contributing to the problem because it had not taken into account the fact that the entire Atchafalaya Basin, which had started out as a large lake a few hundred years before, had absorbed just about all of the sediment it could and was necessarily sending the excess, in ever-increasing portions, down the river. Preweir, the river and the Wax Lake outlet were carrying sediment in proportion to their discharges; postweir, the extra volume of water in the river couldn't overcome the extra sediment.

The weir had not solved the dredging problem, but it had raised flood levels in Morgan City by about eighteen inches. With a big river eighteen inches doesn't sound like much, but to the businesses positioned right on the water, it was. We used some direct measurements and the Corps's own models to demonstrate what was happening. We also found what we thought was pretty shoddy workmanship. After an investigation and debate that lasted about a year, the Corps took out the weir at just about the cost for which it had put the thing in ten years earlier.

We had other run-ins with the Corps over the years, including a major reassessment of the levee systems in the Atchafalaya Basin. The Corps had set up a citizens' advisory panel that turned out to be a divide-and-conquer strategy, or so it seemed, because all the different stakeholders and user groups ended up at odds. Paul Kemp, the natural conciliator, helped the groups recognize the advantages of working together, and once this was accomplished the Corps was dealing with a different kettle of fish. It had to be responsive. All the while Paul, Joe Suhayda, and Mashriqui were helping the Corps with its modeling efforts for this reassessment and finding many problems, some as basic as misplaced gauging stations, major bridges, and large pilings. These made a joke of the model. Another joke: This planning effort, which has cost more than $14 million, has still not issued a final report.

Given this history it would have been very difficult for us to "go it alone" with the Army Corps of Engineers on the matter of the levee breaches during Katrina, which was the worst catastrophe to ever confront the agency.

In the weeks following Katrina, as more reporters started thinking about the official explanation that the breached levees had been designed only for a fast-moving Cat 3 storm—setting aside for the moment the fact that Katrina was not even that strong on Lake Pontchartrain—the inevitable question was, "Why protect against just a Cat 3 storm? Why leave the city of New Orleans in jeopardy against a Cat 4 or Cat 5 storm? Does the Corps think that water from the lake and storm surge from the Gulf of Mexico is somehow less wet than water from the Mississippi River? Would this water not rise as high, do as much damage, and require just as much time to pump out?"

These are not new questions, they are very important questions, and the Corps has offered an assortment of answers. Most of them revolve around an assessment-and-design process that dates from the early 1960s, an era before the serious loss of the wetlands, before modern computers, before reliable storm-surge models. At that time the levee system around New Orleans consisted of earthen embankments like those along the Mississippi River, just not nearly as large or high. None were reinforced with the steel plates called sheet piling or topped with concrete flood walls. Clearly, that system was not protective. When the Bonnet Carre Spillway from the Mississippi River into Lake Pontchartrain was opened for the first time in 1937, the lake had filled up and poured over the levee immediately into adjacent Jefferson Parish. Embarrassing. A storm in 1947 had overtopped lakeshore levees and swamped nine square miles in the city and thirty square miles in Jefferson Parish. Ominous. Sections of the levees on the Industrial Canal had failed or were overtopped (contemporary accounts differ) during Hurricane Flossy in 1956, flooding over two square miles of the Ninth Ward.

A harbinger. Hurricane Hilda had sideswiped southeast Louisiana in 1964. A reminder.

No sooner had the Corps begun thinking about doing something than Hurricane Betsy ripped ashore in September 1965, between Grand Isle and Port Fourchon (about 30 miles west of Katrina's landfall at Buras). This was a strong Cat 4 storm at landfall, and still a Cat 3 at its closest approach to New Orleans, thirty-five miles to the southwest. Even though the storm surge was only eight feet to ten feet, East New Orleans and St. Bernard Parish went under. Water from a levee breach on the Industrial Canal (there's that name again) rose twenty feet in that many minutes. Fifty-eight died, some drowning in their attics. As many as 250,000 were then evacuated. "Billion-Dollar Betsy" was the tipping point, the call to arms, and Congress almost immediately passed the Flood Control Act of 1965, ordering the Corps to build a complete system to protect New Orleans. (I've read several versions of the politics behind this measure. My favorite is the short one: Senator Russell Long, Huey's son and a very powerful man in Washington, asked his old friend, President Lyndon Johnson, to fly down to survey the scene. The president promised to send his "best man." The senator said he was not "the least bit interested in your 'best man.'" LBJ immediately called for his airplane.)

With the president's enthusiastic support Congress then ordered the Corps to protect New Orleans from "the most severe meteorological conditions considered reasonably characteristic for that region." In order to do this, the Corps commissioned the Weather Bureau (now the National Weather Service) to define the hypothetical storm that the strengthened levees would be designed to withstand and dubbed this the standard project hurricane, or SPH. In 1967, the Corps compared the SPH to Hurricane Betsy, a Cat 4, but this is just not right. The Corps now says that, taken as a whole, their defining factors amount to a Cat 3 storm—and a "fast-moving" one, which is less dangerous than a slow-moving one, as I've explained earlier.

All in all, that SPH paper tiger doesn't make a lot of sense. Some of the parameters match today's Cat 3 storm, others a Cat 4. Regardless, is this the "most severe meteorological conditions" that Congress ordered? A definite *no*. The most severe would have been a Cat 5 storm. So, the key question remains: Why was that hypothetical storm chosen by the Corps of such moderate strength and danger? Lieutenant General Carl Strock said on the Thursday after Katrina's landfall, "We certainly understand the potential impact of a Category 4 or 5 hurricane." So why didn't the Corps design the system to protect against such a storm? Why not protect one of the nation's prized cultural and economic jewels against all comers, major storms like the one that had leveled Galveston in 1900, the Florida Keys in 1935, the Texas-Louisiana border in 1957 (Audrey). Why not take the worst-case scenario and design and build to those specifications?

From one perspective, the answer seems to boil down to money. The Orleans Levee District complained that even the relatively modest design standards dictated by the SPH would be too expensive to maintain. It also opposed putting the floodgates at the mouths of the main drainage canals: too expensive to maintain. In the 1980s, the Corps stated that raising the levees around Lake Pontchartrain would be cheaper than the plan to erect barriers at the two main entrances to the lake. So the Corps may have been constrained by money, but Congress was not constrained, and Congress literally dictates the Corps's agenda. Money was not and is not the problem. Political foresight and will was the problem and will be the problem in the years to come.

Four years after Hurricane Betsy the famous Cat 5 Camille just missed Louisiana and destroyed the Mississippi coast with winds of almost 200 mph and a storm surge almost of Katrina's magnitude. A track just twenty miles west for Camille would have both leveled and drowned Greater New Orleans. No one bothered to deny it. This was in 1969. Did the Corps therefore reassess the standard project hurricane? Did it adjust its design? I wasn't here, but apparently not, even though a 1982 report by the Government Accountability Office states, "Subsequent to project authorization and based on the Weather Bureau's new data pertaining to hurricane severity, the Corps determined that the levees along the main drainage canals, which drain portions of New Orleans and empty into Lake Pontchartrain, were not high enough since they are subject to overflow by hurricane surges."

The *Times-Picayune*'s Bob Marshall drew my attention to the Weather Bureau's two redefinitions, in 1972 and 1979. For the bureau, at least, the SPH for New Orleans was now a much stronger Cat 4 storm. As the GAO report indicates, the Corps was aware of the redefinition but opted for rather minimal measures. Pinching pennies, the Corps raised and strengthened the levees at the eastern end of Plaquemines Parish. Steel-sheet piling was used to strengthen the levees along the Industrial Canal. Some of the levees along the lake were raised two feet and linked with the levees along the Mississippi River to close the western side of the westernmost bowl. On the river, the levee at the French Quarter was beefed up with a concrete revetment. The local levee boards, tired of waiting for Corps action on the drainage canals, including 17th Street and London Avenue, reinforced those levees with sheet piling, raising their effective height from plus-6.5 feet above sea level to plus-10 feet. All the work was done to the Corps's official design standards, in order to ensure that the expense could count toward the locals' cost share when the Corps finally built more substantial levees.

That 1982 GAO report was titled "Improved Planning Needed by the Corps of Engineers to Resolve Environmental, Technical and Financial Issues on the Lake Pontchartrain Hurricane Protection Project." What fascinating, disturbing reading it makes today. It states bluntly that even though the levees in southeastern Louisiana were a high priority, the Corps still had not resolved any of the named issues fifteen years after congressional legislation had mandated action; that it had completed only 50 percent of the work; that "there has been no strong effort to complete this project until recently, when preparation of design memoranda was initiated"; that completion was estimated for the year 2008. (By August 2005, this completion date had slipped to 2015.) The GAO report continued, "State and local sponsors generally agreed with our findings, conclusions and recommendations. They believe the Corps has not pursued this project with the expediency necessary to protect the New Orleans area and that only another disaster . . . would expedite project completion."

In 1985, the Corps and the Orleans Levee Board decided to solve, once and for all, the problems posed by the drainage canals in the heart of what I call the Orleans Metro Bowl. What happened next? There's a good deal of contradiction and confusion in the reporting on that subject. In any event, five years later the Corps dropped plans for floodgates at the entrances to the canals and agreed with the Orleans Levee Board to upgrade the "parallel protection plan," that is, the levees and flood walls. Now, post-Katrina, the Corps is going to spend several billion dollars doing what it considered doing twenty years ago: sealing the canals and installing pumps at the entrance structures. If the Corps and the Orleans Levee Board had moved the pumps twenty years ago, the Katrina tragedy would not have happened, because the breaches along the 17th Street and London Avenue canals were the main source of the floodwaters in the heart of New Orleans.

After a flood in 1995 (just rainfall, not a hurricane), the Corps undertook a $145 million upgrading of the pumping stations on the drainage canals in Jefferson, Orleans, and St. Tammany parishes— in theory, that is, but this initiative was never fully funded and, as mentioned, the low embankments at the Orleans Canal pump station that overtopped during Katrina were among those projects. In 1996, an attempt to study the levees along the lake broke down because of bureaucratic infighting. Joe Suhayda recalls a meeting from that era in which someone said about upgrading the levees to handle a Cat 5 storm, "We can't afford it."

Think about all that—or don't, if it makes you too angry. Then, in 1998, Hurricane Georges tacked sharply in the Gulf of Mexico, saving New Orleans yet again—and barely. Waves from the surge in Lake Pontchartrain came within a foot of overtopping some of the levees along Haynes Boulevard close to the Lakefront airport, and the surge in the lake was only seven feet. The maximum surge that struck Mississippi and Alabama was seventeen feet. This action caught the attention of Congress, which instructed the Corps to investigate providing Cat 4 and Cat 5 hurricane protection for coastal Louisiana that would encompass all of the previously authorized projects. On paper, that investigation continues to this day—although it is now mooted by Katrina, of course.

What's the deal with these studies? Why do they always take forever? I conclude that no one at the Corps took any of this seriously enough. Forget the military-management veneer. We're dealing with a classically hidebound civilian bureaucracy. Although the first storm-surge models appeared in 1985, and a highly refined and accurate one (ADCIRC) has been in hand for at least a decade, it was not until 2002 that the New Orleans district joined the modern world and began working with the latest storm-surge models. Before that, as the agency has acknowledged, it based its estimation of the adequacy of the levees on calculations that were forty years old. The Corps's Waterways Experimental Station in Vicksburg, Mississippi, did put a lot of money into developing ADCIRC in the 1990s, but the problem, as we outsiders saw it, was that the old-line engineers in New Orleans didn't have experience working in two-dimensional modeling, nor the ability to communicate with their expert counterparts in Vicksburg. The local Corps engineers complained that Vicksburg didn't answer questions, and that Vicksburg was too expensive!

Overall, the Corps of Engineers answers to whom, exactly? Congressional "earmarkers"? Lobbyists? Special interests? The demands of its own bureaucracy? All of the above and more, probably. While the New Orleans District of the Corps could not get the money to build proper levees, it got $748 million for the questionable locks in the Industrial Canal. Before Katrina the Corps estimated that a complete upgrade of the levees to Cat 5 status would cost at least $2.5 billion, perhaps $3 billion, and require twenty to thirty years. All now moot. The Corps's budget for levee work fell from $14.5 million in 2002 to $5.7 million in 2005. All now moot. Dominic Izzo, the principal deputy assistant secretary of the Corps for civil works in 2001–2007, told the *Baton Rouge Advocate* two weeks after Katrina arrived that the Office of Management and Budget in

Washington—a component of the executive branch—had targeted the Corps's funds for cuts for years, under both Democratic and Republican administrations. All now moot. Louisiana received far more Corps money than any other state—almost $2 billion, with California second, at $1.4 billion—but hundreds of millions of these dollars were for dredging and other projects that have absolutely nothing to do with flood control and not much to do with commerce. It's pork—and now moot. The total budget for the Corps is less than $5 billion annually. Compare the latest highway bill and its 6,371 earmarked projects, including the now-famous bridge to nowhere in Alaska (subsequently crossed out, although the state still got the money, as you may not have read), which came in at $284 billion. All now moot.

TEN

THE INVESTIGATION

On Thursday, September 8, Paul Kemp, Hassan Mashriqui, and I drove into flooded New Orleans to inspect the levees for the first time, escorted by an LSU cop, which was mandatory, given the roadblocks everywhere that were manned by serious military units. Our guy, Sergeant Bill Thomas, just switched on his blue police lights and the rifles waved us through. Over the following month, Bill and his lights saved us many hours. We turned off West Esplanade Avenue, and drove north on Orpheum Road on the west side of the 17th Street Canal, the dry side. For the first time we saw with our own eyes the state of the earthen embankment: pristine, I would almost say, with the grass green and the turf intact, with no drip lines or mud splatters on the concrete flood walls. As clear as day, there was all the proof we really needed that the Corps's claim was wrong. These levees had not been overtopped. From the beginning, all of us had had our doubts about the official line, but now my doubts instantly crystallized into certainty. We stopped the car and I jumped on the levee and turned to the others and said, "See, I told you we were right. Look, no sign of overtopping, none whatsoever."

These levees have three parts. The foundation is the earthen berm built on old swamp soils. Sheet piling—corrugated steel plates eighteen inches wide, fitted together tongue-and-groove fashion—is then driven into the berm to whatever depth is deemed necessary, based on a design plan that should include the geotechnical characteristics of the soil, the height of the wall, the depth of the canal, the geology, and so on. The designers decide. For many years the sheet piling installed after Hurricane Betsy in 1965 stood alone, protruding from the top of the embankment by six feet and serving these purposes: increased height for the entire levee; solid, rooted support for the berm itself; and as an underground barrier to prevent water from the canal from seeping all the way under the embankment, thereby weakening the entire structure. In the 1990s the New Orleans District of the Army Corps of Engineers affixed a concrete flood wall to the top of the steel-sheet piling—the third element. The contractor either pulled out the old steel piling and drove in a new piling or used the existing steel. In either case there is an overlap of a couple of feet between the steel and the concrete. This new structure increased the overall height of these levees to thirteen feet to fourteen feet above mean sea level. Of course, the sheet piling still served to support the whole structure, and to act as a barrier to underground water movement from the canal to the outside of the levees—and to the homes beyond. (The water level in these canals is just about sea level, fluctuating with the tides in the lake, which puts it level with the eaves of many of the homes on either side of the canal.)

I'm not a structural engineer nor an expert on levee design and construction, and I haven't spent as much time on the levees in and around New Orleans as I have in the wetlands, but I know these structures pretty well. In 2001, after our Hurricane Public Health Center was funded, I'd occasionally leave home early, drive to New Orleans, and just cruise the city, trying to feel in my veins the natural ridges, the unnatural canals and levees, what would happen during a flood. I knew about the lower section of the levee at Lakefront Airport—the one that overtopped during Katrina. I saw the weak spot at a joint between the earthen levee and the concrete wall near the Lake Pontchartrain causeway. I had seen sections of levee walls that had sagged downward, suggesting potential soil or differential subsidence issues. (Areas mostly underlain by clay will subside more than areas predominantly underlain by sand—always a concern when building levees or anything else in a swampy setting such as New Orleans.) I know that water coming over the top of a flood wall—overtopping—scours a trench in the soil at the base of the wall on the protected side, the side facing the homes. It's common sense, and it always happens.

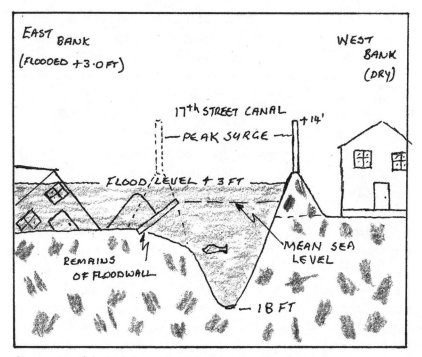

Cross section of the 17th Street Canal breach (view from the north).

There was no such scouring here at the 17th Street Canal. I couldn't believe the Corps was taking this line, because surely one of the engineers—many of the engineers—had toured the levees after Katrina and had seen the *absence* of any scouring or other signs of overtopping. Also, the new hurricane bridge just a few hundred yards inland from the lake entrance to this canal would have blocked any significant wave action in the canal itself. Waves pounding on the flood walls would not have been a factor. Nor is this canal wide enough to create significant fetch. (Wind-driven waves get bigger the greater the distance of open water. With the wind mostly blowing across them during Katrina, these narrow canals could not have supported much in the way of waves.)

What the Corps was saying seemed so far from the truth as I observed in the field that I'll admit the word "cover-up" came to my mind—and probably to my lips—as we studied the scene that Thursday. After all, the Corps and its contractors can be sued, under the

Federal Tort Claims Act. They have a lot at stake here. As the LSU group studied and compared notes, there was no question that we had all come to the same conclusion about this levee: It had somehow failed, structurally. Paul and I looked at each other and almost sighed. Here we go again with the Corps.

We crossed the bridge over the canal—the scene of all the action I described in Chapter 6—and then walked toward the breach itself on the new roadway built by the West Jeff crew, right next to the flood wall, right above the floodwaters. Of course, there were no signs of overtopping on this side of the canal either; the walls are roughly the same height on both sides of the canal. At the breach itself a section of the bank with its green grass and fence still intact had heaved laterally thirty to forty feet, carrying with it several large trees. Literally, this heave acted as a huge bulldozer and pushed everything in front of it forward and upward. The yard directly in front of the breach was now a hummocky terrain, rather than the flat, level yard so typical of this area of New Orleans. One frame house had ended up on the high ground and was fairly dry. In the scour areas on each end of the breach, houses were gone. The huge roots of the cypress trees that had grown here hundreds of years ago were scattered here and there in the scour holes. Clearly, the entire structure of the levee—flood wall, sheet piling, and earthen embankment—had succumbed to the pressure of the water in the canal and heaved laterally, almost as a unit. This breach was about five hundred feet across. Water had poured into the city with incredible power.

I met Joseph Bowles and his sister, Schoener Cole, working their way through what was left of the possessions inside Joe's flooded, ruined house near the end of the breach on the north side. This house had never flooded before, Joe said, and during Betsy this levee, just an earthen berm, with no sheet piling or concrete flood wall at all, had held, so Joe's inclination had been to ride out Katrina, just as he had stayed put for all of the other storms over the decades. Like many people, though, he had evacuated on Sunday evening, when the predictions were dire indeed. He had thought he would find a place in Baton Rouge but ended up in Arkansas, and he didn't know the fate of his house until he came back to see for himself what he had left. Even with all of the photographs telecast around the clock, he hadn't realized his house was right at the now-famous 17th Street breach. He was staying with his sister in nearby Metairie—two of the two million lives that would never be the same.

Our group now drove east to the London Avenue Canal, where there were two breaches, but with only one easily accessible, on the west side of the canal. This breach was about 450 feet across—not as wide as the one at 17th Street. The berm on either side showed no signs of overtopping or scouring. It had heaved away from the canal, shoving a little building 8 feet up and 20 feet back. (This building turned out to be the clubhouse that homeowner Gus Cantrell, a civil engineer, had built for his kids years earlier. He sent us the before-and-after pictures. Inside that house an enormous, extremely solid, and heavy china cabinet wasn't just shoved or moved by the wall of water that had roared through. It was gone.)

We couldn't know for sure yet, but at this breach, too, it certainly looked like something instantaneous and structurally catastrophic had happened on the morning of August 29, and that water from Lake Pontchartrain had poured into the city, soon meeting the water pouring in from the 17th Street breach to the west.

The third of the fatal breaks in the Orleans Metro Bowl is on the east side of the London Avenue Canal, just north of the bridge at Mirabeau Avenue. We were finally able to reach this site a week later, and we needed my Xterra to do so. Just imagine, I said to the others, I need four-wheel drive to get around New Orleans. The reason was all of the sand piled deep over an area two hundred yards or more around this breach. Dunes of sand—an amazing sight. Where had it all come from? Possibly Lake Pontchartrain. When John Pardue and I had crossed the lake on the Saturday after the storm, the echo sounder revealed that the bottom was now very irregular, with lots of dips and valleys. Scour holes? Normally the echo sounder shows a flat, smooth bottom. Since I've sailed over this bottom literally hundreds of times, I pretty much have the bathymetry stored in my head, and it appeared to me that the surge and waves of Katrina had deepened this lake—shallow to begin

with, averaging twelve feet—by two feet in some areas. That missing bottom was now sediment suspended in the water, and in the
canal it would have been held in suspension by the current until it
spilled over the breach, where it would have deposited the heaviest
material, which is the fine sand, first. That's what I was thinking as I
studied the new beach inside New Orleans. But why was there so
much more sand here than at the other breach on this canal or at the
one at 17th Street? This was a bit puzzling, and it was puzzling because my hypothesis was dead wrong, as I learned later when we got
the borehole data for this site. Below this breach the soil from
minus-10 (that is, 10 feet below mean sea level) to minus-50 is thick
beach sand. So this sand deep enough to cover cars was of local origin. It had come from the breach area itself. This would be a cru-
cially important fact for the levee investigation.

Lined up with the middle of this three-hundred-foot-wide breach
at Mirabeau was a slab house that had been shoved thirty or forty
yards. (Or maybe it floated; entire houses can float down rivers in
floods. We see it all the time.) Other slabs were now bare. Again,
there were no signs of any scouring along the intact berm at both
ends of the breach. No overtopping. To all immediate appearances,
yet another catastrophic failure from some other cause.

A block away, Carmen and Dale Owens were working in their almost new two-story brick home. Like all of the homes throughout
the city that had taken in water to eye level or higher, the first floor
was a grim vision of ruined furniture and dried mud and muck on
the floors and walls, juxtaposed with pictures still hanging on the
walls and placed on the mantles. "Depressing" is a pitifully inadequate word for these scenes, even for an outsider who's not picking
though a lifetime's possessions, looking for something to save. No
wonder a lot of the evacuees now scattered far and wide were saying
that they would not even come back to see their former homes. Just
too difficult. Carmen said she understood this attitude, but the bed-
rooms and possessions upstairs were fine. They looked exactly the
way they had when she and Dale had fled late Monday morning,
when the winds were dying but water was suddenly in their house.
They couldn't understand what had happened. This neighborhood

had *never* flooded. That's why they didn't have flood insurance. They did have another house—dry—not too far way, so they had someplace to live. Still, I was amazed by their spirit. (A few weeks later one of Carmen and Dale's neighbors contacted me. They had video shot right after the breach, and it was time stamped. As our forensic studies moved forward this video would prove more and more important. It is, as far as I know, the only video taken immediately after the failure of a levee.)

Back at the breach, we looked into a house that was completely missing one exterior wall. The furnishings inside were a mud-caked shambles, of course, but there in an open closet were all the winter blankets neatly packed into plastic bags, the kids' school sports bags, Barbie dolls, everything in this one little section looking perfectly okay, but with the house around it a complete loss. My daughters loved to play with Barbie dolls, and it always amazed me how they knew which doll was whose and which clothes belonged to each one. Who and where were the little girl or girls who played with these Barbies? Did they get new ones for Christmas? The garage was filled with sand and a very strong smell of death. I said a silent prayer for this family, wherever they may be.

I've said it before, and I'll say it again now. These images stuck with me, and they convinced me to try to get the federal government to own up to the fact that this city was flooded by the failure of *its* levees. As the month passed and the unwatering of the Orleans Metro Bowl was proceeding nicely, helped in good measure by the huge portable pumps flown in by a number of European nations, more and more residents mustered the courage to return to see what they had left, if anything. My images were their homes and lives. And they were angry, too. They wanted to know what had happened. Many of these neighborhoods had never flooded in the sometimes long experience of the owners. These three breaches had effectively ruined the largest part of New Orleans for the foreseeable future. Call it a blame game if you must, but some of us were determined to find out exactly what had happened and to demand justice from the responsible parties.

The Corps had not dug these canals or built the first levees here, but when it added the concrete flood walls in the 1990s, it had conducted a comprehensive assessment of what was here and what was needed. By law and by any moral calculation you choose to perform, the Corps was now totally responsible. Whether the owners or renters of these homes had evacuated or not, they were wiped out, and I believed—and still do, of course—that the federal government needs to compensate them fully. I don't care whether I become a one-man band on this issue (but I don't believe I will). One afternoon when I was a guest on NPR's *To the Point*, Warren Olney started the program with a quote from President Bush about the need to balance compassion with fiscal responsibility. What would I like to see the president do? Olney asked me. I don't miss this kind of opportunity. Warren had really teed it up for me, and I tried to hit that ball long and straight. The feds need to step up and compensate those who trusted the levees—the federal security system—because that system had failed during Hurricane Katrina.

Like many structures, a levee under pressure is only as strong as its weakest link. In different trips to the different breaches over the following weeks and months, we looked for that link. We looked at the panels of the flood walls and the joints between. (The panels were not linked together, but stood independently with a rubber epoxy sealing the crack.) We looked at the steel rebar—that is, what we could find in the rubble—that would usually be tied with wire into a "cage," with this cage then strengthening the concrete itself and uniting the concrete in some way with the sheet piling, so that concrete, rebar, and steel piling function as one unit. We looked at the Corps's choice of an I wall for the flood wall rather than a stronger T wall with batter piles. The term "I wall" is self-explanatory: Viewed on end, it resembles the letter I, supported at its base by the vertical steel-sheet piling driven into the berm. The T wall resembles an inverted T, with a wider base than the I wall; in addition, two piles, one on each edge of the base, penetrate the soil at an angle away from the wall, almost like the legs of the capital letter A. These are the batter piles, and they assure a far more robust structure.

They are mandatory in soft, weak soils. The wide base of the T wall also helps protect the system should there be overtopping. But on these canals we have I walls.

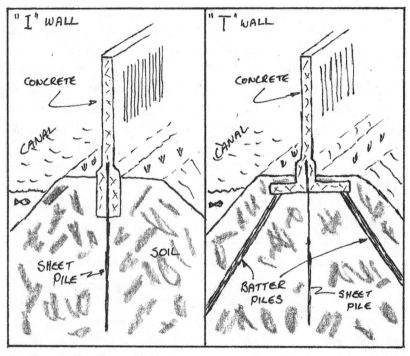

I-wall versus T-wall construction.

If an I wall begins to give way and leans back under the pressure of the water, a gap will open at its base, providing easy access for water to dig down the sheet piling—percolation, this is called. If this water gets all the way down and under the sheet piling, it may emerge on the outside of the berm as a boil. Obviously, this is a dangerous situation, with "boiling" water cutting completely through the earthen embankment. How deep in the soil was the steel-sheet piling in these embankments? Was it the same depth everywhere? Was it deeper than the canal to help ensure that no sand boils or seeps would develop under the pressure of high water levels due to the storm surge? Was any of the piling, in the failed sections, bent or distorted?

We looked at everything—or tried to, because the Corps was necessarily scrambling to rebuild the ruined berms and come up with some kind of makeshift structure that might stand a chance of holding back a serious surge, if we should get another storm, which was always a possibility. It was only September, in an extremely active hurricane season. Barges and trucks were hauling in rocks and other fill material, bulldozers were shoving and shaping new embankments, and all of this rebuilding work was covering up some of the evidence of the failures. Sections of the failed flood wall were buried. The structure of the original heave was being buried. What if the equivalent of the "black box" or the smoking gun was being buried? This was very frustrating, but there was nothing we could do. Every day that passed less and less of the flood walls and other evidence were visible.

And what did the design plans and specifications show? Did the structures, as we could still piece them together, match those designs? How could we ever get those designs?

On Friday afternoon, September 16, I talked with Michael Grunwald of the *Washington Post*, on the recommendation of John Barry, author of *Rising Tide*. I'd met John during our appearance on *Meet the Press* the previous weekend, and we'd agreed immediately that this flood was a failure of the federal government, which should compensate homeowners and businesses for their losses. Barry would soon publish an Op-ed to this effect in the *New York Times*. But now I needed a national reporter who was following the Katrina story and would be open to our tentative interpretation of why the levees had failed. In a few TV appearances I had tried to get the debate going, but no one seemed to realize its significance. I wasn't getting a lot of traction, as they say. The overtopping explanation from the Corps was misleading and self-serving, because it allowed them to claim that the surge exceeded the design capacity, which would let them off the hook. (Who knows, they may still try to argue this, but without a shred of evidence, it won't be easy.) I was concerned that good forensic evidence would be buried at the breach sites or otherwise lost before any congressional investigation could gear up. I thought we had to get the alternative story out there immediately for Congress and the world to consider. What better way than through the *Washington Post*? I hated not bringing in the *Times-Picayune*, specifically Mark Schleifstein, who is a great comrade-in-arms in the hurricane business, but I thought, rightly or wrongly, that the *Washington Post* would be the best mouthpiece. I wanted everyone in Washington, D.C., to see what was going on and above the fold, if at all possible.

John Barry agreed with me and set up a conversation with Michael Grunwald. On the phone Grunwald was very friendly and polite, heard me out, and seemed to understand right away what I was saying and the gravity of the situation. He said he needed to talk to one of his editors, but would try to fly down as soon as possible. Apparently his editor got the picture too, because I picked up Grunwald at the Baton Rouge airport on Monday just after noon, then collected Paul Kemp and Mashriqui, and we drove straight to New Orleans and toured the 17th Street and London Avenue breaches that afternoon. Level-headed Paul Kemp said straight out at one point, "This should not have been a big deal for these flood walls. It should have been a modest challenge. There's no way this storm should have exceeded the capacity." That was what we wanted to demonstrate to our guest from Washington. We returned to Baton Rouge, had a great dinner on Grunwald's newspaper, then set off early Tuesday morning for the Industrial Canal. That afternoon Grunwald called spokesman Paul Johnston with the Army Corps of Engineers one last time to get comments on the alternative theory shaping up with the LSU hurricane experts—and others—that overtopping had had nothing to do with the three failures on the 17th Street and London Avenue canals. I sat there listening to one end of the conversation, during which Johnston repeated yet again that "the event exceeded the design."

Grunwald talked to former Louisiana congressman Bob Livingston, a Republican who had chaired the House Appropriations Committee and was now a lobbyist in Washington. Livingston, who must understand well the symbiotic relation between the Corps and Congress, noted that the earthen levees along the lake had held while these smaller berms topped by flood walls along the canals had failed. "I don't know if it's bad construction or bad design, but who-ever the contractor is has a problem," Livingston said. So does the Corps, I thought, when I read that quote in Grunwald's story, co-written with Susan Glasser. It ran on Wednesday, September 21, with the headline FAULTY LEVEES CAUSED NEW ORLEANS FLOOD, EX-PERTS SAY. And yes, it was above the fold! Since this was my birthday as well, I took the story and its location as a good omen. The fol-lowing day Mark Schleifstein laid out essentially the same contrar-ian point of view on the *Times-Picayune*'s Nola Web site. In that story Colonel Richard Wagenaar acknowledged that the overtop-ping theory was being questioned. He said that the Corps had been ordered by Congress to retain all documents. He added, "My guys want to know what caused this just as bad as everyone else, because we've got two hundred people on the other side of that canal who lost their homes as well—at least two hundred people." He reiter-ated, however, that the design criteria may have been exceeded by this storm. He pointed to debris inside the lakefront levees at Metairie, in Jefferson Parish west of New Orleans, proving that waves had reached at least seventeen feet in that section of the lake.

Not really. We had also looked at that debris, and it told us that the waves were dumping debris on the lake side of the earthen lev-ees, with winds of up to 70 mph lifting this debris and blowing it over the levee. There was no evidence of overtopping here, as per-haps the colonel was suggesting.

Without a doubt, I think, the batch of overlapping stories in the press turned the corner for us and guaranteed that the truth about the levees would come out, sooner or later. Calls and e-mails from reporters picked up, that's for sure. My phone rang at 2:00 A.M. on the morning the *Post* story appeared. I was under the weather and didn't answer, so they called Paul Kemp. Being the tough soldier he is, Paul left his home in Baton Rouge at 4:00 A.M. for a dawn inter-view in New Orleans with ABC—all part of a great team effort from day one until the present. Our angle about the levees and the Corps gained even more momentum when, unbelievably, sections of the St. Bernard Bowl and the Orleans Metro Bowl, both almost drained from Katrina's floodwaters, took heavy water again on Friday, September 23, as powerful Hurricane Rita, passing 150 miles to the south on her way to a landfall in far western Louisiana, threw up a seven-foot surge, and the Corps's breach repairs along the Industrial Canal proved unsatisfactory.

Rita was scary. When she first shaped in the Caribbean the previous weekend, the most cursory consideration of the weather maps put a lump in the throat. This storm, too, gave every indication of floating west, just as Katrina had, right into the Gulf of Mexico for the almost predictable sudden strengthening, and then at some point starting her swing to the north. Of course, any kind of reprise of Katrina's path—or, even worse, one somewhat to the west— might have been the bitter end for the city of New Orleans. The levees are "severely degraded," I told one inquiring reporter, and the city is "extremely vulnerable." To put it mildly. On the Industrial Canal, the quickly repaired levees on the east side were several feet lower than the originals. The Corps said these barriers, composed of rock and limestone chips, would be high enough for the predicted storm surge. They weren't, and some sections eroded as well, with water pouring once again into Lower Ninth, Arabi, and Chalmette. (We had warned the Corps that the limestone chips should have been protected with surface seals.) The smaller breaches on the west side of Industrial Canal were also overtopped again, and water returned to the adjacent neighborhoods, including Gentilly, in the Orleans Metro Bowl. Fortunately, the 17th Street and London Avenue canals had by then been sealed near the lake entrances with sheet piling driven down alongside the bridges—a makeshift mechanism whose function should have been in place all along and that must be a feature, in one form or another, of the upgraded levee system everyone is promising will now be built.

With the levee investigation events followed hard and fast for the next six weeks or so, as everyone came to appreciate how important the answers were. Three groups were officially investigating what had happened: one team sent in by American Society of Civil Engineers (ASCE); another from the University of California at Berkeley, working under the auspices of the National Science Foundation (NSF); and, as of Wednesday, September 28, the Corps's official investigators (the Interagency Performance Evaluation Task Force), with its report not due until June 2006! A fourth team was our group from LSU, but we were unofficial. I didn't like this. Without an official mandate to do a forensic study, I feared hassles from LSU, where some people apparently were getting nervous about the involvement of us "hurricane center people" in the levee failure story. In fact, just two doors down from my office sit some folks who try to get money out of alumni, some of whom have made huge fortunes in the local petroleum and chemical and shipping industries, and word filtered out that some of these alumni were upset about our visibility. My answer was, tough, but I also knew we needed some kind of independent status, so I worked the phones with state people, pointing out that the ASCE and Cal Berkeley teams didn't have their roots in the details of Louisiana geology. And were these people truly independent? After all, former Corps employees were among the members of the ASCE team. What credibility would such an investigation have? I thought the state of Louisiana needed its own official investigation, beholden only to itself, and my main sounding board for this was Terry Ryder, someone I have known for a number of years. Separately, Johnny Bradberry, the head of the Department of Transport and Development (DOTD), had been moving on a track he called "Team Louisiana." I was not surprised. Secretary Bradberry is extremely sharp and knows how to make a decision (so important in this time of crisis), which I guess he learned from years of managerial experience in the oil patch. I knew we'd be able to work together.

As noted, our LSU team has never enjoyed smooth sailing with the Corps, at least not for long. I didn't help our cause when I suggested at a getting-to-know-you dinner with a group of Corps officials at a Baton Rouge steak house that the site of the levee breaches should be treated as a "crime scene." Typical bluntness and perhaps an unfortunate choice of words. All I wanted to convey was the need to look at all the evidence at every breach before still more of it was covered up by the ongoing repair work. We needed to get everything to an off-site building, where all of us could have easy access, including, eventually, the media and the public. Why did the Corps choose that meeting to offer us the use of a valuable centrifuge? Were they trying to get on our good side? Paul Kemp said after the meal, "Well, all we learned tonight was that the Corps likes to eat steak." That cracked me up. We were supposed to meet these guys in the field the next day, but they were no-shows. It was so strange with these engineers: From one day to the next we never knew what we were going to get.

Then someone with the state was told that someone with the Associated Press said that I had called the Corps "nonprofessional." That certainly would have been my thought, but I didn't say that in the interview in question. The reporter might have asked, regarding some action or another (he would have had numerous options), "Isn't that unprofessional?" I might have answered "Yes." Live and learn, but that's one reporter I won't talk to anymore. The damage was done, however, and a state official whose support we needed was upset, so I sent around an e-mail apologizing for any misstatement on my part. (I also sent around e-mails suggesting that the state set up a new coastal restoration czar—a real one, this time, with real powers.) Thank goodness none of this sabotaged the Team Louisiana idea, which was soon ready to go. Before the official announcement I sent Paul Mlakar, head of the Corps's investigative team, an e-mail advising him of the new group and urging full cooperation and sharing of data. Mlakar replied that the Corps had made contact with LSU "last month" about a "joint data-collection effort and have included LSU most intimately in ours thereafter. . . . However, not all in the engineering profession believe that the reason for the disaster is as clear as you suggest." Then, out of the blue, on Saturday morning October 1, we got a call informing us that the Corps was going to begin a survey of high-water marks in two hours. Did we want to join them? How strange: two hours' notice on a Saturday morning, one that also happened to be the first day off most of us had had since the week before Katrina. What we didn't know was that the ASCE and Cal Berkley teams were in town for the first time to kick off their own investigations, hosted by the Corps.

Paul and Mashriqui immediately dropped family plans and rushed down to New Orleans. Paul called me that evening with the news that the Corps had organized a big meeting of all the teams for the next evening, Sunday. I wanted to be there—and I should have been, since I'd be heading the new Team Louisiana. But the damnedest thing happened. I was told there wouldn't be enough room for me at this large meeting of Corps officials and the investigative groups. There was room for Paul Kemp, but not for me? The meeting was at the Corps's district office, where there are some huge assembly rooms. Subsequently, members of both of the other teams confirmed that the room had been crowded, but that there had been space. Of course there'd been space! This was so childish of the Corps. I think the other teams were appalled at what had happened, and they told me that some of the Corps's people had explicitly said that they hoped these other teams wouldn't be like me—that is, full of bothersome questions.

On Tuesday, October 4, we met with staffers for the Senate Homeland Security Committee who were in town for some preliminary fact-finding prior to the committee's upcoming hearings about the federal government's response to Katrina. We put together a CD and a movie that summarized where things stood, in our estimation, and then I was very surprised—more than that, distressed—when, out of the blue, I thought, Paul Kemp brought up the idea that "harmonics" in the canal waters might have caused, or at least contributed to, the collapse of the levees. The Republicans in the room seemed to perk up at this possibility, and I sensed an attempt to get the Corps and the federal government off the hook. Later that day Paul explained that he was just trying to be open-minded because we had not completed our field investigations. (The harmonics argument went nowhere immediately.) We went to dinner with some of the staffers and tried to figure out the political dynamics. My initial conclusion was that there was a split along partisan lines, but, in the end, I decided that the whole group was rather nonpartisan, commendably so.

The following day we drove these folks to New Orleans, and I had a chance to discuss some of the many issues about Katrina that from the perspective of a disaster science specialist were glaring examples of how not to run a response operation. I told them about the ridiculous episode of the previous weekend, when I'd been excluded from the Corps's meeting. Touring the breaches and the drowned city, the staffers were suitably stunned, even though the buildings didn't look to me as dark as they had just a few weeks before. Still, it was unspeakably desolate, with piles of trees and limbs and garbage everywhere (twenty-two million tons of garbage, by one estimate, easily the biggest cleanup job in American history, including the Twin Towers); boats still parked in the unlikeliest spots; mounds of discarded possessions on every overpass; block after block after block with no people whatsoever; street corners festooned with signs advertising cleanup or restoration work (imagine the scams), and lawyers. At one house someone had placed a Santa Claus by the front door. Was that for Christmas '05, or '06? or '07?

Coincidentally, we ran into both the ASCE and the Cal Berkeley investigators at the London Avenue breach. I thought they were none too friendly to us initially, but I was told later that others in our group had good exchanges with them. Paul Mlakar was also there. The Corps was preparing a handbook for everyone, he said. I took the opportunity to ask him, in front of the folks from Washington, about the Sunday meeting to which I hadn't been invited for space reasons. "It was tight in there," Mlakar replied, but he then assured me that LSU would be invited to the forthcoming meetings.

I guess it's clear that the "banning" episode had really soured me. I decided things weren't quite right in New Orleans, and the first chance I got that day I told Marc Levitan about my concerns that the Corps might interfere in the investigative process, that they were exerting an overbearing presence and attitude, and, most important, that there might be interference from some members of the ASCE headquarters staff. I told Marc that if I called Michael Grunwald of the *Washington Post*, say, with the story about what had been going on with the Corps, topped off by the refusal to allow me in the big meeting, that story would be news two days later. If the ASCE were ever seen as a tool of the Corps, it would be putting itself in a position to get hammered. Marc's face dropped. He is well connected with the society, and he knew that I wasn't bluffing, and he knew my analysis was right. Shortly thereafter, Paul Mlakar was a lot friendlier to me.

But get this: On that very day in New Orleans our geotechnical engineer, Radhey Sharma, was invited to join a working session that evening of the ASCE investigative team. Radhey is an ASCE member. In the afternoon he broke away from us and drove away with some of those engineers. A couple of hours later, he called me. Standing right in the doorway of the meeting someone from the ASCE team had rescinded Radhey's invitation, because of "things difficult to make public at this stage." So we doubled back to pick up Radhey on the steps of the building in which the meeting was going on. I think he was suddenly unwelcome because the ASCE team was going to put together a press release for the next day via a conference call with ASCE management in Washington. They didn't want anyone from Team Louisiana hearing that conversation (which lasted for two hours, I understand).

On Friday I was tied up with a crew from the PBS series *Nova*, but Radhey, Mashriqui, and Paul headed down to New Orleans very early for a meeting prior to the ASCE press conference, where a senior Corps official introduced everyone except the LSU team members. Paul Kemp abruptly stood up and pointed out that not everyone in the room knew the group from LSU, and he then asked Mashriqui and Radhey to introduce themselves. My man.

I was working with *Nova* when Paul called with the news that the ASCE would announce that the levees at the London Avenue and 17th Street canals had *not* been overtopped. Vindication for us, that's all there was to it. That evening Mashriqui hosted two of the ASCE members at his home for a barbeque, one from Japan, the other Professor Jurjen Battjes, one of the world's leading levee experts, from the Netherlands. Now we learned that the official statement from the ASCE team had indeed been watered down after the phone call with the front office. The phrase "soil failure" had been deleted from the statement. I listened to everything they had to say, and I came away with the clear impression that at least some of the field engineers were extremely unhappy with the way ASCE was dealing with them, their findings, and the whole situation. A few weeks later one of the ASCE team e-mailed me with the remarkable revelation that all eleven investigators had threatened to resign, standing out there on the levee, unless the interference in the process was stopped. Jurjen Battjes told us how he had disagreed with a further watering down of the statement about the nature of the failure. The wall slid. It failed. That was right in front of everyone's eyes. Finally, Jurjen was simply appalled at the design of the levee systems in New Orleans.

Within just a day or two of the release of the watered-down ASCE statement, Team Louisiana was officially in business under a contract with the Department of Transportation and Development. We were the LSU guys and three private-sector civil/geotechnical engineers with truly vast experience with the local geology—Billy Prochaska, Art Theis, and Louis Capozzoli, whom the rest of us soon called the three wise men. (The contract also included small amounts for surveys, for our stopped-clock program, and for a program to capture the oral history of the survivors—these last two part of the effort to pin down as closely as possible the exact time for each failure.)

Now there were *four* investigating teams in the field—ASCE, Cal Berkeley (NSF), the Corps, and us representing the state—and now everyone would be able to collect all the forensic data. We'd have access to the original design plans and specs for the levees. Or would we? When Paul Kemp soon asked for some surveying data from the Corps that he had helped collect, he was advised to submit a FOIA request—under the Freedom of Information Act. This, Paul replied, is "inappropriate." I was amazed by his self-restraint. I might have said, "Look, asshole. Give us what we need, what you've been saying all along you'd give us." Paul took the milder approach, probably wisely, and received an immediate acknowledgement that the FOIA answer had been wrong. The survey data would be forthcoming. Over two weeks later Paul had to send the Corps another note: Now, where's that surveying data? Meanwhile, we read in the newspapers that the Corps would be making available to the investigators (or some of the investigators?) 235 boxes of material. Some of these documents have been posted to the Web, and some of these have key pages missing, such as calculations on lateral stability at the 17th Street breach.

Even after we had official status as Team Louisiana, we had to fight for every scrap of information. We even had to rely on the media. It's almost embarrassing to admit this, but so it was. Sometimes we would point a reporter in a certain direction, at other times a reporter or television producer would find new data, bring it to us, we would comment, and then they'd release it to us. This is how we were forced to build up most of our background information. Then we found some records in the New Orleans office of the DOTD. Getting data out of the Corps was extremely frustrating. We never seemed to get what we asked for, but we were hearing through the grapevine that the Corps's own "independent" investigators had access to boxes and boxes of stuff.

Nor were we alone in battling for the necessary data. The Berkeley levee warriors, as we soon began calling them, were having their own problems with access to the Corps's documents, even though they were working under the auspices of the National Science Foundation, and even though Bob Bea on that team had started his engineering career with the Corps in south Florida in 1954, building levees, canals, and pump stations. His father was a career Corps employee, so Bob truly understands the unique bureaucratic psyche that confronted us. He also has a visceral connection with the Katrina tragedy, because he lost his home in New Orleans when Betsy flooded parts of the city in 1965. He had waded to his house in the Lower Ninth to salvage what he could, which was nothing, not even his wedding photographs. He sold that house for the price of the land—a seriously discounted price.

I've mentioned the press conference for the release of the preliminary ASCE report on the levee failures. The night before, one of the people helping to set up the event had collared Bob Bea and pointedly asked if he was going to attend. Yes, Bob said. Perhaps he shouldn't, this person said—more than once. That's not the way to deal with Bob Bea. He was there the next day—and so was his antagonist, standing right next to him. Was someone hoping to muzzle this man? Forget it. He soon met with reporters from the *Los Angeles Times* and elsewhere, and all the coverage over the weekend stated quite clearly that there had been a massive failure of the levee flood walls. Bob was joined in this PR campaign for the truth by Ray Seed, another member of the Berkeley team whose father, Harry, was one of the great geotechnical engineers, now often considered the father of geotechnical earthquake engineering. (Harry Seed was awarded the National Medal of Science by President Reagan.) As Ray tells the story, he was fiercely determined to be anything but another "geotech," but now he occupies his father's old chair at Berkeley!

And people thought they could manipulate the investigation and the judgment of Ray Seed and Bob Bea? Instead, these two scientists helped us carry the banner during the fall, supporting our earlier conclusions, helping the world realize that overtopping did not cause the tragic breaches along the 17th Street and London Avenue canals.

Believe it or not, this is how things went with the investigation of one of the most catastrophic levee breaches and floods in American history—an investigation that was not just an academic exercise, because more storms are coming, and that same levee system is still the only one we have.

In order to set the stage for the next phase of the investigation story I need to backtrack briefly. On September 30, NBC News had broken the story about an old lawsuit against the Army Corps of Engineers regarding work that dated from 1993, when the levees were upgraded. In this action the Pittman Construction Company complained that the Corps had not provided enough information about the problem with the soil at the 17th Street Canal, which turned out to be weak and shifting and "not of sufficient strength, rigidity, and stability." These poor soils caused problems pouring the concrete flood walls, which was Pittman's job. Also, the firm alleged problems with the steel-sheet piling. The dispute concerned just 12 of 257 flood-wall sections, those which had tilted a little and were technically "out of tolerance." The Corps had allowed a variance on the

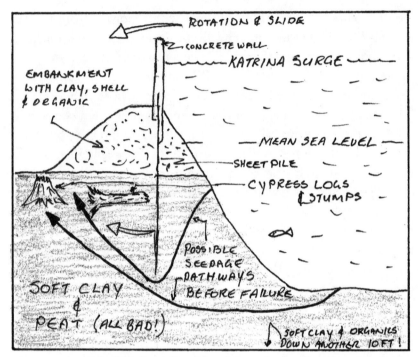

A cross section of the 17th Street Canal breach area showing the soils and predominant failure mode.

work and accepted the job, but the company claimed that it had incurred huge cost overruns and was seeking relief from the Corps.

I had not heard of this lawsuit. None of us at LSU had. At this point in the investigation of the breaches the Corps had not released any design or construction documents (and it would not for another month). As I've said, we were forced to get much of our information with the help of the media, who were now out in force on this story and digging furiously, as this NBC scoop made clear. I also suspected that the Corps was getting "leaky," that at least one of the two hundred or so Corps employees who had lost their homes was divulging information.

These courtroom documents had been filed in 1994, and the administrative law judge had ruled in 1998—in favor of the Corps. For the purposes of the investigation of the Katrina flooding seven years later, the decision itself was irrelevant. Almost irrelevant was whether the twelve sections addressed by the lawsuit were the sections that had failed on August 29, 2005. (Naturally, the Corps hasn't provided the documents we need to make that determination.) The bombshell here was the revelation that a company had complained during construction about the quality of the *soil* in the 17th Street levee.

The NBC team had come to my home about 11:00 P.M. the night before the piece went on the air. I could tell they were excited about what they had. They should have been. As I told them, and as they quoted me, "That's incredibly damning evidence. I mean, really, incredibly damning. It seems to me that the authorities really should have questioned whether these walls were safe." Bob Bea, the Berkeley levee warrior, agreed. "I think it is very significant," he said. "It begins to explain some things that I couldn't explain based on the information that I've had." Indeed, because the soil that comprises the berm that holds the sheet piling that supports the flood wall is, obviously, all-important. If the weakest link of any structure is the foundation, that structure is a disaster waiting to happen, and that disaster will happen at the most inopportune moment, by definition: in the case of a levee, when it is under pressure from high water.

The judge in the Pittman case may have found for the Corps, but all of us investigating the Katrina flooding sensed a breakthrough here. Recall that this entire city was once a cypress swamp, as indicated by the stumps and logs exposed by the upheavals at the breaches. What happens to sheet piling driven into one of these old logs, which are spaced probably every fifteen feet or so? The steel sections could bend or split apart at the tongue-and-groove sections, and there goes the barrier against seepage. What about the soil itself? The Corps's original environmental impact statement for the levees, dated 1982, describes the soil in the lakefront area as "a thin layer of very soft clay underlain by silty sands" and "peat and very soft highly organic fat clays." The original soil material for these levees was this same dredge material. Peat is organic matter. It decomposes, compresses, subsides (the New Orleans problem in a nutshell). It is an excellent path of least resistance. Under pressure such as that in a storm surge, water moves very easily along layers of peat. It can create a slippery surface. Structures built on such soil can tilt, break, slide, float, sink. Peat must therefore be carefully considered before construction, and engineers must look at the "global stability" of the whole. What is the history of the compaction of these berms since they first took shape in the first half of the twentieth century? How closely did the Corps test these soils before the flood-wall upgrading program was initiated in the 1990s? Did it account for the peat in the calculations? Did it account for the effect of adding the heavy concrete flood wall to the sheet piling? Did they pay heed to Engineer Manual No. 1110-2-2502, which has language that basically states that if you build a flood wall to fourteen feet, then it must hold water up to fourteen feet without failure? Did the Corps pay heed to the design memorandum for the MR-GO levees that state those levees should be built to withstand overtopping such that overtopping will not endanger the security of the structures or cause material interior flooding?

In the last chapter I mentioned the 1982 GAO report titled "Improved Planning Needed by the Corps of Engineers to Resolve Environmental, Technical and Financial Issues on the Lake Pontchartrain Hurricane Protection Project." I had found this document late one night while searching the Web, terminally frustrated with the Corps for not releasing its records to us. One of the most damning elements of that report, in retrospect, is the Corps's attribution of schedule delays "primarily to unforeseen foundation problems. . . . Increased construction time for flood walls, levees, and roads as a result of foundation problems discovered after project initiation." There it is, in black and white. The Corps of Engineers was well aware of foundation problems years before it constructed the flood walls along the London Avenue and 17th Street canals. Why, then, did it change some of the designs to call for less robust structures after this date? On Tuesday, October 11, Ray Seed from Cal Berkley fired off a letter to the Corps, pointing to unstable soils as the source of 17th Street and London Avenue failures. He linked the evidence to the Pittman lawsuit.

As the soils in the embankments came under suspicion during the investigation, so did the depth of the sheet piling, with the first point being a very simple one: The steel must be driven below the softest of the soft stuff. Clearly, it should not be *rooted* in the soft clays, peats, and muck that will just not support the whole structure when high water in the canal adds side forces to the equation. Drive the piles until you hit solid earth! If this is minus-80 feet, then so be it! Spring for the extra steel! The very life of a city hangs in the balance. You don't need to be a structural engineer to understand all this.

The second point is also simple: Even if the soils were the best possible, which they definitely were not, the sheet piling should be at least as deep as the bottom of the adjacent canal—minus-19 feet. What was the case with these levees? We eventually determined that the original design memorandum for the 17th Street Canal called for sheet piling driven only to minus-10 feet. Not nearly deep enough. Reporters were telling me that Corps officials were saying that the steel had been driven to minus-17, so I asked them to get the Corps to supply the records, called Pile Push Lengths. As of early February 2006, we still had not seen the numbers, although certain Corps staffers working at the breaches told us that the district office had the data. Of course it did.

Because pulling the sheet piling to determine its depth would destroy the flood wall, we needed a nondestructive test, and still somewhat experimental sonar testing seemed the way to go. We'd also use a cone penetrometer setup to get data on the strength and other characteristics of the soils. We got the funding for part of our investigation in three hours, working with Secretary Bradberry at the DOTD and the state attorney general's office.

For the sonar test, the investigators, Southern Earth Sciences, pushed a probe equipped with a special sound recorder—a transducer—into the soil, no farther than six feet from the wall. The basic idea of such testing is that at each one-foot increment of depth the concrete flood wall is struck with a special hammer, and the transducer in the ground records the signal. As the recorder is driven deeper and deeper, the signal doesn't change much *until* the receiver is lower than the sheet piling. This change should tell the investigators the depth of the steel at that location. We knew that the Corps was conducting similar tests using a different system, and we believed ours was superior, because, for starters, our recorder was quite close to the wall, not as far away as twenty-two feet, as with the Corps's system. However, both groups were going to rely on the same Colorado laboratory, Olsen Engineering, to interpret its data.

That lab told both us and the Corps that the steel ended at minus-10 feet—eight feet shy of the bottom of the canal, and not nearly deep enough. Both we and the Corps reported this number to the media, but probably thanks to the Pile Push Length numbers that the Corps has but have not released to us, it had reason to believe that the engineering firm had misinterpreted the data. The sheet piling was at minus-17, the Corps believed, and in December it orchestrated a widely covered media event at which sections of the sheet piling were yanked dramatically from the levee by a large crane. I was in The Netherlands at the time, studying their excellent flood-control system, but I heard and read later about the joy on the faces of Corps officials. This particular piling had been driven to minus-17. The Corps then said our data was bad. After careful analysis of our methods, we thought the data must have been misinterpreted by the engineering firm, and after a reevaluation, owner Larry Olsen realized that he had indeed misinterpreted our data. Subsequently, he flew down to New Orleans and went out in the field for two days with us and Scott Slaughter of Southern Earth Sciences, all of us hoping to better understand how this embarrassing error had occurred. Also along on those two days were investigators from the state attorney general's office, who regularly accompanied us in the field, in case there was any subsequent ligitation between the state and the federal government. They wanted to observe the retesting of the sonar technique.

We used different techniques to collect a series of sonar data sets. In the end, after some discussions in the field, Scott Slaughter came up with his own methodology for the seismic interpretation, which we believe is pretty much foolproof. Really, though, whether the steel in a given section of the canal levees is minus-10 or minus-17 is almost moot, because even minus-17 is not deep enough, not when the channel is more than eighteen feet below sea level and the soils are mucky clays and layers of peat. As Billy Prochaska, an absolute geotechnical engineering whiz, stated clearly in one of his reports, strength calculations show that the flood walls would fail when the water level in the canal approached 11 feet (the Katrina surge, as it turns out), no matter if the sheet pile was minus-10 or minus-17. Billy believes the Corps's engineers failed to consider the weak soils between minus-10 and minus-25 feet when they did their strength and safety calculations. Later, the Berkeley levee warriors came up with exactly the same results.

Modjeski and Masters, the engineering firm that developed the design for the flood wall on the 17th Street Canal, said in a letter to the *Times-Picayune* that it had recommended that the sheet piling be driven to a depth of minus-35 feet, but the Corps requested a shallower depth. The Corps responded to the paper with a written statement, defending its own actions. One point is certain: As part of its latest temporary patches at the breaches, the Corps has driven the new sheet piling to a depth of at least minus-50, sometimes minus-65.

Then in early February 2006 we learned from documents provided the Cal-Berkeley team that a cross section in the design documents for these levees shows the peaty soils between minus-11 and minus-16 feet, while the soil borings on which the cross section was based found the peat as deep as *30 feet*. Excellent detective work by J. David Rogers pointed out this geotechnical data irregularity. Our engineers agree with the Cal-Berkeley engineers that the Corps's levee designers may have designated minus-17 for the depth of the steel-sheet piling because the erroneous cross section showed that to be the bottom of the peat layer. Was this breach at the 17th Street Canal caused by a simple error in transferring the raw data to the visual depiction in the cross section? Of this we can't be absolutely certain, but the error didn't help.

Every day that fall and early winter, new data was announced or old data uncovered by one source or another. Every day, new statements and new stories hit the press, and with almost every one the Corps's valued reputation for conservative overdesign took a serious hit. For all of the criticism that agency has endured over the years, cutting corners on design has not been one of them, for the most part. The rationale for a project may have been dubious, or the project may not have worked as advertised (the Wax Lake weir described earlier is an example), but rarely has the design been on the cheap. At least, that's been the reputation until now, when *any* reasonably objective observer would conclude that the soil structures for these vital canal levees weren't strong enough, period, and the sheet piling wasn't driven deep enough, period. Terrible errors. Either by itself would have presented problems. Together, they were catastrophic.

At the breach on the west side of the London Avenue Canal (the "clubhouse" breach, as we called it), the sheet piling is minus-10

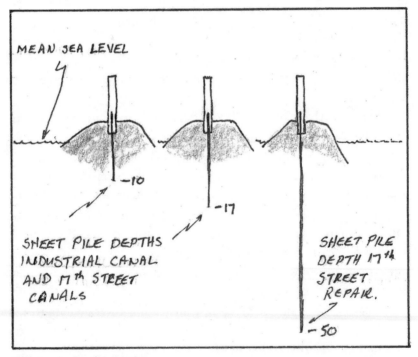

Relative depths of sheet piling.

feet—right to the top of a peat layer—this according to the design memorandum. An enterprising reporter found a consulting engineer for Pittman Construction, the company that lost the lawsuit,

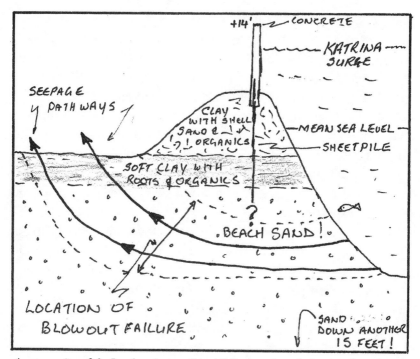

+14' — CONCRETE

KATRINA —
SURGE

SEEPAGE
4 PATHWAYS

CLAY
WITH SHELL
SAND &
?! ORGANICS

— MEAN SEA LEVEL —

— SHEETPILE

SOFT CLAY WITH
ROOTS & ORGANICS

?

. BEACH SAND !.

LOCATION OF
BLOWOUT FAILURE

SAND
DOWN ANOTHER
15 FEET !

A cross section of the London Avenue Canal/Mirabeau breach showing the soils and predominant failure mode.

who suggested that pilings driven just ten feet deeper might have made all the difference. I don't have the impression that that was a deeply "engineered" statement, but it's quite possibly correct anyway. What a crushing thought. There's no doubt that piling driven fifty feet deeper—to a depth of minus-60, say—would have made all the difference. Still a crushing thought, because the need for such design was easily seen, and the work itself easily and inexpensively done. Steel is cheap, and so is the job of driving those extra feet into the ground. How much extra could it conceivably have cost at the time? *Maybe* $10 million.

There's more. The original design memorandum for the wall at the Mirabeau breach on the London Avenue Canal called for the superior T wall design with sheet pilings driven to minus-26 and the letter A-type batter piles to each side. What we got instead was an I wall design, and our one sonar reading in this area suggests that the sheet piling bottoms out at minus-10. Who made the decision to cut corners from this robust design to something that failed catastrophically? And why? Ray Seed, the Berkeley professor, has suggested that budget cuts may have strapped the Corps. "They still have good people—what they have is less of them," Seed said. "It strikes me as potentially dangerous over the long term." He also noted the general shift away from big projects to environmental restoration, plus the trend toward handing over soil boring and testing to private contractors. Donald Basham, chief of engineering and construction for the Corps, replied, "We have not completely contracted out technical expertise."

Responding to these and many other provocations regarding an agency that is technically part of the U.S. Army, Secretary of Defense Donald Rumsfeld announced in October 2005 the creation of an "independent panel of national experts" to study the levee failures under the auspices of the National Academy of Sciences. So, a *fifth* investigating team. This one will use data and conclusions from the teams working for the Corps, the National Science Foundation (the Berkeley group), and the ASCE. Its report will be peer reviewed. This is fine, but I am not sure what anyone else can say. The evidence is very clear. When we have levee walls sliding forty feet laterally there is no appropriate description other than "catastrophic structural failure." Whether the first water there and at the other breaches seeped through the peat, or down and around the sheet pile, or through deeper sands is almost academic. Important for the investigators, but academic. The bottom line is that these levees were underdesigned and failed under winds and surge equivalent to minimal Cat 1 conditions, much less the Cat 3 conditions the Corps claims they were designed to withstand.

On Wednesday, October 26, Colonel Richard Wagenaar, the district engineer for the Corps in New Orleans—the local boss—paid me a visit in my office at LSU, a meeting he'd requested the previous week. A tall man with short hair, he had two other officials with him, and he got straight to the point. How can we sort out our relationship with the LSU people? I explained the history, and described the opposition we had encountered from the day we first stated that the overtopping scenario was transparently wrong. I told him how we'd had to bring in the big guns from the media (Michael Grunwald with the *Washington Post*, specifically) to listen to our thinking and go to the Corps with the story. I told the colonel that we were thinking of the people of Louisiana, trying to understand the causes of the flooding and the impacts. We don't enjoy being on opposite sides of the table, I said, but we felt the need to get the information and the investigation out in the open. So does the state of Louisiana. I explained that if we had wanted to be completely anti-Corps we could have made much more of an issue of the breaches at the Industrial Canal.

The levees along the east side of this large navigation canal, the ones that had failed and flooded and basically destroyed the Lower Ninth Ward, had been overtopped at about 6:50 A.M. Monday morning, but only for three hours, and by only a foot and a half of water. This water began to erode the outside of the earthen embankments (the scouring effect that is so absent on the inner-city canals). The head in the canal pushed four sections of the flood walls outward. As they tilted, cracks developed at the base on the canal side, with water percolating down and then under the sheet piling. At these breaches the levee was built on a layer of organic marsh and peat with very soft clays ten feet thick—the dredge material from the original 1920 excavation of the canal. Like the soils at the drainage canals, this is a very weak medium. Fifteen feet below the top of the embankment is a layer of soft clays with silt and sand lenses—more poor material. Based on the design memorandum that we found in the files of the DOTD, the pilings at the breach extended to a depth of ten feet below sea level. (This we knew from the exposed sheet piling in the breached areas, but we checked elsewhere with our sonar testing.) The canal is dredged to a depth of thirty-six feet below sea level. Thus there was a linear depth of twenty-six feet of canal that was not blocked by sheet piling, allowing for a potential lateral flow of water under the pilings from the canal. Local residents adjacent to the canal had often said that their backyards were at times quite wet, even during dry spells. This suggests serious seepage from the canal in the best of times. At the very least, this sheet piling should have been sunk to minus-70 feet. Every engineer in the region knows that this wide, deep canal is on the receiving end of all the water and pressure coming out of the Funnel, which I derided earlier as one of the world's best storm-surge delivery systems. This woefully insufficient steel could not hold the static loading from the surge, nor was it deep enough to form an effective hydrologic barrier against seepage below. Around 7:45 A.M., a little less than an hour after the overtopping began, the levees at two sections along the eastern side of the Industrial Canal succumbed to the enormous pressure, the scouring, the substandard soils, and the insufficiently deep sheet piling and failed explosively and catastrophically.

The geotechnical collapse was aided by the overtopping and the scouring, but it was not caused by it. Nor was it caused by the barge that ended up inside the failed section. (In the reflooding of the Lower Ninth from Rita, the barge moved again and landed on the front of a small yellow school bus. Six months later it was still there.) A cursory examination showed that something had knocked nine inches off the top of about forty feet of the southern sections of the concrete flood wall. Initially the Corps speculated that the drifting barge did this while the wall was still upright and intact, but closer inspection revealed that this segment was damaged after it had already tilted to a 45-degree angle. The wall failure was prior to the impact from the barge, which floated into the breach well after the major failure.

In a way we were giving the Corps a bit of a break regarding the Industrial Canal failures and the terrible flooding and loss of life that resulted in these eastern neighborhoods. This design and construction were every bit as bad as on the drainage canals in the Orleans Metro Bowl. I told the colonel this. When his turn came the colonel explained that no one in Washington really understood the extent of the problem here. I got the impression that he was isolated and frustrated with the lack of progress and the lack of cooperation from Washington. He was having to clean up a mess that he hadn't caused with little help from his superiors, who wanted to ignore it. He used his hands a lot as he talked. I felt a lot of emotion coming from him. He was really expressing his feelings. I understood that he had found himself in a very tough situation, newly arrived in Louisiana—a month before the disaster—from an assignment in Korea. There was no way he could have been up to speed on the status of the Corps's work in just New Orleans, much less throughout his region. His background expertise is in environmental science and forestry. I pointed out that we at LSU have bureaucracies just like everyone else, and that he had my commitment to work together.

Of course, I emphasized the problems with the data—how we'd been battling to get the basic facts that the Corps had at its fingertips. The other investigators were getting hundreds of boxes of stuff, but we had to go through the media. I even had a new example handy. Just the night before a reporter with the *New York Times* had directed me to a Web page that the district uses to solicit bids from contractors. One of these bid documents had the boring data that we'd been trying to get from the Corps for two weeks! Without any communication from the Corps, how were we supposed to know about it? I assumed that someone in the Corps had tipped the *Times* reporter. Wagenaar knew about some of these problems, because he had in his hand an e-mail in which Paul Kemp had let fly his frustration about the FOIA request and everything else. He had even brought with him the water-level data Paul had requested! He invited me to call him directly with any other problems.

I wanted to make sure the colonel knew about all the goodies that we could contribute to the cause—the surge modeling, geotechnical work, water sampling, sediment sampling, and mortality studies. What we weren't doing ourselves, we could find. I don't think he had known all of that. I couldn't resist the opportunity to present my spiel about the need for a Gulf Coast Reconstruction Authority, a new Tennessee Valley Authority–type entity headed by a czar empowered to make decisions—informed decisions, advised by scientists and engineers who really know Louisiana. I wouldn't go with the National Science Foundation or the National Academy of Sciences, because they don't know Louisiana. How could they? But the Army Corps of Engineers does know Louisiana. It's really the only game in town. If the Corps would join us we could reach out to the governor's office and the congressional delegation and bring some of the environmental groups on board and make something happen. What about the mayor? Wagenaar asked. Yes, someone from the mayor's office must be close to the action. He said he would contact Major General Strock in Washington about this idea.

So far, so good. I thought it was a productive meeting, and we proceeded down the hallway to meet with the dean of the College of Engineering and the chair of Department of Civil Engineering. I immediately got the feeling that the dean thought that Wagenaar had come to LSU in order to raise hell about us. I tried to correct that false impression. I'm not sure I succeeded. Wagenaar said that he and I had tried to sort out the disagreements—not quite the way I viewed the meeting, but so be it—and that the meeting had been fruitful. Anyway, we'd see what happened next—which happened to be a phone call from Brigadier General Don Riley at the Pentagon, who had been briefed by his colonel about the meeting at LSU. The general apologized for my banning from the meeting in early October. No problem, I said. Let's move forward. Some of the Senate staffers whom I'd met in New Orleans would later suggest that this call from the D.C. brass was most likely because they knew I was going to testify before the Senate Homeland Security Committee on November 2. I wanted to believe instead that the colonel and the brigadier general were really interested in moving forward in Louisiana, not just engaging in damage control.

In the days before the Senate committee hearing, I heard reports that the team representing the American Society of Civil Engineers in the field was being urged by the ASCE to go slowly. Then I heard talk from some ASCE folks about "malfeasance" on the part of the levee contractors, later repeated in testimony to the Senate committee by the Berkeley engineering team. At the hearing itself the malfeasance discussion did seem, to my mind, to concentrate on the contractors. When it was my turn I said that the one breach at the 17th Street Canal and the two at the London Avenue Canal had been geotechnical engineering failures, period: bad soils. The same conclusion can be made for the Industrial Canal levees, I said, although surge overtopping no doubt enhanced their collapse. Regardless, most of the flooding of New Orleans was due to "man's follies." Society owes an apology to those who lost their lives. It owes an apology to those three hundred thousand who lost their livelihoods and their possessions, and it needs to step up and rebuild their homes and compensate for their lost means of employment. New Orleans is one of our nation's crown jewel cities. Not to have given the residents the security of proper levees is inexcusable.

The next day the malfeasance suggestion got all of the headlines. This surprised and disturbed me, and I sent around a note asking reporters to make sure that the malfeasance argument did not distract from the larger point. Even assuming, as the Berkeley engineers testified, that contractors or even individuals may have shortchanged their responsibilities, were such actions the main reasons the levees failed, or did they fail because of much more basic errors of conception and design? According to the Corps's design manuals for the levees on the canals, a safety factor of 30 percent was built into the calculations. That is, the design should have withstood forces 30 percent higher than the highest anticipated. That's a joke. They were doing well to handle forces 30 percent *lower* than anticipated. Both our Billy Prochaska and Bob Bea of the Cal Berkeley team have determined that the factor of safety in the levees is less than 1. Simply put, it had a very high probability of failure. It was a disaster waiting to happen, which is what I told the Senate committee in early November. But even the 30 percent safety factor is actually low for any dynamically loaded structure exposed to rapidly shifting forces such as storm surge; for a structure built on questionable soils; for a structure defending the very life of a major city and the hundreds of thousands of individuals within that city. That low safety factor caught the attention of every investigating engineer.

And all to save a few bucks? If not this explanation, what? We're not going to stop investigating until we know the answer, so it doesn't happen again.

The following week, Friday, November 11, two LSU vice chancellors called me into one of their offices and asked that I henceforth pass all media requests through the university's public affairs office. They told me that my critical remarks to the media about the levees were hurting LSU's quest for federal funding across the board. They also said the university had received complaints about my presenting myself as an engineer and talking about engineering issues. Since I am on the faculty of the Department of Civil and Environmental Engineering, I can certainly see how a reporter could assume that I am one, but I have never so claimed, and I always correct anyone who seems to have that misimpression. Moreover, I said, my nonengineer status did not seem to worry the College of Engineering at Rice University, for example, where I'd been invited to talk. No issue with those folks about my talking as a geologist about geotechnical (soil) issues and foundation failures. Other engineering departments had also requested such talks, and a number wanted to team up with our LSU group to apply for funding, with me directing the effort. In short, I said, I hadn't been made aware of any academic institution having a problem with the scope of my activities.

The gag order, as I referred to it, created a few problems with reporters, who now had to obtain permission to talk to me. They thought this was pretty silly, and so did I. Naturally I objected to the university and asked for clarification. The following Wednesday it backed off and set me free.

At this writing the five investigations of the levee failures in New Orleans are still under way. Various preliminary findings have been released, but the definitive conclusions will not be available until well into 2006. That said, we know the broad outline of what happened in each case. No report will contradict them. At the three breaches on the 17th Street and London Avenue canals, overtopping was not a factor at all, as the Corps eventually admitted, so these failures did not reflect the scouring that aided (not caused, aided) the failure of the Industrial Canal levees. Otherwise, the mechanism of the catastrophic structural failure was similar in each case.

In December 2005, we learned that the semiannual inspections of the levees by the Corps and the various levee boards and state agencies had consisted of a five-hour tour of the levee system. In the *Livingston Parish News*, my hometown newspaper, the headline on the story about this inspection read A DRIVE-BY SHOOTING OF NEW ORLEANS. In the *Times-Picayune* one subhead read: "Lunch, not levees." Elsewhere I saw a sneering reference to beignets and coffee. These attacks were perhaps unfair as they related to the levee boards and the state agencies. From the ground the levees looked fine, given what they were. The problems were with basic design and construction, and the problems were underground. No visual inspection was going to reveal them, and they were *not* the responsibility of the local boards or state agencies, who had no good way to even know about them. They were the responsibility of the only agency that had designed them and then supervised their construction: the Army Corps of Engineers.

This fact was driven home hard right at the end of the year, when the *Times-Picayune*, under Bob Marshall's byline, published incendiary documents showing that a design review in the Corps's Vicksburg, Mississippi, office had found errors in the New Orleans District's assessment of soil strength for the 17th Street levees, errors that had led in turn to "overly optimistic" conclusions about the overall strength of the design. As the *Times-Picayune* reported, this had been discovered in 1990, a couple of years before the concrete flood walls were added to these levees, plenty of time in which to make changes. In fact, the Vicksburg officials directed the local engineers in New Orleans to make necessary changes. The *Times-Picayune* pointed out that Eugene Tickner, then chief engineer of the New Orleans District, cited "engineering judgment" and overruled those instructions. Vicksburg backed off. (It remains to be seen exactly how these documents correlate with the others about the erroneous cross section.)

In a letter to the New Orleans District dated August 8, 1990, the chief of the Engineering Division in Vicksburg questioned the designed depth of the steel-sheet piling. Noting the critical nature of the project and the proximity of the adjacent canal, he questioned the validity of the calculations in the lateral-stability analysis—that is, will the wall fail due to the lateral pressure of the water when the surge comes into the canal? This question didn't surprise me. Billy Prochaska had already shown us that the soil strengths used in the design of the 17th Street levees were too high. The designers had averaged the data for weaker and stronger layers, a no-no in the geotechnical engineering of levees. Where the pertinent 1982 borehole data had strengths as low as 100 pounds per square foot, the designers had used strengths as high as 320 pounds per square foot. Standard practice in levee design is to model based on the soil strengths in the weakest layers. Weakest layer, weakest link, common sense. Also, the New Orleans District used soil data from locations over a mile apart. In this part of Louisiana, where the land is the product of delta switching and channel growth and abandonment cycles, one after the other, one on top of the other, we can have a dramatic change in the geology in one mile.

To my mind, these Vicksburg documents are the worst of the smoking guns in the levee investigation to date, although I won't be surprised by anything that follows in the months and years to come. It's sickening to think about this, especially since our analysis at the Hurricane Public Health Center shows that almost nine hundred of the deaths and the great preponderance of the property damage in New Orleans and Louisiana as a whole were in the neighborhoods flooded by these drainage canal flood wall failures.

Toward the middle of February 2006, the *New York Times* informed us that the Corps was spending more than three hundred thousand dollars to create a ⅟₁₅-size physical model of Lake Pontchartrain and environs (basically a pond such as kids sail model boats on in parks), where they intended to simulate the waves and surge during Katrina. Well, good luck. I have worked with such scale models in South Africa and there are real problems with "scaling" water depths, waves, and so on. How do you hope to create a revolving wind field such as a hurricane? I really don't know what the Corps hopes to achieve here, even though it is spending almost twice the money our whole team had for all its levee work. As the *Times* article points out, the process was immediately attacked by critics as an expensive attempt to deflect the blame from the Corps.

ELEVEN

NOW OR NEVER

I guess the acronym was pretty good: the PELICAN Commission, for Protecting Essential Louisiana Infrastructure, Citizens, and Nature. Otherwise, the legislative initiative I came to think of as the Pelican Brief (for two reasons: John Grisham's bestseller about environmental damage and because its effective life of about twelve hours) was a terrible mistake for the state. Let's hope it doesn't set the standard for the thinking that will guide the rebuilding and restoration in the years to come. If it does, we're probably sunk.

My part in this fiasco began on September 14, with an e-mail from John Barry, author and fellow traveler on the major questions concerning what had happened and now needed to happen in New Orleans. John was part of a team being gathered by Senators Mary Landrieu and David Vitter to develop a plan for the restoration and reconstruction of Louisiana that would be the basis for the main federal support legislation. Specifically, John had been invited to be part of the working group focusing on flood protection and restoration of the wetlands; the deadline for the recommendation was one week away. I immediately phoned and asked John if I could be part of this exercise. When I had left the Department of Natural Resources almost exactly ten years earlier, I wasn't invited back to the table, but I thought that someday I might be. This could be a step in that direction. Who wouldn't want to be involved here? These decisions could be critical. The science could be critical. I wanted to bring expertise to the table. I wanted to push hard for my belief that the catalyst to compromise is a thorough understanding of the science. John then asked if I wanted to chair the working group! No way could I take on that responsibility, not with the levee investigation heating up, but count me in otherwise. John ended up chairing it himself.

I missed the first conference call—that same day, the fourteenth—because I was in the field at the levee breaches helping out a *National Geographic* team in the morning and then a French documentary team in the afternoon, which turned out to be one of the saddest moments in the whole catastrophe for me. We went to the Upper Ninth Ward, which was just about dry (this was before Rita flooded it again), with the body search just getting under way. We searched for a site at which to film the last interview, which was to be about my personal feelings, and we did not have to go far to find a totally eerie one: trees and power lines down, some buildings wind damaged, a thick, black-brown, stinky mud underfoot (one of the vehicles got stuck along the way), and the buildings all absolutely black from the mud and with a ring of oil near the top of the floodwater line. We stopped between a small Baptist church and a midsized family home. This home showed no sign of damage—this was the eerie part—and the body-search groups had not come here yet, so the front door and windows were intact. There were even hanging flowerpots on the front veranda, though the plants, like those everywhere, were black and dead from the saltwater and the oil. The flood line was just below the eaves. It struck me immediately—this home has a rich history. Where were the occupants? It was obvious that they had evacuated. Was one of these dogs wandering around their children's pet? My heart was so very, very sad. I felt defeated. Could we have better predicted what had happened in Katrina? No, we couldn't have and academia had not designed or built the levees. That night we said some extra prayers for all those families.

A National Guardsman in a Humvee rolling past asked, "Did you see a body back there? We have a report of a body." No, we hadn't, but the sweetish smell of death was in the air, and I was sure that they would find bodies the next morning as the search crews got started. In the months following, I passed that home many times and never saw any signs of life. (Six months later, still no signs of life.)

That evening I told John Barry about my day in the Upper Ninth. In addition to the science, such images and hands-on, day-to-day experience in New Orleans were what I could bring to the committee. No one else in the group had that perspective. John said he had tried during the conference call to alert the assembled team about these issues, especially as they involved the Corps, but he didn't feel as though he had had any impact. Then he rang off to watch President Bush's speech from the stage in the French Quarter. (I read it instead.) Later that night I received the "welcome aboard" e-mail that had gone out from one of Senator Vitter's staffers to the participants in the call, and I concluded that I was an official member of the team.

The following morning I was leading a group that was flying over all of the major levee breaches, both in the city and out to the east in St. Bernard and Plaquemines parishes. I brought along the cameraman for the French crew, because we had a deal: In exchange for the flight he'd provide me with a copy of that high-resolution footage, which is much better than any of us could achieve with our handycams. But I therefore missed the second conference call of the Pelican working group. That night I studied a report submitted to the group by the Association of Flood Plain Managers. "No adverse impact" is one of the goals of this organization. This principle emphasizes the importance of understanding how natural systems function and then defining, at the local level, how best to manage rivers and drainage systems. In essence, "No adverse impact" floodplain management tries to assure that the actions of one property owner do not adversely affect the rights of other property owners, as measured by increased flood peaks, flood stage, flood velocity, and erosion and sedimentation. This is definitely the right idea. Given that flood damages in the United States continue to escalate, now approaching $6 billion annually, even with the billions of dollars spent for structural flood control and for other structural and nonstructural measures, we really need to change the way we do business. This association has some great ideas and ideals, and their report was a serious piece of work.

I was pretty encouraged, but when I talked with John later that night, he repeated his unease that for a second time he had failed to get his group to hear his concerns about the existing levee system, the multiple failures, the probable causes, and the implications they held for all future plans and projects. It seemed pretty basic to him—and to me, of course—but he wasn't getting through to them. He wanted me to try on the next conference call, but first he wanted me to contact Garret Graves on Senator Vitter's staff, who would actually draft the plan. It was late, but I phoned Garret and presented a brief version of our early concerns about the levee breaches and what I thought they should mean to this team. He heard me out, but he was also tired. Understandable. It was 1:00 A.M. in Washington. He had to interrupt the call, and said he'd get back to me, but did not. After half an hour I decided to put all my ideas and concerns down in an e-mail to the group.

I've said before that I can be naive. I should have paid more attention to a note John had sent me after our conversation but before I had called Graves. This is a group of Hill staffers and lobbyists, John said, and their approach seems to be "piecemeal," a compilation of old Corps proposals, and not a comprehensive reassessment. If I'd thought about what John had said and realized we were working with a group of lobbyists, for the most part, my note would have been a little less frank. But I didn't pick up on this salient fact, and my note was not less frank.

I began with a pretty vivid description of the scene in the Lower Ninth. I laid out the issues with the levee breaches and wrote, "I believe it will be a long, long time before anyone trusts the COE [Corps of Engineers]. . . . No one trusts the COE." I mentioned that we (LSU people) had been working with the Greater New Orleans Planning Commission to develop a design for a floodgate for the infamous Funnel east of the city—the confluence of the Mississippi River–Gulf Outlet and the Intracoastal Waterway. No one wanted to wait fifteen years for the Corps to build the project. And as for the state, its agencies do not have the infrastructure to manage the comprehensive restoration and levee work—a conclusion I based on my brief tenure as the main coastal restoration guy. Fear of corruption would also dog any vast program run by the state. Fact

of life. I therefore mentioned my idea for a new body along the lines
of the Tennessee Valley Authority that could "cut through red tape
because . . . there will be no interdepartmental and intradepartmen-
tal turf battles." This authority would have a czar and a blue-ribbon
panel of scientific and engineering experts and business administration advisers. It would have cabinet-level representation, and it
would have the right to seek its own appropriations and independent financing. It would spread the rebuilding dollars to contractors
throughout the tristate area (Louisiana, Mississippi, and Alabama).
It would pay above minimum wages. It would not allow contractors
to use mainly illegal immigrant labor. It would be a twenty-first-
century solution to a twenty-first-century problem.

The next morning Garret Graves's e-mailed nine-point plan for
a "Marshall Plan–type Commission" was waiting for me and all of
the other working group members. This was based on the team's
discussion of the previous day. The call for "programmatic authority" for the Pelican Commission was in line with my TVA thinking.
The plan called for an independent review of the levee failures and
for Cat 5 levee protection. It advocated an "inter-related" approach
to "hurricane protection, flood control, navigation, and coastal
restoration." It stated that coastal restoration should not be viewed
or construed as "eco-system restoration" but as "protection of our
coast and energy infrastructure" that is in the national interest. All
this was a promising start, but there were also red flags, especially
the "navigation" initiatives, like dredging canals and improving ports
miles and miles away from New Orleans. How did these projects
help restore and rebuild southeast Louisiana? And why wasn't the
closure of MR-GO and stopping all plans for building new locks for
the Industrial Canal in the main plan? Those are basic requirements
for any responsible plan. Everyone knows that. But the point that
really got my attention was this one: "Work should proceed in an
expedited manner—including the possibility of waiving, reducing or
streamlining environmental, cost-share, economic and other considerations." That was radically open-ended. Regarding the environmental "considerations," this statement could lead to weakening
wetlands permitting regulations, leaving the door wide open for de-

velopers to build more homes or factories in drained wetlands—the very wetlands we need for storm buffering in many cases.

Immediately—prior to the planned 9:00 A.M. conference call—I sent the planning team a list of these concerns. On that call with about a dozen people (as best as I could figure) someone called "Bubba" on Senator Landrieu's staff complimented me on my *Meet the Press* interview, and I thought, great, this is starting off well. Then, at John Barry's prompting, I tried to inform the assembled listeners of my observations concerning the levee failures and the Corps's failure to warn people on the day Katrina struck. I asked about the relationship between dredging harbor canals nowhere near New Orleans and flood protection, wetlands restoration, and Katrina relief. That's when an unidentified stern male voice tried to shout me down. "The oil companies have said they will go overseas to build rigs if we don't dredge the canals!" he yelled. *What a lot of bunkum*, I thought—and then it hit me. These people—some of them—are all about their favorite deals! I started to sense that the two callers who seemed to be supporters of the Corps were getting rather annoyed with me. I could hear the contempt in their voices, so I tried to deflect the antagonism by suggesting that deepening the canals was not my concern, but they had better try to encase it in an economic development envelope.

The discussion then turned to the value of a scientific panel. On one of the earlier calls, the group had discussed using the National Academy of Sciences. An unidentified woman suggested that we should set up a committee of scientists from Louisiana, because they know the area and understand the problems. Of course, I agreed. One of the main reasons we set up Team Louisiana for the levee investigation was to get local engineers with local knowledge of the soils and other issues. (This question of turf and reputation can be surprisingly significant even in science. In many third world countries local people frequently have the attitude that any idea or scientist from the first world, especially from the United States, must be better than their own. It's an inferiority complex of some sort. When I returned to South Africa after my graduate studies at LSU I had to fight the feeling that *I* must understand the local problems better than the local scientists, who had lots of experience. Such nonsense—and we have it in Louisiana as well. Some group from the *National* Academy of Sciences must be better than our people, when quite the contrary is the case.)

Slowly but surely, two guys (unidentified, at least for me) seemed to begin dominating the conversation, and before I really knew what was happening the decision had been made that the Pelican Commission wouldn't need any science at all. Maybe I was the problem, I don't know. I was the only representative of science in the group, I was becoming a squeaky wheel, therefore just get rid of science. That was kind of the way it seemed to be going, and I was deflated. Other than John Barry, the woman who wanted some local scientists involved, and me, no one in the group wanted to take this opportunity to do the rebuilding and restoration right. Instead, they wanted their projects. When someone else rang off the call, I followed suit.

Less than twenty-four hours later, Marc Levitan received a call from Randy Hanchey, deputy secretary of the Department of Natural Resources, complaining about my bad-mouthing of the Corps in my e-mails to the group, which he had. (Hanchey worked for the Corps for many years before his retirement in 1998.) The e-mail's path began with Hunter Johnston, a Washington lobbyist and former senator Bennett Johnston's son—and a member of the Pelican working group. Johnston had forwarded one of my e-mails to Ken Brown, CEO of the engineering and architecture consulting firm Brown, Cunningham & Gannuch. Most if not all of the firm's principals are former Corps employees, and they do a lot of work for the New Orleans Port Commission (beneficiary of the controversial lock on the Industrial Canal), numerous districts of the Corps, and many other others. (A few months later—January 2006—the company received a sole-source contract from the New Orleans District of the Corps to look at drainage in New Orleans.) Ken Brown in turn had sent my e-mail to Hanchey, who in turn complained to my colleague. I was being honest but that seemed to get me into trouble at every turn. I then found out who the other members of our little club were. The *Washington Post* reported that they were lobbyists from such powerful firms as Patton Boggs, Adams & Reese, the

Alpine Group, Dutko Worldwide, Van Scoyoc Associates, and a firm owned by former senator Johnston. According to the *Post*, the group also included a lobbyist for the Port of New Orleans, a lobbyist for Verizon Wireless, and three lobbyists who were former aides to House Transportation and Infrastructure Committee chairman Don Young of Alaska.

After this incident involving a senior state employee with very obvious pro-Corps leanings, and having learned the exact makeup of the planning team, I decided to go directly to Garret Graves. On September 16, I sent him an e-mail expressing my concern that what I considered a confidential e-mail within our group had been disclosed to a private engineering company. I questioned if this action should disqualify the engineering company from participating in the reconstruction efforts, and I deplored what seemed to me like politics and deal-making already at work even in Louisiana's greatest hour of need.

I received no reply. A few days later John Barry sent the committee a note reminding us all that "projects need to be integrated and priorities set. Particularly, ties need to be developed between the construction projects and the coastal restoration effort. It seems that we all are hell bent on getting projects funded (money) rather than a comprehensive reconstruction/restoration plan. It may be important to take at least a ¼ step back for a second, and make sure things are approached comprehensively." John's team would have been well advised to heed their leader's wise counsel. As a longtime Louisiana resident as knowledgeable as anyone about these issues, going all the way back to the 1927 flood, John knows what he's talking about. But his committee went on its merry way—around him. Perhaps John's presence (and then mine) were just meant to be some sort of cover? In any event, less than a week later Senators Landrieu and Vitter introduced their Louisiana Katrina Reconstruction Act, seeking $250 billion in federal monies—that's $250 billion over and above the $63 billion already authorized by Congress for emergency relief purposes.

What were our senators thinking? They had taken all the suffering from Hurricane Katrina and turned it into a boondoggle, a porkfest. The request came to $55,000 for every man, woman, and child in the state (pre-Katrina, even more per capita post-Katrina). Everybody was taken care of in this legislation—every commercial interest, that is: energy (oil and gas), construction, ports, shipping, you name it. The $35 million for the seafood marketing campaign caught the eye, as did millions for a sugarcane research laboratory. A long article in the *Los Angeles Times* on October 10 reported that just five days before the bill was introduced one of the energy companies had retained the services of Lynnel B. Ruckert, Senator Vitter's former campaign manager and wife of his chief of staff. Smart move. The bill made $2.5 billion available to the private utilities.

All of this was catnip for the press, who predictably and quite rightly ate it up. They had great sport with this legislation. The *Washington Post*'s outraged editorial was titled LOUISIANA'S LOOTERS. (The alliteration proved irresistible; others in the media picked up on it immediately.) The editorial said, "This is the equivalent of New York responding to the attacks on the World Trade Center by insisting upon a federally financed stadium in Brooklyn." Then and there the legislation was effectively dead, I'm sure. Reporters and columnists pulled out favorite tales of colorful corruption, Louisiana-style, going back to the era of Huey Long and his brother Earl, who was railroaded into a mental institution by his wife. (I learned that one of Huey's mottoes had been "Share the Wealth," which can be a noble sentiment or something else. Likewise "Every Man a King.") Did a single story fail to mention that former governor Edwin Edwards is right now sitting in prison (as is his son)? I wonder if former senator John Breaux enjoyed being reminded of his quip, delivered after supporting some Reagan-era, trickle-down budget proposal, to the effect that "my vote can't be bought—but it can be rented." Funny at the time, I'm sure.

Mississippi governor Haley Barbour was upset that the outrageous request from his neighbor state indirectly hurt his own request for $34 billion, but in the end, Mississippi Republicans in Washington—let's tell it like it is—ended up getting three or four times as much aid per capita for their state as Louisiana received. (Barbour is a former chairman of the Republican National Committee.) No matter. Not three weeks after Katrina struck, with parts of New Orleans still underwater, with the catastrophe still unfolding, with the whole world watching, it was suddenly open season on Louisiana and its politicians.

The section of the legislation I was most familiar with would have directed $40 billion to the Army Corps of Engineers for their ultimate wish list of projects, some of them, like the $740 million for the new lock on the Inner Harbor canal, long discredited as among the worst of the worst boondoggles. The final bill exempted all of the rebuilding work from the regulatory provisions of the National Environmental Policy Act and the Clean Water Act. This was unbelievable. John Barry's and my advocacy of an oversight role for a scientific panel was not included in the legislation.

John was upset with the final package, and said so. I was really upset, and said so. Up to that point in the Katrina story I had thought that the offer of a paid vacation in Las Vegas to New Orleans cops and others was the worst political/PR blunder. Or maybe it had been President Bush's lame flyover. Or the president's lamentation about Senator Trent Lott's demolished shorefront estate in Mississippi. Or Brownie's admission that he had been out of the loop regarding the thousands of people stranded at the Convention Center. Now I was certain that the Pelican Brief would be the worst by far, because it stood the chance of undermining the entire recovery effort.

On September 1, President Bush had said, "I'm confident that with time, you get your life back in order, new communities will flourish, the great city of New Orleans will be back on its feet, and America will be a stronger place for it. The country stands with you. We'll all do all in our power to help you." As the months passed this was becoming more and more doubtful. On December 15, the president announced that he would ask Congress for $1.5 billion to bolster New Orleans's levee system. His own "best man" for Gulf Coast reconstruction, Donald Powell, admitted that there were design and construction flaws that needed to be remedied, and he added, "The federal government is committed to building the best levee system known in the world." Well, this would cost a lot more than $1.5

billion—about twenty times that much. Time will tell if those funds are really forthcoming, and if they're not we can lay a good part of the blame on the Pelican mistake. In December, Senator Larry E. Craig (R-ID) told a home-state newspaper, "Louisiana and New Orleans are the most corrupt governments in our country, and they have always been. Fraud is in the culture of the Iraqis. I believe that is true in Louisiana as well." Pretty harsh words, but in line with lots of similar comments from Washington lawmakers. John J. "Jimmy" Duncan Jr. (R-TN), chairman of a key subcommittee involved in re-construction efforts, told the *Los Angeles Times*, "I don't think I have ever seen an issue flip so quickly as this did." The *Shreveport Times* noted that D.C. and state officials agreed that "the tide of support for helping the state turned when [the] submitted legislation seeking $250 billion . . . had little or nothing to do with hurricane protec-tion." Meanwhile, Mississippi's legislators got high marks for working quietly behind the scenes to steer resources to their constituents.

What a blunder. What a loss. There were other blatant acts of profiteering, but this one got the headlines. It was embarrassing, and when the dung instantaneously hit the fan, the two senators' apologists hurried to explain that the final sum would probably be in the range of $200 billion, not $250 billion. This didn't help. Senator Landrieu's spokesman said to the *Los Angeles Times*, "Standing up the region's economy will help stand up the American economy. The lobbyists and the entities they represent tend to be among the most experienced experts available who have direct real-world knowl-edge of the situation. They are advocating for a position and for a client, but usually from a vantage point of expertise that can be very beneficial to us."

Who, exactly, is "us"?

Throughout the fall I and others with LSU and elsewhere were working on two fronts: continuing to investigate the levee failures that had caused this catastrophe, and developing political support for the ideas that could prevent another one (while hoping that the Pelican Brief hadn't made this impossible). The truth about the levee failures and the plan for the future are absolutely related. Most obviously, as I wrote in my note to the Pelican planning group, I don't believe we can entrust overall control of the incredibly important restoration work to the Corps. Not now. I had my chance to lobby Governor Blanco on this point and many others in December, a couple of days before she briefed a House committee on the situation in her state. This was my first conversation with the governor one-on-one, and she was great: businesslike but warm and friendly, and I have no doubts about *her* motivation or her grasp of the issues. We met for two hours, even discussing my problems with LSU, some of which I've sketched in these pages.

I pressed the critical point that there is only one way to describe the levee breaches, and that is "catastrophic structural failure." I was pleased she used that exact phrase before the committee. Clearly some congressional Republicans are trying to blame the state and local governments for the catastrophe; just as clearly the responsibility lies with the Army Corps of Engineers and the federal government, which had, through its agency, failed to deliver protection from even the modest storm that Katrina was in New Orleans. But even if Katrina had been the Cat 4 storm the Corps portrayed, its excuse that Congress hadn't provided enough money to protect against such a storm just does not hold water, if you'll accept the pun. Switching metaphors, the squeaky wheel gets the oil, and all the Corps had to do was complain, complain, complain, help the state complain, and get citizens' groups to complain. The Corps doesn't seem to have much problem getting the special-interest lobbyists to procure the funding for canals and harbors. If it knew it had such an inferior product in the levees, if it could not supply the level of protection required by the 1965 Flood Control Act with the funds provided, then it should have organized a public information campaign to tell the public that they were living with a ticking time bomb.

I suggested to Governor Blanco that the Corps would have to be involved in the new flood-protection plan, whatever it turned out to be, because there is no way to push this behemoth aside entirely, but it could not have final authority. The state needs to take the initiative and design the best system for the future. In the three months since I'd started pushing my hope for a TVA-like federal reconstruction authority, I'd realized that that just isn't going to happen. That idea was DOA, I'm afraid. What *is* possible is independent state leadership, with federal funding—convincingly independent, to address the state's image problem, now even worse, thanks to the Pelican Brief. The governor had already set up the Louisiana Recovery Authority (LRA) to be the legal conduit for whatever federal reconstruction money Washington still feels like dropping in the can after the Pelican Brief fiasco. The LRA is modeled on the Lower Manhattan Development Corporation that monitored the work at Ground Zero and did, by all accounts I've read, a great job, in no small part thanks to the system of "integrity monitors" put in place by Mayor Rudy Giuliani, private-sector watchdog firms assigned to every construction company involved in the cleanup. As a result, there was not one significant corruption scandal in that effort. This is incredible, given New York's own reputation for funny money in the construction trades. Governor Blanco did not copy this oversight scheme, but she did institute stringent controls for verifying the disbursement of every federal dollar, to the point of irritating some communities waiting for FEMA checks. At a special session of the legislature, the governor also created a twenty-one-member Coastal Protection and Restoration Authority, itself somehow augmenting the old Wetlands Conservation and Restoration Authority, charged with devising a master plan for flood protection and coastal restoration. But the $32 billion for flood protection and wetlands restoration, advanced principally by our old friend Randy Hanchey, was really just a dusted-off version of the Corps's old plans. It even bore a strong resemblance to the $40 billion allocated to the Corps in the ill-fated Pelican legislation. I say throw out the old and start with a fresh sheet of paper. Otherwise we are doomed to repeat the mistakes of the past.

Almost every local and state (but not federal) official has lined up to proclaim that protection from a Cat 5 storm—not just a promise, but a program with guaranteed funding in place—is mandatory for luring people and businesses back to the city. Various Corps officials

have said all along that such an upgrade would take a minimum of
ten years, perhaps fifteen, perhaps more. Congress has already be-
stowed $8 million on the Corps to study how to do it, with a pre-
liminary assessment due in the spring of 2006, and a final plan due
eighteen months later. Randy Roach, the mayor of Lake Charles,
which was badly damaged by Hurricane Rita, said in anger about all
such planning, "We're burning daylight. We have just a matter of
months, not a matter of years. We have studied this. I don't want to
hear about a new study." Indeed, a small group of independent engineers and scientists—no politicians, politically connected members, lobbyists, contractors, or anyone with any financial or political
stake in the work—could sit down and in one week craft an ironclad
plan for saving southeastern Louisiana. Whoever selects this panel
would have a few dozen men and women from which to choose, and
any combination would come up with essentially the same plan.
This is not rocket science. It never has been. It requires only a political system that can get it done. The plan they come up with will
cost $30 billion. It will require ten years to complete. As a political
reality, the Corps will build the projects, but at least it can be forced
to build them to the state's specifications and overall plans. We need
this thoughtful, comprehensive, big-picture plan that can achieve
the goal with a minimum of lost time and wasted dollars. Politically,
we need a clear, effective mission and purpose that emphasizes protection for the people. Emphasize protection from flooding and the
restoration of the wetlands will necessarily follow. But protection
must drive the process, politically. This is the way to confront
Speaker of the House Dennis "A lot of that place could be bull-
dozed" Hastert and others who question whether low-lying, high-
living New Orleans is even worth the trouble to rebuild.

(If Hastert's remark was a calculated trial balloon, it went over
like a ton of lead. He caught a lot of flack, but Randy Lanctot, executive director of the Louisiana Wildlife Federation, of which I am a
card-carrying member, sent around a note suggesting that the
Speaker's basic question about rebuilding, if delivered in the right
spirit, was legitimate. Maybe it just reflected the "practical way
Midwesterners think," Lanctot added hopefully. Hastert is certainly

aware of the vital role played by the ports in Louisiana for the grain producers in his own state of Illinois. *How* do we rebuild? Should the levees be upgraded to Cat 5? Should the lowest levels of the city be raised? To use the buzzword, shouldn't rebuilding be "sustainable"? Recipients of the e-mail agreed that these are the right questions, but they weren't willing to give the benefit of the doubt to Hastert's motivation. Neither was I.)

A few days after our conversation Governor Blanco was off to testify in Washington, D.C., and I was off for the Netherlands to see for myself what the best flood-protection system in the world looks like. The trip was sponsored by WWL-TV, the CBS affiliate in New Orleans that never went off the air and was so important during Katrina. The editorial idea was for me to join veteran anchorman Dennis Woltering, a New Orleans institution with a soft warm smile, to study what the Dutch have accomplished following their own catastrophic flood of half a century earlier. Despite my Dutch heritage I had never been to my ancestral homeland. As a child I had heard how the Netherlands had "turned back the ocean" and "captured the land from the sea," and along with every other kid, I guess, I knew the story of the little Dutch boy who discovered a hole in the levee and saved the day by plugging that hole with his finger. Today Dutch engineers are considered just about the world's leading river flood-and-surge protection experts. I was very anxious to see for myself what they have.

Our host for the week was Jurjen Battjes, a recently retired engineering professor who had been a member of the levee investigation team assembled in New Orleans by the ASCE. Jurjen is tall, pleasant, and very knowledgeable, and he has a wonderful twinkle in his eye. It was Jurjen who asked when he first surveyed the drainage canals in New Orleans with their pumps inside the city, "Why invite the enemy so deep into your camp?"

The Netherlands is about half the size of Maine. Almost a quarter of its land is below sea level—the lowest land 22 feet below—and without the protection of dunes and dykes about 65 percent of the country would be inundated either by storm surges from the sea or by floodwaters from the great rivers (the Rhine, Maas, and Schelde). The vicious winter storm in 1953 resulted in 1,800 Dutch deaths, destroyed 4,000 buildings, and flooded 625 square miles. (Katrina flooded about half as much land.) Such a catastrophe demonstrated the woeful insufficiency of the protection system in place at the time, and the nation mobilized practically overnight to set things right. And how. They have contrived an engineered landscape of flood control structures—dunes, dikes, dams, barriers, sluices, and pumps—that puts to shame anything Louisiana has to offer. The contrast is embarrassing, frankly. The system is now an integral part of Dutch national pride, and rightly so. It demonstrates what determined and highly motivated people can accomplish. It is a standing challenge to the citizens of Louisiana and the United States.

As Jurjen explained to the visiting Cajuns (including one honorary Dutchman), the local policymakers and engineers looked at their old, failed system and presented the nation with a choice: rebuild the existing levees to higher and stronger standards (they had suffered seventy-eight breaches in the big flood), leaving a certain vulnerability, or start all over, in effect, and think really big and outside the box. The Dutch chose the latter option. Cost was barely an issue, because the life of the nation was at stake. (I write that sentence with a heavy heart. With the life of the city at stake in New Orleans, money was always invoked as the reason for not doing this or that.) The complete overhaul would be entrusted to one central agency. Local authorities could be charged with maintenance duties, but overall design and construction would be a national responsibility. One very interesting aspect of the Dutch system from which we could take a lesson is that the design of certain of the larger structures was set up as a competition, with engineering and contracting companies challenged to submit their own designs. The planners believed this was the best way to utilize all available brain power and creativeness. (The motto of our Army Corps of Engineers is *Essayons*, French for "Let us try." Maybe it should now be, in Louisiana, *Maintenant, laissez un autre essayer,* or "Now let someone else try.")

The first and most important decision regarding the new design was prompted by the same problem Jurjen had pinpointed with the drainage canals in New Orleans. The former levee system, long and sometimes sinuous, had allowed surge water to penetrate deep into populated areas. The system had needed to be "shorter." It had needed large barriers across estuaries and other open waterways, thus cutting back on the need for extensive interior defenses. The replacement system has a basic, outer line of defense backed up by a secondary defense of compartments within compartments. Experts in probabilities and risk management determined just what degree of protection was needed where. Highly industrialized areas now have protection against anything short of the ten-thousand-year flood, while rural farmland is more vulnerable. (In New Orleans, the Corps thought its standard project hurricane was, in essence, a two-hundred-year storm.) As in Louisiana, the essence of the problem for the Dutch was that the draining of their peat bogs and marshes initiated the vicious cycle of subsidence, ever more subsidence. Understanding this, their system now allows nearly normal tidal interchanges in some locations, while others are carefully monitored and, if necessary, pumped in order to maintain groundwater elevations, so the decomposition and subsidence rates are held to an absolute minimum.

The most vulnerable and critical link in the Dutch defenses is a channel system known as the Hollandse IJssel that penetrates deep into highly industrialized and settled areas. Less than five years after the flood, they had designed and built a double storm-surge barrier in this channel consisting of vertical sliding gates three hundred feet wide, a ship lock, and a road bridge. These gates, as well as those elsewhere, are beautifully designed with two of everything, in most cases: two surge gates, two sets of locked doors. Of course, some commercial and recreational craft, especially sailboats, have high clearance needs, so these gates feature a narrow section that can be raised, in the manner of a drawbridge. I can see such a structure on the Industrial Canal just off Lake Pontchartrain.

One of the highlights of the trip was the visit to the Ooster Schelde barrier, one of five other major barriers known as the Schema Afsluitingen. The Ooster Schelde is a series of 62 sluice gates, each 120 feet wide and separated by man-made islands. The whole structure is 4 miles long and allows free tidal interchange with the estuary, keeping intact the natural functions and the commercial harvesting of seafood, but the gates can be closed quickly, thanks to their ram-driven hydraulics. Cost: about $4 billion. This barrier and the four others with similar functions face the North Sea, whose tidal range of nine feet and potential exposure to huge waves necessitates far more robust structures than we would need anywhere in Louisiana.

The most impressive and famous of the structures in the Dutch system is the storm-surge barrier at Maeslandt on the extremely busy Rotterdam Waterway. This design was also the product of an open competition. The main element of this barrier is two enormous "butterfly wings," one on each bank of the channel. Each wing looks something like two oil rigs joined at one end by a gigantic

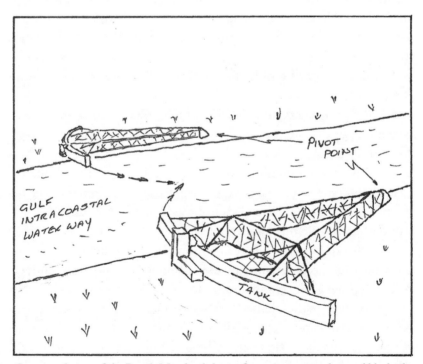

Conceptual view of the Dutch Maeslandt butterfly surge gates as they could be built in the Gulf Intracoastal Waterway at the location of the Funnel.

ball-bearing assembly to form an enormous V as long as the Eiffel Tower is tall. The open end of each V is a large water tank. In normal times each wing lies beside the channel flat on the ground, so to speak, and completely out of the way of all maritime traffic. Called into action, they swing out and meet in the middle of the channel. The two large tanks are then filled with water and sink to the bottom, sealing the waterway from any conceivable storm surge. Otherwise, ships have an unimpeded passageway at all times. The whole system is computer-driven, with backup redundancy for every mechanism. It is an amazing sight, truly an engineering marvel—and it is something we could easily adapt and build in Louisiana. We have some of the top riggers and shipbuilders in the nation and therefore the world. Fabrication of such a structure should be a piece of pie for them. And the cost would be only $700 million, in current dollars.

Are we in Louisiana and the United States even capable of such comprehensive, science-sensitive planning, and then performance? It's a shame I have to ask the question, but we all know that the answer remains to be seen. I returned home from the Netherlands more convinced than ever that such Cat 5 protection in Louisiana is very doable, requiring only the political will and wherewithal. And the job does not have to take fifteen or twenty years. Ten years is enough. I've decided we need the Dutch onboard in some kind of consulting or oversight role. Earlier I criticized the susceptibility of some in Louisiana to the notion that the *National* Academy of Sciences must know something we don't, and I'm not succumbing to that same error now. We have the expertise here, but the fact remains that the Dutch have already done it, and they could serve as a wonderful fail-safe mechanism for us.

We have to give careful consideration to subjecting the design of individual features of the plan to a competition, just as architects routinely engage in competitions for design commissions. Such a process worked in the Netherlands—it is one key reason their system is so excellent—and it can work here. The various agencies that expect a piece of the action can be bluntly informed that the control they have always enjoyed is a luxury we can no longer afford. Encouraged by the independence of this process, private foundations would surely underwrite the competition.

We must immediately move forward on two fronts: a major barrier system and large-scale wetlands creation. No more Band-Aids! If this isn't clear by now to everyone concerned, something is seriously wrong in the state of Louisiana. Any big-picture surge-protection system for this state must include major barrier levees and flood gates in conjunction with creating wetlands and barrier islands. The best procedure is to build the hard structures where they can be protected by an existing "platform" of wetlands, no matter how fragile, and where there's a reasonable supply of good soil-building material for levees. The wetland platforms seaward of the barrier levee and floodgates would be the target sites for future wetlands creation projects, with barrier islands seaward of the expanding wetlands base. Barriers—wetlands—barrier islands: This progression assures the survival of the estuarine bays necessary to keep the commercial and recreation fishing industries alive, as well as to supply the breadth of natural habitats that make up this unique ecosystem.

Here are the main elements of the major barrier system:

- At the main entrance to Lake Pontchartrain, build a flood-control structure with multiple gates in the Rigolets along the I-10 Bridge. (The Dutch often combine a bridge and flood-control structures into one engineered unit.) Maybe this structure is quite similar to the Dutch Ooster Schelde barrier, especially the floodgates, although we will need at least one shipping lock at the highest part of the bridge over the navigation/tidal channel. Maybe it's something entirely new. To find out, put the design up for competition and wait for unfettered American genius to show its colors. This structure could have locks or gated sections to allow shipping free movement. It could address the environmental issues that helped stall the idea forty years ago, allowing normal tidal interchange to and from the lake. There is no good reason

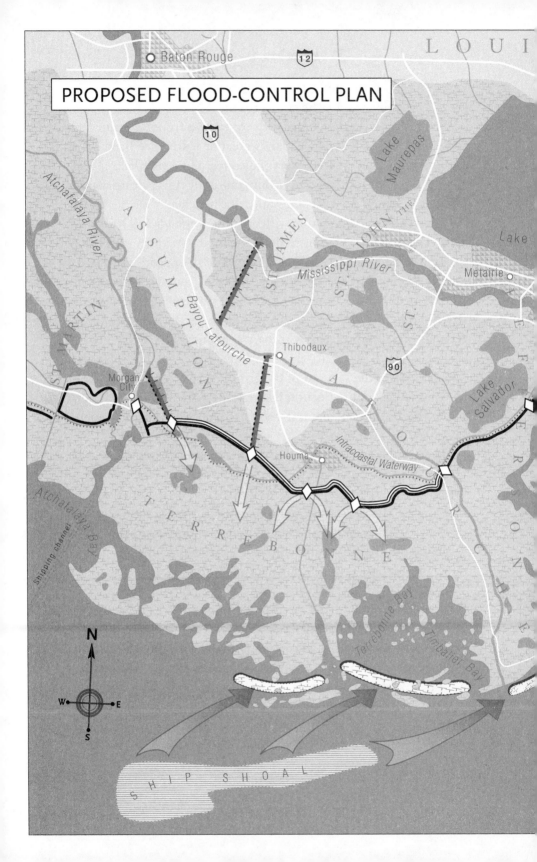

KEY

▬ New Barrier Levee
⌒ New Waterway
▱ Gated Structure
⊗ Butterfly Gate
▦ New Canal
⇒ Diversion

Mined Sediment
to
New
Barrier
Island

the commercial or recreational value of the lake has to be impaired in any way.

These floodgates at the Rigolets and Chef Menteur entrances to the lake have always been considered the ultimate protection for the city. If the water cannot get into the lake from the Gulf of Mexico in the first place, it cannot then be pushed over the levees by the north wind.

As the story is usually written, the Corps's sixties-era plan to build floodgates for Lake Pontchartrain was blocked by environmentalists. Indeed, certain green groups did file suit, asserting that the gates would inhibit tidal flows and therefore damage the fragile ecology of the lake, and an injunction was entered in December 1977, calling for a second environmental impact statement. (The first had been filed in 1974.)

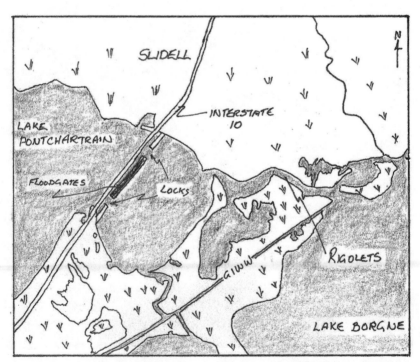

Location of surge floodgates and twin lock system proposed for the Rigolets at the I-10 Bridge. This would protect not only New Orleans but all the parishes bounding lakes Pontchartrain and Maurepas.

However, the local entities and levee boards that would have had to maintain and operate the gates were also wary. In the end, the Corps gave up the gates project and focused on the levees, which were deemed much less expensive to work with, and theoretically just as effective.

Post-Katrina, the shelved barrier plan became an issue in the campaign of various right-wing commentators to hammer environmental organizations at every opportunity. See! they screamed. If the tree-huggers hadn't stopped the barriers, this wouldn't have happened. It's not that simple. According to a statement issued by the Corps in late 2004, its engineers have been revisiting the idea of the floodgates, this time with "environmental modifications" to address the concerns that had prompted the lawsuit forty years earlier. These floodgates must be built. The environmental issues can be resolved.

Such a structure would mean that we would *not* have to raise any of the lakefront levee systems in New Orleans. All we would need to do is "armor" them. The Dutch have great examples of such armor, often a shield of tightly fitted nine-inch-thick concrete blocks with a loose gravel covering, or a layer of asphalt or bitumen mix as protection against surface erosion. These floodgates in the Rigolets would also protect the north shore of Lake Pontchartrain and communities all the way up to the Country Club of Louisiana in Baton Rouge, which could have some flooding with a Cat 5 surge. Therefore, huge areas of St. Tammany, Tangipahoa, and Livingston parishes would benefit greatly.

• The pump stations must be moved to the head of the 17th Street, London Avenue, and Orleans Avenue canals in New Orleans, blocking any storm surge from the lake from even entering the canals. (The Corps has announced its intention to do just this, at a cost of $3 billion.) The job could take a few years; as an interim measure, simple gated structures could be built. We saw several versions of such structures in the Netherlands, most featuring stout wooden gates, hinged and moved into place by hydraulic rams and locked into place with hydraulic pins. These provisional gates could be built in about a year. Obviously, lakefront gates create a problem if we have a storm with high surge and lots of rainfall. With the gates closed to protect against the surge, the existing pumps could not operate should there be flooding from rainfall, so we need new pump stations along the lakefront, fully automated, computer-driven, and with standby generators to make them immune to power failures. No one has to stay behind to operate them. The Dutch even have automatic scoop systems that lift the debris from the pump intakes and require no manual labor.

- During Katrina we saw how water poured from the Industrial Canal into Lake Pontchartrain. A gated structure with either a large lock or a surge barrier plus a lock needs to be built where the Ted Hickey Bridge crosses the Industrial Canal, a hundred yards or so from the lake—something similar to the Hollandse IJssel surge gate.

- Eastward from the Rigolets Barrier system the levees from Orleans East to the Intracoastal Waterway have to be substantially raised and made into major barrier levees. (Likewise, we must have a major barrier levee west of the Rigolets to protect Slidell and possibly parts of coastal Mississippi.) East of New Orleans we need a butterfly-gate type of flood-control structure in the area of the Funnel. It could be a copycat version of the Dutch structure at Maeslandt (and thereby perhaps become a tourist mecca, like Maeslandt). We need substantial levees extending from this butterfly gate and linking with the great levees along the Mississippi River that protect us from river floods. It goes without saying that all levees should have armoring that saves them from both wave attack and erosion should they be overtopped.

- From the Mississippi River westward we need to build one giant barrier levee that basically follows a bulging curve seaward, taking in Houma and some of its surrounding communities (some smaller curves may be necessary to incorporate some communities). With careful location, this levee, about eighty-four miles long, can balance the protection of the communities "inside" and wetlands fronting the system on the "outside." This inland levee would include numerous gated structures including, for example, where the barrier levee crosses Bayou Lafourche. Others would be built at key navigation channels and where river/sediment/freshwater diversions will be built. (See description following.) The barrier levee would then tie into the East Guide Levee of the Atchafalaya River at a point close to Morgan City. This levee can then be extended from the West Guide Levee of the Atchafalaya River all the way to Texas, with navigation gates at the required locations. Ideally, this giant levee would be on the seaward flank of a large navigation channel, parts of which would include the existing Intracoastal Waterway. This channel would allow access for heavy equipment and barges with soil, rock, and other levee-building materials.

Simply put, this levee would be the line in the sand—the real deal, a Cat 5 wonder with gates and locks where needed for navigation and/or sediment diversions for coastal restoration. To some extent this new levee would replace the misshapen network of levees now in place in this area south and west of the Mississippi River. (The existing network creates some funnel effect problems of its own. It should be replaced.) On talk radio the big idea for some time has been the ultimate levee somewhere out in the marshes. On WWL-AM, Bob and Vinny say we could start the big wall tomorrow. I don't know about that, but the final plan for flood protection in southeastern Louisiana—if it is indeed Cat 5 protection—must include some such levee.

• This whole system—barrier levee with navigation/sediment distribution gates—must be accompanied by legislation that stops development in the wetlands anywhere in the newly protected areas. Otherwise our current river flooding problems will be exacerbated, because these gates, and especially those at the entrance of Lake Pontchartrain, will slow down drainage of water out of the lake after major rainfall floods. I know this legislation would not be popular with certain developers, but the idea, remember, is to do it right this time. A good guide would be the principles in the paper submitted to the Pelican committee by the Association of Flood Plain Managers. Don't do anything that will worsen your neighbors' flooding. Likewise, there needs to be a moratorium on the mining of cypress forests for mulch anywhere in coastal Louisiana. Cypress swamps are some of our best defense against storm surge.

Let's acknowledge right now that many communities are going to be outside this new levee system. Some retreat has to take place. Communities outside the new system could be given some level of flood protection, but protection that costs more than the value of the protected infrastructure is, clearly, problematic, and hard to sell to the federal government, which would be paying for this job.

It would also be circumspect to require that all new construction within the new barrier be elevated a given number of feet as determined by the design specifics of the whole system. This would provide an extra margin of protection in the event of some levee overtopping, or to reduce flood damage should there be a rainfall flood that exceeds the capacity of the pumps.

The alternative to the proposed levee cutting across this part of the state is a much longer wall right at the coastline, an unbelievably expensive venture that offers no wetlands protection. I mentioned earlier that the determined citizens of Terrebonne Parish have levied a quarter-cent sales tax to raise money for their share of an ambitious, seventy-two-mile structure known as the Morganza-to-the-Gulf levee. The Corps has already spent $32 million planning this levee, but it was dreamed up without full consideration of how vulnerable the whole coast is to drowning, and without a thought given to the large-scale creation of wetlands seaward of the barrier system. The old project was deserving enough under the old vision, perhaps, but it would necessitate miles and miles of finger-like levees sticking seaward toward the Gulf. So do some of the other old ideas. As the Dutch learned, and as common sense dictates, a long set of levees set out like the fingers of your hand is a poor substitute for one solid levee across your knuckles. The latter is the much safer, less expensive system. (The old projects and studies would be extremely useful and would provide valuable data, background information, and project justification material for the major barrier system. They would allow us to fast-track the new system, because much of the ground work has been done.)

One major difference between Louisiana and the Netherlands is that we do still have a lot of wetlands for storm-surge protection. In order to protect the levee system, and as a hedge against a rising sea level and climate change, we must concentrate on building and restoring wetlands seaward of the barrier, using the sediment resources of the Atchafalaya and Mississippi rivers. Even with the major barrier system, these wetlands are still the outer defense and must be maintained for this purpose, as well as for their commercial, recreational, and environmental uses. Natural systems and some developed areas within the core should also be maintained, in order to accommodate expected overtopping and to avoid the degradation of water quality that the Dutch have experienced. Seaward of these wetlands we need to build barrier island chains, close in to the existing wetlands, using high-quality sand from offshore.

Lieutenant General Carl Strock, head of the Army Corps of Engineers in Washington, was simply wrong when he said that a restoration program would not have helped much with Katrina's storm surge because the storm passed to the east of the wetlands. Come on, General. How did the surge get into Lake Pontchartrain? How did it get into the lower part of St. Bernard Parish? By crossing thousands of acres of open water that just thirty to forty years ago had been healthy marsh and swamp. Maybe General Strock was under the spell of MR-GO, which has created a wonderful channel for the encroachment of saltwater from the Gulf of Mexico into what had been some of the most productive marshes and wetlands in the entire United States. More than eleven thousand acres of cypress swamps have been destroyed, and almost twenty thousand acres of brackish marsh have converted into less productive saline marsh. With proper management instead of desecration these regions would have diminished the surge from Katrina not only in Louisiana but in parts of western Mississippi. Levees protected by healthy marshes survive and protect people; levees exposed to open water are annihilated and leave communities open to devastation.

We need the best levees. We need extensive wetlands. And we

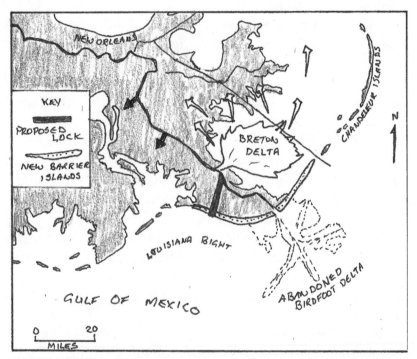

Conceptual plan of major diversions from the lower reaches of the Mississippi River, notably the Breton Delta. Also shown are the new navigation channel and the abandoned Bird-Foot Delta now reworked into a barrier island chain.

need them under one administrative roof. It would be senseless to differentiate between the two elements for either planning or financing purposes.

In Chapter 8 I mentioned the four major wetlands initiatives I set forth in the CCEER white paper in 1994. With minimal modification these are still the obvious projects we need immediately.

Here are the major elements necessary for large-scale wetland creation:

- Below New Orleans, divert the Mississippi River into the Breton and Chandeleur sounds, 32 miles upstream from the present main outlet. The Breton and Chandeleur sounds are dominated by shallow bays that have modest subsidence rates (half a foot per century) and are therefore excellent recipients of river sediment. This new diversion would create five thousand new acres of marshland every year in eastern Plaquemines and St. Bernard parishes. In twenty years we would have 140 square miles of new wetlands to buffer storm surges. In a domino effect, these healthy marshes would benefit the other marshes in St. Bernard Parish. The plan would mean the loss of the bird-foot delta, but it is dying slowly anyway, because of its high subsidence rate (three feet per century) and the absence of sedimentation, since the river discharges most of it into deep waters offshore. This dying delta could be reworked into new barrier islands that would coalesce with the Breton-Chandeleur islands to the east and the shoals and islands of western Plaquemines Parish, thus creating an almost unbroken barrier island arc south and east of New Orleans and its suburbs. The plan would also eventually require, in all likelihood, a set of locks and other control structures at the new outlet. Some oyster beds would have to be relocated.
- Reconnect Bayou Lafourche to the main channel of the Mississippi River fifteen to twenty miles to the east of its junction with the Mississippi and divert 10 percent to 12 percent of the total flow down this channel, which would feed the marshlands all along its course, bring freshwater to 8 percent of the state's population, and create jobs in the fisheries. Dredging the bayou would be necessary, along with extensive plumbing that would include small diversions and siphons—all to the immediate and lasting benefit of six hundred thousand acres of wetlands.

- Increase the flow down the Atchafalaya from 30 percent to 40 percent, while using plumbing to manage the extra water and sediment flowing into the Terrebonne, Atchafalaya, and Teche-Vermilion basins. The east-west–oriented Intra-coastal Waterway is an excellent conduit to move sediment-laden water miles laterally; the boat traffic's propellers keep the sediment in suspension. The canal dredged behind the barrier levee where it did not follow the Intracoastal Water-way could act as a similar conduit. Throughout the system, large- and small-scale diversions and siphons could help mimic the natural annual floods. The system needs to be as "leaky" as possible.

Regarding these first three big-picture items, the knowledgeable, perhaps even dubious observer asks three questions immediately: Is there any history showing that such freshwater diversions actually work? Does the river still carry enough sediment to support the ad-ditional widespread dispersal? Would the new diversion into Bayou Lafourche and the increased diversion into the Atchafalaya leave enough water in the Mississippi to sustain full navigability all the way to the new outlet? The answers are yes, yes, and yes. The granddaddy of freshwater diversions in Louisiana is the Wax Lake Outlet. This canal, between the Lower Atchafalaya River and the Gulf of Mexico, was cut in 1948 as a relief valve for floodwaters that would otherwise hit Morgan City a few miles to the east. The chan-nel was cut through wetlands and a series of small lakes with no con-fining levees for the last ten miles of its length. It was free to flood as it wanted. Since the diversion offered a shorter course to the Gulf than the actual river course, this channel maintained itself; that is, it required no dredging and even started to capture more water from the river. Discharge from the Wax Lake Outlet has averaged about 10 percent of the total flow of the whole Mississippi system. It should be no surprise that seaward of the outlet we have a great evolving natural delta with extremely healthy natural levee and marsh environments, a delta that expands with every flood with no

2002. The Chandeleur Islands took another hit, and then again in 2004 with Hurricane Ivan. However, after each storm the islands displayed a remarkable capacity to repair themselves, though they were a bit shorter and a little thinner. Then came Katrina, who erased them from the map.

Therefore, ask the critics of rebuilding the islands, why fight the inevitable? Barrier islands come and go. Let them. The struggle to save them is too problematic and too expensive. I disagree on both counts. We know from experience and from the storm-surge models that the islands provide excellent buffering. The barrier islands along Louisiana's south coast have, for the most part, been cut off from their sediment supply, mostly due to the navigation and oil and gas canals. Just as we refurbish beaches in Florida and along the East Coast from time to time, some also because they have been cut off from their sediment supply, so we need to and can restore Louisiana's islands. We know that a healthy barrier island with a good sand beach berm—and wide wetlands behind the berm—is a long-lived feature. We need to build the sand parts and the marshes of these islands. The marshes have been missing from the Chandeleurs. We can create the conditions to rebuild them.

Overall, rebuilding the islands would be something of a Sisyphean effort, because there would probably be losses in every big storm, but as the islands are being torn apart, they are in turn tearing down the storm surge to a measurable extent. Not restoring them dooms all remaining wetlands to a far more rapid death. And if that's not a good enough reason, consider that the islands also form the outer edges of the giant estuaries that are the basic framework supporting the very rich fisheries in Louisiana. Lose these and the fishery collapses.

To summarize: The major barrier system and large-scale wetland creation work through these initiatives, and include elements of both attack and defense:

- outer substantial barrier-levee with floodgates
- wetland and barrier island-building and maintenance outside that barrier

- maintain compartments within compartments, where
such exist

To repeat, the core protected area in southeastern Louisiana would *not* have to be evacuated for a Cat 5 storm. This would not be necessary. Other areas outside this core would have a higher level of protection than exists today, but to a lesser degree than the core, and they would sometimes require evacuation. This fact can't be allowed to compromise the commitment to protect the core. So this plan is attractive because it proposes a higher level of flood protection for the principal populated areas than anyone has previously proposed. If, like the Dutch, you never have to evacuate, you can then support a level of infrastructure investment that has not been possible in the past. With this plan in place there would be no reason *not* to rebuild every single neighborhood in metropolitan New Orleans, and every reason to do so. The residents of the Lower Ninth would be as safe as those in the highest redoubts in the Garden District, which were left high and dry after the Katrina flooding. On the other hand, the plan does require political and civic courage. It requires honesty from our politicians and clearheaded, pragmatic acceptance of the facts from the citizens because restructuring the coastal landscape will mean dislocations and disruptions of some traditional fisheries, for example. Resources will be lost while new ones will be gained. Dislocations will be kept to a minimum, and the planning effort must incorporate compensation for those who lose land or livelihood. Such a fair program can assure that we will not waste years in the courts or arbitration proceedings. Am I dreaming? As I said, our citizens will have to accept the facts of life in Louisiana.

Again, this is not rocket science. The science is the easy part. The hard part is overcoming the narrow-mindedness and selfishness of politics and business as usual. For decades the two have undermined plan after plan to restore the wetlands, build new ones, and thereby protect people and property. They have played hell with improving the existing levee system. We must do better now, or we can kiss it all good-bye for good. I was not exaggerating in the introduction when I said that politics and business as usual in Louisiana will eventually put everything below Interstate 10 underwater. Science and engineering can save the day, but not if they're censored or manipulated. If that's to be the case, just shelve them and start packing. It's over.

It is February 2006. The lights are still out in the Lower Ninth Ward, Lakeview, Gentilly, Upper Ninth, elsewhere. At night these neighborhoods are dark, lonely, quiet. The diaspora from Hurricane Katrina has contracted, but only slightly. A few stalwart souls have returned and now live in FEMA trailers in their backyards, if those backyards are large enough. Jack-o'-lantern neighborhoods, these have been called, accurately. They're spooky. They may also be more dangerous than they appear. The ubiquitous layer of sludge is contaminated with arsenic and a lot else we'd be better off without. Short-term health impacts, including skin rashes, respiratory distress, and asthma, are practically a given; no one really knows the long-term impact of exposure to this mud.

Basically, most of New Orleans is still very dead. Large expanses of southeast Louisiana and coastal Mississippi still lie in ruins. Gray Line has started bus tours, and even bike tours, of the devastated neighborhoods. Is this dismayingly morbid rubbernecking or a good way to build awareness and political support for rebuilding the city (in addition to making money)? Your call. (I think they do help.)

The news about FEMA doesn't seem to get any better. Every day it's a new story about some glaring failure before or during the Katrina emergency, a new "probe" about dubious accounting, dubious contracts awarded without competitive bidding, inexplicable delays for folks still waiting for their trailers. This agency has proved that it is not capable of handling a complex catastrophe (or billions of cash dollars, apparently). Therefore, no agency in the federal government is. The military can establish a rough order—as it must—but the Katrina emergency proved that rough order is just the start. Without a radically revised attitude on the part of this and all subsequent administrations in Washington, we are doomed to repeat this debacle in southeast Louisiana, or somewhere else, or both.

What about hurricane season 2006? Just how safe is the greater

New Orleans area? The Corps's district office says it will have everything back to pre-Katrina levels by June 1. I'm not sure what this means, because the whole levee system is compromised. It will *not* be back at pre-Katrina surge-protection levels. The heights of the levees may be as they were, but height, as we saw with the catastrophic failure of the London Avenue and 17th Street levees, is not the only factor in their survival. The Corps says it will have the MR-GO levees rebuilt by June. With what? There are no sources of good material anywhere near those destroyed levee sites. Site inspections by Team Louisiana have shown that the contractors, in many areas, are using a sand base material for the repair. They appear to be scraping up the remnants of the old levees and trying to use this material, plus some they have barged in. Sand is porous and highly permeable, and it lends itself to dangerous seeps—not exactly the material of choice for levees. The contractors themselves are concerned; their field staff told us they are not getting the support or supervision they expected from the Corps. The Berkeley levee warriors and the ASCE team have been quite vocal in the media about these questionable repairs. Are they a strong pointer to the future? I sure hope not. Moreover, the progress out east has been painfully slow. Unless drastic changes are made, these levees will not be fully returned to the pre-Katrina heights, even using the unsuitable materials. There will be no armoring at all. Any wave field that develops in Lake Borgne with an east wind will start to erode these levees instantly.

At the other side of the metropolitan region, way out west at the border of Jefferson Parish and St. Charles Parish, a levee I haven't mentioned because it was not a problem during Katrina could be a terrible problem with the next storm. For a stretch of about 150 feet, the flood wall sections have sunk about 6 inches and are offset one from the next by a few inches at the top. This structure needs help, and fast. At the Industrial Canal above the Lower Ninth Ward, the I wall has been removed and will be replaced by an inverted T wall with batter piles. This is good, because it's a far more robust design. The Corps understands that the whole levee wall was compromised in this area. The three breaches on the infamous drainage canals along the south shore of Lake Pontchartrain have been sealed, but both the 17th Street and London Avenue canals now have, as a result, sections that are much narrower than before. The capacity of the canals to transport floodwater out of the city is therefore seriously diminished. I guess the Corps figures that since very few folks have moved back to the flooded neighborhoods, a bit of rainfall flooding won't hurt too much. But the real concern along these canals is that sections of the flood walls that did not breach during Katrina, but did "give" somewhat, remain in that compromised position. Early data indicates that the soils all along these levees are consistently much weaker than before Katrina, and we know that the soils contributed mightily to the Katrina collapses. So don't let them kid you. For the 2006 hurricane season, some of the levees will *not* be as strong as they were pre-Katrina.

In January 2006, New Orleans's Mayor Nagin appeared before yet another congressional committee to complain about the unending need for him to "grovel and beg" for FEMA trailers, levee money, and everything else. Then he groveled and begged one more time: "I'm puckering up! Help us!" (The mayor is on record as favoring this unique style of communication. It's refreshing, certainly, but not always helpful. I'm thinking of his subsequent avowal on Martin Luther King, Jr.'s birthday that New Orleans should always be a "chocolate" city. He soon retracted the remark and admitted a need to be more circumspect. We'll see.) The mayor's "Gang of 17" business leaders, officially the Bring Back New Orleans Commission, find themselves caught between an enormous rock and a very complex hard place. Open all devastated neighborhoods or redline some forever? How about giving former residents one year to vote with their feet, with those neighborhoods that reach some tipping point of returnees deemed viable, and all others not so? This is an audacious idea but not one likely to make the cut, or I miss my guess. It's not even clear that any government entity has the legal authority for the wholesale condemnation that would have to follow. That question is before the courts, but this hasn't stopped Sean Reilly, a member of the Louisiana Recovery Authority, from saying bluntly that city officials had no business even holding out the hope that every neighborhood would be rebuilt: "Someone has to be tough, to stand up, and to tell the truth. Every neighborhood in New Orleans will not be able to come back safe and viable. The LRA is speaking the truth with the money it controls."

On that score, though, state legislators have made it clear that they're not anxious to give up *their* historic control of the purse strings: The LRA is doing a great job, but *we* are the people's accountable representatives, and we want to stay accountable. (Strange. Politicians these days usually duck accountability. I guess it's the money here that makes them willing to take the chance.) In a special session called by the governor in November 2005, the legislators flexed their muscles by defeating a plan to dissolve the local levee boards in southeastern Louisiana and consolidate their functions under a new state authority, then they defeated a separate plan to create a commission to oversee the boards. The idea was that businesses, before they will return to New Orleans in large numbers, need confidence in a new oversight mechanism for the levees; the legislators took umbrage at the notion that their actions had anything to do with patronage and misappropriation. The Gang of 17 in New Orleans was disgusted. Two months later, in a second special legislative session, the legislators had a sudden and predictable change of heart and gave a nearly unanimous blessing to milestone legislation dissolving local boards in the New Orleans area in favor of regional authorities. The new system takes effect January 1, 2007, and is, in my opinion, a mandatory step forward in the development of the statewide big picture. Meanwhile, I'm reliably informed that the parishes have lost all trust in the Army Corps of Engineers, and in the ability of other federal or state agencies to develop and institute a comprehensive plan.

I'm on record defending the radical idea that the same federal government that drowned New Orleans with the failure of its levees should compensate all of those who lost lives and homes. Instead, the best we have come up with so far is the plan devised by Congressman Richard Baker from suburban Baton Rouge to allot homeowners and lenders 60 percent of the pre-Katrina value of their demolished property. Since the federal government is responsible for 100 percent of the losses, why not compensate for *100 percent* of them? Still, coming from a conservative Republican, this was a pretty radical, progressive idea, and is appreciated as such. Of course, the Bush administration has declared the plan dead, but in February 2006, Governor Blanco announced a state initiative that adds $4.2 billion authorized by Congress for community development block grant funding to the $6.2 billion already guaranteed. Blanco proposed a cap of $150,000 on the money available to each homeowner to repair, rebuild, relocate, or accept as a buyout. A program to register potential homeowners is currently under way.

Let's face it. A just outcome for the homeowners is highly unlikely. Lord knows there are plenty of civil cases shaping up against various defendants, including the Corps, contractors, and insurance companies, but this litigation is guaranteed to last forever, and it is unlikely to deliver full justice to those who have lost everything. The state of Louisiana cannot possibly afford to pay for the program.

It's the strange book that must end just as the story is beginning, in a way, but such is the case here, and at this early juncture I have to be counted among the pessimists. The fight for the future of New Orleans is going to be a long and difficult one. I now picture a big theme park as the end result, a plastic place without much vitality. What an incredible loss. And those with the least resources are sure to lose the most. On this score, I'm really pessimistic. And if the right decisions are not made about the levees and the wetlands, well, forget it. On this score, I'm beyond pessimistic. Consider a recent meeting I attended at the request of Lieutenant Governor Mitch Landrieu (Senator Landrieu's brother) at which I presented the big-picture plan outlined above, using the big official state map as the backdrop. Going in, I was pretty excited. Our two senators, the governor, DOTD secretary Johnny Bradberry, and others had just returned from the Netherlands, and news reports indicated that they were coming around to my ideas for adapting features of the Dutch system in Louisiana. They reportedly even saw the wisdom of cutting the Corps out of the loop for designing the system, depending on competitions instead. On matters of flood control, they certainly saw the manifest superiority of everything Dutch. I viewed my subsequent presentation as a confluence of the lessons learned from the experience of the Dutch, Hurricanes Katrina and Rita, and from twenty years of assorted wetlands restoration initiatives. (Actually, Paul Kemp, who was also at the meeting, summarized the presentation in these terms, and I agree.) But no sooner had I completed my talk than two senior members of Governor Blanco's staff, both political appointees, astounded me (and some of the others, including Paul) with comments about how the storm surge from Katrina had overwhelmed the levee design of the Army Corps of Engineers, and so on. The Corps, now and forever! *Essayons!* I could not believe what I was hearing. Had these folks talked with the boss? They then said they were in the process of developing, along with the Corps, a comprehensive plan for the state. I can tell you exactly what it will look like: the Pelican Brief all over again, in spades.

One aspect of our American way of life that is really missing in the Katrina response and recovery is our pioneering spirit that built this country, at times over almost insurmountable odds. Just three decades ago it took us to the moon. What has happened to it? Have we lost our heart and soul? Are we no longer a nation always ready to help the underdog and the less fortunate? No! The outpouring of public support during the Katrina emergency tells me that we have not lost our founding beliefs. Now we have to sustain that spirit— that pioneering spirit of old—and accept this latest challenge that nature has thrown before us, rebuilding in a sustainable way with the best of science and engineering at our disposal. My motto, one last time: The catalyst to compromise is a thorough understanding of the science.

As a nation, let's take up the "Rebuild!" battle cry. Now is the time to put politics, egos, turf wars, and profit agendas aside. We owe it to the thirteen hundred Americans who died in the Katrina tragedy. We owe it to their survivors and to all future generations. It's now or never. Let's show the world what we're all about, here in America in the twenty-first century.

ACKNOWLEDGMENTS

I want to thank my family for everything they've done for me. Katrina changed many lives and certainly ours. My wife Lorie gave me all her love and support and read early drafts of the book; daughter Julia contributed many ideas about content and cover; and younger Vanessa helped in collating copies and in other ways. Since Katrina I have missed many family events and I thank my family for their understanding. Late one night, Lorie told me she would make up for me when the book pulled me out of our home. That was the kind of encouragement I needed.

I would not have been in the position to write this book if it was not for wonderful friends such as Paul Kemp and Marc Levitan. Paul has always been a great comrade-in-arms, and thanks to Marc's vision we got into the hurricane business. They both also offered valuable suggestions on early drafts of this book.

Hurricanes Katrina and Rita really taxed our research teams, both during the response phase and now in the recovery phase. Our twin hurricane centers' researchers, all extremely dedicated, developed a thorough understanding of the impact of a major storm's hitting New Orleans, and their research was crucial throughout all aspects of this catastrophe. All gave hours and hours of time and many still do. These include Brian Wolshon and Chester Wilmot (*nog 'u suid afrikaner*)—transport and evacuation; Jeanne Hurlbert and Jack Beggs—sociology and public opinion surveys; John Pardue and Bill Moe—water contamination; Erno Sajo—air contamination; Nan Walker, Larry Rouse, and Ric Haag—Earth Scan Lab; Kevin Robbins, Barry Keim, Luigi Romolo, and Jay Grymes—Southern Regional Climate Center; John Snead, DeWitt Braud, Hampton Peele, Lisa Pond, and Robert Paulsell—GIS experts and mapmakers; Paul Kemp, Hassan Mashriqui, Joannes Westerink (Notre Dame), and Rick Luettich (UNC)—ADCIRC surge modeling; Joe Suhayda—surge modeling; Dane

Dartez—storm-surge measurements and field trip organizer; John Pine—hazard assessment and risks; Martin Hugh-Jones—veterinarian; and Jim Diaz—medical doctor and tropical diseases. Graduate students Ezra Boyd, Young Souk Yang, and Carol Hill really helped out as well. LSU vice provost Chuck Wilson offered early encouragement as we faced the media onslaught.

I would be remiss if I did not acknowledge the Hurricane Public Health Centers research associates, Kate Streva and Ahmet Binselam. Both these folks offer so much support and are always willing to go the extra mile. I will never forget their efforts during the first few days in getting the GIS mapping going. They helped to make the HEF center the success it is and I thank them for all they still do to keep things on track.

Brian Ropers-Huilman, William Scullin, Sam White, and Steve Brandt, Center for Computational Technology, really helped move the ADCIRC modeling forward with smooth access to LSU's supercomputer.

During Katrina there were huge demands for GIS data analysis and mapmaking. Fantastic GIS support came from Barrett Kennedy, College of Art & Design; John Anderson, Andrew Curtis, and Farrell Jones, Geography and Anthropology, as well as a number of their graduate students.

I acknowledge Pace Laboratories' Dean McInnis and Sonny Macaisz, who ensured our water sampling in the first hectic days went so smoothly. Sergeant Bill Thomas of the LSU police got us into and out of New Orleans safely.

All of this research would not have been possible without the support of the Louisiana Board of Regents (BOR)—Health Excellence Fund to whom we are extremely thankful, as to Jim Gershey, BOR project manger, who gave us the go-ahead day one to use our funds for response activities. A sincere thanks to all at the BOR.

Thanks to Tom Berg of Hurricane Alley for spaghetti plots on page 68.

My trip to the Netherlands was funded by WWL-TV out of New Orleans and I thank their news manager, Mark Swinney; newsman and anchor, Dennis Woltering; and all the other reporters and support staff there for making this extremely important trip possible. On the ground in the Netherlands, Professor Jurjen Battjes of the Delft University of Technology organized the whole trip, and I am also extremely indebted to Professor Han Vrijling, Bas Jongman, students Elwyn Klaver and Wim Kanning, and cameraman Ivo Coolen.

Louisiana state officials Terry Ryder, Johnny Bradberry, Ed Preau, Susan Severance, Burton Guidry, Will Crawford, Mike Stack, Justin Guilbeau, Amber Thomas, and Giuseppe Miserendino helped move the levee studies forward. I am indebted to the members of Team Louisiana who were willing to step into the fray: Paul Kemp, Wes Shrum, Radhey Sharma, Hassan Mashriqui, Ahmet Binselam, Billy Prochaska, Louis Capozzoli, and Art Theis. I and the state are truly indebted to the University of Berkeley surge warriors, especially Bob Bea and Ray Seed. Governor Kathleen Babineaux Blanco always had kind words of support.

The idea to write a book came as I was putting together an e-mail to friends and family late one night shortly after Katrina struck, an e-mail written partly as therapy to deal with my own feeling of sadness and partly to inform people about what was really happening in New Orleans. John Barry encouraged me to start a book and introduced me to Wendy Wolf at Viking, who, sight unseen, felt the potential in my Katrina story and ultimately brought Mike Bryan to my front door. I thank John for his support and wise counsel, and I also thank CNN's Anderson Cooper, who, during a depressing helicopter flight over New Orleans a week into the event, encouraged me to write. Wendy needs a special word of thanks, not just as my editor but also as someone who grew up in New Orleans and has a real love for the city. Wendy has been so, so supportive and encouraging as well as making sure we met deadlines.

I knew I would not have enough time to write the whole story myself and needed someone who would feel the passion of the story, who could convey that as well as the sadness. Tall, lanky, inquisitive Mike Bryan stepped into our lives on a moment's notice late September 2005. Within three and a half months we had written a book together and he had become part of the family. Mike is a wonderful teacher and friend. Mike lost his dad while we were working on the book and yet still managed to keep his eye on the ball. I am eternally indebted to "Mr. Mike," as my kids affectionately call him.

At Viking I wish to acknowledge the heroic work that was done in production, art, and design by Tricia Conley, Nancy Resnick, Carrie Ryan, Herb Thornby, Clifford Corcoran, and Rachel Burd. Adrian Kitzinger worked quickly to give us the crucial maps for the book. Attorney Jack Weiss, a Louisiana native, helped me understand how things looked from different points of view. My own attorney, Donald Price, reviewed the LSU passages and I thank him for that.

My agent, Joe Spieler, got the passion from the get-go. I thank him for his savvy advice and for sorting out the paperwork—not one of my strong points.

The media did a wonderful job of getting the word out and still does. They were a great source of data during the first few months of our levee assessments. Thanks from all of us in Louisiana.

Last, on a very personal note, my family and I are great believers in prayer, and it is through prayer that I could face some of what I saw and dealt with during the Katrina event. My prayer now is that this book does make a difference.

Ivor van Heerden
Satsuma, Louisiana
March 2006

REFERENCES AND RESOURCES

From my perspective, the hundreds of newspaper, magazine, and television reporters and producers dispatched to Louisiana and Mississippi during the Katrina emergency did a wonderful job and provided a vital public service. Their reports from the scenes are one of the three main sources for the information in this book. I've sometimes cited certain specific stories in the text, but I am not footnoting the hundreds of others because the same facts and quotes appeared in so many different stories. (For the curious, there's always Google.)

The other two main sources of information are my personal experience during the emergency and my background knowledge acquired over the years. My experiences as presented here speak for themselves; of course, this also holds true for my general knowledge of the situation along the coastline. For all errors of fact, blame me and me alone.

Below is a brief—very brief—selection of sources for further reading and research.

BOOKS

Barry, John M. *Rising Tide: The Great Mississippi Flood of 1927 and How It Changed America*. New York: Touchstone, 1997.

CNN News. *Katrina: State of Emergency*. Kansas City: Andrews McNeal Publishing, 2005.

Colten, Craig E. *An Unnatural Metropolis: Wresting New Orleans from Nature*. Baton Rouge: LSU Press, 2005.

Emanuel, Kerry. *Divine Wind: The History and Science of Hurricanes*. New York: Oxford University Press, 2005.

Larsen, Erik. *Isaac's Storm: A Man, a Time, and the Deadliest Hurricane in History*. New York: Vintage Books, 2000.

Nicholson, William C. *Emergency Response and Emergency Management Law.* Springfield, IL: C. C. Thomas, 2003.

Sheets, Bob, and Jack Williams. *Hurricane Watch: Forecasting the Deadliest Storms on Earth.* New York: Vintage Books, 2001.

Van de Ven, G. P., ed. *Man-Made Lowlands: History of the Management and Land Reclamation in the Netherlands.* Utrecht: International Commission on Irrigation and Drainage, 2004.

WEB PAGES

America's Wetlands: http://www.americaswetland.com/

ADCIRC Development Group: http://www.nd.edu/nadcirc/index.htm

CCEER 1994 Plan:
http://publichealth.hurricane.lsu.edu/Adobe%20files%20for%20webpage/CCEER%201994.pdf

Center for the Study of Public Health Impacts of Hurricanes:
http://www.publichealth.hurricane.lsu.edu

Coalition to Restore Coastal Louisiana: http://www.crcl.org/

Hurricane Alley: http://www.hurricanealley.net/

Hurricane Basics: http://hurricanes.noaa.gov/prepare/

Louisiana Environmental Action Network: http://www.leanweb.org/

Louisiana Geological Survey: http://www.lgs.lsu.edu/

Louisiana Water Resources Research Institute: http://www.lwrri.lsu.edu/

LSU Earth Scan Lab: http://www.esl.lsu.edu/home/

LSU Hurricane Center: http://www.hurricane.lsu.edu/

LSU Hurricane Experts: http://www.lsu.edu/pa/mediacenter/tipsheets/hurricane.html

National Hurrricane Center: http://www.nhc.noaa.gov/

NHC Tropical Analysis and Forecast Branch Radiofax Broadcast Schedule:
http://www.nhc.noaa.gov/radiofax.shtml

Southern Regional Climate Center: http://www.srcc.lsu.edu/

"Washing Away" Series, *Times Picayune:* http://www.nola.com/hurricane/?/washingaway/

Weather Underground: http://www.wunderground.com/

INDEX

Page numbers in *italics* refer to illustrations